Society and Education

FOURTH EDITION

SOCIETY AND EDUCATION

Robert J. Havighurst
and
Bernice L. Neugarten

Allyn and Bacon, Inc.   **Boston**

LIBRARY OF CONGRESS CATALOGING IN PUBLICATION DATA

Havighurst, Robert James, 1900–
    Society and education.
    Bibliography: p.

    1. Educational sociology. I. Neugarten,
Bernice Levin, 1916–   II. Title.
LC191.H33   1975   370.19'3   74–19192

CONTENTS

PREFACE

To be a teacher in America requires not only a competence in teaching but also an understanding of how the school fits into the society and what its tasks are.

As we have rewritten this book for the third time in 15 years, we are impressed with the ways in which social change in America has increased and made more complex the knowledge that teachers should have about the society in which they work. The quickening pace of social change has given the schools more opportunities and more problems. The new patterns of work and leisure, metropolitan development and the urban crisis, the "black revolution," the enormously expanded functions of the federal government in the field of education, the emergence of a serious problem of unemployed and out of school youth—these are some of the social changes that require new ideas in education and new ways of teaching.

We have revised every chapter in order to take into account new research that has been published within the past five years. We have had all of the 1970 Census volumes available for this revision, plus some more recent sample studies by the Bureau of the Census. Because various ethnic and racial groups are undergoing a new group consciousness that emphasizes cultural differences and that creates new problems for the schools, we have added several new chapters dealing with cultural pluralism and its significance for the American educational system. The problems of education of the economically disadvantaged in the large cities have become more complex, and this, together with the movement toward decentralization, requires a special chapter.

This edition begins with a new chapter on the changing postindustrial society and its changing values. The emergence of the age-period now called "youth" and the appearance of a counterculture of youth are treated in a separate chapter. The changing roles of women are discussed in a separate chapter on women's education.

In Part I, after a new introductory chapter, we examine the social-class structure of the society, the interaction between social class and ethnic differences, and how the educational system deals with the pervasive problem of inequality in a democratic and pluralistic society.

In Part II we explore the process of socialization of the child and adolescent, and examine the relation of the school to the other socializing agencies, especially the family and the peer group.

In Part III, the school system is seen in the context of the local community, particularly the metropolitan community.

Part IV deals with the school in the wider society, with problems related to population growth, to ethnic and racial diversity, and to the changing status of women.

In Part V the focus is upon the teacher: the various roles of the teacher in the classroom and in the community, the career of the teacher as a member of the largest professional group in modern society, and the new professionalism in teaching.

Throughout the book we have attempted to develop our interpretations from empirical findings and thus to maximize the social-science base on which educational policies and practices can be built. At the same time, a sociological interpretation of education cannot avoid dealing with controversial issues and value judgments. We have not avoided such issues, but we have attempted to make clear where our interpretations are supported by research findings and where they rest upon value judgments.

Full information on all the references cited in the text (and in the suggested readings at the end of each chapter) appear in the Bibliography. To make the Bibliography of maximum value, we have placed in parentheses after each reference the page numbers where the reference has been cited in this book.

We are indebted to a number of persons who have assisted us in various ways in writing the first and subsequent revisions of this book. We should like particularly to acknowledge the influence of our longtime friend and colleague, Professor W. Lloyd Warner, whose research and writing had a major effect upon our thinking about social structure in America. We are indebted to our many graduate students who contributed illustrative materials and who have made many useful suggestions in the light of their own experience as classroom teachers. We are especially indebted to Dr. Betty Goldiamond for her substantive contributions to the chapter on women in education (Chapter 18); to Mrs. Mabel Frazier and to Mrs. Edythe M. Havighurst for their painstaking work in the preparation of the manuscript.

Robert J. Havighurst
Bernice L. Neugarten

Society and Education

PART

I

The Educational
System in the
Social Structure

CHAPTER 1

The Changing Society

This book is about the contemporary, complex, rapidly changing society and its educational system. The aim is to help the teacher study the American society with special reference to its social structure, values, and subcultures as these interact with the educational system.

RECENT ECONOMIC AND SOCIAL CHANGES

Since the turn of the century the productive efficiency of American industry has increased enormously. Industrial productivity per man/hour has multiplied fourfold, and the Gross National Product per person, in terms of dollars of constant purchasing power, has increased sixfold. The real income of the average American family of four (after deducting taxes) increased 80 percent between 1940 and 1970.

The advantages of this increased productivity and prosperity have been delivered to Americans in higher wages, more profits, and more leisure time. In 1900 the average work week in American industry was 58 hours, but in 1970, it was about 35 hours. Workers get more holidays and vacation days with pay, and when they reach 60 to 65, they retire on pension and/or social security benefits.

The task of American industry and business is no longer to produce enough goods and services, but to limit production so as to avoid glutting the market. The major task for the country as a whole is to *distribute* our product more equitably and to *consume* it more wisely. We still have many families living in poverty. At the same time, we have a new task: to find interesting and satisfying things to do in our growing amount of free time. With present life expectancy, with the present norm of retirement at or before age 65, with the present length of the work year and the work week, the average American works the equivalent of about 200 eight-hour days a year for 45 years, or 9,000 work-days. This average American at age 21 can expect to live 52 more years, while at 65 he can expect to live 15 more years. In addition to 7,400 days free from work between ages 20 and 65, he will have at his disposal, after retirement, the equivalent of 5,110 days without work.

When his situation is contrasted with that of his grandfather, it becomes clear that his life-style and his life-values are likely to be different from those of his grandparents.

Bigness and Bureaucracy

During this century, and especially since 1950, there has been enormous growth in size and complexity of most of the organizations in American society. Industrial and business corporations have grown by expansion of their business and by merger with other corporations. School systems have grown enormously in size, due to the postwar increase in birthrate and also to the merger of small school districts. Universities and colleges have expanded, especially the state-supported ones. In 1971 there were 50 universities with enrollments over 20,000. Federal government organizations have multiplied.

The proportion of the white-collar labor force which is employed by large organizations has increased greatly, while the proportion who are self-employed or who work for organizations with ten or less employees has been reduced accordingly. The small food shop or clothing store or hardware store owned and operated by one man with two or three employees has been replaced by the supermarket and the department store chain. The small factory with 100 employees and a corresponding office and executive staff has been bought up by a large industrial corporation. The one-man law office or the two-man partnership has been replaced partially by the large law firm. The doctor with his own office has been replaced partially by a clinic consisting of eight or ten specialists. The church with a pastor and a part-time director of religious education may have grown to have a professional staff of four to six people. Even the one-family farm has lost ground to the mechanized industrial farm corporation.

Values are changing with respect to commercial, governmental, and educational processes, changing in ways which are only dimly understood today. Things which can be done efficiently by large organizations and by computers may come to be valued simply because they are more easily achieved than other things. Forms of learning which can be promoted by computers may come to be favored over other forms of learning. Forms of amusement which can be purveyed through mass media may become the most popular forms of amusement. Ways of working with other people which are most effective in large organizations may become the most highly valued ways of working.

4

Population Increase

The population of the United States grew very rapidly from 1800 to 1920, practically doubling every 30 years. Then it slowed down, due partly to reduced immigration after 1920 and partly to the reduced birthrate during the severe economic depression of the 1930s. But immediately after the close of World War II, the birthrate jumped about 50 percent and stayed up until 1960, after which it dropped slowly again to the level of the 1930s. This fluctuating birthrate has produced a very large group of young adults, beginning about 1967, with results which we are only beginning to cope with. The major problem is the growing unemployment of youth since about 1965.

United States in the World Arena

The relations of the United States to other nations have gone through basic changes, with the United States emerging as a world economic and military power at the close of World War I, and becoming the leader of one of two rival groups of nations after World War II. This rise in power was complicated by the fact that the white race was losing its hegemony over the world, a position it had held ever since the fifteenth century voyages of discovery and conquest gave white Europeans the economic and military dominion over the whole earth. Early in the present century, nonwhite nations began to take power. In 1905, Japan defeated Russia in war. In 1949, the Chinese Communists took control of mainland China and ousted the western powers. The subcontinent of India became independent of the British Empire in 1947. In 1971, the People's Republic of China took a seat in the United Nations. Since 1950, most of the former European colonies in Africa have become independent nations. Thus, the United States' foreign relations have brought the nation into conditions of international equality not only with peoples of different political and economic ideologies, but with peoples of different skin-color.

CHANGING SOCIETAL STRUCTURE

These economic, social, and political changes have been accompanied by changes in the social structure of American society, and changes in its component subcultures. The terms society, culture, and subculture are key concepts for this book. They will be introduced here, and then developed further in later chapters.

The term society is a vague term that may refer to the persons who share a government, or who share an area of land, or who share a set of social relationships. A person may be a member of several societies—of a church society, a society of teachers or of engineers, of an English-speaking society, of a national society such as the United States of America or the Union of South Africa.

Each of these societies has a culture or subculture of its own. By a *culture,* we refer to the patterns and products of learned behavior: the etiquette, language, food habits, religious and moral beliefs, systems of knowledge, attitudes, and values; as well as the material things and artifacts produced—the technology—of a group of people.

A complex society such as that of the United States of America has both an overall culture, a way of life shared by all Americans, and a number of subcultures that are characteristic of subgroups. There are subcultures based upon ethnicity or country of origin—German, Polish, Italian—and others based on geographical differences, such as differences between rural and urban, or between different parts of the country such as the West Coast, New England, and the Deep South.

Members of such groups share a certain subculture when they have in common certain practices, beliefs, or attitudes that are not held by other American groups.

Social Classes as Subcultures

One type of social grouping that crosscuts ethnic, racial, and religious subcultures and is of particular importance to educators is social class. There are middle-class (as well as upper-class and working-class) Catholics, Protestants, Jews, German-Americans, Italian-Americans, blacks, and whites.

Social classes constitute subcultural groups. When people from the same social class meet and converse they soon find they have much in common, even though they may come from different ethnic or religious backgrounds or from different sections of the country. They will find that they live in much the same kinds of neighborhoods, have similar eating habits, dress in much the same ways, have similar tastes in furniture, literature, and recreation, and have about the same amount of education.

Changes in Social Classes

The social classes in America have been changing greatly in recent years, both in relative size and in life-styles. Due to technological development, the "working classes" or blue-collar workers have decreased in numbers compared with the "middle classes" or white-collar workers. In the larger cities and the metropolitan areas, there has been residential segregation by socioeconomic level or social class. This effectively segregates children in schools so that relatively few children attend school with a representative socioeconomic mix of pupils, and it tends to limit communication between youth of various social classes.

Furthermore, the upper-middle class is now experiencing a division between the majority group that follows cultural patterns set in the early years of the century and an emerging group with quite a different life-style described by Charles Reich in his best-selling book, *The Greening of America,* and that often is referred to as "the counterculture." The schools are affected by this emergent "counterculture," and the tension between the two life-styles is reflected in schools and colleges.

Another major change in social structure is the rise in numbers and in power of certain racial and national subcultures, mostly the black, Puerto Rican and Mexican-American groups. For these groups the educational system has the function of preparing their children for social and economic competence that will lead to middle-class positions in the society—or so, at least, is the view of the educational "establishment." In this view, just as the American educational system was the main agency for the "Americanization" of European immigrants from 1860 to 1915, teaching their children English and the mental and vocational skills that enabled them to "make good" in the new society, so the educational system is now the main agency for black, Puerto Rican and Mexican-American children to "make good."

But does the American school system or the American business and industrial system really provide much opportunity for the recent immigrants and for the nonwhite minorities to rise in income and social status? Can the black and Spanish-surname minorities make use of the educational system for their own advancement? We shall be studying this question in various ways in this book. Basically, we shall have to come to grips with the problem of *inequality* in human society.

BASIC INEQUALITIES IN AMERICAN SOCIETY

All human societies that we know about exhibit social inequality: that is, inequality in power, prestige, and material goods. Some societies, including the American society, regard inequality as a social fault, and strive for social equality; but no society has ever *achieved* social equality. "Social inequality is as old as human history, as universal as human societies. Everywhere and in every epoch there has existed some form of stratification with those at the top holding more privilege, power, and enjoying greater rewards than those at the bottom. Inequality, not equality, has been the predominant social rule by which most men at most times have lived." (Reissman, p. 9)

The American society, by its professions of faith and value, has worked for greater equality. The American educational system has explicitly and publicly worked for greater equality. It has not fully succeeded at this task, and some critics say it has failed miserably. The present-day student of education and society should study the record and make up his own mind about this basic issue. Then he can take his place in the continuing effort to realize the ideal of equality.

The facts about human inequality have to be taken fully into account; but this is no easy matter, for the facts do not add up to a simple straightforward story. We know there are inborn differences between individuals with regard to physique, sex, and qualities of the brain and nervous system. Some scientists believe there are inborn differences by race or by sex in the brain and nervous system which differentiate *groups* of people as well as individuals, and which have important implications for the educational system. Other scientists do not believe that such group differences exist. This is a major contemporary scientific controversy which the student of education needs to study and decide for himself.

Forms of Equality and Inequality

There are two forms of equality, quite different in fact, but sometimes confused in educational practice. One is equality of ability, or competence, or income. The other is equality of *opportunity*. To create equality of the first type is a vain hope. We know that individual human beings are almost never born equal in potential ability and never are equal in competence or achievement. But they can approach equality of opportunity to achieve their values, if a society provides a wide variety of choices and maximum freedom to choose. This is what a democratic society tries for, through its educational system as well as through other social provisions; and not only for individuals, but for groups of people.

There are two major forms of inequality in America—economic inequality (poverty) and ethnic inequality (racial and ethnic discrimination). At an earlier time, in the nineteenth and early twentieth centuries, it was widely believed that poverty was the fault of the individual, who could rise out of poverty if he tried hard enough. At the same time, members of certain racial or ethnic groups were thought by many Americans to be biologically inferior. Therefore it was said that these groups could not climb out of their inferiority by their own efforts, nor could society get them out of their difficulty.

Another view has it that both poverty and discrimination are faults of the society and the social structure. Society is the culprit. Americans now appear to view these two forms of inequality as chronic problems of American society. They see society as responsible—not the individuals who are poor, or who are members of a disadvantaged group. This view has given rise to attempted solutions to cure the society by legislation, by tax reform, by education, by religion, so as to give greater opportunity to the disadvantaged. We shall come back to these issues at later points in this book.

CHANGING VALUES

When a society changes its basic social and economic circumstances, its values change. Because the twentieth century is one of rapid and pervasive social change, the American society is going through pervasive and fundamental value changes.

The value changes are seldom as quickly visible as social and economic changes. Indeed, value changes appear at first in only a minority of people who are especially sensitive to the socioeconomic changes. Just now, in the mid-1970s, we are sensing a value change which has been underway for at least a decade. The very affluence of a highly productive industrial society makes people revise their valuation of affluence. When there is plenty of food, comfortable housing, television and automobiles for nearly every family, the people who own these things come to take them for granted, and to value them less highly than when they were scarce and were obtained only by work and sacrifice.

Instrumental vs. Expressive Activities

During the nineteenth and the first half of the twentieth centuries, the dominant thing about American society was its emphasis on the production of material goods. It was a quantity production society. The most highly prized activity of men and women was productive work; a man or woman was judged to be a good person if he or she was a good worker, and work was the principal source of self-esteem.

The most highly prized activities in American history have been *instrumental*: that is, activities that are a means to an end. Americans broke the sod of the prairies and planted grain to obtain more food. They dug for coal, drilled for oil, harnessed the power of the rivers, built railroads and factories, organized banks and corporations—all as instruments of greater material production. America became known for a life-style of *instrumental activism*.

But as production increased beyond their needs, the American people reduced their work week, reduced the value they placed upon work and upon saving, and upon doing things in the present for some material gain to come in the future. Instrumental activity lost some of its attractiveness. Instead, *expressive activity* gained in importance: that is, activity which is itself the goal. A person engages in an expressive activity for the sake of the activity itself, not for something that may result from it. Thus a person who studies a foreign language "for fun" is engaging in an expressive activity, while one who studies the foreign language in order to qualify for a certain job is engaging in instrumental activity.

The transition from the instrumental to the expressive is generating a quest for an enhanced quality of life which cannot be obtained by simply increasing material wealth. Americans are attempting to change to a *quality of life* society instead of the earlier *quantity production* society.

The fact that Americans have much more free time than they had a generation or a century ago gives them more options about the use of their time. The idea of work is changing in significance. For some people, work remains purely instrumental, a means to get money for material things. But for other people, work is partly expressive—something they enjoy doing for its own sake. Work is enjoyed especially by the people who have a good deal of training for their work, as in the professions, or by people who have achieved positions of responsbility, as in the management of business and industry. For such people, work is both instrumental and expressive. When asked about their hobbies, they say, "My hobby is my job." These people often take no vacations, and resist retirement, even though they do not need the money they earn by their extra work.

There are wide differences, but on the average it appears that Americans give less value to their jobs now than they did when earning a living was more time-consuming.

Almost every activity can be instrumental for some people and expressive for others. A quality of life society gives people a good deal of freedom of choice in the ways they use their time. It does not necessarily reduce the efficiency of the society in material productivity, although it reduces the value of material production and of work in the eyes of some people.

Contemporary Emergent Values

There is no doubt that Americans are undergoing a pervasive change of values, but there is much uncertainty about the exact nature of the new values that will emerge and that will direct American life and American education for the remainder of this century. A useful analysis of the current transformation of values is that of Getzels (1972) who describes a three stage scheme moving from

A: Traditional values (pre–World War II) to
B: Transitional values (late 1940s to middle 1950s) to
C: Emergent values (since 1965).

Getzels names four major value-themes, and follows them through the three stages as follows:

A_1, *Work-success* ethic, shifted to B_1, *Sociability* or easy social relations, and is now changing to C_1, *Social Responsibility* or an ethic of working to improve society.

A_2, *Future-time Orientation* and consequent self-denial for a better future, changed to B_2, *Present-time Orientation* or enjoying the present, and is now changing to C_2, *Relevance* or use of both past and present to fashion a meaningful life for the future.

A_3, *Independence* or self-direction changed to B_3, *Conformity* or adjustment to the society, and is now changing to C_3, *Authenticity* or doing your own thing with candor and spontaneity.

A_4, *Puritan Morality* changed to B_4, *Moral Relativism* or the morality of one's social group, and is now changing to C4, *Moral Commitment* to moral principles as a guide for action.

It will be noted that Getzels' emergent values are more instrumental than expressive, but they do have expressive qualities not possessed by the traditional values.

The transformation of values with related changes in behavior has been seen most clearly in the lives of a minority of young people who form the *counterculture*. The most visible expression has appeared on college campuses, with variants appearing in the communes or in the groups of young people who live together and make up a new kind of "family." (We will examine the counterculture in more detail in Chapter 10). It is possible that these young people are the forerunners of the future society.

An alternative possibility is a return to instrumental activism, together with a liberal socio-political ethic which favors greater equality among the social classes and among ethnic and national groups. This second alternative has been set forth by Peter Drucker, political scientist and social analyst. Based on the fact that job opportunities for young people have become restricted since 1970 due to the unusually large number of young in the population, Drucker (1971) argues that young people will compete with each other for these scarce jobs, and those who succeed will be the instrumental activists. Perhaps, then, these young people, rather than those who represent the counterculture, will determine the cultural tone and tempo of the 1980s.

Educational Implications

If values continue to change from instrumental to expressive, substantial changes in the educational system and in educational methods are likely to follow. Among these changes, there will probably be more self-directed education and at earlier ages; less differentiation between the sexes in the subjects studied and the careers chosen; more emphasis on education *as life,* rather than education *as preparation for life;* more selection of *service* careers as distinguished from *production* careers; and more emphasis on the arts and the humanities in schools, colleges, and adult education programs.

PLURALISM VS. ASSIMILATION OF MINORITIES

A pervasive change in contemporary society seems likely to develop out of the changing relations between the numerically dominant Caucasian group and the several racial and ethnic minorities. While Chapters 16, 17, and 18 will be devoted to this subject, we mention it here because it represents a change in American values. The blacks, who are the largest visible minority, are now making headway in economic and educational terms toward a less disadvantaged place in a pluralistic or culturally diversified society. The Orientals are growing in educational and economic status, and are already on a par with Caucasians in these respects. The Spanish-surname groups and the European ethnics are receiving more attention as separate cultural groups, with educational programs that help build pride in their ethnic identity. The simple "melting pot" or assimilation policy which has been ascribed (perhaps erroneously) to American education of the early decades of this century seems now to have little support among educators. Instead, cultural pluralism is coming to the fore. Pluralism means full recognition of cultural differences between racial, ethnic, and national groups, together with the devising of educational strategies whereby economic and social equality can be secured.

CONCLUSION

The educational system is functionally related to the society in which it operates. A changing society will require a changing educational system. In this chapter we have noted some of the major social changes that have occurred since the end of World War II, and some of the changes in values. Subsequent chapters will deal with the educational system as it reflects the changing American society.

EXERCISES

1. Try to sketch the biography of one of your grandparents, with special reference to his or her education and career development. Compare this with your own biography, that which is behind you and that which you think lies ahead.

2. If you live in a city with several visible minority groups, collect data from newspapers, lectures, public meetings, and interviews to assess the desire of these various groups for separate schools, churches, and social clubs.

3. Make a list of instrumental and of expressive activities in your life over the past few months. How closely do these balance each other? How do you think you compare with others of your group?

4. On your campus, what minority groups have a pattern of separatist behavior, and how do they demonstrate it?

SUGGESTIONS FOR FURTHER READING

1. Changes in the value orientations of Americans are described in books of sociological essays that have become best-sellers: *The Lonely Crowd* by David

Riesman and others*; *The Organization Man* by William A. Whyte, Jr.; and *The Affluent Society* by John K. Galbraith.

2. The popular paperback book by Charles Reich, *The Greening of America,* describes a new era in American culture which he calls *Consciousness III.* This book may be read in connection with a book of essays and critiques of the book edited by Philip Nobile and published as a paperback under the title *The Con III Controversy.*

3. For an overview of the cultural pluralism movement, read the *Phi Delta Kappan* for January, 1972.

*For each of these references, see Bibliography for facts of publication.

CHAPTER 2

Social Structure and the Schools of America

In the preceding chapter we defined the concept of culture and pointed out that there are many groups in the United States which have their own subcultures. The subcultures with which educators are most concerned are those of different social classes and those of different ethnic-minority groups. Because every social class contains several ethnic subgroups, and at the same time each ethnic group has two or more social classes, it is the *interaction* of social class with ethnic subcultures that makes the American society so dynamic and makes the work of the schools so complicated.

SOME FIFTH-GRADE CLASSROOMS

Schools reflect the diversity of American society, as can be seen in the following descriptions of fifth-grade classrooms.

A Fifth Grade in the Inner City

Mrs. Gordon stood at the girls' entrance to the grimy, red-brick school, making sure that the girls formed an orderly line ready to march inside when the buzzer sounded. She heard a scuffle behind her and a big eighth-grade girl landed on the ground beside her. "Damn you!" the girl shouted, and then looking up at Mrs. Gordon she said, "Teacher, they pushed me."

"Get back in line," said Mrs. Gordon. "How can we make the little children behave when you big girls act like that?" By this time the lines were moving

into the building. Mrs. Gordon followed them in and up to her own room on the third floor. The noise died down as she strode into the room and with a strong voice said, "Good morning, boys and girls."

Thirty-five boys and girls stood beside thirty-five desks in five rows, and, placing their hands over their hearts, they repeated the pledge of allegiance to the flag, "and to the Republic, for which it stands." Mrs. Gordon liked this ceremony. It was a symbol of unity in a variegated group which she sometimes called her "United Nations." About half of the youngsters were black, mostly very dark-skinned, but some light brown and yellow, barely distinguishable from several Mexicans in the class. There were four Puerto Ricans. Several children with Polish names, and three or four with Scotch names, who spoke a hillbilly English from Kentucky, were the only blondes in the room.

Mrs. Gordon had been teaching in the John T. McManus School in the Canalport district of Metropolis for 15 years. Previously she had taught in two schools which were known as "better schools" because the children came from families of professional men and lived in better houses. Most teachers liked these other schools, but Mrs. Gordon had not. The children had been argumentative with her—they would quote their fathers or mothers, or bring to school something they had read that didn't agree with her statements. The parents were always criticizing everything and everyone from the superintendent to the janitor. So when she heard of a vacancy in the McManus school, where the principal was known as good to work under, Mrs. Gordon had applied for transfer.

The John T. McManus school had been tutor to 13,000 children during its 75 years of existence. At first they were children of Irish immigrants. When the Irish moved out of Canalport to better houses farther from the factories of the neighborhood, the Bohemians and Hungarians moved in. Their children were followed by Italian and Polish children, and more recently these families were moving out, and blacks, Mexicans, and Puerto Ricans were coming in. The McManus school had some distinguished graduates, including three state senators and the present sheriff. At present it had the best eighth-grade basketball team in the city.

There were all types of children in her room, Mrs. Gordon thought. Of course, many were slow about learning. They would drop out of school as soon as they reached 16. But she could teach them a little more than their parents knew. There were a few bad ones. She was keeping her eyes on Juan Gomez, a tough, overage boy with a sullen expression. One day he had been annoying the boy sitting in front of him, and the boy had turned his head sharply and rammed it into Juan's open knife. The gash in his cheek had required five stitches. The principal had warned Juan that if he ever came to school with a knife again he would be sent to the special school for delinquent boys.

There were a few children in her room who would make good—maybe even in a big way, Mrs. Gordon thought. There was Maria, the Puerto Rican girl who had the looks and possibly the talent to become a great dancer. Mrs. Gordon took Maria to the settlement house and asked the Director to place the girl in a dance group. She told Maria's mother that the girl had talent and must be kept in school until she had learned enough English and enough manners to be accepted by the people she would have to work with if she became a dancer. There was also David Widder, the black boy who scored the highest in the class on an intelligence test. He was a good reader and good at arithmetic, and she thought he might become a scientist or a doctor. She told him this, and she told it to his father and mother whom she summoned to school. She told them about Donald Matthews, the highest ranking boy in her first class at McManus, also a black, who had just won a fellowship for graduate work in chemistry at the state university.

Mrs. Gordon knew that the great majority of her pupils would grow up to be hard-working, respectable people, and she was sure that they needed patient teaching and firm handling from her.

A Fifth Grade in a Suburb

Miss Bond was seated at her desk in a corner of the room as her fifth-graders came in from the schoolgrounds. A few gathered in little groups, talking to one another. Looking out the window, Miss Bond could see other children arriving, many of them in automobiles driven by their mothers, with occasionally a child coming in a long black Cadillac driven by a chauffeur. She could see the sloping curve of the lanscaped grounds. Now the last boy sauntered in, and the class was slowly getting to work, most of them at their desks grouped in one half of the room, while a few were sitting at worktables using reference books. It was a large, light, airy room, with green blackboards and green-colored bulletin boards. The fluorescent lights were not needed this morning, but it was cool, and the floor was comfortably warmed by inlaid heating coils.

Forest Park School was a show place, and Miss Bond felt fortunate to be able to work in such a fine building, in the finest suburb of the metropolis.

The children were all engrossed in work now. They were a good-looking lot, clean and sweet-smelling, as though, Miss Bond thought, they had come out of scented bedclothes. There was Estelle Woodford, taking charge of the committee, acting just like her mother who was president of the garden club. Tommy Beauregard raised his hand to ask for help. He was a plodder. She knew that he would work hard through high school and then through an Ivy League college, and then probably work up into the management of the company of which his father was president.

Helen Fischer sat in a corner, studying from a sixth-grade arithmetic book. She had finished the fifth-grade book and was going ahead on her own. The girl was too much on her own, thought Miss Bond. Dr. Fischer was a psychiatrist who had just bought a big house and moved his family out from the city. She would like to help Helen get on more friendly terms with the other children but she hardly knew how to go about it. She had thought of speaking to Mrs. Fairbairn, her PTA room mother, but Mrs. Fairbairn seemed so occupied with her own plans for the year's activities and so sure of how Miss Bond should fit into them that the teacher felt there was no room for her to make suggestions about the welfare of Helen Fischer.

Her relations with the mothers were different from what she had known in her previous job. She felt she had an accepted place with Forest Park mothers, and a respected place, but that she should not step out of it. Only twice had she been in the home of any of her pupils—and then to plan a school program. On these occasions she had been uncertain about what kind of dress to wear, and whether to wear gloves, and she had been uncomfortable. The women spoke of the eastern colleges they had attended, and suddenly the state teachers' college which had meant so much to her had become something to keep quiet about.

A Fifth Grade in a Ghetto School

Stanley King stood by the door of his classroom on the second floor of the Carver School, as the last two boys ran up the hall and dashed into his room. Closing the door behind him, he faced 32 black children. About half were in their seats; the others, mostly boys, were standing talking and a few pairs were shoving each other. He walked quietly to his desk, picked up the ruler, and struck it sharply twice on the table top.

"Get your arithmetic workbooks out for me to see," he said. "And if you have had trouble with any of your problems, this is the time to ask for help. Remember that city-wide test comes next week, and we aim to be just as good as any fifth grade in this building, and better than some." He walked over to Lewis, a big boy at the back of the room who was slow to take out his workbook, and noted that Lewis was behind most of the others in the number of problems he had worked. He leaned over and whispered, "Lewis, you'd better stay in after school for half an hour this afternoon and catch up some of those problems. I know you want to get out to play basketball, and I won't keep you long. But if you don't pass your arithmetic you'll never get to high school, even if you're the best basketball player in this school."

The Carver School served a ghetto area which included a big public housing project, and Mr. King knew the project well from visits he had made to talk with mothers. He was known and respected by children and parents alike as a teacher who did not tolerate "foolin'." The school principal, a black woman in her fifties, had made Carver a school that teachers like to work in. She had brought along three young white teachers as a means of promoting faculty integration, helping them with discipline problems and bringing them into contact with those parents who could make them feel at home. She counted on black teachers like Stanley King to help maintain morale among the teachers, but she also encouraged him to work on his master's degree and to take the principals' examination. "You can go right up in this system," she told him. "There will be more black principals than white appointed during the next five years."

Stanley came from a black family that was well regarded in the community. His father was a post office clerk; his mother had worked in the home of a fashionable white family, but now was doing community work on an Urban League project. Stanley had been active in his church; he had done well in high school and in the local teachers college. His wife worked as a secretary in a law office downtown, but she would soon take time off to have their

17

first baby. They lived in an apartment in a middle-class black residential district.

As he moved around the quiet room, he felt very much attracted to these boys and girls, but he knew that they were making very slow academic progress, and that at least half of them would be two years or more behind national norms in reading and arithmetic when they finished the eighth grade. What should he do about this? Should he join the group of dissidents who were about to demand from the school board a building where they could put all of their experimental ideas to work? Maybe he could find out how to help these youngsters make the most of the talents and values of the black community. He was attracted to the leader of this group, a militant Afro-American whom the school administration and the school board did not fully trust. But he also could visualize himself in the shoes of the deputy superintendent, a hard-working black educator who was called an "uncle Tom" by the more militant blacks in the city.

Stanley King was going to have to make a decision, and he knew he had to make it himself.

These merely illustrate the variety of American classrooms and of American teachers. We might have chosen a typical classroom in a small midwestern city, one in the East Los Angeles Chicano district, or one in a Polish Catholic school in Milwaukee.

The teachers are different in background and in style of teaching, but all of them know they must fit their classroom activities to the life-styles and to the educational needs of the families whose children attend the school. Because life-styles and educational needs are closely related to social class, educators need to understand the social-class structures of their communities and the subcultures of different social classes.

As we shall see in the chapters that follow, by knowing the social-class composition of a school or a classroom, a teacher in the middle grades or high school can anticipate such important characteristics of the group as these:

1. the general level of educational achievement;
2. the educational aspirations, (for example, whether the majority will be interested in job training, or in college entrance);
3. the drive for achievement, and the willingness to postpone gratification (that is, to do things that are difficult or uncomfortable in the expectation that they will bring future gain);
4. some of the experiences the child will have had in his family before he entered school as well as some of the experiences in the family and the neighborhood that he is likely to have during his school years. (For example, children from one social class can be expected to have had a different kind of intellectual stimulation during the pre-school years than children from other social classes.)

While we shall consider the family in greater detail in Chapter 7, at this point it may be said that, compared with race, religion, or ethnicity, social class is in most instances the main determinant of family experiences that contribute to or hinder a child's mental development and that will affect a child's progress in school. (Havighurst, 1971b)

THE SOCIAL-CLASS HIERARCHY

A social-class group consists of people who have similar social habits and values. One of the tests of membership in a social class is that of association, actual or potential. In a small community, the members of a particular social class tend to belong to the same social organizations and to entertain one another in their homes. If they live in a big city, their numbers are so large that only a few can actually associate with one another; yet, even in large cities, if members of the same social class meet as strangers they soon recognize a good deal of similarity in their ways of life, and recognize each other as social equals.

The various social classes are organized into an overall hierarchical structure.

Most persons recognize that they occupy a position on a social scale. They acknowledge that there are other people and other groups that have more or less economic or political power or social prestige than their own group. Within a particular community, people can rank themselves and their neighbors according to power or prestige; that is, they can assign different individuals to particular positions on a "social ladder."

All societies, large or small, primitive or modern, show this phenomenon of rank: the leaders and people of high prestige occupy positions at the top; others occupy intermediate positions; and still others are at the bottom of the social scale. This is true regardless of the political form of government. A democracy has rank; so does an absolute monarchy; so also does a communist society such as the Soviet Union. While the king and the nobility are at the top in a monarchy, the top people in the Soviet Union are the leaders of the Communist Party and the high government and military officials. In a democracy the people at the top are those who have earned or inherited economic power or social prestige.*

*Some people, when they first become acquainted with the idea of social classes, tend to deny their existence in America because they feel they are undemocratic. Yet all of us are aware that differences in social rank exist in any community, whether or not we use the term "social class" in describing them. The reader can refer to his own community and will recognize that there are certain people in it who are considered "the best families" or "the elite," others who are "the leaders" or "pillars of the community," others who are "just nice, respectable people" or "the working people," still others who are "poor, but honest" or "good people, but nobody," and still others who are "bottom of the heap." We Americans speak of people who have "gone a long way up," or "climbed the social ladder," or of people who have "dropped a notch." We speak, too, of marrying "above" or "below" one's own position and of having made "good" or "poor" marriages.

Whatever the terms used in a particular group, such expressions refer clearly to a social organization characterized by different levels of rank and prestige.

19

Dimensions of social class

Kahl (1957) has delineated the major *dimensions* that underlie the American social-class structure (and that sociologists measure when they undertake empirical studies of stratification) as follows:

1. Prestige. Some people in the community have more personal prestige than others, and are regarded by others with respect and deference.
2. Occupation. Some occupations are considered "higher" than others, partly because they are more important to the welfare of the community, partly because they require special talents, and partly because they pay high rewards.
3. Possessions, or wealth, or income.
4. Social interaction. In a large community, everyone cannot interact with everyone; patterns of differential contact arise; and people are more comfortable with "their own kind."
5. Class consciousness. The degree to which people at given levels are aware of themselves as distinctive social groupings. Americans are said to be less class conscious than Europeans; yet Americans, too, think of themselves as "working-class" or "middle-class"; and a large proportion identify "on the side of management" or "on the side of labor."
6. Value orientations. People differ about the things they consider good or important; and groups of people come to share a limited number of abstract values or value systems.
7. Power, or the ability to control the actions of other people. Kahl points out that this variable, while it is important in determining social class, cannot be measured directly. It can be studied indirectly, however, by delineating the cliques of important people in a community; or by studying the people who control the capital wealth of a community.

Although each of the first six dimensions may be considered independently, all seven are interdependent; they interact to form the basis of the social-class structure. Thus, for example, a person is often granted prestige on the basis of his occupation. Similarly, people with high incomes tend to be persons in certain occupations; they tend to interact with people in the community who are like themselves; they are accorded considerable prestige; and they tend to occupy powerful positions with regard to community organizations: civic, political, or economic. In somewhat different words, persons who are high (or low) on one dimension tend to be high (or low) on the others.

Studying the Social Structure

Although various sociologists have chosen to highlight one or another of the dimensions listed above in undertaking studies of social stratification, we are primarily concerned with studies of American communities according to the methods developed by W. Lloyd Warner and his associates (Warner, Meeker, and Eells, 1960). These investigators stressed the dynamics of community organization; that is, they focused upon prestige and the patterns of social interaction that constitute the social life of a community.

The usual procedure was for the social scientist to move into the community and live there for a time, conversing with people and observing the social scene. He discovered the social groups that existed; he talked with the members of various social groups and asked about the social structure of the community. He learned who associated with whom, who were considered the "top" people, who the "bottom," and why. Gradually he pieced together a picture of the community as it was viewed by its members. Seldom did any one citizen see the whole structure of his community clearly, but the social scientist combined the views of many people into a single composite picture representing the consensus. This picture showed groups of people arranged in a network, but arranged also on a social scale from top to bottom in terms of the status assigned them by their fellow citizens.

After the major lines of the social structure has been delineated, and after the positions of a few key people had been agreed upon, it was possible to locate other people in relation to the original persons. Eventually the majority of the population could be located on the social map in this way.*

This method, of course, worked well only in small communities, where it was possible to meet with, or at least find out about, practically every adult inhabitant. Somewhat different methods had to be devised for use in metropolitan areas, as will be described later on in this chapter.

SOCIAL STRUCTURE IN AMERICA

The results of a score of community studies enabled social scientists to draw certain general conclusions about social structure in the United States. In general, there is a basic five-class structure. (See Figure 2.1, page 25.) The proportion of people in each class varies depending upon the size, the age, and the economic character of a given community. Thus, in comparison with the country as a whole, a community in a coal-mining or steel-mill area is likely to

---

*This method of mapping the social system and of discovering the social class of a particular person is called the "method of evaluated social participation," often abbreviated as E.P. First, by interviewing members of the community, the major lines of social structure were ascertained, and the names obtained of a few people who interviewers agreed occupied given positions in the structure. It was then noted with whom these people associated in social clubs, informal social cliques, service clubs, church associations, and so on. Thus other people were placed in relation to the original group. Eventually the majority of the population was placed in this way. Then, if the social scientist wished to know the social status of Mr. X, whose name had not previously been brought into the study, he asked who Mr. X's friends were, what clubs or associations he belonged to, and then found that Mr. X was close to one of the groups already defined on the social map. Mr. X's social participation was thus *evaluated* in relation to that of others in the community, and his place in the social structure was *determined*.

have a higher proportion of working-class people, while a community with a college or university is likely to have a higher proportion of upper-middle-class people. If the economic situation of a community changes drastically, the social structure of that community is likely to change also.

Small Communities

It is very common for Americans, particularly if they live in small, self-contained communities (that is, communities that are not satellites of big cities) to stress equalitarianism and to play down, or deny, the existence of social classes. At the same time they recognize that there are different "types" of people in their community. As a respected citizen of Jonesville, a city of 6,000, explained:

> Almost everyone in this town is rated in some way; people can rate you in just a few minutes by talking to you. It's remarkable how you can size people up in a hurry—suppose I use a rating scale of zero to 100 and rate people on it. You can be sure this is not a hypothetical thing either. Not to the people of Jonesville. People like the Caldwells and Volmers ... rate 100. The Shaws would be up there, too. People like me, oh, a 70 maybe, and people like John (a janitor) about a 40, no better than that. Remember, this is the social rating. If we rated them financially, some of them would rank differently. (Warner and associates, 1949, p. 22.)

This man did not speak of social classes as such; however, he recognized that his community reflected a social hierarchy.

The Small Rural Community.   Studies of extremely small communities, villages ranging from a few hundred in population up to about 1,500, generally showed a three-class structure consisting of an upper-middle class, a lower-middle class, and a few families at the very bottom. Class lines in these communities were relatively indistinct as compared to larger communities, and there was more social intercourse between classes (Barker and Wright, 1954; Havighurst and Morgan, 1951; Bailey, 1953).

The Small City

Cities with a population from about 5,000 to 15,000 tended to exhibit a five-class structure. A good example is a midwestern community that was described under the names of Jonesville, Elmtown, and Midwest (Warner and associates, 1949; Hollingshead, 1949; Warner, Meeker, and Eells, 1960.). This city had a population of about 6,000, and represented the most common type of small city in the north central states—a county seat, with both an industrial and an agricultural population.

In this community, the upper class constituted about three percent of the population. Some of them were the descendants of a pioneer settler who, a hundred years earlier, had acquired large tracts of farmland which had now become the best real estate in the city. Others were executives of a small factory, or they were the owners of the banks, the largest farms, and the most profitable businesses.

The upper-middle class contained about 10 percent of the population and consisted mainly of professional men, business executives, and owners of businesses and of large farms. The lower-middle class, about 30 percent of the whole, consisted mainly of white-collar workers, owners of small retail businesses, a few foremen and skilled manual workers, and the bulk of the prosperous farmers. These people were said by those in the classes above them to be "nice people," but social "nobodies."

The working class, numerically the largest group with 35 to 40 percent of the population, were described as "poor but honest" people who worked as skilled and unskilled laborers or as tenant farmers.

The lowest class, about 15 percent, consisted partly of people who were working hard to maintain a respectable kind of poverty and partly of people who seemed to the rest of the community to be generally immoral, lazy, and defiant of the law.

After the Jonesville studies were made, two other midwestern communities, one of 40,000 and one of 100,000, were studied. In these communities essentially the same picture of social structure emerged (Havighurst et al., 1962; Eells et al., 1951).

A somewhat more complicated six-class social structure had been found, however, in a New England community of about 17,000 called "Yankee City," the first community to be studied by these methods (Warner and Lunt, 1941). In that community, there were two upper-class groups: an "upper-upper," consisting of families who traced their lineage back to colonial times and who had had wealth and high social position for several generations; and a "lower-upper" group or *nouveaux riches,* families who had moved into the community more recently, and whose money had been acquired for the most part in the present generation or in the one just preceding. There was a clear separation between these two groups in terms of their social participation.

The Large City

In a large city it is impossible for the sociologist to analyze social-class differences on the basis of actual social participation (who associates with whom), for only a handful of people are known to each other and any given pattern of face-to-face interaction can involve only a small number of the total population.

In attempting to study the social structure of the metropolitan area of

Kansas City in the late 1950's, however, investigators found that residents made consistent evaluations of various *symbols* of status (Coleman and Neugarten, 1971). Kansas Citians had a highly developed awareness of the status hierarchy in their community; and, although the average citizen could name only some of the persons who were at the top and some who were at the bottom of the social ladder, he nevertheless ranked his fellow residents on the basis of such dimensions of status as area of residence, quality of housing, occupation, club membership, ethnic identification, and so on. Thus, for example, Kansas Citians were particularly aware of the prestige ranking of various neighborhoods and tended readily to "locate" persons on the social ladder according to their home addresses.

As anticipated, the heterogeneity and complexity of the large city produced a much more highly differentiated social structure than in a small town. Thirteen different social strata were visible, each stratum representing a gradation on the social scale. At the same time, the basic five-class system seemed applicable. There were five "core" groups of people, readily distinguishable on the basic social characteristics mentioned above; with each of the other eight groups forming a variant of one of the basic patterns; and with greater differences appearing between the five larger groups than between the 13 smaller ones.*

Large cities then can be described in terms of the basic five-class structure, granted that there will be many subgroups. The proportions of people in the five classes are probably roughly the same as those for small cities. In Kansas City, for instance, the percents of the population in the five social classes were estimated to be, from upper to lower, 2.5, 11, 32, 40, and 14, proportions which agree quite closely with the proportions in smaller communities as shown in Figure 2.1.

In the same way, Hodges (1968) after studying the "Peninsula" area of California (from San Francisco through San Jose) and after studying data obtained from almost 2,000 heads of households in the area, summarized the social structure as a five-class structure.

The Metropolitan Area

In huge metropolitan areas such as New York, Chicago, or Los Angeles, a large proportion of residents will neither be sufficiently acquainted with vari-

---

*The study of Kansas City stands midway, in a sense, between studies of social structure in smaller communities based upon the method of E.P. (see footnote, page 21), and studies of social stratification based on particular indices of socioeconomic status such as level of education or occupation. The essential difference lies in the fact that neither social participation itself, nor the objective indices themselves, but the *evaluations* of these *indices* as made by the residents of the community formed the basis of the study. Thus, as one of the dimensions of status, persons were not ranked according to the economic value of their houses but according to the prestige assigned *by fellow* residents to the neighborhood in which the house was located.

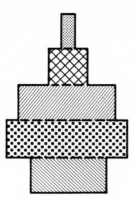

Upper (1 to 3%)

Upper-middle (7 to 12%)

Lower-middle (20 to 35%)

Upper-working (25 to 40%)

Lower-working (15 to 25%)

FIGURE 2.1.   A national view of the social-class structure. (Source:
The percentages presented are derived from a number
of studies of the social structure made in communities
ranging from 5,000 to 500,000 in population; the percentage ranges show how a given class varies in size.)

ous neighborhoods (except in very gross terms) nor with particular clubs and
associations to assign them prestige ranks; and some of the other dimensions
of status used in Kansas City will not be applicable. It is relatively useless to
attempt to study the status structure of the large metropolitan area on the
basis of patterns of social participation or evaluated symbols of status. Instead, the sociologist relies on socioeconomic indices such as occupation,
level of education, or income—indices that have been shown to be highly related to social status positions in smaller communities (Warner, Meeker, and
Eells, 1960).

The same is true in making generalizations concerning the social structure of the society at large; sociologists for the most part must use socioeconomic variables as indices of social status, and social classes are defined
most frequently as groups that vary according to occupation or according to
educational levels. We shall return to this point shortly, after describing social
classes as subcultures, but it should be pointed out that there is good empirical evidence to show that, in this as in other industrialized countries, occupations and/or levels of education follow a consistent prestige ranking. In
other words, to know a man's occupation is to enable one to predict, with a
large degree of accuracy, his social status in his own community and in the
society at large.

In the chapters to follow in this book we shall be referring to social
classes that have been differentiated on the basis of socioeconomic indices
rather than on the basis of direct evidence of status or of evaluated participation. As will be seen from the following descriptions, however, the concept of a social class refers primarily to a way of life and a set of attitudes
and values that are common to members of the group, ways of life that are

only approximated by discrete items of information such as occupation, education, or income.

SUBCULTURES OF THE SOCIAL CLASSES

Finding that people can be described as belonging to different classes is only a first step. How do the class groups differ in behavior, in beliefs, in attitudes, in values? In other words, what is the subculture that characterizes each of the social-class groups?

In describing subcultures we will make use of the five-class structure that has been found to be characteristic of American communities, even though this is an oversimplification, especially of the complex metropolitan area. The following descriptions are based upon studies carried out in large cities (such as Kansas City) and larger geographical areas (such as the San Francisco peninsula) as well as in smaller communities. While they are only thumbnail sketches and thus cannot do justice to the variety of patterns to be found at each class level, they should suffice to point up the most salient differences in styles of life as these differences bear upon the educational system.

It should be remembered that the classes are in many respects more alike than they are different. People of all classes, for instance, share the modern American mass culture; they read the same newspapers, go to the same movies, listen to the same music, watch the same television programs and commercials. Many social scientists such as Riesman (1950) and Hodges (1968) believe that the mass culture is obliterating class differences, particularly between the lower-middle and the working classes.

The following descriptions apply to the majority of people in a given social class, but not to every person in the class. There are many people who share the major socioeconomic characteristics of a given social class, but who do not follow its way of life in all respects. There are also large numbers of persons who will show "status discrepancies," or inconsistencies; that is, they will rank higher on some of the dimensions of status than on others.

Upper Class

Upper-class people generally have inherited wealth, and usually have a family tradition of social prominence that extends back several generations. A few may not be wealthy, but as the respected cousins, nieces, or nephews of upper-class families, they also belong in the upper class. All these people will be listed in the *Social Register* (if the community has one) and will belong to the most exclusive social clubs. They are likely to be well-versed in family history.

Upper-class people belong to the boards of directors of art museums, of symphony and opera associations, or of Ivy League colleges. They tend to support charitable organizations, chambers of commerce, and the Republican Party (in the North). In older New England communities, their support was often silent ("the power behind the throne") and they left the offices in these organizations to be filled by upper-middle-class people. In newer and in larger cities, however, they are likely to be indistinguishable from upper-middles in this respect and are visible as community leaders. Upper-class people usually belong to the Protestant Episcopal, Presbyterian, or Congregational churches in the Midwest, or to the Unitarian or Congregational churches in New England. Relatively few are Catholics or Jews.

Only rarely do upper-class people indulge in conspicuous consumption—showy parties, ostentatious mansions with numerous servants, jewels, and furs. Their houses, gardens, summer places, automobiles, and clothes are more likely to be conservative and inconspicuous (but in "the best of taste").

In the eyes of upper-class people, education is a matter of proper rearing; formal schooling is no more important in this connection than are other aspects of training that children need if they are to fill their adult roles properly. Training for an occupation is not of primary importance, since these children will inherit high status and cannot go any higher by occupational success. Nevertheless, the occupation must be of the "right" type for the upper class. Young men go into business or into one of the higher status professions such as architecture, medicine, law, and (infrequently) the ministry in an upper-status denomination. Boys and girls generally attend private schools and the prestige Ivy League and selective women's colleges.

Upper-Middle Class

About half of the adult members of this class have climbed to their present status from lower beginnings. Hence this class seems to be made up largely of active, ambitious people. The men are business executives and professional men; the women are active in club work, PTA, and civic organizations, and a number work as professionals or technicians. The members of this class do not have aristocratic family traditions. Although some are interested in building up such traditions, the typical comment is, "We do not care about our ancestors. It isn't *who* you are, but *what* you are."

The great bulk of positions of leadership in civic, business, and professional organizations are held by upper-middle-class people—organizations such as Rotary and Kiwanis clubs, the League of Women Voters, the Chamber of Commerce, the Medical Society, the Ministerial Association, the Bar Association, and the National Association for the Advancement of Colored People.

Hodges (1968) has labelled these people the "Americans of 'tomorrow,'" pointing out that they have been the first group to accept many now-standard innovations and gadgets, such as the split-level home, the sport car, the backyard barbecue, and hi-fi music. Their homes are medium to large in size; houses usually have a flower garden or lawn, and a recreation room or a wood-working shop in the basement; apartments are large and located in good residential areas of the city.

The upper-middle-class family may be a quite wealthy family, with money earned in the present generation; more usually the income is "adequate," enough to pay for a comfortable home, a new automobile every few years, a fair-sized insurance and pension plan, college education for the children, and some left over for modest investment in stocks and bonds.

Most such families patronize the theater and the symphony concerts, and they read such periodicals as *Harper's Magazine*, the *Atlantic Monthly*, and the *New Yorker*.

Active church leaders come mainly from this class. The most favored churches are Presbyterian, Congregational-Christian, Methodist, Baptist (in the Middle West) and Unitarian (in New England). There are also numerous Roman Catholic, Lutheran, and Jewish upper-middle-class people. Most members of this class are native-born Americans, and most of them have native-born parents and grandparents.

Upper-middle-class people stress harmonious relations with others; they want to be flexible, tolerant, and nondogmatic. In the California suburban area studied by Hodges (1968), the upper-middle parents were found to be less anxious and more easy-going in rearing their children than lower-middle and working-class parents.

Education is extremely important to people in this group. Many of them have risen into this class through professional careers, and they feel that it is almost essential that their children secure a college degree if they are to maintain upper-middle status in the next generation. The children generally go to public schools, and then to the state university or to privately supported liberal arts colleges including Ivy League colleges in the East.

As was noted in Chapter 1, the upper-middle class is now undergoing a major shift in values, with the major force of the counterculture coming from upper-middle-class young people aged about 15 to 35. It is probably incorrect to speak of upper-middle-class values as though the phrase referred to a tightly knit subculture.

Lower-Middle Class

This large group is often called the "common man" group by those above them in the social scale, although they themselves think of the working-class people below them as being the "common man."

The lower-middle class consists of white-collar clerical and sales workers. Some are factory foremen or members of the "labor aristocracy" such as railroad engineers, conductors, photoengravers; some are small building, electrical, and plumbing contractors. Most farm owners who operate their own farms are also in this class. These people tend to be at the "national average"; their income is at about the middle of the national income range, and the magazines, sports, TV programs, movie stars, and comic strips that they prefer tend also to be the national favorites.

Lower-middle-class people stress thrift and are proud of their economic independence (although Hodges found that lower-middle-class people in suburbia were likely to be living above their means). Their houses are usually comfortably furnished and well kept, but small to medium in size and located nearer the "wrong part of town," or in inexpensive suburban tracts.

This group makes up the bulk of members of fraternal organizations such as the American Legion and their corresponding women's auxiliaries. They are fairly active in the PTA, and they furnish the bulk of membership in the Protestant and Catholic Churches. They also furnish the lay leadership of some churches, especially the Baptist, the Lutheran, and in many places the Methodist churches. Many lower-middle-class people are Catholics, and some are Jews. This class has in it appreciable numbers who are children or grandchildren of immigrants.

Most members of the lower-middle class finished high school, and approximately half their children go on to college, generally a junior college. Schooling is considered essential for a good job, and the children are expected to be obedient pupils. In the suburbs, lower-middle-class and working-class people often live in the same developments and have many characteristics in common. In time, the two classes may become enough alike to be considered together as the "common man" group.

Upper-Working Class*

The "respectable working people," the skilled and semi-skilled "blue-collar" (as opposed to "white-collar") workers, make up the working class. They are often Catholics, but there are also considerable numbers in the fundamentalist Protestant denominations such as the Assembly of God, the Pentecostal, and Holiness churches. They are also frequently Baptists and Methodists and, in the big eastern cities, Jews. At the same time, a considerable minority of this group are not church members, and some are hostile to churches.

Working-class people in small towns and cities live "across the tracks"

---

*In earlier studies of social structure undertaken by Warner's methods, this social class was referred to as "upper-lower," and the bottom class as "lower-lower." While it is not easy to find substitute terms which are free of implied derogation, the present authors have chosen the terms "working class" and "upper-working class" and "lower-working class" as at least somewhat less biased, and as reflecting more accurately the fact that most persons at the lowest social level are also workers. At the same time, to do as certain other sociologists have done and to draw no distinctions within the working class is to obliterate some very significant differences between the large group of stable, blue-collar workers at the "common man" level and the smaller group who in many respects stand apart from all the other levels of society by virtue of poverty and other social and economic deprivations.

or "on the wrong side of town" in small houses that are usually well kept. The working class has enjoyed a considerable increase in real income in recent years, particularly in the big cities, which has enabled increasing numbers to buy homes in inexpensive suburban tracts. Working-class people are as fond of labor-saving gadgets as middle-class people, and frequently show concern about "keeping up with the Joneses" by buying more household equipment, newer and bigger cars, and by frequently remodeling their homes. Wives expect to add to the family income by working, when they are not tied down with children.

Working-class people seldom join civic organizations. The men belong to veterans' organizations and occasionally to fraternal orders. Their wives join the ladies' auxiliaries and are often members of PTA when the children are small. The men enjoy hunting and fishing; but most working-class people spend their leisure time at home, watching TV, working in the vegetable garden, or "fixing up around the house." They seldom read more than the local newspaper and one or two magazines.

Typically, working-class adults put little value upon learning for learning's sake, but they recognize that education is the key to a good job, and they want their children to go further in school than they themselves have gone. At present most of the children from this social class complete high school, and many go on to the local college or junior college.

Lower-Working Class

Most of society looks down on this group, using such terms as "the lower element" or "people of the slums." Lower-working-class people are easy to stereotype because they live in highly visible and often shockingly poor quarters—big city slums or low-income public housing developments; shacks on "the flats" at the edges of cities; or tenant farmers' cabins. Miller (1964) has distinguished four groups within this class: the "stable poor," unskilled workers who have steady jobs and a stable family life; the "strained," who have steady jobs but who have major family or personality difficulties; "the copers," people who have economic difficulties but strong family relations, and who manage to get along most of the time; and the "unstable," people who have both financial and familial or personal problems and who may end up on the welfare rolls as "multiproblem" cases.

According to origin, lower-class people may be divided into at least two groups. There are those who have been at the bottom of the social structure for several generations. There are also the newest immigrants who perform the most menial tasks of the society while they are learning American ways of life. In the past, such people were frequently Irish, German, Swedish, or Polish. Today they are primarily Puerto Ricans, Mexican-Americans or black or white tenant farmers from the poorer rural areas who have moved to the city. Most migratory farm laborers also belong to this class.

Lower-working-class people have few occupational skills and frequently have less than a grade school education. Many have difficulty finding jobs because of their color. Because they are "the last to be hired and the first to be fired" they have difficulty acquiring job seniority. A business recession that has only a slight effect upon the other classes will put many lower-working-class people out of work, swelling the relief rolls. Many people in this class spend a great deal of time seeking work—work that will provide a meal ticket for the family. Many families are constantly in debt. It is not surprising that many of these people believe that diligence and thrift have little to do with getting ahead, and that only by "luck" or "connections" will they ever better themselves.

These people often distrust persons with unfamiliar skills, strangers, or persons who represent government agencies. For insurance against trouble they look to their network of mutual-help relationships with relatives. Lower-class people in suburbia were found by Hodges (1968) to visit their relatives more often than the members of any other class. For many, welfare is seen as a last resort.

Some lower-working-class people are members of fundamentalist Protestant churches, some are Catholics, but many are unattached to any church. They seldom belong to formal organizations, except occasionally to a labor union.

This group began to draw a great deal of attention in the mid-1960s with the "war on poverty," and the large-scale government programs organized under the Office of Economic Opportunity. Its size has been variously estimated. All thoughtful observers agree, of course, that all poor people are not of low social status, in the sense that the term "lower-class" is often used. For example, there are large numbers of older people in the population whose reduced incomes place them in the "poverty" group; and there are the differentiations made by Miller (1964) and others between various types of "respectable" and "unrespectable" poor.

Families of this class produce a large share of "problem" children in the schools: the slow learners, the truants, the aggressive, and the delinquent. These children draw a good deal of attention from the educational authorities. Identified as needing "compensatory education," some get considerable help from remedial reading specialists, counselors, truant officers, and more recently, volunteer tutors.

SOCIAL STRUCTURE: A NATIONWIDE VIEW

Not all sociologists agree that the social structure of the United States is fairly represented by the five-class hierarchy shown in Figure 2.1. For one thing the economic and technological changes occurring in American society are producing raised standards of living and changed relationships between various classes. From certain perspectives, the differences between classes are becoming obliterated. For instance, the lines between upper class and upper-middle class seem to be disappearing, with less emphasis given to lineage in all but the oldest and most conservative communities, and with upper-status people taking active leadership roles in community affairs. Blue-collar workers have had greater relative gains in income over the past two decades than white-collar workers, and patterns of buying and spending have become more similar between these two groups.

From other perspectives, the differences between social classes are becoming sharpened—as, for instance, between the group on public assist-ance in metropolitan and rural areas and all the other groups in the society.

Some observers describe the American social-class structure as a three-class system in which there is a growing upper-middle class that en-compasses the old upper class; then a huge, increasingly undifferentiated "common man" or blue-and-white-collar working class; and a "lower" class of unskilled, public-assistance families, sometimes referred to as the "hope-less" class. Mayer (1963) for one, describes the changing social-class out-lines of America not as a pyramid, but as approximating a diamond in which there are small groups of nonmobile people at both the top and the bottom, with all the rest of society in between, and in which gradations in the undif-ferentiated middle are so numerous and so gradual that class lines are relatively obliterated.

Other sociologists go further. While they do not deny differences in rank, they feel that class lines cannot be drawn at all in an "open" society like our own, where there is so much movement or mobility up and down; where networks of informal social interaction overlap friendship, clique, and membership groups to form a series of gentle gradations; and where, accordingly, the concept of social class itself lacks meaning.

Social classes can be thought of, however, as *conceptually* discrete, even though, in an increasingly urbanized society, the social scientist finds it difficult to establish empirically the boundaries between classes. In this view, social classes can be described in terms of averages; classes differ, *on the average,* by income, by occupational level, by attitudes toward education, and by other value systems that we have been describing. People who rank high on one class indicator such as education will tend to rank high on others such as occupation or income; yet there will be many exceptions. Probably everyone has met such exceptions: a successful businessman who never completed high school; a service station operator who has a college degree; a social worker who lives in the slum neighborhood in which he works; a graduate student who is scraping along on a very meager income.

However, people whose characteristics are very different from the average on many characteristics of their class will be very possibly in the process of moving into the class immediately above or immediately below their own. As we shall show in the next chapter, there is a great deal of movement between classes. A modern democratic society always has open social classes; that is, people are able to move from one to another class according to their ability and effort.

SOCIAL-CLASS SEGREGATION
IN THE SCHOOLS

When a city is as large as 10,000 in population, it generally shows some degree of residential segregation by social class. There is a "country club" district, and a "slum district," and other in-between areas. Therefore, the elementary schools, serving small residential districts, tend to differ in their social-class composition, while the single high school of the city includes pupils from all social classes.

A city of 50,000 or more shows a greater degree of social-class segregation, generally with two high schools, one of definitely higher social status than the other. And a city as large as 100,000 is likely to be sufficiently segregated along social-class lines, residentially, to have elementary schools of almost complete middle-class composition and others of almost complete working-class composition.

Most educators believe that schools of mixed social-class composition tend to produce greater social equality in the society, for children from different social classes are thus given the opportunity to learn each other's attitudes and values. Accordingly some educators have hoped to change social-class segregation patterns in the schools in something of the same way that racial segregation patterns have been changed. We shall return in later chapters to issues of racial segregation, but here it should be pointed out that persons of different social classes often have strong negative attitudes toward other social classes and these attitudes are directly reflected in the organization of the school system.

A striking example is Duluth, Minnesota, a city of 100,000 which has been stable for several decades, with no suburbs and with a complete cross section of social classes. The population is 97 percent white, and the school enrollment in 1972 consisted of approximately 23,000 pupils, including only 390 Indian, 268 black, 74 Oriental, and 56 Spanish-surnamed. Thus the major population differences in Duluth are those of social class, not race or ethnicity.

In 1971 the Duluth School Board approved a social-class desegregation plan to go into effect the following September. The impetus came from publication by the Minnesota State Board of Education of a set of "guidelines" for racial desegregation in the schools of the state. The guidelines defined a segregated school as one that has "a student body consisting of 30 percent or more minority-group students, or 30 percent or more students from low-income families, or 30 percent or more of *a combination of minority-group students and students from low-income families.*"

In that year, six of the 32 elementary schools in Duluth had more than 30 percent low-income pupils. (Those six schools all averaged below the national average—at about the 40th percentile—on achievement tests, while the other Duluth schools were all above the national average—above the 50th percentile). It appeared that Duluth would be a good place to put these guidelines into effect.

The Duluth plan provided that some pupils would be assigned to nearby schools that were more nearly middle-class in composition; pupils from middle-class families might go to the formerly lower-class schools; and similar changes would occur in the high schools.

After the plan was voted, social and political pressures arose against it. The outcome was that in May 1972, the Duluth School Board voted 7 to 2 to postpone indefinitely the plan it had earlier approved. Duluth had found it difficult to pioneer in socioeconomic integration. This illustrates the importance of social-class distinctions in the minds of a great many Americans. The concern seems to be primarily with regard to the lower-working class, whose children are not welcomed in the same schools with other children.

SOCIAL CLASS IN RELATION TO ETHNIC AND RACIAL MINORITY GROUPS

When an ethnic or racial minority grows large enough in numbers, and when the surrounding society offers opportunity for some of its members to secure property and to enter occupations that command power and leadership, that minority group develops a social-class structure like the larger group around it. Accordingly, socioeconomic and social-class differentiations have become clearer among blacks in America in the past two decades. Some indication of this fact is given in Table 3.2 in the next chapter. As of 1970, 19 percent of black men were in white-collar or middle-class occupations, while the remainder were in various working-class occupations.

Social-class differentiations are true within other minority groups, also, especially the Mexican-Americans and the Spanish-surname groups.

The Spanish-surname or Spanish-origin people in America consist of three distinct groups (see Chapter 17), each of them with a characteristic social-class composition: the Americans of Spanish origin in the Southwest range from upper-class to lower-working-class; the Puerto Rican immigrants range from middle-class to lower-working class; and the Cubans, mostly very recent immigrants, are mainly middle-class. (Table 3.2 reports the occupations of two of these groups.)

Ethnic and Social Interaction
in Elementary Schools

The interaction of social-class and ethnic-minority subcultures can be seen in any school that includes a range of social classes as well as a range of ethnic minorities.

A good example of how this interaction affects the school is given by the two schools portrayed in Table 2.1. The Jefferson and the Madison schools are located in adjoining neighborhoods in one of the country's biggest cities. They are so close to each other that the children who live on one side of a main boulevard go to Jefferson, while the children who live on the other side of the boulevard go to Madison. But the Jefferson school is in a somewhat "better" neighborhood: home values are higher, there is a fine open park, and residents describe it as a "good" area to live in.

The ethnic-minority composition of the two schools is shown in Table 2.1. At first glance they look alike. Each has 54 percent white children; both have about equal proportions of blacks. Both have small and nearly equal proportions of Orientals and of American Indians.

But the academic performance of the children in the two schools is strikingly different. Jefferson is substantially above the city average in all three types of tests: mental ability or "intelligence," reading comprehension, and arithmetic. Madison is far below the city average.

What are the reasons for this difference? It is well known that school achievement is related to the socioeconomic status or to the social class of the child's family. (The reasons for this will be discussed in later chapters.) The two schools differ in the social-class distributions of their white pupils—Jefferson whites are about half from upper-middle-class homes and half from working-class, whereas the Madison white children are all working-class. Another difference lies in the Spanish-surname pupils. At present in the United States most Cuban families are middle-class, while most Chicano and Puerto Rican families in large cities are working-class. These differences are probably reflected in these two schools, so that Jefferson, with its 11 percent Cubans, probably has more middle-class pupils than does Madison, with its 2 percent Cubans. As for the black students, investigation of the two schools showed the black families in the Jefferson district had higher occupational and economic status than the black families in the Madison area. All together, then, the differences in school achievement shown in Table 2.1 might have been anticipated.

Furthermore, the difference between the levels of performance in reading and in arithmetic may be explained by subcultural factors. The pupils in both schools do much better in arithmetic than in reading, which is unusual. The probable reason is than 25 to 30 percent of the pupils in each school come from homes where English is not the family language. (This is true of nearly all the Spanish-surname families, and some of the Oriental and Indian

TABLE 2.1.   *Two Schools in a Big City*

	Percentage	
Subcultural Characteristics of Pupils	Jefferson (enrollment, 1250)	Madison (enrollment, 1150)
White (Appalachian working-class)	29	54
White (upper-middle)	25	—
Black	11	16
Oriental	5	7
American Indian	4	6
Chicano	7	3
Puerto Rican	8	12
Cuban (middle-class)	11	2

	Average Percentile Test Scores (on national norms)		
	Jefferson	Madison	All Schools in the City
Third Grade			
Mental Ability	44	23	40
Reading	38	18	34
Arithmetic	63	27	45
Sixth Grade			
Mental Ability	43	21	34
Reading	38	14	29
Arithmetic	77	23	35

Source: Author's research files.

families.) Consequently, we might expect the children of these families to have some difficulty with the reading of English, and to do relatively better in arithmetic.

This comparison between the Jefferson and Madison schools serves to illustrate the complexities of social-class factors and ethnic-group factors as they interact in affecting school performance.

EXERCISES

1. A person's social position as measured by socioeconomic indices (occupation, income, level of education, and so on) does not always coincide with his social position as evaluated by the people in the community. (For example: a poor, but upper-class woman; or a wealthy, but lower-class businessman.) Have you

known such a person? What does his case illustrate about the bases of rank in his community?

2. Obtain a map of your community. Interview a few people, and ask them to point out the areas that are "best," "average," and "worst" neighborhoods. (One of the best persons to interview will be a real estate man.) How much agreement do you find among your informants? On what kinds of factors are their judgments made?

3. Select an elementary school in your community and make an informal investigation of the community from which it draws its pupils. Walk up and down the streets of the neighborhood, observing the houses, lawns, alleys; look at the names on doorbells; go into the stores and notice what kinds of food, clothing, and other goods are sold; and so on. From what social classes would you say the school draws? How heterogeneous is the neighborhood?

4. Think about the community in which you grew up. (If it was a large city, interpret this to mean your neighborhood.) Write a description of that community in terms of its social-class structure. How many social classes were there? Were class lines clearly drawn? What kinds of people occupied positions of highest and lowest status? Does it make sense to think of your community as a system of social classes? Why or why not?

SUGGESTIONS FOR FURTHER READING

1. There are a number of studies of social structure in various American communities. The first and most elaborate was of a New England community, reported in a series of volumes called the Yankee City Series. Volume I of the series, *The Social Life of a Modern Community*,* by W. Lloyd Warner and Paul S. Lunt is the most appropriate for students of education. A midwestern community is reported in *Democracy in Jonesville*, by W. Lloyd Warner and associates. A small agricultural town in a border state is described in *Plainville, U.S.A.*, by James West; the same community studied again is described by Gallaher in *Plainville Fifteen Years Later*. The social structure of the San Francisco peninsula is described in Hodges, *Peninsula People*. For a discussion of the social-class structure in America at large (rather than a study of a particular community), read *American Life: Dream and Reality*, by W. Lloyd Warner. The most comprehensive study of the social structure of a large city (Kansas City) is reported in *Social Status in the City* by Coleman and Neugarten. Chapter 12 in that book summarizes studies of social-class structure in eight different communities.

2. The methods of investigating and measuring social status are described in *Social Class in America*, by W. Lloyd Warner, Marchia Meeker, and Kenneth Eells; *Social Status in the City*, by Richard Coleman and Bernice Neugarten; and chapters 1 and 2 in Kahl's book, *The American Class Structure*. Also, *Class, Status and Power: A Reader in Social Stratification* edited by Bendix and Lipset is a good reference for the student who wishes to explore further the theoretical issues of social structure, or to study different theories of stratification.

*For each of these references, see Bibliography for facts of publication.

3. Changes in the value orientations of Americans are described in books of sociological essays that became best-sellers: *The Lonely Crowd* by David Riesman and others; *The Organization Man* by William H. Whyte, Jr.; and *The Affluent Society* by John K. Galbraith. A controversy arose over Reich's book *The Greening of America,* which argues that a pervasive value change is now in full progress. Pros and cons appear in the paperback compiled by Nobile, entitled *The Con III Controversy.*

4. A number of books analyze value patterns and life styles of particular social classes. For example, C. Wright Mill's book, *White Collar,* is a penetrating analysis of the American middle class. Spectorsky's *The Exurbanites* describes the lives of upper-middle-class suburbanites. Chinoy's *Automobile Workers and the American Dream;* Walker and Guest's *The Man on the Assembly Line;* and Rainwater, Coleman, and Handel's *Workingman's Wife* are all interesting studies of the working class, as is *Whitetown* by Binzen. *Blue Collar World,* edited by Shostak and Gomberg, reports research findings on working-class life prepared by various authors. Baltzell's *Philadelphia Gentlemen* deals with a national upper class.

5. The selection by Mayer in *Society and Education: A Book of Readings,* (Havighurst, Neugarten, and Falk), discusses the "shape" of the American class structure and how it may be changing; while the selection by McKinley describes the dominant cultural themes and values of American society from a historical perspective. The question whether there is a black subculture is discussed by Blauner in an essay entitled "Black Culture: Myth or Reality?" in this same book of readings.

6. Ruth Landes' book, *Culture in American Education,* describes an experimental teacher-training program aimed at helping teachers understand cultural traits of California minorities, especially blacks and Mexican-Americans.

7. Religious groups function as subcultures in American societies. A book by Lenski comparing Protestants, Catholics, and Jews in Detroit shows that different religious subcultures exist within a given social class. Also, Rossi and Rossi have studied the effects of a parochial school system upon the attitudes and beliefs of Catholics. Gordon's *Assimilation in American Life* is a recently published book that deals with religious as well as ethnic factors. Greeley's book, *Religion and Career,* is a study of differences between Catholics, Protestants, and Jews in a large sample of college graduates.

8. A number of recent books focus attention upon problems of poverty in modern America, among them Harrington's *The Other America;* Bagdikian's *In the Midst of Plenty: The Poor in America;* Miller's *Rich Man, Poor Man;* the report of the Conference on Economic Progress, *Poverty and Deprivation in the United States.* One of the important questions about the relation of poverty to social status is whether poverty *makes* people adopt a lower-class culture, or whether people with a certain life style tend to fall into poverty. This is discussed in an article by Havighurst entitled "The Culture of Poverty."

9. The heterogeneity of suburban life is described in Berger's book, *Working Class Suburb;* and in Dobriner's *Class in Suburbia. The Levittowners* by Gans reports on the public schools in a Philadelphia suburb.

CHAPTER 3

Mobility in the Social Structure

In a complex democratic society a considerable degree of movement upward from one social class to another is encouraged. This movement is implied by the ideal of equality of opportunity.

A substantial amount of upward mobility is evidence of opportunity. Data on social mobility—its nature, extent, and location in the society—are necessary for an objective study of the degree of opportunity that exists in modern America.

UPWARD MOBILITY AS SOCIAL LEARNING

Mobility may occur in only one area of life, such as in occupation (when a man moves from the position of factory worker to that of factory foreman) or in living arrangements (when a family moves from a small house in one part of town to a larger house in a "better" part of town). More typically, however, the term mobility means movement from one social class to another, involving the *consolidation* of the various elements of the new social position, including occupation, income, type of house, neighborhood, new friends, and new organizational memberships.

Because the various social classes have somewhat different subcultures, a person moving up on the social scale must learn the subculture of the class into which he is moving. The amount that must be learned will, of course, vary according to the particular circumstances of the family into which the person was born, as well as the social distance he travels.

Mobile people are most likely to move into the class immediately

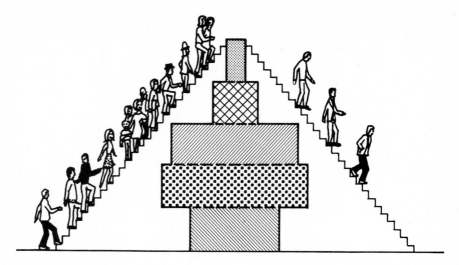

FIGURE 3.1.   *There is both upward and downward mobility in the
social structure.*

above the one of their parents. Only very rarely does a person move "from
rags to riches." However, to illustrate the kinds of things a person may need
to learn when moving up the status ladder, we shall look at a relatively extreme case, such as that of a man who at age eight worked with his parents in
the fields as a migrant farm laborer but who by age 45 had risen to the position of assistant division manager in a large corporation. During his rapid rise
this man would have found it necessary to learn a great deal besides the
techniques and information necessary for his occupation. A list of such
things would almost certainly include:

How to speak middle-class English; that is, with good grammar and with the
appropriate vocabulary, intonation, and inflections of speech.
How to converse with business associates and other upper-middle-class men;
how to agree and disagree with them.
How to choose a home in a "good neighborhood" and furnish it in the proper
style.
How to discuss matters such as current books, theater, art, tennis, golf.
The etiquette and "little" social skills of middle-class life: for example, how
to meet strangers and introduce them to one's friends; how to order a
meal and tip the waiter at a first-class restaurant or club.
How to participate in professional or business associations, as well as charitable and civic associations.

A man who began life as an unskilled laborer would find the learning
of these tasks difficult but not impossible. First, he would probably have
spent a relatively long apprenticeship in school and at work, during which
time he would gradually have acquired the ways of the new class (by watching and imitating friends and acquaintances who possessed the desired

attributes, by reading, and by traveling and observing the ways other people act in new situations).

Second, he would probably have had help from others. Once a person has moved into a higher-status *occupation* and has proved his worth, his colleagues help him to fit into his new *social* world. They may, for example, suggest a good neighborhood in which to live, tactfully point out a good place to buy his clothes, or sponsor him for membership in a club. Third, such a man is likely to have married a woman of higher status or one who was sensitive to status points, and he probably learned from her.

Such a man need not absorb every bit of the culture of his new class. He might keep on feeling awkward at cocktail parties; and he might continue to stumble a bit in vocabulary. However, particularly if he lived in a metropolitan area, the acquisition of a few major symbols of status such as an apartment with a "good address" or the high-status occupation itself would indicate to the vast majority of observers that he was a bona-fide member of the class into which he has moved. The small group who know him personally may think of him as "a rough diamond," but they are likely to respect and prize him for the qualities that brought him to the top, and they may take a proprietary interest in "polishing off the edges."

What has been said about a man's upward mobility applies in general also to a woman. The modern woman can rise socially by the same kinds of learning as have been sketched out above.

An Example of Upward Mobility

Ambition and intelligence may lead to dramatic upward mobility as in the following case.

> Ernest Smith, a black man, was born in a midwestern state, a few months after his father was killed in a farm accident. His mother moved back to her family on a farm in another state; then moved to Chicago when Ernest was ready for school. She found a manual job, and Ernest went to school in a poor neighborhood in the city. He delivered newspapers and later worked part-time in a neighborhood store, where he learned, among other things, that a part-time accountant earned as much as the store owner.
>
> After graduating with a good record from an all-black high school in the inner city, he entered the school of business at the state university. He finished in the early 1930s, just at the time of the Great Depression.
>
> Unable to find work at first, he and his mother were forced on relief for several months. He then found a job clerking and keeping books. Later he was a caseworker for the county, dealing with families on public assistance. Next, he began an accounting business. By the early 1940s he was working in Washington as a budget officer for the federal Fair Employment Practices Commission.
>
> Returning to Chicago in the mid-1940s, Smith took a position with an insurance firm, and over the years he moved up to become senior vice-president

and general manager. When he was 50, he was appointed a regional director of the Office of Economic Opportunity. He lived now with his wife, who was a social worker, in a racially integrated upper-middle-class neighborhood; one child had just finished college and was beginning graduate study; the other was in college on the West Coast. He owned a large boat and was one of the first blacks admitted to the local yacht club.

The newspapers described Smith as having filled a succession of civic and public offices: he had served as a member of the state parole board, as a member of the state Public Aid Commission, as a board-member of a national child welfare association, as a member of a national committee on equal opportunities in housing, and as president of the local chapter of the National Association for the Advancement of Colored People. He was presently a member of the board of trustees of the university from which he had graduated some thirty years earlier.

Other Patterns of Mobility

In the case just described, the individual had high intellectual ability as well as ambition. Other types of talents and personal assets are also good bases for mobility. A working-class boy with dramatic ability develops his talents in high school, may obtain a scholarship in dramatics at a college, and may get a tryout in a Broadway show. If he makes good, his rise in the social scale is almost certain.

Even though most upward social mobility today occurs through education, there are other channels. The self-made businessman who marries a wife who guides him up the social ladder is one example of an alternative pattern of mobility. A girl with unusual beauty may make a "good" marriage. She may marry a man of much higher status than her own; then, if she is skillful, she learns the ways of her husband's social class and finds a secure position in it.

Athletic prowess in a boy often provides a good base for mobility, as in the instance when a boy becomes a professional baseball or football player. Although there are notable exceptions, in most such cases athletic ability is also combined with a college education if the young man is to become a successful middle-aged man.

Examples of Unattained Mobility

Upward mobility often hinges upon education and upon success in high school and college although good academic records do not, of course, always lead to successful careers, much less to such dramatic examples of upward mobility as in the case described above.

Even more frequent are the instances in which young people do not succeed in high school; or others who do not succeed in college, despite promising high school records; or others who drop out of school or college for reasons other than academic difficulty. Two brief cases are illustrative:

DONALD LEWIS

Donald Lewis graduated tenth in a class of 110 in an all-black high school. With an IQ of 112, and scoring at the 83rd percentile of the College Aptitude Test, he had done consistently superior work in science and mathematics. His father and mother were both high school graduates; his father had a stable job as a maintenance man; and they thought Donald had made a good choice when he entered the school of engineering at the state university.

Donald wrote, as a high school senior:

"For as long as I can remember, I have always wanted to go to college and become a mechanical engineer. My family is behind me one hundred percent."

His teachers recommended him highly, though one of them commented, "With a little more aggressiveness, Donald could develop into an outstanding college prospect."

Donald got all C's and D's in his first year at the university and was placed on scholastic probation. The next year he repeated a mathematics course, but did not get a good start and he withdrew from school until the second semester. This time he withdrew after only six weeks. Donald thereupon gave up on his college career. He took a civil service examination and got a job in an office in the city government.

Although it appears likely that Donald will rise above his parents' level in socioeconomic status, nevertheless his failure to complete college is a puzzle to his high school teachers. Donald looked like a good risk for college graduation; he was a conscientious student, with a very good high school record; yet he had failed to meet the standards of a first-class university. It is this kind of experience that leads some educators to argue that a segregated black school may not maintain scholastic standards high enough to prepare even their best students for the competition of a good university. They feel that failures like Donald's are to be blamed upon poor schools, not upon lack of ability or motivation in the student. (We shall return to these issues in later chapters in this book.)

LAURA CARTER

Laura Carter's home room teacher in the twelfth grade wrote:

"This girl ranks high in scholastic ability and she has a burning desire'for a college career. I feel she would be quite successful in college."

Laura is next to the oldest in a family of ten children. Her father, who did not go beyond the eighth grade, is disabled and receives income from a disability pension; her mother, who is a high school graduate, stays at home and looks after the big family. They live on a minimum income.

Laura was a school leader. She was president of her Honor Society and a member of a Junior Achievement program.

Her aptitude tests indicated a strong interest in scientific work; her IQ was

108; and she scored at the 75th percentile of the College Aptitude test. On the basis of her course grades, she ranked second in a high school class of 200. Her counselor commented that she was "a hardworking girl who strives for perfection."

Laura was given a full scholarship to the state university. In her first semester she made the Dean's list, with a fairly easy program of only 12 hours. Then she started into a heavy program of science and mathematics, her grades going down to only average. At the end of that year, she wrote the following letter to her scholarship sponsor:

> Dear Mr. Roberts:
>
> This letter should have come to you much sooner and I apologize. I think I have been postponing it because I know you would not be entirely pleased with the news. I am planning to be married in August and do not plan to return to school in the fall. It is not a matter of money but rather a matter of the way I feel about school at present. I am tired of all the studying and the hard work with no success. Perhaps someone else would be pleased with my grades but it is hard for me to accept the fact that I am only average in the field I have chosen.
>
> I could continue with school after being married; I have seen other women do it. But I no longer have the desire to put in the time and effort for only mediocre results.
>
> I'm sorry I have not done better because I know everyone thought I would. But I'm not sorry I tried. Those two years in Chemistry will enable me to get a job as a lab technician at a decent salary. College has also broadened my views and made me more aware of people.
>
> I'm looking forward with great eagerness to marriage, as for me this signifies the beginning of life as an adult. I have always felt too sheltered in college, too cut off from what I consider to be the world. College is really a different world and I no longer want to be a part of it.
>
> Yours truly,
> Laura Carter

There is no question of Laura's ability to complete a satisfactory college record, but she was caught in a situation that is typical for many girls. The first person in her family to go beyond high school, she was headed for a career in a middle-class occupation. But the boy whom she was dating wanted to be married. She chose the latter.

DOWNWARD MOBILITY

Downward mobility is less frequently observed than upward mobility. There are several types of downward mobility. One is relatively dramatic, in which a man may lose his job and may suffer a marked loss of economic and social status in the succession of poorer jobs that follows. There is not only loss of money but loss of friends. Sometimes alcoholism is involved or some other form of personal maladjustment. Such a man may drop a level or two in the social scale.

Other instances involve intergenerational mobility: the son of a high-status family does poorly in school, rebels against the family's expectations, and may settle for an occupation of lower status. In one such family, for example, the father was a successful businessman, the oldest son is a practicing surgeon, the second son is beginning an academic career as a college instructor; but the youngest son has rejected his family's style of life, dropped out of high school, and is an electrician, supporting a wife and two children in a working-class suburb of the city.

A more frequent type of downward mobility is the slow and almost imperceptible downward movement that may come to people who do not manage to keep up with the rising standards of living. For instance, an upper-middle-class youth who does only an average job in his occupation may find himself, after 10 years of adulthood, falling behind his associates as they are promoted. He cannot afford to move to a better neighborhood, as they do; he does not get invited to the "right" clubs nor to work on civic committees. His wife may not make a good impression on the wives of his associates or upon those who are above him in the business hierarchy. He gradually drops in social status.

UPWARD MOBILITY IN A
DEMOCRATIC SOCIETY

A major goal of American democracy is the maintenance of an "open" society that permits upward mobility and that provides substantial opportunity for all groups of people to seek happiness. For many people who grow up in poor families, opportunity to get a good job with good pay is necessary for life satisfaction. This means that they will strive to become upward mobile.

Because upward mobility is crucial for a healthy democratic society, careful measures of mobility are essential. The simplest measure is a comparison of a person's occupation with that of his father. This measure is fairly good for men in urban occupations, since occupational status is closely correlated with social-class status. But our measures for women are not so good, particularly since more and more women are achieving their adult social status through careers of their own rather than through marriage. A number of occupations in which women specialize are now undergoing revaluation in terms of social status in the eyes of the public; for example, executive secretary in a law office, administrative assistant in a government agency, teacher's aide, child care aide. Perhaps we shall soon have a set of fairly stable occupational prestige ratings for such occupations, but they do not yet exist.

In the next few pages we will examine the best available data on the extent and nature of upward mobility in this country. For a healthy democracy, there should be evidence of a system of opportunity open to all youth, with greater aid and encouragement for economically and socially disadvantaged youth than for youth of more advantaged families, since the more advantaged families provide more opportunity to their children through their own resources. This proposition is a value judgment made by the authors, but it is shared by the majority of social scientists.

Reduction of Inequality

The very stress in America on the desirability of upward mobility underlines the fact of inequality in this society. Social classes are unequal in power, income, and prestige. Incomes are unequal. Intelligence is distributed unequally among individuals. Performance in school, on the playing field, and in the labor force is distributed unequally among individuals, and also among ethnic groups.

Various groups of people evaluate the present state of inequality differently. Many of those who are now relatively comfortable (mainly the middle classes) point to the past when their progenitors were upward-mobile, or when history tells them there was much upward mobility, and claim that America is the "land of unlimited opportunity," as indeed it was known to Europeans who emigrated to America between 1850 and 1914. On the other hand, many people (mainly at the lower-working-class level) see their own positions as evidence of injustice as well as inequality. Some of them know friends, or even their own children, who have climbed up the ladder to a higher status, but they believe that there is not enough of this kind of mobility.

Then there are some upper-working-class or lower-middle-class people who cling precariously to their present status, and complain that youth of minority groups are being favored over their own children in gaining access to higher education and better jobs. This may seem unjust to them.

The liberal political strategy in this complex situation favors some reduction of the existing degree of inequality through higher taxes on the wealthy, and various forms of assistance to low-income families, including scholarship funds and loans for higher education. In general, the argument is that a good society can and should apply principles of *equity* to reduce *inequality*. Equity is what is fair and just to the greatest number of people. The 1965 Civil Rights Act and the Fair Employment Practices Act moved the country toward greater equity, and resultant changes in employment practices gave minority groups greater access to middle-class jobs.

It seems impossible to imagine a society without inequality, though the sources of inequality vary from one society to another. As long as societies exhibit social stratification, we will have the higher strata passing on more opportunity to their children than the lower strata can. Even if we could use a lottery to award university scholarships on a chance basis, thus distributing educational opportunity more equally, the family backgrounds of students would make for inequality of outcomes.

Nevertheless the amount and nature of inequality is influenced, not only by the technology, the natural wealth, and the religious and ethical principles of the society, but by socioeconomic and educational policies. We shall have more to say on these points in successive chapters of this book.

Characteristics of Upward-Mobile People

The people who rise on the social scale are those who have talents, abilities, and motives that happen to be valuable in that society. In the highly instrumental and materialistic American society of the past 100 years, this meant ambition, economic foresight, habits of industry, and verbal or mechanical intelligence. But in the contemporary period of value change, there is likely to be a change in the human qualities which gain favored status for people. We will not try to predict the future, but it will be well to keep this possible change in mind as we examine the mobility data for recent decades.

Mobile Youth

Teachers and other observers often feel confident that they can spot the talented or the ambitious boys and girls, and that they can predict which ones will and will not get further in life than their parents. At the same time there are relatively few studies in which a large group of youngsters have been followed to find which ones actually do, in adulthood, follow patterns of upward mobility and, in this way, to identify the characteristics leading to mobility.

One such study was carried out on a group of boys and girls who in 1951–52 constituted all the sixth-graders in the public schools of a community called River City, and who were then followed until 1964 when they were approximately 23 years old. Some of the original 450 left the city and were lost to the study, but fairly adequate data are available on almost 400 of the group (Havighurst et al., 1962).

Table 3.1 shows the social and intellectual characteristics of the group when studied at age 23. By this time almost all of those who expected to go to college had at least started. Of those who had not gone to college, the men and some of the women had been working for four to seven years. Most of the women had married and were homemakers.

Each person in the group was evaluated in comparison to his family of origin with regard to educational level, occupation, occupational performance, and reputation in the community. On this basis he or she was identified as upward-mobile, stable, or downward-mobile. (The women who had married were assigned the status of their husbands; those who had not married were evaluated in the same way as the men.)

The data on *intelligence* are based on a battery of tests administered when the group was in the sixth grade. The data on *social effectiveness* came

TABLE 3.1. *Characteristics of Mobile and Stable 23-Year-Olds in River City (N = 399)*

			Mean percentile scores[a]	
	N	IQ[b]	High School Grades	Social Effective-ness[c]
Upward-mobile:				
Men	52	71	59	70
Women:				
Not married	11	75	75	77
Married between ages 21 and 24	18	65	75	77
Married by age 20	36	50	51	64
Total	117			
Stable:				
Men	101	42	45	42
Women:				
Not married	10	86	66	80
Married between ages 21 and 24	17	59	71	57
Married by age 20	72	42	47	46
Total	200			
Downward-mobile:				
Men	44	28	26	40
Women:				
Not married	4	42	41	44
Married between ages 21 and 24	4	34	52	—
Married by age 20	30	50	48	42
Total	82			

a Based on the entire group of students.
b Based on a number of tests given in sixth grade.
c A combination measure including popularity, friendliness, and leadership as evaluated by both teachers and peers.

from sociometric tests and teachers' descriptions obtained when the boys and girls were in the sixth grade and again when they were in the ninth grade. The combination measure shown in Table 3.1 includes popularity, friendliness, and leadership as evaluated by both teachers and peers.

Among the men the upward-mobile as compared to the socially stable had been markedly superior in high school on measures of intelligence, school grades, and social effectiveness. The downward-mobile had been the poorest on these measures. Thus, a teacher who knew this group of students could have predicted with considerable accuracy which of the boys would be upward-mobile and which would be downward-mobile.

For the women, however, predictions would have been more difficult.

While the upward-mobile women had been superior in high school to the stable and to the downward-mobile, the patterns were complicated by differences related to age at marriage. With a few exceptions, in the stable and upward-mobile groups the late-marrying women (those who had not yet married by age 23) had been superior to those who married between 21 and 24; the latter, in turn, had been superior to those who married early (before age 20).

At the same time, the girl who was upward-mobile as the result of an early marriage to a higher-status man was higher on social effectiveness than other early-marrying women, though not higher in intelligence or school grades. The early-marrying downward-mobile girls had the same IQ as the early-marrying upward-mobile girls. In short, social effectiveness, but not IQ, differentiated between early-marrying girls who married "above" and early-marrying girls who married "below" their own social status levels.

All in all, the River City study showed clearly two main paths of social mobility. Boys, and some girls, will climb the social ladder by making use of superior intelligence and superior social effectiveness to succeed in school and college and on the job. The more frequent path for girls (as of 1960) was by marrying a relatively successful young man.

INTELLIGENCE, EDUCATION, AND MOBILITY

As we have seen, one of the principal means of upward mobility is through a good education, which implies the possession of above-average intelligence, even though in some cases other factors appear to be more important. Some persons have argued that intelligence itself is a major cause of upward or downward mobility, while others have argued that education is the principal factor.

Jayasuria (1960) found that the vocational aspirations of early adolescent boys and girls in England were more dependent upon intelligence than upon social class. He interpreted this finding to mean that:

> Intelligence acts as a kind of energy arouser which greatly influences the individual's desire to experiment, affects his belief in himself, his desire to excel in all areas, not only in those related to school or to scholastic performance. Greater intelligence thus provides the motivational conditions needed for mobility. This factor is subsequently reinforced by differential educational experience, rather than created by it.

Of the upward-mobile River City boys mentioned earlier, 24 of the 52 were in the upper quarter of their class in intelligence and only 4 were in the bottom quarter. Of the downward-mobile boys, 21 of the 44 were in the lower quarter in intelligence and only 6 in the upper quarter. Among the girls the difference was not so striking because girls who are upward-mobile by early marriage are not more intelligent on the average than girls who are downward-mobile by early marriage. For boys, then, but not for girls, the River City data support the views of Jayasuria concerning intelligence.

How important is education for upward social mobility? In River City, the investigators estimated that about 20 percent of upward-mobile youth (6 percent of the total group) were relying primarily upon intellectual ability and intellectual training. There is no way of estimating how many of these youth would have moved up the social scale if they had not had access to higher education.

Another 50 percent of the upward-mobile (15 percent of the total group) were relying primarily on their social skills or on their drive and ambition. Their mobility was achieved through performance in their work. Many of this group used education as a means of obtaining certain useful skills or knowledge, but they would probably have been upward-mobile without much education if they lived in a society in which higher education was not so easily accessible.

Finally, 50 percent of the upward-mobile girls (9 percent of the total group) had made "favorable marriages." They had married while relatively young, and they had not shown outstanding intellectual ability. Some of them rejected education.

On the whole it seems that education is less a *cause for* than a *means of* upward social mobility. Where education is as available as it is in the United States, boys and girls with intelligence and ambition will find it a ready means for self-improvement.

On the other hand, the lack of educational opportunity has little relation to downward mobility. Most downward-mobile individuals in River City were school dropouts or persons who did not go beyond high school, but the reason was not lack of opportunity for more education. Of the downward-mobile group, 40 percent were girls who were downward-mobile by marriage; 25 percent (5 percent of the total group) were probably downward-mobile primarily because of low intelligence. Another 15 percent (4 percent of the total group) lacked drive or ambition. The rest (19 percent of the downward-mobile and 4 percent of the total group) showed defects in moral character.

A book appeared in 1972 which received wide publicity and which supplements the conclusions just stated regarding the relations of intelligence and education to mobility. This book by Christopher Jencks and a research team at Harvard University is entitled *Inequality: A Reassessment of the Effect of Family and School in America*. The major data base for the study consisted of information on the occupational status of a national sample of nonfarm males born between 1897 and 1936, and of military veterans born mainly in the 1930s. These men were compared with their fathers on occupational status, as a means of determining their social mobility. Since the sample did not include women, or black men, or men born on farms, it can hardly be said to represent American adults of the 1970s. However, its focus on adult occupational status and the money income of white nonfarm men does give useful information about mobility in this subgroup.

Jencks found that the facts most predictive of both adult income and occupational status were *amount of education,* and *socioeconomic status* of the man's father. Intelligence (measured by a typical test given to adults) was also correlated with occupational status and of course with the amount of education. Adult income was considerably less related to family socioeconomic background, amount of education, or IQ than was occupational status. If one were interested primarily in studying the money income of adults, one would find other elements, mainly personality factors, to be heavily involved. But income is not a very good index of social-class status, since business and industrial executives have higher incomes, on the average, than professional workers, even though the two groups have approximately equal social status.

GROUP MOBILITY

We have been considering the phenomenon of individual social mobility, one mark of democracy in the American social-class system. Group mobility also affects and qualifies individual mobility.

Group mobility occurs when a social group moves as a whole in relation to other groups. The mobile group may be a large or a small one. For example, skilled workers in America have gained greatly in economic status relative to minor white-collar workers and relative to farmers. The wages of electricians, plumbers, railroad men, and others of the "aristocracy" of labor have risen more since 1900 than have the incomes of clerical and retail sales-workers, teachers, farmers, and other groups. This economic gain has enabled many of these blue-collar workers to move up, using their money to purchase the symbols of lower-middle-class living.

Upward group mobility tends to favor upward individual mobility of members of the group, but the two movements are not identical. Thus, as the American standard of living has risen, working-class people in America have come to enjoy fancy automobiles, the newest home appliances, high school educations, and paid vacations, all of which would have marked them as middle-class in 1920. Indeed this phenomenon has caused some foreign observers to refer to America as a nation of middle-class people. However, those working-class people who in 1970 possessed certain material and nonmaterial goods that in 1920 would have symbolized middle-class status have not thereby been turned into middle-class people. This is true because many of the symbols of middle-class status have changed in the interim. By 1970, middle-class people quite generally have a college education rather than the

51

high school education that was characteristic of the middle class in 1920. A great many belong to country clubs. They buy high-fidelity and stereophonic phonographs and read the *New Yorker* magazine. Quite a few travel to Europe. These things have now become symbols of a middle-class life-style, a life-style which is not shared by working-class people.

Thus the system of rank continues in a changing society even though the *bases* or signs of rank are shifting.

Mobility of Ethnic, Racial, and Religious Groups

There has been a great deal of group mobility among the various ethnic and religious groups that have come to this country: first, English, then Irish, German, Scandinavian, French, Dutch, Polish, Hungarian, Italian, Bohemian, Serbian, Rumanian, Armenian, Chinese, Japanese and Spanish-American. People came in groups and made settlements either in the new lands on the frontier or in the cities. Gradually they joined the main cultural stream of American life. The schools hastened this process by teaching American ways to their children.

Generally a new immigrant started at the bottom of the social scale and worked up. For example, the Irish, the lowest-status group in the mid-nineteenth century, were employed in digging canals and building railroads in the expanding country. They moved up, leaving room at the bottom for Scandinavians, Italians, and Bohemians, who in turn worked their way up.

Some immigrant groups came into the American social system at a level above the bottom, either because they possessed capital, or because they brought with them a culture which was enough like that of the American middle class to enable them to participate at once at that level. For example, numerous Germans came to America after 1848 because of political unrest and persecution in Germany. Some of them were middle-class people who started businesses and built up cities such as Milwaukee, St. Louis, and Cincinnati.

The Jews came with their religion and with a compound Jewish ethnic culture from Holland, France, Germany, England, Poland, and Russia. Some, with business skills and a willingness to go alone into new communities, moved into small towns and cities where they rapidly rose to middle-class status, though their religious culture set them apart from other middle-class people. Many others remained in big cities where, although they now occupy a wide range of social-class positions, a large proportion work mainly as factory workers. Today the Jewish people themselves comprise a variegated set of cultural subgroups. Some have become "liberal" in their religious views; others have remained orthodox.

The Jews have probably made more use of education as a means of moving up in the American social-class structure than has any other immigrant group, although education alone does not account for their mobility.

According to studies by Fauman (1958) and Glazer (1958), even when education is held constant, Jews as a group still outdistance non-Jews in occupational mobility.

Post-World War II Immigrants.   Japanese immigrants who settled on the Pacific coast and who had lived in "islands" of Japanese culture were dispersed by the relocation measures of World War II. Possessing personal habits that were acceptable to middle-class Americans and having work skills that were valuable, they moved into the cities of the Midwest at lower-middle-class and upper-working-class levels.

The displaced persons who fled into Germany at the close of World War II from Lithuania, Estonia, and Latvia, and who later came to the United States, were mainly middle-class people. So also were the Hungarian refugees of the mid-1950s. Although they took whatever working-class jobs they could get, they quickly integrated themselves into the American culture. Their children adopted American middle-class ways of life relatively quickly.

Differences in Group Mobility

Various ethnic groups in America have differed in the rates with which they have moved up the social scale. Among immigrant groups in the northeastern section of the United States, for instance, the Greeks as well as the Jews attained middle-class status more quickly than French-Canadians or southern Italians (Strodtbeck, 1958; Rosen, 1959). There are probably several reasons for such differences. One is the extent to which the immigrant group possesses certain work skills that are valuable in the economy; another is the degree to which the dominant group is willing to permit newcomers equal access to jobs, housing, and schooling; another is the differences between the immigrant groups in psychological and cultural orientations toward achievement. In a study of six ethnic and racial groups (Rosen, 1959), historical and ethnographic data showed that differences between the groups in achievement motivation, values, and aspirations existed before these groups arrived in the United States, and that these differences tended to persist. The differences are related to the variations among the groups in rates of upward mobility.

The careful reader will have noted that the studies cited on group mobility all deal with the situation *preceding 1960*. Since that time there has been an increase of ethnic separatism on the part of the more recent immigrants, as well as among the blacks, which complicates their group mobility. Some subgroups have been promoting ethnic solidarity at the expense of mobility in the occupational structure. This applies especially to the east and southeast European ethnics, and to some blacks and Spanish-surname groups. This will be examined in detail in Chapters 15, 16, and 17. At this point it may be noted that an ethnic or racial or religious group, when it has been in America for more than two generations, tends to subdivide into social-

TABLE 3.2. Occupations of Male Workers: 1960 and 1970

											Percentage Distribution							
	White		Black		Japanese		Chinese		Filipino		Indian		Southwest Spanish		Puerto Rican			
Occupation	1960	1970	1960	1970	1960	1970	1960	1970	1960	1970	1960	1970	1960	1970	1960	1970		
Professional, Technical, Managerial, Proprietor	22	30	5	9	25	33	36	40	9	20	8	14	9	12	6	9		
Clerical and Sales	15	13	7	10	14	15	15	14	6	12	5	8	8	10	11	15		
Craftsmen and Foremen	21	21	11	15	20	20	7	7	11	13	16	22	17	21	11	16		
Service Workers	6	6	16	16	6	6	25	24	22	21	6	11	8	11	18	17		
Operatives Nonfarm	20	19	27	30	11	10	14	11	17	14	23	24	24	25	42	33		
Laborers	6	6	22	16	6	10	2	3	11	8	18	13	15	12	9	8		
Farmers and Farm Laborers	10	5	12	4	17	5	1	1	24	12	24	8	19	9	3	2		
Number (in thousands)	41,250	44,160	3,327	4,052	114	147	67	114	54	79	64	116	700	923	182	262		

Note: Spanish-origin groups are also included in the columns for whites.

Source: U.S. Census of Population, 1960. Series B2P8
U.S. Census of Population, 1970. Series PC(1). 1A, B, C, D, F.

class subgroups. Some of the members then become more aware of their social-class status and tend to minimize the importance of their ethnic backgrounds. This tends to weaken the ethnic solidarity of many groups.

Mobility of Racial Groups

The black and Oriental groups in the United States are racially distinct, and have fared differently, with respect to social mobility, than the white immigrant groups. Table 3.2 indicates how these groups fit into the socioeconomic structure. The Japanese and Chinese since 1950 have gained greatly in status and are now averaging above the white population in amount of education and in occupational status. The blacks have been seriously disadvantaged, and are only now beginning to show rapid upward mobility. These points will be discussed more fully in Chapters 15 and 16.

EXTENT OF MOBILITY IN THE UNITED STATES

Returning now to individual mobility, its extent can be studied by measuring the degree and kinds of mobility that have occurred within the lifetimes of adults. Such studies have been carried out with several samples of the population, with generally similar findings. Using a five-class system as the frame of reference, social scientists estimate that about one in every four or five persons climbs one step in the class system during his lifetime. (It is only the rare individual who climbs more than one step.)

In the data already presented from River City (see Table 3.1), of the total number of young people followed from the time they were in the sixth grade, almost 30 percent were upward-mobile by the age of 23. This figure is probably an underestimation, for undoubtedly some of these young people are late starters. Further changes are likely to occur by the time the group reaches their middle 40's when most people reach the peak of their careers.

In a study of middle-aged adults in the metropolitan area of Kansas City in the late 1950s, it was found that 36 percent had been upward-mobile at least one social level, while 13 percent had been downward-mobile. (Coleman and Neugarten, 1971). In that study, a representative sample of men and women aged 40 to 70 were interviewed, and their current status as well as the status of their parents was determined. Table 3.3 shows the social class of the adults in relation to their social class at birth and indicates a relatively high degree of fluidity in the society.

Several studies have been made of the family socioeconomic origins of certain occupational groups. For example, Warner and Abegglen made a study in 1952 of the social origins of a sample of business leaders. They found that about 30 to 35 percent of these men had fathers who had been farmers

TABLE 3.3.   Amount of Mobility in Kansas City Adults (Aged 40–70)

Parents' Status	Current Status			
	Upper and Upper-Middle	Lower-Middle	Upper-Working	Lower-Working
		(in percent)		
Upper and Upper-middle	6.5	3.5	.7	.0
Lower-middle	6.5	16.3	5.5	.2
Upper-working	2.0	14.7	23.9	2.3
Lower-working	.2	2.1	9.9	5.7
Total	15.2	36.6	40.0	8.2
Total, upward-mobile	36			
Total, nonmobile	51			
Total, downward-mobile	13			

Note: The table is to be read as follows: 6.5 percent of the total sample are currently of upper-middle-class status and were born into upper-middle-class families; 6.5 percent of the total sample are currently of upper-middle status, but were born into lower-middle families; and so on.

Source: Authors' research files.

or as urban dwellers were definitely below the upper-middle-class level of their sons. The most recent large scale study was made by Blau and Duncan (1967) who studied white men born between 1897 and 1936, using census data as a basis for sampling. They had certain technical difficulties in categorizing occupations, but these investigators found a substantial amount of upward mobility in this group of men. Kahl (1957) assessed the extent of occupational social mobility between 1920 and 1950 in the United States, and estimated that two-thirds of the labor force in 1950 had been mobile relative to their fathers.

Although rates of upward mobility may have changed somewhat in the 1960s and early 1970s, it may be generally concluded that the social structure in the United States is not "hardening" in the sense that class lines have become more tightly drawn or that barriers between class levels have become more difficult to surmount. On the contrary, our social-class system may have become even more fluid during the past several decades than before. A lessening of the social and economic distance between the lowest-status group in American society and the rest of the working class may be occurring, with simultaneously increasing proportions of men and women moving from the bottom. These are largely blacks, although there are also Puerto Ricans, Mexicans, and others. Mobility upward from blue-collar working class to lower-middle and from lower-middle to upper-middle is also likely to continue at a high rate if needs for technical and professional workers in the society continue. (We shall return to this point in Chapter 14, in discussing economic and technological trends in relation to population.)

Factors That Promote Mobility

Among the factors that tended to promote upward mobility in the United States has been the expanding economy and increasing industrialization. Not only has economic production in America increased, but the economy has changed in the direction of increasing the proportion of highly trained people. There are fewer unskilled laborers in relation to skilled; there are more jobs in the professions and in the managerial and technical occupations, jobs which carry with them middle-class status.

Kahl (1957) has analyzed the causes of mobility when seen from this broader perspective of the society at large (rather than from the point of view of the mobile individual or group). As he points out, the man who has advanced in the world as compared with his father may have no idea which of the social forces made it possible for him to get ahead, and he might not care if he were told. But for the social scientist who looks at the society as a whole, it is relevant to study the *causes* or the forces within a society that promote or impede mobility as well as the *patterns* of mobility followed by individuals or groups. From this point of view, Kahl has weighed the relative importance of four factors:

1. Individual mobility, or the fact that some people slip down and make room for others to move up.
2. Immigration mobility, or the fact that immigrants do not enter the system at all levels in proportion to the numbers already there.
3. Reproductive mobility, or differential birthrates, whereby people at the top levels have smaller families than those at lower levels, thus making room at the top.
4. Technological mobility, whereby changes in the economy and occupational distribution result in an upgrading of the work force and in creating new jobs at the upper levels.

By analyzing census and other nationwide data, and by comparing numbers of men in specific occupational categories against the numbers that might have been expected under varying conditions, Kahl arrived at certain conclusions regarding the relative importance of these factors. He described some 67 percent of the labor force in 1950 as having been mobile. Of this 67 percent, 20 percent were mobile by virtue of technological changes in the society; 7 percent because of reproductive mobility (see Chapter 14, pp. 297–298, for further discussion of the effects of differential rates of reproduction upon social mobility); and 40 percent because of individual mobility. While immigration had a greater effect in earlier periods, its effect on the generation just preceding 1950 was almost nil. Since 1950, the influence of reproductive mobility has decreased and immigrants have included more middle-class persons (Cubans, especially). These two factors are less effective in producing mobility than they were earlier. However, technological mobility has increased in importance, due to the increase of technician and professional level jobs and the decrease of unskilled labor jobs.

Net Mobility vs. Exchange Mobility

In an open society with relatively free educational opportunity and with a tradition favoring social mobility, the amount of individual mobility is relatively high. This is the situation in the United States, Great Britain, and the Soviet Union. Upward and downward mobility, considered together, may be called *exchange mobility*. The amount of one kind of mobility over the other may be called *net mobility*.

The amount of exchange mobility may be a better index of equity in a society than the amount of net upward mobility. Exchange mobility signifies openness to individual mobility and therefore signifies that people succeed in relation to their ability and effort. A society may have considerable exchange mobility and yet, if industrialization is not rapid and if upward and downward mobility are approximately equal, there may be very little *net* upward mobility. Glass (1955) found this condition to exist in Great Britain between 1920 and 1950. During that time, given the more rapid economic and industrial expansion in the United States, it probably required less intelligence, drive, and social effectiveness to be upward-mobile in the United States than it required to be upward-mobile in Great Britain. For the same set of reasons, those who were downward-mobile in the United States were probably less able and less ambitious that those who were downward-mobile in Great Britain.

In the British study made by Glass, there was 27 percent of upward mobility and 33 percent of downward mobility, or 60 percent of exchange mobility. The American Kansas City study, covering approximately the same decades, showed 36 percent upward and 13 percent downward mobility, or 49 percent exchange mobility. The American situation involved a substantial degree of technological mobility. A look at Table 5.5 in Chapter 5 shows that technological change has contributed substantially to upward mobility right up to 1970. But the decade of the 1970s may see less upward mobility due to technology, and therefore less net upward mobility in the United States. This would signify a decrease of opportunity, but no decrease of equity.

Equality of Opportunity

A low degree of mobility is interpreted as a hardening of the social structure and a lessening of opportunity. On the other hand, too high a degree of mobility may indicate a revolutionary or chaotic quality in the society. The latter is unhealthy because people cannot count on holding and passing on to their children the gains they have made. No one can say what degree of individual mobility would be most desirable in a modern society, but there would probably be general agreement among Americans that the present amount of mobility in the United States should not decrease.

The level of exchange mobility as of about 1970 will have to be maintained or even increased if the disadvantaged minority groups (blacks, Puerto Ricans, Chicanos) as well as the poor whites get the increased economic opportunity they are asking for. Education will be the principal instrument for increasing opportunity to the disadvantaged groups. But there will be competition between various working-class groups, and the search for equity will be a major concern of American politics and education.

EXERCISES

1. Make a list of things that a girl, born the daughter of a factory worker, would have to learn if she were to become the wife of the vice-president of the company that employed her father.
2. Describe the group mobility of one subgroup in your own community during the past 100 years.
3. From among your acquaintances, describe briefly three who have been upward or downward-mobile. Try to think of people who have experienced mobility for different reasons.
4. Do you think that upward mobility requires that a person should have a certain set of personality characteristics? What characteristics seem to have been common to the mobile people you know or have read about?
5. Interview a dozen adults, selected more or less at random, asking them what they think is happening to social mobility in America. Is it increasing or decreasing, and why?

SUGGESTIONS FOR FURTHER READING

1. One of the most dramatic examples of intergenerational mobility is provided by President Kennedy's family, where within three generations (the President's great-grandfather to his father) the family moved from the lowest to the highest rungs of the social ladder. This family history is, of course, described in various biographies of John F. Kennedy; one, written in colorful terms, constitutes the first chapter of *John Kennedy: A Political Profile* by James MacGregor Burns. Whalen's *The Founding Father* is a biography of the President's father, Joseph P. Kennedy.
2. Novelists have described social classes in America and various types of social mobility. Among the many examples: Christopher LaFarge's *The Wilsons* describes upper-class behavior in a Rhode Island community; John Marquand's

The Late George Apley; H. M. Pulham, Esquire; Wickford Point and *Point of No Return* are penetrating observations of upper-class New England. Sinclair Lewis' *Elmer Gantry, Babbitt,* and *Main Street* deal with middle-class and upper-class people. Budd Schulberg's *What Makes Sammy Run?* describes the rapid rise of a New Yorker who goes to Hollywood; and his *The Harder They Fall* is a "success" story of a prizefighter.

3. There are a number of biographies and autobiographies of immigrant youth that give different versions of upward mobility, such as *The Americanization of Edward Bok* by Edward W. Bok, and *From Immigrant to Inventor* by Michael Pupin. Others are Eugene Lyons' biography of *David Sarnoff* and Carl Rowan's autobiography. Perhaps the best known fictionalized account told as an auto-biographical narrative of an immigrant's mobility is *The Rise of David Levinsky,* by Abraham Cohan.

4. For a description of ethnic group differences in America, see the book by Glaser and Moynihan, *Beyond the Melting Pot;* or Gordon's book, *Assimilation in American Life;* or Lieberson's, *Ethnic Patterns in American Cities.* Handlin's *The Newcomers* is an interesting account of the problems of assimilation in various immigrant groups. Gans' book, *The Urban Villagers,* is a study of an Italian community in the metropolitan area. Two recent studies of Puerto Rican immigrants are reported in Patricia Sexton's *Spanish Harlem* and in Padilla's *Up from Puerto Rico.* Andrew Greeley's *Why Can't They Be Like Us* summarizes the situation as seen about 1970.

5. The book by Coleman and Neugarten, *Social Status in the City,* is an empirical study of the social-class structure of a large midwestern city, with special attention to social mobility.

6. The student who wishes to learn more about inequality in relation to social mobility, might read the book *Inequality* by Jencks *et al.,* and also the essay review of this book by Havighurst, entitled *Opportunity, Equity, and Equality.*

7. A little book by Leonard Reissman, entitled *Inequality in American Society,* gives an incisive analysis of poverty and of racial discrimination as sources of inequality, and argues for major changes in educational and other institutions in order to reduce inequality.

CHAPTER 4

The School as a Sorting and Selecting Agency

Since the landing of the pilgrims in Massachusetts more than 300 years ago, America has been perceived as a land of opportunity. During the eighteenth and nineteenth centuries there was good land to be had at low prices, and there were jobs available in the expanding economy. New cities were being built and new industries were being established. Since 1900 the areas of economic opportunity have shifted to expanding industry and to the expanding technical and service professions, where there has been an enormous increase in numbers of workers, an increase that far exceeded the increase in population. For instance, the proportion of men employed in the professions or as technicians increased from 3.4 percent of the male labor force in 1900 to 6.4 percent in 1950 to 14 percent in 1970. Among women these proportions increased from 8.2 percent in 1900 to 10.3 percent in 1950 to 14.5 percent in 1970.

Industry and trade have also expanded more rapidly than the population, thus creating a greater proportion of executive positions than existed in earlier generations. The proportion of men working as managers, officials, and proprietors (except farmers) in 1900 was 6.8 percent, and this increased to 14.2 percent in 1970.

These are middle-class occupations, and children of middle-class families tend to enter them. At the same time, the numbers of these positions have increased so rapidly that there are not enough children born in middle-class families to fill them and some must be filled by youth from lower-status levels. (Differences in birthrates among various social classes are discussed in more detail in Chapter 15.)

These occupations also require higher education. The professions all require at least a college degree, and executive positions in business and industry are awarded more and more to college graduates.

EDUCATION AS THE AVENUE OF OPPORTUNITY

Education has become the principal avenue of opportunity in twentieth century America: college education for upper-middle-class occupations, and high school education for such lower-middle-class occupations such as clerical work, sales work, and skilled technical work. Realizing that the avenue of opportunity is provided by the educational system, parents have encouraged their children to go further and further in school. Since 1890 the proportion of young people attending high school has multiplied by 13, while the proportion attending college has multiplied by 15. Table 4.1 shows the increase in high school and college attendance since 1910.

Amount of education is a good indicator of socioeconomic status, from lower-working up through upper-middle class, for education leads to economic opportunity. Young people, through education, secure higher-status jobs than their fathers. With greater incomes, young adults from lower-status families tend to associate with persons of higher status and adopt their ways. It may be concluded, consequently, that education provides the channel not only to better socioeconomic status, but also to social mobility in the broader sense.

These statements are so widely accepted that few people, even those most critical of the educational establishment, will disagree with them. A recent review of the research on amount of schooling in relation to success in adult life (Levin, Guthrie, Kleindorfer, and Stout, 1971), affirms the view that *amount* of education (not school marks) is linked with individual and societal improvement. These authors conclude their report by saying: "The evidence is overwhelming in support of the proposition that the postschool opportunity and performance of a pupil are related directly to his educational attainment." (p. 14)

The recent book entitled *Inequality* by Christopher Jencks and his co-workers analyzes the data on the relations between occupational status, income, amount of education, and intelligence as measured by a standard intelligence test. The occupational prestige of American men is highly associated with the *amount* of education they have obtained, although their financial income is not so highly related to amount of education.

A Skeptical Note—Has the Educational Channel
Been Too Narrow?

There is a school of thought in American social science and in American history that is very critical of the account that has been presented in the preceding two pages. Although accepting the research findings mentioned

TABLE 4.1. *Change in the American Educational System as a Selecting Agency*

Educational Level Reached	Number (per thousand)			
	1910	1938	1960	1971
First year high school (age 14)	310	800	908	970
Third year high school (age 16)	160	580	746	870
Graduation from high school (age 18)	93	450	621	790
Entrance to college or a similar educational institution	67	150	328	460
Graduation from college (Bachelor's degree)	22	70	170	210
Master's degree	1.5	9	34	73
Doctor of Philosophy degree	0.2	1.3	4.7	11

Source: United States Office of Education, *Digest of Educational Statistics,* 1971.

here, this group of scholars argue that these findings are incomplete and inadequate. They describe the period from 1800 to the present as one in which the white upper-middle class in America has successfully (and perhaps consciously) conspired to enhance its power and prestige relative to the lower-status groups, both immigrant and native born. Especially through control of the public educational system, these critics argue, the white middle class admitted relatively few lower-status youth to the educational mobility channel, and they limited this channel to students with a narrow range of life styles. In support of this line of thought, they have assembled data to show that the children of the poor and of immigrants have always had a hard time in the schools. Those data show clearly that children of immigrant families were more likely than native-born children to receive failing marks in school and to repeat one or more grades. This, presumably, was due partly to their lack of experience with the English language, and partly to their poverty.

The critics go on to argue that immigrant groups which did rise in social status were able to do so by going into local politics (Irish) or by succeeding in their own businesses (Jews and Greeks), rather than by using their schooling to get preferred jobs. Greer (1972) argues that the school system is treating black students today with the same negative attitudes that were displayed 70 years ago against poor immigrants from Europe. Cohen (1970a) has reviewed the studies of school advancement and retardation of immigrant and native-born children, and concludes (p. 15) that the school system has been "unable to overcome the educational consequences of family poverty, and to recognize the legitimacy of working-class and ethnic cultures." Through the use of intelligence tests, school achievement tests, and vocational guidance, Cohen concludes that school administrators and teachers limited the educational opportunity of these groups. He says (p. 25) "there is more than a little evidence that these practices were employed—if not conceived—as a way of providing the limited education schoolmen often thought suitable for children from the lower reaches of the social order."

This school of criticism ignores or minimizes the evidence provided by growing numbers of Italian, Jewish, Polish, Greek, and Slavic names on law firms, banks, university faculties, as well as among businessmen, city officials, state legislatures, and Congress. College education and in many instances graduate education is necessary to attain these positions.

This last kind of evidence is cited by writers who present a favorable picture of the school system as a provider of opportunity to disadvantaged groups. No doubt this position, the one that has prevailed for so many years, has been overstated by some zealous writers. The situation is like one where different people are commenting on a cup which is partially filled with water. One group says the cup is half-empty, while another group says it is half-full. It might be better for both groups to set aside their political ideologies and join in measuring the amount of water in the cup, then in measuring it again at a later time to see what change has occurred.

HOW THE SCHOOL SELECTS

The American educational system is expected to provide opportunity for social and economic mobility by selecting and training the most able and industrious youth for higher-status positions in society. Insofar as the school system does this job efficiently and fairly, it equips youth for career opportunities and it contributes to the success of democracy.

The degree of selection can be observed in Table 4.1, which shows the number of boys and girls per thousand born in a given year who reach various levels of the educational ladder. It will be seen that the high school is much less selective than it was 40 or 50 years ago; and the college, too, while still selective, is less so than before.

The process of selection is not carried on in a formal sense by the school alone. Several factors determine how far a boy or girl goes in school: the parents' wishes, the individual's aspirations and ability, the financial status of the family, as well as the school's system of encouraging some students and discouraging others. The end result, however, is selection.

This selection process can be seen from the findings of Project TALENT, a large-scale research undertaking in which nearly a half-million boys and girls who were in ninth, tenth, eleventh, and twelfth grades in 1960 were given a large battery of achievement and ability tests; they are being followed up at one, five, ten and twenty years after graduation from high school. In the follow-up of students who graduated in 1960, 42 percent entered a recognized two-year or four-year college within a year after leaving high school. Of these about 22 percent dropped out during or at the end of the freshman year, the great majority to take jobs or because of financial difficulties. Among girls, marriage accounted for 23 percent of the dropouts; among boys, 22 percent reported that they had failed in their academic work (Flanagan, 1964).

One may ask whether or not the educational system does an efficient and fair job of selecting. This is not an easy question to answer, because it is not easy to determine who are the ablest and most industrious youth. The ablest in terms of intellectual ability (at least in terms of IQ) can be discovered more easily than the most industrious.

Intellectual Ability

Intelligence tests are fairly good measures of intellectual ability, even though they do not measure artistic, musical, or social leadership ability. Furthermore, the ordinary paper-and-pencil test of intelligence probably underestimates the abilities of lower-class youth, a point we shall return to presently.

With these qualifications, we may consider first the question: How

TABLE 4.2.   *Amount of Education in Relation to Intelligence*

| IQ Quartile | Percentage in Each IQ Group Achieving a Given Educational Level in the United States (1970) | | | |
	Enter High School	Graduate from High School	Enter College	Graduate from College
IV (highest 25% of population by IQ level)	98	97	87	57
III	96	90	65	23
II	92	75	30	18
I (lowest 25% of population by IQ level)	88	60	10	2

Source: Estimates by the authors, based on recent studies in various parts of the country of college attendance and educational attainment. Latest data from Hilton's analysis of 1967 high school graduates for the Educational Testing Service Growth Study.

well does the educational system select and carry along the ablest youth? The answer is that abler youth in general go further in school and college, but a considerable proportion of able youth do not enter college, and some do not even finish high school. Most of the boys and girls who drop out of school are below average in academic ability, but a considerable proportion are above average.

The overall tendency of youth of higher ability to stay longer in school is shown in Table 4.2 where the estimates are based upon recent studies undertaken in various parts of the country.

Intellectual Ability and Social Class

Although ability alone is a major factor in determining level of education, the picture is greatly modified when we consider the additional factor of social status. Youth from upper-middle-class families are likely to go to college even though they have only average ability, while youth from lower-status families have less chance of entering college even when they have high ability.

Table 4.3 is based on information from a number of different studies concerning the educational experience and social status of boys and girls who are in the upper quarter of the population in intellectual ability, those with IQ's of 110 or above. Under the conditions existing in 1970, about 57 percent of the ablest quarter of youth completed a four-year college program, while about three percent of these able youth did not finish high school.

TABLE 4.3. *The Ablest Youth: Educational Attainment in Relation to Social-Class Background*

	Percentages of Youth Within Top Quarter in IQ Achieving a Given Educational Level (arranged by social class of family)		
	Upper and Upper-Middle	Lower-Middle	Working Class
Do not finish high school	0	1	2
Graduate from high school, but do not enter college	1	2	7
Enter college but do not finish	4	14	12
Complete a four-year college program	20	25	12
Percentage of top quarter in this social class	25	42	33

Source: Estimates by the authors based on recent studies in various parts of the country of educational attainment in relation to IQ and socioeconomic status.

It is clear that the educational system selects and carries along most of the ablest youth of upper and upper-middle status, but that able youth of working-class status tend to stop their formal education before finishing a college course. The reasons for this lie partly in the inability of many working-class youth to pay for a college education, and partly in the lack of motivation for higher education. This lack of motivation is illustrated in the following statement by Kenneth Walters, a filling station attendant. Kenneth had been doing quite well in school when, a few months before his sixteenth birthday, he quit school and went to work. Ten years later, he was asked by an interviewer why he had not continued. He answered:

> Well, there was quite a few of us. At the time I quit school there was five of us children at home. My mother and father never got along very well. They broke up and, well, my brother and I quit school and went to work. We kept our two sisters going to school. But at that time—I'll be honest with you—it didn't make me very mad, because I didn't like school very well anyway. I was kind of fickle about the whole thing. 'Course now being a little older, I wouldn't mind going a little further. One funny thing—the same year I quit school I went to work up at the mill and that summer my grammar school principal—he was a very nice fellow—well, he worked up at the mill too. So there was me, the dumbbell, and him just as high as you can go, I guess, in education—both of us working at the mill. As a matter of fact I think I was makin' a little more than he was. He was just up there for the summer months you know. So he gets all that education—all filled up—and for what?

We shall return, in the next chapter, to a further discussion of motivation as a factor in college attendance. At this point, in summarizing the facts it is clear that the educational system does tend to select and retain the more able pupils, but that it operates much less effectively in this respect with children from the lower social classes than with children from higher social classes.

INTELLIGENCE IN RELATION TO
SOCIAL CLASS AND COLOR

The school system could sort and select more or less mechanically if there were a close relationship between intellectual ability and social status, or between intellectual ability and ethnicity or skin color.

Until recently it was widely believed that there was an inborn intellectual inferiority in people of lower-class status and in people of nonwhite skin color. Many white people developed the idea that whites had the highest innate intelligence and that other races followed in order of their departure from this color, with the darkest-skinned blacks lowest in the scale of intelligence. This idea was supported by some of the earlier intelligence test studies, in which it was found that American black children scored lower than American white children, with children of mixed white and black parentage scoring in between.

However, more critical studies of intelligence testing (Eells *et al.,* 1951) have shown that the ordinary intelligence tests favor children whose parents are of middle or upper-class status. The problems in the tests are ones for which life in an upper-class or middle-class home give superior preparation.

For example, in the following test item,

A symphony is to a composer as a book it to what?
( ) paper   ( ) sculptor   ( ) author   ( ) musician   ( ) man

the problem is probably easier for middle-class children. They are more likely to have heard their parents talking about symphonies than are working-class children.

On the other hand, the following item is probably as difficult for high-status as for low-status children:

A baker goes with bread the same way as a carpenter goes with what?
( ) a saw   ( ) a house   ( ) a spoon   ( ) a nail   ( ) a man

The ordinary intelligence test contains many items of the first type. As a consequence, the test, by bringing in words that are less familiar to him, tends to penalize the child of low socioeconomic status.

Furthermore, children of upper and middle-class families are more often pushed by their families to do good work in school. School training itself helps one to do well in most intelligence tests. Therefore it is now thought that the differences in intelligence test performance between black and white children are mainly due to the fact that more black children are working-class. When middle-class black children are given intelligence tests, they do about as well as middle-class white children.

Most anthropologists and psychologists now believe that there is no innate difference in intelligence between racial or ethnic or religious groups. There are innate differences between *individuals* within these groups, but the average intelligence of the *groups* is the same, it is thought, if the groups have equal opportunity and similar training in solving the ordinary problems of life.

The Theory of Innate Group Differences

The possibility of racial group differences in intelligence has not been ruled out by all scientists. A vigorous controversy developed in 1968–69 over the publication by Professor Arthur R. Jensen, a distinguished educational psychologist, of his conclusions from his own and other research on intelligence in relation to heredity, social class, and race (Jensen 1968, 1969). Jensen believes that intelligence is inherited to a considerably larger degree than most other psychologists believe. He also believes that certain research studies demonstrate a genetic difference between whites and blacks in the quality of abstract intelligence, although this, too, is doubted by most social scientists.

Most social scientists agree with Jensen that the quality measured by intelligence tests is *partially* determined by heredity. The difference between Jensen and others is over the degree to which this quality is determined by heredity and the degree to which it is determined by the experience of a person, or his environment. (In technical terms, what proportion of the variance on an intelligence test is to be attributed to heredity, and what proportion to environmental influence?)

The controversy is not likely to die out, since there is a long history of belief in the superiority of certain races by the members of these races, and whites have been especially prone to believe in their own superiority.

Educational Implications. If there is a real and substantial innate intelligence difference between races, it might be socially desirable to educate the races differently. This is what Jensen and some others suggest. They believe that black children learn well by mechanical kinds of rote learning, but not so well by reasoning ability of a more abstract level. Therefore Jensen suggests that black children should be trained to memorize, rather than to reason things out. This has the implication that blacks should be trained for the less complex, the less creative, and the less prestigeful occupations. Also, this line of thought might be used to argue for segregation of black children in separate schools (Jensen, 1973). (Jensen does not argue, incidentally, that Chinese or American Indian children have lower innate intelligence than whites, or a different kind of intelligence. He believes the evidence shows that these groups have the same level of innate intelligence as whites.)

Peggy R. Sanday (1972) takes issue with Jensen by supporting the following propositions:

1. The magnitude of the genetic contribution to a given trait cannot be measured with present methods if the trait is determined by more than one gene, as is true for intelligence.
2. The methods used to measure intelligence (the ordinary tests) are not equally valid for various socioeconomic groups.
3. When the socio-cultural factors for different socioeconomic and racial groups are equated, the measured intelligence does not differ reliably, or differs very little.

This last proposition is disputed because a variety of published researches give a variety of results. But the most recent studies, where black and Chicano children of middle-class status have been studied in sufficient numbers to give stable results, appear to support this proposition. For example, Mark Golden *et al.* administered the Stanford Binet test individually to three-year-old black children who ranged from middle-class to lower-class welfare families, and found a range of IQ for various groups to be from 116 to 93, almost identical with the range for white children.

In a study of school-age children in Riverside, California, Mercer (1973) found that when the socio-cultural factors (such as home background and education of mother) were kept equal, there was no difference between the intelligence of Chicano, black, and white elementary school children. But Jensen's response to Mercer is that socio-cultural factors are themselves determined at least partly by the innate intelligence of the parents. That is, parents who are more intelligent create a favorable socio-cultural environment for their children; but it is their own innate intelligence passed on to their children that gives the children high intelligence test scores.

Evaluating the Theory of Innate Group Differences.   There are complex technical problems in the statistics used to study the relative importance of heredity and environment in the development of intelligence. There are also complex problems in constructing a test which measures "intelligence" equally fairly in different subcultural groups. These considerations led the National Academy of Sciences to appoint a committee of scientists, including three outstanding geneticists, to report on the state of knowledge in this area. The National Academy of Sciences can speak with something like the authority of the Supreme Court in areas of its competence. The report states:

> With complex traits like intelligence the generalities are understood, but the specifics are not. . . . There are strong disagreements as to the relative magnitudes of hereditary and environmental factors in intelligence. . . . There is no scientific basis for a statement that there are or that there are not substantial hereditary differences in intelligence between Negro and white populations. . . . (National Academy of Sciences, 1967, p. 892–3)

Thus the issue remains moot in the eyes of the National Academy of Sciences. Nevertheless, because it is difficult to avoid taking a position on the matter, the present authors should make clear their own opinions: namely, the theory of innate group differences of intelligence cannot be accepted as a basis for operating schools in a democracy. And, even if it were proved that there is a hereditary group difference, this difference is small compared with the effects of improved environment, and the school is inherently an environmental treatment agency. Whatever the future scientific research may reveal regarding innate group differences, the school system in a democracy must pursue a policy that aims to enhance each child's abilities.

HOW THE SCHOOL OPERATES
AS A SELECTING AGENCY

The school system attempts to treat children in accordance with their intellectual ability on the ground that children of different kinds of intellectual ability need somewhat different educational experience. At the same time, it is true the system has tended to treat children of higher social status *as though* they had higher intellectual ability. This differential treatment in relation to social class is not intentional on the part of most school people; it results primarily from the cultural differences between social classes.

One can see the school system operating to encourage children of higher social status and to discourage children of lower social status in nearly every aspect of the school program, formal and informal.

Ability Grouping

In many schools where there is more than one classroom per grade there is "ability grouping" or "homogeneous grouping," whereby pupils of the same general academic level are supposed to be grouped together. This is aimed at facilitating the work of the teacher. Whenever there is "homogeneous grouping" in a school that draws from a socially diverse population, however, the groups tend to become homogeneous for social class as well as homogeneous for mental ability.

The pattern of grouping varies from community to community. In some schools, ability groups are formed only in particular subject-matter areas, as when those children in a grade who are poor in reading, or those who are particularly good in science, are given special instruction as a group. In such schools, the child may spend only one period a day with a "special" group; the rest of the time, with his regular group. This modification of "homogeneous grouping" tends to counteract the possible social-class biases that may otherwise operate.

To take another example, schools in homogeneous parts of a large city, where the school population is drawn from one or two social classes, may use a scheme of sectioning by ability that brings together those children with the most motivation for education. The children who consistently work hard often seem to teachers to be the abler ones and will tend to be grouped together.

Ability grouping has been severely criticized since about 1965 on the basis of the double-barrelled argument that (a) the ability tests as they now exist tend to favor middle-class children and (b) the tests now in use tend to segregate students by social class and by race. In some places, ability grouping has been ruled illegal by the courts, and school boards in some of the larger cities have abandoned or reduced the extent of ability grouping.

High School Curricula

In the high school there exists another basis for grouping pupils: by type of curriculum. The typical American high school is of the "comprehensive" type, with several different curricula or courses of study. There is the college preparatory curriculum; the commercial; the vocational, which may include agricultural and home economics programs; and the "general" curriculum for those whose vocational aim is not clear and whose ability is not high enough to warrant entrance to the college preparatory program. (The general curriculum does not usually include mathematics or a foreign language, and thus differs from the college preparatory.)

The several curricula tend to draw differentially from the social classes, with the college preparatory curriculum enrolling higher-status pupils and the general and vocational curricula those of lower status.

Types of Secondary Schools

In large city school systems, high schools themselves are often of various types (as differentiated from comprehensive high schools in which several curricula are offered within the same school building). Usually there are the "academic" or "general" high schools, and the "trade" or technical schools.

In the majority of large cities, the comprehensive high schools have attendance districts of their own, and all students living in a given district are expected to attend the school from that district unless they go to a vocational or other special school. The attendance districts tend to be fairly homogeneous in the social class of their residents.

Some basic differences between various types of high schools have been identified and described, for example, in a study of the high schools (public and private) in the Kansas City metropolitan area. Levine, Mitchell, and Havighurst (1970) studied the high school seniors in 55 schools in spring, 1967. The high schools were classified according to the socioeconomic status of the students' families, according to size, and according to public versus private control. This resulted in six types of schools:

Middle-class—with 44 percent or more of the fathers being college graduates.
Socially comprehensive—with fathers showing a wide distribution of social
    status.
Working-class—with 41 percent or more of fathers in manual occupations.
    Two subtypes: mainly white families and mainly black.
Small public—with less than 100 students in the graduating class, and social-
    status distribution similar to working-class schools. Mainly in rural
    areas.
Catholic and other private schools—with a social-status distribution like that
    of the comprehensive school.

73

The seniors were asked whether they expected to go to college. As shown in Table 4.4, the proportion of students expecting to go to college was related both to the socioeconomic type of the school and to the socioeconomic status of the student. That is, a lower-middle-class student (Status III) was more likely to expect to enter college if he attended a middle-class school than if he attended a working-class school. And his likelihood of attending college was greater than that of a working-class student, but less than that of an upper-middle-class student in a given type of school. This can be seen by comparing the figures for Status III with those for Status II and IV for each type of school.

Private Schools.   The parochial type of private school is usually quite similar to a public school in its relation to social class. Most parochial schools are Roman Catholic, and the Catholic Church in most communities is fairly representative of the total population as regards social class. In a large city the Catholic parishes are likely to be differentiated along social-class as well as along ethnic lines, thus producing variation from one elementary school to the next. The parochial high schools are generally of the comprehensive type and draw from all social groups.

The "independent" private schools cater to families of upper and upper-middle class and perform special functions in relation to the social structure. Boys and girls of upper-middle-class families may learn social skills and may make friendships that will help them later to rise to upper-class positions.

Single vs. Multiple-Track School Systems

A formal procedure for selective treatment of pupils has been operating in Europe ever since these countries have maintained a free public school system. This is known as the *multiple-track* system, in contrast to the single-track system of the United States and certain other countries. The single-track school system is one in which there is one general pathway from the first to the last year of school, a track that leads from the first grade to the terminus of the university. All pupils continue in the same pathway until they leave school, whether they drop out as soon as the law allows or whether they go on beyond this point.

By contrast, a multiple-track school system is one in which pupils start out together at the elementary level, but where they are later shunted to one or another track—one leading to the university, another leading to the teacher-training institution, another to the vocational school, and so on.

While in reality both American and European educational systems provide more than one track, it is customary to speak of European systems as multiple-track systems, with elementary schools that lead to commercial, teacher-training, or trade schools, and with only a minority of pupils shifting

TABLE 4.4. *College Expectations in Relation to Social Class and Type of High School: 1967*

Percent of Twelfth-Grade Students in Kansas City Metropolitan
Area Expecting to Go to College
(arranged by socioeconomic status)

Type of High School	I (high)	II	III	IV	V (low)	Total Number	Total Percent
Middle-class	87	87	80	70	—	1422	84
Comprehensive	80	68	61	40	22	4110	58
Working-class							
Black schools*	47	54	58	56	40	780	54
White schools	74	58	55	33	25	741	42
Small	74	58	52	29	30	828	41
Catholic	80	74	69	53	46	804	63
Total (Percent)	81	72	63	42	30		59
(Number)	1149	1634	2896	2412	494	8685	

* These schools were almost entirely black in composition. Other schools had small minorities of black students.

Source: Levine, Mitchell, and Havighurst, *Opportunities for Higher Education in a Metropolitan Area,* Bloomington, Indiana: Phi Delta Kappa, 1970.

over at the age of 11, 12, or 13 to secondary schools leading to the university.

The system in the United States, with the majority of pupils following the track that can lead to the university, is usually spoken of as a single-track system. Certainly the single track has been carried further in America than in other countries, with the choice of pathway, when it occurs at all, being postponed until at least the ninth, and usually until the tenth or eleventh grade, and with the possibility for a pupil to move back and forth from one pathway to another.

The single-track system promotes social fluidity by keeping the way open to higher education for practically all young people up to the age of seventeen or eighteen. This provides time for boys and girls, with the aid of

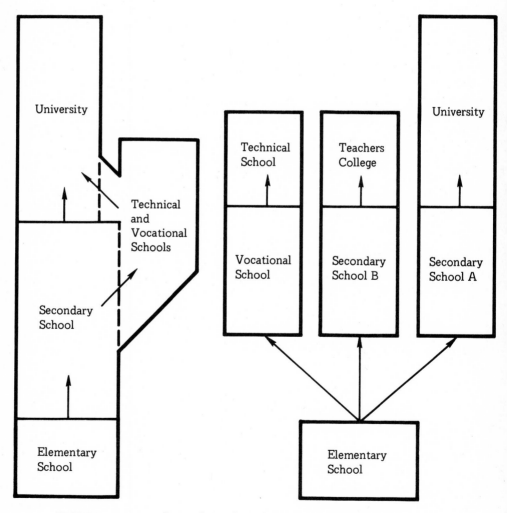

FIGURE 4.1   Single-track and multiple-track educational systems.

teachers, guidance officers, and age-mates, to explore the possibilities of higher education. Many young people of working-class status, if required at an early age to choose between a college-preparatory or a noncollege-preparatory course, as in the multiple-track system, would choose (or their parents would choose) a noncollege course. They might later regret the choice, at a time when it was too late to change.

On the other hand, the single-track system may discourage some working-class pupils from developing their abilities by forcing them into a verbal, academic curriculum, one that they dislike and which may cause them to drop out of school altogether.

Whether the single-track system promotes social fluidity, then, depends upon the particular school. One school may be so heavily dominated by the traditional college-preparatory requirements of mathematics and foreign languages that it alienates the alert and active-minded working-class youth. Another school, still within the single-track system, may offer a variety of alternative curricula, and may provide easy transfer arrangements, so that a boy or girl who starts in a commercial or vocational course can readily shift his program to get enough academic subjects to qualify for college entrance.

It is to be noted that the Russian school system is single-track, and that western European systems have been evolving recently toward the single-track and away from the multiple-track models.

Contrasting European and American Systems

To see more clearly the significance of the difference between a single-track and a multiple-track system, we may compare the school experience of youth in the United States with that of Denmark around 1965. Like other Scandinavian countries, Denmark is a practicing democracy, offers free education to all its youth, and seeks to encourage upward social mobility through education. But, for generations, until the most recent past, Denmark had several different and unrelated schools following the general elementary school. (This is changing now, as in other European countries, with movement toward a more nearly single-track school system.) But the system was still essentially multiple-track in 1965, when the data shown in Table 4.5 were obtained. After a seven-year elementary school, the Danish youth proceeded to one of two junior secondary schools. One of the schools offered vocational courses, while the other offered courses with foreign language and mathematics that prepared him for any of several examinations which would either certify him as a graduate of the secondary school who was ready for employment or admit him to the higher academic secondary school (the gymnasieskolen), from where he could go on to the university if he passed a stiff examination.

Table 4.5 shows how Danish youth aged 14–20 were distributing themselves among the general and university preparatory courses, the vocational courses, and dropping out of school for work or marriage. Data for American youth are presented in parallel columns. It is seen that substantially more Danish than American youth take vocational courses, except for 16 and 17-year-old girls, where the American girls are more likely to be taking courses in home economics or in typewriting and secretarial work. The young Danish men of 17 to 20 years flood into vocational schools, and thus actually have a higher school enrollment rate than do American males.

The Comprehensive High School

The American high school of the so-called comprehensive type carries the single-track system furthest toward the goal of social fluidity, since it

TABLE 4.5.   *Types of Education for Danish and American Youth: 1965*

		Percentage Distribution for Each Age Cohort					
		In General or University-Preparatory Courses, or College		In Vocational Training Courses		Not in School	
Age	Sex	Den.	U.S.A.	Den.	U.S.A.	Den.	U.S.A.
15	M	68	95	16	5	16	0
	F	78	95	5	10	17	0
16	M	47	80	34	15	19	10
	F	56	54	17	40	27	6
17	M	29	60	47	20	24	20
	F	34	39	30	45	36	16
18	M	19	50	57	15	24	35
	F	21	35	36	25	43	40
19	M	12	30	52	5	36	65
	F	12	25	32	5	56	70
20	M	11	25	37	5	52	70
	F	9	20	19	5	72	75

Note: The meaning of being enrolled in a vocational training course is not the same in the two countries. The vocational courses tend to be separated from academic schools in Denmark, whereas many of the federally supported vocational courses in the United States are taken by students in a comprehensive high school.

Source: United States: U.S. Office of Education: *Progress of Public Education in the U.S.A.*, 1971.
Denmark: Erik Jorgen Hansen, *Youth and Education: The Educational Situation of Danish Youth aged 14 to 20 in 1965.* Vol. II, table 1.2. Copenhagen: The Danish National Institute of Social Research, 1971.

contains a variety of curricula under one roof and permits transfers from one curriculum to another fairly easily. Furthermore, this type of school usually brings youth from all social levels together in classrooms and in extracurricular activities, thus encouraging the potentially mobile lower-status youth to learn social skills from middle-class age-mates.

The comprehensive high school may, however, operate to limit mobility. Students choose one curriculum rather than another in line with their social-class positions. Thus, the boys who take an auto mechanics course or a printing trades course tend to find themselves with other boys of their own social background, and they may learn to fit into the adult social structure accordingly.

A comprehensive high school, if it is run like a set of parallel schools, may do little in actuality to promote social fluidity. If it is run with a minimum of barriers between curricula, it may do much to promote fluidity.

Extracurricular Activities in High School

A high school with an active program of clubs, special-interest groups, and social affairs may promote social fluidity by bringing lower-status youth into intimate social contact with upper-middle-class youth. Thus lower-status boys and girls may learn skills and attitudes useful for upward mobility.

In the typical high school, however, the cliques who dominate the social life of the school consist mainly of higher-status youth. Although a few lower-status boys and girls, usually those who are already oriented toward upward mobility, may occupy positions of leadership, most lower-status youth do not participate in many extracurricular activities. Some, feeling excluded and unhappy, drop out of school altogether, thus losing opportunities for mobility.

THE SCHOOL, SOCIAL STABILITY, AND SOCIAL FLUIDITY

From a long-range perspective the school system in a democratic society is called upon to work toward two somewhat different goals: one, to improve society and promote social change; the other, to maintain a certain social stability and continuity over time. When the school system acts as a sorting and selecting agency it promotes movement or fluidity in the social structure by selecting some people for upward social mobility. At the same time it maintains stability of society by some of the ways it helps to keep children in the same social-class levels as their parents (as, for instance, in its ways of grouping pupils). While providing mobility, society must have enough stability so parents with high social status can give thier children a favored start in life, since they will insist on passing on to their children some of the rewards they themselves have gained.

The two goals of education, social fluidity and social stability, must be sought within the framework of certain basic realities about society and about human beings.

One reality is that the structure of society is based on a *division of labor.* There are positions of greater and lesser responsibility and prestige, positions requiring greater and lesser ability and energy. The social structure is changing due to powerful technological forces, with a relative increase in those positions that give generally greater rewards and that require greater ability and training.

Another reality is that of *individual differences* in abilities and temperament. While some types of ability are more socially valuable than others, children with all types of ability are born to parents of low as well as high status. According to generally accepted social ideals in America, a good educational system helps people to develop their socially valuable abilities and to find the positions in society where they can contribute most to the general welfare. Enough has been learned about the distribution of ability to know that we still have a long way to go in America before we reach the place where we are making the best use of all people's abilities. This is a job in which the educational system plays an important role.

It will be possible for the people of each new generation to find the places for which they are best fitted only if the society remains in a fairly fluid state. There must be a good deal of movement of young people from the social positions established for them by their parents to new social positions that they establish for themselves. The educational system helps in this process, while educating the society at large to welcome such fluidity.

As we saw in the preceding chapters, during the twentieth century approximately 35 percent of American adults have been upward mobile at least one step on a five-step scale, while approximately 15 percent have been downward mobile. Is this a sufficient degree of mobility for a healthy democratic society? Does it permit enough parents of middle-class or upper-class status to pass on some of their advantages to their children?

It sometimes appears that the critics of the American school system to whom we referred earlier would not be content unless every child born in a poor family was to move up at least one step on this ladder of social class. Thus, if the society had a stationary population and stable proportions of occupational and income positions at each level of the social structure, "every poor child a winner" policy would have to be balanced by an "every rich kid a loser" policy. Even in a society which is increasing its proportion of middle-status positions and decreasing its proportion of low-status positions, as is true of the United States, there could not be unlimited upward mobility for the children of low-income and low-status families. There are two reasons. One reason is that middle and upper-status families will use their intellectual, social, and economic resources to help their own children maintain the family status and will succeed in perhaps 80 percent of the cases, thus limiting the upward flow of children from lower-status families. Only a violent change in our political and economic institutions could prevent this.

The other reason is that—by definition—half of the children of lower-status families are born with below average native intelligence. (The same is true of upper-status families, again by definition, and assuming no innate differences among the social classes in this respect.) Even if environmental advantages were maximized through the school system for these children, most of them would probably not do well enough in school and in employment to compete successfully with those of more native ability. Not everybody can win.

Thus, a society which offers a considerable degree of opportunity to the "poor but able" and at the same time commands the support and collaboration of the middle and upper-class groups is bound to allow some advantages to the groups of middle and upper status. At the same time, a democratic, pluralistic society provides as much assistance as possible to the low-status groups. But there is bound to be a considerable group of children born to low-status families who do not succeed in moving out of this status, no matter how effective the schools and other instruments for mobility are. Hence the statistics will show more school dropouts, more low test scores, more of what is ordinarily called school failure among lower-status students than among middle and higher-status students. The fundamentally important question of social and educational policy is: Does the educational system provide adequate opportunity for children of low-status and ethnic-minority groups to learn the information, skills, and attitudes that will enable them to compete and to win a "fair" share of middle and higher-status adult positions? The answer to the question—What is a "fair" share?—must be what the majority of people believe is "fair."

The Balance of Social Fluidity and Social Stability

A serious student of American society in relation to education during the period from 1850 to 1950 will discover that various minority groups and groups of poor people found and used a number of ways of working up to higher status. The educational system was one of their principal instruments, used more by some groups than by others. Whether there has been a wholesome and democratic degree of upward mobility in American society, and whether the educational system has been sufficiently effective as the principle instrument of mobility, are questions which may be answered differently by individuals of different socio-political attitudes.

Programs to Increase Educational Opportunity.   There have been many explicit attempts at making the school more effective as a purveyor of opportunity to disadvantaged groups—the poor and certain ethnic-minority groups. In general these have clustered around two contradictory strategies. One calls for integrating the schools racially and in social-class terms, so that disadvantaged children can attend school and be taught together with the more advantaged children. This is based on the propositions that (a) the disadvantaged pupil, when in school with children who perform better and are better motivated for school, will try harder and will learn along with them; (b) the schools and teachers of advantaged children are better than the schools and teachers of disadvantaged children, and therefore through integrating the schools the disadvantaged children will get the same quality schools and teachers as do the advantaged ones. The opposing strategy is that disadvantaged children should be taught with materials and methods most suited to them. This may mean bilingual teaching for those whose home language is not English; or Black Studies for black high school students; or special reading materials and methods for white children from the lower-working class. This strategy leads to acceptance of or demands for separate schools for ethnic minority students.

The federal government was committed by the Civil Rights Act of 1964 to enhancing the opportunities of ethnic-minority group students and by the Elementary and Secondary Education Act of 1965 to increasing the amount of money spent on the schooling of children from poor families. These events caused the Commissioner of Education, Francis Keppel, to authorize a survey of public schools to find out to what degree equal educational opportunity existed for pupils of various racial and minority and income groups. Professor James S. Coleman, sociologist, was appointed to direct the survey, which was carried out by the National Center for Educational Statistics of the U.S. Office of Education. Tests were given to pupils in grades 1, 3, 6, 9, and 12, and information was obtained on teachers and pupils in a sample of 4,000 public schools in the autumn of 1965. More than 645,000 pupils were studied. The test scores of the children were found to be most closely related to the socioeconomic status of their families, and only very slightly to the amount of money spent on the school programs, the age of school buildings, or the class size. (Comparative data on the test performance of the pupils are reported in Chapter 16.) When socioeconomic levels are kept constant across ethnic lines, black pupils get somewhat lower test scores than white pupils of the same social status, but it is not completely clear whether this is due to racial segregation of the schools. Rather, Coleman thinks this is due to the tendency for students to aspire at about the same level with their fellow students, and black students in black schools generally have lower aspirations. Black pupils in integrated schools scored higher than black pupils in segregated schools. Coleman says,

> The higher achievement of all racial and ethnic groups in schools with greater proportions of white students is largely, perhaps wholly, related to

effects associated with the student body's educational background and aspirations. This means that the apparent beneficial effect of a student body with a high proportion of white students comes not from racial composition per se, but from the better educational background and higher educational aspirations that are, on the average, found among white students.... As the educational aspirations and backgrounds of fellow students rise, the achievement of minority group children increases. (Coleman, 1966, p. 307)

Thus the Coleman report supports the argument for integrated schooling, as long as there is a solid core of pupils of middle-class status in the school, or at least a core of well-motivated pupils, to act as a reference group. Daniel P. Moynihan, commenting on the Equality of Educational Opportunity Study, concluded, "The evidence is that if we are going to produce equality of opportunity in the United States in this generation, we must do so by sending Negro students, and other minority students as well, to majority white schools." (Moynihan, 1967, p.9)

The Equality of Educational Opportunity Study and a number of research studies made since 1965 give an answer to the question that some middle-class parents and some white parents ask when they react to a program of school integration that will bring a number of lower-working class minority group children into the school their children attend. "Won't my child's school work suffer if he has to be in the same class with a number of lower-class black children?" The answer to this question, reinforced from several independent researches, is that the achievement of middle-class pupils does *not* decrease when their school or class receives some working-class black or other minority students, as long as the middle-class group remains in the majority.

CONCLUSION

The title of this chapter (School as a Sorting and Selecting Agency) implies a universal function of schools in modern societies. The school system inevitably facilitates the process of separating children into groups that move toward different adult occupations and statuses. This process may be conducted so as to create a great deal of opportunity and encouragement for youth from lower-status families to move up the social scale. This is a goal of education in a democratic society.

In working toward this goal in the United States, the school system has become involved in the major problems of race relations, social-class relations, and the discovery and maintenance of a viable combination of social fluidity and social stability in the society. We shall return to this topic in later chapters.

EXERCISES

1. In a school to which you have access, make a list of the children in a given classroom. Estimate their socioeconomic positions. Compare these positions with such things as their school grades, their extracurricular activities, and their vocational goals.

2. Study the life and functioning of a high school to find out how it fits into the social structure of the community it serves. To what extent does it encourage upward social mobility? To what extent does it fit boys and girls for social positions similar to those of their parents?

3. Interview several high school students of different social backgrounds to find out what their attitudes are toward the school and its various curricula.

4. Outline the kind of school–parent relationship that you think would be best in an elementary school situation in a working-class area of the city. How might this relationship differ from what would be best in a middle-class area? What would you try to accomplish through the school–parent relationship in the one and the other type of community?

5. How would you go about improving the extracurricular program in a high school where these activities have long been monopolized by a small fraction of the students?

SUGGESTIONS FOR FURTHER READING

1. The effect of the social-class structure upon education is treated at length in *Elmtown's Youth* by August B. Hollingshead; in *Children of Brasstown* by Celia B. Stendler; in *Social-Class Influences Upon Learning* by Allison Davis; and in *Growing Up in River City* by Robert J. Havighurst and colleagues. For a somewhat different perspective on the role of the school in relation to the social and economic structure of the society, see the book by Kimball and McClellan, *Education and the New America.*

2. A recent extensive study of high schools in a sample of cities throughout the country has been reported by Herriott and St. John. Their book, *Social Class and the Urban School* documents the discussion in this chapter. Also, a 1969 study of all the public senior high schools in the cities over 300,000 in population (*Profile of the Large City High School*, by Havighurst, Smith, and Wilder) reports on the social-class and racial composition of these schools.

3. A student interested in the history of education might do some critical comparison of the "revisionist" historians with the "establishment" historians in their accounts of the relations between schools and immigrant or disadvantaged youth over the past hundred years. The "revisionist" historians might be represented by Colin Greer, *The Great School Legend*; David Cohen, "Immigrants and the Schools"; and Michael Katz, *Class, Bureaucracy, and Schools.* The principal "establishment" historians whose work is challenged are Bernard Bailyn, *Education in the Forming of American Society;* and Lawrence Cremin, *The Transformation of The School* and *The Genius of Education.*

4. A good summary of the issues and of the research program that attempted to create "culture-fair" tests of intelligence (tests that would not penalize boys and girls from lower socioeconomic level) is given in "Social Class and Intelligence Tests" by W. W. Charters, Jr. that appears in *Readings in the Social Psychology of Education.*

5. The important questions about the relative influence of heredity and of environment in the production of intelligence cannot be answered in simple terms. There is always an interaction of heredity and environment. In the United States, the practical question concerns the relation of IQ to race and to social class. But no two racial groups have the same social-class or social environmental experience. Therefore, information about racial status is mixed up with information about the social environment. A student who is reasonably knowledgeable about statistics and about socioeconomic status could usefully study the recent publications of Jensen and of those who disagree with him. See Sanday, Scarr-Salapatek, Mercer, Stevenson *et al*, and Herrnstein.

6. A reasoned exposition of the controversy over racial differences in intelligence and over the relative power of heredity and of environment in the production of intelligence is provided by Professor Norman Daniels in *Harper's Magazine* for October, 1973, under the title "The Smart White Man's Burden."

7. The interaction of social class, scholastic aptitude, and college attendance has been illustrated in this chapter. For a more comprehensive analysis, one may follow the recurrent reports on *Project Talent* in the book by Folger, Astin, and Bayer (1970). A similar study of Wisconsin high school seniors and their college-going is reported by Sewell, Haller, and Ohlendorf (1970).

8. Goldberg's book, *The Effects of Ability Grouping* gives a good review of the issues and the findings.

9. *Rethinking Educational Equality* is a book of readings, edited by Andrew Kopan and Herbert Walberg, which deals in a sophisticated way with the problem of equality of opportunity in the United States for various minority and ethnic groups at the close of the decade of the 1960s.

CHAPTER 5

The College in the
Social Structure

Increasing numbers of Americans during the present century have come to look upon a college education as a necessity. The vast majority of upper-middle-class occupational positions are now occupied by college-educated men and women, and the number of these positions is increasing rapidly. As a consequence, there is need not only for young people born in middle-class families, but also for young people from lower-middle and working-class families, to obtain college educations. College is the avenue of upward mobility for growing numbers of young people.

The decade of 1960 to 1970 saw a doubling of college enrollment, as is noted in Table 5.1. Since 1970 the rate of increase has fallen off, and it appears that college enrollment will stabilize in terms of the percentage of youth going to college. But this does not mean that the college scene must become less changeful than it was in the 1960s. Rather, the 1970s are a period of questioning the values and the functions of the college in American society, backed by a readiness to make basic changes.

It is assumed that there is need for a variety of types of educational experience for young people from 17 to 21. There is general agreement that the academic high school and college should be only one of the avenues to adulthood, though still a very broad one. For example, James A. Perkins, formerly president of Cornell University, speaking in 1970, said:

"First, we in education, particularly in higher education, must reduce our propaganda that a four-year liberal arts experience is a necessity for everyone. This style of education, though essential for many, is probably not meaningful for more than one in five, and may be harmful for half the rest. The junior college is an effective alternative but only one alternative. We must continue to experiment. Second, we must recognize that specific vocational or professional purpose is a legitimate and necessary objective for the majority of students that come into our colleges and universities. . . . Third, we must reduce the emphasis on the idea that higher education can take place only inside institutions." (1970, p. 247)

This statement by a college president might be called an example of the "post-1970 realism" concerning the general matter of college enrollments. During the 1960s, undergraduate college enrollments increased regularly at a rate of about eight percent a year. But the rate of increase dropped to less than two percent in 1971 and 1972. This reflected an increase in the total 18-year-old group of less than two percent a year. The number of persons in the 18-year-old group will stay approximately constant until 1978, and then it will decrease slowly, due to the decrease of births in the 12 years following 1961. Unless the rates of high school graduates and college entrance rise substantially, there will actually be an absolute decrease in college enroll-ments after about 1978, and the projections in Table 5.1 will prove to be wrong.

A Commission on Non-Traditional Study was created in 1971 with Samuel B. Gould (Chancellor emeritus of the State University of New York)

TABLE 5.1.   College and University Enrollment, 1940–1980

Year	Enrollment Undergraduate and First Professional	Percent of 18–21 Age Group	Enrollment Graduate and Advanced Professional	Percent of 22–24 Age Group
1940–41	1,388	14.5	106	1.5
1955–56	2,348	27.6	250	3.7
1960–61	3,227	33.8	356	5.2
1965–66	4,945	40.1	582	7.3
1968–69	5,851	40.8	800	9.6
1970–71	6,533	46.1	900	9.4
1972–73	7,290	48.0	930	9.0
1975–76*	8,180	50.1	1,157	10.4
1978–79*	8,980	53.2	1,339	11.1

Note: Enrollment figures are in thousands. Enrollment figures are for opening fall enrollment, and generally include extension as well as resident students. First-professional-degree students include those working for M.D., LL.B., D.D.S., and similar degrees. Some of these students already have a bachelor's degree. Advanced-professional-degree students are working toward the Ph.D. or a similar doctoral degree. In recent years, approximately 20 percent of the under-graduate enrollment consists of part-time students, who are also employed. Thus the percentages in column 3 should be reduced about 20 percent to get the figures for full-time resident college students. Furthermore, many people enrolled in college are over 21 years old. The actual percentage of youth aged 18–21 in college was about 35 percent in 1972–73. Columns 3 and 5 are percents of the numbers in these age-groups.

Source: U.S. Office of Education, Digest of Educational Statistics 1972.
*Projections of the U.S. Office of Education.

as chairman, and with financial support from the Carnegie Corporation. The Commission was created by the Educational Testing Service and the College Entrance Examination Board, both agents of the higher education establishment. Mr. Gould said, at the beginning of the Commission's life, "We believe that change can and should come from within the present system of higher education as well as from without, . . . we will explore vigorously the means to bring about effective change and to provide new, high-quality alternatives to traditional patterns of study and degree-granting. We will also identify and develop a variety of specific models for opening up access to higher education on a national scale." (Educational Testing Service, 1971a)

A more explicit commitment to the broad societal goal of the good life is recommended by Amitai Etzioni, professor of sociology at Columbia University. Discussing *Higher Education in an Active Society* he writes: "Like generals preparing to fight again the last war in the next engagement, many features of the American system of higher education are past rather than future oriented. At present, the American college and university system is best at preparing students for a society which is committed primarily to the production of commodities, while the society is reorienting toward a growing concern with the Good Life." (Etzioni, 1971, p.II-1) He proposes a broader general education experience for all American youth which will include a year of national service for youth between high school and college, and a guarantee to every high school graduate of two years of college education, through an open admissions policy.

DECREASING SELECTIVITY IN COLLEGE ADMISSIONS?

Policies and practices concerning admission to college have undergone a radical change during the years just before and after 1970. It became clear in the late 1950s and early 1960s that competition for entrance to the more favored colleges was increasing, and that colleges were becoming more selective in their entrance requirements. The reasons were the increasing numbers of young people of college age and the rising cost of maintaining a college. The latter factor operated to keep private colleges from expanding to any great degree and forced public-supported institutions to take most of the increased enrollment. Although it was possible for any boy or girl who had average ability to get into a college, it was much more difficult than formerly for the person with average ability to get into one of the growing number of selective colleges. Even the state universities were establishing strict entrance requirements, whereas most of them in 1940 had been admitting any student in the state who had a high school diploma.

The crowding of the colleges, due to the increased numbers in the 18–21 age cohort, which took place after 1965 permitted the private colleges to raise their tuition fees, forced the state governments to expand the state colleges and universities, and induced the legislatures to vote funds for a network of local state-assisted community colleges.

About 1968 there occurred a remarkable change in college admissions policies. The use of standardized achievement and aptitude tests to select those students to be admitted to the selective colleges and universities came under serious attack. It was clear that these tests were operating to limit access to such colleges by black and white youth from working-class families. These youth were being forced by relatively low aptitude-test scores and by low family incomes to attend public colleges with the lowest admission requirements. Also, a few experiments with the admission of such young people to selective colleges showed that some of them, at least, could succeed in these colleges if they were given special consideration.

By 1970 there was a broad movement toward admissions procedures that would admit at least a substantial minority of students who could not qualify by the earlier aptitude test requirements. For example, the City College of the University of the City of New York, long known as more highly selective than even some Ivy League colleges, adopted an open admissions policy which admitted, up to the capacity of the College, any applicant with a high school diploma. More common was the practice of other colleges to create a quota of places in the entering class for students who could not meet the previous aptitude test requirements.

A striking example of this change of admissions policies was the creation by the College Entrance Examination Board of a Commission on Tests with the following assignment: "The Commission is asked to describe a comprehensible set of testing activities supporting open access to higher education under conditions in which, as stated earlier, 80 percent of high school graduates and 70 percent of 18-year-olds, together with significant numbers of adults, will make up the college-bound population. The exact figures may be debatable, and the time at which this level will be reached may be even more so. The important point is that our reference is to mass higher education and to the full range of people making up the potential post-secondary population." (College Entrance Examination Board, 1970, p. 2)

It was not proposed that there be no admission requirements or no tests, but rather that new tests or other methods be developed to select young persons of potential ability and of merit for the kinds of post-secondary education which they can use most profitably.

It is too early to say how the new selective procedures will differ from the old ones. They will certainly take account of personality as well as cognitive qualities. They will pay less attention to formal academic records and more to qualities of creativity and commitment to societal betterment.

Thus the ground was prepared in the early 1970s for a democratization of college-level education that would require a vast increase of financial support for higher education.

FACTORS RELATED TO COLLEGE
ATTENDANCE PRIOR TO 1970

During the period from 1950 to 1968 the increase of college attendance represented the application of a policy that able youth should go to college, independent, as far as possible, of their family income.

For example, a recent report from Project Talent (1964) concerning high school graduates of 1960 showed that general picture, although the actual percentages were a bit different from those given in Table 4.2 in the preceding chapter. The Project Talent report showed that, 18 months after high school graduation, 94 percent of the top quarter of high school graduates had entered college. Of those above average but below the top quarter, 53 percent had entered college. A study of high school graduates of 1961 in Minnesota showed that 88 percent of the top 10 percent entered college (Hood and Berdie, 1964).

Academic Ability. The present authors estimate that 87 percent of the youths who are in the top quarter in scholastic ability now enter college. This leaves 13 percent of the top quarter, or 3 percent of the total age group, who ought to go to college if scholastic ability were the major determinant. Who are these young people, and why do they not go to college today? The majority of them come from working-class homes or from lower white-collar homes. The majority of them are women. If they are to go to college, most of them will need financial assistance, and many, if not most, will need substantially more motivation for higher education.

Of the third highest quarter in intellectual ability, some 65 percent now enter college. The remaining 35 percent of this ability group come mainly from working-class and lower-middle class families and a good many of them are black, Puerto Rican, or Mexican, whose IQ scores probably underestimate their true learning ability. Also, more than half of them are women. If the schools undertook a major program of financial aid and of motivation aimed at this particular group, perhaps as many as a third to a half of them might be persuaded to enter college, or another 5 percent of the total age group.

The great increase of college enrollments since World War II did not at first lower the scholastic ability of students who are in college. Thus Berdie, who studied the scholastic ability of college freshmen in Minnesota between 1930 and 1960 says, "The intellectual ability of the Minnesota college students today is no different from what it was thirty years ago" (Berdie et al., 1962, p. 39). In spite of a tremendous increase in the absolute and relative numbers of students attending college, the mean ability scores of these students had remained remarkably constant. Similarly, Darley (1962) summarized the data from a national sample of 167 colleges and found that the average scholastic aptitude of college entrants did not change significantly between 1952 and 1959.

Since 1965 it is likely that there has been some reduction in the average scholastic ability of college entrants, as measured by the ordinary test of scholastic aptitude. This is documented by K. Patricia Cross (1971) in her study of the effects of "open door" admissions policies which have come into play since 1965. These policies have encouraged young people in the lower half of the scholastic ability range to enter college—especially community colleges where they can live at home and "try themselves out" in a one or two-year program.

There are various factors besides ability that determine whether or not a person goes to college.

Sex.   Whereas 52 percent of high school graduates are girls, more boys go to college. Roughly 57 percent of entering college students are men and 43 percent are women, and this ratio is about 58 to 42 for college graduates.

Race.   Smaller proportions of black youth go to college than is true of white youth, but this is largely due to the lower average socioeconomic status of blacks. The latter have increased their college attendance rates very greatly since 1965. The number of black students in college increased by 190 percent between 1964 and 1971, but still only 9 percent of college students were black in 1971, compared with 12 percent of the college-age black population.

Region of Country.   There is a wide variation among the states in the proportions of young people going to college. California, Utah, and Colorado have led the states for a number of years, while several of the states in the Deep South and Appalachia have had the lowest percentages entering and graduating from college. Presumably these differences reflect differences in prosperity for the most part, although value systems independent of socioeconomic status might also play a role.

Socioeconomic Status.   Young people from high-status families usually have both the financial means and the motivation to attend college.

The relationships between college attendance and social-class background of students have been explored in a number of researches during the past decade. Sewell (1970, 1971) and his research group in Wisconsin have studied the post-high school experience of a sample of Wisconsin high school seniors of 1957. They found that socioeconomic status has approximately the same amount of influence over college attendance as scholastic aptitude. They also found that the influence of parents and of friends is important in determining college attendance, even after allowing for the influence of socioeconomic status. That is, lower-class students are more likely to attend college if their parents and friends urge them to do so. Levine, Mitchell, and Havighurst (1970), as noted in Chapter 4, found that high school students of working-class background were more likely to go to college if they attended a high school in which the majority of students were of middle-class backgrounds than if they attended working-class high schools.

Basic facts from many studies such as the ones just cited concerning social status and college attendance are shown in Table 5.2, where data are presented concerning the social-class origins of college entrants. Since 1920 the proportions of working-class youth who enter college have risen markedly; but so, also, have the proportions of upper and middle-class youth.

If the factor of intellectual ability is added to this general picture, the three-way relationship between intellectual ability, socioeconomic status, and college attendance becomes clear, as stated in the preceding chapter. With relatively few exceptions, the boys and girls who are both high in intellectual ability and high in social status go to college. The proportion who go to college is considerably lower, however, in groups who are lower on one or both characteristics.

Who Will Go to College?

While the factors we have been discussing are related to college attendance in overall terms, the question of who does and who does not go to college can also be considered from the point of view of the young person himself. The probability that a particular boy or girl will go to college depends upon four factors: (1) mental ability, (2) financial ability, (3) propinquity to college, and (4) individual motivation. In other words, a young person will or will not attend college depending upon the extent to which these four factors determine his decision.

Of the four, mental ability is the factor that can be influenced least. Still, there is evidence that ability to do college work is influenced by school preparation as well as family experience. A substantial increase in financial aid in recent years has had the effect of sending more young people to college. Propinquity to college has also increased for a great many people. Not only has urbanization operated to give more people easy access to colleges and universities, but more institutions, such as junior colleges and branches of state universities, have become available.

Motivation for College

There is an interaction of financial ability with desire for a college education which is coming more and more to control the individual's decision about going to college. When young people about to graduate from high school are asked whether or not they intend to go to college and, if not, why not, the great majority of those who do not intend to go say they are not

TABLE 5.2. *Social-Class Origins of College Entrants*

Social Class	1920	1940	1950	1960	1970 Males	1970 Females
Upper and upper-middle	40	70	75	80	90	86
Lower-middle	8	20	38	45	70	57
Upper-working	2	5	12	25	48	32
Lower-working	0	0	2	6	20	10
Percent of total age group entering college	6	16	22	33	53*	41*

* When 1970 figures for males and females are averaged, the percent of the total age group who enter college is approximately 47.

Sources: 1920—estimated by the authors from scattered data.
1940—estimated by the authors on the basis of several studies of the occupations of fathers of college students.
1950, 1960, and 1970—composite figures from several studies of social class and college attendance.

interested in going or they cannot find the money that is necessary. A summary of the situation as of 1970 is given by the Carnegie Commission *(New Students and New Places)*. The most recent study, made in the mid-1960s, indicated that approximately 20 percent of high school seniors claimed expense as the greatest obstacle to college attendance. But roughly the same size group give reasons such as "not interested enough" or "prefer to work." (Carnegie Commission, 1971, p. 28).

Motivation or personal incentive for a college education arises from at least the following four factors:

1. *Need for achievement.* There seems to exist in some people a basic need for achievement that drives them toward accomplishing as much as they can in almost everything they undertake. This need for achievement is a deep and possibly unconscious drive. Not only may the person be unaware of the extent to which this need operates within him, but the extent of the drive may not always be apparent in the person's school record.

2. *Identification with persons who have gone to college or done well in school.* It is likely that a boy or girl will do his best in school if he has identified closely with another person, usually a parent, who has done well in school. The process of psychological identification is well known whereby a child takes an older person for his model and tries to do and to be all the things that model represents to him.

3. *Social pressure.* In addition to the unconscious pressure that stems from identification, there are also a number of social pressures upon an individual of which he is fully aware. Family members, friends, teachers, and other persons in the community have expectations concerning school achievement, high school graduation, and college attendance, and these expectations act as pressures upon the individual.

4. *Intrinsic pleasure in learning.* A person who enjoys studying and learning will do as well in school as his ability permits. Probably intrinsic pleasure is a more important factor in artistic and musical achievement than in school achievement at the elementary and secondary school levels. It is likely, however, that intrinsic pleasure in learning is a factor of some importance when it comes to making decisions about entering college and in achievement in college.

The Counterculture?

Another piece in the complex puzzle of American higher education in the 1970s is the attitude that members of the counterculture take towards college attendance. If this group grows very much in size, it will exert a large influence over schools and colleges by the choice its members make of particular colleges, and by their decisions to go to college or not. During the 1960s they found their main base in the colleges, either as students or as dwellers on the fringes of the campus. But in the early 1970s it appears that some of this group are drawing away from the colleges to live a more isolated life, in the geographical sense.

TYPES OF COLLEGES

There is a great variety among the 2,500 colleges and universities of the United States, not only in the nature of their educational programs, but also in the social composition of their student bodies. It is possible to categorize colleges and universities into several main types. No given institution will fit in every respect one of the following types, nor is this an exhaustive list, but the types are useful in considering how colleges vary in the ways in which they fit the social structure.

Cosmopolitan University.   This university is either a midwestern or western state university or a large municipal university. It charges a small tuition fee to residents of the state. Although it has a liberal admission policy, it maintains fairly high academic standards by failing a large proportion of the freshman class every year. In socioeconomic status its students, as shown in Table 5.2, come from almost the whole range of social levels. Campus life tends to be dominated by upper-middle and a few lower-middle-class students.

      The social life of this campus is extraordinarily diverse. There are conventional fraternities and sororities that draw upper-middle-class youth and a few mobile youth from lower-middle and working-class homes. The church foundations provide social centers for those young people of all status levels who do not care for the activities of the more sophisticated social organizations. A Student Union offers organized activities and informal recreation for boys and girls of all degrees of social affiliation and sophistication.

Opportunity College.   This college appears in several versions, always characterized by low costs, easy admission standards, and a predominance of students from working-class families. It may be a city community college, with all its students commuting to school. Or it may be a small "self-help" college, with a number of cooperative work enterprises in which students earn their board and room.

      This college tends to draw ambitious youth, usually of high average but seldom of superior academic ability. The sons and daughters of salespeople, office clerks, railway brakemen, construction workers, factory workers, and tenant farmers predominate. Opportunity College is primarily a place for youth who hope to be socially mobile by learning middle-class vocational skills more than by learning middle-class social skills. (A case study of this type of college is given by Clark, 1960.)

Black College.   The traditionally black college was founded in the South during the latter part of the nineteenth century, and most of the border states established one or more public colleges for black students. There were, in 1973, 107 black institutions, including two universities—Atlanta and Howard—which offered the Ph.D. degree. In 1970 there were 33 public institutions, several of them by that time having 10 to 50 percent white students. The other 74 black colleges were private colleges, mainly church-related. These have been the main source of educational opportunity for southern black youth. Their students come mainly from black middle-class and upper-working-class families. There are a handful of high-status elite schools, who send more than half of their graduates on to graduate and professional schools.

Ivy College.   This is the generic name for the high-status colleges with long and respected tradition which are highly selective in their admission policies. Ivy College may be an eastern school that ranks at the top of the liberal arts hierarchy; or a midwestern church-related college where there is a long waiting list. Both types have fine records of sending students on to graduate work.

Ivy College is the only type in America that has a literal majority of students from upper and upper-middle-class families. Added to these are a minority of ambitious, hard-working boys and girls from lower-middle-class families and a scattering of working-class youth who are strongly motivated for academic and professional success. Social life centers around clubs, fraternities, and informal dormitory activities.

For the minority of upward-mobile youth in Ivy College there are tremendous learning opportunities, both intellectual and social. The intellectual opportunities are open to all, through a stimulating academic program and through personal relationships with competent scholars. The social opportunities tend to be more restricted for these mobile young people, with only those of attractive social talents, or with special artistic or athletic abilities becoming members of the prestigious campus cliques and organizations.

Warnell College.   There are several hundred Warnells, a generic name used to represent those liberal arts colleges found in cities of 10,000 to 100,000, where they are regarded as the chief cultural asset of the community. Most of these colleges are church-related, either now or in the past. They are essentially middle-class institutions, as much lower-middle as upper-middle. By location and by tradition they tend to remain culturally homogeneous. They may be largely Methodist, or Presbyterian, or Baptist, or Lutheran, or

Catholic. There are some black Warnells in the South, and a small but in-creasing number of black students attend the northern Warnells. Jewish students are present, but in a small minority.

Warnell is a much more comfortable place than Ivy College for boys and girls of lower-middle and working-class status. It is the easiest kind of college in which to learn upper-middle-class social skills.

Composition of Student Bodies

Table 5.3 represents the estimated proportions of young people from different social classes who make up the student bodies in these various types of colleges and universities. The estimates have been arrived at on the basis of a variety of studies, both formal and informal, relating to occupa-tional and social-class levels of students in attendance at various institutions, admission policies, dropouts, educational standards, and so on. (Examples of such studies are Clark, 1960; Sanford, 1962; Berdie et al., 1962; Astin, 1969; Folger, Astin, and Bayer, 1970.)

The American college system is adapted to a fluid and variegated social structure and to a society in which a relatively high proportion of young people go to college. The diversity and fluidity of the society are reflected in the colleges. Empirical studies of college characteristics supple-ment the descriptions just given. Stern (1963) identified the following six factors in the college environment which are related to student characteris-tics: intellectual orientation, social effectiveness, play, friendliness, con-straint, and dominance-submission.

The Carnegie Commission on Higher Education (1971) has classified colleges and universities somewhat more by the nature of their instructional program than by the nature of their students. This classification is as follows, with the percentage distribution of undergraduate students for 1968, when the total undergraduate enrollment was 6,483, 000.

Doctoral-granting institutions	27 percent
Comprehensive colleges	31 percent
Liberal arts colleges I (Ivy)	2 percent
Liberal arts colleges II (Warnell)	8 percent
Two-year institutions	29 percent
Specialized institutions	3 percent

Higher Education Around the World

The period since World War II has seen a major expansion of higher educa-tion in all parts of the world, in the economically developing nations as well as the more developed nations. This expansion has two driving forces behind it. One is the technological development and the urbanization of the country, which increases the proportions of professional, technical, and

TABLE 5.3. *Estimated Social-Class Composition of Students in Various Types of Higher Institutions*

Family Status	Percentage Distribution				
	Cosmopolitan University	Ivy College	Opportunity College	Warnell	Black College
Upper and upper-middle	20	75	5	30	15
Lower-middle	45	20	35	50	35
Working	35	5	60	20	50

TABLE 5.4. *Comparative Enrollment Rates for all Higher Education*

Country	Age Group	Percent of Age Group Enrolled				
		1950–1	1955–6	1960–1	1965–6	1968–9
Austria	19–24	–	3.0	4.5	6.4	8.3
Denmark	19–25	5.0	5.4	7.7	9.6	10.9
France	18–23	4.8	6.0	8.7	12.5	13.9
West Germany	20–25	3.8	4.4	5.8	8.3	9.0*
Italy	19–25	4.2	4.1	5.5	8.7	10.0
Netherlands	18–24	4.4	5.2	7.4	8.6	9.0
Spain	18–24	–	2.6	3.8	6.0	7.1*
Sweden	20–24	4.8	6.3	8.6	12.6	16.9*
United Kingdom	18–22	5.2	6.3	8.7	10.7	13.5*
Yugoslavia	19–25	2.7	2.9	6.1	9.2	11.5*
Canada	18–23	6.5	8.1	13.6	18.9	28.0*
Japan	18–22	4.9	7.1	8.1	12.0	14.1
United States	18–23	16.8	21.1	25.9	31.4	35.0

Note: The age group varies from a five-year to a seven-year range, and the normal duration of a higher education course leading to the first degree is three or four years. Graduate students are included in the enrollment figures. These facts suggest care in making comparisons between countries even though the general magnitudes are correct.

Source: Organization for Economic Cooperation and Development (OECD), Paris, 1971. *Analytical Report on Development of Higher Education.*

* Estimated

managerial positions in the labor force, most of which require post-secondary school education. The other is the broad social demand for higher education as a means of increasing economic opportunity for youth of low-income or disadvantaged minority groups. Related to this second force is the world-wide movement for more education and more participation of women in the work force.

Table 5.4 summarizes data on the growth of post-secondary education enrollments in various countries since 1950. The "enrollment rate" is obtained by dividing the overall enrollment in post-secondary institutions by the number of people in the age group which contains most students. This age group varies, ranging from a five-year cohort in some countries to a seven-year cohort in others. Actually, diplomas or degrees may be obtained for as little as two years' work in some countries (as the United States), while the Ph.D. degree requires as much as seven years of full-time study in some countries. Of the countries not included in the table, the Soviet Union, Australia, and New Zealand have relatively large post-secondary enrollment rates, comparable to that of Canada.

HOW MANY SHOULD GO TO COLLEGE?

A much larger percentage of the youth of the United States attend college than of any other country. The proportion is increasing in the United States, giving rise to a question, "In relation to the welfare of the society and the happiness of its youth, how many young people should go to college? Is there danger that too many may go?" (For further figures on number of college students, see Chapter 14, Table 14.1.)

Three Answers to the Question

A number of educational commissions have tried to answer the question of how many should go to college, and three major alternatives have been proposed:

1. *Two-thirds of the youth population to enter college; one third to complete a bachelor's degree.* This is the policy and the prediction recommended by the Carnegie Commission on Higher Education. It flows from the Commission's policy of *universal-access* higher education. This means that financial means and college places should be available to all young people who want to graduate from high school and to enter college. The Commission says:

> We now expect the percentage of college-age population actually in college at any moment of time to level off at about 50 percent in the year 2000,

99

although there are many uncertainties about its ultimate resting point. The 50 percent level will make it as possible for young persons of equal ability from the lower half of the socioeconomic scale to attend higher education as it is now for young persons from the upper half, and for all states to reach an average at the present level of the highest states in terms of high school graduation rate (90 percent) and entry of high school graduates into college (75 percent). (1971, p. 2)

This is the most expansive proposal yet made by a responsible and influential group of people.

2.   *Those who are in the upper two-thirds of the population in intellectual ability and who want to go to college.* This answer takes account of the fact that many able boys and girls do not wish to go to college. About two out of ten in the top quarter of ability do not have a strong desire to go; and motivation for college attendance becomes lower as we go down the scale in intellectual ability. This would bring about 50 percent of the age group into college, with less than half of this group graduating from a bachelor's degree program.

3.   *Those in the upper quarter of intellectual ability who possess a strong and clear motivation for college education.* Again, taking account of the facts of motivation for college-going, this proposal would bring at the the most 20 percent of the age group into college and would graduate about 15 percent.

The situation in 1974 was close to the second of these alternatives. About 46 percent of the age group entered college; many dropped out after one or two years, and approximately 22 percent graduated with a bachelor's degree after four or more years.

THE SOCIOECONOMIC FUNCTIONS OF COLLEGES AND UNIVERSITIES

During the twentieth century, colleges and universities in the United States have grown rapidly in order to keep pace with the development of a modern economy.

The modern technological society depends on the work of a large number of people in such occupations as research chemist, industrial engineer, accountant, laboratory technician, nurse, physician, teacher, banker, and specialist on computing machines. These are called "tertiary occupations" to distinguish them from the primary occupations of agriculture and mining and the secondary occupations of manufacturing and construction. They are occupations in which the worker receives a salary or fee rather than an hourly or weekly wage, or profits.

Table 5.5 shows how these occupations have increased since 1910 in the United States. In this table it can be seen that the biggest increases are in the category of professional and technical occupations and in the category of operatives and other semiskilled workers, which contains factory workers. These increases have been paralleled by decreases in the numbers of unskilled workers and of farmers. The important thing about the changes in occupational distribution shown in Table 5.5 is that the professional and technical occupations, which are growing rapidly, require a college education; while those that have been decreasing in numbers do not require formal schooling.

Several American economists (Schultz, 1961; Becker, 1964; Denison, 1964) attribute a large part of the twentieth-century economic growth of the United States to the increased knowledge and skill obtained through education by the people in the working force. They believe that, in expanding per capita production, the development of human capital through education is as important or more important than the development of physical capital such as factories, steel mills, power plants, and highways. The college and university may be seen as an investment made by a modern society with the aim of increasing economic production.

Since about 1920 the colleges of the country have been increasingly regarded by business and industry as agencies for recruiting and training the people who will occupy their most important positions. The highly educated person has become the central figure and the principal resource of modern society.

The vast and rapid economic growth of the United States has been both the cause and the result of the vast expansion of secondary and higher education during the twentieth century. At the same time, the expansion of education and of the economy has made possible a very large degree of upward social mobility. Working-class youth have made a major and increasing use of secondary and higher education as a means of achieving economic advancement. The selective process in American secondary schools and colleges has worked to recruit very large numbers of poor but able youth and to promote them into a new American elite.

There is some doubt expressed recently as to how efficient and how fair the educational system has been in promoting mobility. The writings of Katz (1972), and Berg (1970), have argued that gaining educational credentials has not been a sure guarantee of economic and occupational advancement. Now, with the vastly increased output of college graduates, education may not be sufficient to cause upward mobility for all youth who go to college for this reason.

Factors Affecting College Enrollment in the Future

Technology and economic growth have required expansion of secondary and of higher education, and in accordance with the demand, numbers

TABLE 5.5. *Occupational Distribution in the United States, 1910–1970*

Occupational Class	Percent of Men					Percent of Women				
	1910	1930	1950	1960	1970	1910	1930	1950	1960	1970
Professional and technical	3.1	4.0	6.4	10.7	14.0	9.2	13.6	10.0	12.2	14.5
Managers, proprietors, and officials	7.9	9.0	12.9	13.4	14.2	1.6	2.2	5.7	5.0	4.5
Clerical	{9.2	{12.8	{7.2	7.1	7.1	{13.9	{28.8	{26.2	29.8	34.5
Sales			{5.7	6.1	5.6			{8.3	7.6	7.0
Craftsmen and foremen	14.5	16.4	17.7	18.7	20.1	1.2	0.8	1.1	1.0	1.1
Service workers	2.0	2.7	6.4	{6.5	6.6	24.9	21.6	22.0	{14.8	16.5
Private household workers				{0.1	0.1				{9.8	5.1
Farmers and farm managers	19.9	15.2	9.4	6.4	3.2	3.5	2.5	1.5	0.5	0.3
Farm laborers	14.0	9.5	5.3	3.5	1.9	16.4	5.4	5.5	3.9	1.5
Operatives (semiskilled)	11.2	14.4	20.8	19.4	19.6	27.9	23.7	19.1	15.0	14.5
Nonfarm laborers (unskilled)	18.2	16.1	8.1	8.1	7.3	1.4	1.5	0.5	0.4	0.5
Number employed (millions)	29.5	37.9	42.2	44.5	49.0	7.8	10.7	17.5	22.2	29.7

Source: *Statistical Abstract of the United States, 1971,* Department of Labor, Bureau of Labor Statistics, Bulletin 1630, July, 1969.

of college students have risen sharply, as can be seen in Table 5.4. But will the technology of the next 20 years require further expansion of college enrollments beyond the 1970 level? The spring and summer of 1970 saw a softening of the job market for college graduates. By that time the 1950–1970 shortage of school teachers had disappeared, except in a few special fields. The aviation industry was reducing its manpower. General economic growth had slowed down, and these conditions continued on through 1974. Thus it was becoming clear that a college degree would not have the automatic economic value that it possessed in the 1960s.

But college enrollments are affected by other forces as well as the laborforce demand for college graduates. There are three of these forces which operate in an affluent, highly productive society:

1. The prestige of being a "college man" or a "university woman." A good many middle-class families send their children to college because it is the appropriate thing to do for people in their social class. This probably applies more to girls than to boys, since a considerable (but decreasing) proportion of girls expect to marry and keep house and rear children and do not expect to use a college education as a means to earn a living.
2. The "cultural value" of a college education. A good many educators and at least some college students see college as a place to cultivate one's mind and one's sensibilities so as to become a "better person" or a better citizen. This may become a greater force as American society moves from its present emphasis on *material productivity* to what some people expect will be an emphasis on *quality of life.*
3. The *custodial* function of the college—to give a young person a few years in a safe and preferably a nurturant environment before he assumes adult responsibilities. This function becomes especially important in a society that does not have many employment opportunities for adolescents, does not expect them to marry and rear children at this age, and does not have employment for them at home.

These three factors plus the overriding factor of the demand of the labor force all appear in varying combinations in the writings and the speeches of educators and educational commissions which deal with higher education in the 1970s.

The Carnegie Commission on Higher Education does not expect the less favorable job market for college graduates to discourage many young people from going to college.

"The prospect of a higher-paying job is by no means the only reason for attending college. It may not even be the most important reason in many cases. The cultural advantages, the opening of new avenues of intellectual interest and appreciation, and the enhanced social prestige associated with the college experience are likely to continue to stimulate rising enrollment rates even if the income differential associated with college graduation declines. Quite apart from genuine individual aspirations, the social pressures impelling young people to go on to college are strong indeed.... Perhaps most important, in a less favorable labor market for college graduates, employers are likely to raise their selection standards and require a bachelor's degree even more widely than is now the case. This would have an unfavorable effect on job opportunities for high school graduates who, in a deteriorating employment market, would be likely to experience prolonged unemployment. On the other hand, college graduates are not likely to be unemployed on any substantial scale but rather will have to accept less attractive jobs than they have been able to get in the past." (*New Students and New Places,* 1971, p. 53)

A similar expansionist view is taken by Dael Wolfle, chairman of the Commission on Human Resources and Higher Education, created by the Russell Sage Foundation to examine especially the relation of higher education to the manpower problems and issues facing the nation. In his own book, Dr. Wolfle says: "The United States has been blessedly free of rigid attitudes about what kind of employment is suitable for a college graduate. Some jobs carry higher prestige than others; some pay better; some have other advantages; but the typical college graduate has thought it better to accept the best job available than to be out of work. For their part, employers have usually wanted to employ the best-qualified applicant they could find, and that has often been interpreted to mean the one with the most education. Thus there have regularly been jobs for college graduates, and the concept of a surplus of college graduates has had little meaning. Nor do I anticipate an overall surplus in the 1970s. There will be enough new graduates for the jobs that require college degrees, and the rest of the graduates will be employed in work for which a college degree is optional but not required." (*The Uses of Talent,* 1971, p. 49)

The rather rose-colored picture painted here is different from the rather grim view presented by Peter Drucker in a magazine article bearing the title, "The Surprising Seventies." He believes that college graduates of the 70s will feel a severe shock on their entry into the labor market. He says, "During each year of the next decade, we will have to find jobs for 40 percent more people than in each of the past 10 years. . . . The first implication of this is, of course, that jobs are likely to be of increasing concern to the young during the next 10 years. The shift from "abundant jobs for college graduates" in 1969 to a "scarcity of jobs for college graduates" in 1971 is not, as most commentators believe, merely a result of the 1970–1971 minirecession. It is a result of the overabundance of college graduates, which will continue until the end of the decade even if the economy starts expanding again at a fast clip.

"At the same time that many more young, college-trained people are out looking for jobs, the largest single source of jobs available to them in the sixties—that is, teaching jobs—will almost completely dry up." (Drucker, 1971, p. 37)

The more conservative view, by 1973, was reflected in the final reports of the Carnegie Commission, which noted that college graduates in the 1970s would have to adjust to a less expansive labor market. Some of these people will have to accept jobs that do not ordinarily require college-educated persons.

> Perhaps somewhere in the vicinity of 1 million to 1½ million college-educated persons, as a *very rough guess*, will face this frustrating experience. But the same number would probably have ended up in about the same types of jobs if they had not gone to college. They are no worse off occupationally—and often may be better off in other ways—for going to college than they otherwise would have been. The problem, then, may be concentrated on about one-half of the 25 percent of the college-educated persons who will enter "educationally upgraded" positions. The potential problem is thus one more nearly for 10 percent than it is for 100 percent of college-educated persons.
>
> This is not to say that the resultant frustration will not be a negative experience for the persons involved—it will be. We only indicate the general proportions of the problem, and note that it is not a new problem. (*College Graduates and Jobs*, 1973, p. 4)

Colleges and Credentialism

From another quarter has come a slashing attack on a proposition that is central to the American ideology of higher education—namely, that a college education contributes directly to success in an occupation. During the 1960s the growing skepticism about the American society and its social institutions was directed by several critical persons into a series of investigations of the relationship of occupational success and college experience.

There are two aspects of this question. One is the relation of college grades to occupational success, and the other is the relation of the possession of a college degree to later occupational success. Both aspects depend on a definition of occupational "success," and a number of definitions have been used, such as amount of money earned, status of the job, ratings by one's peers.

There have been a number of careful studies of the relationship between college grades and postcollege achievement. Donald P. Hoyt has reviewed 46 of the studies and concluded: "Although this area of research is plagued by many theoretical, experimental, measurement, and statistical difficulties, present evidence strongly suggests that college grades bear little or no relationship to any measure of adult accomplishment." (1965, Summary) This is hardly surprising, since college grades have never been expected to measure the nonintellectual factors which are so important in a complex adult career.

The question of the relations between the *amount* of schooling and a

105

person's occupational performance has recently been raised critically by Ivar Berg in a book aptly titled, *Education and Jobs: The Great Training Robbery.* He finds that many people are employed in jobs that utilize less training than they possess, and that learning "on the job" is more effective than preparation in school or college in producing success. Also measures of aptitude are better than amount of education in predicting performance and earnings. This throws doubt on the validity of a diploma or a college degree as a means of selecting people for complex jobs. While many employers use the high school diploma or the college degree as a device for screening applicants, this may be a crude and unfair method. On the other hand, the study by Jencks and his associates (1972) of *Inequality* indicates that the amount of education is a good predictor of adult occupational status, and a fair predictor of adult income.

Commenting on this situation, a task force appointed by the Secretary of Health, Education, and Welfare, headed by Frank Newman of Stanford University and supported financially by the Ford Foundation, concluded:

> It is time to halt the enormous and growing power which colleges and universities have as sorting and screening institutions. One necessary course of action is to reduce the reliance on educational credentials as admission tickets to careers. We must develop mechanisms and criteria for measuring an individual's potential for a job that are more relevant than those now universally assumed to be valid. . . . The more immediate need, however, is to break the credentials monopoly by opening up alternative routes to obtaining credentials. The monopolistic power of existing colleges and universities cannot be justified on the grounds of their effectiveness in screening for occupational performance, nor on the grounds that being the sole agencies for awarding degrees and credentials is necessary to their educational mission. Internal reforms now under way—a de-emphasis on grades, more independent work, credit for off-campus experience, modest expansion in the use of equivalency examinations— are important but not enough. New paths to certification are needed. (Newman, 1971, p. 42)

Referring to this situation in what is often called a "learning society" where people must continually learn new occupational roles, Walizer and Herriott analyzed the personality characteristics necessary for competence in the more complex occupational roles of the modern society. They listed the following: "tolerance for ambiguities; creativity; an open, receptive mind; critical thinking ability; flexibility; freedom from authoritarianism and opinionated thinking; recognition of achievement via independence; ability to think abstractly and reflectively; and ability to assimilate new information in a logical manner" (1971, p. 5). These characteristics should be taught or encouraged, they believe, in an effective college.

THE 1970–1975 CRISIS

The answers to the questions—How many should go to college? Who should go to college?—are being worked out in the critical 1970–1975 period primarily by the national Congress and the state legislatures, because it is clear that privately supported colleges and universities cannot meet their previous share of the demand for higher education.

The question is being answered partly by the facts of the need of the labor force for numbers of college-trained people; partly by the desires of young people and their parents for a college education; partly by the creation of colleges and especially community colleges at places which are within commuting range of more and more young people; and partly by the readiness of the federal and state governments to aid students financially.

The number who actually do attend college also depends on the number in the age cohort which produces college students—usually taken as the 18–21 (inclusive) group. This group has increased from 12.3 million in 1965 to 14.4 million in 1970 and will reach 16.3 million in 1975, after which it will remain fairly constant until 1980, and thereafter will decrease, due to the decreased numbers of births after 1961. If the present proportion of the age cohort who attend college remains constant, college enrollments will increase 13 percent between 1970 and 1975, then will stabilize for a time, and will actually decrease somewhat after 1980. But if the proportion of the age cohort who attend college continues to increase, there will be corresponding increases in college enrollment.

Many educational experts who study enrollment statistics expect that the percentage of young people entering and graduating from college will continue to increase, roughly in accord with the expansionist view that the Carnegie Commission takes. Others expect the percentage of young people attending college to remain constant during the 1970s, while a few expect actual decreases in college-going. These differences stem from different expectations about the motivation of young people to attend college during a period when college graduates are having difficulty finding the kinds of jobs they believe a college experience entitles them to.

If the *proportions* of youth who attend college are to be increased, there must be substantial scholarship funds, and building of colleges in the home areas of the students. These additional students will generally have little or no financial support from their families, and they will need a great deal of encouragement.

Scholarships and Social Fluidity

The extent to which scholarships and loans promote social fluidity depends on the extent to which financial need, as well as ability, is taken into consideration. A considerable proportion of scholarship awards made before 1955 went to middle-class youth who would have gone to college anyway. The winner of a Harvard National Scholarship, for example, was often an upper-middle class boy who used the scholarship to go to Harvard instead of to his own state university where the expense would have been less.

The scholarship award situation changed slowly during the 1950s, as major scholarship funds began to stress the policy of aiding youth who needed financial help. By 1960 a concerted effort was being made to award scholarships on the basis of family income. The National Merit Scholarship Corporation awarded its scholarships on the basis of ability, but regulated the amount of the award according to the student's family income, with students from wealthy homes getting a Scholarship Certificate which had no money value. The colleges which offered the most valuable scholarships introduced the practice of requiring the parent of a scholarship applicant to fill out a form indicating the amount of his current income, the value of his insurance, capital assets, etc. As a result, very few students from families whose incomes were over $10,000 were given scholarships of much value, and the majority of awards went to young people from lower-middle-class families whose incomes were at or slightly above the median level for all American families.

Data from the National Merit Scholarship Corporation on the family incomes of 12,418 finalists who graduated from high school in 1964 throw some light on the effects of a highly selective scholarship program on educational opportunity for youth of low-income families. Nichols (1965) reported that Merit Finalists numbered 0.6 percent of high school graduates in 1964. Of this group, 1.8 percent reported family incomes less than $3,000; 3.8 percent less than $4,000; 11.1 percent reported less than $6,000; and 22.9 percent reported less than $8,000. The median family income in the United States was about $6,000. Thus about 1,300 young people from families below the median income won Merit Scholarships. Eighty-nine percent of the scholarships went to boys or girls from families with income above the median. Many of them were awarded only a token stipend because they did not need the money.

The intention of the Carnegie Commission and of most other policy-making groups is to increase socioeconomic opportunity and social fluidity through a vast government-financed program of scholarship grants and loans to students from families of below average incomes.

The Higher Education Acts of 1965 and 1972

Two significant laws passed by the Congress in 1965 and 1972 committed the federal government to basic support of higher education through two mechanisms. The first was a system of financial grants and loans to students. The second was a system of grants to colleges and universities, both public and private.

Student Assistance.   It is now generally agreed that the federal government will continue to increase its financial aid to students during the foresee-
able future. The Carnegie Commission on Higher Education has recommended
that the financial barriers to college attendance be largely removed so that
enrollment rates are independent of the socioeconomic status of the student's
family, and depend only on his scholastic ability and motivation for higher
education.

This can be achieved, the Commission says, through a combination of
direct grants to students and low-interest loans to students. Estimates of the
cost of this program are of the order of $4 billion a year by 1975 (in dollars
of 1970 purchasing power). The main load would be carried by the federal
government, with state government funds and private scholarship funds accounting for possibly 20 percent of student aid. Since student loan funds
would result in substantial repayment income after about 1980, the actual
layout by the government will be greater in the 1970–80 decade than later.

The 1972 Act provides a grant of $1,400 for every student who can
show that his family cannot pay for his college education. There will be a
sliding scale, depending on the family financial status and the number of
children in the family who want to attend college. Initially, the rules will
probably set a family-income level which will bar assistance to students from
most middle-class families. The details of the plan will be worked out in relation to the amounts of money actually appropriated by the Congress from
year to year.

A major issue developed in 1973 with the publication by the Committee for Economic Development of a report on the *Management and
Financing of Colleges* which proposed that public colleges and universities
should double or triple their tuition rates so that these would cover 50 percent of institutional costs, as they do at typical private colleges. At the same
time the CED recommended increased federal and state support of student aid
funds. Representatives of public institutions argued that this would tend to
increase student enrollment at private colleges, since the tuition costs would
be about the same at public and private institutions.

Direct Grants to Colleges.   The other aspect of the 1972 Act may have far-
reaching consequences which are only dimly perceived at present. Most colleges and universities, private as well as public, will receive grants of money
which they may use as they wish, related to the size of their enrollment.
Initially, these grants will amount to approximately $1 billion a year, but this
level of support will probably increase. One consequence of this may be a
stabilization of tuition charges to students. This would benefit students from
middle and upper-class families, as well as students from low-income
families.

Other Aspects of Government Assistance.   There is no likelihood that government scholarship grants will cover the entire cost of college attendance

for all students from low-income families. But there will probably be a substantial student-loan program, financed by the government, through some form of Educational Opportunity Bank. The Carnegie Commission has recommended that such a bank be established, to make loans to students up to $2,500 in any given year, up to a limit of $6,000 for a four-year period.

Graduate Advanced Professional Education.   Since the costs of graduate education are greater, the *educational opportunity grant* would be increased to $2,000 a year for two or three years, and the student could borrow from the Educational Opportunity Bank as much as $2,500 per year, up to a total of $10,000. Doctoral candidates, with high ability, after two or three years of graduate study would be eligible for a $3,000 annnual predoctoral fellowship. Other federal government programs for support of graduate programs will continue.

EXERCISES

1. Select a college you know. Analyze the student body in terms of socioeconomic backgrounds. What is the relation of socioeconomic background to fraternity membership, participation in athletics scholarship awards, participation in church organizations, and enrollment in various curricula or courses of study?

2. Of the four factors which determine whether or not a person shall go to college, which ones can be most easily changed in your home community? How would you go about changing them?

3. To what extent do you believe that there is danger of too many people going to college in the United States? What arguments can you use to support your position?

4. Suppose you were counseling a high school boy of about 110 IQ, who was not certain whether or not he should go to college. What advice would you give him, and how would you support your argument?

5. Assume that the state university and the private colleges of your state will receive applications for admission from 100 percent more youth in 1975 than in 1960. Suppose you were a member of a State Commission on Higher Education. What admission policies would you favor for the private colleges? For the state university? Why?

6. Everybody is now aware that the supply of college graduates exceeds the demand for them in the adult work force, after a long period of under-supply. But there is very little agreement as to what should be done about it. An interesting paper could be written by a student, based on the analysis and recommendations of the following authors: Peter Drucker, Dael Wolfle, David Riesman, Frederik Terman, Allan Cartter, James Harvey.

7. The actual state of college enrollment is a resultant of several forces: the amount of student financial aid, the market and salary level for college graduates, and the general feelings of students from low-income and minority groups

about the value of higher education. Students may study the interplay of these forces by comparing the expansionist recommendations of the Carnegie Commission on Higher Education during the 1970–73 period with the actions of the federal government and with the facts of the job market at any given time during the current decade.

SUGGESTIONS FOR FURTHER READING

1. There have been a number of recent studies of the nature of college students and their motivation for attending college. Some of these are: *The American College* edited by Nevitt Sanford; *Who Goes to College?* by Ralph Berdie, et al.; *A General Pattern for American Higher Education* by T. R. McConnell; *Factors Affecting Admission of High School Seniors* by Elmo Roper; *Changing Values in College* by Philip E. Jacob.

2. Colleges are seen as a positive force for the improvement of American society in the publications of the Carnegie Commission on Higher Education (Clark Kerr, Chairman). Special attention might be paid to the following reports: *New Students and New Places; A Chance to Learn: An Action Agenda for Equal Opportunity in Higher Education; The Open-Door Colleges; Policies for Community Colleges; The Campus and the City; College Graduates and Jobs; Adjusting to a New Labor Market Situation; Higher Education: Who Pays? Who Benefits? Who Should Pay?; Opportunities for Women in Higher Education; Toward a Learning Society; Priorities for Action; Final Report of the Commission; The American College and American Culture,* by Oscar and Mary F. Handlin; *A Degree and What Else?; Correlates and Consequences of a College Education* by Stephen B. Withey and colleagues; and *Models and Mavericks; A Profile of Private Liberal Arts Colleges,* by Morris T. Keeton. On the other hand, a negative view is presented in: *Education and Jobs: The Great Training Robbery,* by Ivar Berg. Critical and relatively neutral studies of the functions of colleges in the social structure are given by Christopher Jencks and David Riesman in *The Academic Revolution;* Frank Newman, *Report on Higher Education;* Wolfle in *The Uses of Talent.*

3. A useful general essay on the factors that produce inequality of opportunity for higher education has been presented by William H. Sewell in his 1971 presidental address before the American Sociological Association. (Sewell, 1971).

4. For a recent and thoughtful book addressed to the problem of how standards of excellence can be achieved in a democratic society which subscribes to equalitarianism ("everyone has a right to go to college"), read John W. Gardner's book, *Excellence.*

5. Bernard Berelson's *Graduate Education in the United States* is a readable book which describes the history of graduate education, the issues that have developed through time, and those that are currently controversial. (Included also is a discussion of the problems surrounding the preparation of college teachers.)

PART
II

The School as a
Socializing Agency

CHAPTER 6

Socialization and the Child's Life Space

In the first section of this book we focused attention upon the school in the social structure and upon the way the school functions to promote both social stability and social mobility. In this section we move to the function of the school as a socializing agency in the life of the child and how the school relates to other socializing agencies, particularly the family and the peer group, in providing the experiences by which the child gradually learns to take his place in society.

We shall deal in the present chapter with certain basic concepts such as socialization, social role, social loyalty, social life space. In the chapter to follow we shall focus the discussion directly upon the family, the school, and the interaction between them.

THE INFLUENCE OF THE SOCIAL ENVIRONMENT

The mind and the personality of the child develop, not according to immutable processes inherent in the child's genetic endowment, but according to the influences that particular social experiences have upon him. While normal development of mind and personality requires a normal physique (body, brain, and nervous system), the kinds of intellectual and social traits that develop depend primarily upon the interaction between the social environment and the child's biological potentials, upon what the child learns formally and informally, from social interaction.

The Socialization Process

Of special importance to educators is the general process of social learning whereby the child learns all the many things he must know to become an acceptable member of society. We refer to this process as the socialization process; we say that the child is gradually "socialized" (that is, he becomes a member of the group and takes on the ways of life that are the group's ways); and we say that society, through its agents (parents, teachers, and other persons), acts to "socialize" the child.

Biologically the human organism is predisposed toward social living and social learning. Because of his biological immaturity and his extended growth period, the infant is dependent upon other people. The human organism is also characterized by adaptability and by intelligence; by the ability to learn a great variety of modes of behavior, and to learn any one of a great variety of cultures and subcultures.

Socialization has facetiously been referred to as the lifelong process of "housebreaking." While the term is often applied to learning experiences that occur within the first years of life, to patterns of feeding, sleeping, toilet-training, control of aggression and sexuality, it is more accurate to think of socialization as a lifelong process. The child who learns how to read and write, the adolescent who learns to speak the special language used by his peers, the woman who learns how to behave as a mother and the man who, at 60, learns how to retire from work "gracefully" are all being socialized. Various social groups constantly provide new learning situations and expect new responses from the individual; all through life the individual is constantly fitting his behavior to social expectations.

Socialization is not only a matter of controlling or restricting the child's behavior. It also has active and constructive aspects: it produces growth; it encourages, stimulates and motivates; it produces an infinite variety of desires and strivings in the individual; it leads to development and to achievement of all kinds. Socialization is thus both a molding and a creating process.

Social Roles

Every individual becomes socialized by learning a set of social roles. A social role may be defined as a coherent pattern of behavior common to all persons who fill the same position or place in society and a pattern of behavior *expected* by others. The pattern may be described without reference to the particular individuals who fill the role. Thus, for example, all women behave in certain patterned ways when they fill the role of mother, so we speak of the social role of mother. All teachers are expected to behave in certain ways within the school room, regardless of how they may behave when they are filling other roles such as father or mother, husband or wife, friend, or church member.

A very young child learns first how to behave in the role of child; he learns that his parents take care of him and make decisions for him; that he may behave in certain ways, but not in other ways. Soon he learns to differentiate other social roles: that of being a girl or a boy, then brother or sister, then playmate, then pupil. As he grows older and as his circle of social interactions widens in scope, he takes on an ever-increasing number of social roles and incorporates the role behaviors into his personality. (See Figure 6.1). In this sense, the social self consists, in large part, of the behavior the individual expresses in his various social roles. In this sense, too, the well-socialized individual is one who fills his various roles successfully. While every person has his idiosyncratic pattern of role behaviors (thus no two persons fill the role of teacher in exactly the same ways), still the well-socialized person is one whose behaviors are appropriate to the expectations set by the social groups with which he interacts.

Socializing Agencies

The major socializing agencies in the life of the child are the family, the peer group, the school, the college, the church, the youth-serving organizations, political and economic institutions, and the mass media. Some of these agencies are formal and some informal. The school is an example of an agency formally organized for the purpose of inducting the child into his society; the peer group is an example of an agency that is informally organized. Before looking more closely at each of these agencies, let us look further at the general course of socialization, especially with regard to the timing of significant experiences in intellectual growth.

SOCIALIZATION IN THE
EARLY YEARS OF LIFE

Although individuals keep learning new ways of behavior all through their lives, it is also true that early learnings tend to be crucial ones because they set the pattern for subsequent learnings.

Educators in particular have long been concerned with the timing of different kinds of socialization: at what age, for example, the child is "ready" to be taught to read; whether there are natural sequences that should be followed in providing particular learning experiences; how much can early experience be "undone" by specially planned education or retraining; at what point in the child's development are certain types of teaching most strategic or most economical in achieving desired outcomes. These questions have taken on new urgency in recent years as, on the one hand, educators and social scientists seek new ways of producing excellence in young people who pursue intellectual and scientific careers; and, on the other hand, as the

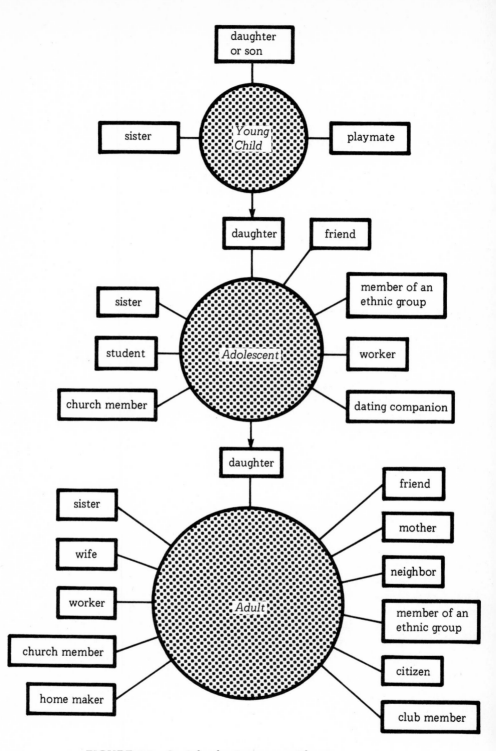

FIGURE 6.1   Social roles increase with age.

educational system has been increasingly urged to provide "compensatory" education for disadvantaged groups in the society.

There has been an upsurge of research in child psychology and child development with regard to growth in cognition, curiosity behavior, and creativity, and with the effects of early stimulation upon cognitive development. At the same time there has been a great multiplication of educational experiments in schools all over the country. To take but one example, the program called "Head Start," initiated in 1965, in which special educational opportunities were provided to preschool children of poor socioeconomic background, was predicated on the assumption that, to have maximum effects upon subsequent intellectual development, it is important to enrich the experiential environments of children as early as possible. Some educators question this approach on grounds that perhaps more can be accomplished if special educational experiences are provided at later ages when children are more mature and presumably more able to benefit. (An evaluation of Head Start is reported in Chapter 7.)

Still others point out that the quality of the social environment is important at both early and later years of the child's life, and that special enriched programs at the preschool level need to be followed by special programs in successive school years.

It is too soon to settle the differences in opinion just described, but outside the school setting itself evidence is accumulating which points to the overwhelming importance of early socialization upon later development and learning.

Bloom (1964), for example, after analyzing the data from approximately 1,000 different studies dealing with the development of various human characteristics from infancy to adulthood, concluded that variations in the environment have the greatest effect during the early years of life—that is, during the period when the child is growing and changing at his most rapid rate. By implication, after early childhood, drastic changes in environment are required if changes in the direction of growth are to be produced. With regard to mental growth, in particular, it is likely that many of the children who in the past were considered "dull" or even retarded were, in effect, made so in early life by restricted environments, to the extent that they were never able to succeed at the tasks expected of normal individuals. To put it another way, we have in the past been prone to blame the effects on heredity without first taking a close look at the effects of environment; and we have been prone to underestimate, in particular, the effects of early environment upon later achievement.

Differences in Early Environments

A dramatic illustration of this point is provided by a recent follow-up of a group of children first studied in the 1930's by Skeels and Dye (1939).

119

These events took place in the child-caring agency of the State of Iowa, during the 1930's.

> Thirteen infants ranging in age from 7 to 30 months who were considered unfit for adoption because of mental retardation (mean IQ, 64.3) were removed from an orphanage and placed in an institution for the feebleminded. Another group of 12 children who came from comparable family backgrounds but who seemed of better intellectual endowment (mean IQ, 90.0) remained in the orphanage where they were periodically observed and tested.
>
> The orphanage nursery, as it was being operated prior to the study, was limited to a rather small play room with additional dormitory rooms. . . . The children were cared for by two nurses assisted by two young girls. . . . Contacts with adults were largely limited to feeding, bathing, dressing, and toilet details. . . . The girls who assisted the nurses accepted the work as a necessary evil and took little personal interest in the children as individuals. Few play materials were available. The children were seldom out of the nursery room except for short walks for fresh air.
>
> At age two the children moved on to "cottages," where 30 to 35 children of the same sex under age six lived in charge of one matron and three or four untrained girls aged thirteen to fifteen. Their waking hours were spent (except during meal times and a little time outdoors) in an average sized room, a sun porch, and a cloak room. . . .
>
> The duties falling to the matron were not only those involved in the care of the children but also those related to clothing and cottage maintenance, cleaning, mending, and so forth. . . . The result was a necessary regimentation. The children sat down, stood up, and did many things in rows and in unison. They spent considerable time just sitting on chairs for there was inadequate equipment. . . .
>
> The experimental situation in the school for the feebleminded provided quite a different environment. Generally one, and no more than two, of the experimental children were placed in wards that contained only older, brighter girls. The attendants and the older girls became very fond of the child placed in their ward and took great pride in the child's achievement. There was considerable competition between wards to see which one would have "their baby" walking or talking first. The girls would spend a great deal of time with the children, teaching them to walk, talk, play with toys. . . . They spent their small allowances to buy them special foods, toys, picture books, and materials for clothing.
>
> Similarly, attendants frequently took the children on excursions, car rides, and trips. In addition, it was the policy of the matron in charge to single out certain of these children whom she felt were in need of individualization, and permit them to spend a portion of time each day visiting her office. This furnished new experiences, including special attention and affection, new play materials, additional language stimulation, and contacts with other office callers. . . .
>
> The children were sent to the school kindergarten as soon as they could walk. . . . As part of the school program, the children each morning attended chapel exercises, including group singing and music by the orchestra. The

children also attended the dances, school programs, moving pictures. (Adapted from Skeels and Dye, 1939.)

Findings: The results of this experiment were unexpected. All experimental children (who had been considered mentally retarded by the trained members of the orphanage staff as well as by a psychiatrist) achieved the normal range of intelligence within 6 to 52 months. The average gain in IQ was 27.5 points, with three children gaining 45 points or more. A year after the experiment ended, two of these children were above average in intelligence and only one had an IQ below 80.

The children who remained in the orphanage, on the other hand, fell increasingly behind in intellectual development. Except for one child, all suffered losses ranging from 8 to 45 IQ points.

The radical improvement in the experimental children cannot be attributed solely to environmental enrichment. Nine children who became greatly attached to one or two adults gained an average of 34 IQ points, while the four children who did not develop close personal attachments to an adult made an average gain of only 14 points. A parent surrogate whom the child learns to love and imitate is apparently an important factor in optimum development.

When these results became known, the orphanage staff made heroic efforts to improve conditions by adding more personnel to the staff, cutting down the numbers of children in the cottages, and initiating a preschool program in the nursery. Nevertheless, the damage to the orphanage group could not be undone; and the differences persisted between the children who had received special attention in infancy and the children who had not.

Follow-up: Twenty-one years later all the children were located and restudied (Skeels, 1966). Every one of the thirteen children of the experimental group had eventually been placed in a family and was now found to be living a normal life. They had completed, on the average, twelfth grade; four had entered college, and one had received a B.A. Eleven had married, and nine of these had children.

In contrast, of the orphanage group (originally the better endowed), one had died in adolescence after prolonged institutionalization for mental retardation, and three others were still inmates of such institutions. One was in a mental hospital. Of the two who had married, one was divorced. In conformity with state law, three girls, classified as retarded, had been sterilized before they had been permitted to leave the institution. On the average, this group had completed less than third grade in school. Half were unemployed; and of those who were working, all but one held the lowest of menial jobs.

While the Skeels findings are dramatic, they should be interpreted cautiously since they do not themselves prove that the effects of early enrichment are permanent. The two groups studied by these investigators were not only different in early childhood experiences, but they were different also with regard to the experiences which intervened between early childhood and the time of follow-up some 20 years later.

The Milwaukee Project

Another important experiment in early socialization, not yet completed nor fully reported (as of 1974) is the "Milwaukee Project," of Dr. F. Rick Heber and others in the Department of Psychology of the University of Wisconsin at Madison. Beginning in 1966, the research team worked in a slum area of Milwaukee, an all-black residential area, and located 50 mothers of newborn children, all women who were below 75 IQ on a standard intelligence test. Forty of these mothers agreed to cooperate with the project, which meant, for a random half of them, placing the child in an Infant Education Center and receiving some occupational and home-making and baby-care training. The other half of the mothers (the control group) were only interviewed occasionally and their children tested. The experimental group of children were picked up in their homes early each morning and kept at the Center until late afternoon. The children were taught intensively by a staff with a ratio of one teacher to two children. The teaching program consisted mainly of cognitive tasks aimed at the development of language, reading, and arithmetic. By the summer of 1972, the experimental group averaged about 125 in IQ, while the control group averaged about 85 in IQ.

This is the most gain that has been shown in any of the several careful preschool experiments thus far reported. The crucial question is—Will this gain hold up during the next four or five years, or will the experimental group fall back to the level of the control group? Other studies, none as intensive and early-beginning as this, found that much of the experimental gain was lost during the first four years of school. One explanation for this is that the intensive training in language and reading necessarily involves teaching some of the elements that appear on intelligence tests (naming pictured objects, recognizing words). Thus the experimental child is initially "coached" to do better on an intelligence test than is the control child.

The question of the long-term effects of early deprivation or early enrichment is still not fully answered, although the works of Skeels, the Milwaukee experiment, and other studies such as the Harvard-Brookline Early Childhood Project (to be described in Chapter 7) give strong evidence, first, that the child's social and intellectual development is a direct reflection of the environment in which he grows up; second, the quality of the social environment in the first years of life is of particular importance; third, it is difficult to overcome the effects of early social and intellectual deprivation on later intellectual development.

DEVELOPMENT OF SOCIAL LOYALTIES
AND SOCIAL VALUES

Another aspect of social development that is of special importance to educators is the child's formation of social values and social loyalties, his feeling of allegiance to the various groups of which he is a member, his desire to collaborate with others, and the merging of his self-interests with group interests.

The case for the significance of early experience is less clear-cut when we move from intellectual development to the development of social values and social loyalties, although the latter also develop throughout life concomitant with socialization itself. In one important sense, the socialization process may be regarded as having been successful when the individual seeks to become a member of groups that are approved by society and when he develops appropriate feelings of belonging. The typical individual, as he goes from childhood to adulthood, develops feelings of loyalty to his family, then to his play group, his church, his school, his ethnic group, his local community, his occupational group, and his nation.

The Bases of Social Loyalties

Feelings of loyalty have their bases in simpler forms of social participation, the processes of communication and collaboration. A baby comes to anticipate satisfaction when the mother's voice is heard. Soon, by gesture and by sound, mother and child develop a language in which they communicate. After a short time, the child not only communicates with the mother, but he collaborates with her, as in feeding and dressing. Out of such rudimentary forms of communication and collaboration the child moves on to more complicated forms.

The child usually develops affection for those persons who help him to gratify his needs. For such persons the child feels a close bond, a willingness to cooperate, and, eventually, a willingness to make sacrifices for the other person's welfare. Involved also is the process of identification, in which the child tries to be the other person. There are differing theories regarding the basis for early identification. Some psychologists believe that the young child identifies first with the person who gratifies his needs; others believe the child identifies with the person whose status he envies and who withholds from him the things he wants (Kagan, 1958; Bronfenbrenner, 1960; Burton and Whiting, 1961.) In any case the child imitates, consciously and unconsciously, the behavior of the person with whom he identifies; he takes on that person's attitudes, values, and ideals. As he grows older, the child identifies not only with family members, but with persons outside the family, and identifies his own interests with those persons' interests.

These, then, are the elements from which feelings of group allegiance develop: communication, collaboration, affection, identification, and the merging of one's own interests with those of another.

Expanding Social Allegiances

Having learned to collaborate with others in the family situation, the child moves into the neighborhood play group and into the schoolroom group. Here he learns to communicate and collaborate with age-mates and, if these experiences are satisfying, he develops feelings of loyalty to these groups. This basic pattern repeats itself in more complex forms in the formation of loyalty to church, ethnic group, school, and community.

Social groups build upon this pattern, with or without awareness, in inculcating feelings of loyalty in their members. Formal and informal rituals are used in most social groups to promote feelings of group solidarity. Among age-mates there are the initiations, the secret passwords, and the oaths of loyalty. Schools have their own symbols and rituals, among them school songs, school assemblies, convocations, and homecoming day.

Churches have religious holidays, music, holy communion, baptism, and confirmation, as well as the rituals of the weekly services. Fraternal orders such as the Masons, the Elks, the Eagles, and the Knights of Columbus have their symbols, their initiation ceremonies, and their rituals. Some ethnic groups maintain special rituals honoring their past or present leaders, special events and special holidays. Our nation celebrates Independence Day, Thanksgiving Day, and Washington's Birthday. We have our national heroes, our patriotic songs, and our pledge of allegiance to the flag.

Loyalty to Secondary Groups

The family, the play group, the school group, and the local church are *primary* groups; that is, groups in which interaction between members is face-to-face. The maturing individual also develops loyalty to *secondary* groups whose members may be spatially separated and who may never meet, but who nevertheless share common experiences and common interests. Occupational groups, ethnic groups, religious groups, political groups, and other national and international groups are examples of secondary groups.

There has been comparatively little study of how secondary loyalties are developed, but presumably imitation, identification, and rational thought processes become increasingly important with the age of the individual. The socialization of political attitudes in children and adolescents, for example, has been relatively neglected by social scientists; but a book by Hess and Torney (1967) describes a developmental process in the formation of political attitudes and political loyalties that occurs in early and middle childhood. Attitudes toward figures such as the President may initially be reflections of attitudes toward authority figures in the family. Only later do the images of governmental figures become differentiated as the child gains more knowledge of the functions of various governmental offices and of the particular persons who occupy given offices. The majority of Americans maintain allegiance to the same political party throughout their lives, following the political choices of their parents (Lane, 1959).

Rational and abstract learnings become increasingly important in reinforcing earlier emotional experiences. A teacher (or a lawyer or a doctor) decides that his own welfare and the general welfare are served by promoting his professional group, and thus he forms new feelings of loyalty to this secondary group.

THE CONCEPT OF LIFE SPACE

Socialization can also be seen as learning to participate in an ever-expanding social environment. The social environment, in turn, can be viewed in terms of the life space in which a child or an adolescent lives and grows. The concept of life space, as it is used here, involves physical space, and the objects contained within that space, the people who inhabit that space, and the psychological sense of freedom or constraint in exploring and expanding one's social and intellectual environment.

The child learns to use objects in ways defined by his society—chairs are to sit on, not to climb on; books are to be read, not to be chewed. The natural objects of the environment are also to be used in socially defined ways. Depending upon the community setting, trees are or are not to be climbed; grass may or may not be walked on; and animals of various kinds may or may not be played with.

From the same point of view, physical space itself takes on socially defined limits and uses. Thus a child may live in certain rooms in the house, but perhaps not in others. He may, if he grows up in a small town or on a farm, be free to explore hills and fields; or he may, if he grows up in a city, be confined to the backyard or to the neighborhood in which he lives.

The life space of the growing individual expands—from the crib, to the living room, to the street in front of the house, to the neighborhood, and then to the community. From here it enlarges partly through the child's travel experience and partly through his vicarious experience by way of movies, television, magazines, books, maps, and geography lessons. At the same time his psychological and intellectual life space expands to include new ideas, new attitudes and new values.

It is an obvious point that individuals from earliest childhood onward differ enormously with regard to their physical and psychological life space, and that each of the socializing agencies plays a significant role in creating these differences between individuals.

The degree of freedom or restraint placed upon the child's life space will vary from one family to the next, and will depend on a wide variety of factors: the child's age and sex, the neighborhood, the educational levels and the social values of parents (these, in turn, are usually related to the social class of the family). In some families children are subject to rigid parental control, while in others they experience more flexible and equalitarian relationships and are freer to disagree with parents. While from a historical perspective, given the changing curriculum of the school and the influence of the mass media, it is likely that children have larger life spaces than their predecessors, still the variety is enormous. It is not unusual today, still, to find an adolescent in the city, especially a girl and especially one from a lower socioeconomic ethnic group, whose whole life has been circumscribed by the local neighborhood in which she has grown up.

It is an obvious point also that neighborhoods and communities vary in the extent to which they foster fearfulness or feelings of "openness" and self-confidence in their residents.

In a study of families who live in a large public housing project in Chicago, mothers often reported to the interviewers that their ten-year-olds were not allowed out of the apartment alone, except to go back and forth from school; or they were limited to playing on the small balcony of the apartment. Often these children were not allowed even to play in the playgrounds below, because, as one mother said, "I can't keep my eyes on him all the time, up here on the tenth floor; and he might get into trouble with some of the bad kids that live in this project."

Another mother said, "I tell her she can't walk through this neighborhood. It isn't safe. Especially she is not to play in the elevators or on the stairs of this building. That means she can watch television, and she can do her school work, and she can wait for me or her daddy to take her out. Of course I don't get out much because of the younger kids...."

One interviewer reported an extreme case in one of these families: "There are four children, all under five. Each time I arrived, all four were lined up on the bed, watching television and not moving. I couldn't get even the oldest one to respond to me, even after several visits and after I tried repeatedly to bribe him with candy. I couldn't lure him from the fixed position on the bed."

A middle-class mother, on the other hand, lived within several blocks of the same housing project, described to the same interviewer the activities of her 10-year-old daughter: "She has to check in after school, of course, but then she usually goes down the block to play with her friend . . . or else the two get on their bicycles. (Interviewer: Where do they go?) Oh, around the neighborhood. Sometimes they ride over to the lake. They have to stay on the streets, of course, and they have to be home by five o'clock. They don't go into any deserted areas. But they're sensible by this age, and I don't worry. Then one day a week she takes the bus after school and goes to her piano lessons . . . and on Saturdays she goes down to the Art Institute for her art class. . . ."

Variation by Type of Community

It goes without saying that a child brought up on a farm has a relatively wide physical space to live in, but the life space may be a simple one in social complexity. On the other hand, the life of a child in a rural community—or, for that matter, in one neighborhood of a large city as compared to another—may be bound up closely with that of the adults; this may provide richness and variation of social experience if, for instance, the child shares in adult work and leisure, household chores, weddings and funerals, church meetings and other meetings.

Barker, Wright, and their associates have been engaged in research along these lines of describing the psychological and social environments of children (Barker and Wright, 1954). One of their first studies was reported in the book entitled *One Boy's Day* (Barker and Wright, 1951), where, in a midwestern village of 725 people, Raymond, a seven-year-old boy, was followed through a typical day, from the time he woke up in the morning until he went to bed at night. Raymond's physical life space, that day, consisted of nine square blocks, and all his physical movement occurred within a radius of two and a half blocks. He had that day some kind of personal contact with 24 adults, and he played, briefly or for a longer time, with 12 children varying in age from one to eleven. In his classroom at school were 27 other pupils, all quite similar to him in religion, skin color, and social class.

Raymond's day may be contrasted with the day of a seven-year-old who lives in a mixed residential area on the south side of Chicago. Jerry walked five blocks to a big school where he was one of 1,000 pupils. On the way to school he passed stores, taverns, and restaurants; he crossed a busy street where a policewoman directed traffic. After school his mother took him in the automobile to his friend's home a mile away so that the boys could play together and then downtown to pick up his father. On the way they passed beaches, factories, a railroad roundhouse, a slum area, a new housing project, then the skyscrapers of the Loop.

In this typical day, Jerry experienced a greater variety of objects and physical settings than Raymond. While he probably did not have actual face-to-face dealings with more people than Raymond, the people were more varied. The 35 children in his schoolroom, for instance, were of different races, religions, and social classes. There are more social contrasts in his life space than in that of Raymond.

Comparison of Small Towns in England and in America.   Not all small towns, of course, will provide the same ecological setting, nor will they have the same effects upon the child's or adolescent's social participations. Barker, for instance, applied his techniques of measurement in a small English town, Yoredale, that was similar in many respects to Midwest, Kansas, the small American town he had studied earlier. He found some striking differences in the extent to which the residents of different ages participated in the social life of the community and in the settings in which social interaction occurred (Barker, 1960). He compared the numbers of people involved in various "behavior settings" (a behavior setting is a place outside the home where certain expected patterns of activities and social interaction take place, even though the particular persons change from one time to another—for example, behavior settings in which residents of Midwest spent relatively great amounts of time are such places as a grocery store, a drug store, the post office, a school classroom, the church, and so on); and compared the extent to which residents of varying ages are engaged in "responsible positions" (a responsible position means a position in a behavior setting that is essential to the effective functioning of the setting—for example, proprietors and clerks of stores, chairmen and soloists at entertainments, presidents and secretaries of clubs, and so on).

Barker found major differences between the American and the English communities. Yoredale's population was 1,300; Midwest's, 700. In proportion to its size, Yoredale had half as many behavior settings as Midwest; and within those settings, fewer responsible positions. In a year's time, Midwest provided and required more than three times as many responsibilities of each of its residents, on the average, as Yoredale required. Particularly striking differences existed with regard to the adolescent age group. Adolescents in Midwest filled three and a half times as many responsible positions in community settings during a year as did Yoredale adolescents. "On the average, every Midwest adolescent acts in a play, works in a store, teaches a Sunday school class, plays in a basketball league game every three weeks; Yoredale adolescents occupy such positions every eleven weeks."

The Neighborhood School and the
Child's Life Space

Before leaving the topic of the effect of the local community or local neighborhood upon the child's life space, another comment is relevant. The life space of a young child generally has two principal centers: the home and the neighborhood school. In small cities, the school playground is likely to be used by the neighborhood children all year round, and in most neighborhoods whether in small or large cities, the child's friendships tend to be built around the school and his schoolmates. The school becomes more familiar to the child than any other physical space except his home. It is often the case, also, that the mother of a young child views the school as the most important institution in her life outside the home. She wants to have easy access to the school and to be able to talk with the child's teacher or the school principal as the occasion arises.

Thus for both the child and his parents the local school has been an important place. The tradition of easy access between home and school, and between home, school, and peer group was interrupted after 1965 by proposals to bus children away from racially segregated to racially integrated schools. This usually meant taking a child away from a familiar area near his home and transporting him to a strange place too far away to maintain this easy access. It often meant also that the child's friendship patterns were interfered with. In spite, therefore, of a widespread belief in the desirability of creating racially integrated schools, the program of busing children to schools miles away from their homes ran into major resistance from both black and white parents in many communities, and the resistance seriously weakened the pro-busing advocates. This will be discussed further in Chapter 15.

THE MASS MEDIA

The media for popular education and entertainment are obviously important influences in socialization and important components of the life space. Four of the communication media are particularly significant to children and adolescents: comic books, movies, radio, and television.

After World War II the radio was supplanted in the American home by television as a quasi-universal medium of amusement and communication. In the United States, television became an arm of the advertising and the amusement industries, subject only to a small degree of inspection and licensing by the federal government. In this, the United States differed from Europe and the British Commonwealth, where the government paid for television and regarded it as a medium of public education.

The obvious educational possibilities of the media have long been recognized by school systems and by educational publishers, as well as philanthropic foundations. Accordingly, every one of the media has been used, at least experimentally, for educational purposes. Comic books were produced to teach history and literature. Educational films were produced; educational radio brought outside experts in nature study, literature, drama, geography, and mathematics into the classroom. Educational television then came to replace educational radio. The field of audiovisual education has thus developed into a specialty, with courses for teachers, and with audiovisual libraries in all except the very small school districts.

Public Television

By the middle of the 1960s it had become clear that commercial television, although performing a substantial public service through its news and cultural programs, was not becoming a satisfactory educational institution. Two major philanthropic foundations, the Ford Foundation and the Carnegie Corporation, supported national commissions; and both commissions advised the creation of a major publicly financed television system to serve educational and cultural needs of the society. Congress passed the Public Broadcasting Act of 1967 and set up the Public Broadcasting Corporation with an initial appropriation of $5 million. Shortly thereafter, the Federal Communications Commission, the American Telephone and Telegraph Company, and the

Public Broadcasting Corporation agreed to provide the electronic channels for National Educational Television at rates far below the commercial rates. The Public Broadcasting Laboratory was created with government support to produce educational and public service programs. Both the Ford Foundation and the Carnegie Corporation have granted money to these public agencies to supplement their relatively low government appropriations.

Two major educational programs for children have been developed since 1969, *Sesame Street* and *The Electric Company*. A careful evaluation of the first year of *Sesame Street* has shown that preschool children learned a good deal in comparison with children who did not view the program. (Ball and Bogatz, 1970). However, it also appears that middle-class children have learned more from *Sesame Street* than children from economically disadvantaged families. Middle-class mothers expose their children as early as age two or three to the program, and encourage them to respond. Although *Sesame Street* is definitely useful for children of low-income families, once again, as has been true of other formal and informal learning activities, middle-class parents have taken greater advantage of the opportunity than have others.

Meanwhile, cable television has loomed up as the next technological breakthrough. This could provide perhaps as many as 70 separate television channels in place of the four or five that have been available in most cities. While at the time of this writing, certain new technological and financial problems are arising, the Federal Communications Commission is now in the process of making rules and regulations for the expansion of cable television, millions of dollars from the commercial television industry are being invested, and there is pressure from educational organizations to preserve some 20 percent of cable television channels for public and educational use. (NEA Division of Educational Technology, 1971)

Influence of Commercial Television and Movies on Children and Youth

No matter how much or how little the educational system makes use of television and other electronic media, the media systems will continue independently to exert a pervasive influence on the behavior and on the emotional and cognitive development of children and youth. Some 15 years ago, Schramm, Lyle, and Parker (1960) studied a sample of children and families in the United States and Canada and reported that the average child between the ages of 3 and 16 spent one-sixth of his waking hours watching television. This means, when we add in the amount of television viewing during the vacation periods, that the average child spends as much time looking at television as he does in school. In response to the question: "Is television good or bad for children?" the investigators said, "No informed person can say simply that television is good or bad for children. For *some* children, under *some* conditions, *some* television is harmful. For other children under the same conditions, or for the same children under *other* conditions, it may be beneficial. For *most* children, under *most* conditions, *most* television is probably neither particularly harmful nor particularly beneficial."

It may be asked whether the influence of television has changed since 1960, with the much greater freedom now in television and motion pictures to show scenes of violence and sexuality, and to use language that would not have been permitted in that earlier period.

The Surgeon General of the United States appointed an advisory committee on television and social behavior who studied the matter from 1969 to 1971. They reported that the scientific data were not conclusive on the question whether television violence causes aggression in children, although they went on to say that there was good evidence to indicate a relation between violence on television and aggressive behavior among children who already had a tendency toward aggressive behavior. The committee reported that the findings "converge in three respects: a preliminary and *tentative* indication of a *causal relation* between viewing violence on television and aggressive behavior; an indication that any such causal relation operates only on *some children* (who are predisposed to be aggressive); and an indication that it operates only in *some environmental contexts*." (U.S.P.H.S., 1972) (Italics are ours.)

There is somewhat more concern on the part of critics over the violence and the sexual explicitness of current movies. It is claimed by some that these are causing pervasive changes in the customs and values of the society, while others argue that the social mores were already changing toward more free sexual and aggressive behavior and the contemporary movies are simply satisfying the changing tastes of the public. A book by Lawrence Alloway (1972) on violence in the movies supports this latter conclusion. It is of course to be noted that the most violent and sexually explicit movies are supposed to be barred to the view of persons under age 18.

Whatever the effects may be, the appeal of television is even greater now than it was in 1960, and television sets are more widely distributed, especially in low-income homes. Morrisett (1973) says:

> Preschool children up to the age of six are the single heaviest television viewing audience in the United States. And while viewing falls off slightly after children enter school, those between six and thirteen are still very heavy television viewers. For the preschool child, estimates ranging as high as an average of fifty hours per week of watching television have been given. Even if one discounts these estimates, it becomes clear that for young children the one activity that engages most of their time, aside from sleeping, is watching television.

Having in this chapter described some of the socialization processes that occur in the life of the child, and how the child's life space is influenced by his social surroundings, we move in the following chapters to an examination of the major social institutions—the family, the school, the peer group—as these interact in the socialization process.

EXERCISES

1. What are some of the goals of socialization in American society? What kinds of personal and social traits would you say our society attempts to produce in its members?

2. Give an example from your own experience (preferably, experience within the classroom) where identification was important in understanding a child's behavior.

3. Select any one group of which you are a member. What are some of the formal or informal ways used by the group to inculcate loyalty in its members?

4. Describe a child whose socialization experiences you regard as inadequate. What can be done to provide compensatory social experience?

5. Describe two school situations that tend to restrict the child's life space. Be specific. Describe two school situations that tend to enlarge the child's life space.

6. Ask several children you know (preferably of the same age) to trace on a map the area with which they are familiar. Using crayons, one color can be used for streets covered every day; another color for streets covered as often as once a week; another color for streets and places visited once a month. How much variation do you find from child to child?

7. Ask several children (or adolescents) to write a diary-account of their activities on a typical school day (or a weekend). Ask them to describe everything they do, from the time they get up in the morning to the time they go to bed. Compare their reports for similarities and differences. What insights do you gain concerning the life space of each child?

SUGGESTIONS FOR FURTHER READING

1. For a comprehensive survey of research on the socialization process, see the review by Edward Zigler (1970) entitled "Social Class and the Socialization Process." See also the chapter "Sociological Correlates of Child Behavior" by Clausen and Williams in the NSSE Yearbook, *Child Psychology*. The political socialization of children and adolescents is described in the book by Hess and Torney, and in the collection of papers edited by June L. Tapp.

2. Television, comic books, radio, and movies are important aspects of the culture that operate on the child. The chapter by Eleanor Maccoby, "Effects of the Mass Media," in Hoffman and Hoffman's *Review of Child Development Research* is a good overview of this topic.

3. The black adolescents described in *Children of Bondage* by Allison Davis and John Dollard were followed up 20 years later and described in an interestingly written book, *The Eighth Generation*, by John H. Rohrer and Munro S. Edmonson. Problems of identification and identity are stressed throughout.

4. For the full description of one day in the life of a seven-year-old boy (the boy Raymond, mentioned in this chapter), read *One Boy's Day*, by Roger G. Barker and Herbert F. Wright.

5. The book of readings, *Education and Culture*, edited by Spindler, contains a number of interesting selections on the American culture and how it is transmitted to children in the school situation. See especially chapters 7, 8, and 9 by Spindler and by Lee.

6. For general information and for varying points of view on socially disadvantaged children and the causes of their disadvantage, read Riessman's *The Culturally Deprived Child*; or Bloom's *Stability and Change in Human Characteristics*; or Bloom, Davis, and Hess, *Compensatory Education for Cultural Deprivation*. A variety of publications have recently become available describing practicable programs for socially disadvantaged children and youth. Some of these are: *Urban Education in the 1970s*, edited by Harry Passow; Grotberg, "Institutional Responsibilities for Early Childhood Education;" Weikart, *Longitudinal Results of the Ypsilanti Perry Preschool Project*. Articles on disadvantaged children by the following persons, Hess and Shipman; Cervantes; Ahlstrom and Havighurst, are to be found in *Society and Education: A Book of Readings*, edited by Havighurst, Neugarten, and Falk.

7. *Adult Status of Children with Contrasting Early Life Experiences* has been published as a monograph by Harold M. Skeels. It is the complete account of the study which was cited in this chapter.

8. There have been recurrent studies of the experience of children and youth with television, beginning in the early 1950s. The publications of Maccoby, Schramm, and Bogatz (for the Educational Testing Service) give the reader an overview down through the evaluations of *Sesame Street* and *The Electric Company*.

CHAPTER 7

The Family and the School

The family, as the major socializing agency in the society, acts to teach the child the culture and subculture. The child not only learns the overt behaviors, he learns also the social, moral, and economic values; how children relate to adults, and how men relate to women; how to curb his aggressiveness and yet to cultivate his competitiveness; how to develop loyalties and how to seek for self-achievement. The overall expectancies and way of life of the group are transmitted through the family. Ethnic, religious, racial, and social groups maintain their differences through time to the extent to which different families provide their offspring with distinctive patterns of thought and action.

The family functions also to "prepare" a child for school and, thereafter, to influence his attitudes toward school.

THE FAMILY

The family as a social institution has undergone marked changes over the past 100 years. In contrast to the rural or frontier family, the modern urban family remains the unit of economic consumption but is no longer the unit of economic production. Formal education, as well as many types of informal education, have been taken over by the school, the mass media, and other agencies. Even the function of character building has been taken on more and more by nonfamily agencies such as the church, the school, and special youth-serving organizations such as the Boy Scouts and Girl Scouts, the 4-H clubs, Future Farmers of America, the YMCA and YWCA.

The modern family is characterized by a high degree of mobility, social and geographic. There is a constant attempt to improve the material standards of living, and a great deal of moving from one house to another, from one part of the country to another. This geographical transiency is found not only among low socioeconomic groups, such as migrant agricultural workers or blacks who move from south to north; it is also present to a marked degree among middle-class groups, as witnessed, for example, by the movements of young business executives from one community to another at various stages of their careers, or by the movement of older people from farms to cities and towns, and from cold climates to warm.

Despite the historical changes and the loss of some of its functions, the family has lost none of its importance as the primary socializing agency in the life of the child. It is the individual's first and most influential social system and provides him with his most influential social training situations.

THE FAMILY AS A SOCIAL SYSTEM

The family obviously differs markedly from other social systems. Compared with the play group, the school group, or the work organization, the family is a smaller and more closely-knit system; relationships are intimate and face-to-face; the old and young are related in a well-defined hierarchy of status; and while its members will change somewhat through the years, the family provides the individual with a primary group membership that endures throughout his life.

There is great diversity among American families and there is no single pattern that characterizes "the" American family.

The modern middle-class family, for example, is becoming increasingly democratic in its relationships, with a growing sense of equality between child and parent and between husband and wife. At the same time responsibilities and privileges for each member are well-differentiated. Each person fills a social role as husband, father, wife, mother, child, or sibling in which behavior is determined to a large extent by the role expectations established by the larger groups to which the family belong. Thus, in the typical German family, at least until very recently, the father was the authority figure; while in a rural black family in America, it was usually the mother. In many families the mother shares with the father the role of breadwinner, while an older child may act in the role of mother to the younger siblings.

Emerging Family Patterns

The household consisting of biological father, mother, and the children, and sometimes grandparents, living together as a unit until the children grow up, seems so "normal" to middle-class Americans that they often forget that relatively few people, in the past or in the present, live in this type of family setting. And, although this may seem to most Americans the only morally proper form of family life, other forms are now appearing in this country.

One variant form is the household headed by a woman, a form that has existed in many times and places. In the United States it is often seen in low-income urban areas, where it has been unwittingly encouraged by welfare laws which stipulate that federal welfare payments for dependent children are not to be made if there is a father in the home. It is also increasingly seen in middle-class levels, where more and more children, as a result of the rising divorce rates, are reared in father-absent homes.

If the family is regarded as a household group responsible for feeding and sheltering its members, then all family members need not be biologically or legally related to each other. There are now in the United States a number of expanded family units which consist of friends who set up a home together, do mutual baby-sitting, and in some cases constitute themselves as *communes*. Ron Roberts (1971) defines an expanded family as any of several combinations of adults and children in one or more houses, sharing a number of housekeeping and economic functions. There are also expanded families consisting of adults of one sex only, such as the contemporary women's lib communes, which may be analogous to the *beguinages* of medieval Europe that housed single working women who wished to live free from male interference.

Using the definition of an expanded family which has been given above, one estimate places the number of people in such groups in the United States in 1972 as about 500,000, containing possibly 100,000 children.

SOCIAL CLASS DIFFERENCES IN FAMILIES

Obviously enough, families differ one to the next in social organization, attitudes and values, child-rearing practices, and in countless other ways. In addition to the idiosyncratic differences that develop from the interaction of individual personalities over time, there are other differences related to such broad social factors as ethnicity, religion, rural or urban location, and so on. Differences exist also between families in which the father is employed in an entrepreneurial setting and those in which he is employed in a bureaucratic setting (Miller and Swanson, 1958). For reasons that we have tried to make clear in the first chapters of this book, the factor that is of particular importance to educators is that of social class.

While the differences in family life between the various social classes are many, we have chosen here only a few illustrations.

Parental Roles in the Middle-Class Family

The "typical" middle-class family lives where the husband's job dictates (secondarily, where the children's schooling dictates). Although men's and women's roles are changing rapidly due to the increasing education of women, the increasing numbers of middle-class women who work, and the changing perceptions of women's roles associated with the women's liberation movement, nevertheless in the "typical" family, the father is perceived as the primary economic provider and as the "head of the family," with major responsibility legally, financially, and morally for the welfare of family members. Talcott Parsons, a leading sociological theorist, described the father-husband role as primarily an "instrumental" one; that is, as maintaining the family's position in relation to the outside world and coping with the extrafamilial environment (Parsons and Bales, 1955). The wife-mother role, on the other hand, is primarily an "expressive" one; that is, as maintaining the integrated relationships within the family and as primarily concerned with the expression of emotions, discipline, values, and so on.

Middle-class women are becoming more instrumental in their behavior, while middle-class men are becoming more expressive, but the "typical" middle-class home has both parents present and sharing in the tasks of child-rearing. As described in our earlier descriptions of middle-class values (see Chapter 2) there is likely to be considerable stress placed upon the child's achievement in school, upon competence-building, and in general upon activity, accomplishment, and practicality.

Poverty and Family Structure

Families in which the parents' roles are quite different from those just described are found in very poor groups in a modern society. It seems probable that poverty places people in situations where they are compelled to behave in certain ways and to adopt certain attitudes that mark them as different from the mainstream of the society. If this is true, then it may be accurate to speak of a culture of poverty which consists of ways of behaving and believing that tend to be shared by poor people in a modern industrial society, and that are passed from parent to child. The anthropologist, Oscar Lewis (1961, 1966) described such a culture among the poor in Mexico City, in San Juan, Puerto Rico, and among Puerto Ricans in New York City. The principal characteristics of this culture are these:

There is a large proportion of one-parent families usually headed by the mother or grandmother.
Children at an early age have to take responsibility for their own care and that of younger children.
People have a low level of aspiration for educational and occupational achievement.
People have a poor self-image.
People believe that they cannot control their environment. They believe that other people with more power exert the controls.
People believe that "chance" or luck determines much of what happens to them.

People spend their income for present needs and do not save for the future.
(Getting by is more important than getting ahead.)
People have a low degree of control over their aggressive impulses.

There is considerable controversy over the concept of a culture of poverty—first, whether or not it is a culture that is maintained from one generation to the next and is therefore relatively slow to change (this involves the question of whether or not this cultural pattern would disappear as soon as poverty could be made to disappear); and second, whether there is in truth a pattern of life common to most or all families who live below the poverty level, or whether variations are greater than similarities. When challenged on this point, Lewis amplified his position by saying that he expected the culture of poverty to be fully exemplified in only some 20 percent of families who live below the poverty line. He wrote, "In my experience, the people who live in slums, even in small ones, show a great deal of heterogeneity in income, literacy, education, political sentiments, and life styles." (Lewis, 1969, pp. 5–6)

It is likely that the concept of a "culture of poverty" applies only in a general way to the poor among groups who are as different as urban Anglo, black, Appalachian-Ozarkan white, Spanish-American white, Puerto Rican, and American Indian. The family structure of low-income blacks is quite different, for example, from that of low-income Appalachian whites, or Navaho Indians.

Father Absence and School Performance

Families with no father present in the household are relatively frequent in the lowest income groups. There seems also to be a direct association in low-income groups between the absence of the father and the child's school performance. For instance, in a study of the children of low-income families in New York City, Deutsch and Brown (1964) found a relationship between father's presence and the child's school grades and academic ability. For both boys and girls, the IQs of children with fathers in the home were higher than those of children who had no father in the home.

A father's influence may be important to a boy at certain critical points, such as that of dropping out of school. For example, in a study of black and white dropouts in Connecticut high schools in 1959, it was found that 38 percent of the black males came from broken homes. Perhaps as a result, only 29 percent of the black male dropouts discussed their decision to drop out of school with their fathers, as compared with 65 percent of white male dropouts. In fact, 26 percent of the black males as compared with only 8 percent of white males did not discuss this major decision with anyone at all.

THE CULTURE OF THE SCHOOL

In a sense the family can be said to "launch" the child into the school environment. What are the main features of that environment? How does the culture of the school become a potent socializing force upon the child? And how do the cultures of the family and the school interact?

The school has a subculture of its own—a complex set of beliefs, values and traditions, ways of thinking and behaving—that differentiate it from other social institutions. Education in the school, as compared with that in the family or in the peer group goes on in relatively formal ways; and even those activities that are least formal (as in children's play at recess) are evaluated in terms of their contribution to the learning situation. Groupings are formed, not on the basis of voluntary choice, but in terms of aptitudes for learning and teaching.

Differentiation develops gradually according to achievement. In the elementary school, achievement proceeds along two lines; the first is the "cognitive," or the learning of information and skills; the second is what Parsons calls "moral" or social—learning respect for the teacher, consideration of fellow-pupils, good work habits, initiative, and responsibility. In the secondary school, the emphasis is upon types, rather than levels, of achievement. With its variety of subject matter, personnel, and activities, the high school offers the student a wider range of choices along both the cognitive and the social axes of achievement.

Compared with other social institutions, the school has not only its own rules for behavior, but also its own rituals and ceremonies involving both children and adults. There are the school assemblies, the athletic events, and the graduation ceremonies; the school songs, school insignia, and school cheers. All these are an accepted part of the culture of the school.

The orientation of the American school is predominantly that of the middle class. There is strong emphasis upon the character traits of punctuality, honesty, and responsibility. Respect for property is stressed. There is a premium upon sexual modesty and decorum. While both competitiveness and cooperation are valued to varying degrees, there is always stress upon mastery and achievement. These middle-class values are expected to be binding upon both children and adults.

Formalism

The formality of the school is well exemplified in the extent to which rights and duties are distributed according to age. Not only does age-grading operate in formal aspects of the school, with each grade group having a different curriculum and a different teacher, but it operates also in more informal ways. Thus, in most elementary schools a child must have reached seventh or eighth grade before being eligible to help out in the principal's office or to act as a traffic patrol boy. In most secondary schools, a boy or girl must be a junior or a senior to participate in certain extracurricular activities.

Time itself is formalized in special ways. With the day divided into periods, every person is expected to be in a given place, engaged in a given activity, at every period. Some activities occur on Mondays, others on Fridays.

Authority rests with the adult personnel of the school, and children are in clearly subordinate positions. This is to be seen in the very way in which the physical space of the school is arranged. Certain rooms in the building are set aside for teachers; and within the typical classroom the teacher's desk occupies a special part of the room.

The right to privacy is also differentially assigned. In most schools, for instance, the teacher may inspect the child's desk at will, but the teacher's desk is kept locked.

There are a number of schools in which formalism has been reduced; schools, for example, in which age-grade lines are not strictly drawn, as when six and seven-year-olds are grouped together into a "primary" section, or when special-ability groupings may include boys and girls who vary in age by three or four years.

Some schools have dropped the formal system of letter grades as methods of reporting student progress; others have broken down the traditional lines between school subjects, giving longer periods of the school day to "basic curriculum," "social studies," or "language arts."

Formal vs. Informal Education

In examining the culture of the school, and studying the interaction of the school culture with the other cultures in which the individual participates (family, peer group, religious group, etc.), it is useful to make a distinction between *formal* and the *informal* education. Scribner and Cole, (1973) two anthropologists who have studied the process of education in various societies, describe formal education as:

> "(1) organized deliberately to fulfill the specific purposes of transmission, (2) extracted from the manifold of daily life, placed in a special setting and carried out according to specific routines, and (3) made the responsibility of the larger social group."

Informal education on the other hand, is carried on without explicit intention or definition, and is "caught" by the learner rather than "taught" by the teacher. It has the following characteristics:

1. It fuses the cognitive and the affective. What is learned has a high affective charge, because the teachers are significant persons to the learner.
2. *Who* is teaching is more important than *what* is taught.
3. It fosters traditionalism rather than social change.

While modern societies pay more explicit attention to formal than to informal education, there is much of the latter that goes on in the schools. The extracurricular activities, the sports, the peer culture, and pupil-teacher relationships all are important parts of the informal education.

When the formal and the informal education a particular child experiences are coherent and supplementary, the child is provided with an integrative educational experience. Broadly speaking, this occurs for most middle-class and upper-working-class children in America. Much greater discontinuity, or even conflict, is likely to exist, however, for students from a cultural group which relies heavily on informal education for the rearing of its children, such as native American Indians or even isolated Appalachian whites. The very formation of the school may create a cultural conflict for such children.

The Open Schoolroom and Informal Education. The school has officially been designed and conducted as an agency of formal education. But since about 1960, the American development of the "open classroom," based on the British model, and the appearance of "free schools" and "alternative schools" indicates that the schools are responding to the general value change toward more expressive activity. (These points are discussed further in Chapter 13.) Expressive activity is likely to be fostered by informal education, which, in turn, is likely to conflict with the continuing bureaucratization of the school system.

Bureaucratization

Not only is the school system formally organized, but it is becoming more and more bureaucratized, as are other organizations in the modern society. Bureaucratization involves the centralization of authority and the standardization of work routines. Given the growth in school populations and the economy that is gained from larger organizations, bureaucracy and centralization are becoming characteristic of school systems everywhere. The cult of efficiency that grew up in American school systems in the first half of this century (Callahan, 1962), and the way in which business principles were taken over by educators are increasingly apparent in the tendency of some educators and some laymen to measure the efficiency of a school system in terms of the numbers of pupils, classes, and teachers in relation to costs. The stress on efficiency and increased bureaucratization adds to the formalism of the school as a social system.

141

Variations in School Culture

Individual schools differ in many intangible ways. In one school the relationships between teachers and pupils are unusually intimate and friendly; in another, unusually formal. In one school, competition is played up; in another, it is played down. In one case, students may feel fierce pride in their school and its accomplishments. In another, there may be a feeling of resignation among both children and adults, as if mediocrity is all that can be expected in any school endeavor.

Much of what is "caught" comes not from the formal curriculum but from the pervading culture of the school. Relevant here, for example, is the study by Coleman (1959, 1960) with regard to the impact of the adolescent subculture upon academic achievement. In various midwestern high schools, students gave highest priority to athletics, school activities, and social popularity rather than to academic achievement. In a school in which the football player or cheerleader is given more prestige than the scholar, students are "catching" certain attitudes from their peers which may offset the attitudes they are catching from their teachers.

Interaction among Students

There is always a social organization among the students of any school, one that has its own system of rank and prestige, and one in which different students have quite different patterns of activities.

The size of the school itself has been found to make a difference in this regard. Barker and his associates (1962), in comparing the social and intellectual environments of small high schools to a large high school in the same state, found that the students in the small schools were more likely to participate actively in extracurricular activities and to hold positions of importance both in their schools and in the community. The students in the small schools, furthermore, were more likely to report satisfactions relating to the development of competence, to being challenged, to engaging in important activities, and to achieving more cultural values. The students in the small schools had, as well as more opportunity, more pressure put upon them to participate—the small schools had much the same variety of positions to be filled as did the large school, but fewer students to fill them.

Social Prestige Hierarchies. Social-class background, as we have discussed it in an earlier chapter, operates to greater or lesser extent in creating a system of prestige among students, with children from upper social classes often being in advantaged positions in the eyes of their peers. Athletic ability, participation in extracurricular activities, physical attractiveness, personality attributes—all these are factors that combine to produce a system in which certain students are at the top of the social hierarchy while others are at the bottom. This hierarchy can be seen especially among adolescents. There are some who "rate" and some who do not.

Gordon (1957), for example, made a detailed study of the social system of the high school in a midwestern suburban community referred to as Wabash. By using a composite index of social status within the school, he placed each of the 576 students within the social network; then proceeded to show how students' behavior was related to those positions. The index of social status was based upon three factors: school grades; participation in formal student organizations; and the number of times the student was chosen as a "best friend" by other students.

The prestige value assigned to the various formal organizations differed. Thus, of the 50 different organizations in Wabash High, the seniors assigned the top ranks to Student Government, Varsity Basketball, Varsity Football, National Honor Society, Cheer Leaders, and Crest Coronation (Yearbook Queen's Court). The lowest ranks went to the Roller Skating Club, the Outdoor Club, the Pencil Pushers (creative writing), the Riding Club (horseback riding), and the Knitting Club. Directly related to the ratings of the organizations was the prestige assigned to their various offices. Competition to fill these offices was a major preoccupation for a majority of students.

The student who belonged to a sufficient number of prestigious organizations and filled a sufficient number of offices warranted the title, "big wheel." For boys, the sources of this status were primarily athletic achievements, although by extreme effort, achievements in other activities might be combined to produce the "big wheel." The label itself denoted a pattern of expected behavior as well as a particular status in the eyes of the group.

One twelfth-grade boy, a self-styled "big wheel," said: "Everyone enjoys privileges but no one intends to take advantage of them, although I feel that sometimes I do. . . . I'm constantly absent or late to class.

Today was an example. At 1:07 I strolled into class without a word and took my seat. I thought Andrews wouldn't say anything, but he stopped and asked me for an excuse. I gave my usual answer of, 'Why, am I late?' He says, 'Are you late? Seven minutes!' To this I just said, 'Oh, do you want me to get an excuse?' He gave up. . . . What are the kids' reactions? They all think it's a big joke.

Who are the "big wheel" seniors? I think I am one, since I have carried on many more activities than anyone else. . . ."

Girls were "big wheels" too, and the most prized status of all was formalized in the position, Queen of the Yearbook. The Queen was crowned in a public ceremony called the Yearbook Coronation, the major social function of the year.

The social careers of the twelfth-grade girls were climaxed with the election of the Queen who was selected by a school-wide vote from a slate of nine candidates nominated by the senior boys. The eight candidates who were not chosen Queen served as Maids of the Queen's Court.

The Queen's throne was a slippery place, made so by the intense competition for the office. Girls "hoped" to be Queen, but they definitely worked

to *"make the Coronation Court"* as hard as boys worked to make the basket-
ball team. . . .

Many of the features of Wabash High are still to be found in high
schools over the country. While Gordon described a single overall prestige
system, in other schools the social interaction between students is more
differentiated. Clark (1962), for example, has described three adolescent subcultures to be found within the typical comprehensive high school: the first
he calls the "fun" subculture—the sports, cars, dating, beauty queen value-
pattern, with a derogation of intellectual values; the second, the "academic"
subculture—the serious students who are more oriented toward their studies
and to academic extracurricular activities than to anything else, sometimes
called by others, the "grinds" or "curve-raisers"; the third, the "delinquent"
subculture—the students who rebel against the school and the adult value
pattern, and who want to get out of school, the group who, in some slum
schools, have the switchblade knife as their symbol. A fourth type of student
Clark described as being marginal to all three orientations—these are the
"faceless" students who never speak up, who go unnoticed during school
hours, who show apathy and withdrawal.

FAMILY PREPARATION FOR SCHOOL

We have looked briefly at two socializing agencies, the family and the school,
sketching in some of the ways in which each has a culture of its own. By
implication, it is the ways in which the two cultures interact in the life of a
given child that is of overriding importance to educators. Many educators
phrase the issue by saying how well the child will do in school will depend
in large part on how well his family has prepared him.

It has long been observed that children from lower socioeconomic
groups provide by far the greater share of a school's behavior problems,
academic failures, and dropouts. These phenomena were explained away in
earlier periods as due, first, to lower native intelligence of these children; and
second, to lack of concern on the part of their parents. Today, we know that
neither of these explanations is adequate.

Parents of all classes realize the importance of education; and good
schooling for their children is highly prized. It became even clearer during the
1960s that a massive effort must be mounted to assist children of low socioeconomic status to do better in school. The question was not whether or not
to make such an effort, but *how* to do it. The answer centered around the
relative importance of the family and the school in the mental development
of the child.

Factors Which Determine School Achievement

There are four factors which determine the level of achievement of a child in school. One is the inborn ability of the child. Another is the kind of family life or family training he experiences. A third is the quality of the schooling he receives. The fourth is his self-concept or aspiration level which grows out of his family and school experience. After several years of school experience, the child himself can determine how hard he shall work in school and toward what goals.

Inborn or biological differences of intelligence exist, but between individuals, not between large social or racial groups. Inborn differences in intelligence exist among children in a single family; and every school class of 30 children includes 30 different levels of intellectual potential.

Once a child is born, a good family experience can operate so that a child with only average inborn ability does well in school. A very good school can operate so that a child with only average innate ability does well; and it can operate also to compensate a child for a poor family background.

Since the late 1950s studies of the relations between family factors and mental development have led to a revision of earlier beliefs about the relative importance of family and school, with greater emphasis now being given to the family factor. As already mentioned in the preceding chapter, research on the cognitive development of children summarized by Bloom (1964) points to the family as the major influence and to the preschool years as the crucial ones for mental development.

In recent years efforts have been made to determine some of the specific ways in which different family experiences affect a child's development and behavior; for it is clear that social-class differences in these factors are present when the child first enters school. Hess and Shipman (1965) have summed up the results of a number of observations on this problem as follows:

> Children from deprived backgrounds score well below middle-class children on standard individual and group measures of intelligence (a gap that increases with age); they come to school without the skill necessary for coping with first grade curricula; their language development, both written and spoken, is relatively poor; auditory and visual discrimination skills are not well developed; in scholastic achievement they are retarded an average of two years by grade six and almost three years by grade eight; they are more likely to drop out of school before completing a secondary education; and even when they have adequate ability, are less likely to go to college. (Hess and Shipman, p. 869)

The likely explanation for these differences is that different families create environments that influence children's intellectual growth and educational motivation in different ways. Thus, when one parent ignores his child's

145

questions but another parent makes a point of reading to his child every day, the first has created an environment that operates against learning; the second, one that promotes further learning. The socioeconomic level of the family continues to emerge in various studies as the principal factor in determining not only the young child's, but also the adolescent's school achievement. Thus Bachman (1971) studied a national sample of high school boys in 87 schools and found that boys in families high on the socioeconomic ladder were the most educationally advantaged.

Social Class and Cognitive Style.   The child-rearing practices of a given social class favor a more rapid cognitive development than those of another social class. This is a conclusion reached by Edward Zigler, one of the leading researchers in the field of child development. In a systematic review of the social class influence on cognitive development (1970) he concludes: "There are real class differences in intellectual functioning and these are produced by class differences in environment. . . . We tend to take this view rather than the other, that the average level of intellectual functioning probably does not differ from one class to another and that the observed relation is an artifact of measurement, a product of the unfairness of intelligence tests for lower-class populations." (p. 92) According to Zigler, there is a general *developmental sequence* in cognitive function which is common to all social classes, but the middle-class children move along this sequence more rapidly than lower-class; and lower-class persons may end at a lower level as adults.

Differences in Language Environment.   The presence or absence of adequate parental techniques for helping the child understand his world or cope with complex situations may have permanent effects. Bernstein (1961, 1969) has analyzed the language used by working-class and by middle-class children, and he has found considerable differences. Children of both classes learn adequately the language of ordinary conversation, which is grammatically simple, uses stereotyped expressions, does not permit precise statement of ideas or emotions, and relies upon gestures, inflection, and further explanation to make meaning clear. Bernstein calls this language "public," or "restricted." Middle-class children learn, in addition to the "restricted" language, what Bernstein calls the "formal" or "elaborated" language—the grammatically complex language of the schoolroom, which permits precise expression and provides greater potentiality for organizing experience than the "restricted" language. The child who learns only the "restricted" language, in Bernstein's view, is limited in his ability to learn new things and to interact with other people because his language restricts his ability to organize experience. The child who masters the "elaborated" language possesses a tool which permits expression of complex ideas and distinctions between feelings and ideas.

In an effort to understand why some children learn a more elaborate language than others, Hess and Shipman (1965) studied the ways in which mothers teach their own four-year-old children. They found that the techniques used by mothers vary by the amount of education the mothers have had—and thus also by social class. The middle-class mothers, as compared with the working-class mothers, talked almost twice as much to their children in teaching them, and used more abstract words, more adjectives, more complex grammar, and longer sentences. Furthermore, they more frequently gave explicit instructions, let the child know what was expected of him, and praised him for his accomplishments.

The children from the middle-class homes learned much better than the children from the working-class homes; and the middle-class children were more frequently able to explain correctly the principle behind the task they had learned.

These investigators suggest that homes which produce children who are, from the educator's point of view, educationally disadvantaged, are homes that are "status-oriented," or oriented toward control of the child by ascribed roles. In such homes, a child is expected to obey his parent because children *should* obey parents. "Status-oriented families present the rules in an assigned manner, where compliance is the *only* rule-following possibility. In these situations the role of power in the interaction is . . . obvious, and coercion and defiance are likely interactional possibilities."

Middle-class families, on the other hand, are likely to be "person-oriented"; the feelings and desires of the child are taken into account, and explanations are given to him. This procedure requires a more elaborate language and permits responses from the child other than simple obedience. For example:

> A child is playing noisily in the kitchen with an assortment of pots and pans when the telephone rings. In one home the mother says, "Be quiet," or "Shut up," or she issues any one of several other short, preemptory commands. In the other home the mother says, "Would you keep quite a minute? I want to talk on the phone."
>
> In one instance the child is . . . asked to attend to an uncomplicated message and to make a conditioned response (to comply); he is not called upon to reflect or to make mental discriminations. In the other example the child is required to follow two or three ideas. He is asked to relate his behavior to a time dimension; he must think of his behavior in relation to its effect upon another person. He must perform a more complicated task to follow the communication of his mother in that his relationship to her is mediated in part through concepts and shared ideas; his mind is stimulated or exercised (in an elementary fashion) by a more elaborate and complex verbal communication initiated by the mother. (Hess and Shipman, 1965, p. 872.)

The second mother has required her child to think about his behavior and to take the needs of others into consideration. A child who is consistently taught in this manner is likely to enter school with the capacity to choose among alternatives and to reflect before he acts. On the other hand, a child who is taught merely to obey is likely to be impulsive rather than reflective.

Attitudes Toward Learning.   Children grow up not only with different language environments but with different attitudes toward school and school achievement. Frankie, a four-year-old enrolled in an experimental reading-readiness program for children from impoverished fatherless families, was a difficult child from the outset, aggressive, restless, and with an unusually short attention span. The mother, interviewed in the slum apartment where she lived with Frankie and two younger babies, pointed to the stout leather belt that she kept handy, and said:

> "I don't have to use it so much any more. Just two or three times a week. I can give him a certain look, and he knows what I mean." She controlled his behavior also by his fear of the "bogeyman"—a fearful creature which came in the window and stood over him when he had been "bad."
>
> When the interviewer asked how important it was to her for Frankie to do well in school, the mother said, "Very important. Very important! I tell him, I say, 'Frankie, when you go to school, I want you to learn,' I say, 'because it's important.' I say "You do what the teacher tell you to do, you hear, when I send you to school, 'cause I want you to go school and learn—you learn good, see? And if I get any reports on you from your teacher, I'm going to spank you good, see? That's what they got teachers for, to teach you . . . and you have to pay attention, see?' Frankie is smart, he's very smart. Only he just won't pay attention. Even though I whips him all the time."

It should be stressed that Frankie's behavior cannot be laid to his mother's lack of concern that he do well in school. She had gone to considerable effort to get him enrolled in the preschool program, and she was highly aware of the advantages education would bring. Parents such as Frankie's mother seldom are equipped, however, to help their children to succeed in school.

To illustrate this point further, we present the response of another mother who, when asked how she would prepare her four-year-old boy for school, answered:

> "First of all, I would remind him that now he was big enough to go to school and that we were proud of him. Then I would tell him that he was going to school to learn, that his teacher would take my place, and that he would be expected to follow instructions. Also that his time would be spent mostly in the classroom with other children, that he would enjoy it, and that any questions or any problems that he might have he could consult with his teacher for assistance. (Anything else?) No, anything else would probably be confusing for him at his age."

The attitudes of the two mothers just quoted are not isolated cases, but illustrate the fact that differences in the types of punishment used by parents and in the types of behavior they punish are reflections of actual differences in values between social classes.

Kohn (1963) is one among others who claim that middle-class values center on self-direction for the child, while the working-class values stress conformity to authority.

Families and Competence in Children

An empirical study of the development of competence in children before they reach school-age has been in progress for several years, although by 1974 it had not yet been published in definitive form. White and his colleagues at Harvard University organized the Brookline Early Education Project, studying children in the Boston suburb of Brookline from birth until they reach school age. They identified a small group of exceptionally competent children, whom they call A's, and an equal sized group of exceptionally incompetent (but not abnormal or mentally handicapped) children whom they call C's. Their initial conclusion is that all children develop much the same during the first year of life, but that in the second and third years, which are critical years for the development of all-round competence, differences begin to appear. The family, and especially the mothers, seem to make the difference. The A mothers allow their children a good deal of freedom to explore the home environment, and are not worried about accidents, clutter, or the child's interference in home routines. The A mothers nurture language growth by talking freely to the child and reading to him. By contrast, the C mothers seem more concerned with good housekeeping and try to keep the child from interfering. They put the child into a playpen with some toys, or they switch on television to keep the child quiet, rather than trying consciously to converse with the child. The A but not the C mother arranges a setting that sparks and nurtures the natural curiosity of the one-to-three-year-old. (White, 1973)

The World School Survey

The importance of the child's socioeconomic background in determining school achievement has been heavily underscored by the major international study carried out between 1967 and 1974 by the International Association for the Evaluation of School Achievement. Information was gathered from 250,000 students and 50,000 teachers in 20 countries. The students were 10, 14, and "pre-university." They were tested with identical but local-language versions of tests in mathematics, reading, science, and literature. The countries varied in their average scores on the several tests, but within each country it was found that the scores were closely related to socioeconomic status of the students. (Husen, 1967; Thorndike, 1973)

149

While family socioeconomic status is statistically correlated, overall, with children's school achievement, there are many exceptions. The exceptions show that the causes of the relatively low achievement of lower-class children are characteristics of individual families and are *not* universally connected with low socioeconomic status. This was demonstrated in a study of children from a working-class population in New York City's Harlem, where high achieving and low achieving fifth grade pupils were compared (Davidson and Greenberg, 1967). Eighty boys and 80 girls were selected from 12 elementary schools, all of whom met the following criteria:

Parents were of low socioeconomic status according to occupation, educational level, and type of dwelling unit.
Parents were all born in this country.
Child attended school in a northern city since first grade.
IQ between 75 and 125.
Age between 9 years, 11 months and 11 years, 4 months.

The 40 boys and 40 girls who were high achievers averaged at the 6.45 grade level in reading and the 5.4 level in arithmetic. The 40 boys and 40 girls who were low achievers averaged 2.85 in reading and 3.35 in arithmetic.

The two groups—the high achievers and the low achievers—were compared on a number of psychological and social characteristics. High achievers were superior to low achievers on a number of psychological characteristics, as would be expected. But the striking thing was the relationship of certain home or family characteristics *within* this working-class group to school achievement. An experienced interviewer visited in the homes and talked with the mother about the child and about the mother's behavior. He was not informed as to the achievement level of the children. The families of high achievers were rated as substantially superior to that of low achievers in "Concern for the Child's Education," "Thinking and Planning for the Child as an Individual," "General Social-Civic Awareness and Concern of the Parent," "Structure and Orderliness of the Home."

Thus, *within* the black lower-class group some children score above the national norms on educational achievement, and they tend to come from homes that prepare them well for school achievement. It was also noted that certain socioeconomic differences within the working class differentiated the high from the low achievers. Parents of the high achievers had more education, higher status occupations, and took better care of their apartments than parents of low achievers.

COMPENSATORY EDUCATION

By 1965 it had become clear to most educators that the great majority of children from low-income families, particularly from low-income black families, were achieving poorly in the schools, and were probably headed for a lifetime of poverty. There was also convincing evidence that these children were severely handicapped by the time they reached school age. Hence there arose a number of proposals and experiments for working with such children to help compensate for their unfavorable start in life and for their disadvantages in school. Thus arose the concept of *compensatory education*. The federal government put relatively large sums of money into this field, first through the War on Poverty and the Office of Economic Opportunity, beginning just before 1965, and then through the Elementary and Secondary Education Act of 1965.

It was then and still is uncertain what balance of effort should be placed on preschool children or school-age children. If stress is laid on the preschool years, it emphasizes the family factor and seems to imply that the lower-working-class family, and especially the black working-class family, is inadequate for rearing children in a complex urban society. If stress is placed on work with school-age children, it emphasizes the school factor and implies that it is primarily the school that should be improved.

When stress is placed upon the family factor, some persons see an inference that blacks themselves are to blame, even though these persons also recognize that society, through slavery and racial discrimination, is responsible for the situation of the black working-class family. They look not to the schools but to other economic and political institutions of the society to remedy the situation. On the other hand, some black leaders and civil rights workers, as well as some whites who are emotionally identified with the working class, tend to charge the schools with the responsibility for present defects in the achievement of black as well as other working-class children.

In the late 1960s and early 1970s, efforts to improve the situation for disadvantaged children were proceeding in a context of emotional tension, for various groups held different interpretations of the basic causes and therefore of the basic solutions to the problem.

Those who emphasized the family factor wished to expand preschool classes for socially disadvantaged children, educational work with their mothers and fathers, spread of birth control knowledge among lower-working-class people, and a variety of forms of assistance and support through social workers. For this group, the school system could go on with its present programs for school-age children, but making improvements such as smaller classes and remedial instruction for disadvantaged children.

Those who emphasized the school factor were demanding new forms of education, not merely more of the old forms. They called for new and radical changes in the schools and asked that the schools find new ways of teaching lower-working-class children. Among this latter group was Kenneth Clark, the eminent black psychologist who played a strategic role in marshalling the evidence for the Supreme Court decision of 1954 to end segregation in the public schools. Clark called for school experimentation on a broad scale, insisting that educational compensation can and must be accomplished through the schools. (Clark, 1971)

151

A slashing attack on what they regard as "institutional racism" has been made by Baratz and Baratz, who place their emphasis on the school rather than the home. They regard the "inadequate mother hypothesis" as a mistaken interpretation of cultural and language differences between middle-class and lower-class people—the mistake being made by middle-class educators and researchers such as Bernstein, Deutsch, Hess, and others, who, they claim, are mistaken also in their interpretation of cultural difference in language usage as a "linguistic deficit." They say,

> "It is important to understand that the inadequate mother hypothesis rests essentially on the grounds that the mother's behavior produces deficit children. It was created to account for a deficit that in actuality does not exist—that is, that ghetto mothers produce linguistically and cognitively impaired children who cannot learn. Black children are neither linguistically impoverished nor cognitively underdeveloped. Although their language system is different and, therefore, presents a handicap to the child attempting to negotiate with the standard English-speaking mainstream, it is nonetheless a fully developed, highly structured system that is more than adequate for aiding in abstract thinking.
>   . . . The mother's involvement in reading activities is also presumed to be extremely important to the child's development and future school success. The conclusions of many studies of the black ghetto home stress the absence of books and the fact that ghetto mothers rarely read to their children. Although the presence of books in the home may be quite indicative of middle-class life styles, and stories when read may very well give pleasure to all children, there appears to be no evidence which demonstrates that reading to children is essential for their learning to read, or that such reading will enhance their language development." (Baratz and Baratz, 1970, pp. 35–36)

The controversy among various researchers in child development and researchers in linguistics leaves the issue undecided.

Preschool Compensatory Education vs. School Improvement

The available facts lead the present authors to the conclusion that while some form of assistance should be provided by the society to disadvantaged children, it remains unclear just what forms this assistance should take. The growing evidence of the importance of the second and third years of life leads to emphasis on teaching mothers how to help their children at home. However, the Milwaukee project of Heber (cited in Chapter 6) argues for the use of child-care centers in low-income areas of big cities, for taking very young children out of the home, and for setting up intensive (and expensive) child development programs.

For children aged four and five, there is a strong argument for pre-school education aimed at both mental and social development. This argument is now so well accepted by the public that by 1972 approximately 40 percent of children aged three, four, and five were enrolled in preprimary programs. Most of them were five-year-olds in kindergarten, but there was a growing proportion also of three and four-year-olds in school. One aspect of this argument is that school is and should be different from the home, and that especially children of low-income families should have schooling as early as age four or five. One educator, noting that experiments have failed to improve the learning of children of low-income families when they are kept in their own homes, has said, "The child must learn to live in two worlds, the school and the home . . . and to distinguish between them. . . . The child should feel that he belongs to the school, which is there to help him learn and see himself as a successful learner." (Smilansky, 1973)

Compensatory preschool education will probably be continued into the school grades if the findings of recent major long-term studies are confirmed. The work of Weikart at Ypsilanti, Michigan, is an example. Children who began preschool at the age of three or four had made substantial gains in IQ, compared with a control group, and performed better in the primary grades. But their superiority over the control group diminished when they reached the age of 10 or 11.

Assuming that in the future a substantial gain in school achievement could be made to hold up over the middle-childhood years, it might be asked who should pay the cost of providing a year or more of prekindergarten education. Intensive preschool efforts like those followed in the more successful experimental programs cost more per child than the average elementary school program. The argument in favor of supporting such preschool programs with public funds is that only by this means can the society come fairly close to true equality of educational opportunity for lower-class children. One group of researchers has computed the money value of the mother's educational services to her child in relation to the extent of the mother's education. They concluded that the school system should devote about twice as much money to the education of a lower-class child, compared with an upper-middle-class child. This would tend to compensate the lower-class child for the lower value of the mother's educational services. (Levin, et al., 1971)

Although the majority of experts in the study of child development agree that socially disadvantaged children do profit from preschool education if it is intensive enough and continues over at least a year of time, there is some basis for arguing that the schools might do a much better job by working on compensatory education programs at the primary grade levels. This, of course, would cost much less extra money, since the school program is already being paid for, and the extra cost of a compensatory program would be relatively little as compared with a preschool program.

A choice between the two strategies has not yet been necessary during what has essentially been a tryout period for both. Since about 1964 substantial amounts of money have been put into preschools for socially disadvantaged children, but with most experiments being financed by the federal government or private foundation money. Even larger amounts of money have been put into compensatory education for low-income children and youth at school age. Since 1965 more than $1 billion a year has been spent on compensatory education in public schools under the Elementary and Secondary Education Act.

However, the time has come in the midseventies to gather the evidence concerning the effectiveness of the two strategies, and to determine how much money and human energy should be placed on the one and on the other. For this reason, we should turn attention to evaluating various forms of compensatory education.

Evaluation of Preschool Compensatory Education

Several variants of preschool programs have been tried, in which children in the experiments are matched with similar children not in the experiments. The age of children ranges from two to five. Some experiments involve training the mothers; others take the children to a preschool site where a variety of educative procedures are used. The most widespread program is Head Start, which was operated in some instances on a six to eight-week summer basis, and in other instances on a year-round basis. Children were tested for mental ability as well as for physical health when they entered Head Start programs. They were tested again at the close of a program, and the results were reported to state and federal agencies.

Evaluation of Head Start. The Office of Economic Opportunity, which supported the Head Start program, employed Westinghouse Learning Corporation in collaboration with Ohio University in 1969 to answer the question: Have Head Start classes made an intellectual and psychological difference to poor children who are now in the first, second, or third grades? This evaluation reported that when Head Start graduates were compared with other children of poor families who had not had Head Start, there was very little advantage for the Head Start group. However, many of the Head Start programs had been summer programs of brief duration and it was generally agreed that such a program should operate for a full year in a child's life before much could be accomplished. In any case, Head Start was retained after 1969, placed under the new Office of Child Development in the Department of Health, Education, and Welfare, and it was being supported in the early 1970s with funds over $350 million a year.

The Director of the Office of Child Development from June, 1970 through July, 1972 was Edward Zigler, Professor of Psychology at Yale University. In 1973, he wrote an article entitled: *Project Head Start: Success or Failure?* in which he gave a limited positive evaluation. He acknowledged the Westinghouse findings, but argued that Head Start's main goal was *social competence,* and that this had been improved substantially. He said:

> Whether Head Start is seen as a success or a failure is determined by the factors one chooses to weigh in making such an assessment. Thus, if Head Start is appraised in terms of its success in universally raising the IQs of poor children, and maintaining these IQs over time, one is tempted to write off Head Start as an abject failure. On the other hand, if one assesses Head Start in terms of the improved health of the tens of thousands of poor children who have been screened, diagnosed, and treated, Head Start is clearly a resounding success. The problem appears to be that, as a nation, we are not clear about the exact nature of the Head Start program or its goals. I believe that a realistic and proper assessment of Head Start demonstrates that it has been a success. Furthermore, I think that what we have learned from Head Start to date can give clear direction to those responsible for future compensatory efforts. (Zigler, 1973, p. 3)

He went on to stress the importance of the social competence gained by the Head Start pupils.

> If I am correct in my suspicion that compensatory programs have a larger impact on motivational and emotional factors than on cognitive factors, we will never assess the magnitude of this impact by continuing to overemphasize cognitive measures in our evaluations of compensatory efforts.

Evaluation of School-Age Compensatory Education

Under Title I of the Elementary and Secondary Education Act of 1965, federal funds were given to every public school which had a substantial proportion of children from families below the officially defined poverty level. These funds amounted to $150 per year or more for each pupil in this category. Some school systems, such as New York City, had already been experimenting with enriched education for socially disadvantaged pupils during much of the decade of the 1960s, but now a wide variety of new compensatory programs were developed by the many school systems in the country. The name given to certain special programs in the primary grades under ESEA was *Follow Through,* meaning a follow-through of the assistance given to children in preschools. There were other programs, including *bilingual education* for children whose home language was not English, and *Upward Bound,* for junior and senior high school students.

The President's National Advisory Commission on the Education of Disadvantaged Children kept a close watch. Its 1969 report gave a limited positive evaluation, described 21 outstanding Title I programs which had been reasonably effective, and concluded:

What is clear is that among the thousands of different programs and approaches labeled as compensatory education, some efforts are paying off and others are not. Some of these programs can be evaluated in terms of positive, easily identifiable changes such as improvement in reading scores; in this report the Council identifies a number of such programs which have proven successful by such measurements.

More recently, in 1973, the Department of Health, Education, and Welfare made a systematic review of evidence of the effectiveness of compensatory education. This included careful studies made in the states of California, Colorado, Connecticut, Rhode Island, and Wisconsin; studies in New York City, Los Angeles, Sacramento, Indianapolis, and Cleveland; and U.S. Office of Education evaluation of Follow Through and of ESEA Title I programs. The general procedure was to measure the average growth on reading and arithmetic tests of a group of disadvantaged children over a period of at least one and preferably three or four years, comparing this with the average growth of .7 grade equivalent per year which is usually the most that groups of disadvantaged children gain in one year of school. (That is, data from all over the country indicate that, at the most, children from families below the poverty level average a growth rate of .7 of a grade in one year compared with 1.0 grade equivalents for the national average of all public school children.) Therefore a fair test of the effectiveness of compensatory education is to measure the growth of children in such programs, and to find what proportion gain *more* than .7 grade equivalents per year. Some of the results reported in the HEW study are these:

The following are the preliminary conclusions which can be drawn from the data at this time: children receiving compensatory help show very small but consistent improvement in learning compared with matched children without compensatory help; and, the more disadvantaged the children are, the more effective this compensatory help has been in improving their academic performance compared with similar children not receiving any help. . . .

The most complete data are those available from the State of California. California has collected pretreatment and posttreatment standardized test achievement data on children receiving Title I services for the last four years. Achievement data were collected for about 80% of all participants in compensatory reading programs and analyses were conducted using data covering about 50% of the participating children. Only that achievement data which met specified quality control criteria were included. Over the four years covered by the data, 54% to 67% of children receiving compensatory services showed a rate of reading achievement gain larger than the usual maximum for disadvantaged children. Analysis and results for mathematics were similar and even slightly better. We judge this to be clear evidence of success. (Lynn, 1973)

The extra cost of the various school-age programs ranged from $150 to $1,000 per pupil. Comparison of various programs indicated that $300 was the cost of the most productive programs, with no great advantage for the more expensive ones.

The conclusions from this evaluation (which, incidentally, had been made by an agency of the federal government that was recommending a major program of compensatory education to the Congress in 1972) was:

We know:

that compensatory education can be made to work for poor children—therefore we will use this approach;

that poor children are most in need of educational help—therefore we seek to focus on the schools which contain substantial proportions of poor children;

that children need most help with the basic skills, reading and arithmetic— therefore we have stipulated that the funds be used for this purpose;

that successful programs often require substantial departures from typical educational practice and usually cost more—therefore our provision for about $300 per child in compensatory services;

that children learn less effectively when there is a great degree of economic or racial isolation—therefore our provision for a "transfer bonus" which will encourage districts to reduce economic and racial concentrations within schools, and our desire to provide priority in funding for districts which are making efforts to increase desegregation and reduce economic isolation;

that the federal compensatory education program has not been successful as a whole;

that funds have not reached poor children in the correct proportion and that the formula grant aspects of the program have permitted significant amounts of funds to be spent in ways which have had only minor educational consequences for disadvantaged children—therefore we seek a project grant program which will permit us to attempt a coherent, focused and concentrated compensatory education effort. (Lynn, pp. 7–13)

The program being recommended was approved by Congress, and at the time of this writing, the federal government is continuing its support of compensatory education at about the same level as in the late 1960s. The issue— stated above—namely, whether funds are better spent at preschool or at school-age, is yet to be resolved.

CONCLUSION

In summary, the family and the school operate always together in socializing the child. While most families expect their children to work conscientiously at school tasks and to conform to school expectations, still there is general agreement that thus far the schools have fallen short of succeeding with lower-working-class children.

The child is the product of his family and, figuratively speaking, "brings his family with him into the schoolroom." At the same time the child becomes also the product of the school, and eventually he "takes the school with him into the family." The relative influence of the family factor and the school factor in the mental development of the child remains unclear; it is also not clear how the interaction between the school and the family can be improved to insure long-run advantages for all types of children.

EXERCISES

1. Pick two or three children whose families are likely to be very different. Pay a visit to each home. What were the most striking differences you observed? What were the most striking similarities?

2. It is sometimes said that by the time a child enters school it is "too late" to make any real changes in his personality. A teacher may say, especially of a lower-class child, "I can't undo what the family has done." Do you agree with this point of view, generally speaking? Why or why not?

3. Interview the parents of three or four children whom you know, to investigate the methods of child-rearing that have been used. What similarities and what differences do you find?

SUGGESTIONS FOR FURTHER READING

1. For an account of how the family acts to produce differences in personality between children of different social classes, read *Father of the Man* by Allison Davis and Robert J. Havighurst.

2. *The Changing American Parent* by Daniel R. Miller and Guy E. Swanson and *Patterns of Child Rearing* by Robert R. Sears, Eleanor E. Maccoby, and Harry Levin are reports of two large-scale studies of child-rearing practices. For an account of how methods of child rearing have changed in America in the past 100 years, read chapters 9 and 10 in *Childhood in Contemporary Cultures,* edited by Margaret Mead and Martha Wolfenstein. See also the article by Urie Bronfenbrenner, "Socialization and Social Class Through Time and Space," in *Readings in Social Psychology* by Eleanor E. Maccoby, which is an analysis of the findings from various studies of child-rearing over the past 25 years. Margaret Mead (1971) has recently commented on the relations between preschool experience in the family and the child's experience in school.

3. There are a number of good textbooks on the family as a social institution. A useful survey of recent research on the family as an agent of socialization has been prepared by Clausen (1966). A book of readings on the *Family in Transition* (Skolnick and Skolnick) deals with the changing family in the 1970s.

4. *Family Worlds* by Hess and Handel describes five different families, each treated as a case study. It also introduces new ways of observing and interpreting family interaction.

5. For more information on the social and economic conditions of the lower-working-class black family, read the "Moynihan Report" which appeared as a booklet (which stirred a major controversy in 1965 and 1966) published by the U.S. Department of Labor, entitled *The Negro Family: The Case for National Action.* See also *Marriage and Family Among Negroes,* by Jessie Bernard; or Billingsley's *Black Families in White America;* or Scanzoni's *The Black Family in Modern Society.* Frazier's book, *The Negro Family in the United States,* while written sometime ago, remains a classic in the field.

6. The controversy over the existence of a *culture of poverty* makes interesting reading. Some people argue that simply increasing the income of poor people will result in major changes in their way of life, while others argue that this way of life is more deeply ingrained and will persist at least through more than a generation even though the family's economic status improves. For arguments pro and con, see the article by Havighurst on "The Culture of Poverty" in *Society and Education: A Book of Readings,* Second Edition (Havighurst, Neugarten, and Falk, 1971).

7. In *Society and Education: A Book of Readings* (Havighurst, Neugarten, and Falk), there are two readings that stress the relation of family background to school performance (Cervantes) and the facts that lack of cohesiveness in the family is related to deliquency (Ahlstrom and Havighurst).

8. The influence of poverty on children's language is a matter of some controversy. Bernstein's pioneer research, referred to in this chapter, is confirmed by Jerome Bruner (1971) in a thorough summary of psychological research on the relation of intellectual development to social background of young children. In this he makes some useful distinctions between children's flexibility in the use of language and other qualities of their language which Labov and other linguists believe do not depend on social-class background. (Labov, 1972)

CHAPTER 8

The Peer Group

The child grows up in two social worlds. One is the world of adults: his parents, teachers, club leaders, the store clerks, friends of the family, and the policeman. The second is the world of his peers or age-mates: his friends, play groups, clubs and gangs, and school groups.

THE NATURE OF THE PEER GROUP

For any given child, of course, "the" peer group means a succession of specific groups of children with whom he interacts, just as "the" family is, for any given child, one particular family. Peer groups are of many different kinds—from the informal play group to the organized Scout troop or organized gang, from the clique of three or four members to the wide school group—and the average child will interact with a variety of particular peer groups as he grows up. Each group has its own rules, implicit or explicit; its own social organization; and its own expectations for group members.

While there is great variation from one group to another, we may speak of the peer group in general terms, much as we do the family or the school. From this broad point of view, the peer group of the child and the adolescent constitutes a world of its own with its customs, traditions, manners, and even, at times, its own language.

The adult is always, to a greater or lesser degree, excluded from the peer group of the child and adolescent. At the one extreme, a peer group may be in open conflict with adults, as in a delinquent gang in a slum neighborhood whose activities may be in express defiance of community standards of law and order; or as in groups of adolescents whose standards of dress, speech, and behavior, while by no means delinquent, nevertheless come into

160

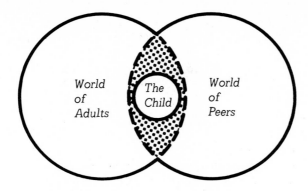

FIGURE 8.1   *The child lives in two worlds.*

conflict with the expectations set by parents. The situation in which a teen-age boy or girl argues with his parents that, "The other kids stay out until midnight, why can't I?" has its countless variations. Yet the variations are on the same theme, that of reconciling two sets of expectations: one set from the world of one's peers, the other from the world of adults.

At the other extreme is the situation in which the peer-group expectations are in full accord with adult expectations and are even a direct outcome of adult planning, as in a neighborhood play group formed under the watchful eyes of mothers; or a Boys Club organized through a settlement house, or an urban renewal project; or a high school Hi-Y group meeting under the leadership of a respected teacher. Even in such situations, the adult is to some measure excluded, with youngsters reserving certain areas of communication and interaction to themselves. The child or the adolescent feels comfortable with age-mates in a way that he is not comfortable with the adult, however acceptant and understanding the adult may be. There are always certain thoughts, values, and behaviors that youngsters share only with other youngsters.

That the peer group constitutes a social world of its own is well known and accepted by most parents and teachers. Yet the importance of the peer group as a socializing agency is less often recognized. Unlike the family and the school, the peer group is not a formalized, institutionalized agent of society. It has no legal definitions, no formally ascribed functions or duties. Yet it pervades the life of the child to a greater extent as he grows older, and it performs increasingly important functions in teaching him the ways of his society.

The Peer Group as a Learning Situation

In the adult world the child is always in a position of subordinate status. In the peer world, he has equal status with others and he learns from

161

persons who are not removed from him by wide differences in age, maturity, or prestige. Deference and respect for authority are largely irrelevant issues. The child with his peers is in a position where he is relatively free to express his own attitudes, judgments, and critical faculties. He is relatively free to explore personal relationships and to test himself out against others.

One of the special characteristics of the peer group is the transitory quality of relationships. The average school-age child forms one or two close friendships and becomes a member of a small play group that he thinks of as "his" group. These relationships may be intense, but not necessarily long-lasting. An eight-year-old for example, may suddenly switch his allegiance from one child to another and report to his family that it is now Richy, rather than Don, who is the paragon of all virtues. A twelve-year-old girl said, in similar vein, "I used to think Ellen and Nancy and I would always be friends. We spent a lot of time together, and did our homework together, and all. But now Ellen seems kind of silly, and we get into a lot of arguments. So I've become friendly with Kathy and Jill, and I like them lots better. They're my best friends now."

There are, of course, long-enduring friendships formed in childhood. Still, unless he lives in a relatively isolated setting where he has so few age-mates that he is forced always into the company of the same group, the average child moves about in the world of his peers. He forms new relationships and breaks old ones as his own levels of social and emotional maturity shift in relation to others, as his interests change, and as his needs for new social experiences change. This transitory quality of relationships occurs within the peer group as a concomitant of what we have called the lack of emotional commitment.

A third differentiating characteristic of the peer group as a socializing agency is that its influence tends to become more rather than less important with the advancing age of the child. Unlike the family, whose influence becomes less monopolistic with time, the peer group becomes more influential. The eight or ten-year-old wants to do things "like the other kids do." By the time he is sixteen this desire may become an obsession. In adolescence, the peer group takes a certain precedence in many ways over any other group that influences the individual.

FUNCTIONS OF THE PEER GROUP

As a socializing agency, the peer group serves the child in a number of ways. Adults generally expect the peer group to teach a child how to get along with others, as witnessed by the distress of parents and teachers over a child who is not accepted by other children and who is therefore denied many opportunities for social learning.

Teaching the Culture

While a peer group may be said to have a subculture that is particularly its own (a point to which we shall return presently), it nevertheless reflects the adult society and reinforces most of the values held by the adult society.* A child learns through his peers the prevailing standards of adult morality—competition, cooperation, honesty, responsibility—which, while they may at first be childlike versions, become adultlike with increasing age.

The peer group teaches children their sex roles, building upon, but changing and elaborating the earlier teaching of the family. A child learns from his peers what behavior is acceptable and admired in a boy, and what is accepted and admired in a girl. Thus the peer group is a powerful agency in molding behavior in accordance with current versions of manhood and womanhood.

The peer group is also an important source of information in areas other than social relations. Our modern sophisticate, aged 10, has obtained much of his up-to-the-minute knowledge of outer space and satellites from television, it is true; but it is after discussion with his age-mates that the information takes on value and becomes part of his intellectual equipment. It is the peer group that often decides what knowledge is important, and what is not.

Certain areas of teaching and information-giving have become the special province of the peer group: for instance, to teach a child by actual experience how rules are made, how they can be changed and, concomitant with this, an understanding of the individual's responsibility in a group situation. It also has been left to the peer group, by and large, to impart sex education to the child. (The latter situation is now changing, as the family, the school, and other institutions are taking responsibility for sex education.)

Aiding Social Mobility

The peer group also operates, in many cases, to teach social mobility. A working-class boy or girl who, through an organized youth group or through the school, becomes friendly with middle-class boys and girls, learns

*The distinction should be drawn between an organized gang and other types of peer groups. The gang may be defined as an organization of preadolescents or adolescents that does not relate itself positively to adult leadership. A gang may or may not engage in delinquent behavior, but in the eyes of most adults, gangs are undesirable because they are at least potentially antisocial, if not actually so. The efforts of most social agencies in dealing with gangs are directed toward the transformation of gangs into "groups" by providing adult leadership and thus to guide their activities into socially acceptable channels. While gang activity is receiving a great deal of publicity recently in a period in which juvenile delinquency is regarded as an increasingly grave social problem, it must be kept in mind that only a small proportion of children or adolescents are ever members of a gang.

from them new ways of behaving. He may be encouraged to acquire the values and goals of his new friends.

The opportunity for working-class children to become acquainted with middle-class children is most often found within the school. Many educators, recognizing the power of age-mates in aiding social mobility, use this as a strong argument in favor of heterogeneous schools. They feel that one of the ways the school can help to foster mobility is to bring children of varying social backgrounds together in the same classrooms; and thus to provide the opportunity for working-class children and adolescents to learn from age-mates, as well as from adult school personnel, a middle-class way of life.

In a study which bears this out, it was found that a student's desire to attend college, and the likelihood that he would actually get into college, were both strongest if the student's best friend planned to go (Alexander and Campbell, 1964). The friend's influence was more important than the family's desires or the family's socioeconomic position.

Peer Group Serving as Reference Group

Every person wants to look well in the eyes of certain other people, and does not care what impression he makes on still other groups for which he has no respect or interest. The groups to which he wants to be favorably known and seen are called his *reference groups*. He sees himself through their eyes; he judges himself as they would judge him; he learns from them his attitudes and aspirations.

Most people have several reference groups. Their family is generally the first, and most important when they are quite young. Then come their friends, their teachers, their peers, their neighbors, and their fellow citizens. Their peer group is generally quite important to them by the age of seven or eight, and it becomes more important as they move into adolescence, reaching its greatest effectiveness as a reference group when they are 15 to 20 years old.

Still, the parents remain an effective reference group for some purposes. Brittain (1963) studied the relative importance of friends and of parents on various issues. He found that peers are more influential in deciding some things, like what course to take in school; but parents are more influential when, for instance, a girl decides which of two boys to date.

The peer group helps the adolescent to become independent of adults—especially of parents. However, this independence is not monolithic. As we have just noted from Brittain's study, the adolescent, instigated and supported by his peer group, becomes independent of parents in some matters, but not in others. It appears that the adolescent peer group acts as a kind of shock absorber in the relations between adolescents and adults. It defends youth from too stringent demands for scholarly behavior or for adultlike behavior, but it also presses youth to become more mature in their behavior. The research evidence is mixed on this matter. The so-called "adolescent society" is not simply a group which glorifies athletic skills, social skills, and student leadership.

THE GROWING INFLUENCE OF THE PEER GROUP

While the peer group operates informally, as we have said, its influence has grown more important over the last 100 years in America. There are a number of factors involved. Since more and more children and adolescents live in urban rather than rural settings today, since the number of youth organizations of all types have grown, and since adolescents spend increasingly more years in school rather than at work, children and adolescents are thrown together in groups of age-mates to an ever increasing extent.

In our society adolescents as an age group play a relatively insignificant part. Their labor is not required in economic production, and they remain in positions of economic dependence upon the family for longer and longer periods. As adolescence tends to be prolonged, and as youth are excluded from participation in the adult society, young people turn more and more to the peer group for recognition. In return, the peer group takes on an increasingly larger role in the socialization process.

Adolescent Values

Part of the importance which the peer group assumes for the adolescent has been documented by James Coleman (1961b) in a study of student bodies in 11 different high schools. Even though the schools were carefully picked to reflect a wide range of differences in terms of the size of the community and the social-class backgrounds of the students, there was considerable agreement on major values from one adolescent group to the next as expressed in responses to questionnaires. Thus, for boys, the importance of being a "brilliant scholar" was secondary to being a "star athlete" in all schools in the study; and, for girls, it was less important than being an "activities leader." For both sexes, it was better to be popular than to be intellectually outstanding.

Coleman summarized his data, at one point, in the following terms: "Despite wide differences in parental background, type of community, and type of school, there was little difference in the standards of prestige, the activities which confer status, and the values which focus attention and interest. In particular, good grades and academic achievement had relatively low status in all schools." (Coleman, 1959, p. 338)

It appears that, within the adolescent society, while no special social stigma is attached to intellectual brilliance, neither is there any special value attached to it. There are, however, stigmas attached to disinterest in sports and to an excessive and apparent zeal for study.

These studies, made about 1960, may not give an accurate picture of the present situation. Coleman, in his description of what he calls the Youth Culture in the 1974 report of the President's Panel on Youth, gives a somewhat different statement, more like that given by Margaret Mead in her book *Culture and Commitment: The Generation Gap.* (See Chapter 9.) They suggest that the youth of the 1970s may be ahead of the adult society in anticipating the values of the society of 1990.

The Peer Group in Other Societies

The peer group can be understood better when its characteristics are examined in contrasting societies. Some interesting studies have been made in the Scandinavian countries, aimed at testing some of the conclusions that have been drawn from American studies. Bengt-Erik Andersson studied a sample of 14 to 16-year-olds in Goteborg, Sweden in 1963 and 1965. He found the attitudes and educational aspirations of this sample to be related to four social environments: the home and family; the school; the local community; and the peer group. There was no one dominant environmental force. Some youth were more oriented toward peers, while others were more dependent on their families. Youth could not be considered as one homogeneous group controlled by peer group norms. (Andersson, 1973)

Another source of information about peer group influence comes from the study in the Soviet Union reported by Professor Urie Bronfenbrenner of Cornell University. The natural tendency of an age group of children to work together has enabled the Russian schools to treat the school class as a "collective" which takes on certain responsibilities as a group. For example, the responsibility to get to school on time, or to do a certain amount of homework, or to assist a class of younger pupils. Also, a school class may be divided into two or more subgroups which then compete with each other on tests, on punctuality, or on service to the school community (Bronfenbrenner, 1970). Thus the energy of the individual pupil is turned toward cooperation with a group of peers rather than striving for individual achievement and recognition.

Status in the Peer Group

Most parents and teachers are aware occasionally that the specific characteristics which give a youngster high status in the eyes of his companions may be different from the qualities they themselves consider important. The following example, although unusual, illustrates this point:

The elementary school in which I teach (school population about 700 pupils) has, in addition to regular classrooms, several "ungraded" classrooms, three for boys and three for girls. The Hanley School is composed of 70 per cent blacks and 20 per cent Italian-Americans. The remaining 10 per cent is composed of various nationalities including Mexican and Puerto Rican children. We have heterogeneity at Hanley, not in economic status, but in race, religion, and nationality.

Leadership among pupils is not based on intellectual attainment, but on age, size, and knowledge of sex. These factors seem to grow and thrive in our ungraded sections, since these children may not be graduated until they are at least 15½ years old and have reached an achievement level of at least fourth grade. These children become the models of behavior for our much younger school population in the regular grades. This results in an atmosphere where these ungraded pupils are not penalized for their IQ's (below 80), but are instead admired for their muscular, social, and sexual precocity. The ungraded leader cannot compete academically, but physically he has no peer. A leader is tough—he might not be able to read or write well, he may have the vocabulary of a hoot owl, but if he's tough, who cares?

There are some other interesting factors. In the ungraded sections, girls take cooking and sewing. As class projects, they cook their own breakfasts— orange juice, milk, wheatcakes, susages, and so on, with the food being provided by the Board of Education. Since many of the children in the regular grades come to school without breakfast, this aspect of being in an ungraded room seems like paradise. The girls also take up sewing, again with materials provided by the school, and make their own clothes, putting on a fashion show at Easter time. The rooms in which these girls work are large and the enrollment is small—not exceeding 20 pupils in one group—and the class atmosphere is informal. The younger children in the regular grades, sitting at immovable desks and working haphazardly at academic tasks, see the ungraded rooms as the "Elysian fields."

But do these ungraded boys and girls at Hanley see themselves as they are seen by the regular-grade children? During the last few weeks I have asked, during conversations with these ungraded children, if they would like to be in the regular grades; and out of the total number asked, over 90 per cent answered "Yes." By and large they felt stigmatized by being placed in the ungraded sections—that it was unfair, that they were "as smart as anybody." Though they enjoyed their work in woodshop and kitchen, still the regular classroom with its routines, its discipline and strict order, its emphasis on academic achievement, was the greener field.

I have focused my observations mainly on the ungraded sections because most of the teachers in our school feel that the pupils in the ungraded sections are the instigators, conspirators, and the reasons for most of our problems in school. The basis of my focusing so much attention on the ungraded is not to distort the situation as it exists, but rather to point out the fact that the ungraded pupils, who in the eyes of many of the teachers are just vegetables, are in reality the models and leaders of the school; they are the ones who are followed and imitated by pupils in the regular grades.

One more interesting point. In checking our records, I find that where tru-

ancy is involved, pupils of the regular grades are truant many more times than the ungraded pupils. This is, I believe, due to the fact that these ungraded children—who would be lost in the shuffle if they were competing with children their own age in high schools—have an important stake in school. Their status as leaders in the elementary school is not taken lightly. They find untold satisfaction in the position of being socially successful.

While this example illustrates how a group of children may operate on certain values that are different from those of adults, it would be a mistake to conclude that such differences are either more common or more important than the basic similarities between the social values of children and adults. The characteristics that make for success in most peer groups are generally the same that make for success in adult groups—courage, good sportsmanship, loyalty to the group, and the ability to strike a balance between conformity and individuality.

Social-Class Factors.   The peer group also reflects the social-status structure of the wider society. Social-class differences not only operate in the adult society but operate also in the society of children and adolescents.

The first study of social-class differences in the child's society was made in Jonesville. There Neugarten found that fifth and sixth-grade children (all of whom were together in the same school), when asked who were their best friends, most often named children above them in social class, then, second, children from their own social class. Few choices were made downward in the social scale, with the result that most working-class children were chosen only by others of their own social status. Similarly, as regarded reputation, children ascribed favorable personality traits to children of the higher social classes; and unfavorable personality traits to the children from lower social classes. There was a consistent relationship between social class and reputation: as one moved up the social scale, from lower-working to upper-middle-class, children received consistently higher proportions of mentions on favorable characteristics and consistently lower proportions on unfavorable ones.

Among tenth and eleventh graders in Jonesville, social-class differences were also clearly operative, but in somewhat more complex ways. Here, where a large proportion of working-class children had already dropped out of school, adolescents also chose upward or horizontally on the social scale, but seldom downward, in selecting their friends. Adolescents of upper social status, while less uniformly regarded by their classmates in favorable terms, were nevertheless in the limelight so far as social visibility is concerned. Working-class adolescents were rarely mentioned, either positively or negatively (Neugarten, 1949).

THE PEER GROUP AND THE SCHOOL

The school is expected to help the child to bridge the gap between the child's world and the adult world. This is, in one sense, the expressed function of the school as a socializing agency. While this is also a function of the family, the important difference between school and family in this respect is that the school deals with children and moves them along toward adulthood, not as individuals, but as groups. Consequently, the influence of the school upon the individual child is always mediated in the setting of the peer group. It is from this point of view that the school and the peer group are inextricably bound together in their influences upon the child.

Peer Group Structure in the School

One of the first tasks of a child or adolescent when he enters a new classroom is to find out where he stands in relation to classmates and his teacher. According to Glidewell (1966) there are three dimensions of status in the school group: (1) social acceptance or liking by the group; (2) leadership or ability to influence other students; and (3) competence in school work. During the elementary school period, a child's status on these dimensions remains moderately stable. These dimensions tend to correlate positively in the elementary school. For example, Schmuch (1963) found that elementary school children who saw themselves as being well-liked by their classmates, whether they actually were or not, were more likely to view themselves positively and to utilize their abilities than were children who saw themselves as being disliked.

The "Ins" and the "Outs."   In secondary schools one can usually find "the leading crowd," the "brains," the "wild ones." Among these groups an informal hierarchy will exist so that everyone will know which group has the greatest prestige and which the least. However, the members of any one group, the "Ins," so to speak, while recognizing this hierarchy, will be able to maintain among themselves a certain security in their group membership. The group, with its common values, gives the individual an identity and a sense of belonging.

Not all students, of course, are members of groups; some never become identified with any particular clique, but remain on the fringe, perhaps with one or two friends, perhaps not. These are the "Outs," and their marginal positions may have deleterious effects. Some of these individuals may have no need for group association; but for others, this lack of group identity will affect self-confidence and may retard the normal process of social and emotional development.

169

Skin Color. Although the situation may be changing slowly, it appears that, in the early 1970s, friendships do not frequently cross racial lines. Gottlieb and TenHouten (1965) found that, in three high schools in a northern city, racial composition of the school strongly affected the extracurricular activities as well as the prestige ratings of activities for black students. In the school where blacks constituted less than five percent of the student body, they participated primarily in the highly structured, school-sponsored extracurricular activities such as sports, vocational clubs, and band and chorus—activities that do not require a great amount of support from other students. The blacks in this school placed considerable emphasis on being good students and participating in student government in order to achieve leadership; though they participated in sports, they did not give sports a high leadership ranking.

In the school where blacks constituted almost half of the student body, a separate social system had developed parallel to that of the white students. Fewer black students thought it a prerequisite for leadership to be a good student, but being an athlete and being a party-goer received higher ratings than in the first school. The black students were not as dependent upon the formal activities of their school as were the blacks in the first school, although their memberships were still heavily concentrated in the structured activities. In this school, there was greater consensus between white and black students on what activities were important for leadership.

The third school was 99 percent black, and the black students tended to rank a larger number of activities and memberships as important for leadership, indicating that they were no longer concentrating their energies in a small number of extracurricular activities. The tiny minority of white students, on the other hand, was concentrated in a few school-sponsored groups—much the same as were the blacks in the first school.

The group morale of black students in high schools and colleges has increased in the late 1960s and early 1970s, with the result that black students have become more visibly self-segregating in schools with a mixed racial population. They have formed "Black Student Associations" and asked for special recognition with separate lounge rooms as well as courses in Black Studies.

Small Friendship Groups. Within the larger peer structure there is always a substructure of small friendship cliques, consisting of youth who associate for a variety of reasons, including personal attraction, living close together, or common recreation interests and hobbies. The members of such a group tend to be rather similar in home background, school achievement, and school conduct. Sugarman (1967, 1968) has studied these groups in four London secondary schools for boys. He asked boys (age about 14–15): "At school, which other pupils do you usually go around with?" He then defined a "peer group" for his purposes as a group of three or more boys who named each other as associates. In this way he was able to define 66 small peer groups with 230 members. The members of a particular small peer group were quite similar in terms of their conduct as noted by teachers and their school achievement in relation to their IQ. Sugarman was interested in the problem of how participation in a small "peer group" influences the behavior and attitudes of pupils. He finds no simple answer to this problem.

The School as a Reference Group

Among people who interact again and again, certain norms develop and tend to influence the behavior of these people. This is the *reference group postulate,* and it can be seen to operate especially in secondary schools. This postulate leads to the hypothesis that a school from which most of the pupils will graduate and go to college would influence its pupils to adopt this pattern of behavior, whereas a school whose pupils drop out early would influence pupils to drop out.

Where an entire school is seen as a reference group, it must be assumed that students and teachers have a general consensus about the desirable forms and outcomes of the school program. There may be subgroups of students who do not share this consensus, but they have little prestige and little power. The average student feels a pressure from the school as a whole to adopt certain attitudes about his education, or his clothing, or his career, or his political activities. Examples are: a school with a strong tradition of musical and dramatic performance will lead its students to value music and dramatics; a school with a strong athletic record will lead its students to value sports, both as participants and spectators; an all-black school with black militant students and faculty will lead its students into black separatist actions and attitudes.

Reference-Group Influence on College Attendance. Since high school graduation and college attendance are becoming more and more frequent, especially for middle-class students, it might be expected that high schools with a substantial middle-class population would exert a reference-group effect upon their students to cause them to graduate from high school and go to college. A study of high school seniors in the Kansas City metropolitan area was designed to test this hypothesis.

The high school seniors in nearly all of the high schools of the Kansas City area were asked by Levine, Mitchell, and Havighurst (1970) to answer a questionnaire in the spring of their senior year, telling about their home backgrounds and telling whether they expected to enter college the next autumn. The 55 high schools in the study were categorized as described in Chapter 4.

The college expectations of those high school seniors are reported in Table 4.4. This shows that the socioeconomic type of school interacts with the socioeconomic status of students to influence their educational plans and aspirations. For example, students from middle-middle-class families (Level II) show decreasing percentages planning to enter college as we go from "middle-class" to "socially comprehensive" to "working-class" type schools, and the same rule applies to students from lower-middle-class families (Level III). This is true for both sexes.

Very similar findings were reported by Alan Wilson (1959) from his study of college aspirations of boys in eight public schools in Oakland, California.

Student Rights and the Peer Group

Student protest and student conflict emerged in the late 1960s as a major concern of students and of educators in colleges and high schools. There is hardly a school or college that did not experience a student strike, or a student protest, or a conflict between groups of students, though the exact numbers are difficult to determine because it is difficult to define "incidents" in such a way that comparable data can be obtained from the many institutions. One careful survey of secondary schools in cities over 50,000 population found that 85 percent of the schools which responded to a questionnaire had experienced some type of disruption in the three years ending in June, 1970. (Bailey, 1970). These could be called peer group activities only in a loose sense. They seldom involved all students as a single united group, and sometimes they consisted of fights or conflicts of students from rival ethnic or racial groups. The three principal issues around which the student protests centered were student dress-appearance codes, special nonacademic provisions for ethnic minority groups, and national government policy on Vietnam and poverty.

Student activism around issues of this sort would hardly have been possible 10 years earlier. Thus it appears that the general social unrest which emerged in the 1960s over American foreign policy and domestic problems was reflected in student activism. However, there was an additional factor in the growing sentiment for protection of the rights of minorities or of hitherto disadvantaged groups. Student rights came to the fore, along with women's rights, after the movement for more equitable treatment of blacks and other ethnic minorities had been recognized as a legitimate and respectable cause.

Student rights at the high school level took the form of greater freedom for student dress and physical appearance, greater freedom of the student press, and more care to maintain privacy of information in high school files about students. The Commission on the Reform of Secondary Education in 1973 made recommendations in favor of greater student freedom (Brown, 1973):

1.   Students should have complete freedom of expression in their own publications.

2. Student school records should contain only factual information neces-
    sary to the educational process, and made available at all times for re-
    view by students and their parents, but not released to others unless the
    student consented.
3. Corporal punishment should be abolished.
4. Academic scholarship should not be a requisite for participation in vari-
    ous kinds of student activities.
5. Youth aged 14 and over should not be compelled to attend school.

Analogous changes have been made in many colleges concerning the
rights and responsibilities of students. Student publications have been freed
from faculty supervision. Coeducational dormitories have been established.
Students have been placed on many academic committees with responsibility
for curriculum and other issues. The office of student ombudsman has been
created in some colleges to provide a student spokesman who has access to
the administration on matters affecting student individual and group welfare.

Students have been made aware of their "rights" through publications
by the American Civil Liberties Union (1965, 1968, 1973). Several key court
cases have been decided in favor of students against school and college ad-
ministrations. Speaking in general terms, we can say that the right of the
school and college authorities to deal with students *in loco parentis* (in the
role of the parents) has been substantially reduced. Students have much more
power than formerly. It is not yet clear whether students will get together
and organize this power for general improvement of their education, or will
use this power largely to protect their individual freedom and privacy.

It seems that the area of student rights in relation to high school and
college attendance needs further clarification, with the development of
ground rules which the courts and the educational system can live with.

YOUTH-SERVING AGENCIES
AND PEER GROUPS

The peer group is so important to children and youth that the adult part of
society works through it whenever the opportunity appears. This is especially
noteworthy in the case of churches, and of "youth-serving" organizations.

Churches and the Peer Group

It is regarded as important by the churches to provide a social life for
youth within the church group which gives some moral direction and training, some religious instruction, and some experience of fellowship within the
church.

Social Class and Participation of Youth in Churches.   Churches reach
more young people of middle-class than of lower-class families. This has

been found in several surveys, including one in the midwestern community of River City (Havighurst *et al.,* 1962). In this study, all of the clergymen were given a list of names of all boys and girls age 17 and 18 who had been in the ninth grade of the public schools a few years earlier (in 1954–55), and who were still in the community. The clergymen were asked to indicate all youths who were known to them as participants in their church, to rate the frequency of their attendance, and to give their judgment of the significance of religious belief, affiliation, and participation to the individual. These ratings were placed in three categories:

1. The church has some importance in the life of this person.
2. This person is known as an occasional participant in the church, but does not show by his attendance or participation that the church has any importance to him.
3. This person is unknown to any clergyman as a participant in church.

Table 8.1 shows how social class and sex are related to church activity and interest in this community. Of the total group, 61 percent were known to a clergyman, and 35 percent were judged by the clergy to find some importance in the church. In general, as social status declined, the proportions who found church important decreased, and the proportions who were unknown to the clergy increased. An exception was the high proportion of boys from the upper and upper-middle-class (40 percent, or 8 of the total 20) who were unknown to clergymen.

Religion-Oriented Agencies.   Besides the youth organizations of individual churches, there are several large-scale organizations that have a religious orientation, and that have had broad support from religious groups. Chief among these are the Young Men's Christian Association (YMCA), Young Women's Christian Association (YWCA), and the Jewish Community Centers. These organizations all provide settings for the social and physical development of boys and girls, settings in which the aim is to promote character development. Usually such an organization will have a building with gymnasium, swimming pool, indoor recreational facilities, and, often, dormitory quarters for older youth.

Originally these agencies were widely separated from the school. They offered programs on Saturdays and on weekdays in after-school hours. Then, about 1915, the YMCA began experimenting with clubs of in-school youth at the secondary school level. Many of the club leaders were high school teachers. The Hi-Y Clubs thus formed are often closely associated with the school program, even though their meetings are generally held in YMCA buildings or in members' homes. A boy does not usually need to be a member of the YMCA to belong to a Hi-Y Club. In communities that did not have a YWCA, the YMCA launched into work with girls. There Tri-Hi-Y clubs for both boys and girls were started. Later a type of boys' club at the grade school

TABLE 8.1. *Percent of Youth Having Relationships with the Church in River City: By Social Class*

| | Social Class | | | | | | | | | |
| Relationship to the Church | Upper and Upper-Middle | | Lower-Middle | | Upper-Lower | | Lower-Lower | | Total | |
	M	F	M	F	M	F	M	F	M	F
Church is important	30	63	43	55	31	39	14	16	30	40
Known to clergy, but church is not important	30	32	30	29	19	31	14	33	21	31
Unknown to clergy	40	5	27	16	50	30	72	51	49	29
Number	20	19	56	56	86	84	58	51	220	210

Source: Authors' research files.

level was formed, under the name of Gra-Y. Often these clubs meet in the school building after school hours.

The YMCA has grown into a huge organization, with programs and buildings around the world to serve men and boys of various ages. The other organizations have also grown tremendously, and all have strong programs for the social and physical development of youth. The specific religious emphasis of earlier programs has tended to decrease, concomitant with the growing secularization in the middle class of America.

Since 1940, a new group of religion-oriented youth organizations has emerged. These are nonsectarian, with a Protestant Fundamentalist theology. They encourage their young people to carry the Bible with them to meetings, and to rely upon it entirely for religious guidance, without using other books that might favor one interpretation of Christian theology over another. There are four principal organizations of this kind—Youth for Christ, Young Life, Youth on the March, and Word of Life. Meetings are held on Sundays and weekdays; there is a social as well as a religious fellowship; and summer camps provide an important part of the program. Possibly these new organizations perform somewhat the same functions that were performed by the YMCA and YWCA in earlier years, before the latter organizations became more secular in orientation.

During the 1960s and 1970s, there was a further development of youth religious activity which attracted attention partly because it seemed to be allied to the "hippy" or counterculture. One form was the production of the musical play *Jesus Christ, Superstar,* which had a wide appeal among a wide variety of people, but also was roundly condemned as "sacrilegious" by other groups. Even more unusual is the "Jesus Freak" group, many of whom dress and live as hippies in some respects, and are seriously religious in their conversation and in their life style, and who call themselves the "Jesus people."

Other Youth-Serving Agencies

An important group of youth-serving agencies has less specifically religious motivation. These agencies are primarily interested in bringing adults into active and supportive relations with youth peer groups. There are, for example, the Boy Scouts, Girl Scouts, Campfire Girls, Girl Reserves, Junior Achievement, Junior Optimist, Key Club, and DeMolay (sponsored by the Masonic Order). Somewhat similar to these are such organizations for rural youth as the 4-H Clubs, Future Farmers of America, Future Homemakers of America, and Junior Grange.

These organizations do not have buildings of their own, but form small units under local leaders and meet in churches, community centers, schools, and homes. Generally they are unrelated to the schools, although the Future Farmers and Future Homemakers are school clubs organized by the vocational agriculture and vocational home-economics teachers as part of a government-supported program. The 4-H Clubs are organized under the United States Department of Agriculture through its county farm-services program.

In the big cities there have been a number of youth-serving organizations established in underprivileged areas. For example, settlement houses, in addition to providing recreational facilities for boys and girls whether they are club members or not, usually organize clubs for children and adolescents. Boys Clubs and Girls Clubs have been established in slum neighborhoods, independent of settlement houses. The sponsors and financial supporters of these agencies are usually people of middle-class or upper-class status who give time and money to provide better opportunities for underprivileged youth and to reduce juvenile delinquency.

These organizations seldom have any connection with the schools, and they serve children from both public and parochial schools.

The earliest youth-serving agencies were designed for boys and girls aged about 12 to 16. It was expected that boys and girls of this age wanted to associate with each other outside of the family circle and under the leadership of adults who were neither parents nor teachers. In most of these agencies, boys and girls were organized into separate groups.

On this basis there was a tremendous growth of youth-serving organizations with the bulk of the membership aged 12 to 15. By age 15 there was a tendency for boys and girls to drop out of these organizations, in spite of vigorous efforts by leaders to keep them as members. Programs were developed for older youth, such as the Explorers (Scouts). Some of these kept the sexes separated; others included both sexes. With more and more young people staying in school through the twelfth grade, and with many having no after-school employment, there is clearly a large pool of youth aged 15 to 18 or 20 who have a good deal of spare time, yet who do not take part in youth organizations. It has become a major source of concern to the leaders of youth-serving organizations to do a better job of "holding youth" in the middle and late teens.

At the same time there has been a downward reach of youth-serving agencies into the age range from 7 or 8 to 12. This is accomplished partly by lowering the entrance age in some organizations. More generally, however, this is done by setting up new organizations for younger children, organizations which are closely related to the child's family. The Boy Scouts, for instance, organized the Cub Scouts, with a Den Mother in charge of a group of 6 to 10-year-old boys, a woman who generally has her own son in the group. The Girl Scouts organized the Brownies on a similar basis. The YMCA not only has organized classes for boys as young as 9 to 10, but has also started the Indian Guide organization for younger boys, with fathers and mothers of the boys leading the groups that meet in their homes.

This downward reach of the youth-serving agencies into middle childhood probably reflects two attitudes on the part of parents: first, the realization that the peer group, if left unaided and unwatched by adults, either would not develop adequately or would move in undesirable directions. In the big cities many middle-class parents feel that children need their help in forming peer groups. In smaller cities, children are somewhat freer to associate informally and there is perhaps less need for formal organizations. Nevertheless, the youth-serving agencies for young children have also flourished in small cities, again mainly in the middle class. This movement illustrates the intense desire of middle-class parents that their children become socially well-adjusted during the elementary school period.

It was perhaps a foregone conclusion that the development of youth-serving agencies in America would be closely related to the social structure. In the first place, there is a tendency for youth of higher social status to belong to more organizations than do lower-status youth. This has been seen in a number of national surveys of organizational membership of boys and girls.

There is also a tendency for boys with mobility aspirations to belong to more groups than do boys without mobility aspirations. In the surveys referred to above, it was found that boys with occupational aspirations above the level of their fathers' occupations are much more likely to belong to three or more youth groups than boys who aspire to the same level occupation as that held by their fathers.

Recent Changes in Youth-Serving Organizations—
The Boy Scouts

In the years since 1960 there has been a general tendency of the groups from age 8 to 14 to grow and for the groups aged 15 and over to decrease in size. Also there has been a determined effort to recruit members from low-income and from minority-group families. This is seen in the recent history of the Boy Scouts, which provides a good example of the youth-serving groups. In 1968, the Boy Scouts organization asked a research-survey organization (Daniel Yankelovich, Inc.) to interview a national sample of 2,800 boys, aged 8 through 18.

It was found that one of every two boys in the sample belonged to an organized group or club. At the time of this interview, 23 percent of the boys were in Scouting, and 33 percent had formerly been in Scouting. As is shown in Table 8.2, membership in Scouting tends to be concentrated in the Cub Scout age group, 8–10. Membership in Scouting is more frequent in upper-middle-class families and in suburbs, though all income levels and races are substantially represented. It was also found that, among the non-Scouts, desire to be in Scouting was greatest among younger boys, nonwhites, lower income, and those living in nonmetropolitan areas. When asked why they were not in Scouting, 17 percent out of the 77 percent non-Scouts said there was no Scouting program available to them, and another 17 percent said they were not interested. This latter subgroup were mainly in the 15–18 age group.

TABLE 8.2.   *Memberships in Various Boys' Organizations: Percentage Distribution*

Belong to:	All Boys	8–10	Age 11–14	15–18
Boy Scouts of America	23	56	28	5
YMCA	8	8	8	7
Boys' Clubs of America	7	6	8	6
4-H Clubs	6	8	8	3
Future Farmers of America	5	—	2	6
Police Athletic League	4	2	4	4
Junior Achievement	1	—	1	1

Source: Research on a national sample of boys, "Is Scouting in Tune with the Times?" Daniel Yankelovich, Inc., New Brunswick, New Jersey: Boy Scouts of America, 1968.

About 25 percent of boys expressed some negative feelings about Scouting. The characteristics they did not like were, in order of frequency: Is too organized; Initiative is restricted; Is too childish; Is boring; Is out of date; Teaches things boys won't use. The Boy Scout organization leaders are now working to increase their appeal, especially to the 15–18 age group, through the Explorer program.

INNER-CITY YOUTH ORGANIZATIONS

One of the phenomena of city life that troubles many adults is the delinquent or semidelinquent "gang" of youth. Beginning at age 10 or thereabouts, the boys of a neighborhood cluster together in groups of six or eight or more. Often they choose a name for themselves, such as the Tigers or the Nighthawks. They may organize a baseball team, or carry on athletic activities of one sort or another. More frequently they retain a kind of loose organization that brings them together afternoons and evenings at a particular street corner, just to talk and play. Girls seldom organize into such groups though they often maintain a loose relation to boys' gangs in the neighborhood.

Characteristic of the gang phenomenon is the lack of an adult leader. The boys seem to use their gang as a way of avoiding adult domination, if not actually fighting against it. Sometimes the gang of boys aged 10 to 12 breaks up as it grows older and reorganizes in groups in adult-led organizations such as YMCA, Settlement House Club, Hi-Y, and CYO. When the gang does not break up, but persists into the middle and late teens, there is danger that it will become a delinquent gang, hostile to organized authority represented by police, school teachers, businessmen, and church leaders.

Since about 1965 there has been a major development of aggressive organizations made up of racial and ethnic minority groups in the big cities, commencing with boys in the midteens and continuing on through the twenties. Some have grown into national organizations, such as the Black Panthers, and La Raza. Others have limited themselves to individual cities, and have become powerful in the local political and social life. The Chinese in San Francisco have developed such a group. Thus the teenagers of a big city find available to them a strong political and social organization made up of young working-class men of their own racial or ethnic group. These organizations develop programs of service to their own minority group. Their activities are viewed with a certain ambivalence by the police, the city government, and the middle-class business interests. They have a considerable potential for constructive service and for developing leaders. They are likely to be strongly represented in the local community colleges. But they have strong separatist tendencies, which may bring them into conflict with middle-class groups and their ideology of integration.

EXERCISES

1. Are there any learning experiences offered by the peer group that could *not* be offered by other socializing agencies? Explain.

2. Give an example, from your own experience, in which the peer group's standards of behavior for a child (or adolescent) were at variance with adult standards. What did the child do to resolve the conflict?

3. Thinking back over your own experience as a school child, were children in your elementary school more or less democratic as regards social-class differentiations than your high school group? Cite examples.

4. Describe briefly a case in which a boy or girl dropped out of school before graduating. How did the attitudes of his classmates toward him affect his decision to leave school? Was there anything the school might have done to change the situation for him?

5. Have you been in a school which had conflicting peer groups? If so, what were the differences among the groups, and how did the various groups relate to the authority of the school or the teacher?

6. Examine the material on "student rights" put out by the American Civil Liberties Union and other freedom-promoting organizations. Do you think this goes "too far"? Compare your ideas with those of E. T. Ladd in his article on "Regulating Student Behavior Without Ending Up in Court."

7. Locate a youth-serving agency in your community and find out how it serves children and youth of different ages, sex, and social class.

8. Select a minority group which you know something about and compare the formal and informal teaching within this group to the formal and informal teaching of the school.

SUGGESTIONS FOR FURTHER READING

1. The influence of the peer group is treated in most textbooks on child and adolescent development. See for example chapter 12 in Martin and Stendler's *Child Behavior and Development*. See also the chapter by Campbell, "Peer Relations in Childhood," in *Review of Child Development Research*, edited by Hoffman and Hoffman.

2. Jean Piaget, in *The Moral Judgment of the Child*, describes how children learn through games (and thus through the agency of the peer group) how rules are made and changed, and how children move through various stages of maturity in the development of moral judgment. See especially chapter 1. Also, Kohlberg (1966) summarizes his theory of moral development as it is affected by the school.

3. A very useful book of readings edited by Muuss (1971) contains articles on the influence of the peer group in adolescence, especially articles by Brittain, Gronlund, Bronfenbrenner, Costanzo and Shaw, Coleman, and Himes.

4. The National Education Association (1971), through a Task Force on Student Involvement, has issued a *Code of Student Rights and Responsibilities*. The issue has been widely discussed in recent journal articles such as that by Professor E. T. Ladd of Emory University entitled "Regulating Student Behavior without Ending Up in Court."

5. Edgar Friedenberg in his interestingly written little book, *The Vanishing Adolescent*, sounds a note of caution for those who would like to increase adult control over adolescents. Friedenberg views adolescent conflict with adult society as necessary if the adolescent is to mature and become independent.

6. *The Adolescent Society* by James S. Coleman describes in nontechnical language a study of the students in ten different high schools, and the implications for education of the differences between adult and adolescent values.

7. For a review of research on peer socialization in elementary schools, see the article by John C. Glidwell, Mildred B. Kantor, Louis M. Smith, and Lorene H. Stringer, "Socialization and Social Structure in the Classroom."

8. Read C. Wayne Gordon's *The Social System of the High School* for more details of the social organization that exists within a socially comprehensive high school.

9. The great mass of research on religious development of youth has been abstracted and summarized in a comprehensive handbook entitled *Research on Religious Development* edited by Merton P. Strommen. There are chapters on "Religion in Public Education", "The Religion of Youth", and "Changes in Religious Beliefs of College Students."

CHAPTER 9

The Transition from Adolescence to Adulthood

The American educational system has come to dominate the lives of most young people. As shown in Table 4.1 in Chapter 4, of the 14–17 age group, 95 percent were enrolled in school in 1972. Almost 80 percent of both sexes complete a high school course, and about 50 percent enter a college. This situation contrasts with the beginning of the century, when only 11 percent of the 14–17 age group were in school, and only about 3 percent entered college.

Thus most young people spend far more time in school than their grandparents, and substantially more than their parents did. This means less time in employment, less time associating with a variety of adults, and more time in what might be called "preparing for" adult living.

A federal government Panel on Youth, reporting to the country in 1973, starts as follows:

As the labor of children has become unnecessary to society, school has been extended for them. With every decade, the length of schooling has increased, until a thoughtful person must ask whether society can conceive of no other way for youth to come into adulthood. If schooling were a complete environment, the answer would properly be that no amount of school is too much, and increased schooling for the young is the best way for young to spend their increased leisure, and society its increased wealth.

But schooling, as we know it, is not a complete environment giving all the necessary opportunities for becoming adult. School is a certain kind of environment: individualistic, oriented toward cognitive achievement, imposing dependency on and withholding authority and responsibility from those in the role of students. So long as school was short, and merely a supplement to the main activities of growing up, this mattered little. But school has expanded to fill the time that other activities once occupied, without substituting for them. These activities of young persons included the opportunities for responsible action, situations in which a youth came to have authority over matters that affected other persons, occasions in which he experienced the consequences of his own actions, and was strengthened by facing them—in short, all that is implied by "becoming adult" in matters other than gaining cognitive skills. (Coleman *et al.*, 1974)

The report of the panel, chaired by Professor James S. Coleman, shook the educational world, because it recommends for the society "not merely to design new high schools and colleges, but to design environments that allow youth to be more than students."

YOUTH AS A SEPARATE STAGE OF LIFE: AGE 15–24

As we shall see in the next few pages, it is useful to think of the age period from 15 through 24 as a stage of life which is a transition between early adolescence and adulthood. This period is different from what is ordinarily called adolescence, for the latter has usually a biological meaning, referring to puberty and the immediate postpubescent years up to about age 18. For the period of *youth*, we are dealing with a psycho-sociological period of transition.

The proposal to designate this as a separate stage of life was made in 1972 by Keniston, in his book entitled *Youth and Dissent*.

In the prologue to this book, Keniston says:

Millions of young people today are neither psychological adolescents nor sociological adults; they fall into a psychological no man's land, a stage of life that lacks any clear definition. . . .

The very fact that so many millions of young people are in a stage of life that lacks even a name seems to me one of the most important psychohistorical facts about modern societies. In this essay I argue that the unprecedented prolongation of education has opened up opportunities for an extension of psychological development, which in turn is creating a "new" stage of life. . . .

The opening up of youth as a stage of life to millions of young people seems to me a human advance, whatever its perils and dangers. A prolonged development can make possible a more autonomous, more individuated position vis-a-vis the existing society and can permit the individual to achieve a degree of inner complexity, differentiation, and integration not vouchsafed those whose development is foreshortened or foreclosed. Furthermore, the extension of human development means that we are creating —on a mass scale—a "new" breed of people whose psychological development not only inclines them to be critics of our own society, but might even make them potential members or architects of a better one than ours.

This transition period, according to Keniston, is one of tension between the selfhood of the young person and the existing social order. The resolution of this tension leads to adult status. During this transition period, which for individual persons may be as short as 5 years or as long as 15, a youth settles a set of questions for himself and thereby becomes an adult: questions of his relation to the existing society, of his vocation, of his life style and characteristic social roles.

Major Transformations in Consciousness and Behavior

A number of psychological and interpersonal transformations occur during this transitional stage of a person's life. Keniston describes six major transformations.

1. *Individuation.* The youth acknowledges and can cope with social reality, or failure to do so results in *alienation*—either from self or from society. Alienation from self means abject submission to society, "selling out." Alienation from society means ignoring society, and loss of social effectiveness.
2. *Sexual development.* The youth learns to combine sexual feelings with intimacy with another person.
3. *Mutuality in interpersonal relations.* The adolescent moves from close relationships with a few "soul mates," to a general positive relation to others. Others are perceived as worthy, even though they may be quite different from oneself.
4. *Relationships with elders.* Older people become more real and three-dimensional. The youth learns to see parents and others as complex persons, to be emulated in some ways and not in others.
5. *Principled morality.* The young person becomes capable of operating on the highest level of moral judgment—that of moral principles which can lead him to challenge the existing moral order. (However, according to the psychologist, Kohlberg, who has described the hierarchy of stages of moral development, most contemporary Americans, whether youth or adults, do not move beyond the stage of conventional moral reasoning, that stage where they conform to the general moral judgment of the society. (Kohlberg, 1973)
6. *Intellectual complexity.* Youth passes beyond simple views of truth and falsehood to a more complex and relativistic view of what can be known and what is true. This is a complex form of Piaget's highest stage of cognitive development, in which the person "thinks about thinking" and develops intellectual creativity. Like the highest level of moral judgment, this level is seldom reached by most adults, but the potential for it comes during the period of youth.

EXPERIENCE OF YOUTH DURING
THE TRANSITION PERIOD

Every society must absorb successive generations of children and must socialize them into adults who can carry on the business of the society. This process is sometimes more troublesome than at other times, as seems to be true in the 1970s in the American society.

Change in Size of the Youth Group

Fluctuations in the absolute and relative size of the youth group are a striking feature of the American population during the twentieth century. The birthrate was very high (above 30 per 1000 population) from 1900 to 1910, and then dropped steadily (to about 18 per 1000) in 1933, influenced partly by the economic depression of that decade. The birthrate remained at the relatively low level of less than 20 per 1000 until 1945, when it shot up to 25 per 1000 by 1955, remaining at about that level for about eight years. Then it dropped again in 1968 to a level below the 1933 depression figure where it has remained until the mid-seventies. During this time the death rate decreased steadily from 17 per 1000 in 1900 to 9 per 1000 in 1955, where it has remained to the present.

The result of these phenomena is shown in Table 9.1 where the absolute numbers of the 15–24 group are shown as well as the ratio of the 15–24 group to the 25–64 group. This ratio clearly presents the problem. The

TABLE 9.1. *Population Aged 15–24, 1890–2000*

Year	Number (millions)	Percent of Total	Percent Change in Preceding Decade	Ratio, 15–24/25–64
1890	12.8	20.4	—	.51
1900	14.9	19.5	+16	.47
1910	18.2	19.5	+22	.45
1920	18.8	17.6	+ 3	.39
1930	22.5	17.0	+20	.39
1940	24.0	18.2	+ 7	.36
1950	22.2	14.6	− 8	.29
1960	24.1	13.4	+ 9	.29
1970	36.4	17.8	+51	.41
(est.) 1980	41.2	17.8	+13	.39
(est.) 1990	37.9	14.6	−8	.31
(est.) 2000	48.1	16.7	+26	.35

Source: U.S. Bureau of the Census: U.S. Census: 1960 *Final Report* PC1-1B. Table 47. 1961. U.S. Bureau of the Census: *Current Population Reports* Series P-25, No. 470. Table 2, Series D. Nov. 1971.

15–24 group is ready to move into the productive labor force, to do the work of the society. But the American society has increased its man-hour productivity so much since World War II that it needs fewer workers to do the necessary work. Even though the society has increased its gross production, especially in the 1950–70 period, the vast increase in size of the 15–24 group from 1960 to 1970 was more than the labor force could easily absorb. As Table 9.1 shows, the ratio of 15–24 to 25–64 jumped from .29 in 1960 to .41 in 1970, and will stay at that level through the decade of the 1970s. This spells crisis for the youth, and for the rest of society alike.

The situation is further complicated by the change in women's roles and the fact that young women are spending more time in the work force. The proportion of women aged 20–24 who were employed rose from 40 percent in 1960 to 47 percent in 1970, while the proportions of employed civilian men 20–24 decreased from 72 to 61 percent.

Youth in School and College

It is well known that school and college enrollments have increased greatly since World War II, both absolutely and proportionately. Table 9.2 shows the relative increases, for men and women, white and nonwhite. Chapter 4 reported the increased rates of high school and college graduation.

As enrollment has grown, and as the population has become more urbanized, the schools and colleges have grown larger. In 1970, there were 120 two-year colleges each with over 5,000 students. Among four-year institutions, 50 had 20,000 or more students, and another 60 had more than 10,000. These large institutions tend to group students by age, thus practically limiting their social experience to people of their own age. Students in large schools may be grouped also by scholastic achievement level. Remembering also that relatively few students with below average scholastic achievement get into college at all, the upshot is that the youth of the 1970s tend to be segregated by narrow age groups, by school achievement level, as well as by socioeconomic level and by ethnicity.

Youth in the Labor Force

The decade 1960–1970 saw a substantial percentage increase of women 16–21 in the labor force, but relatively little change in the proportions of young men who were at work or seeking work, as is shown in Table 9.2. However, there was a very large increase in the percent of young people of both sexes who were unemployed. Effective unemployment (idleness) existed for 14 to 17 percent of the age-group 16–19, and dropped only slightly at age 20–21. Unemployment was about twice as high in relative proportion among nonwhites as among whites.

In addition to those who are unemployed and looking for work there

TABLE 9.2. Changing Status of Youth: 1960–1970

	Percentages of Total Group		Percentage Shift Over 10 Years
	1960	1970	
(Ages: 16–21 inclusive)			
In School			
or			
College			
White Male	60	62	+ 4
Nonwhite Male	47	56	+19
White Female	48	55	+14
Nonwhite Female	42	50	+20
In Labor Force			
White Male	58	62	+ 6
Nonwhite Male	51	49	− 3
White Female	38	49	+29
Nonwhite Female	30	40	+33
Unemployed (As percent of age group in labor force)			
White Male	10	12	+21
Nonwhite Male	15	25	+63
White Female	8	13	+72
Nonwhite Female	17	32	+83
(Ages: 14–19)			
Married			
White Male	3.1	3.8	+23
Nonwhite Male	4.3	1.5	−65
White Female	13.3	9.6	−28
Nonwhite Female	12.1	8.1	−33

Note: Percentages in a column do not add up to 100, because a person may be both in the labor force and in school.

Source: U.S. Bureau of the Census, Series P-23, No. 40, 1972. *Characteristics of American Youth: 1972.* Series P-20, No. 225, 1971, for marital status data.

is a considerable group of youth who are not at school and not looking for work in the mid-1970s. A few of them are unable to work for one reason or another, but the bulk of this subgroup are simply idle. They are not actively looking for work, and therefore are not officially "unemployed." Many of them have looked for work, and have become convinced that the search is useless; therefore they are not in the "labor force." There is also a large subgroup of young women who are keeping house, most of them married, and therefore are not in the labor force and not employed.

Among the age-group 16–20 there are a good many who are employed part-time and are also students in high school or college. Youth unemployment is very high in the United States, much higher than in Britain, Japan, Australia, Northern Europe, and Russia. The difference is partly due to the fact that there are juvenile wage scales in several of those countries, and no minimum wage laws. Thus employers are able to use younger workers profitably, where they cannot do so in the United States. But there are other causes as well. Griliches writes: "High unemployment among young Americans is therefore in part a reflection of our commitment to providing many more years of schooling than is common in other countries and is in part the price we pay for a very fluid educational system which encourages people to move back and forth between full-time work and full-time education." (Griliches, 1973)

Hugh Folk, analyzing the economics of youth unemployment, sees little prospect of improvement in the situation and says:

> The extraordinarily large unemployment rates of the least preferred groups of workers in the last few years and the large trends in these rates create grave doubts about the capacity of the competitive labor market to provide jobs in anything like sufficient numbers to lead to a reversal of the trends. During a period when adult unemployment rates have been at rates as low as any in peacetime, the dispreferred youth groups have experienced unemployment rates that are probably somewhat higher than those of the Great Depression. While much of the higher unemployment is short term and intermittent, it is no less a problem. It will not do to exaggerate the social implications of high unemployment among school youth, but at the same time it must have its due. (Folk, 1968, p. 107)

Government Programs to Increase Employment of Youth. During the 1960s there were several federal government programs to provide work experience for youth and to train young people for jobs. The Neighborhood Youth Corps has provided part-time work for students, and full-time summer jobs. The avowed aim of the NYC In-School Program has been to help keep youth in school or college. More direct influence on youth employment was anticipated from the Job Corps, which brought young people seeking work together for intensive job training and counselling. This proved to be quite expensive, and was less successful than had been hoped. And the number of youth actually assisted was small in comparison to the numbers of unemployed youth. For example, in October, 1969, there were 1.1 million unemployed youth, but ony 110,000 youth in Neighborhood Youth Corps or Job Corps programs.

Characteristics of Youth Culture

The decade of the 1960s saw the emergence of a diverse array of patterns of activity associated with youth. These include style of dress, new forms of music, small intense subgroups with political, or religious, or mystical orientation. These diverse activities are called by James Coleman a "youth culture, . . . not because they constitute a homogeneous culture, nor because they characterize all youth, but because taken together, they are activities initiated by youth and pursued more by youth than by adults."

Coleman sees certain common characteristics of these youth activities, and lists them as follows:

1. *Inward-lookingness.* Young people look very largely to one another. Their friends are other young people and a large fraction of their communications come from young people. This is not psychological introversion. It is a social movement of youth with youth.
2. *Psychic attachment.* This pertains to the attachment of youth to other youth. This is a pattern of closeness, intimacy, and extreme openness among a small group of close friends, often aided by marijuana. A similar but less pervasive pattern is the commune. These groups meet psychic needs that were formerly met within a large extended family.
3. *Press toward autonomy.* A high regard for youth who successfully challenge adults, or who act independently of adults. This is facilitated by a number of offbeat communication media—such as a radio station run by young people, or an independent newspaper—that provide a means for anti-establishment youth to build a following.
4. *Concern for the underdog.* This finds its expression mainly in political support by youth for minority causes. This leads to political alliances with minority groups, with women's liberation, and to support for Third World political causes.
5. *Interest in change per se.* As "outsiders" to the conventional adult system, many young people feel that they have no stake in maintaining the status quo. Consequently, they are friendly to change, which they see as possibly improving things.

THE COUNTERCULTURE

As young people share these characteristics, they have been said by Keniston and others to be creating a counterculture. This counterculture is seen by some as the hopeful "Wave of the Future"; but by others as mindless and generally destructive rebellion. The counterculture is a reaction to the rationalism, technology, organization, and discipline of the postindustrial society.

Whichever interpretation one adopts, the counterculture is an active force in the changes that are now taking place in American society and in American education. Its most visible expression has appeared on college campuses, though it is seen in a more extreme form in the communes or in the groups of young people who live together and make up a new kind of "family."

After studying the values of college students for several years, Daniel Yankelovich, a psychologist, has written a book which describes the counterculture as a system of beliefs and behavior which attempts to place *nature* and the *natural* at the center of existence. To be natural means:

> To place sensory experience ahead of conceptual knowledge. To de-emphasize aspects of nature illuminated by science; instead to celebrate all the unknown, the mystical, and the mysterious elements of nature.
> To stress cooperation rather than competition.
> To devalue detachment, objectivity, and noninvolvement as methods for finding truth, to arrive at truth, instead, by direct experience, participation, and involvement.
> To reject mastery over nature.
> To dispense with organization, rationalization, and cost-effectiveness. (Yankelovich, 1972a, p. 35)

These values are a mixture of the conservative and the radical, and do not fit any current political program or party.

Yankelovich's conclusions are based on various studies of college students of which the following is an example. In October, 1968, a sample of 718 young men and women, aged 18–24, were asked to say whether they agreed or disagreed with a number of value-statements. About half of this sample were college students, and the others had not attended college. The college students were asked to select one or the other of the following statements as representing their views about college education.

> 1. For me, college is mainly a practical matter. With a college education I can earn more money, have a more interesting career, and enjoy a better position in society.
>
> 2. I'm not really concerned with the practical benefits of college. I suppose I take them for granted. College for me means something more intangible, perhaps the opportunity to change things rather than make out well within the present system.

Those who chose the first statement—58 percent of the students—were called "practical-minded." The remaining 42 percent, who chose the second statement, were called "fore-runners."

Some of the results of this survey are shown in Table 9.3. This indicates some of the characteristics of the counterculture. It is concerned with political change in a mildly liberal direction, but is not leftist. It is too pacifistic, too esthetic, too individualistic, to be very far to the political left.

Roles vs. Goals

Another way of examining contemporary value changes is to compare the emphases laid by young people on the *present reality* as compared with *future goals*. It appears that young are increasingly concerned with the question of *identity*. They want to know *who* they are, before they become concerned about their future goals. In a book entitled *The Identity Society*, Dr. William Glasser, a psychiatrist, makes a basic distinction between *roles* and *goals*. Roles are part of the present, while goals point to the future. Roles are expressive, goals are instrumental. When a young man or woman feels comfortable in his roles, and has discovered an identity for himself, he can work for goals that are inherent in the roles he has chosen. Glasser has a theory of history which predicts that mankind is now moving toward a *civilized identity society*. This is made possible by man's achievement of material affluence—a standard of living which permits people to enjoy themselves and to live a satisfying life, free from the compulsive drive to work so as to amass material wealth and power over other people. The new role-dominated society gives people a chance to concern themselves more and more with their identities and how they may express them. Dr. Glasser writes, "Not everyone can work at a job he would enjoy identity with, such as doctor, artist, or teacher; but now anyone can pursue a recreational goal (such as bowling or bridge-playing) or a volunteer goal (such as working at a hospital or fund-raising) that reinforces his identification as a worthy person. A young doctor's view of himself in the new identity society illustrates the changed situation:

"I am a doctor not because I can make money and find a very secure place for myself high in the power structure, but because I think I can practice medicine to become involved with my fellow man. I'd like to work in an inner-city hospital, in the Peace Corps, in a "free" clinic, in research, or for the Public Health Service. I expect to get paid enough to live, perhaps to be comfortable; but, to me, being a doctor is much less to gain money, prestige, and power than it is to reinforce my own role, my belief in myself as a human. As I struggle helping others, I will enjoy the satisfaction that comes when I do this well.

The dean of my medical school has confirmed that before 1950, students who answered the standard question 'Why do you want to become a doctor?' by saying, 'For the human involvement it provides' (the role answer) were often rejected as candidates for a physician's training. They were suspected of being deviants or troublemakers. The student who answered that

TABLE 9.3. *Beliefs and Values of Young People, 1968*

| | Percentages | | |
| | College Students | | |
Belief or Value Statement	Fore-runners	Practical Minded	No College
Agree with those who call ours a "sick" society.	50	32	44
Would you describe yourself as a "hawk" or a "dove"? (Refers to the war in Vietnam)			
Hawk	20	37	47
Dove	69	45	37
Don't know	11	18	16
Do you feel this country is doing, for black people:			
Too much	7	15	20
Enough	22	47	45
Too little	71	38	35
Do you feel that the differences between your values and your parents' are:			
Very great	24	11	15
Moderate	51	49	41
Very slight	25	40	44
Which of the following social changes would you welcome?			
More emphasis on law and order	39	78	91
More emphasis on self-expression	90	68	69
More emphasis on the arts	84	45	42
More sexual freedom	48	35	19
Less emphasis on money	80	53	57

To which of these ideas do you personally subscribe?

Hard work will always pay off if you have faith in yourself and stick to it	59	80	75
Hard work keeps people from loafing and getting into trouble	18	34	54
The individual who plans ahead can look forward to success and achievement of personal goals	46	64	65

Which of these definitions of success reflect your personal values?

Living the good Christian life	36	54	75
Having the love and respect of your family	69	82	82
Doing your own thing	73	57	58
Bringing about needed changes in society	71	53	49

Source: Daniel Seligman—Daniel Yankelovich, "A Special Kind of Rebellion." Fortune. Vol. 69, No. 1. January, 1969. © 1968 Time Inc.

he wanted a secure profession (the goal answer) was accepted. This attitude began to shift about 1950. Since then, many medical schools have been admitting students who proclaim interest in public service." (Glasser, 1972a, p. 31)

The Two Forms of Counterculture

It is useful to distinguish two forms or wings of the counterculture, which have some things in common, but disagree in important ways. Keniston calls them the "cultural" and the "political" wings.

The cultural wing are the *hippies*, who withdraw from the dominant society, create their own small communities, and live on the margin of socio-political life. The other wing are part of the New Left, who are *instrumental* in promoting a revolutionary program of creating a new and *expressive* society. Keniston believes that the two wings come from different kinds of upper-middle-class homes. The members of the New Left or political wing tend to be recruited from the children of social workers, ministers, professors, lawyers, and artists, and from the more liberal members of those professions. On the other hand, he says the recruits to the expressive and esthetic or hippie wing tend to be drawn from the families of advertising men, merchandisers, personnel managers, entertainers, and media executives. (Keniston, 1972, p. 395)

The counterculture, then, is not a single, coherent, and organized force with a socio-political organization which is ready to "convert" the rest of society to its life-style. It is, rather, a loose array of "fore-runners" who are not altogether sure of their direction but are moving toward a "quality of life" society. Its youthful members create the most excitement for education.

CATEGORIES OF YOUTH

Although we have described youth as a stage of life, the young people in this stage are similar only in some ways, and diverse in others. Their differences are important in thinking about and planning the educational programs that are most attractive and most useful to them.

There are three broadly definable groups:

A. The Fore-Runners—20 percent.
B. The Practical Minded—60–65 percent, apprentices to a technocratic society.
C. The Left-Outs—15–20 percent, a burden in a technocratic society.

The *Fore-Runners*, as defined by Yankelovich, have been described in Chapter 1 and in the preceding pages of this chapter. There has been some

TABLE 9.4.   *Description of Youth Subgroups*

		Estimated Size (percent of age-group)
Fore-runners	A_1 Nonpolitical. Mainly upper-middle-class	10
	A_2 Political	10
Practical-minded	B_1 Professional, managerial, middle-class	10–15
	B_2 Stable white-collar and blue-collar, lower-middle and upper-working-class	50
Left-out	C_1 Apathetic. Marginal to labor force. Unskilled. Mainly lower-working-class	10–15
	C_2 Seriously delinquent	5

eloquent writing about the good qualities of this group, and also some critical and negative evaluations of their potential.

The apprentices of the technocratic society are the *Practical-Minded* group, as described by Yankelovich. This group are the most likely to resist the leadership of the Fore-Runners and to attempt to retain the early twentieth century instrumentalism and materialism. Although they are not all "unmeltable ethnics" as defined by Michael Novak, they all have some of the characteristics he describes so positively. He comments: "When one says the word 'youth' . . . one ought to think of the sons and daughters of the working class first, and of college students second." (Novak, 1971, p. 24).

The *Left-Outs* represent a substantial group in the society, who must be assisted toward a more individually and socially satisfactory youth if our society is to maintain even a fairly healthy condition.

Interaction with the Educational System

In Table 9.4 we break down the three broad groups each into two subgroups with a crude indication of their social-class origins.

The high school receives the entire age-cohort, but most of the C_1 and C_2 groups drop out before high school graduation. Approximately half of the B_2 group complete high school and go to full-time employment, or in the case of many girls to homemaking. The other half of the B_2 group follow a one or two-year course in a community college. Groups B_1 and A_1 and A_2

generally enter a four-year college or university, where most of them get a bachelor's degree, and a substantial proportion go on to get a master's or doctor's degree.

There is some sex difference, as indicated in Table 9.5. More B_2 girls stop their formal education at the close of high school. A growing proportion of B_1 girls, on graduating from college, postpone childbearing and take jobs. Each of the six subgroups has one particular social class as its principal component, except for B_2 which is made up of lower-middle and upper-working-class youth. We noted in Chapter 2 that the social distance between lower-middle and upper-working class is small, meaning that they tend to have similar life-styles and educational objectives.

OBJECTIVES FOR YOUTH

We have just viewed a socio-psychological picture of American youth in the decade of the 1970s, and we note that this is a unique group in many respects. Not since the early 1900s has there been such a high proportion of the population in the 15–24 age group, ready to move into adulthood, and this time the labor force appears unable to receive such a large group into wage-earning roles, due to the decrease of unskilled jobs in the economy.

The obligation of the society is, through its educational system and through other institutions, to induct all youth into adult roles which promise to give youth satisfactory life styles and opportunity to become happy and responsible people. This indicates a set of broad objectives for youth, which extend beyond those ordinarily stated for schools and colleges. The following list of objectives is adapted from the Youth Panel Report.

> *In general,*
1. to aid youth to develop a sense of identity and self-esteem.
    With respect to self-development, to assist youth to develop
2. cognitive skills and noncognitive qualities necessary for economic independence and for occupational competence;
3. capability for effective management of one's own affairs;
4. capabilities as a consumer, not only of goods, but also of the cultural riches of civilization;
5. capability to engage in intense concentrated involvement in an activity.
    With respect to social relationships, to provide settings that give
6. experience with persons different from oneself, not only in social class and subculture, but also in age;
7. experience of having others dependent on one's actions;
8. experience with others in activities directed toward collective goals.

How should the contemporary society use its resources to achieve these objectives, keeping in mind the various types or categories of youth?

TABLE 9.5.   *Sex Differences in Youth Groups*

		Estimated Size of Group (percent)	
		Male	Female
Fore-Runners	A$_1$ Equal numbers of both sexes.	10	10
	A$_2$ If Women's Liberation groups are included, equal numbers of both sexes.	10	10
Practical-Minded	B$_1$ Increasing proportion of women postpone child-bearing and take jobs.	15	10
	B$_2$ Substantial differentiation of sex roles. Increasing numbers of women in labor force at this age. Relatively large numbers of women married and keeping house.	48	53
Left-Out	C$_1$ Women are likely to be mothers, some unmarried.	12	15
	C$_2$ Few women in this category.	5	2

SCHOOL AND COLLEGE TAKE ON CUSTODIAL FUNCTIONS

The Coleman Panel has underlined the fact that school and college have taken on new functions in relation to youth, quite different from the functions of such institutions at the beginning of this century.

In the earlier period, schools and colleges simply carried on and supplemented the functions of the family in protecting children and youth while they were vulnerable to exploitation by unscrupulous employers or others or while they were living away from the home in order to continue their education. Thus the secondary school and the college acted in the role of the parents, *in loco parentis*, to protect and control youth up to the age where they should be able to take care of themselves, which was vaguely between

197

14 and 20, depending on the social class of the family and the individual characteristics of the youth.

The adult society, acting on its view of what was good for the young, made laws which prevented child labor, or controlled it in terms of the time a young person could be employed, and in terms of a limitation to "safe" occupations; and made school attendance compulsory up to a certain age. This was much needed in a period when there was an enormous demand for unskilled labor with low wages. But, as the demand for unskilled labor decreased, and as adult workers organized unions to protect themselves against what they regarded as unfair labor practices and to raise their incomes, children and youth were increasingly squeezed out of the labor force—except where the family was the economic unit, which meant except for farm families and a few small business owners.

It appears, now, that some of the laws limiting and regulating the employment of youth operate so as to limit youth more than is desirable. Also, it appears that a juvenile wage or reduced minimum wage for youth may be recommended by society's leaders in promoting a broader experience for youth.

Furthermore, the actions of the boarding school and the college in regulating the living arrangements of students living away from home have come under criticism since about 1960. Some young people claimed that they were being treated "like children" and demanded more freedom in their living arrangements. Some colleges made substantial changes, including dormitories occupied by both sexes, freedom for upper-class students to live in apartments and rooms outside of the college residence halls, student communes, and certain other arrangements which even in the 1970s seemed "far out" to some parents as well as to some college administrators and to some students.

What are loosely called "extracurricular activities" also became more student-controlled. College and high school student publications were freed more and more from faculty censorship and supervision. The concept of "student rights" was allied to the concept of civil rights. Students were accorded more and more the "right to privacy," which meant that their academic records were treated more and more as confidential, not to be shown to others except when the student gave his "informed consent."

In effect, youth have been seen and treated more and more as adults by school and college teachers and administrators, and the doctrine that the school and college should operate in loco parentis has lost some of its force.

The move toward reducing the custodial function or changing its nature has caught more attention as a matter of public policy since the publication of the Coleman Youth Panel and the Report of the Commission on the Reform of Secondary Education. Both of these reports have urged a decrease of sheer custodial effort, balanced with a development by the society of more maturity-promoting experience for youth, in or out of the formal educational system.

PROPOSALS FOR EDUCATIVE INSTITUTIONS

For the age-group 15–24, in the remainder of the 1970s and in the 1980s, there is need for a major development of youth-serving programs which are aimed at achieving the *Objectives for Youth* which have been presented here. Both the President's Panel on Youth and the Commission on the Reform of Secondary Education have both called for new educative institutions, which probably will be quite different from the secondary schools and colleges of 1970. Furthermore, educators are likely to argue that schools and colleges can and should broaden their programs so as to meet the needs of all kinds of youth.

The following summary of proposals for change in the institutions that affect youth have been advanced by the Panel on Youth as a basis for pilot programs that should be tried experimentally, and expanded as they prove their value.

There are seven broad sets of recommendations:

"The first recommendations concern modifications of the high school, in some cases supporting existing innovations in schools, and in others proposing new directions. Two of these, closely related, are the development of more specialized schools, as distinct from current comprehensive ones, and a reduction in size of high schools. A pattern of simultaneous attendance at more than one specialized school makes possible both the benefits of specialized schools and the benefits of small size.

The second proposal is a general encouragement for those innovations which involve a mixture of part-time work and part-time school, all the way from a daily cycle to a trimester cycle. Where those experiments are already in progress, the report calls for a careful evaluation of the results on the objectives discussed earlier, and not only the narrow objectives of cognitive skills and job skills.

The third proposal recommends pilot programs involving a much more intimate intermixture of school and work, carried out at the workplace. The proposal is to incorporate youth into work organizations with a portion of their time reserved for formal instruction. The change envisioned would mean that persons of all ages in the work organization would engage in a mixture of roles including learning, teaching, and work.

The fourth set of proposals involves youth communities and youth organizations. The proposal is for the federal government to serve as a paying customer for certain public services carried out by youth organizations, thus strengthening both their financial base and their direction and purpose. It is proposed that the principles of residential youth communities, in which youth provide most of the services, have most of the authority, and carry most of the responsibility, be experimentally extended to non-residential settings. A youth community can provide early assumption of responsibility, and thus fulfill certain of the objectives that are necessary for the transition to adulthood.

A fifth area of proposals concerns the dilemma of protection vs. opportunity for youth. We feel that current laws and administrative procedures are overbalanced in the direction of protection, and propose two changes toward greater opportunity. The first is an extensive review of the administrative procedures and regulations designed to protect workers under the age of 18. These procedures currently act as a strong disincentive to some employers to hire youth under age 18. Second, we propose board experimentation with a dual minimum wage, lower for younger workers.

A sixth proposed change is the introduction, on a pilot basis, of broadly-usable educational vouchers from age 16, equivalent in value to the average cost of four years of college. Such vouchers would be usable for a wide range of skill training as well as higher education. The existence of such vouchers would put the decision for further training in the hands of youth who will themselves experience the consequences, and would likely encourage wiser management of one's affairs than do current institutions.

Seventh, the report proposes a much wider range of opportunity for public service, through federally funded public service programs. Current programs, some of which are strikingly successful, should be modified in these ways:

1. Increased in numbers far beyond their miniscule quantity now, which is less than 20,000 for an age-cohort of about 4,000,000;
2. Availability from age 16, rather than from age 18, as is true with most current programs;
3. Availability for commitments of one year, rather than two, which is the current standard. (Coleman, pp. 147–148)

It is clear that most of these changes would make the secondary schools and the community colleges into much more diversified institutions than they now are. Some school and college administrators and teachers would prefer to avoid these programs, leaving them to be established and operated by a State or Area Youth Authority, supported with public funds. Then the schools and colleges could maintain academic programs aimed primarily at the development of cognitive skills and preparing students for the professions. Also, some social scientists and some policy makers doubt that the school and college personnel can carry on these nonacademic operations. There will probably be a good deal of debate in educational circles as well as in state and federal legislatures as to the form the new experiments should take, and what kinds of people should carry them through. The need is to develop educative institutions which ordinary men can run, and incompetent men cannot ruin.

DRUG ABUSE

A major aspect of the life of youth since about 1950 is the so-called "drug culture"—the vastly increased use (or abuse) of psychodelic (consciousness-expanding) drugs by youth. Also, high school and college youth have taken to using amphetamines, or psychostimulants. Alcohol consumption has increased in this age-group. The use of "hard" drugs, such as heroin and other morphine derivatives, by youth has also increased a great deal in recent years.

In a Gallup Poll of college students made late in 1970, 42 percent said they had tried marijuana, almost double the 1969 figure and eight times the 1967 percentage. At the same time (1970) 14 percent said they had taken LSD or something like it.

These are not figures for "addiction" to drugs. But experimentation with drugs can lead to addiction. Dr. Louise Richards (1971) reported a study in New York City of heroin addicts, where the typical age at first use was 16. In 1969, the average age of death of addicts in New York was 26 years. Heroin abuse killed a total of 650 people in New York City in 1968, and more people in the 15–35 age group than did murder or any other single cause, including automobile accidents.

With such a widespread use of the milder forms of drugs, it is clear that this cannot be attributed to one or another form of deviant or disturbed personality. But psychiatrists and psychologists find that, as with alcohol, a social use of the mild drugs goes on to addiction in people with certain kinds of personality. Persons who have a "weak ego," who are insecure and dependent and have low self-esteem, seem to be most vulnerable to drug abuse. (Richards, 1971, p. 19)

Whether the legal restrictions on the sale or possession of marijuana (cannabis) should be removed is a controversial issue. Some people with substantial experience argue that marijuana is less dangerous and habit-forming than alcohol. (Marin and Cohen, 1971; Coles *et al*, 1971; Snyder, 1971). However, these people tend to distinguish sharply between marijuana and the other drugs, seeing grave danger in LSD, amphetamines, and the hard drugs. The situation is regarded as rather serious by federal government agencies, which have set up a Special Action Office for Drug Abuse Prevention in the Department of Health, Education, and Welfare.

There is a good deal of disagreement among responsible and knowledgeable people concerning the most effective and appropriate ways of dealing with drug abuse. The British procedure is very different from the American. In England, addiction is treated as a medical problem, and addicts may legally obtain drug prescriptions from physicians. It is claimed that a number of people in England carry on relatively normal lives, supported by mild doses of drugs under medical supervision. However, the amount of drug consumption has increased substantially in England also, in recent years.

DELINQUENCY

As adolescents pass through the period of youth on the way to adulthood, many of them present delinquent behavior, and most of these outgrow it. One might see it as a kind of contagious disease, like mumps, which most youth catch and get over, with very few permanent disabilities. But to treat it so lightly would be a mistake, for two reasons: first, it hinders a youth from developing into a competent adult, even though he does not become a criminal; and second, some youths become seriously delinquent and go on into an adult life of crime or serious social maladjustment.

Delinquency is one form of reaction by youth to the opportunities, stimulations, and demands of a society. Boys try this pattern more frequently than girls. In all societies for which delinquency data are available, boys outnumber girls in the delinquency statistics by a ratio ranging between 4 to 1 and 10 to 1.

Boys at the beginning of adolescence are likely to do some mischief to property in the neighborhood, and may be warned by the police. When legal automobile driving age is reached, there are many arrests for breaking traffic laws. Approximately one in three juvenile arrests are traffic cases.

In a typical year in the 1960s, about 20 percent of the youth arrested were charged with serious offenses, as follows: burglary, 12 percent; automobile theft, 7 percent; robbery, 1 percent; aggravated assault, 1 percent; criminal homicide, 0.1 percent. In the 1960s juveniles, rather than adults, were responsible for most of the auto thefts, about half of all burglaries, and half of all larceny cases. The peak ages for arrests of youth are 16 and 17.

After the first experiences with minor delinquency, most young people leave this behind as they grow into more responsible and socially approved roles. But the fact that juvenile delinquency has increased tremendously all over the world, in urbanized and industrialized societies, suggests a need for improved social institutions aimed toward assisting youth to grow up.

Socioeconomic Status and Delinquency

Rates of juvenile delinquency are highest in the lower-class areas of the large cities. A study of delinquency was made in Philadelphia of a cohort of boys born in 1945 who lived in Philadelphia from their tenth to their eighteenth birthdays. Of nearly 10,000 boys in this cohort, 35 percent incurred one or more police contacts. About half of this group were arrested a second time, and most of them continued to have more trouble with the police. Of the whites in the cohort, 29 percent were classified as offenders, compared with 50 percent of the blacks. But it was socioeconomic status that was most highly correlated with repeated delinquency. (Wolfgang, et al, 1972)

The Philadelphia data are supported by a number of research studies made in large and small cities after 1950. For example, Table 9.6 shows the relation between social class and delinquency among boys in River City. In this midwestern city of 43,000, Havighurst et al. (1962) found that slightly over 20 percent of the boys had enough contact with the police to be placed into delinquency categories I, II, or III. Another 20 percent were on unofficial police records for such minor offenses as truancy, speeding in automobiles, faulty automobile brakes, breaking windows, or trespassing on property, offenses which are placed in category IV.

School Failure and Delinquency

There is a good deal of research evidence which links low academic performance in school to alienation and to delinquency, when IQ and socioeconomic status are kept constant. It appears that the school has not worked well as a socializing agent for these youth. Kelly studied one thousand semi-rural high school boys in Oregon and found the same degree of relationship between school alienation and delinquency in middle-class as well as working-class boys (Kelly, 1971). In a New York City study covering a large sample of delinquent youth in the 1950s, it was found that 95 percent of the 17-year-olds adjudged delinquent had dropped out of school, and 85 percent of the 16-year-olds were school dropouts.

Family Experience

All students of juvenile delinquency ascribe some causal effect to the family which neglects or rejects a child. The classical study by Sheldon and

TABLE 9.6. *Delinquency and Social Class in River City*

	Boys Classified as Delinquent: by Category				
Social Class	I (most serious)	II	III	IV (least serious)	All Boys in Age Cohort
Upper and upper-middle	0	1	0	2	22
Lower-middle	2	2	4	14	64
Upper-working	5	6	7	19	91
Lower-working	9	9	5	11	70
Total	16	18	16	46	247

Eleanor Glueck (1950, 1956) found the following five family characteristics to be closely related to delinquency:

Overstrict, erratic, or lax discipline of boy by father.
Lack of supervision of boy by mother.
Lack of affection of father for boy.
Lack of affection of mother for boy.
Lack of cohesiveness in the family.

On the basis of an interview with the parents or observation of the home situation it is possible to rate the family on these five characteristics. More recent research continues to verify this finding.

Apparently, much delinquency is caused by a combination of poor family relationships, low socioeconomic status, school failure, and below-average intelligence. These were all involved in the Kansas City study reported by Ahlstrom and Havighurst. The Kansas City study was an attempt to reduce delinquency through a program of work experience during the high school years. The target group was 13 and 14-year-old boys screened in 1961 and 1962 as socially and educationally maladjusted from among all seventh grade inner-city classrooms in Kansas City, Missouri public schools. The ratio of black to white youths was three to two. The boys were divided into experimental and control groups. Experimental boys, beginning in the eighth grade, received special attention through half days of classroom work geared to their abilities and their assumed needs, interests, and personal orientations, and half days of supervised work experience; these boys had their own teachers and work supervisors. Control group boys were enrolled in regular school programs and their progress was followed. The study was longitudinal and complete records were maintained on the school, work, community, and family adjustment of the boys, both while they were in school and up to the age of 18 or 19. Work experience, as the independent variable, included three different developmental stages involving different kinds of work experience, supervision-guidance, and rewards. As the Kansas City Study group grew older, some of the boys adjusted well to school and work, while others became more and more maladjusted and delinquent. It was found that the *cohesiveness* of the family was closely related to the boys' adjustment—those with cohesive families were much better adjusted to society and showed less delinquency. (Ahlstrom and Havighurst, 1971, p. 47)

TYPES AND CAUSES OF
JUVENILE DELINQUENCY

Juvenile delinquency is not one simple pattern of behavior but a complex phenomenon that takes a variety of forms and has a variety of causes. One type of delinquent behavior is related to abnormal personality. This has been studied by psychiatrists and psychologists. They have identified a personality type, often called a "psychopathic personality." This person displays extremely aggressive and uncontrolled behavior, behavior that may even go as far as murder. Children who show such extreme behavior have usually been raised by parents or other persons who neglected them and failed both to love and to discipline them consistently. Another type of personality disturbance consists of a severe and pervasive anxiety which makes a child do strange things, such as setting fires or compulsive stealing. It is estimated by researchers that no more than 10 percent of male delinquents show an unusual degree of emotional maladjustment.

Delinquency as a Subcultural Phenomenon

The most common type of juvenile delinquency in the United States and other industrialized countries seems to arise from certain disjunctions in the society itself. People in power in the society regard certain types of behavior as undesirable and they label it "delinquent," although the same behavior may appear "natural" to other people who belong to special subcultural groups. From this point of view, delinquent acts are primarily carried out by subgroups of youth who are at odds with the value system of the greater society in which they live. In a sense these young people are alienated from society and, feeling rejected by the community at large, they do not wish to obey its rules.

Most sociologists see juvenile delinquency as resulting from the fact that many children grow up in a disadvantaged American subculture. Working-class boys and girls are more likely than middle-class to become delinquent because in their culture they readily learn to become delinquent.

There are several theories of delinquency as a subcultural phenomenon. They all rest upon the following propositions:

1. Delinquency is learned and generally occurs as group behavior.
2. When delinquency is learned, the learning includes both motives and methods of committing crime.
3. Juvenile delinquency is one way of expressing needs and values, not in themselves delinquent, which are shared by all youth.

Delinquency as an Expression of Working-Class Culture. One of the theories of delinquency as a subcultural phenomenon explains it as a "natural" form of behavior for working-class boys. According to this theory, working-class boys grow up with standards of behavior which get them in trouble with the authorities who represent middle-class standards. Kvaraceus and Miller (1959) favor this theory and list the following characteristics of working-class culture which tend to get a boy in trouble with the authorities: high value placed upon toughness, outsmarting others, seeking excitement, maintaining one's autonomy, and attributing events to fate. In contrast, the middle-class culture places high value upon the following traits: achievement through hard work, responsibility, desire for education, respect for property, cleanliness, ambition, belonging to formal organizations, and ability to defer present pleasure in favor of future gratification.

The male gang is frequently found in working-class culture; the subculture provides the value system, teaches boys to become delinquent, and then fortifies their delinquency.

Since most working-class boys do *not* become delinquent, it is pointed out by Kvaraceus and Miller (1959) that not all working-class families have typical working-class values, and that some boys from working-class families learn middle-class modes of behavior in school, in church, or in recreational settings. With the aid of education, these boys move out of the working class. Many other boys accept the working-class culture but are not aggressive enough to become involved in serious delinquency, even though they participate with delinquents in many gang activities.

Status Discontent.   A second theory in which delinquency is viewed as originating in the social structure is the "status discontent" theory of Cohen (1955). In this theory it is assumed that all or practically all boys have accepted most of the goals of *middle-class* society, but that some boys are unsuccessful in achieving these goals. All boys would like to have money, a job, and, as they grow older, a girl friend, then a wife and family. Most middle-class boys and many working-class boys make steady and sure progress toward these goals by doing satisfactory work in school, by getting along well in the school peer group, and by getting a job and earning money. These boys have adequate mastery of the means for achieving their goals.

However, a minority of boys—most of them from working-class families—do not have the intelligence, or the study habits, or the work attitudes, or the social skills that are necessary to achieve these goals legitimately. Because they have the same desires as their peers, they become discontented with their disadvantaged status. These boys then seek illegitimate means to get what they want. They turn to the delinquent gang for moral support and for guidance in ways to get money, excitement, power, and the feeling of masculinity.

The Opportunity Structure.   A third theory emphasizes not the *inability* of working-class youth to measure up to middle-class standards, but the unfair or unequal distribution of *opportunity* between middle-class and working-class youth. Cloward and Ohlin (1960) argue that, if opportunity is not available by legitimate means, boys will band together in delinquent groups to seek illegitimate means of achieving their goals.

Delinquency as a Phenomenon of Idleness

Some sociologists view delinquency not as an outcome of a delinquent subculture but as the product of a social structure that fails to operate effectively to provide pathways of growth to adulthood. According to this view, it is the *absence* of a constructive social situation rather than the *presence of* a destructive social situation which is essentially responsible for much lower-class delinquency (Matza, 1964).

The great increase of juvenile delinquency since World War II may be more closely related to the growing numbers of unemployed and out-of-school youth than to any subculture that causes boys to become delinquent. Idleness leads boys into trouble. With nothing socially constructive to do, boys easily turn to theft, car stealing, and fighting. According to this view, if middle-class boys were out of school and out of work in large numbers, they, too, would show high delinquency rates.

THE PREVENTION OF DELINQUENCY

Since the causes of delinquency are multiple, it is natural that a variety of procedures has been proposed for its prevention. The report of the U.S. congressional committee studying juvenile deliquency summarizes in the following terms the various types of programs and the theories of causation underlying them:

> Programs specifically established to prevent delinquency by treatment of incipient offenders vary widely in plan and underlying theory of causation and cure. Among the favored assumptions as to what will help are the following:
>
> Having an adult friend or sponsor who will stick to the delinquency-prone boy or girl through thick and thin and will secure needed services in his behalf will render the child less likely to become delinquent.
>
> Delinquency-prone children can be identified by teachers at an early age (the schools know all the children and their ways, it is said) and referred for treatment to either a particular agency set up for the purpose or to the on-going service agencies.
>
> Delinquency results largely from disturbances in the parent-child relationship; hence, these disturbances should be recognized by all services (health, schools, day nurseries, police, etc.) that have contact with the families, and prophylactic measures should be taken.
>
> Delinquency frequently results from or is a sign of emotional disturbance, and this disorder can be remedied by individual or group therapy.
>
> Delinquency results largely from a breakdown in the cohesiveness of neighborhoods and in the controls exercised by parents and neighbors. A reduction in delinquency can be secured by restoring these lost or diminished social attributes and functions.
>
> The chief source of delinquent conduct and the chief bearers of the delinquent tradition in slum areas are certain of the established street-corner clubs or gangs. Direct work with these groups is required to carry them fairly peacefully through the tumultuous years of adolescence, to teach

them democratic ways of conducting their organization, and—perhaps—to break the chain of transmission of delinquent customs.

The usual social and mental health services of a community are not effective in delinquency prevention because they do not operate in concert and are inadequately staffed, quantitatively and qualitatively.

Delinquency can be reduced by assuring that all intellectually capable children, even though they are handicapped by language and culturally impoverished homes, should learn to read well and acquire other basic intellectual skills.

Lack of opportunity for paid work is an important factor in juvenile delinquency, partly because denial of a chance to earn money puts an adolescent in a childlike status and does not permit him to progress smoothly toward adulthood. (United States, 86th Congress, 1960, p. 27.)

Work-Study Programs

Since normal progress in school achievement is predictive of favorable growth through adolescence, programs to improve reading and other aspects of school performance are regarded as preventive of delinquency. But a considerable group of children reach age 13 to 15 without having made satisfactory school progress. They are the ones who will form Group C_1 and C_2 of Table 9.4.

The natural thing to propose for this subgroup is a growth-promoting experience that is not primarily academic. An example of a carefully designed experimental work-experience program is reported by Ahlstrom and Havighurst (1971). The 400 eighth-grade boys constituted about 10 percent of inner-city male youths and about five percent of all male youths in the city. They looked like "losers" when selected at the age of 13 or 14. They came through the next five years as would have been predicted. Ten were killed by violence or accident; 30 others were knifed or shot. Fifty-five percent showed serious social maladjustment. Sixty-five percent had been arrested on charges other than traffic violations. Sixteen percent had accumulated eight or more charges of delinquency. Twenty-three percent had been confined in juvenile institutions. The arrest rate for offenses which would have been felonies if they had been committed by adults was about 40 percent per year for study-group boys, compared with about 20 percent for the total metropolitan area male population of this age.

On the other hand, 43 percent of the group came through with reasonably good adjustment, and seemed to be headed for a fair level of adult adjustment to the society. The control and experimental groups differed relatively little, indicating that the work-experience program had not improved the situation for the experimental group to any marked degree. Actually, a considerable number of the control group went out and got part-time jobs on their own initiative. It appeared that work experience in itself was a good thing, but the school-designed work experience program was not much superior to what the boys could create for themselves.

The experience of observing and studying the 400 boys as they moved through adolescence brought the authors to two conclusions of a very general nature concerning the provisions that a good society should make for such youth. The first is aimed at strengthening the family as the group which gives the boy his basic moral training. This applies especially to the early school grades and to the preschool years. This means basic reform of welfare legislation and institution of procedures which will encourage low-income men to stay with wives and children, and it means some kind of floor under wages that guarantees a family an adequate income. The second policy proposal was that some sort of public service employment program should be established which would provide these young people with training in work attitudes and habits, vocational skills, and the opportunity to be useful to the local community and the state. This was very similar to the recommendation of the Coleman Panel on Youth.

EXERCISES

1. Develop your theory of the sources of the counterculture, taking into account especially the analysis made by Keniston in the epilogue of *Youth and Dissent.*

2. Write a paper arguing for or against the following proposition: Education at the secondary school and college levels should be mainly concerned with the development of knowledge and intellectual skills necessary for the professions and for business leadership.

3. Assuming that everybody at age 16 was given a voucher, equivalent in value to the average cost of education through four years of college, to be used at his discretion for schooling or skill acquisition at any subsequent time; describe how you think four quite different persons, two women and two men, might use these vouchers.

4. From your observation and experience in your own institution, what is the drug situation?

5. Read what you can find on delinquency among girls. What differentiates it from delinquency among boys?

6. Read several newspaper accounts of delinquent gangs and try out on these descriptions the Cloward and Ohlin theory of "differential opportunity." Does the theory explain the types of delinquency found in these gangs?

7. Find an example of a work-experience program for predelinquent or delinquent boys; describe and evaluate it.

8. Looking at the students in your college or university, how would you place them in relation to the categories shown in Table 9.4. What groups seem to be increasing and what groups decreasing in numbers?

9. Student unrest at high schools and colleges has been explored and explained

in many different ways. Read one or more of the following, and give your criticism, from your point of view:

The accounts by Margaret Mead, Joseph Adelson, Richard Peterson, and Jerome Skolnick in *Readings in Society and Education*, edited by Havighurst, Neugarten, and Falk.

The *University Crisis Reader*, a set of readings edited by Wallerstein and Starr.

The account by Theodore Roszak in *The Making of a Counter Culture*. The several articles in a special issue of the journal *Youth and Society* entitled *The Youth Culture*, September, 1971.

The *Radical Probe*, by Michael W. Miles.

The report on youth protest in urban high schools in the study by Havighurst, Smith, and Wilder.

The *Changing Values on the Campus*, by Daniel Yankelovich.

A *Special Kind of Rebellion*, by Daniel Seligman.

Up Against the Ivy Wall: A History of the Columbia University Crisis, by Jerry Avorn, et al.

SUGGESTIONS FOR FURTHER READINGS

1. For students who want to get further into the subject of this chapter, the books recommended are: *Youth and Dissent*, by Keniston; *Youth: Transition to Adulthood*, by Coleman; and Daniel Yankelovich's *Changing Values on the Campus*.

2. The 1975 Yearbook of the National Society for the Study of Education, entitled *American Youth in the Seventies* carries the analysis of the counterculture further than has been done in this chapter.

3. Five recent books on *communes* are analyzed in a survey essay by Jesse R. Pitts in the journal, *Contemporary Sociology* for July, 1973.

4. Chapter 7, "Non-Formal Sources of Secondary Education" in the *Reform of Secondary Education* (Brown) recommends that a wide variety of paths leading to a high school diploma or its equivalent should be opened up, with public funds and with secondary schools actively participating in the programs.

5. *Alternative Paths to the High School Diploma* by Bailey, Macy, and Vickers describes a regional learning service which has been set up in Central New York State to enable young people to earn an External High School Diploma without going through a regular school program.

6. For discussions of the revolution in values which is now taking place in the United States, read some of the following:

William Glasser, *The Identity Society*.

Mitchell Goodman, *The Movement Toward a New America: The Beginnings of a Long Revolution*.

Thomas Green, *Work, Leisure, and the American Schools*.

Margaret Mead, *Culture and Commitment*.

Charles A. Reich, *The Greening of America*.

Theodore Roszak, *The Making of a Counter Culture; Where the Wasteland Ends*.

Peter Schrag, *The Decline of the WASP*.

7. For a look at youth unrest and youth culture in several modern societies, see the collection of essays edited by Allerbeck and Rosenmayr, which contains articles from writers in England, France, Germany, Italy, Soviet Union, and the United States.

8. The values of a work-experience program for boys in the prevention of delinquency are explored thoroughly in the book *400 Losers* by Ahlstrom and Havighurst, which describes a five-year experimental study in Kansas City.

9. Recent books with empirical data as well as theoretical discussions of nature and causes of delinquency include: Marshall B. Clinard, ed. *Anomie and Deviant Behavior;* David Matza, *Delinquency and Drift;* Walter B. Miller, *City Gangs: An Experiment in Changing Gang Behavior;* John M. Martin and Joseph P. Fitzpatrick, *Delinquent Behavior;* and James F. Short, Jr., and Fred L. Strodtbeck, *Group Process and Gang Delinquency.*

10. Compare the theories of delinquency causation in *Delinquent Behavior* by William D. Kvaraceus and Walter B. Miller, *Delinquent Boys* by Albert K. Cohen, and *Delinquency and Opportunity* by Richard A. Cloward and Lloyd E. Ohlin.

11. For a person who wants to get a thorough orientation to the subject of drugs and drug abuse, the following are recommended:

Richard Blum and Associates: I. *Society and Drugs;* II. *Students and Drugs.*
Notre Dame Journal of Education: *Drugs and Education.*
Today's Education—NEA Journal: *Students and Drug Use.*
Louise D. Richards: *Drug-Taking in Youth.*
Snyder: *Uses of Marijuana.*
Coles et al: *Drugs and Youth.*
Marin and Cohen: *Understanding Drug Use.*
Thornburg: *The Adolescent and Drugs: An Overview.*

PART
III

The Educational System in the Community

The chapters which constitute Part I of this book dealt with the school in the social structure of a modern democratic society. Here, we shall return to a consideration of the relation of the school to society, but from a different set of perspectives. We shall ask, first, what is the proper role of the school in the local community; then, given the growth of metropolitan communities, how does the school relate to the local community which has become the whole metropolitan area; finally, how does the school relate to other social institutions and social systems within the metropolitan community?

CHAPTER 10

The Community School

Ever since the school came into existence as a specialized agency for the socialization of the young, questions have been raised about the proper relations between school and community. Three general answers or points of view have been posited. The first is the traditional one, so called because it was the prevailing one in America up through the nineteenth century. According to this view, the school should be walled off from the problems of the local community and should limit itself to teaching essential mental and vocational skills. The other two answers, "the school as a model of the community," and "the community school," have emerged within the present century. According to the latter two views, the school has broader functions that bring it into close relations with the surrounding community.

WHAT IS A COMMUNITY?

In assessing these views, two rather different meanings of the term "community" are relevant. While the school is located in the local community, it is also preparing children for life in the wider national and international community. The difference between the two uses of the term is perhaps made clearer by a distinction between "primary" and "secondary" communities.

A *primary community* is one in which people are related by face-to-face association and cooperation. It is often said of such a community that "everybody knows everybody else." While this may not be completely true, it is true that everybody can see face-to-face anyone with whom he is likely to have significant dealings.

A *secondary community* is one in which people are related indirectly by trade and business connections or by belonging to the same religious, professional, or economic group. People in secondary communities are interdependent, but they seldom or never meet each other face-to-face. The big city is a secondary community, as is a state, a region, or a nation. The world is becoming more than ever before a secondary community.

School curricula and school activities are related both to the local primary community and to the wider secondary community, but the three concepts of the school listed above refer to the school's relation to the local community.

A.   THE TRADITIONAL SCHOOL

When the school is seen to have only the highly specialized job of teaching intellectual and vocational skills, it becomes separate from the community. This point of view, overstated somewhat for the sake of contrast, is that the school should do its job just as the municipal water works does its job. It should work quietly, inconspicuously, and efficiently, and it should limit itself to its special functions. According to this view, to ask the school to do other things, such as teaching children to develop good social relations with one another or to form good food habits, would be like asking the municipal water works to do the job of the police department. The best possible education is seen as taking place when children study lessons that are chosen for their value as mental discipline; or for the information that will be useful in adult life.

Most schools in America have moved a long way from the traditional point of view, even though many of the values inherent within it are still recognized and sought after, and even though the point of view still has vigorous proponents. For example, Carl Bereiter, an educator who has done effective work with the teaching of socially disadvantaged preschool children, doubts that the school can do all of the things that broad "humanistic" ideals call for—namely, to cultivate the personal independence of each pupil and to

FIGURE 10.1   The traditional concept of school-community relations.

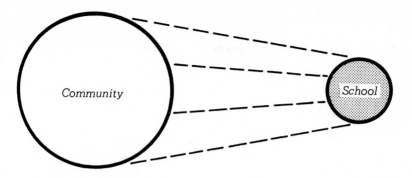

FIGURE 10.2   *The concept of the school as a model of the community.*

develop each person to the fullest. Instead, he proposes that the school accept the limited but valuable function of cognitive training, and leave the rest to other agencies. He proposes the following policy:

1. Restrict the responsibility of the schools entirely to training in well-defined, clearly teachable skills. This should require only about a third of the cost in money, personnel, and time that schooling now costs. That which would be lost would be largely good riddance; and with exclusive concentration on training, the schools could probably do a much more efficient job than they do now.

2. Set children free the rest of the time to do what they want, but in doing so get them out from under the authority of the schools. Provide more economical forms of custodial care and guidance, as needed.

3. Use the large amount of money thus saved to provide an enormously enriched supply of cultural resources for children, with which they can spend their newly found free time. These resources should reflect humanistic values to the fullest, but they should not carry any burden of educational intent in the sense of trying to direct or improve upon the course of personal development. They should simply be resources and activities considered worthy in their own right. (Bereiter, 1971, pp. 21–22)

B.   THE SCHOOL AS A MODEL
OF THE COMMUNITY

A second possible relation of school and community is one in which the school is a simplified model of the community. According to this view, children learn how to live as adults by learning first to live within the school community. This was John Dewey's point of view, and he said:

When the school introduces and trains each child of society into member-ship within such a little community, saturating him with the spirit of ser-vice, and providing him with the instruments of effective self-direction, we shall have the deepest and best guarantee of a larger society which is worthy, lovely, and harmonious. (Dewey, 1915, pp. 27–28)

The Elementary School Level

In a school of this kind the pupils have a busy and varied day. It is considered good for children to eat and play together as well as work to-gether, and to share a wide range of activities. The elementary school of this type is likely to have a garden tended by the children, and pets in the class-rooms. The kindergarten or first grade may have a miniature store where pupils can buy, sell, and learn to deal with money. As the pupils grow older they take responsibility for organizing much of their own work. They form committees to carry out class projects. They organize parties and start clubs. When classes are over they may have a period of supervised after-school play that keeps them off the streets and city playgrounds and confines their choice of playmates to their schoolmates.

The High School Level

At the high school level, this type of school often has an effective stu-dent government that has a good deal of power to deal with school activities, athletics, and minor problems of discipline. The high school tends to be a social unit, with its own parties and entertainments. Such a school usually offers a good program of dramatics and music. (This type of school occasion-ally takes the form of a boarding school with large grounds and sometimes a farm, where pupils do a share of the daily work.)

In schools of this type, it is expected that children and adolescents will be better citizens of the community because they have learned the lessons of democratic community life within the school itself.

Three Different Versions

In viewing the school as a model of the community, there are at least three different versions that are distinguishable, each focussed on a different institution of the larger society. The school can be perceived as a family, as a factory, or as a corporation.

The family model is to be seen in preschools, primary grades of private schools, small rural schools, and some of the new "open schools," which are described in Chapter 13. The teacher has a nurturing role, much as a mother or father; the children learn from each other. A good many primary schools in England have recently adopted this model for children aged five to seven.

The factory model sees incoming students as raw material and then as products turned out by the school. Students are "processed." Or, seen in another way, students may be treated as workers in a factory, with the teacher as a foreman who directs their work. The children all do much the same work, though some work faster or do a neater or more accurate job than others. They are encouraged to compete with each other, somewhat as factory workers who are paid on piecework rates, according to the amount of their individual production. The routines and demands for conformity in the factory-type school are often made more pleasant for children by a paternalistic teacher and principal.

The corporation model is a relatively recent introduction, appearing generally after 1950. Teachers and students are grouped together for collectively planned and organized work. Team teaching by teachers and teamwork by students are emphasized. There is much group planning and evaluation. In some "corporation schools" there is a nongraded structure which permits pupils to move through the school on more individualized schedules than could be tolerated in the factory model. The school makes use of technology —tape recorders, computers, programmed instruction and prepackaged instructional units or "modules." The school schedule and the school curriculum are flexible, and students grow accustomed to change and to moving about as part of the corporation plan.

Presumably the corporation school teaches its pupils to live in a society with much interdependence among people, where each person contributes his specialized abilities and interests to the common enterprise.

C.   THE COMMUNITY SCHOOL

A third relation between the school and the community is one that offers the closest structural unity possible, with the school operating directly as an agent for community betterment and with students, either children or adults,

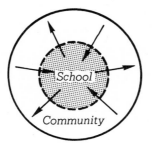

FIGURE 10.3   The concept of the community school.

taking part in community activities. This is the *community school* as it has developed in the United States since 1930.

The Community as the Agent of Education

People who think about education in broad terms, as a process of teaching children the concepts and attitudes of their society, and of teaching them how to behave in their social, civic, and economic relations, tend to think of the whole community as an educative agent. From this point of view, the school alone cannot do the job of education, nor can the school and family together. Education is the result of living and growing up in a community, and educators should be interested in finding the best combination of school and community experiences for educational purposes.

There are two broad characteristics of the *community school:* (1) it teaches children to discover, develop, and use the resources of the local community; and (2) it serves the entire community, not merely the children of school age.

The Community School in a Rural Setting

These features are seen clearly in a number of community-school experiments first undertaken in small rural communities. For example, in the late 1930s the Sloan Foundation supported educational ventures in rural communities in Kentucky, Florida, and Vermont, aimed at improving diet, housing, and clothing (Olson and Fletcher, 1946). Children were taken off the standard readers and arithmetic books that had been traditional in those schools and were given new reading material dealing with nutrition, housing, and clothing. At the same time community projects were started within the schools. In Kentucky, children were taught to eat new foods; tomatoes were grown and introduced into the diet; goats were raised to produce milk. In Florida, a small model home was built out of local building materials. Children learned these new practices at school, then took them home to their parents; and parents were drawn into the school setting.

The Community School in an Urban Setting

If the community school were only a rural phenomenon, it would have limited usefulness in a society that is steadily growing more urban. It appears, however, that big cities also make use of the community school concept. The Flint, Michigan public schools, for example, have developed a community-school program that could be adapted to fit any industrial city.

Although the community-school program in Flint, an automobile manufacturing city, began during the Depression of the 1930s, it has gained momentum since then and is now a regular part of the program of the Flint Public

Schools. The program started with the use of the schools in the evenings and on weekends for providing recreation and diversion for men out of work and their families. When full employment returned, the program became even more popular. Most of the elementary schools are open evenings and Saturdays. All of the 20 or more elementary schools built since 1950 have a "community wing" consisting of a community room, a kitchen, a gymnasium, and an auditorium.

The Flint community school also provides the facilities for regular sessions of the neighborhood Teen Club (one of 43 such groups with a card-carrying membership of 13,000); for 7,000 children on tot lots during the summer; for meetings in the community room of men's clubs, P.T.A.'s, and various other organizations; for square dances for parents, teenagers, and the younger ones, and other recreational activities held in the large gymnasium; for a Christmas party attended by 700 adults in a school with an enrollment of only 500. (Buehring, 1958, p. 36)

The community school program in Flint has changed and developed through the years, but the 1958 description is still generally accurate.

The urban community school has one or both of two characteristics. First, as illustrated in Flint, the school is made to serve the educational, cultural, and social needs of its immediate local community.

The second, a more controversial characteristic and one that most often applies to the whole school system of a community rather than to one or another particular neighborhood school, occurs when the school takes part in the reshaping and renewing of the urban community. For example, the school may adopt attendance or districting policies which are aimed at serving the purposes of urban renewal. If, as is often the case, one of the purposes of urban renewal in a given community happens to be that of maintaining racial balance in the schools, then the urban community school system adopts practices that work toward racial balance. If another of the purposes is to reduce dropouts from high school and to reduce youth unemployment, then the urban community school develops a program of work experience, remedial teaching, or other methods to serve those purposes.

The urban community school cooperates with nonschool agencies. If it appears, for instance, that parents are becoming concerned about educational standards in the city schools and are thinking of moving to the suburbs, the urban community school attempts to act constructively by involving those parents and other citizens in discussions and decisions about school policies and practices.

THE COMMUNITY SCHOOL MOVEMENT

The community school idea has been a vital concept in American education since the 1920s. It has also become an organized *movement*, and deserves to be described as such.

221

The organized Community School Movement began about 1940 in Flint, Michigan, when Charles Stewart Mott, an automobile manufacturing executive, set up the Mott Foundation and the Mott Foundation Projects. The lighted-schoolhouse program in Flint was undertaken with funds given to the Board of Education. This program attracted visitors who developed similar projects in their own communities. As the Flint program became known, the Mott Foundation began to hold semiannual "community school workshops," the first in 1955. By 1967, 12,000 people had visited Flint individually or in groups to see community education in action.

In 1964 the seven state universities in Michigan were assisted by the Mott Foundation to train men and women as leaders in community education. Funds were provided for internships, and more than 500 interns had been trained by 1972. By this date there were 25 centers for community education at universities ranging from Florida to California. At each of these centers it was possible to get full-time or part-time training for posts as Directors of Community Education. The Movement had developed to the point where there were nearly 2,000 "community schools" in the country, with 1,700,000 persons taking part in their programs.

A monthly newsletter, *The Community School and Its Administration*, was begun in 1962, and a quarterly, *Community Education Journal,* in 1971. The National Community Schools Association was founded in 1966 and had 1,200 members by 1972.

The Educational Park

The community school, as indicated, becomes the educational service center of the community. With activities going on at night and on Saturdays as well as school days, it attracts people of all ages who have educational interests. Facilities can be used economically if they are maintained in one center. These considerations have produced the *educational park,* which is a physical structure providing educational functions for a community of 10,000 to 100,000 people. Ideally, the park would be an area of several acres, with buildings to house educational activities serving students from preschool to old age, and with bus services for students who live beyond walking distance.

The educational park is created most easily in a new suburb on the edge of a growing metropolis, where the necessary land can be reserved and then put to use as the community grows up around it. An example is the area in the northeast corner of the Bronx, New York City, which was formerly a large amusement park. When that amusement park was torn down, the city planners created a new community called Co-op City, with mainly private housing but also some public housing, and with an educational park containing a variety of educational facilities. One advantage of an educational park is that it provides for socioeconomic and racial integration, since all students attend the same school complex.

Local Community Control?

In the inner city of the great metropolitan centers of the country, there are now many enclaves, small and large, where people of a given racial or ethnic or subcultural group live. They may be Chinese, or Filipino, or Greek, or Italian, or Chicano, or Cuban, or Puerto Rican, or Polish, or American Indian, or black, or Appalachian white. During the 1960s, with the Civil Rights Movement and a general revival of separatism and cultural pluralism, many of these groups became concerned with their own cultural identity. Also many such groups were dissatisfied with the progress of their children in the public schools and, as was only natural, they tended to blame the teachers and the school authorities. Generally such parents felt that the teachers were strange, and did not "understand" their children.

One response of school administrators who were concerned about establishing better relations with these culturally diverse subgroups was to offer to share with them the important decisions about the local schools: for example, to seek advice from local leaders on the appointment of a new principal, or to discuss the possibility of bilingual instruction, or of using teacher-aides who could speak the native languages. These responses from school administrators led to a variety of forms of decentralization of power and of decision-making, with parents and community members assuming responsibility.

The movement for local community control of schools has produced a good deal of controversy, as will be described in subsequent chapters. It can be seen positively, however, as an effort to implement the concept of the community school in areas of big cities.

EXERCISES

1. Think of a local community that you know well. What are two or three ways in which the school could actually assist the community?

2. Of the three types of school described in this chapter, do you favor one over the others? Why?

3. Analyze the work of the agencies and organizations that serve the children of a particular school grade in a particular community. Which ones fit in well with the school program? Which ones tend to compete with the school?

4. Compare the role of the teacher in a "traditional" school with the role of the teacher in a "community school." How are they the same? How are they different?

5. Study the content of the course of study in your city to see how the history and government of the local community is taught. Organize a teaching unit for pupils which deals with the metropolitan area as the unit. Choose a particular

grade level, such as third grade, where pupils might be studying the local community, or eleventh grade, where community civics is being studied.

SUGGESTIONS FOR FURTHER READING

1. Read chapter 12, "Contrasting Conceptions of the Social Role of the School," in *Social Foundations of Education* by William O. Stanley *et al.,* for a concise presentation of various points of view regarding the proper place of the school in the community.

2. *This Happened in Pasadena* by David Hulburd, written in journalistic style, tells the story of what happened in one school system when a small group of citizens began an attack upon it. Bruce Raup's book, *Education and Organized Interests in America,* although written some time ago, is a revealing account in more general terms of how various groups bring pressure to bear upon the schools.

3. A special issue of the *Phi Delta Kappan* for November, 1972 was devoted to community schools. In addition to twenty articles on one or another aspect of community schooling, there is an article on "The Literature of Community Education" by Pearl C. Brackett.

4. There is a large body of literature on the community school and its development *The Use of Resources in Education,* by Elsie Ripley Clapp, for example, is an account of work carried on over a seven-year period in two public rural schools, one in Kentucky and one in West Virginia. *These Things We Tried,* by Jean and Jess Ogden describes educational work with adults in three rural communities in Virginia. For a survey of the major writings about community schools, see *The Community School,* 52nd Yearbook of the National Society for the Study of Education, Part II, especially chapters 3, 4, 5, and 17. A recent comprehensive treatment of community schools and colleges is given in *Community Education: A Developing Concept,* edited and largely written by Maurice F. Seay.

5. Read chapter 7, "The Clash of Class Interests in School Politics," in Vidich and Bensman, *Small Town in Mass Society,* for an interesting account of the relations between the school board, the principal of the high school, local businessmen, and farmers in a small rural community in New York State.

CHAPTER **11**

Metropolitan Development and Educational Problems

The community of the future is the metropolitan area—a complex of central city, suburbs, industrial areas, highways, parks, and open spaces that are bound together by economic and cultural ties. Metropolitan development brings with it a host of educational problems. In this chapter the relationships between the school and the community and the relation of educational policy to social policy will be explored with special reference to the metropolitan community.

URBANIZATION

Urbanization and technification are the most characteristic aspects of modern society. Urbanization is the process of making people into city-dwellers. "Technification" is a word we shall use to denote the process whereby machines and natural resources of energy are employed to increase production. Until 1800 the people of even the most powerful societies were mainly engaged in getting food and fuel from the land—some 80 percent of the working population were tillers of the soil, or sheep and cattle tenders, or fishermen, or foresters. Then the growing technification of society enabled fewer and fewer people to raise more and more food, until, today, less than 10 percent of the working force in the United States produces enough fuel and food to provide a high standard of living for all the population.

The farm, the home, the office, as well as the workshop, have all been technified, and with this process has come increasing urbanization. Larger and larger proportions of the population have come to live in cities. From 1880 to 1970 the proportion of Americans living in towns and cities of 2,500 or more increased from 30 percent to over 73 percent. This growth in urbanization is shown in Table 11.1.

Growth of Metropolitan Areas

The cities themselves have spread out to include within their economic and social nets smaller communities or suburbs and sections of open country. This growth has been facilitated by the automobile and the highway, which have made it relatively easy for people within a radius of 10 or 20 miles to travel quickly from one part of a metropolitan area to another.

By 1950 a "standard metropolitan area" had been defined in the United States Census and had become a significant unit of population. A metropolitan area includes a central city or cluster of cities and the surrounding area that is functionally related to the central city. In the Census a city of 50,000

TABLE 11.1   Growth of Urban Population in the United States

	Distribution of Total Population (by percent)			
			Urban Population in:	
Year	Rural (under 2,500)	Total Urban (2,500 and over)	Cities over 100,000	Metropolitan Areas
1790	95	5	—	—
1810	93	7	—	—
1830	91	9	2	—
1850	85	15	5	—
1870	74	26	11	—
1890	65	35	15	—
1910	54	46	22	46
1930	44	56	30	54
1950	36	64*	29	59
1960	30	70*	29	63
1970	27	73*	28	69

* Current U.S. Census definition of "urban" adds about five percent to numbers based on pre-1950 definition.

Source: U.S. Census of Population: 1960, Selected Area Reports. Standard Metropolitan Statistical Areas. Final Report PC(3) 10, p. 1; and U.S. Census of Population: 1970, Final Report PC(1A), General Characteristics of the Population.

or more is counted as a central city of a standard metropolitan area (SMA); and the unit includes the whole county surrounding this city, plus any contiguous county that is economically and socially integrated with the central county. A number of SMA's contain two or more cities, such as Minneapolis-St. Paul, New York-Newark-Jersey City, and San Francisco-Oakland-Berkeley-Richmond.

There were 243 metropolitan areas in 1970, with 140 million people, or 69 percent of the population. Although metropolitan units as a whole gained 24 percent between 1960 and 1970, central cities gained only 5 percent while the suburban areas gained 28 percent. In fact, some of the central cities actually lost population. Of the five cities with populations of one million or more in 1950, only Los Angeles gained, while the others lost or remained practically constant. Among cities which lost population between 1950 and 1970 were Boston, St. Louis, Detroit, Philadelphia, Washington, Chicago, Cleveland, Pittsburgh, Cincinnati, Baltimore, with losses ranging from 27 to 5 percent. New York City stayed the same. On the other hand, Houston increased 107 percent during this 20-year period, and several other cities in the Southwest and on the West Coast grew considerably. This was partly due to the fact that these younger cities had extended their city limits to include areas that were sparsely populated at the time, areas that would have become suburban cities if the earlier pattern of drawing city limits had prevailed.

The population increase in metropolitan areas accounted for most of the increase in total population of the United States. In fact, the actual population outside of metropolitan areas *decreased* between 1960 and 1970 by 5 percent.

METROPOLITANISM AND THE SCHOOLS

Two-thirds of the school children and school teachers in the United States are located in metropolitan schools. Metropolitanism refers not only to economic and social processes that go on in the metropolitan area, but also to an emerging way of life which is neither urbanism nor suburbanism. It is a way of life in which people come to feel at home in the complex metropolitan area; to enjoy the cultural facilities of the central city; and to be able to live comfortably at various stages of the life cycle in one or another section of the metropolitan area.

The growth of the metropolitan area and the changing character of the school system can be described in five stages: the medium-sized city, the industrialized city, the growth of suburbs, the appearance of the metropolitan complex, and urban renewal.

The Medium-Sized City

A small trading center grows over a period of years to a medium-sized city of 25,000 to 50,000. Enough geographical stratification occurs in this period to give rise to differentiation among elementary schools along socio-economic lines. One or more "poorer" schools appear, where educational motivation and educational achievement of students are inferior as compared with schools in "better" parts of the city. People who can afford it and who are concerned about the education of their children try to avoid living in the districts of the "poorer" schools.

During this period there is only one public high school, drawing a cross section of youth in terms of ability, educational motivation, and socioeconomic status.

The Industrialized City

As Handlin (1959) illustrates in his detailed account of the growth and development of New York City, if the medium-sized city is located in a strategic place with respect to transportation, raw materials, or markets, it attracts large numbers of in-migrants and it becomes an industrial and commercial center of several hundred thousand. By this time the areas near the center of the city become industrialized, or the dwellings deteriorate and their owners move away from the center to more peripheral areas of the city. Slum areas develop, and choice residential areas appear on the outskirts of the city.

During this period the schools take on the qualities of the areas in which they are located. Some elementary schools become entirely working-class in character; others, middle-class. At the same time, a number of high schools are built, generally to serve youth from given geographical districts which contain eight or ten elementary schools. The single comprehensive high school serving all kinds of youth is now replaced by high schools with contrasting socioeconomic compositions. Some schools get a reputation for college preparation; others begin to specialize in vocational education.

The Growth of Suburbs

By the end of World War I a number of American cities were moving into a third stage, with the appearance of choice residential suburbs, at first strung out along the railway lines that led into the city. These suburbs were exclusive residential areas, expensive to live in, with greater "living space" and with superior schools provided at no greater cost to the taxpayer than in the central city. These suburbs were heavily upper-middle-class, with fringes of upper-class and of lower-middle-class residents. Their schools, elementary and secondary, were relatively homogeneous along socioeconomic, racial, and ethnic lines.

During this phase, which, for cities already industrialized by 1920, lasted from World War I to World War II, some of the suburbs developed well-known public schools along "progressive" lines. Known throughout the educational world were the school systems of Winnetka, Bronxville, Manhasset, Shaker Heights, Clayton, and Pasadena. Despite the fact that the people in these suburbs were known to be politically conservative, in educational matters they were progressive; and their schools tended to retain many of their progressive features during the conservative reaction in education that followed World War II.

Because the suburb is a part of the metropolitan complex, the fact that it draws mainly middle and upper-class people results in an increase in the proportion of lower-class population who live in the central city. As population expands, and as more persons move into metropolitan areas, the working-class areas of the central city expand, creating obsolescence and reduced monetary values in former middle-class residential areas. Slum areas expand. The area of solid middle-class residences becomes smaller and is often cut up into small islands within lower-class areas.

The Appearance of the Metropolitan Complex

At the close of World War II there was a shift toward greater complexity within the metropolitan area. While the suburbs grew much more rapidly than the central cities, suburban growth consisted of two contrasting patterns. First, the prewar pattern of the migration of middle-income people from the central city to the suburbs was intensified. This pattern dominated until the mid-1960s. At the same time, a new and offsetting pattern appeared of working-class migration to the suburbs. The result has been greater segregation within the total metropolitan area by income. (Greater segregation by skin color has also occurred, as will be described in more detail below.)

INCREASED SOCIOECONOMIC AND RACIAL
SEGREGATION IN THE SCHOOLS

As the total population of a metropolitan area grew larger, and as neighborhoods became more segregated in terms of social-class, ethnic, and racial composition, these trends were of course reflected in the schools. By the 1970s, individual schools were more different from each other and more internally homogeneous with respect to these factors than they had been before World War II. The proposition that segregation is increasing may need further clarification, for obviously there are also current trends working in the opposite direction, as we shall see when we come to the topic of urban renewal.

Socioeconomic Segregation

The growth of working-class suburbs and the development of islands of middle-class housing within the inner city have reduced the extent to which large areas are homogeneous and have reduced the size of neighborhoods which are wholly working-class in composition. Nevertheless the evidence is that overall: (1) The percent of all middle-class children who attend schools in which 80 percent or more are middle-class has increased since 1920. (2) The percent of all working-class or blue-collar-family children who attend schools in which 80 percent or more are working-class has also increased since 1920.

The increased socioeconomic segregation within neighborhoods is illustrated by the following account of what happened in a particular elementary school in Chicago between 1955 and 1961.

> *Leibnitz School in 1955 was attended by 1,250 pupils coming mainly from lower-middle and upper-middle-class families of German, Dutch, and Swedish origin. The district was situated about seven miles from the city center, and close to transportation lines. Parents of some of the pupils had attended the same school.*
>
> *Then came a period of rapid change. Some of the three-story apartment buildings were cut up into smaller units and rented to southern white and black families who were moving into the city in large numbers. By 1960 the school enrollment was 2,400, and the school was running on a double-shift schedule. An observer looking at the school in the autumn of 1961 reported as follows:*
>
> *Transiency at the Leibnitz School is calculated at 70 percent, which means 1,900 pupils transferred in or out of the school during the year from September, 1960, to June, 1961. At times of heavy turnover the children waiting to transfer in or out are seated in the auditorium, in some cases with their parents; in some cases, without. One clerk sits at a desk on the stage and processes transfers and records from incoming children; another clerk sits on the opposite side of the stage and processes papers for the outgoing children.*
>
> *The records of transfers out of the school during the past several years show that most of the children leaving the school have transferred to schools farther out from the city center, or in the suburbs.*

Racial and Ethnic Segregation

Not only has there been increased economic segregation of school populations, but also increased racial and ethnic segregation. In the northern cities, all-black neighborhoods came into being, and school enrollments inevitably reflected this fact. For instance, the 1958 report of New York City's Superintendent of Schools (New York City, 1959) showed a net loss of 15,000 white pupils per year for the preceding five years, pupils who had moved out

TABLE 11.2.   *Proportion of Population in SMSAs* That Is Nonwhite: 1900–1970*

Year	Percent in SMSAs* Who Are Nonwhite	Percent in Central City Who Are Nonwhite	Percent outside Central City Who Are Nonwhite
1900	7.8	6.8	9.4
1910	7.3	6.9	8.1
1920	7.2	7.3	7.0
1930	8.1	9.0	6.4
1940	8.6	10.1	6.0
1950	10.0	13.1	5.7
1960	11.7	17.8	5.2
1970	12.8	21.4	4.9

* Standard Metropolitan Statistical Areas.

Source: U.S. Bureau of the Census. U.S. Census of Population: 1960. *Selected Area Reports. Standard Metropolitan Statistical Areas. Final Report.* 1970 data from *Final Report PC (IA), General Characteristics of the Population.*

to the New York suburbs. Blacks formed 20 percent of the school enrollment, and Puerto Ricans 15 percent. Of 704 public schools, 455 had 90 percent or more of their pupils of one group, either black or white or Puerto Rican (Morrison, 1958). Only one in five schools could be said to be "integrated" in the sense that it had more than 10 percent of pupils who did not belong to the majority group for that particular school.

This process of segregation within big cities has intensified since 1960, as we shall see in later chapters. New York City, with 20 percent of the public school enrollment consisting of blacks in 1958, reported 36 percent blacks in the public schools in 1972–3.

The segregation of racial and ethnic groups has been the result of the inmigration to metropolitan areas of blacks, and persons of Spanish origin, and their concentration within the central cities. This trend is shown in Table 11.2, which shows the proportion of nonwhites living in metropolitan areas, central cities, and suburbs over the past 70 years.

Because blacks coming into the big cities have settled mostly in segregated residential neighborhoods, an increasing number of schools in the central cities have consequently become all black, especially elementary schools. Furthermore, the rapidity of black in-migration, the general inability of these new families to pay high rents, and the widespread practice of residential segregation that has limited their dispersion throughout the metropolitan area have resulted in a close concentration of the black population, much denser than that which characterized the same neighborhoods earlier. Another important fact is that the black in-migrants have tended to be relatively young men and women who were just starting their families.

As a consequence, after about 1950 the black areas of the large cities experienced a very rapid increase of child population which soon over-crowded the schools in these areas. By the early 1950s schools which had formerly stood partially empty in many of the central cities were full to over-flowing with black children.

Meanwhile, other sections of the central city fared differently. Some areas near the center of the city became so run down that slum-clearance projects removed whole blocks of tenements, often leaving a school district with only half as many dwellings and again with empty schools. Some areas of stable European ethnic composition, especially Poles and Italians, main-tained their populations as the younger generations took over homes from their parents. Schools in such areas stayed comfortably full. In still other areas on the outer edges of the central city occupied by middle-class people, the school-age population decreased as grown children left the area to estab-lish their own homes in suburbs. Thus the schools in the latter areas lost enrollment and stood with as many as a quarter of their rooms empty.

All these movements of population were taking place during the 1950s and 1960s. At the same time, the total school enrollment of the central city was increasing, due to the postwar birthrate increases and due also to the in-migration of black families who were at the height of their childbearing cycle. These factors created problems of housing school children. Some schools in the crowded areas went on double shift, at the same time that other schools in nearby areas stood partially empty.

Diversification of Secondary Schools

The movements of different social-class, ethnic, and racial groups within metropolitan areas over the past several decades has produced schools which are increasingly diverse, one from another, and which, on the whole, are more internally homogeneous than before. Because the high schools draw their students from a relatively wide geographic area, individual high schools are somewhat more heterogeneous than individual elementary schools. Also, a few big city high schools may serve the entire city, although selectively, by making admission to the school dependent on high grades or special talents.

High Schools in 45 Large Cities

A recent study made under the auspices of the National Association of Secondary School Principals (1971) reported on the relation between socio-economic status and other student characteristics in the 670 public high schools in the 45 cities over 300,000 in population. The schools (all in the central cities) were placed in socioeconomic categories on the basis of infor-mation provided by the principal concerning parental social status. Once they were stratified according to the socioeconomic level of their student

TABLE 11.3 Characteristics of Large-City High Schools, 1968–9, by Socioeconomic Composition (670 High Schools in 45 Largest Cities)

	Percent of Schools in Category	Average Percent of Entering Students in College Entrance Curriculum	Average Percent of Entering Students Who Are Dis-advantaged Economically	Average Number of Foreign Languages Offered at Fourth Year Level	Average Percent of Entering Students Two Years or More Retarded in Reading
A. Middle class predominates	21	80	0	3.0	5
B. Socially heterogeneous with strong middle-class component	30	55	5	2.6	15
C. Lower-middle and upper-working class	28	35	15	2.0	25
D. Working class predominates	21	25	35	1.3	55

Source: *Profile of the Large-City High School,* by Havighurst, Smith, and Wilder, National Association of Secondary School Principals, 1971.

bodies, these schools were seen to vary in other characteristics, as is seen in Table 11.3. The two higher status categories (A and B) have higher proportions of students in college preparatory programs, more foreign languages offered at an advanced level, and lower proportions of entering students who are two or more years retarded in reading skills.

The same 670 schools were distributed among ethnic categories according to Table 11.4. The most frequent types were schools whose students were nearly all white or nearly all black. Only 11 percent of the schools had a racial mix in which no one group predominated, and where students were fairly evenly mixed between white and black, or between Puerto Rican, black, and Anglo-white.

STRATIFICATION IN THE METROPOLITAN AREA

While socioeconomic stratification has proceeded within the central city, there has been a similar process in the suburbs since World War II. Even though most of the suburbs do not include the lowest socioeconomic group found in the central city, the suburbs too have become differentiated into communities which are predominantly upper-middle, lower-middle, or working-class.

The New York metropolitan area shows this decentralized stratification more clearly than other centers, partly because of its size, and partly because it contains several large industrial cities, such as Jersey City,

TABLE 11.4.   *Ethnic Composition of Large-City High Schools, 1968–69 (670 High Schools in the 45 Largest Cities)*

Student Body	Number of Schools
White (non-Spanish): 81 percent or more	287
White (non-Spanish): 61–80 percent	98
Black: 81 percent or more	132
Black: 61–80 percent	25
White and black: 21–60 percent of each	51
White and black and Puerto Rican: 21 percent of each	20
Spanish American: 41 percent or more	14
Predominantly Oriental	6
All others	37
Total	670

Source: *Profile of the Large-City High School,* by Havighurst, Smith, and Wilder, National Association of Secondary School Principals, 1971.

Bayonne, Newark, Paterson, Passaic, and Elizabeth, none of which is part of the central city of New York. Members of the lower-working class live in Manhattan, Brooklyn, the Bronx, and in the Jersey industrial cities. Craftsmen and foremen live out beyond the lower-working class and also in some of the residential suburbs such as Mineola on Long Island, Tuckahoe in Westchester County, and Roselle Park in Union County. The upper-middle and upper classes live in Manhattan (on the upper East Side), in Westchester County to the north, Nassau County on Long Island, and Essex and Bergen Counties in New Jersey.

Suburban stratification is partly due to the decentralization of industry that has gone on since World War II. Formerly there were a few small industrial cities around the fringes of big cities. For example, Chicago Heights, Harvey, Whiting and Gary grew up south of Chicago; Passaic and Elizabeth, outside New York City; and Alameda and Richmond, outside San Francisco. After the war various economic factors led to further decentralization of industry. "Light" industry such as the manufacture of electronic equipment, plastics, pharmaceuticals, airplanes and airplane parts became established in suburban areas. This in turn pulled workers from the central city into new working-class suburbs. These people are mainly skilled craftsmen and white-collar workers with relatively high incomes who drive automobiles to work and are not dependent on public transportation. Examples of this type of community can be seen in various parts of the country: in the new suburbs northwest of Chicago; in North Kansas City; in Edwardsville and other suburbs across the Mississippi river from St. Louis; in some of the new suburbs in central Long Island; and in the northern and southern suburbs of Los Angeles.

At the same time, if there is a substantial black population in the metropolitan area, as is true in Chicago and Detroit, a few black working-class suburbs come into existence. Also when a large black slum area develops in the central city, black middle-class people find their way into mixed black-white middle-class residential areas in the central city, and into middle-class suburbs.

The Socioeconomic Ratio (SER)

In studying the facts of socioeconomic segregation and the changing patterns in central cities and suburbs, it is useful to employ a ratio of white-collar to blue-collar workers, a ratio that can be worked out for the families of children in a given school, or worked out from census data for the people who live in a particular school district or neighborhood. There are several ways of calculating such a ratio. In Table 11.5, the upper-middle-class occupations (UM) have been weighted twice as heavily as the lower-middle (LM); and in the other direction, the lower or unskilled working-class occupations (LW) have been weighted twice as heavily as the upper-working class (UW).

TABLE 11.5.   *Socioeconomic Ratios: United States and The Chicago Area*

Year	United States	Chicago SMSA*	Chicago Suburbs	Chicago City	Chicago City Whites	Blacks
1940	.66	.71	.77	.69	.75	.17
1950	.71	.77	.86	.73	.84	.18
1960	.80	.92	1.28	.69	.82	.25
1970	.99	.97	1.36	.66	.78	.33

* Standard Metropolitan Statistical Area.

Note on the Computation of the SER: This is a crude socioeconomic index, based on easily obtainable census data on occupations in the male labor force, aged 14 and over. The occupations are placed in four categories, as follows:
  A. Upper-Middle Class (UM):
       Professional, technical, and kindred
       Proprietors, managers, and officials
       Farm owners and managers (one-fifth of total)
  B. Lower-Middle Class (LM):
       Sales and clerical occupations
       Farm owners and managers (two-fifths of total)
  C. Upper-Working Class (UW):
       Foremen, craftsmen, and kindred
       Operatives and kindred
       Farm owners and managers (two-fifths of total)
  D. Lower-Working Class (LW):
       Service workers, including private household workers
       Laborers, including farm laborers

The reason for this is that UM is higher on the social scale than LM, while LW is lower than UW. To use the weights gives a more accurate indication of socioeconomic composition of a given geographical area or a given school. The ratio thus becomes (2 UM + LM) / (UW + 2 LW).

Looking at the socioeconomic ratio (SER) for the United States, we see that this ratio has been increasing since 1940, and especially since 1950. The numbers illustrate the fact that the proportion of white-collar jobs in the American economy is increasing while the proportion of blue-collar jobs is decreasing.

The SER for the total Chicago Metropolitan Area shows a similar increase. At the same time, it is clear that socioeconomic differentiation has been increasing between the central city and the suburbs. In 1940 the SER for the city of Chicago was only slightly below that of Chicago's metropolitan area. By 1950, the city SER had increased from .69 to .73, but the suburbs had increased from .77 to .86. Clearly, the central city was lagging, and the flight of middle-class people to the suburbs was in full course.

The decades after 1950 saw even greater changes. The city of Chicago decreased in SER from .73 to .66, while that of the suburbs jumped from .86 to 1.36. The average socioeconomic level of the central city was decreasing in the face of a country-wide increase, and especially in the face of a sharp increase in the Chicago suburbs.

Racial aspects of this phenomenon can also be seen in Table 11.5. While the SER of white males in the inner city moved from .75 to .78 between 1940 and 1970, the SER for nonwhites (almost all of whom were blacks) moved from .17 to .33. Since the proportions of nonwhites in Chicago had increased meanwhile from 8 percent in 1940 to 34 percent in 1970 (not shown in the table), it was the in-migration of nonwhites with relatively low SER (as compared to whites) that caused a substantial part of the growing differentiation between the city and the suburbs. Much the same trends have been true in other metropolitan areas of the United States.

EFFECTS OF NEIGHBORHOOD DIFFERENCES
ON THE SCHOOLS

As we have shown in earlier chapters of this book, the school achievement of pupils reflects differences in socioeconomic levels. For example, as reported in the survey of the public schools of Chicago (Havighurst, 1964), Table 11.6 shows how the elementary schools in Chicago's 21 school districts reflect the socioeconomic differences of the neighborhoods in which they are located. The measure of socioeconomic status is based upon median family income and median level of education of adults in the various school districts. While there are a number of exceptions, the average IQ for the school, the performance of first-graders on a reading readiness test, and the achievement level of sixth-graders in reading and arithmetic (as measured by a standardized achievement test) are related quite closely to the socioeconomic level of the families who live in the school district.

Differences in School Climates

A whole complex of relationships involving curriculum, student relations to teachers, relations between parents and teachers, and other aspects of the school climate also reflect differences between neighborhoods. The complex inner working of any school is affected by the neighborhood and by the types of children and parents the school serves.

In studying the elementary schools in the city of Chicago by means of interviews with teachers and principals and by observation of pupils, the staff of the Chicago School Survey (Havighurst, 1964) identified four types of schools:

1. "High-status schools," generally found in high-income areas, usually in neighborhoods at the edges of the city or in upper-middle-class suburbs.
2. "Main-line or conventional schools," usually located in areas where lower-middle-class families predominated.
3. "Common-man schools," located in areas where most of the families were stable working-class, both black and white.

237

4. "Inner-city schools," located in slum areas of low-income, high-transiency families, both black and white, where rates of delinquency were high.

TABLE 11.6   Socioeconomic Status, School Achievement, and Race by School Districts (Chicago, 1963)

Chicago (City) School Districts Ranked by Socioeconomic Status[a]	IQ	Percent of First-Grade Pupils Who Were Average or Above on Tests of Reading Readiness	Grade-Level Achievement of Sixth Grade in Reading and Arithmetic	Percent of Elementary Pupils Who Are Black
1	111	75	7.5	0
2	104	74	6.8	37
3	112	89	7.8	0
4	108	74	7.4	7
5	101	67	6.4	77
6	107	78	7.1	1
7	107	74	6.8	0
8[b]	95	48	5.8	85
9[c]	94	44	5.8	48
10	109	85	7.2	0
11	109	79	7.2	16
12	96	48	6.0	67
13	93	47	5.7	100
14	103	65	6.7	1
15	99	52	6.3	69
16	91	41	5.5	92
17	89	33	5.4	81
18	92	45	5.5	96
19	93	45	5.6	61
20	90	42	5.5	100
21	90	34	5.3	81
City wide	99	55	6.2	52

[a] The actual school district numbers are not shown here.
[b] This district contains the University of Chicago, where many children of higher socioeconomic status attend the University Laboratory School, a private school, and are thus not included in the public school population.
[c] This district includes the North Side "Gold Coast," where many children attend private schools.

Source: Havighurst, (1964), The Public Schools of Chicago, table 2, p. 39 (adapted).

The four types were distinguished from each other by the nature of the academic program in the school, the attitudes of parents and pupils toward the teachers, the nature of discipline in the school, and the teacher's concept of her role. For example the "high-status" schools were those in which teachers felt the total academic climate was rewarding to the teacher, and where they felt they were really teaching almost all the time. The "inner-city schools" were those in which teachers said an academic climate was lacking, where children's behavior was frequently unrewarding to the teacher, and where they often felt that they were "not teachers, but policemen."

The schools were readily distinguishable not only by staff members of the survey, but by teachers themselves. Doll (1971) found that Chicago teachers could decide relatively easily the type of school in which they worked by rating their school on ten different characteristics, two of which are shown below.

The ten characteristics referred to curriculum and texts (as in Item #1 in the chart); the teaching role; attitudes toward nonacademic duties expected of teachers; degree to which teaching emphasizes academics; student

Check the statement which applies to your school:

1. Curriculum is enriched with extra work. Texts one year or more above grade level can be used.	Curriculum is used as planned. Texts at grade level can be used.	Curriculum is altered downward. Difficulty in the use of grade level texts.	Curriculum does not fit students' needs. Texts one to two years below grade level must be used in many cases.
2. Climate of school set by academically oriented pupils. Children with discipline problems can be easily handled within framework of the school. Discipline problems are mild.	Children with discipline problems are seldom leaders of student behavior but can exert influence in some cases. Discipline problems can be handled within the framework of the school.	Children with discipline problems may be leaders for some students and they sometimes upset academic classroom situations. Majority of discipline problems can be handled within the framework of the school; a few cannot.	Children with discipline problems are influential in setting climate of the school. Many children with discipline problems require the help of outside agencies such as police or Family Service.

hostility; parents' attitudes toward school; students' and parents' respect for teachers; students' exposure to cultural experiences in their everyday lives; students' values; and school climate (as in Item #2).

The check marks made by teachers tended to fall consistently in one or another of the four columns. "High-status schools" were described most frequently by checkmarks in the first column; "conventional schools," in the second column; "common-man schools," in the third; and "inner-city schools," in the fourth. These relationships were not totally consistent, as might be anticipated, for the characteristics of any given school vary not only according to the socioeconomic level of the neighborhood, but also according to the manner in which the school principal sets the general tone of the school, and according to the relationships between individual teachers and between teachers and parents. Some "inner-city schools" were characterized by relatively high morale among teachers and by relatively infrequent discipline problems.

Socioeconomic Ratios in Various High Schools

In Figure 11.1 the social compositions of three general types of high schools are shown. School A is a typical high school in a town or small city which has only one high school; it therefore receives all the children of secondary school age. The high school population will not be distributed in the same way as the elementary school population in this community because some of the high school students drop out of school without graduating. Hence the SER is not .6, as it would be for the average elementary school, but instead is approximately 1.0.

School B is a high school in an upper-middle-class suburb, where there are very few working-class people. This type of school is sometimes called a "comprehensive" high school because it offers several curricula, including commercial and vocational courses, but it is not representative in the sense that its students represent a cross section of the American social structure.

School C is a high school where the SER is low, for the school serves a working-class area where there are no upper-middle and only a few lower-middle-class families. In such an area there may be a majority of lower-working-class residents, but since their children tend to drop out of school early, the composition of the high school shows a preponderance of pupils from upper-working-class homes.

There is probably a critical point in the SER of most big-city schools, a point at which middle-class parents are likely to become anxious and will consider removing their children from the school and moving to a higher-status area. This is not to imply that parents think in terms of the socioeconomic ratio itself; but rather that middle-class parents begin to fear the effects of the growing proportions of working-class students upon their own children. They may fear a drop in the academic standards of the school, or

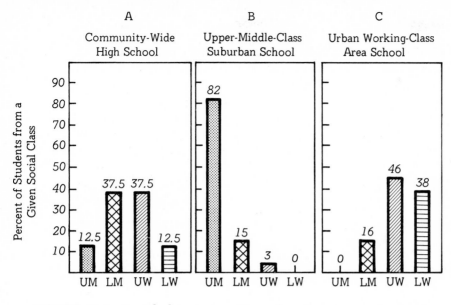

FIGURE 11.1   *Social class composition of various types of second-ary schools.*

changes in curricular offerings, or unwelcome influences upon their own children's motivations for school achievement.

It might be noted that such attitudes on the part of parents are not altogether unfounded. A study by Wilson (1959) supports the generalization that when student bodies vary in their proportions of middle and working class, students develop different educational and vocational aspirations. The study showed that in predominantly lower-status schools, *higher*-status children have lower educational and occupational aspirations than in predominantly higher-status schools, and in predominantly higher-status schools, *lower*-status children have higher aspirations than in predominantly lower-status schools. Wilson says, "The *de facto* segregation brought about by concentrations of social classes in cities results in schools with unequal moral climates which likewise affect the motivation of the child . . . by providing a different ethos in which to perceive values" (Wilson, 1959, p. 845).

The point at which a school becomes undesirable in the eyes of middle-class parents (the critical point in the SER) is subjective, depending upon the attitudes and experience of a particular parent, and depending also upon such factors as the tradition of the school, the racial composition of the school, the type of curriculum, and the quality of the teachers. However, there seems to be relative consensus among middle-class parents on the question of when a school has become a "poor" school and when they begin to move out of the school district.

A High School in a Rapidly Changing Area

An example of what happens when the SER reaches the critical point is seen in the case of Benjamin Franklin High School, located in a large city.

Franklin High School is situated in what was formerly a middle and upper-class area, some six miles from the center of the city. In 1910 this was the school with the best academic record in the city, sending a high proportion of its graduates to college, and winning most of the prizes for academic excellence on the part of its students. The school's SER in 1910 was probably about 1.5.

Between the two world wars many of the upper-class people moved out to the suburbs, and some of the upper-middle-class residents took over the old upper-class mansions, while other upper-middles moved to a high school district farther from the center of the city. Several areas of middle-class houses deteriorated, and some of the old, large apartment buildings were "converted" into small, low-rent apartments. A considerable number of working-class people moved in. On one edge of the high school district an area of old apartment buildings was turned over to black occupancy after the apartments had been "converted." By the beginning of World War II the SER of Franklin High was about .80.

Immediately after World War II, there was a further influx of working-class blacks into the formerly middle-class area, although there were also some new apartments, and some well-to-do blacks who began to buy the old upper-class mansions. The SER of Franklin High gradually dropped to .60 by 1955. With a large rate of dropouts of working-class pupils in the ninth and tenth grades, this meant that the SER of the ninth grade was .35, while that of the twelfth grade was 1.5. The SER for the ninth grade was well below the critical point for middle-class parents, and they began to move away from the area when their children were ready to enter high school.

At about this time the community sensed that a crisis had occurred. An organization was formed by the middle-class people in the district whose goals were "community conservation" and urban renewal. With the aid of government funds, deteriorated houses were torn down and replaced by middle-class houses. The high school was reorganized on the basis of a multi-track program, with the upper track consisting of college-going (and largely middle-class) pupils, thus achieving a high SER for this subgroup. These measures partially stemmed the outflow of middle-class families, and brought some new middle-class families with young children into the area.

URBAN RENEWAL

During the 1950s the civic ills accompanying metropolitan growth led to social action called urban renewal, which is the fifth stage of metropolitan development. At its minimum, urban renewal consists of tearing down the worst of the slums and building large blocks of public housing for low-income families. Beyond that minimum, urban renewal consists of planning the growth of metropolitan areas from the center out to the suburbs, with parks, shopping centers, libraries, churches, and schools organized to serve people where they live; and with industry, the central business district, and the centers of residence linked by fast, comfortable transportation, public and private. Billions of dollars are now being spent on bold new physical structures for shopping plazas, garden villages, high-rise apartment housing, and expressways.

As already mentioned, more than two-thirds of American children go to school in metropolitan areas, and two-thirds of all teachers work in these schools, schools which can hardly be insulated from the momentous events just mentioned. In fact, organization of school systems and the programs of schools are likely to be determining factors in the forms which urban renewal takes.

By 1965 many of the worst slums had been cut out of the major American cities. A slum section of over 400 acres in St. Louis was cleared. Much of Boston's oldest housing was torn out to make room for expressways. Hundreds of acres of tenement houses were torn down on Chicago's South Side, on New York's Lower East Side, and in the area in Washington south of the Capitol. Los Angeles cleared the area on which the new Civic Center was built. The Golden Triangle of Pittsburgh was modernized with new office buildings, hotels, and expressways.

Not only are slums cleared; a major aspect of urban renewal is the attempt to arrest and reverse the process of decay of the city center. This means the building of a second generation of ultramodern skyscrapers to take the place of those erected in the early 1900s. It also means the building of expressways to provide easy automobile transportation for commuters who do not use old-fashioned public transit services. Furthermore, there must be new and attractive apartment housing within walking or taxi distance of the downtown offices and stores for those people who have the money and the inclination to live in upper or middle-class style without going out to the suburbs or the city fringes.

Meanwhile the federal government has continued to award large sums of money to what is now called "Housing and Urban Development." An Act of 1965 provided a variety of aids for housing, including substantial numbers of new low-rent public housing units, rent supplements to aid low-income families to secure better private housing, and subsidized low interest rates for housing for people of moderate income. At the same time there is substantial money for the improvement of metropolitan areas through the purchase of land for recreational, conservation, and other public uses, and for the construction of community centers, health stations, and water and sewer facilities.

Housing and Urban Development programs have been focused on the entire metropolitan area, so as to relate the central city more efficiently to its suburbs. This policy was foreshadowed by Robert C. Weaver, the first Secretary of Housing and Urban Development. Before joining President Johnson's Cabinet, he wrote:

> I am not impressed by those who prophesy the demise of cities. I am convinced that the recent decline in the population of central cities has been due, in large part, to the concentration of new construction in the suburbs and the scarcity of competing living facilities in the central cities.
>
> The city today is, or should be in my opinion, the heart, and in a sense the soul, of a metropolitan area. The suburbs around it, to a large degree, draw their life and their spirit from the city's economy and culture. The city should be revitalized as the anchor holding together our metropolitan areas. It does not perform this function effectively today. (Weaver, 1964)

MOVEMENT TOWARD METROPOLITAN COOPERATION AND GOVERNMENT

Most of the 243 metropolitan areas of the country contain, in addition to the large city, many small towns and villages with their own governments. The average number of local governments per SMSA in 1967 was 91. This situation grew up historically, and it still maintains some advantages for some of the outlying communities. But the growth of suburbs and the growing interdependence of suburbs and central city have produced more and more cooperation among governmental units, as well as some consolidation of smaller units aimed at simplifying the governmental structure of the metropolitan area. Creation of a single government for an entire metropolitan area is being discussed as possibly a desirable solution of problems of metropolitan fragmentation.

The one-government or metro-government approach is already appearing. Nashville and Davidson County, Tennessee combined their city and county governments into a single county-wide unit in 1962. The school districts were also combined into a single county-wide school system. Jacksonville, Florida and its surrounding Duval County merged in 1967 into a single government and a single school system.

A "federation plan" was adopted in Toronto, Canada, in 1954, where the area-wide government includes thirteen municipalities. There is a metropolitan school board which provides school sites and buildings and makes equitable per-pupil payments to the six locally elected school boards. The six school boards operate the elementary and secondary schools.

Educational Programs and Metropolitan Development

It now appears that a number of metropolitan areas are ready for fundamental programs of urban renewal which will involve substantial cooperation between school systems within the area. Certain educational functions, such as educational television, special schools for handicapped children, and community colleges may be paid for by the entire area, or by combination of school districts. Several large cities have already joined with suburbs to form a single area-wide school district, such as Nashville-Davidson County, Tennessee; Miami-Dade County, Florida; and Las Vegas-Clark County, Nevada. In a number of other metropolitan areas active consideration is being given to cooperative programs involving central city and suburban school districts.

On the other hand, as will be noted in some detail in the next chapter, there is an opposite tendency. Some of the larger city school districts are splitting up into smaller autonomous districts as a means of increasing local community control of the local schools.

Financing of Metropolitan Schools

A glaring weakness of the educational structure in most metropolitan areas is the inequality of financial support for schools between the central city, on the one hand, and the wealthy suburbs, on the other hand. Where public schools are paid for mainly by local property taxes, it happens that some wealthy suburbs have twice as much taxable property for each pupil as does the central city. Thus one district may support its schools with $1000 or $1200 per pupil, while a neighboring district in the same metropolitan area, although it taxes its property owners at a higher rate, still provides only $700 per pupil. This is obviously unjust, and produces great inequalities in education.

One solution is for the state to take over more of the financial responsibility for public education, and to pay 50 percent or more of the school bill, paying a single rate per pupil to all districts. Some recent court cases have resulted in judicial decisions along these lines, and they seem to be moving toward a rule that the entire public school bill, or nearly all of it, should be paid from state rather than local funds. This will probably tax the people of the state at equal rates, no matter where they live.

Another solution of this problem is to combine the school districts of a metropolitan area into a single district for financing, but allowing differences of administration and program in different local communities. An important instance is that of Richmond, Virginia, where the courts have ordered the city and county school districts to combine for the purpose of equalizing financial support and also for securing racially integrated schools. At this writing (1974) the Richmond case, and several similar ones, are moving toward the U.S. Supreme Court for a final settlement of this issue.

This chapter has been concerned with metropolitan areas rather than the central city of the metropolitan area. But the most pressing school problems are in the central cities, which will be considered in the next chapter.

EXERCISES

1. Trace the history of the standard metropolitan area you know best. In which of the five stages is it?

2. Compute the SER of a school that you know. In which direction is the ratio moving? What do you predict will be the SER of this school five years from now?

3. How are the schools governed in the metropolitan area you know best? What problems do you see ahead in educational policy for this area?

4. Describe the steps being taken for urban renewal in a metropolitan area, and discuss the relations you think the schools should have to urban renewal in this area.

5. Write a paper on the various planning agencies that exist in your SMSA with special emphasis on educational planning and its relation to the government planning.

6. Write a report on public housing in your area and discuss its contribution to making the area a more or less desirable place to live.

7. If you live in a city of less than 50,000, study it and its county as an example of tension between urban and rural styles of life. How do the schools fit in? Do they tend to work toward urbanization?

SUGGESTIONS FOR FURTHER READING

1. There are a number of recent books dealing with the growth of metropolitanism and the problems of the city. A general discussion can be found in *The Exploding Metropolis* by the Editors of *Fortune*, which was published as a paperback. The book by Bollens and Schmandt, *The Metropolis,* is particularly relevant, as is also *The Anatomy of a Metropolis* by Hoover and Vernon, and *The City is the Frontier,* by Abrams. The book, *Metropolis, 1985* by Raymond Vernon is one of a series describing the New York Metropolitan Region Study. Jean Gottmann's *Megalopolis* gives a striking account of metropolitan development in the chain of urban areas that stretches from Boston to Washington, D.C.

2. An interesting set of readings about suburban life will be found in *The Suburban Community* edited by William Dobriner. Compare this book with *The Exurbanites* by Auguste C. Spectorsky.

3. For a general consideration of metropolitan aspects of educational systems, see the two volumes edited by Troy V. McKelvey, entitled *Metropolitan School Organization*. These volumes and the Yearbook of the National Society for the Study of Education entitled *Metropolitanism: Its Challenge to Education* argue for the establishment of a single educational authority for a metropolitan area.

4. A thorough treatment of the problems of financing public schools in large cities is to be found in the book by Seymour Sacks entitled *City Schools/Suburban Schools: A History of Fiscal Conflict.* Sacks and several colleagues at Syracuse University analyzed the financial systems for 37 of the largest American cities in relation to their support of education.

5. The American metropolis is rather different in its history and structure from the great cities of other parts of the world. To see the range in types of cities, the following books are useful: *The Urban Community: A World Perspective* by Nels Anderson; *The City* by Rose Hum Lee; *Images of the City* by Anselm L. Strauss: and *The City in History* by Lewis Mumford.

CHAPTER 12

Local Community Control
and Administrative
Decentralization in
Big-City School Systems

As the metropolitan areas have increased in size and population, their central cities have generally experienced a lowering of per capita income and socioeconomic status in relation to the area as a whole. Moreover, the central city is structured residentially by socioeconomic status as well as by race and ethnicity. Therefore the elementary schools and even high schools tend toward a *de facto* segregation. This has been documented in Chapter 12.

This process of racial and socioeconomic segregation was not seen as inevitable in 1960. At that time it appeared possible to work out attendance areas for individual schools that would produce a fair degree of integration. Under the pressure of the 1954 Supreme Court decision on racial integration in the schools, the northern, western, and border state cities worked to integrate as many of their schools as possible. These developments are described in Chapters 15 and 16.

However, it became clear by 1965 that economic and ethnic segregation was increasing, rather than decreasing, and that the process of segregation was out of control in big-city schools. The policy of integration was then supplemented by a drive for *compensatory education*, which was aimed at helping economically disadvantaged children to achieve better in school through remedial teaching, smaller class size, preschool teaching, and improved school facilities. But we have seen in Chapter 6 that Head Start and other compensatory measures produced only limited and unsatisfactory gains in school achievement.

ACHIEVEMENT OF PUPILS IN THE PUBLIC
SCHOOLS IN THE BIG CITIES

Most of the big-city school systems gave standardized tests of reading and arithmetic achievement to their pupils, and compared their scores with the national averages. The results of these testing programs were made public, at first for the school system as a whole. These results showed a sharp decrease in achievement scores after 1960. Up to that date, most city school systems had shown test results approximating the national averages for all youth. Then the scores dropped steadily, year after year, until the averages for most large cities were about at the 40th percentile on the national scale. That is, the average pupil in the big-city school system scored below 60 percent of pupils in the nation, instead of below 50 percent, as had been true in 1960. These facts were published in the newspapers, along with facts about the growing proportions of black and Spanish-surname pupils. Then, as public pressure for more information mounted, the school systems released the test results for individual schools, together with data on the proportion of black and white students in each school; or proportions of black, non-Spanish white, Spanish surname, and other ethnic groups. Such data were generally being published by 1965. All this time, the proportions of white students were decreasing, and the proportion of middle-class white students were decreasing even more, though these data on socioeconomic status were not generally published in the news media.

Even though the school systems began to receive substantial federal funds under Title I of the Elementary and Secondary Education Act to improve the work of the schools in low-income neighborhoods, there was not much improvement in test scores. The ESEA funds paid for a great deal of experimentation, as well as for reduced class size and for more remedial teaching, between 1965 and 1970, but the results were generally disappointing in terms of the hoped-for improvement of pupils' performance on tests of reading and arithmetic.

Sources of the Problem

In the discussion and analysis of the problem of low school achievement in the big cities, there were two basically different views which gave rise to different policies for solution of the problem.

Source is the Home.   One view held that the parents were primarily responsible for the poor or good performance of their children. If they read to their children, conversed with them in a wide-ranging vocabulary, supported the teacher in the matter of homework, and set an example of orderly and self-controlled behavior, their children would do well in school. On the other hand, if the family did not read, nor have books and educational equipment at home; if there was no father-person to give discipline and to serve as a model for boys; if the work habits of the adults were irregular; and if there was much aggressive and uncontrolled behavior tolerated in the family, the children would do poorly in school. Since a wide range of research studies showed that family socioeconomic status was more highly correlated with pupils' school achievement than anything else in the pupil's experience, it was natural to argue that changes in the home and family experience of the pupil were necessary for much improvement in his school achievement. Then, when remedial work in school, smaller classes, and other methods did not produce much improvement, this reenforced the tendency to place the responsibility on the home.

It was natural for school teachers and for middle-class people in general to take this general position, and therefore to argue that the schools are doing all they can for such children, or that the schools should focus on preschool work and involve the mothers of the children and teach them to help their children more effectively.

School is the Source.   A second view is that the school is to blame for the poor academic achievement of low-income children. It is claimed that school teachers, mostly middle-class persons, do not understand these children, and therefore cannot teach them effectively. It is charged that school teachers expect most minority group children to do poorly, hence they do not set high standards for them. There appears to be a widespread view among nonacademic people that all children are pretty much alike at the age of five or six, and all can learn what the school teaches if the school is doing its job.

The Rational and Informed Answer.   Anyone who has attempted to make an objective study of the situation knows that neither of these two answers is adequate, though there is some truth in both of them. There is no sound reason to doubt that many low-income families, though not all of them, do not give their children adequate help and support for school achievement. The parents simply do not know how to help their children in this connection. On the other hand, many teachers lack understanding of children and youth from low-income families, and do not know how to work with them. The appropriate thing is to make careful studies of a variety of procedures to help low-income parents do a better job with their children, and to study a variety of school programs aimed at helping socially disadvantaged pupils.

Roles Taken by Persons Facing This Problem

These procedures require time and patience, but the situation seemed to demand immediate action, and the action that was generally adopted did not provide for time or patience. The action was some combination of local community control and administrative decentralization. The people involved as leaders in the action can be identified by one or another of the following seven roles: (Each one speaks for himself in the following paragraphs.)

1. The Low-income and minority group parent.   *My children are not learning much in school. They do not like school. When I visit school, the teachers and the principal don't pay any attention to me. Even if I speak English they don't seem to understand me. I wish we had teachers that I could talk to. I could tell them how to make it a better school.*
2. The radical individualist.   *There are too many rules and too much bureaucracy in large-scale organizations. The schools are bogged down. They cannot individualize their instruction. They tend to stereotype pupils according to ethnicity and social status. The system tends to become top-heavy with highly paid administrators. We need to break up the bureaucracy and to restore power to the people.*
3. The sociologist antibureaucrat.   *A rational social structure can be developed by people who share common interests in a relatively small geographical area. The smallness of the community area simplifies this task. Also, their relative socioeconomic homogeneity makes it easier for them to make policy decisions. They do not have to take account of the educational needs and goals of other socioeconomic groups. Big institutions, big cities, big bureaucracies are bad. Smallness is an advantage.*
4. The separatist leader.   *This is a racist city, dominated by white racists. They will exploit minority groups as long as they can get away with it. We minority groups need time to build our own power bases in our own neighborhoods, and that means we need to control the schools in our neighborhoods. We need members of our group as teachers and administrators, just as we need business and political leaders. We need to build confidence and pride in our own group ability. Later on, when we have consolidated our power, we will deal with the white oligarchy from a position of power, and work toward integration on equal and democratic terms.*
5. The middle-class political leader.   *The educational situation is obviously bad. There is much dissatisfaction in the city. The present administration has lost the confidence of the public. We need administrative reorganization which will bring decision-making closer to the local communities. At the same time, we need to have a central authority in the Board of Education or in the Mayor's office which coordinates the complex interdependent activities of the local schools and fits in with responsible future planning for the city and the metropolitan area.*
6. The liberal political scientist—sociologist—educational scientist.   *The contemporary highly productive economy is involved in major socio-political changes which require a thorough and basic institutional reorganization in order to achieve democratic goals in the coming social and economic situation of 1985. The educational system has major importance, and should be organized or reorganized to assist in the broad social metropolitanization of the society, in such ways as to aid in the achievement of democratic social goals.*
7. The teachers' union leader.   *Teachers are best able to serve the community*

251

by maintaining a powerful collectivity which is motivated by professional ethics and goals and provides a base for a satisfactory career. We must have a strong system-wide union with strong chapters in every school. We must work for civil liberties for the economically disadvantaged people. We must work for better schools and a better financial base for schools. We must protect the jobs of teachers against unfair pressures and discrimination. We must keep the career line open for teachers to transfer from school to school in line with their own interests and abilities.

The Practical Alternatives

It is not difficult to discover people active in these roles in every large city. They seek to influence the educational system in the direction their roles suggest. As a result there emerge three broad policy-program alternatives which compete for popular support and for support by decision-making bodies—city boards of education, state legislatures, and the school administrators and teachers organizations. These three policies are not completely distinct. They overlap enough to allow for compromise solutions of the problem.

A.   Local Community Control and Responsibility for the Schools.   This position was taken by leaders of disadvantaged minority groups, even though some of them had hoped that schools would be integrated, and that minority group children would benefit from such programs. But, as it became clear about 1965 that racial or ethnic integration would not come soon to the big cities, they turned to the position that minority children could profit better from schools that were controlled and directed and largely staffed by members of the minority groups. Such schools could work directly to meet the needs of the minority group. Furthermore, parents would be treated with more consideration by the school teachers and administrators.

B.   Administrative Decentralization in Large School Systems.   This position was taken by a number of vocal and influential people who disliked the bureaucracy of large organizations, including school systems. They pointed to examples where individual pupils and teachers and school principals could not get thoroughly reasonable things done because of the "red tape" of an overgrown bureaucracy of clerks and assistant administrators, enmeshed in an enormous bundle of rules and regulations. For example, a high school senior spent four months trying to get out of a mathematics course for which he had been incorrectly scheduled. He had gone to four different persons, each of whom told him that the power to change his schedule lay elsewhere. Finally, he simply avoided the class and took a failure, which prevented him from getting a college-entrance diploma. Again, a principal tried fruitlessly for a whole semester to get the central supply office to take back a set of expensive books on art history and to give him in return a potter's wheel and some photographic equipment. There was no regulation that permitted this kind of transaction.

Several major studies of administration of school systems came out with the recommendation that a big school system should be broken into smaller systems, each with a maximum of autonomy. Each might have its own superintendent, and its own school board. The power to make decisions should be placed in the local neighborhood school, if possible, or in a district office covering 10 or 20 schools. A central board of education should have only general oversight, and possibly the function of allocating money equitably, and of employing and transfering teachers for the entire system. It was argued that decentralization into smaller administrative units would bring the schools closer to the local communities, and encourage them to develop programs needed by the local community. This position had several variations, ranging from a single central education authority which delegated decision-making powers to districts and individual schools under its authority, to a number of practically autonomous district education authorities. In the latter event, it would be rather similar to the Local Community Control position.

C. Reformation of the Present System.   This would reduce the bureaucracy, and delegate the power to make decisions to the "proper" levels in the system while conducting a continuous research program to evaluate all aspects of the school system. This is likely to appear to be a conservative and defensive position on the part of the Establishment. To make it function there must be an effective research and development program in the school system, which has the confidence of the community and of the school system personnel.

Attempted Solutions, 1965–1975

Local community control and administrative decentralization have both been tried out in one form or another in several of the big cities since 1965, with results which are not yet clearly understood. Mistakes have been made, and the administration of public school systems may profit from those mistakes.

The outstanding case is that of New York City, where local community control and administrative decentralization were both tried. They were jumbled together, more through accident than through planning. The local community control experiment in New York preceded the administrative decentralization process. The two will be described separately.

THE OCEAN HILL–BROWNSVILLE CASE

This particular case, located in New York City, caused a series of teacher strikes lasting almost two months in the autumn of 1968. People in all of the roles just mentioned were involved. The case is amply documented. A book has been written on it by Martin Mayer, a journalist, resident in New York, and for five years chairman of a local school advisory board which preceded the present system of community school districts. Mayer introduces his account by saying: "The teacher strikes of 1968 seem to me the worst disaster my native city has experienced in my lifetime. . . . What happened in New York in the fall of 1968 was not inevitable, and those who are saying that it was—especially those in the great foundations and in the Mayor's office—are much more to be blamed for what happened than any of the participants. . . . At no point did these forces demonstrate any understanding of what was happening in terms other than their own preconceptions, and at no point did they exert the authority, leadership, or even influence which their status and social roles obligated them to exert." Mayer blames leaders for making mistakes which might have been avoided. Others see the conflicts as inevitable.

The New York City effort at decentralization has a long history. For many years the New York City Board of Education maintained a set of Advisory Boards for districts of the city, some 30 in all. The members of these boards were appointed by the City Board of Education. The boards were intended to facilitate communication between the local communities and the central Board of Education. Most of these boards were relatively inactive, though a few of them, at one time or another, had been active in relating the schools to the needs of the local district.

For several years, the New York City Schools had been taking vigorous action in favor of racial integration. A policy of open enrollment with free transportation of pupils out of segregated neighborhoods to integrated schools, together with the pairing of schools with largely black and largely white attendance, had been in force. But the influx of black and Puerto Rican immigrants and the outflow of white middle-class population defeated these measures. By 1970 the New York Public Schools had 34 percent black students and 25 percent students of Puerto Rican or Spanish origin. Two of the five boroughs of New York City, Queens and Staten Island, remained predominantly white and non-Spanish, thus leaving the other three boroughs—Manhattan, the Bronx, and Brooklyn—with large minorities of white and non-Spanish students.

In 1961 the State Legislature ordered the New York City Board of Education to revitalize its system of 30 local advisory school boards. Several of them became active in the early 1960s, working to improve the schools in their own districts. Local groups became active, each working on its own local situation.

There were two local groups working for improvement in the Ocean Hill area—a slum area between Brownsville and Bedford-Stuyvesant in Brooklyn. This area had a population that was 70 percent Negro and 25 percent Puerto Rican. In 1966, the United Federation of Teachers started a teacher-parent joint action program that used picketing and other demonstrations to secure the removal of an unpopular school principal and the provision of some special services from the Board of Education for the local schools. Meanwhile, a group of social workers and parents affiliated with Brooklyn CORE (Congress of Racial Equality), aided by a white worker priest, Father John Powis of the Church of Our Lady of the Presentation, formed an unofficial "people's board of education" for the Ocean Hill area. These two groups came together and secured a grant of $44,000 from the Ford Foundation in the summer of 1967 to pay the costs of a "demonstration district" to include two junior high schools and six elementary schools in the Ocean Hill–Brownsville area. The Ford Foundation made grants to two other local groups to aid them in exploring the possibilities of local community action in the school system. These were in the Two Bridges area of the Lower East Side of Manhattan, and the area in East Harlem served by Intermediate School 201.

The Ocean Hill group formed a "planning council" consisting of several teachers in the local schools and parents active in the "people's board of education." Their first action was to employ a Unit Administrator, who would be paid by the Board of Education to administer the demonstration unit of eight schools. They worked hard at this during the summer of 1967, with Father Powis and a black activist teacher, Herman Ferguson, helping them. Since it was summer vacation, the teacher delegates were seldom present at meetings, and the planning group went ahead to employ as administrator, Mr. Rhody McCoy, a black schoolman who was acting principal of a school for disturbed boys in Manhattan. A plan was drawn up to elect a Governing Board of 24, one parent and one teacher from each of the eight schools, five community representatives to be chosen by the parent members of the board, two representatives chosen by school supervisors in the district, and one delegate from a university to be chosen by the board as a whole. The council advertised an election for August 3, and set up ballot boxes in the schools. The voting was light, and for two more days members of the council collected votes by calling on parents. Eventually, about a quarter of the parents voted. The elected parent representatives were all mothers, and several were on welfare. They named five community leaders to the board, including Father Powis, Assemblyman Samuel D. Wright, who was a lawyer and representative of the district in the State Legislature, and Rev. C. Herbert Oliver, a black pastor of the Westminster Bethany Presbyterian Church, recently arrived from Alabama.

One of Rhody McCoy's first acts as administrator was to authorize checks for sums of $39 to $100 a week for 17 mothers of school children, most of whom were candidates for parent positions on the local board. Seven of the 17 were winners, and their pay continued as "parent representative" until February, 1968, during which time they received $15,000 from the Ford Foundation grants. These payments were made through Father Powis's church, which acted as fiscal agent for the grant, and there was no public announcement of them. Rev. Oliver was chosen chairman over Assemblyman Wright. Four of the principals asked to be transferred out of the district, and a fifth vacancy was created by the opening of a new Intermediate School. McCoy proposed and the new Board approved the appointment of five men to fill the vacancies. Only one of the five was on the city school system's list of persons who had passed examinations for the principalship. This list contained several hundred names, with only four blacks. Two of the five new principals were black, one was Puerto Rican, and one was Chinese. Those whose names were not on the civil service list were given the title of "Demonstration Elementary School Principal" which could be assigned to anyone without a licensing examination, temporarily.

This was the first of many actions of Rhody McCoy or his Governing Board that had doubtful legality. The New York City Board of Education did not state just what the powers of the Governing Board or the Unit Administrator were, but simply accepted their recommendations, at first, though later the City Board refused to approve some of the actions of the district Governing Board. All but one of the new principals won approval from the teachers, parents, and other administrators with whom they worked. Nevertheless, the Council of Supervisory Associations (a kind of union consisting of principals, assistant principals, bureau chiefs, and other supervisors) instigated a lawsuit to oust the new Ocean Hill principals as illegally appointed. The Council was joined in this lawsuit by the teachers' union, even though it had generally opposed the Supervisory Associations.

The teachers' union, which had originally favored the Ocean Hill experiment and helped to set it up, had changed its position by the fall of 1967, and forbade union teachers to become members of the Governing Board. The reason for this was that the parent and community members of the board tended to be critical of at least some of the teachers, and made them feel uncomfortable in board meetings. It was becoming clear that the governing board would soon move to replace those teachers against whom there was hostility from parents or pupils.

Also, in November, all 18 of the district's assistant principals applied for transfers, claiming that some of them had been harassed (by anti-Semitic insults, among other things) and that McCoy was not supporting them. This meant that all the schools had to be staffed with new assistant principals, some of them inexperienced. The result of these changes, surrounded with uncertainties about the power and responsibilities of the various persons and groups involved in the experiment, was internal chaos in most of the schools.

People in all the diverse roles mentioned earlier involved themselves in Ocean Hill-Brownsville, and the situation was so complex and ambiguous that there were no general rules or general authority that might have enabled competing interests to state their positions in an orderly democratic procedure.

The New York City Board of Education had not spelled out the powers of the Ocean Hill Governing Board. Thus, although this was technically a case of delegation of administrative authority which was retained by the City

Board, the Ocean Hill Board took the position of local community control and defied the New York City Board of Education at times.

Summary of Events in Ocean
Hill–Brownsville, 1967–69

The Governing Board that was elected in 1967 functioned through the following three years, without teachers' union representation, since the teachers' union forbade its members from serving on the board. The first few months under the Governing Board were taken up with efforts to get the schools to operate smoothly, with new principals and acting principals. Progress was being made, and a number of new programs of compensatory education were started. Then, in April of 1968, there were setbacks. The assassination of Martin Luther King enhanced hostility toward white teachers. A fire in the new intermediate school one afternoon forced the children out of the building for two hours, after which they swarmed back, without adequate supervision by teachers, and produced a minor riot. There was criticism of some teachers who had gone home instead of staying to maintain order. About this time, the Governing Board became more aggressive, though a minority led by Assemblyman Wright urged patience and conciliation. The majority of the governing board recommended "the removal from our district" of 13 teachers, five assistant principals, and the one surviving preproject principal. This started a confusing train of events, in which the Governing Board insisted on its right to discharge personnel, without formally bringing charges against them. Eventually, the teachers' union called out all teachers in the demonstration district, and some 350 of the 500 teachers were out on strike for the last month of the school year.

During the summer of 1968 efforts were made by Mayor Lindsay, by State Commissioner of Education James Allen, by the City Board of Education, by the Ford Foundation, and by the Ocean Hill–Brownsville Governing Board to settle the dispute over the removal of the 10 teachers. (Of the original 13, one was reinstated by the governing board, and two accepted transfers out of the district.) The Board of Education appointed a retired black judge, Francis Rivers, to examine charges which McCoy had agreed to bring against the teachers. On August 26, Judge Rivers found the charges inadequate and denied McCoy the right to transfer out any of the 10 teachers. The Ocean Hill Governing Board voted not to accept Judge Rivers' findings, and also not to reinstate about 100 teachers who had struck against the district the preceding May–June.

Accordingly, the United Federation of Teachers responded with a citywide strike, and nearly 54,000 of the city's 57,000 teachers stayed out on the opening day of school in September. After two days of negotiation, the Board of Education signed an agreement with the union that sent the teachers back to the schools. But the union teachers in Ocean Hill were systematically

threatened at a teachers meeting by community residents of Ocean Hill, including about 50 men, some wearing helmets and carrying sticks. In some
schools the teachers were given police protection, but not allowed to teach.
A second and a third strike were called, altogether keeping the schools of the
city effectively closed for two months.

Finally, the State Department of Education, the State Board of Regents,
and Mayor Lindsay settled the strike and started the schools going again in
mid-November by placing the Ocean Hill–Brownsville district under the direct
supervision of the State Department of Education, while a State Supervisory
Commission would maintain the rights of the teachers in the local schools.

The Ocean Hill schools gradually settled down, with the governing
board headed by Rev. Oliver continuing to function, with some turnover of
principals and teachers, until 1970.

The growing hostility between the local community control people and
the United Teachers Federation resulted in a deep division within the groups
that had originally been united in favor of racial integration and liberal socio-
political policies. This was illustrated by the action of the New York Civil
Liberties Union in publishing a report on October 9, 1968, in the midst of the
teachers' strike, attacking the teachers' union and arguing that the teachers'
union and other groups had brought on the chaos of Ocean Hill by efforts to
undermine local community control of the schools. The New York Civil
Liberties Union is a strong local branch of the American Civil Liberties Union,
but does not speak for the national organization on the issue of local community control. The New York branch report was entitled *The Burden of
Blame: A Report on the Ocean Hill–Brownsville Controversy.* This was foreshadowed by an article by the journalist Nat Hentoff in *the village VOICE* on
September 26, entitled *Ad hoc Committee on Confusion* which attacked a
group of socialist leaders for their advertisement in the *New York Times* in
support of the teachers' strike. Hentoff was one of the leaders of the New York
Civil Liberties Union who favored local community control. Answering
Hentoff also in *the village VOICE* for October 3, 1968, Michael Harrington,
National Chairman of the Socialist Party, USA, said, "I am for opening up
new channels of innovation and popular participation. But there can be no
decentralization in New York City based on breaking the union; there can be
no decentralization based on vigilante control of the schools; there can be no
effective decentralization apart from a long-range program to end the slums."

The *Burden of Blame* created a controversy in the New York Civil
Liberties Union. According to a report by Clark Whelton, published in *the
village VOICE* on March 27, 1969, members who dissented from the *Burden
of Blame* piece attempted to call a special membership meeting to censure the
board of directors for its action with respect to the school strike. This was
not allowed, but the board of directors did hold a public forum, attended by
1,000 people, where speakers argued for and against the actions of the New
York Civil Liberties Union in taking sides on what the critics called a

"political" rather than a "civil liberties" issue. An informal ballot taken as people left the meeting showed 411 in favor and 115 opposed to the *Burden of Blame* stand. It was said that scores of resignations from the Civil Liberties Union had been received, principally from members of the teachers' union.

Furthermore, there were some background factors in the New York situation that heightened the controversy. The most important of these factors was the ethnic composition of the teaching and administrative staff. Less than 10 percent of the New York City teachers in 1967 were black or Puerto Rican, and the principals were almost entirely white and non-Spanish. Furthermore, the large numbers of teachers who had passed examinations for principal or assistant principal and were on the eligible list for promotion were mainly white and non-Spanish. There were to be no new examinations which would give opportunity to members of minority groups until 1972. And the teaching and administrative staff were mainly Jewish, with a substantial minority of Irish and Italian. Thus any move for basic change in school personnel was bound to have racist overtones. The local community Governing Board would almost surely move to bring some minority group teachers into the schools, and this would mean removing white teachers. Actually, the 10 teachers whom the Governing Board tried to discharge in the autumn of 1968 were all Jewish, and two of them were UFT chapter chairmen. An extreme black separatist and activist was employed as a teacher in the Ocean Hill junior high school where he taught a course in Afro-American studies. Over the radio, during the worst tension, he read the following poem, which he dedicated to Albert Shanker, head of the union.

"Hey, Jew boy, with that yarmulka on your head
You pale-faced Jew boy—I wish you were dead."

On the day after the assassination of Martin Luther King, the black principal of the junior high school called an assembly, and in his opening remarks he said that the white teachers might leave, if they wished; they remained. Two members of the local Governing Board spoke as did the forementioned teacher, who was vice-president of the African-American Teachers Association. He is reported to have told the pupils:

"Brothers and sisters, you have to stop fighting among yourselves. . . . You've got to get your minds together. . . . If you steal, steal from those who have it—stop fighting among yourselves."

Following the assembly there were a number of acts of violence. A young white woman teacher was attacked by students who punched her, tore her hair, and ripped her dress. A white male teacher was knocked unconscious and had to be taken to the hospital. (Goldbloom, p. 53.)

DECENTRALIZATION OF NEW YORK
CITY SCHOOLS

While the Ocean Hill–Brownsville case was going on, Mayor Lindsay of New York City appointed a commission to study the school situation and to propose a plan for decentralization. This was an important move toward school reform on the part of the liberal Establishment. The mayor was liberal and the Ford Foundation was a supporter of liberal reforms. This Commission reported in November, 1967. Its report, entitled *Reconnection for Learning,* recommended the formation of between 30 and 60 autonomous, elected school boards, to work with only limited control by the central city board. *The New York Times* welcomed this report with an editorial which said, among other things:

> In a report whose broad principles we strongly endorse, the Bundy panel on decentralization of the city school system calls for an almost total shift of administrative power from the central Board of Education to largely independent community school boards.
>
> If this proposal is radical, it is justified by the fact that the situation is desperate. If the cure is drastic, it is necessary because a long succession of moderate reform efforts has failed to halt the deterioration of New York City's gigantic school system. . . .
>
> The Bundy panel has presented a valid alternative to New York City's continued educational crisis and decline. The *status quo* has been given its chance—and has failed the test of the classroom. Something new and revolutionary is needed. The Bundy report is a brave attempt at an answer. (*New York Times,* Nov. 9, 1967)

Thus the liberal *New York Times* joined in the liberal call for administrative decentralization of a radical kind which would have left the central city Board of Education with very little power or function.

The "Bundy Report" went to the State Legislature, with a recommended plan by the Mayor that differed slightly. But the UFT opposed it, as did other groups, on the ground that it would prevent progress toward racial integration. The New York State Board of Regents developed an alternative plan. In the spring of 1968 the Legislature refused to approve any of the plans, but passed the Marchi Bill giving some little powers to the existing 30 advisory school district boards, and requiring the New York City Board of Education to produce a definitive plan for decentralization for action by the Legislature in 1969. The Board then proposed a plan which was approved by the State Legislature in the spring of 1969. This plan kept the senior high schools under the single City Board and provided for the creation of some 30 community school districts, each to be headed by a locally elected board that has general operating authority over the elementary, intermediate, and junior high schools of the area. The City Board of Education continues to operate the senior high schools and also has other functions for finance and general supervision. Each new district should have at least 20,000 pupils, according to the legislature.

The districts defined by the Board of Education are very similar to the elementary school districts already in existence, each of which had a District Superintendent. Elections of local boards were held in the spring of 1970, with about 15 percent of eligible voters voting. This was a disappointment. In some districts it was complained that Catholic parents organized to elect a board that would be sympathetic to their efforts to get public aid for parochial schools.

A major criticism of the decentralization plan is that it divides the city into districts of some 20,000 to 30,000 pupils who are mainly of one ethnic group, and will prevent the kinds of programs aimed at integration which the all-city Board of Education had going until 1969. For example, the borough of Manhattan is divided into six districts, only three of which have a mixed ethnic population. In 1970 Manhattan had 82 percent black or Spanish origin pupils in public schools. Two districts are predominantly Puerto Rican, and one is almost entirely black.

The three "demonstration districts" of 1967–69 have all been included in larger districts and thus have lost their special character. The Ocean Hill–Brownsville demonstration district became a part of District 23, in Brooklyn, which contains 24 schools and 22,000 pupils. The local school board which was elected in 1970 chose as its chairman Assemblyman Samuel D. Wright, who had opposed Rev. Oliver for chairmanship of the Ocean Hill governing board, and later came out in opposition to the governing board's 1968 activities. A New York Times news article for August 9, 1971 reported that the board was about to dismiss three of the acting principals appointed by the Ocean Hill governing board, leaving only one principal who was also a principal under Rhody McCoy, who was no longer in the district.

A New York Times article for June 30, 1974 reported that 30 percent of the system's top administrative posts (paying $30,000 a year or more) were held by blacks and Puerto Ricans and the proportion of minority group principals increased from 6 percent in 1969 to 19 percent in 1974. But voter participation in elections for local community school boards dropped from 15 percent in 1970 to 11 percent in 1973.

The decentralization of elementary school administration has perhaps not existed long enough to permit a reasoned judgment. But there has been no record of improved school achievement, and the local district school boards have not won wide approval. Indeed, second thoughts on decentralization have been expressed by Kenneth B. Clark, a distinguished black psychologist who was a member of the New York Board of Regents which approved the New York City plan. Appearing before the New York City Charter Revision Commission, he was reported in the New York Times for November 27, 1972 to have said that he had become a "vehement foe" of school decentralization.

Dr. Clark said that the movement for decentralization had become a political one, which neglected the educational welfare of the children. On the "very limited standard of academic achievement," he declared that decentralization of school administration had been and would continue to be "a disaster."

DECENTRALIZATION IN OTHER CITIES

Most of the big-city school systems have moved toward a more decentralized administration since the community control movement got under way in the late 1960s. Few have gone as far as New York City, perhaps partly because the New York experience has not been very successful. On the other hand, one city—Detroit—seems to have gone even further than New York City toward complete decentralization of administration.

Detroit

Under the general push for decentralization of educational administration that was noted above, the Detroit Board of Education divided the city into nine districts, each with a district superintendent with considerable responsibility. However, the City Board of Education retained full authority. This did not satisfy those who wanted as much decentralization as possible, and they turned to the State Legislature which passed the Detroit Decentralization Law that was signed by the Governor in August, 1969. This law decreed that the Detroit School Board should divide the school district into not less than seven nor more than eleven regional school districts, with not more than 50,000 nor less than 25,000 students in each district. Each regional district should have an elected school board. This board should have the power to employ a superintendent and to employ, assign, promote, and discharge teachers, subject to veto by the central city board. The regional district board should determine the curriculum and the testing programs for its districts. The Detroit Board set up seven districts, and changed school attendance boundaries for 12 of the 22 high schools in such a way as to secure greater racial integration.

This was welcomed by liberal proponents of integration in the schools, but resistance appeared immediately, led by whites who opposed the high school boundary changes that would produce greater racial integration. The whites who wanted to retain the present high school attendance boundaries joined with blacks who favored greater black community control of schools in black areas. They introduced a new bill into the State Legislature for eight regional school districts, each with an elected school board, together with a 13-member central board of education, a majority of whom come from the regional boards. The eight districts were drawn along lines that tend to preserve and increase racial segregation in the schools. This bill was supported by black legislators on the ground that black control of schools in black communities was more desirable than the effort to increase racial integration in the schools. The bill passed the legislature with a large majority in June, 1970. The new law provided that any student might attend any school within his own district, if there was room for him. Critics of the law predicted that this would operate to allow white students to leave integrated schools, more than to encourage black students to enter integrated schools.

Thus a temporary coalition of conservative white legislators and black legislators seeking greater local political power defeated a program aimed at fostering social integration in Detroit, and imposed a system of decentralization on the Detroit schools that tends to perpetuate racial segregation.

Nevertheless, Detroit had a somewhat easier time with respect to ethnic hostility, since about 40 percent of Detroit's 11,000 public school teachers were black in 1970, and 30 percent of the administrators. The proportion of black students in the public schools was about 63 percent. All but six of the 320 schools had a biracial faculty in 1970. Detroit included the high schools in its decentralization plan, thus giving the regional school boards more power than the New York community boards have. However, the matter was not settled, because some black parents carried the issue to the federal courts, where Judge Stephen J. Roth ordered the state to combine the mainly white Detroit suburbs with the Detroit city schools through a vast system of cross-district bussing so that most schools would have no more than 25 percent black students. The principle behind this ruling was that public education is the responsibility of the state government, which must make it available to all on equal terms. On July 25, 1974, the U.S. Supreme Court overturned this ruling, stating that bussing pupils from one district to another for the sake of racial integration is unconstitutional.

Chicago

The Board of Education in Chicago responded to the pressure for decentralization by dividing the school system into three regions or areas, each with an Area Superintendent who is responsible to the General Superintendent and the Board of Education. However, a considerable amount of authority has been transferred to these three offices. Then, in an important move, the Board ordered each school principal and each district superintendent to form an *Educational Advisory Council* consisting of a majority of parents, with teachers elected by teachers, and community representatives. The powers of these councils have been definitely stated. Most important, they are to be "consulted" on the appointment of principals, which virtually gives them a veto power. They do not have the right to depose a principal. However, in fact several local councils have exerted pressure enough to cause some principals to ask for transfers, and in a few cases to cause the area superintendent to step in and transfer the principal. The Advisory Council for each school has some authority over a relatively small fund which is used to supplement the basic school program by activities and materials which are best suited to the local situation.

The Chicago Board of Education retains all administrative authority, and *delegates* some of this authority to areas, districts, and local schools. Thus, the Board can and does act for what it considers the welfare of the entire city, which may mean creating new schools at any place in the city, making and changing rules for attendance at individual schools, adopting compensatory education programs and applying them to selected schools. The Board has been able to take certain steps toward racial integration which are no longer possible in New York and Detroit.

However, there continues to be pressure for greater decentralization of administration in Chicago. The Citizens Schools Committee, a liberal citizens' organization, in May, 1972 called for further decentralization, saying that the present system is "a highly centralized, massive, inefficient, and inflexible organization which is incapable of performing its job satisfactorily due to the sheer distance and lack of communication between its decision-makers and the classroom."

HOW TO STUDY PROBLEMS AND ISSUES INVOLVING INTERACTION OF SOCIAL SYSTEMS

The controversy over local community control of schools has been presented in some detail, with the Ocean Hill–Brownsville case to illustrate its complexity. This is an important subject in itself, and anybody trying to understand contemporary American education will spend a good deal of time studying this issue of local control. Moreover, the material on the preceding pages shows the need for:

1. Getting all the relevant facts together, and looking critically for evidence of accuracy and completeness in the various sources.
2. Trying to *see* and *feel* the situation from the points of view of the persons or groups or roles that are most involved in the situation.

This second principle was at least recognized in the list of seven "points of view on local community control." People in these roles are bound to see the situation differently, to see part of the truth clearly, and often to ignore or to falsify other parts of the reality. Looking back at this particular case we have reported actions and statements from people in the following roles: city board of education member; local community board of education member; classroom teacher; school principal; member of a politically active ethnic group; member of the teachers' union; member of an administrators' association; member of a liberal civic group; journalist with a socio-political ideology; official in the city government; official in the state government; educational scientist. It may be noted that we have neglected to report the situation from the points of view of heavily involved but less articulate groups: parents and students.

EXERCISES

1. If you live in a large city, get the relevant information about the administrative structure of the city school system, and make notes of the kinds of decisions that are made at various levels in the system.

2. Compare the kind of informal local control of the neighborhood elementary school in a middle-class area, through PTA and informal relations between parents and school staff, with the more formal procedures in a lower-working-class area which has an elected School Advisory Council.

3. Select a controversial issue involving the school system you know best, and describe the social roles of the various interested people, and their attitude on the issue in question.

SUGGESTIONS FOR FURTHER READING

1. Articles related to the content of this chapter and published in *Readings in Society and Education*, edited by Havighurst, Neugarten, and Falk, are: James S. Coleman, *The Struggle for Control of Education*; Amos Wilder, *Client Criticism of Public Schools: How Valid?*; Robert J. Havighurst, *Decentralization Versus Local Community Control in Large City School Systems*.

2. Practically every issue of the *Phi Delta Kappan* in the year 1973 had one or more articles on an administrative decentralization of large school systems. The January, 1973 issue had several useful articles on this subject.

3. The Report of the Mayor's Advisory Panel on Decentralization of the New York City Schools has been published under the title *Reconnection for Learning* by Praeger in New York .

4. Decentralization of big-city school systems is analyzed in terms of political forces by Jay D. Scribner and David O'Shea in chapter 13 of *NSSE Yearbook on Uses of the Sociology of Education*. They pay special attention to Los Angeles and New York City. Decentralization in Detroit is described in detail by Robert L. Green in chapter 10 of this Yearbook.

5. Ornstein has collected data on administrative decentralization in 62 school systems with more than 50,000 students, finding only two cases of local community control. His first three chapters in *Race and Politics in School/Community Organizations* analyze the issues very well.

CHAPTER 13

School Systems Interacting with Other Social Systems in the Metropolitan Area

In the preceding chapter we considered some of the educational problems that have arisen as a result of metropolitan growth. In this chapter we will again deal with the metropolitan area, but with the school system interacting with other social systems to perform the functions of education.

SOCIAL SYSTEM DEFINED

A social system is a network or system of social interactions—or, more strictly, a system of the *actions* of individuals—organized to carry out one or more essential tasks of society. The principal units of the system are roles and constellations of roles (Parsons and Shils, 1952). The educational system is one among many social systems, such as local government, business organizations, social welfare agencies, and churches. It is a set of roles and role constellations which has been devised for the purpose of systematically teaching children and adults a variety of information, skills, and attitudes that people are not likely to learn efficiently in the family or in work situations. A police system, to take another example, is a set of roles and role constellations designed to keep order in the community and to enforce the law.

When there is social change, various social systems alter their functions and alter their relations with each other. Thus we are accustomed to describing changes over the last 100 years in the functions of the family, and the relations between family and the school; or in the relations between the church and the school; or government and school.

Role Analysis

To understand how a school system operates, one may study its various functions, its subsystems, and the roles of which it is composed. Students of school administration sometimes make such studies using the method of systems analysis. Getzels (1963), for instance, has pointed out that one can study the school system in this way, quite independent of the particular persons who fill the roles; that is, by studying how teachers carry out their teaching responsibilities, how they relate, say, to pupils, to other teachers, and to administrators; and similarly, to study the principal, the superintendent, and the school board, all in terms of the way in which their roles are performed. Such a study would provide a picture of how the school operates as a social system and how the system maintains itself, even though different individuals move in and out of particular roles. The type of analysis has been illustrated briefly in Chapter 9 of this book.

Similarly, one may study the interactions *between* social systems in terms of role analysis: how, for instance, the high school principal or the superintendent relates to the chief of police in the community, to the mayor, to the chairman of the Board of Health, to ministers, to representatives of the Chamber of Commerce; how teachers generally relate to other institutional representatives; and so on. Any social system "relates" to any other by the interactions of the people who fill the roles in the two systems.

In recent years the functions of education have become more complex than they were before about 1930, mainly because the society has become more industrialized, urbanized, and affluent. This has not only produced the metropolitan area as a spatial unit for economic and cultural life, but it has also worked to make schools and other systems larger, more bureaucratic, and perhaps less efficient.

BIGNESS OF SCHOOL SYSTEMS

Throughout this century, the individual school, the school system, the college, and the university have all grown bigger. This reflects not only the urbanization of the country, but also the conviction among educators that a big school is better than a small one. As the one-room school is disappearing, so also is the small school district. In the first nationwide survey of local school districts in 1932, the United States Office of Education found 127,244 public school districts (see Table 13.1). The midwestern farm states had thousands of small districts, usually each with three citizens serving as

TABLE 13.1.   Numbers and Sizes of School Districts Since 1930

	1931–32	1961–62	1967–68	1971–72
Number of public school districts	127,244	35,555	22,010	17,995
Number of public schools	270,000	107,000	97,890	90,821
Number of one-teacher schools	143,000	13,133	4,146	1,815
Total public school enrollment below college level (in thousands)	26,300	38,253	44,140	46,081
Average enrollment per school district	207	1,075	2,000	2,560
Number of non-public schools	12,992	18,891	19,300	18,142

Sources: Biennial Surveys of Education—U.S. Office of Education; and U.S. Office of Education, *Digest of Educational Statistics, 1972.*

school trustees. Thus these states had more members of school boards than they had teachers. The numbers of school districts fell steadily to about 18,000 in 1972.

Meanwhile, the average school district increased in enrollment from 207 in 1931 to 2,560 in 1971. The number of school systems with 3,000 or more pupils more than tripled in just the 20 years between 1951 and 1971. This resulted partly from the sharp rise in school enrollments after 1952, when the postwar birthrate began to affect the schools.

Consolidation of rural elementary schools together with the growing urbanization slowly increased the size of high schools. The average high school had 87 students in 1900, but 520 in 1970.

Colleges and universities grew in even more striking fashion. In 1900 the average size of colleges and universities was 243 students. By 1930 the average was 780, and by 1970 it was 3,140. During this period the number of small institutions varied considerably, but there was a steady growth in numbers of medium-sized and large institutions. By the autumn of 1971, there were 60 universities each with 20,000 or more degree-credit students.

Increasing Financial Investment in Education

During the current century there has been a great increase in the funds spent on education.

Traditionally, American schools have been financed locally. Even though the states had responsibility for a system of public education, they generally passed this responsibility on to the local community—the town, township, or county. In the field of higher education the states were slow to move, although most of them were supporting a university by 1900.

In 1929 public school education was supported 75 percent by local school districts. Then local schools began to be supported from state funds, with federal funds limited to assisting vocational education. By 1972, local districts were paying only 52 percent of the cost of public elementary and secondary education; the states were paying 41 percent; and the federal government 7 percent.

The relation of education costs to the gross national product is shown in Table 13.2. Approximately four times as much of the national product was spent on education in 1970 as was spent in 1900. According to many economists this was an investment in the development of human capital that paid very good dividends (Schultz, 1960, 1963). People obtained more education; they became more efficient producers, increased their own earning power, and increased the productivity of the economy in which they worked. With about eight percent of the gross national product now going into education, the United States invests relatively more in education than most other countries.

RELATIONS AMONG EDUCATIONAL SUBSYSTEMS

The educational subsystems of a metropolitan area consist of the various public school districts in the area, the system of Roman Catholic schools, the system of Lutheran schools, other church-related school systems such as

TABLE 13.2   Cost of Education in the United States, 1900–1971
(In Millions of Dollars, Current Prices)

School Year	Elemen- tary Schools	Second- ary Schools	Colleges and Uni- versities	Total	Gross National Product (in bil- lions of dollars)	Percent of GNP
1899–1900	233	19	40	292	17	1.7
1929–30	1,950	750	535	3,233	104	3.1
1959–60	12,590	5,435	6,616	24,700	483	5.1
1963–64	24,900		11,000	35,900	585	6.1
1967–68	37,300		19,906	57,200	785	7.3
1969–70	45,300		24,700	70,000	932	7.5
1970–71	49,500		27,400	76,900	974	7.9
1971–72	53,900		29,900	83,800	1,050	8.0

Note: The gross national product is for the calendar year in which the school year begins.
Sources: U.S. Office of Education, Digest of Educational Statistics, 1972; and Schultz, 1960.

the Christian schools and the Seventh-Day Adventist schools, and the independent private schools.

These subsystems have had a tradition of working separately. However, in the 1960s and 1970s, needs for cooperation have become apparent among the public school districts, and also between public and private schools.

Cooperation Among Public School Districts

Among public school districts a variety of shared educational projects have made their appearance, including television, special schools for handicapped children, junior colleges, and in-service teacher training programs. Most of this cooperation is presently taking place among suburban districts, without the participation of the central city district; but in some instances it involves all the districts within the metropolitan area.

The first step in some metropolitan areas may be to create an area-wide organization such as a metropolitan area planning commission, followed soon thereafter by the creation of a metropolitan education authority. The functions assumed by the education authority might include planning new suburban school districts; administering a basic state aid fund so as to help equalize educational opportunity for all the children; administering an area-wide educational research and evaluation council; administering programs of special education for the entire area; maintaining a public university, including a teacher-training institution; recruiting and selecting teachers; administering a teachers' pension system; administering an educational television station.

In some instances voluntary cooperation among school districts has taken the form of a study council or a superintendents' study group in which a local university works with the school superintendents of the area. This may lead to a more formal arrangement for voluntary cooperation, such as the Educational Research and Development Council of the Twin Cities Metropolitan Area, Inc.

The superintendents of the Minneapolis–St. Paul area, together with members of the School of Education at the University of Minnesota, formed the Council in 1963. It consists of 35 public school districts in the seven-county metropolitan area, schools which serve 44 percent of all the pupils in the state of Minnesota.

During the first three years of the Council, a number of research studies were completed on the organizational climate and structure of schools, school output measures, program evaluation, and school staffing, and surveys dealing with finance and taxation problems and school expenditures. The Council has also undertaken various developmental activities including workshops for teachers and administrators, programs for the mentally retarded children in the area, and the utilization of computer methods in school record and school accounting systems.

Cooperation Between Public Schools and Church Schools

Cooperation between the public school and church school systems has taken various forms over the years. Because of the American tradition of separation between church and state, there have long been laws against public support of church-operated schools. For this and other reasons, the several church school systems (the so-called parochial schools) have tended to operate in isolation from the public schools. At the same time patterns of collaboration have grown up with regard to religious instruction, independent of instruction in the other areas of school curriculum.

The Issue of Religious Instruction.   A number of Protestant churches offer a weekday program of religious classes which usually meet one period a week in the latter part of a school day. In some communities the Roman Catholic Church gives similar instruction to pupils from public schools. Sometimes the children leave the school building and go to their own churches for this instruction; at other times they remain in school and are instructed by teachers provided by the church. In some communities, a group of churches have banded together to employ teachers who teach an inter-denominational religion; and the instruction is given in the regular school classroom. There are a variety of such "released-time" arrangements, in which those children who do not attend the religious classes are provided for in some other way by the school, often by being placed in a study hall. The "released-time" program was first put into practice in 1914 in Gary, Indiana. The program spread so that by 1950 it included some 2,000,000 children in more than 2,000 communities.

This type of weekday religious instruction in the public schools and on school time, but with varying degrees of church responsibility, has been a matter of controversy in America. Some people have opposed it on the ground that it infringes the constitutional principle of separation between church and state.

In 1948 the United States Supreme Court passed down a decision on a test case involving a "released-time" program in Champaign, Illinois, in which children were taught religion in the school buildings and on school time by teachers employed by some of the local churches. Attendance records in the religious classes were reported to the school authorities. Children who did not attend the classes were required to sit in study hall during that period. It was argued by attorneys in this case that the minority of children who would not attend the religious classes would be ridiculed by the other children who attended these classes. For this reason, it was argued the existence of the religious classes meant in effect that the state, through the school, would be putting pressure on children to take part in a church program, and that the state would thus be supporting the church.

The Supreme Court ruled that this particular form of church and school collaboration is unconstitutional; and, in so ruling, said:

> Religious education so conducted on school time and property is patently woven into the working scheme of the school. The Champaign arrangement thus presents powerful elements of inherent pressure by the school system in the interest of religious sects. The fact that this power has not been used to discriminate is beside the point. Separation is a requirement to abstain from fusing functions of Government and religious sects, not merely to treat them all equally. That a child is offered an alternative may reduce the constraint; it does not eliminate the operation of influence by the school in matters sacred to conscience and outside the school's domain. The law of imitation operates, and nonconformity is not an outstanding characteristic of children. The result is an obvious pressure upon children to attend. (U.S. Reports 333 U.S. 227, 1948)

As a result of this Supreme Court ruling, some "released-time" programs of religious education have been abandoned. Most of them, however, were retained but were carefully kept within limits so that the school could not fairly be accused of putting pressure on children to attend. The Court of Appeals in New York State held in 1951 that a "released-time" program was constitutional if the children whose parents so desired were dismissed from school to get religious instruction elsewhere.

The Effects of the Elementary and Secondary Education Act of 1965. A new chapter in the history of relations between public schools and church-supported schools began in 1965, with the passage of the Elementary and Secondary Education Act. This bill represented a workable compromise in the effort to get federal aid for general education that had been discussed for 30 years. Previous bills had lost out in Congress due to the opposition of Congressmen who generally opposed expansion of federal government activities, as well as the opposition of Congressmen from big-city districts where there was a large proportion of Roman Catholics. The latter group of Congressmen was not opposed to federal aid to education in principle, but they represented districts in which many Roman Catholic parents were opposed to paying extra taxes for support of the public schools while they also had to pay for the education of their own children in parochial schools.

The 1965 Act authorized a substantial amount of federal aid to church-supported education and thus won the votes of big-city Congressmen. Essentially, the Act provides aid to the *education of children,* whatever schools they may attend. The assistance must be given *through the public schools,* but not necessarily *in the public schools.*

Title I of the Act provides money (about 50 percent of the previous per-pupil expenditures in the state) to improve educational programs for children from low-income families. The following two paragraphs from Section 205 of the Act specify that a public educational agency may receive federal money provided the State Department of Education determines, among other things:

(2) that, to the extent consistent with the number of educationally deprived children in the school district of the local educational agency who are enrolled in private elementary and secondary schools, such agency has made provision for including special educational services and arrangements (such as dual enrollment, educational radio and television, and mobile educational services and equipment) in which such children can participate;

(3) that the local educational agency has provided satisfactory assurance that the control of funds provided under this title, and title to property derived therefrom, shall be in a public agency for the uses and purposes provided in this title, and that a public agency will administer such funds and property. (United States, 89th Congress, 1965, pp. 4—5.)

The leaders of public schools and private schools are now working together to answer such questions as the following: How is the state to spend this money on improving the education of children who are in private schools? Most of these children will be found in Catholic schools. Should the public school system employ teachers and assign them to Catholic schools to reduce class size? Should the public school system employ social workers, nurses, and other personnel and assign them to parochial schools? Should the public schools provide instruction in certain subjects for these children under a "shared time" or dual enrollment program?

In addition to the provisions of Title I, Titles II and III of the Act provide for approximately $200 million per year of expenditure *through* the public school system, to assist the education of children, regardless of the school they attend and regardless of their family income level. Title II provides money for textbooks, library books, visual aids, and other teaching materials, to be *loaned* to private schools by public schools. Title III provides for the support of supplementary educational centers, which will offer educational assistance to pupils regardless of their school membership. The centers may provide classes and services for gifted and for handicapped children, counseling services, and other enrichment programs. Also, the centers may make equipment and the services of specialized personnel available to private schools. Public school authorities and private school authorities may be jointly responsible for the direction of these centers.

Thus the period from 1965 to 1975 is one in which public and church-supported schools are learning to cooperate. This is being done more easily in some states than in others; several states have laws which make it almost impossible for public schools to give *any* assistance to pupils in private schools. These laws are now undergoing critical study and revision.

The Question of "Shared Time." The Act is giving a good deal of impetus to programs of dual enrollment or "shared time," which is an arrangement whereby a pupil is enrolled and regularly attends a public school part of the time and a private school part of the time. Though this practice is an old one in a few communities (Pittsburgh has had it for 50 years), it has been promoted lately as a means whereby the expanding Roman Catholic schools can meet the expense of their growing enrollments. By teaching pupils only certain subjects, and permitting them to study other subjects as regular students in public schools, the parochial schools can operate at less expense.

Thus the trend of social forces is to push the public and church school systems closer together, and to create new patterns of cooperation within the educational subsystems of the metropolitan area.

The Issue of Parochiaid

Since about 1965 there has been a mounting movement in some of the large cities in favor of what is called *parochiaid*. This means some form of financial support from public funds for church-related schools. The political forces favoring this kind of policy are based largely on Catholic voters who must pay local taxes to support public schools while they send their own children to parochial schools and pay for these schools. They hope to find some way whereby public funds can be allocated to church-related schools within the bounds of the Constitution which requires a strict separation of church and state. The forms of indirect assistance under the Elementary and Secondary Education Act are welcomed, but are seen as insufficient.

The cost of maintaining church-related schools has risen more sharply even than the cost of public schools, largely because the church-related schools have not been able to recruit enough nuns and priests to staff the growing schools, and have therefore employed more lay teachers who must be paid salaries commensurate with salaries in the public schools. In this situation, church-related schools have raised their tuition fees, thus forcing some low-income parents to transfer their children to free public schools. The number of church-related schools has decreased in a good many cities with large Catholic populations. This means that the public schools must receive more pupils, at a greater cost. It has been demonstrated in several cities that the closing of parochial schools will increase the public school cost substantially more than it would cost the city or the state to keep the parochial schools going with a relatively small subsidy.

These considerations have led to the passage of laws in several states which provide a significant support directly to church-related schools. Such laws have been passed in Pennsylvania, Rhode Island, and Illinois. However, the Pennsylvania law was declared unconstitutional by the United States Supreme Court. The other state laws have not been put into operation, pending the discovery of a legal way by which public funds can be transferred to nonpublic schools.

THE USE OF EDUCATION VOUCHERS TO ASSIST NONPUBLIC SCHOOLS

Another way by which nonpublic schools may receive public financial support is through the use of *education vouchers,* a device which has been much discussed and debated since about 1968. This idea grew out of the movement for *alternative schools* which has developed vigorously in the big cities, and will be described in the next section of this chapter. With so much dissatisfaction over the existing school system, it was natural to ask for a substantial amount of experimentation with new schools, and this might be better done by people outside the present school system than by those who have adjusted and perhaps are tied down to the usual procedures.

One obvious way to promote experimentation and new methods is to support with public funds an array of new schools developed by innovators, and favored or accepted by parents and students. This led to the *voucher idea.* Basically, this idea is that parents and students are the best judges of the kind of education they need, and that public funds should be entrusted to them, to use for their education in an open market where they have a choice among schools. This should provide better education than the present system which gives the educational bureaucracy a monopoly.

The voucher method would give a family a voucher for each school-age child, which is worth a certain amount of money—approximately the amount that is spent on the average pupil in the public schools. The family then "shops around" among "schools" that meet certain criteria, and assigns the voucher to the school of their choice. The school is supported by the vouchers it collects, plus any other money it can obtain from private sources. Parents could send their children to the local public school by giving their vouchers to that school, but the public schools would have to compete in the market with a variety of nonpublic schools.

This idea aroused active support and active opposition from people with a wide variety of attitudes toward education. Vouchers were approved by very conservative people, and also by very radical people, since the scheme could presumably free them to find or create the kind of education they most desired.

The Office of Economic Opportunity, in its role as supporter of educational experiments designed to reduce poverty and to increase educational opportunity, has made several grants of money to support tryouts of the voucher idea. Also, the OEO supported an analysis by Professor Christopher

Jencks of Harvard University of the pros and cons of the voucher concept. This analysis explored seven possible voucher plans, or sets of ground rules for distributing money to voucher schools. Jencks points out the probable advantages and disadvantages of each plan. The simplest one, advocated by "free-market" conservatives, would provide every child with a flat grant which his family could use to pay tuition at the school of its choice. The school could select pupils freely among applicants, and therefore could reject applicants because of low IQ, behavior problems, ethnicity, or any other criteria. The school could charge a high tuition, far above the value of a voucher, thus limiting its enrollment to children of wealthy families who would get some benefit from the vouchers. Jencks opposes this form of voucher plan, saying:

> Our overall judgment is that an unregulated market would redistribute resources away from the poor and toward the rich, would increase economic segregation in the schools, and would exacerbate the problems of existing public schools without offering them any offsetting advantages. For these reasons we think it worse than the present system of public schools. (p. 171–2, Mecklenburger and Hostrup, 1972)

Jencks favors what he terms the "regulated compensatory model." This would require a school that participates in the program to accept at least as high a proportion of black or other minority group students as had applied, and to fill at least half of its places by a lottery among applicants in case there are more applicants than places. It would also give a higher value voucher to low-income children than to middle and high-income children.

Opinions and attitudes toward vouchers are varied, no doubt partly due to the fact that the concept has several different operational meanings. A Gallup poll, made in 1971, asked adults the following question:

> In some nations, the government allots a certain amount of money for each child for his education. The parents can then send the child to any public, parochial, or private school they choose. This is called the "voucher system." Would you like to see such an idea adopted in this country?

The overall response was 38 percent in favor and 44 percent opposed, with 18 percent expressing no opinion. However, among parents of children in parochial schools the response was 66 percent in favor, 33 percent opposed, while public school parents were 39 percent in favor and 51 percent opposed. Polls of educators made by educational organizations showed a strong opposition to voucher plans, on the part of 70 to 80 percent of administrators and teachers. On the other hand, an opinion survey of citizens made in Seattle during the period of public discussion of vouchers, showed 39 percent favorable, 37 percent opposed, and 24 percent undecided.

The OEO made grants for "feasibility studies" of vouchers to school systems in Seattle, Gary (Indiana), San Francisco, and San Jose (California). The only one which concluded that the plan was feasible was the San Jose study, where an elementary school district (Alum Rock) in that metropolitan area concluded that a plan limited to public schools was worth trying. Accordingly, the OEO made a grant to fund the Alum Rock voucher program for two years—1972–1974. This experiment is limited to public schools in the Alum Rock School District. Parents choose between 21 competing school *programs*, not schools. They allocate their vouchers (equal to the average per-pupil expenditure in the district, plus a supplement of one-third for children who are eligible for federal school lunch programs (and who come from low-income families). Several schools offer three or four different programs, giving some choice to parents who prefer the local neighborhood school. And children may be bused (at OEO expense) to any other school with a program they want. Names of some of the school programs are: Cultural Arts; Multicultural (bilingual); Math-Science; Open-Activity Centered; Individual Learning; Continuous Progress Nongraded; Three R's Plus; Basic Skills; and School 2000. The voucher program was made available to 4000 pupils, and some 40 percent chose nontraditional programs for the 1972–73 school year.

The OEO contracted with the Rand Corporation for nearly $1 million to make a thorough evaluation of the Alum Rock Voucher programs after 1974. It might be said that one experiment with vouchers limited to public schools in one school district is a small result from all the talk, controversy, and money expended on vouchers from 1968 to 1974. However, the voucher concept facilitated an extensive consideration by American educators and opinion leaders of the need for basic innovation in the school system.

FREE SCHOOLS

One result of the drive for greater individual freedom and for more expressivity in education has been the Free Schools Movement, which has flourished especially since 1968. Though a number of public school systems are working with the concept, by far the majority of free schools are marginal to the established educational system. They are operated usually by a combination of upper-middle-class parents who want more freedom and spontaneity in the school for their children, working with one or more teachers who are uncomfortable within the Establishment. This group forms a loose-knit organization, rents space in a church or empty business building, and operates by sharing the costs among the parents, and by keeping costs at a minimum through volunteer assistance by some of the parents. This requires a considerable donation of time and money, since there is no state support for these schools, even though parents must pay their regular taxes on their property, much of which goes to support the local public or state school system.

People active in free or open schools held conferences, and set up the *New Schools Exchange Newsletter*. By 1971 this newsletter and others were claiming the existence of some 2,000 open schools. Even though many of these schools existed for only one or two years, depending on the pertinacity of their principal supporters, new ones came into being, and the number probably has remained fairly constant since 1971, though there are doubts about the actual number. According to an apparently objective report by Robert D. Barr, co-director of the *Educational Alternatives Project* at Indiana University, there were about 350 operational schools in 1972, serving about 13,000 students. The average school size was 33 students.

Apostles of the Free School Movement in the United States generally have a tendency toward philosophical anarchism—followers of Rousseau. Thus, the late Paul Goodman (1970), a self-defined anarchist, wrote: "We can, I believe, educate the young entirely in terms of their free choice, with no processing whatsoever." John Holt has written persuasively for maximum freedom for children to direct their own education. In a 1971 book, he answers a question directed to him by an educational journal: If America's schools were to take one giant step forward this year toward a better tomorrow, what should it be? His answer:

> It would be to let every child be the planner, director, and assessor of his own education, to allow and encourage him, with the inspiration and guidance of more experienced and expert people, and as much help as he asked for, to decide what he is to learn, when he is to learn it, how he is to learn it, and how well he is learning it.
>
> It would be to make out schools, instead of what they are, which is jails for children, into a resource for free and independent learning, which everyone in the community, of whatever age, could use as much or as little as he wanted. (p. 5)

Of course, there are many criticisms of the anarchist writers. For instance, Professor B. F. Skinner, the famous psychologist at Harvard University, writing in the *Phi Delta Kappan* for September, 1973 on "The Free and Happy Student" says, "The modern version of the free and happy student to be found in books by Paul Goodman, John Holt, Jonathan Kozol, or Charles Silberman is also imaginary." True personal freedom can only be gained by disciplined study of the real world, he argues, and this requires the assistance of a teacher. "The natural, logical outcome of the struggle for personal freedom in education is that the teacher should improve his control of the student rather than abandon it. The free school is no school at all. Its philosophy signalizes the abdication of the teacher. The teacher who understands his assignment and is familiar with the behavioral processes needed to fulfill it can have students who not only feel free and happy while they are being taught but who will continue to feel free and happy when their formal education comes to an end."

Robert D. Barr, Editor of *Changing Schools,* newsletter of the National Consortium on Educational Alternatives, summing up his judgment on the free school movement in the *Phi Delta Kappan* in March, 1973, wrote:

> The free school movement failed during the sixties to become the wave of the future, and, if we are honest, I think we must all admit that it probably never will. . . . The movement has demonstrated that dedicated, creative people, with much courage and little money, can achieve significant goals. In the long run such vitality and energy and anger and sacrifice should only help to diversify and enrich education for American youth. (p. 454—7)

ALTERNATIVE SCHOOLS

The pragmatic response of the Educational Establishment to the challenge of the Free Schools has been the *Alternative Schools.* Instead of maintaining a monolithic school, as the critics see it, the pragmatic reformers proposed to open up the school system by creating a number of alternatives and giving students and their parents some options. The advantages are described by Mario Fantini, at one time a radical reformer when he was on the staff of the Ford Foundation, who later became the head of one of the major teacher-education institutions of the State of New York and wrote a book entitled *Public Schools of Choice: Alternatives in Education.* In a talk he gave at a conference of a *National Consortium on Educational Alternatives* he said:

> At one time during the Sixties I considered myself a change agent. That is, I had a certain concept of reform—say like team teaching or educational technology, and I would go into a school system and try and manipulate the situation so it would come out my way. Now I feel this is a wrong strategy to use. . . . The idea of providing alternative learning options is based on an entirely different conception of change. For rather than "pushing people around," you provide options that attract people to them. They choose. They make decisions. . . . In an area as important as education, I want a situation where every parent, every student and every teacher is making decisions for themselves. . . . The program of learning options I am proposing would enable every teacher, parent, and child to make selections about school experience. (p. 3)

The United States Office of Education has made several substantial grants to support the development of alternative schools within public school systems. In addition, a number of city school systems have deliberately created alternatives at no extra cost simply by turning over building space to groups of teachers who wish to develop new courses or curricula. There is hardly a city school system that does not now offer several different secondary school curricula within its academic-type program, in addition to technical and vocational training which have existed as alternatives in the past. At the primary school level, the variety is not so great, but a number of cities have deliberately created *open schools* and made enrollment optional for pupils living anywhere in the city.

The most extensive program of alternative schools exists at Berkeley, California, a city of 116,000 where is located the University of California at Berkeley. This city has a working-class residential area as well as a large middle-class area, and has elected a liberal Board of Education consistently since about 1960. The public school enrollment is 45 percent non-Spanish white, 44 percent black, and 11 percent Oriental or Mexican-American. *Saturday Review* for September 16, 1972, described the second year of a five-year experiment with alternative schools. The U.S. Office of Education has provided $7 million over a five-year period, and the Ford Foundation granted the school system more than a half-million dollars for some programs that are run outside of school property. There are 24 quite different programs, some at the secondary and some at the primary age levels. They enroll 4,000 students, while the other 12,000 students attend the "regular" schools. There are four broad categories:

1. Multicultural schools, specializing in mixed racial-ethnic composition.
2. Community schools, related closely to the families of a small local community.
3. Structured skill-training schools, quite traditional and rigorous in their standards, but using new technology, such as teaching machines and computer-assisted instruction.
4. Schools without walls, where the students do most of their school work out in the city.

Alternative schools at the present time are likely to cater to one or another racial or ethnic group, in keeping with the popularity of the movement for *cultural pluralism*. This means racial and ethnic integration in some places, and separate classes or schools for different ethnic groups in other places. It reflects the ambiguity of the movement for cultural pluralism, which seeks mutual appreciation and understanding by the various ethnic and racial groups, and at the same time seeks to strengthen the feeling of ethnic identity and pride on the part of children of various subgroups.

INTERSYSTEM RELATIONS IN THE METROPOLITAN AREA

In order to study relations between educational and other social systems which operate in a metropolitan area, the social systems can be divided into two categories, *critical and supporting* systems. The distinction is a loose one. A supporting system is one which performs its functions in a routine, efficient manner, and is not undergoing major change in its functions: for example, the water department in an ordinary city. The critical systems at any given time are those faced with new demands or new functions because the community is changing. If, for example, the water supply runs low, due to drought, population growth, or other circumstances, as was the case in New York in 1965, the water department quickly becomes a critical system. Also, if the water department is asked to take on a new function, such as that of preventing dental caries among the population through fluoridation of the water supply, this change of function may become controversial in some communities so that the water department may become a critical system.

In the following list, those systems designated as critical are those presently concerned with pressing social problems:

Critical Social Systems (and some of their subsystems)

Educational systems (public school districts; system of Roman Catholic schools, other church-related schools; independent private schools; teachers organizations)

Government systems (city, county governments; special districts; court systems)

Welfare agency systems (Welfare Council; Bureau of Public Assistance; private charities; settlement houses; youth-serving organizations such as YMCA, Scouts, Boys Clubs)

Economic systems (banks; department stores; industrial corporations, Chamber of Commerce; AFL-CIO Council; real-estate board)

Culture agency systems (public library; museums; television and radio stations; park districts)

Transportation systems (rapid transit; airport; department of streets; expressway systems)

Church systems (Church Federation; Roman Catholic Diocese; area or city-wide organizations of specific religious denominations)

Civic organization systems (Civil Rights organizations; foreign-policy organizations; League of Women Voters; Urban League; Citizens Schools Organizations)

Supporting Systems

Health maintenance systems (Board of Health; medical societies; hospitals)

Communication (newspapers; TV and radio; telephone systems)

Public service systems (fire; police; water departments; Commission on Human Relations)

Political organizations

Sociability systems (country clubs; "service" clubs; lodges)

Certain social systems operate effectively when they operate relatively independently. Again, the water supply system is an example. It performs a technical and mechanical function, which is clearly defined; and it is seldom called upon to cooperate with other systems. On the other hand, the educational system is an example of one that must cooperate with other systems, because its functions are complex and similar to the functions of other social systems.

School and Library Systems

For example, the school and the library systems have overlapping functions which are worked out in various ways in different communities. The story of school and library cooperation in the City of Chicago is a good example. Much of the early part of the story is told by John A. Vieg (1939) who studied the schools of metropolitan Chicago in the 1930s.

> In 1910 there were no school libraries in Chicago. At that time the Chicago Public Library provided a large number of fifty-book collections on long-term loan to classrooms in the schools. During 1916–17 the Library set up libraries in six high schools and maintained them for a short time, then closed them.
>
> After several years, a formal cooperative agreement was made by which the Chicago Public Library provided books, magazines, supplies; selected librarians and supervised them; and the Chicago School Board paid the salaries of the librarians. This agreement continued from 1923 until 1937, when thirty-eight high schools and two junior college branches had libraries under this plan. There were no elementary school libraries during this period, but the classroom loan collections were continued. Although the cooperative agreement was in effect for more than a decade, there was some dissatisfaction. For example, the 1935 annual report of the Chicago Public Library says that the services of the librarians were not fully appreciated by the schools.
>
> After 1937, the Board of Education assumed the cost of books and magazines and later took over the selection and supervision of librarians. A complete library system that included almost all of the elementary schools was established in the Chicago Schools during subsequent years. Thus the school libraries became integral parts of the school system, though the long-term loan collections from the Public Library continued in the elementary schools on a declining basis, with 32,000 books out on loan in 1962.

In this case, the new function (school libraries) was introduced into the school system through intersystem cooperation, and then the cooperation was gradually discontinued as the school system took over the responsibility.

THE "INDEPENDENCE" OF SCHOOL SYSTEMS

For many years, it was a basic principle among school administrators that the school system should be protected from invasion by other social systems. Professor Strayer of Columbia University, the most influential leader among school administrators during the period from 1920 to about 1945, repeated frequently what he wrote in his report on the Chicago School Survey in 1932, "It is always a mistake for the schools to be organized so that agencies other than a board of education are responsible for the administration of vital and indispensable services in the schools" (Strayer, 1932, p. 145).

This principle of school administration may be interpreted broadly to mean that the schools should control the administration of all services they perform—even the new and marginal services such as the school lunch program, recreation services in city parks, job placement of students taking part in work-experience programs, delinquency-prevention programs, transportation of pupils. Yet in these and other programs, other social systems have an interest, and their personnel may not cooperate if the school system is regarded as aggressive or uncooperative.

A push for cooperation between city government and school government has become more pronounced since about 1950 with the advent of federal legislation and federal funds for urban renewal. Civic improvement, under the conditions of the 1950s and 1960s, was obviously tied up with improvement in the city schools. The schools, however, were suffering generally. They were overcrowded as a result of the postwar population boom; their buildings were aging; and many of their best pupils and teachers were being lost to the growing suburbs.

Role of Federal Government

Early in the 1960s, the federal government stepped in with substantial funds aimed at improving the quality of the city's population as workers, parents, and citizens. The Manpower Development and Training Act, the Vocational Education Act of 1963, the Economic Opportunity Act, and the Elementary and Secondary Education Act of 1965 all pumped money from Washington into the city school systems, and all aimed at improving the quality of city life. These funds stretched the functions of the school system into forms of more direct service to the city. Education was seen increasingly by civic leaders as serving to improve the city, not only through its effects on the mind and character of the pupils, but also through its effects on the economic system and the social structure of the city. The school system became an instrument for attracting and holding desirable groups of people within the central city, for stabilizing racially integrated neighborhoods, and for solving or holding in check the problems of an alienated and economically marginal minority of slum dwellers.

A contemporary leader among school administrators, Professor Roald Campbell of the University of Chicago, called on school superintendents and school boards to be more cooperative with city government. Speaking at the 1965 White House Conference on Education he said:

> ...Americans have long thought that education should be removed from politics; hence school government, particularly at the local level, has

been more or less independent of city government. Some city councils can adjust the school budget, many cannot. Some mayors or city councils name the school board members, many do not. Even where city government influences school board selection and school budget allocations, seldom does city government play any role in establishing the program of the schools. The courts have often sustained the point that school boards are created by the state, that the state has delegated to such boards powers necessary for the operation of the schools, and that board members are state, not city, officials.

Thus, there is historical and legal precedent for the feeling of independence found in school board members and administrators. Unfortunately, this feeling can get in the way of cooperation with other agencies when the problems require collaboration. . . .

All of this suggests that local government, particularly in our cities, needs serious reexamination. In that process we ought to assess the relationship of school and other special government to general government. Clearly, we need to insist on political responsibility in both general and school government. (Campbell, 1965.)

POLITICAL PERSPECTIVES CONCERNING EDUCATION IN METROPOLITAN AREAS

Examples in this and previous chapters point to the fact that educational issues have close relations to political issues. It seems doubtful that any major educational issue can be separated and solved as purely a matter of doing research on the issue and working out the best solution in the light of the research findings. Even so basic and "educational" a problem as that of how best to teach children to read has proven to be tied in with political problems of local community control of the schools and of the selection and assignment of teachers. However, research is useful and even essential to guide policy makers, who need to know what educational methods and systems are more likely to achieve the goals that are agreed upon through political processes.

The political issues involving education find people grouped into three familiar categories.

Conservatives.   They accept the status quo, sometimes with a look backward to a period when they think society was in better condition. They accept change if care is taken. They believe that individuals get their just desserts in society, due to their talent, ambition, effort, laziness, apathy, criminality, or other characteristics which are more or less inborn.

Liberals.   They believe the democratic principles of the contemporary society are good, but have not been effectively applied to the changing reality. Therefore a continual series of progressive changes is necessary to increase justice and enhance the opportunity of people (especially poor people) through various educational and other social institutions. They believe in working with the existing institutions, which need to be improved rather than abolished.

Radicals.   They believe the present social structure and social institutions are evil and must be overthrown, in order to increase justice and freedom. A few of them call for a violent revolution, but most of them say they believe the desired changes can be brought about through nonviolent political and socioeconomic action. At this point the radicals break apart into two very different groups:

a. *New Left.* Those who work toward basic political changes which would change the institutional structure but maintain strong social and economic organizations under political parties which work for the interests of poor people and economically disadvantaged minorities.

b. *Anarchists.* Those who are opposed to institutional control of human behavior and want to minimize all social institutions. Followers of the philosophy of Jean-Jacques Rousseau, they tend to be politically conservative, or uninterested in the usual political groups.

The Anarchist Critique

Perhaps the most urbane of the anarchists was the late Paul Goodman, whose major book was entitled *The New Reformation: Notes of a Neolithic Conservative.* He wanted to reduce the extent to which large-scale organizations control individual lives. He wrote: "The drive to local liberty has become the strongest revolutionary political movement of our times, both in this country and internationally. As I have been pointing out in this book, it is a protest against galloping centralization, oligarchy, military and cultural imperialism, bureaucracy, top-down administration, and mandarinism, all of which are regarded as illegitimate authority. And the slogans of liberty have been community control, decentralization, participatory democracy, national liberation, Black Power, Student Power, neighborhood city halls, 'maximum feasible participation.' People want to control their own place." (1970, p. 180)

Others of this group, not so consciously conservative, have been called by Fred M. Hechinger, the *New Romantics.*

> The line of the New Romantics is not much different from that of those Old Romantics, such as Paul Goodman. It sees compulsory schooling, not as an opportunity to make education the escape hatch from ignorance and oppression, but as a form of unnecessary baby-sitting or vicious imprisonment. To John Holt, compulsory schooling seems a conveyor belt designed to turn out little cogs for the system's big machine. Edgar Friedenberg,

285

perhaps the most radical and the most honest of the abolitionists, recognizes the schools as a barrier to his own revolution of complete liberation. A deluge of unleashed children clearly seems to him nothing less than the great hope of an American cultural revolution. But it is the current hero of the anti-school movement, Ivan Illich, who has given the party line its target label—the 'de-schooling' of society. . . .

A major flaw in the abolitionists' thinking is that they seem able to acknowledge only two alternatives of social organization: unhappy order and happy chaos. Organized education thus can only be a cause of unhappiness. In this script, all school children are unhappy, even if they are not conscious of it. (1971, p. 2)

Bureaucracy is the villain for the anarchists, and a number of their books consist of mordant critiques of the bureaucratic aspects of school systems. The radical critique tends to find the cause for the difficulties of educational systems in the contemporary urban-industrial society to lie in the dominance of American society since the early nineteenth century by middle-class capitalism rather than by more democratic populist forces. For instance, Michael Katz, in his book entitled *Class, Bureaucracy, and Schools: The Illusion of Educational Change in America,* contends, in his introduction, that American public education "is, and was universal, tax-supported, free, compulsory, bureaucratic, racist, and class-biased."

The Liberal Policy

In the contemporary situation the liberals are entrenched in positions of power within the educational establishment. They have worked for reforms within the existing socio-political institutions—some of the educational reforms being fairly drastic. These reforms require time for their effects to become established, but the political pressures may rise and force new action or innovation on the basis of very slender evidence.

However, the leading liberals do have influence and power, and are very much in charge of the educational innovation activity, so much so that the radicals spend a good deal of their energy criticizing the liberal reforms as inadequate, or racist, or class-biased.

EXERCISES

1. Study the relations between the school system and some other social system in your metropolitan area where there has been cooperation. What has happened in this connection?

2. How do the public and private educational systems in your area cooperate? What are some of the problems?

3. If a "shared time" or dual enrollment plan is operating in your community, pay it a visit and find out how it is working. For background, you might read the U.S. Office of Education Bulletin entitled *Dual Enrollment in Public and Non-public Schools,* by James E. Gibbs, Carl J. Sokolowski, August W. Steinhilber, and William C. Strasser, Jr.

4. Make an analysis of the public school systems in your metropolitan area. To what extent and in what ways do they cooperate? Has there been any consolidation of school systems? Is there now any talk of consolidation of school systems?

5. Give several reasons why you think that the federal government should take a *more* active role in education. Give several reasons why you think the federal government should take a *less* active role in education.

6. For a student who is interested in the educational press, it might be interesting to make a study of possible biases of the principal publishers of popular educational books and of journals which have educational interests. One might make a list of books which are critical of the educational establishment and have been published since 1967, and note who their publishers are. Such publishers as *Basic Books, Simon and Schuster, Doubleday, Harper,* and *Random House* would appear frequently. One might also note who has been invited to review these books in such journals as *New York Review of Books, New York Times,* and *Saturday Review.* One might study the record of *Random House, Publishers,* in relation to the *New York Review of Books* to test the charge which has been made that the *New York Review* uses a stable of authors to review each others' books, nearly all of whom agree with each other in being negatively critical of the educational establishment and in *favoring Random House* books. (Edgar Friedenberg, Jonathan Kozol, John Holt, Herbert Kohl, Paul Goodman, Ronald Gross, Peter Schrag). One might compare the reviews of the books by these authors with the reviews (and reviewers) of the same books appearing in the *New York Times.* For background information on the alliance between *Random House* and *The New York Review of Books,* read "The Case of the New York Review of Books" by Philip Nobile, in the April, 1972 issue of *Esquire.* One might also look for deviations in the "line" of the *Saturday Review* with respect to educational issues over the past 10 years, during which there have been several different education editors.

SUGGESTIONS FOR FURTHER READING

1. For a summary of examples of cooperation among systems in metropolitan areas, read chapter 13, "The Cooperative Approach," in Bollens and Schmandt, *The Metropolis.*

2. Chapter 9, "Church, State and School" in *Social Foundations of Education* by William O. Stanley *et al.* is an excellent discussion of questions about religion and the public schools.

3. The United States Office of Education publishes annually a *Digest of Educational Statistics.* Read the most recent editions to learn what kinds of information you may expect to get from this source.

4. Articles related to the content of this chapter and published in *Readings in Society and Education,* edited by Havighurst, Neugarten, and Falk are:

   Donald N. Michael, *The Next Twenty Years.*
   Donald G. McKinley, *The Ethos of Industrial America.*
   Paul Goodman, *The Present Moment in Education.*
   1970 Gallup Public Opinion Poll, *Public Attitudes toward the Public Schools.*

5. The voucher concept and its educational applications are described and analyzed in a book by Mecklenburger and Hostrup entitled *Education Vouchers? From Theory to Alum Rock.*

6. Recent criticisms of the "mainstream" of American education are commented on from various points of view in paperback books published under the auspices of the National Society for the Study of Education. These are published by Charles A. Jones Publishing Company, Worthington, Ohio. They are:

   Farewell to Schools? ? ? edited by Daniel U. Levine and Robert J. Havighurst.
   Reactions to Silberman's Crisis in the Classroom, edited by A. Harry Passow.
   Pygmalion Reconsidered—A Critical Review of Pygmalion in the Classroom by Rosenthal and Jacobson, edited by Janet D. Elashoff and Richard E. Snow.

7. The Council for Basic Education, through its *Bulletin* is an articulate conservative spokesman. The Council's Occasional Paper, No. 21, entitled *The Schools and the Press* (1974), reports a symposium on the reporting of educational news in the press, with some critical comments directed at some of the newspapers.

PART

IV

The Educational
System in the
Wider Society

CHAPTER 14

Education, Population,
and Economic Trends

In the preceding section of this book we have been discussing the school in the context of the local community, defining the community as neighborhood, town, city, or metropolitan area; and we have looked at some of the ways in which the school relates to other social institutions within that context. In this section we take a somewhat different perspective of the relations between education and society and consider how, within the context of the wider society, changes in population, in economic and technological developments, in relations between ethnic and racial groups all bring about a continually changing set of functions for the educational system.

POPULATION GROWTH

Americans have suddenly become aware of what is called the "population problem." There was no problem, as far as people could see, in the nineteenth and first half of the twentieth centuries; or if there was, it was the opposite from today's, for it centered around the need for new immigrants and for improved infant and child health so as to keep the population growing rapidly, and to "develop" the country. The American population doubled in size every 30 years from 1800 to 1920. Then in the 30 years after 1920 there was only a 42 percent increase, and in the 20 years after 1950, a 34 percent increase.

This slowdown in rate of population growth did not prevent people from warning of a "population explosion," and strong social and political forces were organized to limit the birthrate and to limit the rate of immigration. There is now growing advocacy of a policy of "zero population growth,"

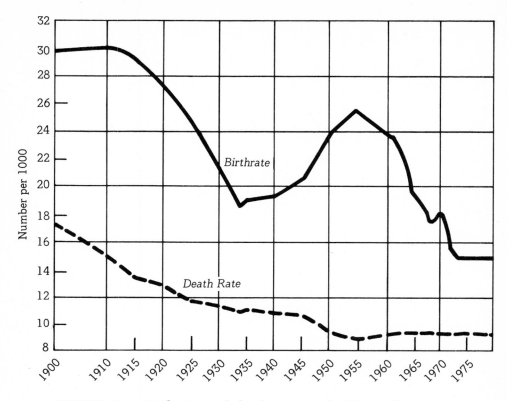

FIGURE 14.1   Birthrates and death rates in the United States, per
1,000 inhabitants. (Data from Dewhurst and associ-
ates, 1955, and from Statistical Abstract, 1973)

aimed at conserving natural resources and creating a high quality of life for a
population not much larger than at present.

There is also, of course, a world population problem of pressing importance. Some countries are seriously overcrowded, while others need people
to develop the land. While the broader study of population growth and population problems is an important part of the general education of Americans, we
will concentrate in this book on the interaction of population change on the
one hand, and the educational system on the other hand, as they are occurring
in the United States. We shall see that the population structure of the country
has profound effects upon the lives and life satisfactions of young people. In
fact, the 1970–80 period may produce a severe educational crisis due largely
to a temporary imbalance between the numbers of young adults and the numbers of middle-aged adults.

As shown in Fig. 14.1, birthrates and death rates (the annual numbers
of births and deaths per 1,000 people) have decreased since the early decades

of this century. But the birthrate has not had the steady downward trend which is characteristic of the death rate. The birthrate dropped during the economic depression of the 1930s to the lowest level in the country's history. Then immediately after the close of World War II, the birthrate jumped up and stayed up for about 15 years, until 1960. This was followed by a sharp drop to an even lower rate than that of the 1930s.

Factors Influencing the Birthrate

While there are many factors that influence the size of individual families, the birthrate for the country as a whole appears to be mainly a result of the interaction of two factors: (1) economic productivity and (2) practice of birth control.

Productivity has increased so greatly that the average worker today produces in one hour as much as the average worker in 1850 produced in six hours (Dewhurst and associates, 1955. U.S. Bureau of Labor Statistics, 1965).

From 1900 to 1970, the productivity of nonfarm workers increased approximately fourfold. This increase in productivity has occurred in agriculture as well as in industry. Increased productivity in industry at first tended to decrease the birthrate, because as machines replaced human labor the economic value of having a large number of children in the family was reduced. Children, unlike adults, could not handle machines, and their labor was not needed. With the spread of information regarding birth control, the number of children per family decreased, first in the cities, and later on the farms.

World Population Growth

The data from various countries add up to a phenomenon of world population growth which is becoming a source of grave concern to many people. It took thousands of years to reach the one-billion mark in world population, a mark reached about 1825. The second billion was reached only a hundred years later in 1925; and the third billion, only 35 years later, in 1960. A United Nations agency in 1971 predicted a world population of five billion by 1985 and more than six billion by the year 2000.

There is a problem of producing enough food for the rapidly increasing population of the more densely populated countries, such as India and several countries in Southeast Asia. However, this problem was partially solved by the breeding of very high-yielding varieties of corn, wheat, and rice, which has increased the food supply dramatically. Still, slow starvation is a threat over much of the world.

Even the most productive countries face an impossible situation if they continue to increase their population at their current rates. Thus, the United States, after 650 years at the present rate of growth, would have one person for every square foot of land—hardly enough to stand on, and certainly not enough to sleep on, or to live on.

CHANGES IN AGE DISTRIBUTION

Since 1850 there has been a marked shift in the age distribution of the American population. In the first half of the nineteenth century there was a large proportion of young children in the population and a very small proportion of persons over 60. In recent decades the distribution has changed, and the proportion of adults has increased markedly. Roughly speaking, 52 percent of the population were under 20 in 1850, 44 percent in 1900, and 39 percent in 1970. This means that there are more adults to do the work of the society. They have the advantages of modern technology. Thus, children and adolescents have been freed from the necessity of working and have been given more time that can be used for education.

Table 14.1 shows what has happened in terms of school and college enrollments. At first, children remained in school until the age of 14, then until 16; then more and more remained through high school graduation at 17 or 18. Finally, since 1920, there has been a great popular movement into the colleges.

By 1970, almost 80 percent of the youth of America were graduating from high school, and almost 60 percent of this graduating group were entering college. Thus in 1972–73, undergraduate college enrollments were the equivalent of 48 percent of the age-group 18 through 21. Somewhat less than half of this group would complete a four-year course, but many wanted a two-year course leading to a job at the technician or lower managerial level in the labor force.

These proportions are far higher than in any other country; so much higher, that educators in other countries find it difficult to believe that American standards of work in secondary schools and universities are as high as their own. American educators, on the other hand, point to these figures as proof that America offers greater educational opportunity than other countries; and that there is a huge reservoir of human ability that can be developed to far greater extent than has been attempted in any other country.

IMMIGRATION

The American population and, in turn, the American educational system have been affected in a major way by great streams of immigration throughout the nineteenth and twentieth centuries.

TABLE 14.1   *Secondary School and College Enrollments in Relation To Total Age-Groups*

Year	Number Enrolled in Secondary Schools per 100 Persons 14–17 Years of Age	Number Graduated from Secondary Schools per 100 Persons 17 Years of Age	Undergraduate Degree Credit Students per 100 Persons 18–21 Years of Age
1889–90	7	3.5	3.0
1899–1900	11	6.4	3.9
1909–10	15	8.8	5.0
1919–20	32	16.8	7.9
1929–30	51	29.0	11.9
1939–40	73	50.8	14.5
1949–50	77	59.0	26.9*
1955–56	84	62.0	27.6
1959–60	86	65.0	31.1
1961–62	90	70.0	33.9
1964–65	93	72.4	40.0
1969–70	94	78.0	44.0
1970–71	95	78.0	46.0
1972–73	96	78.0	48.0

* Includes a half-million veterans of the armed services, almost all of whom were over 21 years of age.

Source: U.S. Office of Education, *Digest of Educational Statistics*, 1972. U.S. Bureau of the Census, Series P-23, No. 44, March 1973.

Once the United States had been formed and the new nation had begun to grow, this country became a haven for the poor and the persecuted. The severe economic depression which followed the Napoleonic Wars in Europe brought many dispossessed people to America. Immigration from the British Isles consisted generally of poor but industrious people who were looking for better economic opportunities. The great Irish famine of the 1840s resulted in a large fraction of the Irish population emigrating to America. The political upheavals of Germany after 1848 caused many Germans to emigrate, some of them middle-class people.

Jewish immigrants came from all over Europe, seeking both religious freedom and economic opportunity. Swedes, Norwegians, and Danes came in large numbers after 1850, and for 50 years French people migrated into New England from French Canada. Then came Finns, Lithuanians, Estonians, Letts, Poles, Bohemians, Russians, and Hungarians. By 1910 the tide of immigration was running strongly from South and Southeastern Europe; and between 1900 and 1914 Italians, Bulgarians, Rumanians, Yugoslavs, Greeks, Armenians, and Portuguese brought the total of immigrants to an average of almost a million a year.

Meanwhile after the Gold Rush of the nineteenth century, Chinese, Japanese, and, later, Filipino and Hawaiian immigrants had been entering the western part of the continent; and later, as the southwest developed, there was an influx of Mexicans.

After World War II there was an upswing in immigration which lasted until 1952, when new restrictive legislation was passed by the Congress. Another upswing began in 1957 after counteractive legislation was adopted. Additional restriction-easing legislation was introduced in 1958 and 1959 and this, coupled with the large number of European displaced persons wishing to enter this country, made the immigration in the decade of the 50s one-and-a-half times greater than in the preceding decade. (Approximately two and one-half million immigrants entered the United States from 1951–1960, compared to the one million from 1941–1950.) More than one million immigrants entered the United States in the four-year period 1961–64.

In 1965 Congress passed legislation which eliminated the "quota" system based on national origins; although the total number of immigrants allowed into this country each year will not increase, persons will no longer be admitted on the basis of their nationality.

DIFFERENTIAL RATES OF REPRODUCTION

Another population phenomenon of significance for the educational system is the fact that birth and death rates vary with socioeconomic status. This variation is due to several factors. Death rates tend to be lower for people of high socioeconomic status because such people can afford better food, care, and medical attention than can people of low socioeconomic levels. Birth rates tend to be higher for people of low socioeconomic status, because these groups are less likely to make use of birth-control methods and because, especially if they are rural people, they still regard a child as an economic asset. Their children frequently quit school by the age of 16 and help to support the family.

Crude birth and death rates are not as accurate a basis for measuring population change as is the net reproduction rate (the number of female births in a given period compared to the number of female births within a similar interval of time in their mothers' generation). A net reproducton rate of 1 means that for every 100 females born in a certain year, there will be, when these women have grown up and passed the childbearing age, exactly 100 girl babies. A country with a long-term net reproduction rate of less than 1 is losing population (unless there is immigration to offset the deficit in births). In the United States, as shown in Table 14.2, the reproduction rate

TABLE 14.2.   *Net Reproduction Rates in the United States*

Year	Net Reproduction Rate
1905–1910	1.34
1920	1.25
1930	1.08
1930–1935	0.98
1935–1940	0.98
1943	1.23
1947	1.51
1950	1.44
1954	1.65
1959	1.72
1960	1.72
1961	1.70
1962	1.63
1965	1.38
1968	1.17

Source: Taeuber and Taeuber, 1958; Statistical Abstract of the United States, 1971.

fell below 1 for a brief period, but not long enough to cause an actual decrease of population.

The net reproduction rate in the early 1970s is once more below the level that will permit a natural increase in the population of the United States. This is seen by examining the figures for the "fertility rate," which is the number of births per woman in her lifetime. This rate must be at least 2.11 just to mantain the present level of population in the face of present mortality rates. But the fertility rate dropped to 2.03 in 1972 and 1.9 in 1973, the lowest in the history of the American population.

Reproduction Rates and Social Mobility

In the United States, as in almost all modern industrial societies, there has been an inverse relation between fertility and such socioeconomic factors as education of parents and occupation of fathers. Estimates of the net reproduction rates of various occupational groups have been made on the basis of birthrates occurring about 1940. These show that professional workers were at that time failing to reproduce their numbers by a very considerable margin. They were producing only about 75 children for every 100 adults in their generation. The same was true of business owners and executives. On the other hand, unskilled workers were producing about 125 children per 100 adults. Farmers and farm laborers were the most prolific of all.

This set of facts has had a considerable influence on the degree of upward social mobility presently existing in the United States and, therefore, has special relevance for the educational system. When the higher-status groups do not reproduce themselves in a society, they leave vacant spaces behind them after each generation, spaces that will be filled by people moving up from lower-status levels.

Some computations based on the net reproduction rates of the various social classes in the United States during the 1920–40 period showed that approximately one in eight young people of the lower-middle class and the two working classes would have to move up one step on a five-step scale of social status, in order to replenish the classes above him, due to the failure of the upper and upper-middle classes to reproduce their numbers.

However, since 1950 the birthrates have increased somewhat for middle-class families, and have decreased somewhat for the working-class families. Thus the young people reaching adulthood in the 1970–80 period will not be favored so much by a differential reproduction rate which would increase their chances for upward mobility.

EFFECTS OF POPULATION CHANGES AND ECONOMIC TRENDS UPON THE SCHOOLS AND COLLEGES

Changes in population size and distribution, when combined with changes occurring in the economic sphere, have produced a new set of educational problems for America that take on special significance when seen in historical perspective.

The Great Depression of the 1930s

After 150 years of almost continuous economic expansion, the American economy suffered a decade of near paralysis, now known as the Great Depression of the 1930s. Nothing like it had been known in America, where previously the periodic "panics" and business cycle depressions had been partially relieved by the opening up of new land to homesteaders and by the general onward sweep of industrialization.

So severe was the depression in this country that 20 percent of workers were unemployed for several years, industrial production fell to 55 percent of its 1929 level, prices plummeted, and farm mortgages were defaulted to the extent of billions of dollars.

The depression brought the marriage rate to its lowest point in many years. This tended to reduce the birthrate, which was cut further by the unwillingness of many married couples to have children during such bad times. In 1933 the situation was so desperate that a quarter of a million boys went "on the road," scrounging a living wherever they could find it. America awoke to the fact that it had a youth problem.

At this time the Civilian Conservation Corps was created with government funds to put boys into camps where they could do useful work, get vocational training, and at the same time send home $20 a month from their $30 pay. Shortly afterward, the National Youth Administration was created to provide work projects in high schools and colleges whereby needy youth could earn enough to pay their school expenses.

Effects on the Schools. During this period, the schools and colleges took on a major new function, that of custodial care of youth. Since there was little or no work available for youth, boys and girls were encouraged to stay in school, aided if necessary by government scholarships and work projects. The idea was to keep young people out of trouble—in cold storage, as it were —until society could find a use for them. (The situation in the 1970s, described in Chapter 9, calls for more "active" learning by youth until they can achieve adult roles, but for different socioeconomic reasons.)

During the depression, teachers' salaries were generally reduced and salary checks were often delayed because there were no funds in city and county treasuries. Nevertheless, teaching jobs were much sought after by people who had some training or experience in teaching but who had been employed in business or industry. For many people there was more security in teaching than in depression-ridden business. Soon there was overcrowding in the teaching profession, and young people were not encouraged to enter it. For ten years after 1932 the intake of young teachers was small; and the total number of elementary and secondary school teachers stayed nearly constant from 1930 until 1950. After 1950 the postwar increase in birthrate raised the school enrollments rapidly and created a vast demand, first for new elementary school teachers and then for secondary school teachers. Thus, by the mid-1960s there was a large group of teachers in the age range 25–40 and a relatively small group over 40.

Postwar Economic Expansion and Population Growth

Beginning with World War II and continuing thereafter, until the late 1960s, the American economy experienced an enormous expansion. This meant nearly full employment, high wages, and a generally increasing economic standard of living. It also meant increasing numbers of positions in executive and professional occupations, especially in the areas of science and health.

At the same time, the great increase in birthrate flooded the schools with children. Since there had been little or no building of new elementary schools between 1930 and 1950, the schools were crowded to overflowing after 1950. Many city elementary schools had to go on "double shift," with one group of children and teachers occupying classrooms in the morning and another group in the afternoon. There was a surge of new school construction, at first of elementary schools and then of secondary schools.

The swelling of school enrollments greatly enlarged the cost of education to the community. With the numbers of elementary and secondary school children having remained relatively constant at about 28 million in the years from 1940 to 1950, the numbers jumped to 31 million in 1955 and to 48 million in 1965 and 52 million in 1971. To meet these increased costs, most states have increased their payments from state funds to local school districts.

Teacher Shortages and Oversupply

The demand for new teachers was intense during the 1950–65 period, and this no doubt helped to increase teachers' salaries, which rose rapidly. But the demand for new teachers began to fade, after 1965, except for those who could teach certain special subjects. The school enrollment had reached a maximum by 1972 and was due to decline by 1975 because the birthrate dropped after 1960. But colleges continued to turn out prospective teachers, and, by 1970, there was suddenly an oversupply of college graduates with teachers' licenses. This came together with the mild economic recession of 1970–71, which reduced the general demand for college graduates in the job market and therefore restricted job opportunities outside of the teaching field. Given the reduced birthrate which will reduce school enrollment throughout the 1970s, it seems clear that there will be an oversupply of young adults available for teaching jobs for the next 10 or 15 years, at least. Whereas some 5 million young people found teaching jobs in the period from 1955 to 1970, no more than 2 million jobs will become open during the decade of the 1970s, this number due largely to retirement of elderly teachers.

Table 14.3 shows how the percentage of persons employed as teachers relative to the population aged 20–64 has varied since 1890. This percentage was relatively constant at about 1.2 to 1.4 from 1890 to 1950. Then there was a sharp rise to 2.1 in 1970. This constituted a 75 percent increase in the proportion of teachers in the adult population between 1950 and 1970. The percentage will drop to about 1.94 in 1980. Meanwhile, the proportion of college teachers will continue to rise until about 1980.

Effects on Colleges and Universities

The direct effect of the low birthrates of the 1930s followed by the high birthrates of the 1950s was to produce an abnormally small college-age population after 1950 which extended to about 1965. Table 14.4 shows how the age group 15–19, the group supplying the college entrants, fluctuates between 1950 and 1980. This factor caused a sharp increase in college enrollments after 1965.

In addition, there is the more general factor that increasing *propor-*

TABLE 14.3. *Percentage of the Population 20–64 Who Are Teachers*

Year	Elementary and Secondary School Teachers	College and University Teachers
1890	1.22	.04
1900	1.18	.06
1910	1.14	.07
1920	1.25	.08
1930	1.32	.11
1940	1.25	.14
1950	1.18	.22
1955	1.34	.25
1960	1.70	.31
1965	1.96	.43
1970	2.10	.55*
1975	2.08*	.63*
1980	1.94*	.64*

* Estimated by the authors.

Source: U.S. Office of Education, *Digest of Educational Statistics*, 1973.

TABLE 14.4. *Distribution of the Population by Age-Groups, 1900–1985*

Year	Age Group Distribution (percentages)							Total (thousands on July 1)
	under 5	5–9	10–14	15–19	20–29	30–64	65 and over	
1900	12.1	11.6	10.5	9.9	18.4	33.4	4.1	76,094
1910	11.6	10.6	9.9	9.8	18.8	35.0	4.3	92,407
1920	10.9	10.8	10.0	9.0	17.5	37.1	4.6	106,466
1930	9.3	10.2	9.8	9.4	16.9	38.9	5.4	123,077
1940	8.0	8.1	8.9	9.4	17.2	41.7	6.8	131,954
1945	9.3	7.8	7.7	8.4	17.0	42.2	7.5	139,928
1950	10.7	8.8	7.3	7.0	15.8	42.2	8.1	151,677
1960	11.3	10.4	9.4	7.4	12.1	39.8	9.2	179,323
1965	10.1	10.5	9.8	8.8	12.9	38.2	9.6	194,237
1970	8.4	9.7	10.2	9.4	15.1	37.3	9.9	204,800
1975	9.4	8.0	9.2	9.6	16.9	36.8	10.1	217,375
1980	10.6	8.8	7.5	8.6	17.4	37.0	10.1	233,798
1985	10.8	9.9	8.3	7.0	16.4	37.4	10.1	252,093

Source: Data for 1900–1970 from Bureau of Census reports. Projections are taken from the U.S. Bureau of the Census *(Population Estimates and Projections)*, Series P-25, No. 476, Feb. 1972. The projections are based on "assumption C," that fertility will decline slightly from the 1960–70 level.

tions of young people have been entering college over the past 100 years. As we have seen in Table 5.1, approximately 34 percent of young people were in college by 1960, and approximately half of them were graduating from a four-year course. The proportion entering college went on increasing to 46 percent by 1972 and approximately 22 percent of the total age-cohort were graduating from a four-year course. A cohort is the group of people born in a given year, or a given period of time, and who enter some stage of life together. One of the major questions now confronting higher education is whether the proportion of young people entering college will go on increasing during the 1970s or whether this proportion will stabilize. In either case, there will be an increase in the number of college students due to the increase in the absolute size of the college-age group.

Effects on the Young Adult Cohort

Just as we have been considering the relation between variation in size of a 5 or 10-year age group and college enrollments, we may consider the relations between a 10-year cohort (the age group 20–29), and the labor force into which this cohort is entering. This can be understood better by referring to Fig. 14.2, which shows how the numbers of 20–29-year-olds have been related to the numbers of 30–64-year-olds. The older group is the established productive group, which receives the 20–29 group as a cohort which is just moving into adulthood, with a particular composition in terms of numbers, training, and attitudes toward work and toward the society. When the younger group is as much as half as large as the older group, as was true during the first 15 years of this century, it is in a very subordinate position in terms of its ability to "compete" with older people for scarce or desirable jobs, since it has such large numbers who are competing among themselves. This was not seen as a particularly disadvantageous situation for young people in 1900–1915, since not only were there many jobs for unskilled young men and women on the farms and in the towns and cities, but the American economy was growing rapidly, and becoming industrialized, with a great demand for new manpower at all levels of skill and training.

The ratio of the 20–29 cohort to the 30–64 group reached its lowest point in 1960, at .3, and was below .35 for a dozen years, from 1952 to 1965. Thus this was a period during which young adults were readily absorbed into the adult productive group, especially since this coincided with a time of great industrial development. There was an especially heavy demand for recruits to four rapidly expanding professions—engineering, scientific research, nursing, and teaching. It is estimated that the number of people in these four occupations increased 40 percent in the single 10-year period between 1955 and 1965, while the size of the 20–29 age group increased by only 11 percent. Thus, young people in this period profited from the opportunities

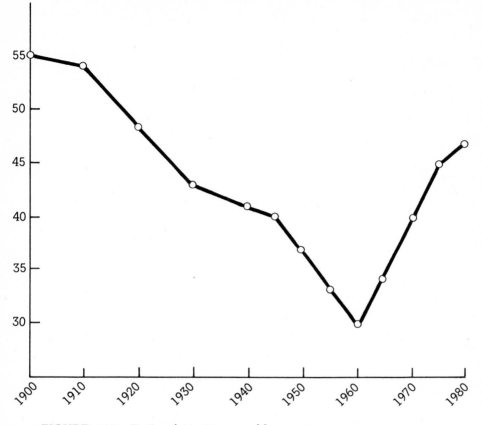

FIGURE 14.2   Ratio of 20–29-year-olds to age-group 30–64.

to attend college and to seek jobs in the occupational areas where shortages existed.

Figure 14.2 also tells us that the 20–29 group is now moving into a much less favorable situation in relation to the 30–64 group, and therefore will not be so readily absorbed by the labor force. They will not be readily absorbed for two reasons: first, there are more of them to compete for the more desirable entry positions in the labor force; and second, there are fewer jobs for unskilled workers than there were in the earlier period, thus forcing some young people who might have settled for an unskilled job to get more education so as to be able to compete for jobs requiring at least a high school education.

It looks as though working-class youth with a desire for upward mobility and with the required college-level training for middle-class occupations will have to compete more strenuously in the labor market than in the 1960–70 period. This is seen when one compares the proportion of an age cohort graduating from a four-year college course with the corresponding proportion of places in the contemporary labor force that require or expect college preparation. A look at Table 5.5 in Chapter 5 makes this comparison possible. Some 14 percent of the jobs in the labor force are in the "professional and technical" category, which generally assumes college-level training or more. This is to be compared with the figure of 22 percent of the age cohort now graduating from college. At first sight this might seem to imply that something like 8 percent of the age cohort, upon graduating from college, will *not* find the jobs they want. However, another 14 percent of the male fraction in Table 5.5 and 5 percent of the female fraction are "managers, proprietors, or officials," a category which covers a wide range of jobs in the business world, from corporation and bank presidents and factory superintendents down to owners of small business and county officials, many of whom do not now have more than a high school education. The clerical and sales categories consist largely of people with a high school education, though some of these sales positions involve large financial dealings and would be regarded as appropriate for people with a college degree. Let us presume that many college graduates will be absorbed into the category of managers and proprietors, with a jump in average educational level from the present high school graduate level to the college graduate level in the 1970s. Then, it may be estimated that the 22 percent of an age cohort *now graduating* from college will match fairly closely the proportion of the labor force that would be required or expected to have a college education.

At present, about 46 percent of an age cohort *enter* college. If more than half of them remain in college no more than one or two years, they will not be able to compete with the college graduates who not only get professional and technical jobs, but who also will be taking "proprietors and managers" jobs. What kind of jobs will these college dropouts expect and be prepared for? To some extent they will be prepared for technical jobs at the "technician" level, for some of the higher status service jobs, such as those of policemen and some civil service jobs. Numbers of women college graduates may drop out of the labor force to raise children and keep house (although the present trend is contrary), but these women are likely to move back into the working force when they reach middle age in line with the present trend.

Looking again at the college graduates, and knowing that this group is having difficulty, for the first time, in finding appropriate jobs, we may expect that the shock of emerging from college with a teacher's license or an engineer's degree to find jobs unavailable at these levels will become painfully familiar to a good many young people during the 1970s. But, if it is true that the changes in values described in Chapters 1 and 9 are indeed in process, and if a good many young people are less *instrumental* and more *expressive* in their approach to life than was true in an earlier day, perhaps they will not be so much concerned about the size of their incomes, and about the nature or

social-class level of their jobs as the more instrumental middle-aged generation might expect.

Dael Wolfle, foreseeing this kind of situation, was quoted in Chapter 5,
"The United States has been blessedly free of rigid attitudes about what kind
of employment is suitable for a college graduate. Some jobs carry higher
prestige than others; some pay better; some have other advantages; but the
typical college graduate has thought it better to accept the best job available
than to be out of work." On the other hand, as already mentioned, Peter
Drucker believes that the college graduates of the seventies will become
more concerned about such things. He writes, "Economics is not likely to fade
out of the public consciousness. The graduates from today's youth culture
are likely to find themselves far more worried about jobs and money than
they now suspect." (Drucker, 1971, p. 39)

What would be the result of a further expansion of college and university education to two-thirds of the youth population, with one third
securing a bachelor's degree—the policy recommended by the Carnegie Commission on Higher Education? It appears that the decade of the 1970s may
give us a foretaste of this policy, if we move to perhaps a 60 percent college
entrance rate and a 30 percent college graduation rate.

Societal Development and Postgraduate Education

In the preceding paragraphs we have considered the likelihood that young
people with a four-year college course will have greater difficulty getting
"appropriate" jobs than they have in the past. There is also a real problem for
those who are now completing postgraduate training with the degrees of
M.A., M.Sc., or Ph.D. A staff member of the U.S. Office of Education writes:
"There is no doubt that Ph.D.'s in all areas are facing the worst job market in
decades." (Harvey, 1972). A National Science Foundation study reported that
in 1971 scientists (with various degrees) had an unemployment rate of 5.3
percent (N.S.F., 1971a). The National Science Foundation predicted a total
available supply, in 1980, of 315,000 to 336,000 Ph.D. level scientists and engineers, with a utilization of only 270,000 to 297,000. Thus there may be a gap
of 42,000 between the supply and the demand.

Estimates and projections are not as reliable for the demand for men
and women with a master's degree, and an oversupply might not be so
serious, since a master's degree generally requires no more than a year's postgraduate work, with that much "income foregone," and many people study
for a master's degree while holding a full-time job.

This looming surplus of people with the most advanced training is
shown in Table 14.5, which reports the numbers of earned degrees in higher
education over the past century. The sharpest increase has come during the
1960–70 decade, with a jump of 320 percent in the number of Ph.D. degrees
awarded per year, and a corresponding increase of 230 percent in the awards

TABLE 14.5.   Numbers of People in the United States Earning Various
Degrees in Higher Education (thousands)

| | Degree Earned | | | | | |
| | Bachelor's or First Professional | | Master's Degree | | Doctor of Philosophy | |
Year	Male	Female	Male	Female	Male	Female
1869–70	9.4		0		—	
1879–80	12.9		0.87		0.05	
1899–1900	27.4		1.58		0.37	
1909–10	37.2		3.77		0.42	
1919–20	48.6		4.30		0.56	
1929–30	122.5		15.04		2.23	
1939–40	186.5		26.73		3.29	
1954–55	288.0		58.00		8.50	
1955–56	196	112	39	20	8.0	0.9
1960–61	256	146	54	24	8.8	1.0
1965–66	331	224	93	48	16.1	2.1
1969–70	456	328	135	84	25.5	3.8
1970–71	473	344	156	99	27.3	4.0
1974–75*	532	427	199	126	40.6	6.0

* U.S. Office of Education: *Projections of Educational Statistics to 1980*, 1970.

Source: U.S. Office of Education: *Digest of Educational Statistics*, 1971.

of the master's degree. Between 1961 and 1970, the total number of Ph.D.'s awarded was approximately 170,000, which was half the total number awarded by American universities from 1861, when Yale granted the first degree, through 1970.

The column in Table 14.5 which is marked "Bachelor's or First Professional" degrees, includes medical and dental doctor's degrees, as well as those in optometry, veterinary medicine, podiatry, pharmacy, and the degrees of Bachelor of Laws (LL.B.) and Bachelor of Theology and other degrees from professional schools. Most of these graduates had two to four years of college work before entering professional school, and therefore are at the master's degree level or above, in terms of length of their higher education. In some of these areas there is also an oversupply. An important exception is that of health services, where there is still a shortage.

The Carnegie Commission in 1970 reported, "The United States today faces one serious manpower shortage, and that is in health care personnel. This shortage can become even more acute as health insurance expands, leading to even more unmet needs and greater cost inflation, unless corrective action is taken now." (*Higher Education and the Nation's Health*, p. 2). The Commission recommends an increase of 50 percent in medical school entrants and 20 percent in dental school entrants. Young people are attracted to this field, and there is at present an oversupply of qualified applicants. But any major expansion of health service personnel waits upon federal government support for new and larger schools of medicine, dentistry, optometry, etc.

RESPONSES OF AN AGE COHORT TO CHANGING SOCIAL REALITY

We have seen that the period since 1960 has seen *changing* proportions of children and of young adults in relation to the basic adult productive and supportive group aged 30–64. There have been a series of *imbalances* and more will come during the 1970–80 decade. These imbalances go back to major fluctuations in the birthrate, which produced markedly different-sized age cohorts to follow each other through the life span. When an age cohort of 10 years has some inner consistency, but differs drastically from the cohort which precedes or follows it, one may expect the "life history" of this cohort to differ a good deal from the life histories of its predecessor and its successor.

A 10-year cohort has a kind of life of its own, and perhaps even a subculture of its own, due to the fact that it confronts a different social reality from the reality met by the cohorts which go ahead or come after it.

The 10-year cohort born in 1946–55, and aged 20–29 in 1975, is especially interesting, partly because it is the cohort just now coming of age, and partly because it is so different from its immediately preceding 10-year cohort. Consequently, it will be useful to compare these two 10-year age groups, and also to speculate on the life course of the latest such group, those born in 1961–70. This can be done with the aid of Table 14.6.

This figure illustrates what appears to be an important difference between Groups A and B (1936–45 and 1946–55). Group B comes onto the adult stage in a period of unusual instability, which faces this group with a variety of cultural alternatives. The 1970–80 decade is a period of testing cultural alternatives against the social realities of the job market, the black revolution, the new politics, and the new sexual morality.

EXERCISES

1. State departments of education make surveys and forecasts of the school-age population to aid local school boards and the state university in making future plans. If your state has such a report available, obtain a copy. What will be the future needs for schools in your own community? What will your state university need to do?

TABLE 14.6 *The Life Span of Three 10-Year Cohorts*

	Cohort A	Cohort B	Cohort C
Born	1936–45	1946–55	1961–70
Age in 1975	30–39	20–29	5–14
Number (in 1970)	26 million	37 million	37 million
Ratio 20–29 /30–64	.34	.45	.38 (est.)
Significant experiences			
Cost of education to society	relatively low	ever increasing	stabilized
Entry to labor force	easy: much needed (1952–1965)	difficult: oversupply. (1962–1975)	? (1977–1990)
18-year-old vote (1970)	not affected	involved: the pioneer cohort	taken for granted
Free Speech Movement (Berkeley) Columbia U. student riots (1967–68) Kent State incident (1970)	age: 22–34 "spectators"	age: 12–24 actively involved	"just past history"
Youth political action: McCarthy and McGovern (1968 and 1972)	age: 23–36 active	age: 13–26 active	"just past history"
Vietnam service and protest (1965–72)	age 20–36 involved	Age: 10–26 involved	history
Drug Culture (1967–72)	age: 22–36 marginal	age: 12–26 involved	?
Attitude toward parental generation	mutual accommodation	cannot trust anyone over 30	?
Watergate (1972–74) Energy Crisis (1973–74)	age 28–37 involved	age 18–27 involved	2–11 ?

2. One of the major issues with respect to higher education during the next decade is the relative value and importance of expanding public community colleges (with two-year programs) compared with expansion of the state system of four-year universities. What is the situation with respect to this issue in your state?

3. Interview some young men and women whom you know fairly well, who are college graduates and have jobs at a "lower" level than might be expected by a college graduate. What are their attitudes toward their jobs and toward their education?

SUGGESTIONS FOR FURTHER READING

1. The Carnegie Commission on Higher Education has paid a good deal of attention to the problem of oversupply of college-trained people and has recommended some selective limitations on expansion of college enrollments. A parallel Commission on Human Resources and Higher Education has been supported by the Russell Sage Foundation (Folger, Astin, and Bayer). Both Commissions have taken an optimistic view of the problem of oversupply of college graduates in relation to the demand of the labor force for people with such qualifications. A useful comparative view of this problem from a European base is given by Ladislav Cerych, who writes on "A Global Approach to Higher Education" in a publication of the International Council on Educational Development. He points out that European students expect the university to guarantee them appropriate jobs, and that European employers resist the employment of persons on jobs for which they are "overqualified" by more advanced degrees.

2. A wealth of factual information about the social and economic characteristics of the nation is to be found in the Twentieth Century Fund Report, *America's Needs and Resources: A New Survey* by J. Frederic Dewhurst and associates. Read also the pamphlet by Michael, *Cybernation: The Silent Conquest.*

3. To obtain background information on the population history and the present structure of population in the United States, any one of the following books is a good reference: *Population Problems* by Paul T. Landis and Paul K. Hatt; *Population Problems,* fifth ed., by W. S. Thompson and D. T. Lewis; *Length of Life* by Louis I. Dublin, Alfred J. Lotka, and Martin Spiegelman; *The Population of the United States* by Donald J. Bogue; and *The Changing Population of the United States* by Conrad and Irene Taeuber.

4. The paper by Michael in *Society and Education: A Book of Readings* (Havighurst, Neugarten, and Falk) is a provocative discussion of technological innovations in American society and of the likely effects of cybernation (the use of computers and automation).

CHAPTER 15

Education and the Black Minority

This chapter and the two to follow deal with the broad problems of the society with regard to cultural pluralism: the changing position in American society of various racial and ethnic groups—blacks, Orientals, Chicanos, American Indians, and other groups—and the ways in which these broad changes are affecting and are affected by the educational system. We shall focus in the present chapter upon the black minority; then in Chapter 16, upon other minority groups; then, in Chapter 17, upon questions of integration, separatism, and cultural pluralism when seen from the broader perspective of the changing society.

URBANIZATION AND MIGRATION
OF THE BLACK POPULATION

A major problem of American society is that of relations between blacks and whites, a problem that has come to a head since 1965 and is now at the center of national politics. In one way or another every social institution—family, business, industry, education, religion, government, sports, communications—is being affected by the changing relations between the races. Black voters have become increasingly active and organized, and the issues around the education of black children and youth dominated the national election of 1972.

To understand the educational situation of a minority group we need to know something about the group in terms of numbers, residence, and socioeconomic status. The black population has been growing at a slightly more rapid rate than the white population. It was 9.9 percent of the total U.S. population in 1950, 10.5 percent in 1960, and 11.1 percent in 1970.

During the period since World War I the black population has become urbanized, and it is now more urbanized than the white. In 1910, 73 percent of blacks lived in rural or semirural settings, but this situation is now reversed, with 81 percent in 1970 living in towns and cities of 2,500 or more (Table 15.1). Urbanization has taken place with about equal speed in all regions of the country except the South. Blacks have moved from the South to the North, East, and West, and have moved into industrial centers. Table 15.2 shows how the proportions of blacks have changed in populations of

TABLE 15.1.   Residence of the Black Population

Geographic Area	Percentage Distribution					
	1950		1960		1970	
	Black	White	Black	White	Black	White
In metropolitan areas	59	63	67	66	74	68
In central cities	44	35	53	31	58	28
Outside central cities	15	28	14	35	16	40
Outside metropolitan areas	41	37	33	34	26	32
In rural areas	38	36	27	31	19	27
In the South	68	27	61	27	53	28
Total number (millions)	15.0	135	18.8	159	22.7	178

Source: U.S. Census. Statistical Abstract of the United States, 1972.

TABLE 15.2.   Nonwhite Population Trends in the Big Cities

	Percent of the City's Population			
	1920	1940	1960	1970
New York	2.7	6.1	14.0	23.4
Chicago	4.1	8.2	22.9	34.4
Philadelphia–Camden	7.4	13.0	26.4	34.7
Los Angeles–Long Beach	2.5	3.9	12.2	21.1
San Francisco–Oakland	1.1	1.4	14.3	32.8
Detroit	4.1	9.2	28.9	44.5
Boston	2.2	3.1	9.1	16.3
Pittsburgh	6.4	9.3	16.7	20.7
Washington, D.C.	25.1	28.0	53.9	72.3
Atlanta	31.3	34.6	38.3	51.6
Birmingham	29.3	40.7	39.6	42.2

Note: Blacks constitute 90 percent of the nonwhite population as a whole. Nonwhite includes Orientals, who are present in noticeable numbers in San Francisco and Los Angeles, but not in other cities on this list.

major American cities. The northern cities had slow increases between 1900 and 1940, then very rapid increases after 1950. The southern cities have seen relatively little change since 1940.

The urbanization of blacks and their migration to industrial centers have posed new problems in intergroup relations. As long as most blacks lived at a subsistence level in the rural South, they tended to be ignored by the rest of the country. But as soon as they moved into the cities they became highly visible.

A minority of blacks became integrated into the social and economic life of the cities. They followed the familiar pattern of other immigrant ethnic groups. They worked hard and saved their money; they secured as good an education as possible for their children; their children moved up the socio-economic ladder into professional and business occupations. Thus a black middle class developed.

But the majority of newly urbanized blacks have not had this experience. They and their children are still set aside from the mainstream of American life. They are segregated residentially, they are discriminated against with regard to housing and jobs and their children attend segregated schools. This larger group of blacks have become a burden on the conscience of a democratic society.

In metropolitan areas in 1965, 75 percent of black elementary school pupils attended schools in which more than 90 percent of their fellow pupils were blacks. In these same areas, 83 percent of the white pupils attended schools with more than 90 percent white enrollment.

ECONOMIC DEVELOPMENT

The occupational distribution of whites and nonwhites in 1970 can be compared from the data in Table 15.3. Among men, it will be seen that smaller proportions of nonwhites are to be found in the higher-status occupations (professional and technical, and managers) and higher proportions in the lower-status occupations. The same is generally true of women.

Another index of their relatively disadvantaged position of blacks is the fact that unemployment has long been, and continued to be, higher than among whites. Since 1950, the unemployment of blacks age 20 and over has been about twice as high—roughly 6 to 10 percent as compared to 3 to 5 percent for whites. The differences have been particularly striking among young people aged 16 to 19, where unemployment among whites since 1960 has fluctuated from 11 to 13 percent, but among blacks, from 24 to 29 percent.

At the same time, the occupational statuses of blacks have improved substantially over the past decade, as seen from Table 15.4 where *changes* in occupational groupings are shown. As indicated in that table, nonwhites constituted 11 percent of all employed persons in 1960 and again in 1970. If non-

312

TABLE 15.3.   *Occupational Distribution of White and Nonwhite Workers. 1970*

| | Percentage Distribution | | | |
| | Men | | Women | |
	White	Nonwhite	White	Nonwhite
Professional and technical	14.6	7.8	15.0	10.8
Managers, officials, and proprietors	15.3	4.7	4.8	1.9
Clerical	7.1	7.4	36.4	20.8
Sales	6.1	1.8	7.7	2.5
Craftsmen and foremen	20.8	13.8	1.2	0.8
Operatives	18.7	28.4	14.1	17.6
Nonfarm laborers	6.2	17.5	0.4	0.7
Private household workers	0.1	0.3	3.4	17.5
Other service workers	6.0	12.8	15.3	25.6
Farmers and farm managers	3.6	1.7	0.3	0.1
Farm laborers	1.7	3.9	1.5	1.5
Number (millions)	44.16	4.80	26.03	3.64

Source: *Employment and Unemployment in 1970,* Bureau of Labor Statistics, U.S. Department of Labor. Special Report No. 129. 1971.

whites were "equivalent" to whites—that is, if they were occupationally distributed the same as whites—they should have approximately 11 percent of the jobs *in each category.* It will be seen that this is far from the case, and that nonwhites are under-represented in the higher-status occupations, and over-represented in the lower-status occupations. Nevertheless, there has been a major gain for black workers between 1960 and 1970. Nonwhites almost doubled their holding of professional and technical jobs, going from 4 to 7 percent of all the jobs in this category; and they increased their holding of other higher-status occupations (from "operatives" on up). Thus in the past decade there has been an overall shift upward in the occupational distribution of blacks.

IS THERE A BLACK SUBCULTURE?

In thinking about the educational situation of the black population in the United States, it is important to understand the relative importance of two bases for grouping: one based on social class and the other based on race. According to one view, blacks and whites of a given social-class level are very similar in life styles and therefore social class is the major determinant of subcultural differences. The contrasting view is that color or race is a primary factor; that blacks behave and think differently from whites, no matter what their economic status; thus that race is a major determinant of subcultural differences.

Ethnicity and racial differences is a topic treated at various points in this book, especially in Chapter 17, but it needs some attention here so that we may better understand the educational system as it affects the black population. The question of concern in this chapter is to what extent should the educational problems of the black population be viewed in terms of the *social-class* structure of the society?

The data on this question are not easily disentangled, but the answer is beginning to be clear. It appears that at very low income levels blacks are different from whites with regard to cultural values and attitudes. As we go up the income or social-class scale, blacks and whites become more similar, even though certain attitudinal differences persist. A recent study of the low-income population of Pittsburgh illustrates this point. Three "poverty neighborhoods" in Pittsburgh were studied in 1968. At each address, the per-

TABLE 15.4.   *Occupational Changes among Nonwhite Workers, 1960–1970*

	Percent Nonwhites	
	1960	1970
Total employed persons, both sexes	11	11
Professional and technical	4	7
Medical and other health	4	8
Teachers, except college teachers	4	10
Managers, officials, and proprietors	3	4
Clerical	5	8
Sales	2	4
Craftsmen	5	7
Construction craftsmen	7	7
Machinists, other metal craftsmen	4	6
Foremen	2	5
Operatives	10	14
Nonfarm laborers	27	23
Private household workers	50	42
Other service workers	20	19
Protective services	5	8
Waiters, cooks, butchers, etc.	15	13
Farmers and farm workers	16	11

Source: *Social and Economic Status of Negroes in the United States:* 1970. U.S. Bureau of the Census. *Current Population Reports.* Series p-23. No. 38. July, 1971.

Note: Blacks make up 90 percent of nonwhites. The next largest group are Orientals.

son who called himself or herself head of the household, or the spouse of the head of the household, was interviewed by a student of the same color as the respondent. Persons were grouped into two economic levels: the "poor," having a median family income of $4,143, and the "not-poor," having $6,764. To determine whether there were differences in subculture, the following questions were asked.

Who is head of this household?
When you think about the future, how far ahead do you have a clear idea of what your life will be like? (Future orientation)
Can you count on most people you meet? (Trust in people)
Which of the following statements do you think is the primary cause of poverty?
Lack of an individual's effort?
Circumstances beyond an individual's control?
Both have equal weight?
Neither are primary reasons? (Work ethic).

The researchers found striking differences between the black and white groups, but little difference between the nationality groups among the whites (Irish, Italian, Anglo-American). Concerning the three value-themes stated above, blacks were lower on "trust in people," "future orientation," and "individual responsibility for poverty."

Among the blacks, furthermore, there were differences according to how persons classified themselves when asked "What is your nationality?" They responded that they were: Negro, black, Afro-American, colored, in that order of frequency. Those who called themselves "colored" gave responses more nearly like the white pattern.

At the same time, the racial differences were substantially less among the "not poor" group than among the "poor." The authors conclude as follows:

> There are many Black and White people whose response patterns are very similar. There are several instances where racial differences diminish with higher income levels. Large proportions of those calling themselves Colored give responses similar to the White pattern. Many in the White poor group conform to the typical Black response pattern. This provides an indication that there is heterogeneity within the two subcultures delimited. However, in spite of the shared elements and the internal diversity, the variables examined here indicate the greatest differentiation to be along racial lines. (Johnson and Sanday, 1971, p. 141)

Comparisons of blacks and whites at middle-class levels have not been made so systematically, but it appears that there is relatively little difference. Values appear to be much the same for both middle-class groups, especially those that have to do with the education of children.

THE BLACK REVOLUTION

The "Black Revolution" is not a revolution as people have understood that term in the past, although it is something like the Industrial Revolution in the peaceable yet drastic quality of the social change it carries with it. The Black Revolution was first taken seriously by many Americans on August 28, 1963, when 200,000 black and white Americans marched to the Lincoln Monument in Washington, to demonstrate the urgent need for action for the blacks of North America.

This may be regarded as the end of Phase I of the Black Revolution which had started 10 years before, in a courtroom in Topeka, Kansas. There, lawyers supported by the National Association for the Advancement of Colored People argued that black children were deprived of their rights under the U.S. constitution, by being required to attend a segregated all-black elementary school. In the southern states, there were two school systems, for both elementary and secondary levels, maintained by the state, one for whites and the other for blacks. Segregated schools were also generally accepted though not required by the state, in the border states between the North and South, and in southern Illinois, Missouri, and Kansas. In many medium-sized and smaller cities in the border areas, like in Topeka, the local school board maintained one or more elementary schools to which black pupils were assigned. (When black pupils finished elementary school, they attended the district high school which was almost entirely white.)

When the U.S. Supreme Court ruled in 1954 that the Topeka school system must close its black school and send its black pupils to schools with white pupils, this was the beginning of the educational system's direct involvement in the Black Revolution. But other things were going on, too. Black workmen in northern cities were gradually moving into jobs as foremen, where they were supervising racially mixed work crews. Black clerks were being employed by big-city department stores. Black secretaries were getting jobs in law offices.

In southern states black people began to protest against the racial segregation in public facilities, restaurants, and places of business—a practice that had existed for decades. On December 1, 1955, Mrs. Rosa Parks quietly started a protest in Montgomery, Alabama, against segregation on city buses, a protest which finally succeeded.

Martin Luther King, who later won the Nobel peace prize, rose to leadership during this period, and his methods of nonviolent resistance to southern segregation practices spread throughout the South.

In another area of American life, the Brooklyn Dodgers baseball team had hired Jackie Robinson, a black athlete, in 1947, thus setting a precedent quickly followed by the other teams in professional baseball, football, and basketball.

Organizations to support the Black Revolution have grown in strength and in number after World War II. Principal prewar organizations were the National Association for the Advancement of Colored People (NAACP) and the Urban League. Later came the Congress of Racial Equality (CORE) and the Southern Christian Leadership Conference organized by Martin Luther King. These were not aligned with any political party and did not have any political program beyond that of getting civic and economic and educational opportunity for blacks.

More militant organizations were formed during the 1960s. These were SNCC (Student Nonviolent Coordinating Committee), the Black Panthers, and a number of associations of black teachers, black students, black psychologists, and other professional groups.

The first phase of the Black Revolution terminated about 1965, when, on June 4 of that year, the President of the United States, Lyndon B. Johnson, speaking to the graduating class of Howard University, said:

> Our earth is the home of revolution.
>
> In every corner of every continent men charged with hope contend with ancient ways in the pursuit of justice. They reach for the newest of weapons to realize the oldest of dreams; that each may walk in freedom and pride, stretching his talents, enjoying the fruits of the earth. . . .
>
> But nothing in any country touches us more profoundly, nothing is more freighted with meaning for our own destiny, than the revolution of the Negro American.
>
> In far too many ways American Negroes have been another nation: deprived of freedom, crippled by hatred, the doors of opportunity closed to hope.
>
> In our time change has come to this nation, too. The American Negro, acting with impressive restraint, has peacefully protested and marched, entered the courtroom and the seats of government, demanding a justice that has long been denied. . . .
>
> We seek not just freedom but opportunity—not just legal equity but human ability—not just equality as a right and a theory, but equality as a fact and as a result (Johnson, 1965).

DESEGREGATION OF SCHOOLS

Racial desegregation of schools was a major aspect of the Black Revolution. The period since 1954 can be divided into three phases.

Phase I. 1954–1965

The Supreme Court decision in the Topeka case rested in part upon the argument that segregation had damaging psychological effects upon black children, even when the school facilities themselves were "equal" to those of white schools. The consensus of social scientists was—and is, still—that segregation of blacks has been an obstacle to their competence in an urban, industrial, democratic society. This conclusion is based on research on the social psychology of race relations (summarized by Pettigrew and Pajonis, 1964; and by Katz, 1964). The research conclusion is that where the races are systematically segregated, black children are taught by their parents that they cannot expect to be treated as equals by most white people, and they also learn from parents and other black children that their schools are inferior, and that they themselves are likely to be inferior. Their teachers, whether black or white, tend to look upon them as slow learners, and therefore lower their standards of expectation.

It is argued by these researchers that black children, in order to overcome or avoid a self-concept of inferiority, should associate with white children as early as possible in life, in situations where they will sometimes be superior and sometimes inferior. They should be taught under a biracial school staff.

These propositions, when read in the midseventies, have a "dated" quality. They report the thinking that prevailed at the time of the Supreme Court decision of 1954. But the economic and educational situation of the black population has changed so much during the 1960s and early 1970s, that a substantially different set of propositions have now come to the forefront. These propositions will be developed during the remainder of this chapter.

Initially, after 1954, the focus of attention by educators and by government officials was upon the process of desegregation. There were two aspects of this problem—that of *de jure* segregation and that of *de facto* segregation. The first is the problem in southern states where state laws long prevented white and black children from attending the same schools. The second is the problem of industrial cities mainly in the North, where, because most blacks live in segregated housing areas, many schools are attended entirely by black children.

When the U.S. Supreme Court in 1955 ordered the southern states to proceed with desegregation of their schools "with all deliberate speed," there was at first a period of rapid change in 17 southern and border states. Within two years, 3,008 out of 9,015 school districts in these 17 states had at least some white and some black children attending desegregated schools. The border states complied with the Court order most readily, and the major cities of these states, which earlier had maintained separate schools for blacks, changed with relative ease. This was true of Baltimore, Nashville, Louisville, St. Louis, and Kansas City.

In the Deep South, and in certain of the larger cities, notably New Orleans and Little Rock, the process of desegregation went more slowly and resulted at times in open conflict. The U.S. Office of Education reported that, at the beginning of the 1965 fall term, at most 7.5 percent of black pupils in the Deep South were attending schools with white children. In Mississippi, it was less than one-half of one percent.

During this period, de jure segregation was generally replaced by de facto segregation, and by a variety of devices to avoid desegregation. In the South, little headway was made in placing black and white pupils in the same schools. Virginia, for example, made it legal for the state to pay tuition of pupils in private schools where public schools did not exist, and Prince Edward County proceeded to close its public schools. Black children and families were left to fend for themselves and had no public schooling for several years. Eventually, the courts declared the county's procedure illegal, and required the establishment of a single public school system to serve both races, with no payments from public funds to support attendance at private schools.

Border Cities.   In the larger border cities—Baltimore, Washington, Cincinnati, Louisville, St. Louis, and Kansas City—there was immediate compliance with the court order in formally desegregating the schools. However, the residential distribution of blacks was such that segregation continued, on a de facto basis, for the vast majority of black pupils. The 1954 decision coincided in time with the largest north and westward black migration that has ever happened, when incoming blacks filled up whatever vacant houses were available in these cities, in neighborhoods that were partly but not entirely black. This made it financially easy for whites who were living in local school districts inhabited also by blacks to sell or rent their homes and to move to suburbs or other sections of the city where there was no immediate prospect of integration.

Small numbers of black pupils moved into previously all-white schools, partly in the suburbs where the number of black families was relatively small and they did not "threaten to overwhelm" the white families.

Northern and Western Cities.   In northern and western cities, the major in-migration of blacks led rapidly to de facto segregation, supported by new patterns of residential segregation.

Conscious attacks on the segregation program began in a few cities. New York City pioneered. The Board of Education on December 23, 1954, unanimously approved a statement which included the following paragraphs:

> The Supreme Court of the United States reminds us that modern psychological knowledge indicates clearly that segregated, racially homogeneous schools damage the personality of minority group children. . . .
> In seeking to provide effective democratic education for all of the children of this city, the members of the Board of Education of the City of New York are faced with many real obstacles in the form of complex social and community problems. Among these problems is the existence of residential segregation which leads to schools predominantly of one race on the ele-

319

mentary and junior high school levels. In addition, prevailing racial attitudes and misinformation of some white and Negro parents reflect out-worn patterns of segregation as well as limited educational and vocational horizons which make it difficult for them to accept school procedures contrary to their attitudes.

In spite of these and other difficulties, the Board of Education of the City of New York is determined to accept the challenge implicit in the language and spirit of the decision of the United States Supreme Court. We will seek a solution to these problems and take action with dispatch implementing the recommendations resulting from a systematic and objective study of the problem here presented. (New York City Board of Education, 1954.)

In Detroit, the Board of Education in 1958 appointed a Citizens Advisory Committee on School Needs, under the chairmanship of George Romney, who was later to become governor of the state. This Committee made a variety of recommendations, and a Committee on Equal Educational Opportunities was set up to study the problem of racial segregation and make recommendations.

In most northern and western cities, however, the official policy of the school administration was that the schools should be "color blind." This meant that the school system was to take no formal notice of the color of pupils or teachers, to keep no records of color, and under these conditions to strive to do the best job possible of educating all children in accordance with their needs and abilities.

Phase II. 1965–1970

The second phase of desegregation was a period during which major legal and financial efforts were made to improve public schools for the children of low-income families, regardless of their race. By 1970 it was generally agreed that the money had not moved the country measurably toward the achievement of either of the two overriding goals—neither toward racial integration of black pupils, nor better educational achievement of pupils from low-income families.

The major legal forces were the Civil Rights Act of 1964 and the Elementary and Secondary Education Act of 1965, which together gave government officials and public school educators a great deal of power. The Civil Rights Act of 1964, among other things, required all state and local agencies as well as private persons or agencies *who receive federal government funds* to give written assurance that "no person shall be excluded from participation, denied any benefits, or subjected to discrimination on the basis of race, color, or national origin." The requirement that school systems receiving any federal payments must submit "assurances of compliance" with the law had the effect of stimulating desegregation in the schools.

The Elementary and Secondary Education Act of 1965, by providing large sums of federal monies to local school systems, strengthened the pressures enormously, and provided financial incentives for compliance.

The Deep South.   Given these new legislative changes, most of the school systems of the South had begun the process of integration by 1966. *The New York Times* of September 4, 1965, reported, "Under the threat of a loss of Federal assistance, the South is admitting probably 7 percent of its Negro children to classes with white children this fall—a percentage that compares reasonably well with the national average. And for the first time school desegregation has come to the Black Belt and to hundreds of rural southern towns, with virtually no violence or resistance." Faculty desegregation also got under way in some southern cities.

Border Cities and Northern Cities.   The drive for integration in the border cities and northern and western industrial cities reached a peak in this period. Civil rights organizations joined together, and were aided by federated church groups acting through such agencies as a Council on Religion and Race. Civic organizations became involved. The most prominent domestic issue in the country during this period was the issue of change in the schools. The majority of big cities saw school boycotts aimed at inducing the board of education to take more active measures to hasten desegregation. A number of state legislatures passed laws requiring the public schools to reduce segregation as much as possible. Several city school systems began to publish annual data on the numbers of black and while children in the various schools, and also the numbers of black and white teachers.

    The majority of school boards, while issuing statements saying that they favored integrated school experience for as many pupils as possible, added, however, that there were limits beyond which the school system could not go in fostering integration. They said the major limiting factor was the "neighborhood school policy," which places a high priority upon the pupil's attending school near his home. Since the big cities have a great deal of residential segregation by race, the neighborhood school policy makes it difficult to get integrated schools, especially at the elementary school level.

    Nevertheless, during the latter half of the 1960s, the more positive forms of integrative procedure were being pushed forward and tried. This was partly due to a mounting series of court decisions, for after 1965 the courts were increasingly throwing their weight against *de facto* segregation. In New York and New Jersey, the courts upheld the actions of school boards in fixing boundary lines of schools so as to produce an ethnic balance among students. The New York Court of Appeals distinguished between an obligation on the part of the school board to reduce *de facto* segregation and the *right* (not the duty) of the school board to correct racial imbalance. The court held that an otherwise reasonable and lawful zoning plan does not become unlawful because racial factors were taken into consideration. When the

United States Supreme Court declined to review the case, other New York and New Jersey courts made similar decisions. In 1965 the State of Massachusetts went further than any other had gone up to that time by passing a law aimed at the *elimination* of racial imbalance in the public schools.

In addition, in the Civil Rights Act of 1964, Congress had authorized the Attorney General to bring desegregation suits against local school districts in certain circumstances where racial discrimination was being practiced and threats of such suits began to loom up in various localities.

In spite of all this artillery supporting the forces of desegregation, the proportions of black pupils in schools that were all-black or nearly so went on increasing in the big cities. Table 15.2 makes it clear that the black population was becoming more densely concentrated in many of the cities. During the decade 1960 to 1970 the black population increased between 50 and 100 percent in New York, Chicago, Los Angeles, Oakland, Detroit, Boston, and in other cities now shown in the table. It simply was not possible to get a racial balance in more than a few of the schools in these large cities, unless mass transportation of as many as a third of the pupils were to be undertaken. The migration of white families to the edges of the cities and to the suburbs was defeating the policy of school integration.

Examples of Successful Integration.   There were a few examples of successful integration of school systems in some middle-sized cities, which served to show that the job could be done if conditions were right, but also served to show that the conditions were not likely to be right in the large cities. A set of four cities appear to have succeeded, by 1970, in the task of integrating their schools. All four are upper-middle-class suburbs of big cities, with black minorities of less than 25 percent—but minorities large enough to have filled several elementary schools with black pupils before the integration program was installed. All four have one or more universities located within the community. All four have a rather liberal political stance. The black populations in all four cities are above the average of the national black population in socioeconomic and educational status, and they contain very few families of the lower-working class. The four cities are Berkeley, Pasadena, and Riverside, California; and Evanston, Illinois. The Evanston case will be described as an illustration. A city of 80,000 on the northern edge of Chicago, Evanston is the home of Northwestern University. The city contains a number of light industrial plants which employ a large part of the local population. The black population has been resident for a long period, having initially been brought in as unskilled workers and domestic servants to serve the upper-middle-class suburbs along Lake Michigan to the north of Chicago. Their median family income in 1959 was more than double the median family income of all black families in the United States.

In 1962, there was one all-black elementary school, and there were others that were more than 30 percent black. In 1964, the school board passed a resolution stating that the school district would eliminate racial segregation from the schools. On the basis of two years of study, a plan was presented to the community for revising the school attendance boundaries so that every school would have some black pupils, ranging from 11 to 36 percent, and averaging 21 percent. After a year of community discussion, this plan was put into effect in September, 1967. It involved bussing at school expense some black pupils to schools that were some distance from their homes. Also, about 400 white pupils were enrolled by their parents in the formerly all-black school, which was changed to an integrated laboratory school. Most of these 400 children were transported to the school by bus, with their parents paying.

Funds were secured from the Rockefeller Foundation to carry out an objective evaluation, and the Educational Testing Service was employed to conduct the study in close cooperation with the research department of the local school district. A detailed report on the program was published in 1971. With respect to academic achievement, the report says:

> After desegregating all elementary schools, white pupils' performance in standardized achievement tests remained constant. Black pupils have made slightly greater gains in most subject areas. Bussing did not adversely affect black or white pupils. Indeed, bussed black pupils from segregated classes showed greater mean score gains than their non-bussed classmates. A predictable and high rate of learning was manifested among black girls who had always attended white majority schools. (Educational Testing Service, 1971, p. 47)

The report also mentions the fact that black parents have taken an increasingly active part in school-related activities. They became more active members of the parent-teacher associations, and of the groups that nominated candidates for election to the school board. A questionnaire sent to a sample of black parents asked for their reactions after four years of desegregated schools. Almost all parents strongly favored the educational experience in desegregated schools. Only a handful felt their children had been inconvenienced by the exigencies of riding a bus daily to school.

It will be noted that the white children all stayed in their neighborhood schools except for the group whose parents chose to send them to the integrated laboratory school. Thus the white parents experienced little disturbance of their own school arrangements. (Perhaps the greatest opposition to bussing for purposes of desegregation in many communities has come from white parents whose children were bussed to schools some distance from their homes.)

Rise of a Black Separatist Movement.   While some limited progress was being made with desegregation in cities where conditions were favorable, little or no progress was made in the large cities of the North and West. This may have been partly the result and partly the cause of the rise of the black separatist movement which grew up during this period, and deprived the integration movement of much of its momentum. Historians of the future will debate the significance of the black separatist movement in its effects upon the educational system, but there is presently little doubt that it split the black leadership of the country in the late 1960s. It made the situation especially difficult for white educators who were working to establish integrated schools, and who now found their support from the black community weakened. Black separatism played an important part in the changing educational scene in the period next to be described, but a fuller discussion will be postponed until Chapter 17.

Phase III. 1970–1975

The situation with respect to formal desegregation of schools in 1970 is shown in Table 15.5 which reports the U.S. Office of Education's survey of racial and ethnic enrollments. This table shows there was less segregation of black students in the South than in other parts of the United States. This condition had been produced by actions taken by school districts in the southern states to combine formerly all-black and all-white schools into mixed schools that reflected the local population ratios. Because many of the schools were in rural counties which had long transported pupils by bus, there was no major change in the school-attendance routine for most families except that the children would now attend a biracial school. As Table 15.5 shows, 39 percent of the southern black pupils attended schools in 1970 where they were in the minority, and another 22 percent attended schools which had more than 22 percent white pupils. The U.S. Commission on Civil Rights commented on this situation as follows:

> However, these statistics reflect only physical desegregation of schools. The figures fail to take into account other serious, but often more subtle, aspects of segregation and discrimination. These include segregation of activities and facilities within schools; unequal discipline based upon race; and demotions and/or dismissals of minority faculty and school administrators. These problems represent forms of discrimination which almost inevitably will become the focus of legal and administrative action in the seventies. (U.S. Civil Rights Commission, 1971, p. 6)

The problem of desegregating schools in the official sense—that is, putting white and black pupils in the same school building with both groups having at least 20 percent of the enrollment—is now primarily a problem for the large cities, where residential segregation has increased to such an extent that a child who attends a neighborhood school is almost sure to be in a

TABLE 15.5. Change in Extent of Racial Segregation in Public Elementary and Secondary Schools. 1968 to 1970

Area	Black Enrollment (thousands)	Black Percentage of Total	Black Pupils Attending Schools with Minority Enrollments of:				
			0–49%	50–79%	80–89%	90–98%	99–100%
Continental United States and Alaska							
1968	6,282	14.5	23	9	4	11	53
1970	6,707	14.9	33	18	6	15	28
32 Northern and Western States							
1968	2,703	9.5	28	15	7	20	31
1970	2,890	9.8	28	15	7	21	30
6 Border and D.C.							
1968	636	17.1	28	8	4	14	46
1970	667	17.3	30	10	4	13	44
11 Southern							
1968	2,943	26.6	18	3	1	3	75
1970	3,150	27.2	39	22	6	11	22

Source: National Survey of Racial and Ethnic Enrollment in the Public Schools, Table 2-A. HEW press release. Washington, D.C.

Note: The five percentages on the right in each row total to 100, and show how the black pupils are distributed among schools containing various proportions of black students.

school that is nearly all-black or all-white. This is as much or more of a problem in the cities of the North and West as it is in the southern cities.

Since 1970, most of the desegregation controversy has been fought out in the courts, and in large cities where the courts have ordered desegregation as a result of lawsuits brought on behalf of black pupils and their families. Court orders have been served on school boards in Los Angeles, Denver, Memphis, Detroit, Richmond, Charlotte, and Austin. In effect, the courts have ordered the school boards to balance the racial composition of all schools. Where the school board has failed to devise a satisfactory plan, the court has outlined the essentials of such a plan.

In general, these plans have involved substantial amounts of bussing of white as well as black pupils, often to school buildings distant from their homes. The lower court orders have been appealed to the Supreme Court, which ruled unanimously, on April 20, 1971, that school districts must use bussing, racial quotas, pairing, and gerrymandering of attendance zones to remove all vestiges of state-imposed segregation.

Two other court orders of great import required the several suburban school districts in the metropolitan areas of Detroit and of Richmond, Virginia, to cooperate with the central city on a program to integrate the schools of the area, since the central city had such a heavy concentration of black pupils that it alone could not establish and maintain integrated schools.

On July 25, 1974, the United States Supreme Court, by a 5–4 decision, ruled that bussing of pupils from one legal school district to another district for the sake of racial integration in a given metropolitan area is unconstitutional, and therefore the Detroit order of a lower court should not be enforced. Chief Justice Burger, in the majority opinion, wrote, "Where the schools of only one district have been affected, there is no constitutional power in the courts to decree relief balancing the racial composition of that district's schools with those of surrounding districts."

President Nixon entered the situation as an opponent of bussing. On March 24, 1970, before the Supreme Court decision, and again on March 16, 1972, he said clearly he was opposed to bussing for the purpose of achieving racial balance in the schools. In his broadcast of March 16, 1972, he said,

> The great majority of Americans, black and white, feel strongly that the bussing of school children away from their own neighborhoods for the purpose of achieving racial balance is wrong.
>
> The great majority, black and white, are determined that the process of desegregation must go forward until the goal of genuinely equal educational opportunity is achieved.
>
> The question, then, is "how can we end segregation in a way that does not result in more bussing? . . .
>
> I believe that the majority of all races want more bussing stopped and better education started.

It remains unclear what Nixon had in mind as an effective method to end segregation.

EFFECTS OF SCHOOL INTEGRATION

By 1973 there was much confusion concerning the effects of racial integration in the schools. This uncertainty, interacting with the attitudes of people about bussing pupils as a means of achieving integrated schools, made it difficult to establish a consistent policy. Some light was thrown on the situation in a 1973 article by Gary Orfield, who had been a Scholar in Residence at the U.S. Commission on Civil Rights. Orfield summarized the research studies on the effects of desegregation upon school achievement test performance, then moved to the effects of school integration on social attitudes, pointing out that little is known on a reliable basis concerning the latter. He found that research scholars generally agree on the following conclusions.

> 1. Integration of a lower-class child in a predominantly middle-class school does more than anything else to narrow the gap in achievement scores, but the gap remains large.
> 2. Newly desegregated school systems seldom show substantial increases in minority student performance level during the first year of integration.
> 3. The test scores of white students are not affected by the desegregation process.
> 4. Social class integration is usually impossible for minority group students without racial integration.
> 5. Racial and class integration are desirable objectives of national policy, everything else being equal. (Orfield, 1973, p. 4)

Taking cognizance of Armor's review (1972) of various studies of integration, studies showing little effects, but studies based mostly on only one-year intervals; and taking cognizance also of a rebuttal of Armor's findings by Pettigrew (1973), Orfield called for a systematic study of the impact of school desegregation when the period of desegregation is several years. Later, the Civil Rights Commission contracted with the Rand Corporation to design such a study.

Meanwhile, a study favorable to desegregation was reported in 1974 by the National Opinion Research Center at the University of Chicago. This study was financed by the U.S. Office of Education to assess the effects of the Emergency School Assistance Program, which provided funds to southern schools in 1971–72 to aid them in desegregation. The NORC study reported test scores on 32,000 fifth and tenth graders, black and white, in 600 southern schools. There was no decrease in school achievement by white students, but male black high school students gained half a grade level in school achievement tests over their status in previous years. The report concluded that this gain was due more to improved racial climate than to improved instruction.

Desegregation of School Facilities

Wherever there have been racially segregated schools, the teachers have tended to be segregated: that is, black schools have had black teachers, and white schools, white teachers. The Civil Rights Act of 1964, however, now makes this illegal, and the Department of Health, Education, and Welfare, and the Justice Department have put pressure on school districts to redistribute their teachers so as to have integrated faculties in all schools.

One of the effects of desegregation has been loss of jobs by black educators. This occurred mainly in the South, as the dual school system was changed to a unitary system. For example, there were 107 black secondary school principals in the state of Virginia in 1965, but the number had dwindled to 16 in 1971. The closing or reorganization of black secondary schools often meant a demotion of a black principal to the principalship of an elementary school or to a job as a classroom teacher.

Black classroom teachers did not experience such a drastic reduction, but they also suffered some loss. For example, the Atlanta branch of the Department of Health, Education, and Welfare's Office of Civil Rights reported on 108 school districts in six southern states which completed formal desegregation in 1970. They found the number of black teachers had decreased from 9,015 in 1968–69 to 8,092 in 1970–71. At the same time, the total number of teachers in these districts increased by 615. Thus, blacks lost 923 places and whites gained 1,538.

There have been other practical difficulties, due mainly to the seniority and tenure rules that exist in most school districts. A teacher gets tenure not only in the job as teacher but also as a teacher in a particular school. The older teachers have had a long time in which to transfer from one school to another and to wind up in a school of their liking. Also, teachers generally find homes near the school where they expect to teach for a lengthy period. Then, when the order comes that the school faculties are to be integrated, this means that many teachers will be transferred to schools they know little or nothing about, and to schools that are distant from their homes.

As a consequence many teachers have objected to the faculty integration program, and have worked through the teachers' associations or the teachers' union to fight the program. Teacher resistance in most cases has been great enough to force compromises—such as the assignment of all *new* teachers to inner-city schools in accordance with an integration plan, or controls on transfers from one school to another so that new transfers will work toward integrated faculties.

The federal government has applied mild pressures on school boards, but so far has not made a major issue of desegregating faculties.

BLACK STUDENTS AND PROFESSORS
IN HIGHER EDUCATION

Black enrollment in colleges and universities has increased greatly both in proportion of the total enrollment and in absolute numbers. In 1964, there were 234,000 black students in institutions of higher education, compared with 680,000 in 1971—nearly a threefold increase in seven years. About 8.5 percent of all college students in 1971 were black, compared with 12 percent blacks in the total college-age population. (At that date, 24 percent of blacks aged 20–21 were in college, compared with 30 percent of whites.)

Despite this vigorous advance in college attendance by black youth, they are still substantially below white youth in proportion to their numbers in the population. The difference between the two racial groups in college attendance would appear to be due primarily to difference in family income. In 1971, 11 percent of the appropriate age group of young black men graduated from college, compared with 26 percent of young white men. At the same time, 8 percent of black women graduated, compared with 19 percent of white women.

A striking example of the change in the social attitude toward black students is seen in the fact that 45 black midshipmen were accepted in the first-year class of the U.S. Naval Academy at Annapolis in 1971, compared with 21 the year before, and 5 in 1960.

The economic value of higher education for blacks has been demonstrated in recent studies, especially since black students tend to come from families of relatively low incomes. Epps sums up the situation as follows:

> We already know that low-income students constitute an unusually large proportion of the total black college student population. Recent surveys report that more than half of the black college students come from families with annual incomes of less than $6,000. Only about 15 percent of white college students report such low family incomes. . . .
>
> In spite of the fact that employment discrimination severely limits the earning power of college educated blacks in America when compared with college educated whites, the average lifetime earning power of black male college graduates is approximately twice that of black males with less than eight years of elementary school.
>
> Recent census data indicate that in the last few years there has been a rapid increase in the returns blacks receive from investment in education. This increase is already being reflected in earning power. Unlike the situation of a few years ago, the gap between median black and white family incomes was smaller in 1968 for blacks with a year or more of college than it was for those with lesser amounts of education. The implication of this new trend is that the gap between blacks and whites will close most rapidly for those blacks who are fortunate enough to obtain one or more years of college education. Thus, it appears that the attainment of higher education

will continue to be one of the most important requirements for occupational and economic success. (Epps, 1972, pp. 102–103)

The increase of black students took place mainly in the large cities and in the public-supported universities, and in colleges that are predominantly white. The latter fact has affected enrollment in the black colleges in the South, although the black institutions continued to enroll a majority of the black undergraduates in the country. In 1947, 90 percent of the bachelor's degrees earned by black students were conferred by black southern colleges. After 1970, it was less than 50 percent.

Speaking on the significance of this change for the black colleges, the President of Clark College in Atlanta, Dr. Vivian W. Henderson said:

> Negro colleges will by and large continue well into the future as Negro colleges. The historic Negro college will have the responsibility for educating a diminishing but significant proportion of black youth enrolled in higher education. A significant proportion of black youth will enroll in newly developed community colleges which will be substantially black because they are located so as to make higher education more accessible to "disadvantaged" youth. Negro colleges will be slow in attracting white students not because of policy or lack of quality but because institutionalized and entrenched racism is a barrier to freedom of movement to white youth. (Henderson, 1971, pp. 1, 4.)

The period which saw this expansion of the numbers of black students in predominantly white colleges also saw a substantial increase in the number of black professors in these colleges. According to Williams (1971) the first black to join the full-time faculty of a major white university was Allison Davis, the educator and social psychologist who was appointed to the University of Chicago faculty in 1942. Williams then makes the point that now, 30 years later, black academics can come and go from black schools to white schools with much the kind of mobility that white academics have had.

In general, universities and colleges have deliberately given preference to minority groups (and to women) in their recruiting of new faculty members since about 1967. This has created a "brain drain" away from black colleges, which may or may not be reversed in the 1970s.

Blacks in Graduate and Professional Schools

Numbers of blacks in graduate and professional schools have not expanded as rapidly as the numbers of undergraduates. The Carnegie Commission on Higher Education noted that only two percent of the practicing physicians in the United States in 1969 were black, and there was only one black attorney to 5,000 black Americans, whereas there was one white attorney for every 750 white Americans. Table 15.6 gives the most recent available information

TABLE 15.6. *Minority Group Students in Postbaccalaureate Training, 1971*

Category	Percent of Total Number of Students				Total Minorities	
	American Indian	Black	Oriental	Spanish Surname	Percent	Number
Study A						
Graduate and professional students	0.3	4.1	1.8	1.2	7.3	39,869
Medical students (not undergraduates)	0.1	4.2	1.8	0.8	6.9	3,044
Dental students (not undergraduates)	0.1	3.6	1.8	0.8	6.2	1,041
Law students (not undergraduates)	0.3	3.9	0.5	1.1	5.8	3,764
Study B						
Graduate students	0.3	4.0	2.0	1.0	7.4	22,869
Percent of minority group in total population (1970)	0.4	11.1	0.8	4.4	16.7	

Studies: A. U.S. Dept. of Health, Education, and Welfare. Office of Civil Rights Publication: OCR 72-8 and 73.
       B. *Survey of 103 State Universities and Land-grant Colleges.* Autumn, 1970. U.S. Office of Education.

Note: These percentages are based on the total numbers of students in the country in the respective categories.

on the of minority group members who have been working for the M.A., the Ph.D., and the postbaccalaureate professional degrees in such schools as law, medicine, dentistry, and optometry. It will be noted that Oriental students far exceed the other minorities relative to their numbers in the total population. There are two different studies, which tend to confirm each other.

Expanding Black College Enrollments

The widespread effort in the late 1960s to recruit black students for college attendance has been quite successful, as has been noted. This has been accomplished in three ways:

1. Publicizing the desire of the colleges for black students, and actively recruiting in black or predominantly black high schools.
2. Offering scholarships and part-time jobs to black students from low-income families. Scholarship funds from private philanthropic foundations were targeted especially for needy black students in the 1960s. It is not clear whether federal government student-aid funds have been administered by college officials so as to favor black students, but there has been no major complaint on this matter. Probably, if questioned, a good many college officials would defend a limited preference for aiding minority group students on the ground that it tends to right past wrongs.
3. Offering "black studies" programs. These vary from two or three elective courses, such as "Afro-American Literature," "Introduction to Sociology (Racial and Cultural Minorities Emphasis)," "United States History (Afro-American Emphasis)," to a full major of 30 to 40 units out of a total of 120 units needed for a bachelor's degree. The advantage of these courses is that they strengthen the "black identity" and the ethnic confidence of the black student. At least one or two such elective courses were being offered in probably two-thirds or more of the colleges as of 1973.

From the beginning of the black studies movement, concern was expressed about the quality of these courses, the qualifications of the instructors, and the performance of the students. Some critics charged that these courses were likely to be overly simple, and would give poorly prepared students some easy college credits. But proponents met this charge head-on. President Charles Hurst of Malcolm X College in Chicago announced that such courses gave "better education than can be obtained anywhere else." (Hurst, 1969). And writing on behalf of the black studies program at San Francisco State College, Nathan Hare, the temporary chairman of the Department of Black Studies, commented as follows:

> Far from restricting black students (even majors) to the study of their culture alone—and hence, further crippling them in acquiring the skills needed to overcome (or overthrow as may be their pleasure) their handicaps in a technological society—the major motivation of black studies is to entice

black students (conditioned to exclusion) to greater involvement in the educational process. Black studies is, above all, a pedagogical device. That is why we have courses in black mathematics, black science, black radio and television, etc. this fall at San Francisco State. We intend to solve the problem of a black shortage in technical and scientific fields, not to aggravate it. (Hare, 1969, p. 30)

Although white educators tended to hold themselves aloof from criticism of these courses, there were vigorous criticisms from black educators and black leaders, mainly from men who had made a success of their lives in an integrated section of the society. Thus Bayard Rustin, executive director of the A. Philip Randolph Institute, New York City, and leader of the March on Washington, wrote in 1969: "What the hell are soul courses worth in the real world? In the real world, no one gives a damn if you've taken soul courses. They want to know if you can do mathematics and write a correct sentence."

In a different vein, W. Arthur Lewis, Professor of Economics and International Affairs at Princeton and one of the leading black scholars in his field, wrote:

Any Afro-American who wishes to become a specialist in black studies or to spend some of his time on such work, should be absolutely free to do so. But I hope that of those students who get the opportunity to attend the 30 best colleges, the proportion who want to specialize in black studies may, in their interest and that of the black community, turn out to be rather small, in comparison with our scientists, or engineers, accountants, economists, or doctors.

Another attitude which puzzles me is that which requires black students in the better white colleges to mix only with each other; to have a dormitory to themselves; to sit at separate tables in the refectory, and so on. I have pointed out that these colleges are the gateway to leadership positions in the integrated part of the economy, and that what they can best do for young blacks is to prepare them to capture our 11 percent share of the best jobs at the top—one of every nine ambassadorships, one of every nine vice-presidencies of General Motors, one of every nine senior directors of engineering laboratories, and so on.

Now I am told that the reason black students stick together is that they are uncomfortable in white company. But how is one to be Ambassador to Finland or Luxembourg—jobs which American Negroes have already held with distinction—if one is uncomfortable in white company? Anybody who occupies a supervisory post, from foreman upwards, is going to have white people working under him, who will expect him to be friendly and fair. Is this going to be possible, after four years spent in boycotting white company? . . .

Blacks in America are inevitably and perpetually a minority. This means that in all administrative and leadership positions we are going to be outnumbered by white folks, and will have to compete with them not on our terms but on theirs. The only way to win this game is to know them so thoroughly that we can outpace them. For us to turn our backs on this opportunity, by insisting on mingling only with other black students in college, is folly of the highest order. (Lewis, 1969)

Relaxed Admissions Policies

The many colleges and universities with selective requirements for admission found that a relatively large fraction of their black applicants could not meet their entrance requirements, which usually consisted of a certain minimum score on the standard college aptitude test, combined with a certain minimum rank in the high school graduating class. Since it was well-known that the college aptitude test favored middle-class over working-class students, and since a large proportion of black applicants were from working-class families, there seemed to be justification for a different entrance procedure, especially if this was combined with intensive remedial instruction during the first few months of the college year, or during the preceding summer.

Under a growing pressure from the proponents of greater opportunity for economically disadvantaged students, even this reduced selectivity was abandoned by some outstanding institutions, and an "open admission" policy was adopted, admitting students with a high school diploma in the order of their application until the entering class was full. This policy was adopted by the City University of New York in 1970, with attendant publicity and controversy.

Associated with relaxed selectivity was a policy adopted by some colleges of seeking a "quota" of minority-group students—often 10 percent. At the same time, there has been a special effort by many outstanding colleges and universities to recruit faculty members from minority groups and from women, who have qualified recently as a "sociological minority." The purposes behind these policies are clear and generally approved as leading toward the righting of old wrongs. But resistance to these policies was bound to appear, and has appeared in two forms:

a. **Do these policies lower academic standards?** A number of outstanding university scholars argue that relaxation of admissions standards will either lower the intellectual quality of higher education or will cause a great deal of frustration for students who are first admitted and then failed. However, the director of research for the American Council on Education, Alexander W. Astin, has made a thorough study of the relation between test scores, high school grades, and college dropouts, and has come to the conclusion that a considerable fraction of students do "make it" in college in spite of low aptitude scores or low high school grades. He concludes, furthermore:

In my judgment, the model of selective admissions based on test scores and grades is inappropriate for institutions of higher education. Presumably, educational institutions exist in order to educate students. Their mission, then, is to produce certain desirable changes in the student or, more simply, to make a difference in the student's life. Given these goals, they should strive in their admissions practices to select those applicants who are most likely to be favorably influenced by the particular educational program offered at the institution. (Astin, 1969, p. 69)

b. **Are the policies fair to nonminority persons?** A group of prominent scholars announced in June, 1972, their formation of a "Committee on Academic Nondiscrimination and Integrity." They charged that discrimination in favor of minority and female candidates for academic appointments and for graduate and undergraduate admissions violates the rights of nonminority persons and men.

Although the committee favors "affirmative action to remove the present effects of past discrimination," it objects to preferential admissions standards and financial aid for minorities in colleges and in graduate and professional schools. It also, objects to preferential faculty employment practices.

EQUALITY OF OPPORTUNITY OR EQUALITY OF ACHIEVEMENT?

To what extent has the educational system met its responsibility for enhancing the opportunity of black people to share in the life-styles they prefer? It is clear that black youth had substantially increased educational opportunity and job opportunity during the 1960–70 decade. There may never be another decade during which an almost complete about-face was exercised by the educational system of the country with respect to an ethnic group. This has been tied to an expansion of job opportunities which has made it much easier for young black men and women to find jobs, if they are high school or college graduates. But unemployment remains high for black youth who do not have a high school diploma.

There has also been a substantial reduction in the proportions of black pupils who attend racially segregated schools. This reduction has taken place mainly in the southern states where the dual system of schools has been abandoned, and where black and white pupils now attend the same schools in the small cities and rural areas. But schools have not been desegregated to any substantial degree in the large cities of the South or the North or the West. Due to residential segregation, the schools in the large cities are heavily segregated.

The problem which looms ahead for the black population is how to take advantage of greater educational and economic opportunity so as to achieve educational and economic equality with whites. In order to do this, the black population will have to achieve roughly the same proportions of high school graduates, college graduates, and postgraduates as the white population, given the fact that, at least for the present, educational training is essential for admission to practically all middle-class jobs. Furthermore, the diplomas and degrees earned by black men and women will have to have equal validity to those earned by whites.

A controversy is now developing. In view of open admissions policies to the colleges, black studies programs, and employment quotas favorable to minority group members, whites doubt the quality of the education many blacks are receiving. Some people argue that the *opportunity* provided by these special measures is all-important, and that black students will justify by their adult performance the faith that the society has shown by giving them special opportunities. Others argue that special programs for black students, if they require less intellectual effort than parallel programs for whites, will lead to widespread failure and discouragement for blacks as they move into the reality of adult life.

This problem has been posed, by Moynihan, for example, by noting that the Black Revolution is a movement *for equality* as well as for opportunity.

> As Nathan Glazer has put it, "The demand for economic equality is now not the demand for equal *opportunities* for the equally qualified: it is now the demand for equality of economic *results*. . . . The demand for equality in education . . . has also become a demand for equality of results, of outcomes."
>
> The principal challenge of the next phase of the Negro revolution is to make certain that equality of results will now follow. If we do not, there will be no social peace in the United States for generations. (Moynihan, U.S. Department of Labor, 1965, p. 3)

Some of the proponents of basic school reform have in effect argued that the schools must keep on experimenting with better methods until lower-working class youth are equal in educational achievement to the youth of other social groups. This can and must be done, they say.

Unless black and white children achieve equally well in school, when they come from homes of equal socioeconomic status, there will be no peace in the educational world. The black leaders cannot accept a situation in which black children are regarded as inferior in school performance because of their color; and white educators cannot rest until they succeed in working out educational procedures that are equally effective with black and white children.

An effective spokesman for this group of black leaders is Kenneth B. Clark, Professor of Psychology in the City University of New York and in 1971 President of the American Psychological Association, who said:

> It is my considered judgment that the basic explanation for the continued chronic academic underachievement of minority group children in our pub-

lic schools is a rather embarrassingly simple explanation that these children are not being taught professionally in their classrooms, as indicated by being held to standards which normal human beings, in terms of the normal distribution curve, would be able to meet. They are not perceived as human beings who are capable of meeting these standards; they are believed to be uneducable. They are being treated, either malignantly or benevolently, as if they were uneducable. . . .

I believe that it is only through rigorous, tough-minded, hard-nosed educational programs and accountability imposed upon the public school system—only with single standards of academic expectations and performance, including rejection of all the nonsense of ghetto idioms and ghetto needs and ghetto negatives, which is another way of disparaging these children and denying them their right to be taught to meet competitive standards of aggressive society; only through rejection of such sentimentalism; only with a tough, hard penetrating analysis of all compassion and addressing ourselves to the business of education, can American education really free itself of racism and can American education really contribute to stabilizing our society. (Clark, 1971, pp. 37, 42)

STRATEGY FOR THE NEXT DECADE

All in all, despite the objective gains in relative status of the black population since 1960, the speed of improvement is not satisfactory to the majority of blacks nor to a minority of whites. Various social and political strategies are being debated, and various positions with regard to policies of separatism and policies of integration in the society as a whole. What happens in the schools will depend upon, and will influence, the resolution of these broader issues.

We shall be dealing with these questions again in Chapter 18, where we shall consider black separatism along with questions of separatism for other racial and ethnic groups. Meanwhile we conclude the present chapter by repeating that the social and educational situation with regard to blacks is one that is changing rapidly; that the effects upon school systems have been profound; and that the forms of the problems and the forms of the solutions for the 1980s are by no means clear.

EXERCISES

1. Work out a teaching unit for elementary or high school on *The Negro in American Life*. What books and pamphlets would you assign students? What topics would you suggest for individual projects? How would you treat contemporary black protest movements?
2. Investigate a school which has had a successful program of racial integration. Talk with some of the teachers and parents as well as the principal. Analyze the reasons for success.

3. Investigate a school in which efforts at racial integration have been unsuccessful. What are the reasons for failure?

4. Read the special Winter, 1968 issue of the *Harvard Educational Review* on "Equal Educational Opportunity" and organize or write a debate illustrating the major points of views presented in it.

SUGGESTIONS FOR FURTHER READING

1. An important address by Pettigrew entitled "Racially Separate or Together?" is reprinted in the book, *Society and Education: A Book of Readings,* (Havighurst, Neugarten, and Falk). There is also an article by Pfautz on "The Community School in the Black Community," and one by Frederick D. Harper on "Black Student Revolt on a White Campus."

2. School-community crises with regard to integration have been analyzed by school survey teams working in large cities, such as Odell's *Educational Survey Report* on the Philadelphia Schools; or Havighurst's *The Public Schools of Chicago: A Survey Report,* or Passow's *Toward Creating a Model School System in Washington, D.C.* See also the report of the Commission on School Integration, entitled *Public School Segregation and Integration in the North;* and Klopf and Laster, *Integrating the Urban School.*

3. Smith's book, *They Closed Their Schools,* tells the story of the closing of public schools in Prince Edward County, Virginia, an extreme example of a community which attempted to avoid, then delay, school integration. The story is told in the personal terms of the people involved.

4. Read the booklet entitled "Equality Through Integration," a report on Greenburgh School District No. 8. It describes the ways in which a New York school district, located 25 miles north of New York City, was transformed from one that was segregated and inferior to a model of integrated and quality education. The booklet is distributed by the Anti-Defamation League.

5. For a comprehensive and clearly written review of the research literature on the effects of desegregation on the intellectual performance of blacks, read the article by Irwin Katz, "Review of Evidence Relating to Effects of Desegregation on the Intellectual Performance of Negroes," *American Psychologist,* 1964. A more recent summary and analysis of research on the relations between school integration and the educational achievement of minority-group pupils has been published by Nancy St. John (1970). Another summary of desegregation research has been prepared by Meyer Weinberg (1970). Orfield (1973) gives a definitive summary.

6. Two of the best sources providing historical perspective on the development and effects of race prejudice in the United States are Gossett's *Race: The History of an Idea in America* and Van den Berghe's *Race and Racism: A Comparative Perspective.*

7. A very good summary of the history of higher education for blacks has been written by Alan Pifer, President of the Carnegie Corporation, in a lecture he delivered in Johannesburg, South Africa in 1973, under the title: *The Higher Education of Blacks in the United States.*

CHAPTER 16

Education and Other
Minority Groups

Several so-called minority groups, besides the black group, stay somewhat aloof from the dominant Anglo-American culture, which is often called by them the "mainstream." They make the American society a *pluralistic* society, for they preserve their own subcultures in various ways. Some speak a non-English language at home. Some have special social or political organizations for maintaining their foreign national cultures. Some practice a form of religion which pervades their social life so completely that they avoid the public schools for their children. Some have prospered financially, but most of these minority groups have below-average incomes. The children of some groups achieve as well in the schools as the children of "mainstream" America, yet the children of most minority groups do relatively poorly on tests of school achievement, as was demonstrated in the Coleman Study of Educational Opportunity.

The largest of these groups is that of "Spanish origin" or "Spanish surname," who make up almost five percent of the total American population. The racially different groups of Japanese and Chinese Americans, the Filipinos, and American Indians altogether make up 1.1 percent of the population. The religious sects of the Amish and Hutterites, who maintain a stable and separate life for themselves, are very small in numbers. Nationality groups from southern and eastern Europe, some of whom maintain strong cultural associations, vary in number as shown in Chapter 17. Most of these European nationality groups have blended into the "mainstream," and are no longer described as "minority groups."

Each so-called minority group is related to the American educational system in a unique way. In the pages which follow we shall describe the larger and most visible of these groups, discuss their educational situations, and indicate what changes are taking place in the education of their children and youth. For lack of space in this book the smallest groups will be omitted from this discussion even though their educational situations are equally interesting.

AMERICANS OF SPANISH DESCENT

Within 50 years of the discovery of North America by Columbus, expeditions of Spanish soldiers and priests explored the Rio Grande country. Later, the Spaniards moved north from Mexico along the coast of California, setting up missions and military outposts, as well as large *haciendas* owned by wealthy families. What is now the southwestern corner of the United States was a part of Mexico until the Mexican War of 1848. After that war, which resulted in annexation of Texas and the southwestern territory to the United States, the Spanish and Mexican settlers who remained there became American citizens.

Thus there is an old American population of Spanish origin* which has as long a history of residence in this country as the New England colonists. Some of these people became business and professional leaders and legislators, so that Spanish surnames figure prominently in the history of the past hundred years in the Southwest. Cities such as Albuquerque, Santa Fe, San Antonio, El Paso, Los Angeles, and San Diego indicate by their names the Spanish influence; and many Spanish surnames are carried on the rosters of the Chamber of Commerce, the upper-middle-class service clubs, and the country clubs. In New Mexico, Spanish and English are both official languages. The "old Americans" of Spanish origin constitute a large proportion of the group labelled "USA and other" in Table 16.1 and number somewhere about one million. They are relatively older in age and their higher educational level testifies to a relatively high socioeconomic status. There have also been some isolated Spanish communities which did not move into the "mainstream" but led an impoverished existence in the mountains of New Mexico and on the dry farms of the areas near the Mexican border. They retained their language and religious customs and have only recently come into close contact with the "Anglo" culture. This group is small in number.

---

*The U.S. Census uses the phrase, "Spanish origin" for people in the states of California, Arizona, New Mexico, Texas, and Colorado who report a Spanish or Mexican family relationship. The Census category "Spanish surname" applies to people, wherever they reside, with such surnames. The latter therefore omits people who may have a parent or grandparent of Spanish-American lineage, but who have non-Spanish names because of intermarriage, just as it includes people who have no such parental lineage but who are married to persons with Spanish surnames.

Mexican-Americans of the Southwest

By far the largest group of Spanish-Americans are those who identify themselves to the census taker as being of Mexican origin, though 83 percent of them were born in the United States, as is noted in Table 16.1. Over five million strong, they provide more than 20 percent of the children in Los Angeles public schools (Table 16.2). Almost all of them are legally American citizens, though a few have come across the Mexican-American border as "wetbacks" and are liable to deportation if they should get in trouble with the law and be found to lack citizenship papers.

The name Chicano probably comes from the colloquial term "Mechicano" (Mexican) which has been used by Mexican-Americans in the Southwest to refer to themselves. The vast majority of the adults of this group are semiskilled and unskilled workers. They or their parents have had experience as agricultural workers, often as migratory workers following the crop cycle through the states of the west coast and mountain regions. In the past 20 years they have tended to settle permanently in the large and middle-sized cities of the Southwest, partly because their work of planting and harvesting crops has been taken over largely by machinery, and partly because they were able to get steady employment and thus could give up the migratory life.

The occupational distribution of Mexican-American men is shown in Table 16.3. About 18 percent are white-collar workers, compared with 23 percent of the total Spanish-American group. With 8 percent working as farm laborers in 1971, this group is the most rural of the Spanish-American population.

Because many Mexican-Americans are or have been migratory laborers, they have not been in a good position to get regular schooling for their children. The local school districts tended either to set up temporary classes for these children for a few months each year, or to ignore them. Before school desegregation began in the 1950s, there was a tendency to place these children in segregated schools. For example, Chicano children were formally segregated in California until 1947, and in Texas until 1948.

At present, due to residential patterns, Chicano children are segregated in elementary schools especially. The Department of Health, Education, and Welfare found that, in 1970, 20 percent of the Chicano elementary and secondary pupils were attending schools which had 90 to 100 percent minority-group pupils, and another 35 percent were attending schools which had 50—90 percent minority-group pupils.

Since a considerable proportion of Chicano families use Spanish as their home language, many of their children come to school with little or no facility in English. Chicano children of low socioeconomic status have the poorest knowledge of English. Texas has the greatest problem in this connection, with three out of five Chicano children who do not speak English as

341

TABLE 16.1. *Population of Spanish Descent, 1970*

Place of Origin of Family	Total Number (thousands)	Residence		Born In:					Age Distribution				Median Years of School for 25–34 Group
		In Five Southwest States*	Rest of USA	USA	Puerto Rico	Mexico	Cuba	Central and South America	−10	10–24	25–64	65 +	
Mexico	5,073	86	14	83	—	17	—	—	28	34	35	2.9	10.8
Puerto Rico	1,454	4	96	44	56	—	—	—	30	32	36	2.1	9.9
Cuba	565	14	86	17	—	—	82	1	16	27	53	4.1	12.4
Central and South America	556	31	69	36	—	—	—	64	24	28	46	3.1	12.4
United States and other	1,583	53	47	85	1	1	2	11	24	28	43	5.4	12.4
Total	9,230	60	40	71	9	9	5	6	27	32	38	3.3	12.4

* California, Arizona, Texas, New Mexico, Colorado.

Source: U.S. Census: *Persons of Spanish Origin*, Series PC (2)-1C. 1970. *Persons of Spanish Surname*, Series PC (2)-1D. 1970.

	Percentage					Total Number
	Indian	Black	Oriental	Spanish American	Anglo	
Los Angeles, 1969						
Elementary schools	0.2	25	3.1	23	49	364,000
Junior high (grades 7–9)	0.1	23	3.5	19	54	145,000
Senior high	0.1	20	3.8	18	58	141,000
Bell Gardens, Montebello School District, 1969 (a suburb of Los Angeles)						
Elementary schools	3.1	XX	0.1	22	75	5,167
Junior high	3.6	XX	0.2	15	81	1,634
Senior high*	1.0	XX	0.4	45	54	4,749*

Source: City of Los Angeles, Board of Education: *Racial and Ethnic Survey, 1969.* Montebello School District. *Pupil Data Report.*

* Montebello Senior High plus Bell Gardens Senior High School. Bell Gardens is in the Montebello District. XX Very small.

TABLE 16.3. *Occupations of Employed Males of Spanish Descent (Age: 16 plus. 1971)*

Occupation	Percent of Employed Males		
	Total, Spanish Descent*	Mexican-American	Puerto Rican
Professional and technical	7.2	4.5	6.2
Managers and owners (nonfarm)	6.4	5.4	4.8
Sales	2.7	2.2	3.0
Clerical	6.9	6.2	5.8
Craftsmen and foremen	18.2	19.7	13.3
Operatives, including transport	27.6	27.7	33.4
Laborers, except farm	12.1	15.0	13.5
Service workers	13.6	11.1	18.2
Farm owners and managers	0.3	0.1	0
Farm laborers	5.0	8.2	1.7

* Includes Cubans and old Americans of Spanish descent, as well as Mexican-Americans and Puerto Ricans.
Source: U.S. Census. *Persons of Spanish Origin.* Series PC (2)-1C. 1970.

well as their Anglo classmates. (On the other hand, many Chicano pupils, especially from high-status families, speak English quite well.)

School authorities in the Southwest responded to this situation initially by barring Spanish speech from the school classes and playgrounds as far as possible. They argued that pupils would benefit from the no-Spanish rule.

However, with the rise of sentiment by Chicano parents and pupils, as well as changing attitudes on the part of educators, this rule has now been moderated or dropped in many districts. For example, one Texas district reported to the Civil Rights Commission: "Effective September 1, 1968, students were allowed to speak correct Spanish on school grounds and classrooms if allowed by individual teachers. Teachers may use Spanish to 'bridge a gap' and make understanding clear." (U.S. Commission on Civil Rights, 1972, p. 15). We shall return to this issue of bilingual education later in this chapter.

Sentiment in favor of a positive approach to Mexican history and culture has also been growing. For instance, a graduate of a San Antonio high school was quoted as saying, about 1969, "Schools try to brainwash Chicanos. They try to make us forget our history, to be ashamed of being Mexicans, of speaking Spanish. They succeed in making us feel empty, and angry inside." (U.S. Commission on Civil Rights, 1972, p. 11). Educators are now attempting to deal with the problem implied, apparently with the help of middle-class Chicanos who are pressing for more attention to Mexican history and culture. Many middle-class and working-class Chicanos seem to have adopted with approval the slogan *La Raza* ("The Race", referring to Indian ancestry) although most Chicanos have little or no Indian ancestry. Present day Mexicans speak proudly of the intermarriage of Spanish colonists with Indians in the seventeenth century.

The United States Commission on Civil Rights has summarized its study of the education of Chicanos as of 1972 as follows:

> The basic finding of the Commission's study is that school systems of the Southwest have not recognized the rich culture and tradition of the Mexican-American students and have not adopted policies and programs which would enable those students to participate fully in the benefits of the educational process. Instead, the schools use a variety of exclusionary practices which deny the Chicano student the use of his language, a pride in his heritage, and the support of his community. (United States Commission on Civil Rights, 1972, p. 48)

As we shall see later in this chapter the present broadly sweeping movement for cultural pluralism is changing these practices in the Southwest, as elsewhere.

Puerto Ricans

Puerto Ricans represent in the industrial North and Northeast what Chicanos represent in the Southwest—a supply of unskilled and semiskilled labor, a growing middle class with political power, and a set of problems and challenges to the schools. As can be seen in Table 16.1, Puerto Ricans make up 16 percent of the population of Spanish descent, slightly over half of whom were born in Puerto Rico. They form a relatively youthful population, and have the lowest amount of schooling among the Spanish-surname group.

Puerto Ricans come and go freely between the mainland of the United States and the island of Puerto Rico. (The number residing on the mainland are about half the number residing on the island.) Puerto Rico is a United States "commonwealth" and not a state, but its citizens have the rights of United States citizens, and they are voting citizens whether they reside on the island or on the mainland.

The socioeconomic status of Puerto Ricans on the mainland reflects the economy of the island. That economy has grown about 10 percent a year over recent years, due to the investment of mainland capital and rapid industrialization. Nevertheless, the per capita income of the island averages about $1,000 (1970 dollars), much less than that of the United States as a whole. There has been a relatively high unemployment rate among the working classes in Puerto Rico, due largely to the modernization of agriculture which resulted in large numbers of rural people moving to the cities in search of work. Thus the average Puerto Rican immigrant to the mainland has been a rural person with relatively little education. Racially, the Puerto Ricans include persons with 100 percent Spanish ancestry to persons (a minority) with African ancentry. Most Puerto Ricans are seen as white.

More than half of the mainland Puerto Ricans live in the New York City metropolitan area, and there are large populations in Philadelphia, Washington, D.C., and Chicago. As noted in Table 16.3, 20 percent of the males have white-collar jobs, very few are farm laborers, and the largest occupational group are factory and transport workers.

School Performance of Puerto Rican Pupils.   Table 16.4 shows the standing of Puerto Rican pupils in 1966 relative to Chicano and other minorities. The data are drawn from the Study of Educational Opportunity referred to earlier. In that study, a large national sample of public school pupils were given brief tests of intelligence, reading (English), and mathematics, with scores given in terms of "school grade equivalents." The sample was fairly representative for all the groups except American Indians, who were drawn largely from a few boarding schools. The minority-group children are compared in the table with white students in nonmetropolitan areas. For example, the ninth grade Mexican-Americans made average scores on the reading test that were 2.2 grade levels below the white ninth graders. Puerto Rican pupils were slightly but consistently below Mexican-Americans. This may be due to the more recent arrival of the Puerto Ricans to the urban centers and perhaps to the greater prevalence of Spanish speaking in their homes.

Within the most recent years there has been a considerable increase in high school graduation and college entrance among Puerto Rican students,

TABLE 16.4.   Test Scores of Minority Group Children

Minority Group	School Grade	Grade Levels Behind White Students of Nonmetropolitan Areas		
		Verbal Ability	Reading Achievement	Math Achievement
Indian	6	1.3	1.8	1.8
Mexican-American	6	1.6	2.2	1.7
Negro	6	1.5	1.8	1.9
Puerto Rican	6	2.3	2.8	2.3
Oriental-American	6	0.5	0.7	0.7
Indian	9	1.4	1.9	2.1
Mexican-American	9	1.6	2.2	2.3
Negro	9	1.9	2.6	2.5
Puerto Rican	9	2.2	2.9	3.1
Oriental-American	9	0.3	0.5	0.1
Indian	12	2.5	2.6	3.0
Mexican-American	12	2.5	2.7	3.2
Negro	12	2.8	2.8	4.3
Puerto Rican	12	2.6	3.1	3.9
Oriental-American	12	0.6	1.0	0.0

Source: Coleman. *Equality of Educational Opportunity.* Adapted from Tables 3.121, 1, 2, 3.

and in the entrance of Puerto Ricans into teaching and school administration. This parallels the movement of Puerto Rican leaders into city government and other civic positions in New York City, Chicago, and Philadelphia. At the same time, a national Puerto Rican organization know as ASPIRA has developed, which aims to stimulate activity among Puerto Ricans for more and better schooling.

Cubans

Emigration of Cubans to the United States was small until the Castro-led revolution in the late 1950s put property owners and middle-class Cubans at an economic disadvantage and led to a major migration to the United States.

The out-migrants from Cuba comprise about eight percent of the Cuban population. About half of this group—some 300,000—are living in the area of South Florida. Other groups numbering in the thousands are living in New York, Philadelphia, Chicago, Milwaukee, Indianapolis. In 1970, the median schooling of Cubans in the United States was slightly beyond high school graduation, which makes them superior to Chicanos and Puerto Ricans in this respect. Their median age as of 1970 was 28, considerably older than the other Spanish-surname groups. Among males, 33 percent were in white-collar jobs in 1969, compared with 44 percent for Anglos. Even though the Cubans as a group may have economic handicaps, many have business and professional skills, and many have become relatively prosperous in the American economy. The median income for a Cuban family in 1969 was $5,957, compared with $7,894 for the total United States population. (Special Committee on Aging of the U.S. Senate, 1971)

Due probably to the fact that the Cuban immigrants have a higher average socioeconomic status than most immigrants, their children tend to do better in school, in spite of the fact that almost all of them speak Spanish at home. Achievement test data in Chicago and Miami show the children of Cuban families to score higher than other children of Spanish descent.

ORIENTAL-AMERICANS

Three groups of immigrants from the Orient are present in substantial numbers, although they represent small percentages of the total population of United States. As Table 16.5 shows, they are Japanese, Chinese, and Filipinos, in that order, making up about 0.7 percent of the total population. Due to recent changes of immigration rules which admit more Orientals, the Filipino and Chinese groups increased very rapidly in numbers between 1960 and 1970. All three groups are city dwellers, and are employed mainly in commerce and industry. The Filipinos are quite different from the Japanese and Chinese, with much lower socioeconomic status and lower educational levels.

The Japanese and Chinese-Americans have a higher percentage in

TABLE 16.5.   Location of Oriental, Indian, and Spanish-American Populations

Group	Number in 1970 (thousands)	Percent Growth 1960–70	Residence (percentages)			
			Central City of SMSA	Suburbs of SMSA	Urban Places Not SMSA	Rural
Japanese	591	27	48	33	7	12
Chinese	435	84	68	23	5	4
Filipino	343	95	48	31	6	15
Indian	793	51	20	12	13	55
Spanish descent*	9,073		56	28	4	12

Source: U.S. Census. General Population Characteristics, United States Summary: 1970. PC(1)-1B. p. 262

* Adapted from U.S. Census: 1970 PC(2)-1C (percent growth data not available).

white-collar jobs than the whites, as is noted in Table 3.2. Up to 1940 there was a great deal of discrimination against both groups, both in employment opportunity and in residential opportunity. The Chinese tended to live in Chinatowns of West Coast cities and New York and Boston. The Japanese-Americans were concentrated on the West Coast before World War II, and were severely limited by state laws and customs. There was objection to their renting or buying houses in "white" areas. But this died down after the war, and many Japanese, somewhat more than the Chinese, moved to other parts of the country where they merged readily into the business and professional life of the community.

School Performance of Oriental Pupils

As shown in Table 16.4, Japanese and Chinese-American pupils do about as well as white pupils on standard tests of school achievement. In the National Study of Equality of Educational Opportunity, the Oriental children were between one half and one grade level below the whites in reading achievement, and in mathematics in grades 9 and 12 they were at the same level as white children.

On the mainland United States, in areas of relatively high concentration of Oriental population, as in Los Angeles and San Francisco, it is well-known that the Chinese and Japanese pupils are seen by teachers and classmates as good students and as good persons to have as friends, and both the elementary and secondary schools that have a high proportion of Oriental pupils are generally regarded as "good" schools.

In Hawaii, where the Oriental and white groups meet on rather equal socioeconomic terms, the Japanese and Chinese students are superior to the whites in school achievement. In a study of test scores of tenth and twelfth grade students in the state of Hawaii in 1966, Japanese and Chinese students ranked above the other groups, followed by whites, Filipinos, and native Hawaiians.

Filipino Pupils

With immigration restrictions relaxed during the past 20 years, Filipinos have moved in large numbers into Hawaii and into West Coast cities. The 1970 Census showed more Filipinos than Japanese in the San Francisco–Oakland area, with 33,000 in Los Angeles–Long Beach, and more than 10,000 in New York and in Chicago. Many of these are young people who appear to be doing well in service occupations. It is too soon to tell how this group will fare in the cities of the mainland, although they seem to be handicapped in relation to Japanese and Chinese in Hawaii. As shown in Table 3.2, Filipinos have lower socioeconomic status than the Japanese and Chinese.

THE AMERICAN INDIANS

The American Indians numbered 793,000 in 1970. There are also some 35,000 Eskimos and Aleuts living in Alaska who are treated as Indians by the state and federal governments. Indians have grown rapidly in numbers in recent decades, due partly to the fact that the U.S. Public Health Service has brought modern health services to most of the Indian communities. With their numbers more than doubling between 1950 and 1970, they are the fastest-growing ethnic group in the country.

Indian people are diverse in tribal customs, religious beliefs, and ways of earning a living. When white men first came into contact with Indians in the various geographical areas that are now the United States, there were about 200 tribes who formed several different language groups. The Eastern Indians were generally farmers; the Plains Indians were buffalo hunters; the Southwest Indians were dry-land farmers, food gatherers, or small-game hunters. Along the Pacific coast, the people were fisherman; and in Alaska, hunters of seal and caribou and salmon fishers.

When the warfare between Indians and whites came to an end about 1870, the government took the role of guardian over the Indian people. It recognized each tribe's ownership of land, but tried to teach the adults better farming and cattle and sheep-growing practices. At the same time, Indian children were placed in boarding schools where they were expected to learn white American culture. It was hoped that Indians would soon become like other Americans and would become assimilated into the surrounding society.

This policy did not work out. Only a minority of Indian people accepted the ways of white society. Most held to Indian ways and to tribal indentifications. Because they were confined to reservations and ruled by agents of the federal government, their ways of life changed, and were no longer Indian in the traditional sense, but neither were their ways of life American. Indians became marked by poverty, due mainly to the fact that they were generally given poor and infertile land for their reservations.

American Indians today are a disadvantaged minority group. On the average they are low in income, educational level, and occupational levels, and their children are low on school achievement. However, a few are doing very well when measured by these three indices, and overall, American Indians as a group are slowly improving their position in society.

Indians have a moral claim on the public conscience somewhat different from the moral claims of other minority groups because they are the original Americans whose lands were taken from them by force or by shady bargaining. For this reason, the American Indians might now expect the best possible treatment from the wealthy society that surrounds them. There is a real desire on the part of most government leaders in the United States to make up for past mistakes by giving the Indians better treatment. But there is no general agreement on what is the best program for improvement of Indian life.

Educational Policy Before 1925

Because official government policy after 1870 was for the assimilation of Indians into the dominant white culture, both in schools run by the federal government and in schools run by churches and missionaries, the aim was to teach Indian children to be like white children. Consequently, the schools at first were almost entirely boarding schools, with the Indian child living away from his family and tribe. The Carlisle Indian School founded in 1878 at Carlisle, Pennsylvania, to serve children from midwestern and western tribes was typical. The curriculum was designed to teach Indian children to speak, read, and write English, to live like white people, and to practice a trade. Part of the educational program was the "outing system," which provided an Indian youth a three-year apprenticeship with a white family after completion of school training. The government paid $50 a year for his medical care and clothing; his labor in the home or on the farm was expected to compensate for his room and board.

By the early 1900s there was a good deal of opposition to the boarding school as the principal institution for educating Indian children, opposition based partly on the resistance of Indian parents to having their children moved away from the family. Accordingly, a number of federally operated day schools were opened on the reservations. At the same time, many Indian children were encouraged to attend local public schools on or near the reservations. By 1920, more Indian pupils were in local public school than in federal schools, and by 1928, the number of federal schools were fewer than in 1910.

Following World War I, federal appropriations for Indian education were increased, efforts were made to increase the proportions of Indian children attending school, and secondary school work was made more available at schools near reservations.

Indian Education, 1925–1965

The New Deal of the 1930s saw a change in Indian education toward relating schools more closely to Indian life, with the new Commissioner of Indian Affairs, John Collier, exerting a decisive influence. In 1934, the Indian Reorganization Act was passed, giving more power and more responsibility for self-government to Indian Tribal Councils. A large number of day schools were built by the federal government on reservations, and the native language was used in the early grades. More emphasis was placed on learning about native Indian culture and history, and on arts and crafts.

Because the Indians were wards of the federal government, reservations were not subject to state or local taxation, and they were given very limited services by the states in which they were located. Educational costs were paid by the federal government, except for those Indians who moved to towns and cities where they paid rent and property taxes just like other citizens.

In 1934 Congress passed the Johnson-O'Malley Act, authorizing federal funds to states where there are numbers of Indian families living away from reservations. And because a good many Indian children continued to live on reservations but were bussed to nearby public schools, the federal government provided funds for the construction of buildings and for instruction in schools attended by large numbers of Indian reservation pupils.

World War II had a great influence on Indian life. Some 25,000 Indians served in the armed forces. Older Indian men and women left reservations to take jobs in war industries or other jobs in towns and cities. The end of the war brought Indians back to the reservations with more knowledge of outside affairs and more interest in education, especially high school and vocational education. For example, the Navaho tribe, containing about one-fifth of all Indians and previously the most isolated tribe, moved explicitly to get literacy training for its teenage youth, many of whom had never been to school.

The federal government's policy on Indian affairs went through a major change beginning in 1951, when the Congress adopted a policy to curtail activities of the Bureau of Indian Affairs and eventually to terminate federal protection of Indians. This included termination of reservations by dividing the land and other resources among members of the tribe. This policy was cancelled after only a few years because it became clear that most Indian tribes wanted to retain common ownership of land and a reservation base for their tribal culture. Nevertheless, the Bureau of Indian Affairs (BIA) schools were closed down on a number of reservations or turned over to state and local public school districts. Indian pupils went increasingly to local public schools. Frequently, they had the experience of being in all-Indian elementary schools, then after the sixth or eighth grades moving to mixed schools, where they were in the minority.

During the 1950s, the Bureau of Indian Affairs established an Employment Assistance Program for members of Indian tribes. Individuals were subsidized for vocational, apprenticeship, and on-the-job training, and were assisted in finding jobs through relocation centers in several areas. This program has continued and expanded. Between 1960 and 1968, some 38,000 young Indian men and women received vocational training and employment assistance.

Thus, the aim of encouraging Indian people to participate more successfully in economic and educational life of the white society has been continued and strengthened, although now with more attention to the desires of the Indian people. The period from 1962 to 1968 saw the financing of

Community Action Projects by the office of Economic Opportunity. These brought young Indian leaders into responsible positions on the reservations and provided better housing, recreational facilities, and educational improvements.

Indians in Urban Centers

Since 1950, there has been substantial migration of Indians into urban centers of America. Like other urban migrants, many Indians leave their home communities because of limited employment opportunities. And like many other migrant groups, Indians find urban communities to be alien environments. Their cultural background, with its strong emphasis on close personal interrelationships and strong traditional family and tribal values, does not prepare Indians for depersonalized and sometimes hostile encounters with other urban residents. Their educational and vocational skills are, for the most part, inadequate or inappropriate for the available job opportunities. When they seek those few jobs for which they are prepared, they often face bigotry and discrimination. However, with increasing numbers of Indians already in the city, with improved job training and housing, and with personal advisory service provided by the Bureau of Indian Affairs and private agencies, many Indians are making good adjustments.

As noted in Table 16.5, 32 percent of Indians were living in metropolitan areas in 1970. The largest urban Indian concentration is in the Los Angeles area where about 35,000 Indians are living and about 1,500 children and youth are in school. Next largest is probably Minneapolis, with approximately 12,000 Indians and 1,700 Indian school pupils. There are some 18,000 Indians in the San Francisco Bay area, and about 10,000 each in Oklahoma City, Tulsa, Phoenix, and Chicago. Because so many are young men and women who have come to the cities only recently, they do not have many school-age children. In most cities, the ratio of children to adults is quite small. In another 10 years, Indian school-age population in the cities will probably be several times as large as it is today.

The Administrative Structure of
Education for Indians

In 1970, there were about 220,000 Indian children between ages 5 and 17, with the largest numbers distributed in seven western states (Alaska, Arizona, California, Montana, New Mexico, Oklahoma, and South Dakota) and in North Carolina.

Table 16.6 shows the distribution of Indian pupils, age 6 to 18, among various types of schools according to the BIA school census of 1967–1968. This shows that about 90 percent of the 6 to 18 age group were enrolled in school.

TABLE 16.6.   *School Attendance of Indian Children and Youth (Age 6–17 inclusive, 1968)*

In schools operated by the Bureau of Indian Affairs	51,000
In public schools where their attendance is financed by the federal government	100,000
In public schools financed by state and local school districts	40,000
In mission or other private schools	9,000
Not in school	20,000
Total	220,000

Source: Fuchs and Havighurst, p. 34.

The boarding school enrollment in BIA high schools doubled between 1959 and 1967, due partly to increased numbers of Indian youth and partly to the fact that more Indian youth were staying in school until age 16 or 18.

Contemporary Problems of Indian Education

As seen by most observers, the principal problem of Indian education is that Indian pupils as a group fall well below the national averages on standardized tests of school achievement. This has been true ever since school tests were first given in Indian schools. For example, a nationwide testing program carried on by the BIA in 1951—1954 showed Indian children to be below national norms after the fourth grade. Similar findings were reported by Coleman in the national study of Equality of Educational Opportunity (See Table 16.4), where Indian students averaged 1.8 years behind white students in reading and mathematics when in the sixth grade, and 2.9 years behind when in the twelfth grade. Furthermore, at least half of Indian pupils are a year or more over the normal age for their grade.

This low school achievement is *not* because Indian children are less intelligent than white children. Several studies based on intelligence tests that do not require reading ability show Indian children to be at or slightly above the level of white children. For example, on the Goodenough Draw-a-Man Intelligence Test, a test of mental alertness that does not require language facility, Indian children show about the same level of achievement as white children. The 1,700 Indian children who took this test in 1969 under the auspices of the National Study of American Indian Education showed an average IQ of 101.5, slighty superior to the average of white children. (Fuchs and Havighurst, 1972, Ch. 4)

The problem of Indian education has a good deal in common with the problems of education of other economically disadvantaged minorities. Many Indian children live in homes and communities where the cultural expectations are different and discontinuous from the expectation held by school teachers and school authorities. Although there are exceptions, the average Indian family teaches its children many valuable attitudes and skills, but it is not effective in teaching them the skills of school-learning.

Secondary School and College.   The Indian population has been improving its educational status very rapidly since about 1950. This shows in the increased proportion of Indian youth attending high school and graduating from high school. Two studies of progression through school, both undertaken in 1968, showed that about 55 percent of Indian youth who had been eighth-graders in 1962 had graduated from secondary school. At that time, about 73 percent of white students were finishing secondary school. When one remembers that most Indian families are poor, and that children of poor families are less likely to complete high school than children of well-to-do families, the record of Indian students seems quite good.

An increasing proportion of Indian youth are entering college and finishing a four-year curriculum. This proportion probably multiplied eight-fold between 1960 and 1970. It is estimated that approximately 3,000 Indian students entered college in 1970 and that about one-fourth of this number will graduate from a four-year degree program. The number of Indian youth reaching age 18 in a given year is presently about 18,000. This means that 17 percent of the age-cohort are continuing their education beyond high school, compared with about 38 percent of the age-group of all American youth, and that 4 percent are graduating from a four-year course, compared with about 22 percent of the total American age-group.

This is a remarkably large proportion, compared with the youth of other low-income groups, including low-income whites. One reason for the relatively high number is that scholarship funds are widely available for Indian students. Many Indian tribes have placed some of their money in scholarship funds, and the BIA has substantial scholarship money. In 1969 BIA scholarships were granted to 3,432 Indian students; the average grant amounted to $868.

Teachers for Indian Pupils.   Since the majority of Indian pupils attend public schools, they have the same teachers as other pupils have. However, schools operated by the Bureau of Indian Affairs have about 1800 teachers who passed a federal civil service examination and were assigned to BIA schools. The BIA made a study of its teachers in 1968 from which the following facts are drawn: there were 1,772 teachers, 61 percent women, and 15 percent Indian. Salaries in 1968 ranged from $6,176 to $12,119, depending on training, standing in college class, and teaching experience. This was higher than salaries in neighboring public schools, due partly to the fact that these teachers are on duty for 12 months, with the three summer months taken up with inservice education, student home visits, preparation for the following year, and vacation. Employment in Alaska is accompanied by a 25 percent cost of living supplement.

Indian teachers tend to stay longer in service than non-Indians. It is likely that substantially more Indians will seek teaching jobs, both in BIA schools and local public schools, as their numbers of college graduates increase. Of school administrators in BIA schools, 28 percent are Indian.

Federal Government and Indian Education—
Current Situation

A special subcommittee of the U.S. Senate issued a report on Indian education in 1969. As the title of the report indicates (Indian Education: A National Tragedy—A National Challenge), the committee's conclusions were critical of BIA's educational program and policy. The main recommendation of the committee was for greater self-government by Indians in their educational affairs, from the local community to the Washington office of the BIA, with more Indians placed in positions of responsibility.

No doubt this is taking place. More Indians direct educational policy from BIA offices and there are more local Indian school boards and advisory committees with more authority and power. The BIA has contracted with some local Indian groups to give them control over use of BIA funds and over the appointment of teachers. Furthermore, directors of BIA schools have been instructed by the BIA to work for creation of local advisory school boards and to listen to them.

A major breakthrough in policy was established by the Congress in the *Indian Education Act of 1972,* which provides funds for programs developed by local school districts and institutions of higher education which serve more than a handful of Indian students. This money is especially useful to urban school systems with a small minority of Indian students.

Programs for which money is requested must have been developed:

(1) in open consultation with parents of Indian children, teachers, and, where applicable, secondary school students, including public hearings at which such persons have had a full opportunity to understand the program for which assistance is being sought and to offer recommendations thereon, and

(2) with the *participation and approval* of a committee composed of, and selected by, parents of children participating in the program for which assistance is sought, teachers, and where applicable, secondary school students of which at least half the members shall be such parents. . . (U.S. Govt. 1972)

Pan-Indianism

There are more than a hundred Indian tribes today, and they exhibit a wide range of cultural differences. However, people from many different tribes now feel that they have much in common, and they cooperate in the National Congress of American Indians, which in turn gives expression to pan-Indianism.

The leaders of pan-Indianism tend to be younger people. Established tribal chairmen and tribal council members tend to be more tribe-centered and somewhat distrustful of pan-Indian programs. Furthermore, the appeal of pan-Indianism is strongest in the cities where intertribal contacts are maximized.

Probably the majority of Indian leaders favor an emphasis on educational and economic improvement tribe by tribe and reservation by reservation, with increasing Indian representation and participation in the Bureau of Indian Affairs both in Washington and in the area headquarters. The reservations will probably remain as an economic and cultural base for most Indians.

Freedom of Choice for Indians

As Indians gain greater control over the programs and policies of schools their children attend, they will face more directly the problem of education for a minority subculture in the dominant urban industrial society. They will have to decide how far the schools should push Indian youth toward assimilation into the dominant culture, or the "mainstream." They will have to decide how native languages should be treated in schools and how much attention should be given to the history and culture of Indians and of the local tribe. The policy of the federal government and of state and local school districts will be to maintain schools which encourage freedom of choice for Indians.

EUROPEAN IMMIGRANT GROUPS

As indicated at the opening of this chapter, most of the European immigrant groups who came to this country, more than 35 million persons since 1840, are no longer regarded as minority groups, even though they maintain certain subcultural patterns that distinguish them from the mainstream. In a sample census taken in 1969, people were asked: "What is your origin or descent?" Almost half of them, 93 million, answered for themselves and their immediate family members by naming a European nationality. At that time, approximately 9 million had been born in a European country. Yet the vast majority spoke English in their homes, and they were not visibly different from those who answered the question by saying they were of American stock.

As is argued convincingly by Michael Novak in his *Rise of the Unmeltable Ethnics,* there is a great deal of ethnic consciousness among the European immigrant groups and European ethnicity is an important element in contemporary American society. We will discuss ethnic diversity at length in the next chapter. Meanwhile it should be noted that the children of these groups do just about as well in school as the children of people who call themselves "old Americans." The immigrant groups from east and south Europe—Poles, Italians, Greeks, and Slavs—are mainly members of the lower-middle and the upper-working classes. Their children perform in school very much as children of native Americans of the same social classes.

EDUCATIONAL PROGRAMS FOR MINORITY GROUPS

It is clear that the ethnic groups with lowest school performance are the black, Spanish descent, and Indian groups. Compared to the Anglo-white and to the Chinese and Japanese-Americans, they lag behind in school performance and in level of education attained. To compare the three groups to each other, it is desirable to find them all in the same region of the country. Although this has not been entirely possible, the data shown in Table 16.7 approach this condition. The table shows that black pupils in California and in Texas were staying longer in school than Chicanos and Indians. In California, 34 percent and in Texas, 27 percent of an age-cohort of blacks entered college in 1971. Next in order came the Chicanos, with 28 and 16 percent. Of the national Indian population, 18 percent entered college as of 1968. (The data on Indians are nationwide, but Indian concentrations are greatest in the Southwest, and thus the Indian data are roughly comparable to the other data in Table 16.7.)

A visible minority group whose children perform below average in school constitutes a problem both for the educational system and for the minority group itself. Consequently, the Spanish-descent groups and the American Indians are now getting special attention from educators while the Japanese and Chinese-Americans and European ethnics are not seen as problem groups by school administrators.

For the Spanish-descent and Indian pupils, there is an educational dilemma that is greater than for other minority groups. As is true for the blacks, more of them need to work toward the kinds of occupational choices and careers which will enable them to compete successfully in the "mainstream" of American society. But for these two groups, in order to achieve better in school they need to master the English language. This seems to imply in turn an educational program aimed at "assimilation" into the dominant society, and therefore to lose the particular values and life-styles which mark their subcultures and of which they are proud. Somehow, a way must be found to help them maintain or enhance their self-concept as members of a minority subculture and at the same time to achieve economic and social competence in the wider society. We shall discuss this dilemma further in Chapter 17 on pluralism, but here it needs to be pointed out that the Spanish-descent and Indian groups have a vigorous national or tribal cultural tradition, while very few blacks identify with the African cultures.

The educational emphasis for these groups is on teaching them to read and speak the English language competently. There are three procedures: bilingual education, English as a second language, and remedial reading.

Bilingual Education

The Bilingual Education Act (Title VII of the Elementary and Secondary Education Act of 1968) authorized federal government funding of bilingual education programs for pupils of low-income families who have limited English-speaking ability. Normally instruction in all subjects is conducted both in the mother tongue and in English. Study of the history and culture of

TABLE 16.7.   *School Holding Power for Anglo and Ethnic Students. 1971*

	California				Texas			
	School Enrollment (thousands)	Percent Still in School			School Enrollment (thousands)	Percent Still in School		
Group		Eigth Grade	Twelfth Grade	Enter College		Eighth Grade	Twelfth Grade	Enter College
Anglo	3,323	100	86	47	1,618	100	85	53
Chicano	646	94	64	28	505	86	63	16
Black	388	97	67	34	380	99	64	27
All American Indians*	220	95	57	18				

Source: U.S. Commission on Civil Rights. *The Unfinished Education.* pp. 14, 17; 1971.

* Data for all American Indian youth, circa 1968, *To Live on This Earth,* by Fuchs and Havighurst, Chaps. 5, 13.

the minority group is encouraged. For this program Congress appropriated $25 million to be used in 1970—71. The Office of Education has defined bilingual education as follows:

> Bilingual education is the use of two languages, one of which is English, as mediums of instruction for the same pupil population in a well organized program which encompasses part or all of the curriculum and includes the study of the history and culture associated with the mother tongue. A complete program develops and maintains the children's self-esteem and a legitimate pride in both cultures.

The pupil is first taught to read in his native language, which is then used as a medium of instruction. The pupil is taught to *speak* English directly, not through reading. The first emphasis is on building a vocabulary that is adequate for the age-level of the pupil, but without emphasis on formal grammar. Reading English follows in the later grades.

Bilingual education may be carried on for any age, but generally it is started in the primary grades. A survey by the Commission on Civil Rights of bilingual education in the Southwest showed about 10 times as many elementary school pupils in such programs as there were secondary school pupils.

Bilingual education programs have had their principal use with Spanish-American pupils, but they are catching on with some schools where Indian children of a single tribe are present in substantial numbers.

English as a Second Language (ESL)

This is a program designed to teach the English language, while most of the instruction in the class is given in the home language of the pupils. This is essentially a matter of teaching English as a foreign language. The advantage of this program is that the skills of reading and the other school subjects can be taught in the native language, without forcing the child to try to learn those skills in a strange language. This is not a cultural program; it does not make use of the cultural heritage of the minority group. The Commission on Civil Rights found that in the Southwest, in 1969, some five percent of Chicano pupils were receiving some type of ESL instruction, more than twice the proportion receiving bilingual education.

Remedial reading

This is a long-established procedure used with pupils who are far below average in their reading skills. It pays no attention to the home language of the pupil, and is generally used in all kinds of schools. The Commission on Civil Rights found that 10 percent of Chicano students, both elementary and secondary school levels, were getting remedial reading instruction.

Language Programs for Other than
Spanish-American Minorities

It is interesting to note that the programs which rely on the use of the home language in the school as a medium of instruction tend to be limited to Spanish-speaking pupils. The Japanese and Chinese minority groups do not appear to need or to want their languages used in the schools. Most Japanese-American families speak English at home. But Chinese-American families are likely to speak the mother tongue at home. Yet the children of Chinese and Japanese families appear to read with only a slight disadvantage compared with white children. A mixture of national and social-class culture seems to give Chinese and Japanese children a good base for school achievement in English. But the Chicano and Puerto Rican and Filipino *lower-class* subculture may not provide the kind of experience and stimulation that will get the pupil ready to start his school work in English. The European ethnic groups mainly speak English in the home, unless the parents are foreign born. Hence the schools are not likely to be pushed to give instruction in the European language.

It is clear that a number of minority ethnic groups are maintaining themselves outside of the dominant American culture, though this places them at a disadvantage. However, they do not wish to be assimilated into the "mainstream" of American society, though they want their children to learn some of the skills that will improve their learning power. This leads to the concept of cultural pluralism, which is the subject of the next chapter.

EXERCISES

1. If you have friends or acquaintances who are Chinese or Japanese, discuss with them the fact that their group does better in school achievement than other minority groups. To what extent is this due to the difference between the Chinese and Japanese subcultures, on the one hand, and the Spanish-American and Indian subcultures on the other hand?

2. Write a paper which either supports or opposes a program of bilingual education aimed to assist the children of a particular non-English-speaking minority. What are the advantages and disadvantages?

3. Select a particular Indian Tribe in which you are interested, and write a paper on the education of the children and youth of that tribe.

4. If you live in a city with a number of Indian families, study the situation of the Indian group—their residence, occupations, family structure, and school performance.

5. If you are a member of a minority ethnic group, describe your own experience in the schools.

SUGGESTIONS FOR FURTHER READING

1. A good collection of articles on education for various ethnic groups is provided in the January, 1972 issue of the *Phi Delta Kappan*. Edited by James A. Banks, it carries the theme title: *The Imperatives of Ethnic Education*. Another book which argues for a multi-ethnic approach to education is *Red, Brown, and Black Demands for Better Education* by G. Louis Heath.

2. For a more intensive study of the education of Spanish-American students, read the following: Thomas P. Carter, *Mexican-Americans in School: A History of Educational Neglect*, College Entrance Examination Board; Julian Samora, ed., *La Raza, Forgotten Americans*, University of Notre Dame Press.

3. For information concerning the changing place of Orientals in the American society, read the following: Carey McWilliams, *Brothers under the Skin*, Little, Brown, 1951. Morton Grodzins, *Americans Betrayed: Politics and Japanese Evacuation*, University of Chicago Press, 1949.

4. The complex problem of the relation of an Anglo teacher to a class of Indian pupils is described and analyzed in a useful way by an Indian teacher, Robert Dumont, Jr., in a paper entitled "Learning English and How to Be Silent: Studies in American Indian Classrooms," in the book edited by Hymes, Cazden, and John, *Functions of Language in the Classroom*.

5. The broad and developing field of *Ethnic Studies* is surveyed and analyzed by a dozen writers on one or another ethnic group in the *43d Yearbook* of the National Council for the Social Studies, published in 1973.

6. A general overview of the data on minorities is given in Marden, *Minorities in American Society*.

7. A National Study of American Indian Education was made in 1968–70 by a consortium of educationists and anthropologists from eight universities, directed by Robert J. Havighurst of the University of Chicago and financed by the U.S. Office of Education. A summary report of the study has been written by Estelle Fuchs and Robert J. Havighurst, with the title, *To Live on This Earth: American Indian Education*.

CHAPTER 17

Cultural Pluralism, Social Integration, and The Educational System

The people of the United States are:

100 million, Anglo-Saxon
25 million, Teutonic
23 million, Negro
16 million, Irish
9 million, Italian
9 million, Latin-American (Spanish origin)
8 million, Slavic
6 million, Scandinavian
5 million, Polish
5 million, French
1.4 million, Oriental
.8 million, American Indian
.5 million, Finn
.5 million, Lithuanian
.5 million, Greek

The people of the United States are:

130 million, Protestant
54 million, Roman Catholic
7.5 million, Jewish
3 million, Eastern Orthodox Catholic
2.3 million, Mormon

.5 million, Christian Scientist
.4 million, Seventh Day Adventist

Although the Anglo-Protestant group has always been in the majority, the American society has always contained a number of different nationality, racial, and religious groups. Relations between these groups have at times been tense, yet the general attitude of Americans has been to anticipate a reduction of group differences through various forms of common activity within a framework of a democratic society. Thus it was common to speak of America as a "melting pot."

However, in recent years the attitude toward the continued existence of subgroups and subcultures has become more approving and more appreciative. Educational systems are now expected to assist various groups to maintain their cultural differences and to achieve their cultural goals within a cooperative framework. Thus James E. Allen, Jr., former United States Commissioner of Education, in recommending support for ASPIRA, the Puerto Rican organization, wrote:

> The day of the melting pot is over. No longer is it the ideal of each minority to become an indistinguishable part of the majority. Today, each strives to maintain its identity while seeking its rightful share of the social, economic, and political fruits of our system. Self-help and self-determination have become the rallying cries of all minorities.

Separate and different group cultures and traditions are now regarded as healthy in a complex democratic society. They enrich the society. At the same time, the "mainstream" of the society is open to new recruits, and offers many rewards to members of minority groups who join the mainstream and who consequently reduce their participation and allegiance to a minority group. Thus, there is an inherent tension between the societal forces which push for a democratic cultural pluralism and those which work toward a democratic social integration.

In the period from 1965 to 1974, the slogans of pluralism have been popular, but integration continues to be an important social goal. By social integration we mean the mixing of various racial and cultural groups through association in business, education, government and cultural affairs, and some degree of intermarriage with the goal being one common culture. By democratic cultural pluralism we mean the amicable coexistence of a variety of racial, ethnic, religious, and economic groups, each group keeping its subculture fairly intact and intermarrying little or not at all with other groups. If equal respect and equal opportunities and privileges are accorded to all groups, a condition of democratic pluralism may be said to exist, as it does in Switzerland, with its French, German, and Italian cantons, and as in Holland where religious subcultures set themselves apart in political and civic as well as social and religious affairs.

A brief look backward at American history is valuable in understanding where the United States stands at present.

PLURALISM IN NINETEETH CENTURY AMERICA

The United States was a pluralistic society from its very beginning with the 13 colonies representing a variety of European nationalities and a variety of religious groups, with Indians who were being pushed out of their lands, and with Africans who were held and sold as slaves. This pluralism could hardly be called democratic. For many of the European immigrants who came to America in the nineteenth century, there was blatant discrimination. For example, the large Irish immigration between 1840 and 1860, resulting partly from famine in Ireland, produced a lower class of Irish in the United States, who were given only the most menial jobs. Advertisements in the newspapers for an office boy or for a parlor maid often carried the letters "NINA" (No Irish Need Apply). Subsequent to this period, immigrant Hungarians, Poles, Italians, Croatians, and Russian Jews arrived and lived in poverty under brutal conditions of employment.

What saved the situation for the newcomers and led to their upward mobility were the constant demand for unskilled and semiskilled labor in the expanding economy, the free schools that enabled many immigrant children to move into white-collar jobs, the almost free land on the frontier, and the expansion of local government and business which created roles into which many of the immigrants could move with little formal schooling. A mixture of social integration and cultural pluralism was at work. Each wave of European immigrants who arrived without money or position improved its status rapidly, although leaving behind in its rise, after one or two generations, some members who were not so fortunate.

Two groups, however, did not share equitably in the nineteenth century blend of democratic pluralism and social integration: the American Indians, who were pushed into inferior lands and decimated by the U.S. Army if they chose to fight; and the freed African slaves.

The period of American social history up to about 1900 was dominated by a policy which the sociologist Milton Gordon calls *Anglo-conformity*. This policy assumed the desirability of maintaining the social institutions of England, the English language, and English-oriented cultural patterns as dominant in American life. (Gordon, p. 88). The society was also heavily Protestant, and there was much prejudice against Catholics and new Catholic immigrants. The German, Scandinavian, and Irish immigrants who predominated during the 1840 to 1890 period were accepted with some misgivings. Most of the Irish and some of the Germans were Catholic. The Scandinavians were regarded as clannish and they maintained their home languages. Still, the country was large, a growing industry needed labor, and the frontier was open. The society became in fact more pluralistic than before.

THE MELTING POT

Around the beginning of the twentieth century, there developed the concept of a new, composite American nationality being formed through the agency of frontier life as it spread across the middle of the country and onward to the west. The historian Frederick Jackson Turner in his influential book, *The Frontier in American History,* said the western frontier acted as "a solvent for the national heritages and separatist tendencies" of the European immigrants. (Gordon, p. 118). Yet the vast flow of immigration from southern Europe after 1880 made it clear that neither Anglo-conformity nor the frontier life could be a feasible social or political model. The eastern cities were filling up with a polyglot population. This reality had to be reckoned with in any conception of the structure of American society.

An English Jewish writer, Israel Zangwill, stated the new theory through his popular drama, *The Melting Pot,* first produced in America in 1908. The hero of the play is a Russian Jewish immigrant, who falls in love with a Gentile girl. The hero, in the rhetoric of his day, proclaims that, "America is God's Crucible, the great Melting Pot where all the races of Europe are melting and re-forming! Here you stand, good folk, think I, when I see them at Ellis Island, here you stand in your 50 groups, with your 50 languages and histories, and your 50 blood hatreds and rivalries. But you won't be long like that, brothers, for these are the fires of God you've come to— these are the fires of God. A fig for your feuds and vendettas! Germans and Frenchmen, Irishmen and Englishmen, Jews and Russians—into the Crucible with you all! God is making the American." (Zangwill, 1909, p. 37)

The melting pot theory accepted the eastern and southern European immigrants as good "material" for making Americans, just as good as the English and north European stock.

Education and the Melting Pot Theory

About the middle of the nineteenth century, free public education entered the picture, in theory aiding the "Americanization" process by teaching everybody English and American social ideals. Although the public school system was influential, it was probably not as effective as was claimed by some of the public school leaders of the 1880–1920 period. Many children of immigrant families achieved poorly in school and dropped out as early as possible to go to work at unskilled jobs. Furthermore, Roman Catholic parish schools were established which taught not only the Catholic religion but taught also the European ethnic culture of the particular parish being served.

Integration and Pluralism after 1920

After the close of World War I, the socioeconomic condition of the country changed markedly. Restrictions were placed on immigration, thus opening the job market in heavy industry to migrants from the South and the Appalachian states and to Mexican-Americans from the Southwest. Puerto Ricans came to the eastern cities. These groups did not integrate readily into the "mainstream." At the same time, technological development reduced the proportion of unskilled jobs in the labor market and increased the proportion of jobs which required high school and college education. Industrial productivity increased so much that after 1950 the economic-industrial complex could not employ all the available labor, thus producing a substantial group of unemployed who had to live on welfare payments.

In effect, the socioeconomic changes of the society between 1920 and 1965 worked to restrict opportunities for groups with the lowest incomes to integrate themselves into the mainstream of economic, social, and civic life.

THE RISE OF CULTURAL PLURALISM

The idea of the melting together of many diverse cultures into a single American culture was not widely approved by leaders of American thought, nor was it clear that it was actually happening. Horace M. Kallen criticized the melting pot theory in his book *Culture and Democracy in the United States* (1924). He used the term "cultural pluralism" to describe his program for America as a democracy of nationalities cooperating voluntarily. Other social philosophers, social scientists, and popular writers favored this concept. Among educators, the field of *intergroup relations* assumed considerable importance. Teaching units on intergroup relations and recommendations for more favorable treatment of minority groups found their way into high school social studies and history courses. The late 1940s and early 1950s saw much activity along these lines, supported by such organizations as the National Conference of Christians and Jews and the American Jewish Committee.

Then came the 1954 Supreme Court decision against racially segregated public schools, followed in the 1960s by the Civil Rights Act and by the Civil Rights movement which broke down many political and economic barriers against blacks. As noted in Chapter 15 however, the blacks were not brought into the melting pot. With the exception of a few middle-class families they were segregated residentially in the large cities and their children continued to be segregated in school. Nevertheless, the 1960s saw substantial improvement in the economic, educational, and political situation of the black population. These were obtained largely it seemed, by black organizations asserting their rights and using political and legal measures to influence the government and the business community.

The relative success of the blacks appears to have stimulated other minority groups to organize for group action—especially the Chicano and Puerto Rican and American Indian groups. The middle 1960s saw the creation of several Chicano groups: Cesar Chavez developed the United Farm Workers Organizing Committee in California; Reies Lopez Tijerina started the Alianza Federal de Mercedes in New Mexico; Rodolfo Gonzales organized the Crusade for Justice in Denver. These worked for better housing, better wages, better health and educational services. Among the Puerto Ricans, ASPIRA worked for better educational and social conditions. Several small Indian groups were organized, including the American Indian Movement which came to public attention with the occupation of the building of the Bureau of Indian Affairs building in Washington in 1972, and with the occupation of the village of Wounded Knee in South Dakota in 1973. Meanwhile, the Black Muslims also grew strong in several cities, with separate schools and separate business activities alongside their religious institutions.

European Ethnic Movements

The east and south European immigrants had not shown much sign of discontent with their lot in the United States. As industrious workers, they had generally established themselves securely in upper-working class and lower-middle class positions by 1940. Most of them lived in the large cities and in the industrial north central and northeastern regions.

After World War II the migration of blacks, Chicanos, and Puerto Ricans to the big cities began to crowd the European ethnics, both in terms of housing and in jobs. Middle-class people moved to the suburbs or to middle-class enclaves in the central city, leaving the working-class whites to come to terms with the new in-migrants. Tensions arose, with white ethnic working-class people appearing as opponents to the expansion of residential areas for blacks and for Spanish-Americans. Mark Krug pointed to this rivalry as a partial cause of the emergence of white ethnic group activism. He quoted Barbara Mikulski, a young Democratic politician and a leader of the Polish-American community in Baltimore, who said, "We anguish at all the class prejudice that is forced upon us. Ethnic Americans do not feel that black people are inferior, but regard them as territorial aggressors in their residential and employment turfs." Krug went on to say, "Encouraged by the example of the black community and strengthened by their unity of interests, white ethnic minorities have become more united and more militant in protesting their grievances." (Krug, 1972, p. 322)

The United States Catholic Conference, through its Division for Urban Life, and Monsignor Gino Baroni, Director of Program Development for the Task Force on Urban Problems, issued a Labor Day Statement in 1970 which said that the white ethnic working class was being called upon to solve the urban problem of relations with blacks and Spanish-Americans, without help from the middle-class white population. The statement said:

> We reject the widespread accusation that these people are the primary exponents of racism in our society, although we do not deny that racism exists in their ranks. We find that race relations in America's big cities have come to mean increasingly the relations between the blacks and/or the browns on the one hand and white ethnic working-class people on the other. This happens because, increasingly, business and institutional leadership no longer lives in the city and the upper-middle class has either fled or is fleeing to the suburbs. It is obvious, therefore, that if there is to be a resolution of the racial crisis which currently grips our society, a critical role will be played by white ethnic working-class communities. (Baroni, 1970, p. 2)

An eloquent voice on behalf of the ethnics of southern and eastern Europe was Michael Novak's in his book, *The Rise of the Unmeltable Ethnics*. He spoke of the 1970s as the "Decade of the Ethnics" and regarded the rise in ethnic consciousness as part of a more general cultural revolution in America. His basic proposition was that ethnic identity has similar elements from one ethnic group to another and it is a desirable antidote to the poisons of the modern industrial society. He says, "The rise in ethnic consciousness is, then, part of a more general cultural revolution. As soon as one realizes that man is not mind alone, and that his most intelligent theories, political decisions, and works of genius flow from 'intelligent subjectivity,' attention to the roots of imagination, value, and instinct is inevitable. When a person thinks, more than one generation's passions and images think in him." (Novak, p. 37). The ethnic group, for Novak, lives in the individual in a mystical, nonrational way. He defines an ethnic group as "a group with historical memory, real or imaginary. . . . Ethnic memory is not a set of events remembered, but rather a set of instincts, feelings, intimacies, expectations, patterns of emotion and behavior; a sense of reality; a set of stories for individuals—and for the people as a whole—to live out." (Novak, p. 56)

What Is Cultural Pluralism?

The racial minorities and the white ethnic minorities who make up about one-third of the population of the United States have become actors on the stage of "cultural pluralism." The action has become so vigorous since 1960 that it is a major concern in domestic politics, in social ethics, and in education. Some of the functions of a viable cultural pluralism are:

1. To provide substantial opportunity to the members of each subculture to achieve life satisfaction in their own life-style.
2. To provide education and training for every member of every subculture of a kind and quality that will enable the individuals to earn a fair living—to avoid poverty.

3.   To provide employment or access to the labor force on equal terms to all members of the society.
4.   To provide opportunity and encouragement for the youth of every sub-culture to associate with youth of other groups in activities of mutual interest.
5.   To maintain freedom of individuals and groups to practice separatism, though perhaps at some sacrifice in terms of material standard of living.
6.   To permit subgroups to maintain a separate economic system as long as this does no damage to the general welfare of the society.
7.   To permit subgroups to carry on their own separate educational systems, though they must bear the extra expense.
8.   To make all subgroups responsible for contributions to the general welfare of the society.

This definition agrees with the answers which Milton Gordon secured from officials of eight agencies for intergroup relations when, in 1963, he asked them "What would you say is meant by cultural pluralism?" (Gordon, p. 16–17)

Integration, Pluralism, Separatism

Cultural pluralism lies between integration on the one hand and separatism on the other. The boundaries are not clear. Although the melting pot concept is the extreme of integration, cultural pluralism can shade into a stable form of integration in which various subcultures are quite distinct in some areas of life, but are merged together in other areas of life. At the other extreme is a multigroup society characterized by separatism in which each group keeps itself apart through laws and customs which prevent intermarriage and through a rigid limitation on the extent of its relations with other groups. Separatism has grown in force since about 1960.

Because a policy of separatism has different educational implications from a policy of pluralism or integration, we shall keep the educational implications in mind as we discuss separatism and pluralism in the rest of this chapter.

CULTURAL SEPARATISM

Two different groups favor a policy of separatism:

1.   Those who want to be left alone to work out their own life styles which they see as superior to others. This position is characteristic of certain small religious sects such as the Amish, the Hutterites, the Seventh Day Adventists, and the Black Muslims. They attempt to keep separate schools, and to do as little business as possible with the mainstream society. In 1884, when the Roman Catholic bishops made a decision that

Catholic children were not receiving proper religious education and called for every parish in the country to set up and operate its own parish school, this was a separatist act.

2. Those who use separatism as a temporary means for building strength and identity within the minority group, after which the group will be ready to move into a pluralistic situation with power and confidence. This is the position of spokesmen for substantial groups of low-income blacks, Puerto Ricans, and Chicanos. It grows out of a conviction that the existing form of pluralism is not satisfactory, and will not become more satisfactory unless certain minority groups can gain the power and the self-assurance with which to negotiate with other groups for a fair distribution of the opportunities and privileges of the larger society.

People in this second camp argue for "local control" of their schools because they feel the existing educational establishment will not move fast enough or far enough. For instance, one such advocate has criticized the educational establishment as one that believes "that a public school system that fails poor black children can be tolerated, while a public school system that fails white middle-class children cannot. The black community, therefore, has decided that it has to make the decisions about what can and cannot be tolerated for its children because society as a whole has largely failed the black community in this respect. . . . In a sense, schools should relate to the people who use them in much the same way that any other producer relates to a consumer. I would like to see schools in Spanish-speaking neighborhoods be forced, because of their relationship to the community, to put up signs saying *Se Habla Espanol* as quickly as every store in the community had to put one up in order to stay in business. (Haskins, 1969)

Rise of a Black Separatist Movement

As described in the preceding chapter of this book, there was widespread disappointment in the black group when, during the 1960s, so little progress was made toward racial desegregation in the cities of the North and West, and when black children were not improving much in their school performance, even with substantial increase of expenditures under the Elementary and Secondary Education Act. By 1970 there was a considerable sentiment in the black community for "black schools, with black teachers and administrators, and a fair share of the school dollar." The argument has been summarized by Barbara Sizemore, a black administrator in the Chicago school system, who later became Superintendent of Schools in Washington, D.C. She said that separate schools and a separate subsystem for blacks are desirable at the 1970 moment, because we are at a stage in the Black Revolution when the condition is necessary and desirable, though it should not be permanent. She argues that desegregation has not helped black pupils, and has operated against the welfare and effectiveness of black educators. She wrote:

371

> In most places where desegregation models have been implemented
> blacks lose jobs. Most blacks have been recruited into teaching because
> they were systematically excluded from participation in the professsional
> slots in the business-industrial-military complex. Recent research indicates
> that hundreds of black teachers have been demoted, dismissed outright,
> denied new contracts, or pressured into resigning because of desegregation
> and that new teachers hired to replace them include fewer and fewer blacks.
> Moreover, the black principal has been desegregation's primary prey.
> Desegregation, then, serves to create more jobs for whites at a time when
> the economy is shrinking and industry constricting. (Sizemore, p. 281)

The rationale is that the minority group should separate and organize itself
so as to enhance its own socioeconomic status, its own solidarity, and its own
control over the conditions of cooperation with the majority group; then,
eventually, the minority group can integrate with the majority group on equal
and favorable terms.

This argument, subtle and powerful, holds that meaningful integration—with true equality of the races—can only come when blacks have
achieved a group identity, pride in their race, and bargaining power based on
unified black communities. Consequently blacks in America should stay to
themselves, study African culture and history, learn that they come from
African centers of civilization and high culture which flourished at a time
when much of western Europe was inhabited by savages. They should have
black teachers for black schools, and they should demand separate black
colleges within the universities.

Black separatism was strengthened in the period from 1965–1970 by
the rise of black politicians to power in the northern and western cities, and
by their need to maintain a black voting constituency. Many black aldermen,
state legislators, and congressmen, elected to office by the growing black
populations in the cities, accepted the fact of segregation and strove to improve segregated communities, including improvement of segregated schools.
This position came to the fore in 1972, when black political leaders of the
country met in Gary, Indiana in a National Black Political Convention, and
adopted a platform statement which included an anti-integration and anti-
bussing resolution. Their statement was quickly repudiated by the Black
Caucus of the U.S. Congress in its own Black Bill of Rights. Thus, while the
separatist groups were pushing for black schools, congressmen in the Black
Caucus stood behind integration and bussing to achieve integration.

The leaders of black separatism tend to be young people who mistrust
the established civil rights organizations—the NAACP and the Urban
League—and call those leaders "Uncle Toms." Black separatism favors the
use of the term "black" to describe people of African descent, and uses the
term "Negro" as an epithet practically synonymous with "Uncle Tom."

The emotional appeal of the "black identity" argument is great for
some young people. One of their major prophets is Frantz Fanon, born in the

French West Indies in 1925, educated in Paris, where he became a psychiatrist. Fanon died at the age of 36 from leukemia. His book, *The Wretched of the Earth,* states the proposition that the nonwhite peoples of the world can only come out from under white domination by discovering their own racial identity and then overthrowing the white-dominated world by violent revolution, leading to a worldwide classless society.

According to this view, Martin Luther King was wrong in advocating integration, and the song "We Shall Overcome—black and white together" is romantic nonsense.

Black Separatism or Integration?

All in all, there are three combinations of separatism-pluralism-integration, each with substantial support in the black community, and each with its educational policy.

A. **Pluralistic Separatism.** The separatist movement that picked up momentum after 1965 is based on the conviction of some black leaders that whites will not *voluntarily* give up a fair share of power and opportunity to blacks, but must be forced to do so. They have concluded that black power can only be achieved through the formation of black interest groups—educational, economic, political, and social—from which whites are excluded. They assume that blacks have enough common interests to pursue a unified strategy aimed at common goals.

Accordingly this group does not push for integrated schools—instead they push for all-black faculties for black schools, for more money for black schools, and for black studies in high school and college. In general, this group consists of younger leaders with a following among lower-working-class blacks, welfare groups, and a vocal minority of black college students. This was the group who held the center of the stage at the 1972 National Black Political Convention in Gary, Indiana, already referred to.

This separatist position had some white liberal support during the period around 1970. One example was the proposal by Christopher Jencks in a 1968 article entitled "Private Schools for Black Children," in which he proposed that black leaders and black parents should be assisted with public funds to set up private schools. Although these schools would be open to white students, he did not believe that many whites would apply. He argued for this plan on political rather than educational grounds. He said, "It seems to me that we should view the present urban school crisis primarily as a political problem, and only secondarily as a pedagogic one. So long as militant blacks believe they are victims of a conspiracy to keep their children stupid—and therefore subservient—the political problem will remain insoluble. But if we encourage and assist black parents with such suspicions to set up their own schools we may be able to avert disaster. These schools would not, I predict, be either more or less successful than existing public schools in teaching the three R's. But that is not the point. The point is to find a political *modus vivendi* which is tolerable to all sides." (Jencks, 1968, p. 132)

B. **Radical Separatism.**   The radical separatist or black *nationalist* position has its principal exponent in the Black Panther Party for Self-defense, which was founded in Oakland, California in 1966 by Huey P. Newton and Bobby Seale, community college students. The Black Panthers were variously perceived in 1970 as: a black racist organization; a communist organization; a revolutionary organization; a fascist organization; an educational and welfare organization devoted to welfare work in the city ghettoes. A friendly white observer wrote:

> The Black Panther Party is not dedicated to the violent overthrow of the Government. That it is a revolutionary organization is obvious. But it is also a political party, a legitimate political apparatus that has operated from the beginning within the legal framework of the existing social order. This fact must be understood. Black Panthers are not bomb throwers or rioters or rebels without a cause, or anarchistic madmen. The Party stresses political education and condemns all spontaneous rioting and insurrectionary violence. (Stevens, 1970, p. 45)

This same observer stated that, in the two and one half years from 1968 to the summer of 1970, 28 Black Panthers were shot to death by police.

On the other hand, the liberal John Fischer, editor of *Harper's Magazine,* denounced the Panther Party as a fascist gang. (Fischer, 1970)

Black nationalists may be placed into three categories with respect to their political aims: those who wish to establish a new nation, probably in Africa; those who wish to have five of the 50 United States assigned completely to black citizens; and those who want black hegemony over the black residential enclaves that exist in this country.

C. **Pluralistic Integration.**   There is an equally strong and passionate position supported vigorously by most civil rights leaders and probably supported also by the majority of black citizens that argues for integration.

The case for integration was put forth by the so-called Kerner Commission, (the National Advisory Commission on Civil Disorders appointed by President Johnson). This commission, which included both blacks and whites, reported in 1968, "Our nation is moving toward two societies, one black, one white—separate and unequal." Saying that improvement of the black part of the society is effectively blocked by racial discrimination, the report said the black ghetto is a responsibility of the white society, "White institutions created it, white institutions maintain it, and white society condones it."

The commission went on to argue, however, that separatism can never produce equality for blacks. It "could only relegate Negroes permanently to inferior incomes and economic status." The goal of America, the commission said, "must be achieving freedom for every citizen to live and work according to his capacities and desires, not his color."

Pluralistic integration is the position of middle-class black leaders and is generally supported by liberal whites. The National Association for the Advancement of Colored People, and the National Urban League take this position, which is diametrically opposed to separatism. A vocal proponent of this position is Bayard Rustin, who argues that the well-being of America's blacks is tied to the well-being of whites and other groups, and primarily depends on improvements in the economy which produce more jobs and higher incomes for all. In an article entitled "The Failure of Black Separatism," Rustin argues that blacks cannot be effective working alone. They should join with other minorities and with the trade union movement to give political power to the democratic Left in America. The leaders of the Urban League and the NAACP have consistently taken a position for social and political integration, although they do not stress the trade union aspect. Kenneth Clark takes the same position and, as mentioned in the preceding chapter, says that it implies integrated education and insistence on the same educational programs and standards for black and white students.

A leading social psychologist, Thomas Pettigrew, in an address entitled "Racially Separate or Together?" analyzed the various points of view held by both blacks and whites, and pointed out that many of both races favor a policy of separatism, but for different reasons (Pettigrew, 1971). The white separatist, he says, believes:

1. That both racial groups are more comfortable when separated.
2. That blacks are inferior to whites—perhaps by heredity, but in any case, in fact. Therefore integrated schooling and other forms of integrated interaction will lower the standards for whites.
3. Strife and unrest can be kept at a minimum by separation of the races.

The black separatist believes:

1. That both racial groups are more comfortable when separated.
2. The central problem is white racism. White liberals should fight against this, and black leaders should work in separate institutions, such as schools, businesses, and churches, to improve the situation for blacks.
3. Equal and mutually beneficial relations with whites are only possible when blacks have gained personal and group autonomy, self-respect, and power. Equality and interdependence are goals which cannot be achieved until blacks have a period of separatism during which they can develop themselves.

Pettigrew disagrees with both sets of beliefs and argues, as a psychologist, that:

375

1.   Separatism is a cause, not a remedy, for dissatisfaction and discomfort in interracial situations.
2.   The belief of whites in their racial superiority is decreasing, as shown by scientific studies during the past three decades. The recent confrontations between whites and blacks have resulted in further reduction among whites of a belief in racial superiority.
3.   Studies of the results of desegregation in busses, jobs, restaurants, and hotels, and in churches and schools, show that increased contact reduces racial friction and strife.
4.   Doing nothing about integration means leaving the present institutional arrangements (segregated schools, housing, and churches) to continue to cause discrimination and prejudice.

For these reasons Pettigrew argues against black separatism, and urges a strong program of social integration.

Spanish Group Separatism

While there is a good deal of protest against discrimination on the part of some Chicano and Puerto Rican educational leaders, there is very little serious talk about separatism. Criticism of the educational system is generally directed toward the school's refusal to use the Spanish language constructively. Occasionally, however, the criticisms are broader, as in the case of Professor Eduardo Seda Bonilla, Director of Puerto Rican Studies at Hunter College of the City University of New York, who writes:

> An educational system geared to the goal of Americanization has become a gate to hell for Puerto Ricans, Chicanos, blacks, and American Indians, because it attempts to disintegrate their identity and force them into the American way. It spells self-hatred, endo-violence, and dehumanized uprootedness. (Bonilla, p. 295)

Antonia Pantoja, founder of ASPIRA (the Puerto Rican organization), was a panelist at a recent Conference in New York City where the principal speaker said that the Puerto Rican subsociety should have control—fiscal, administrative, and pedagogical—of its children's schools. She said that the Puerto Rican adolescent must make peace with his own community, and with his own family, and that this required more attention to his Puerto Rican background. The report of the panel discussion goes on:

> To those who accused her of preaching separatism, anti-Americanism, she replied, "To hell with that. These are the same people who think that somehow segregation is OK because it is imposed from without, but separation is all wrong when it is sought from within."
> "I have to be at peace with myself," she declared, "before I can become part of the whole. But the whole message of the school system has been, 'Don't speak Spanish,' and every other kind of effort has been made to root

out the sources of strength and pride that Puerto Rican children bring with them to school." She urged that the community rally around their language, and certainly not be put off by those academics who say that even this is flawed, that it's not Spanish but Puerto Rican. Miss Pantoja ended by condemning the dominant institutions of the society for their lack of fundamental respect for the Puerto Rican and said that this, more than anything else, prevented parents from full participation in the schools. (ASPIRA, 1968, p. 59)

Despite such attacks upon the schools, most Chicanos and Puerto Ricans have worked, not for separatism, but for a more equitable form of cultural pluralism in the United States.

American Indian Separatism

Indian separatism can be either a protest movement or a desire to live a separate group life and to manage the institutions of society in the name of the tribal group. The latter is feasible where the Indian group has a land base that is relatively free from encroachment by the dominant society. A good example of this second kind of separatism is seen in the Navajo tribe, which has 130,000 members, most of them living in a large area in northeast Arizona and northwest New Mexico. The tribal government, with its political and economic capital at Window Rock, Arizona, deals from a position of power with state and county governments, with the U.S. Public Health Service, and with the Bureau of Indian Affairs. On the reservation are located the Rough Rock School and the Navajo Community College, both operated with Navajo boards of directors and supported by money from the Bureau of Indian Affairs, from foundations, and from tribal funds.

The Navajo example is more nearly one of pluralism than separatism. While operating schools and other institutions for Navajos and as far as possible by Navajos, the Navajo people move freely away from their reservation and tend to participate easily in the dominant society, although they also return often to their families on the reservation if they do not find things satisfactory elsewhere. Navajo college students are widely dispersed.

Separatism of the protest variety is seen mainly in cities where there is an Indian population that suffers from poverty, lack of steady employment, and poor school achievement on the part of children. These are local protest movements, and are seldom linked with similar movements in other communities. Still, a slogan of *Red Power* has been raised and several attempts have been made to organize a national Indian organization and to develop an "American Indian Identity." These attempts have not yet succeeded, due at least partly to the absence of a single Indian language or tradition, and to the diversity of tribal cultures.

A separate institution of higher education was established in 1971 in the Deganawidah-Quetzalcoatl University at Davis, California, by a group of

American Indians and a group of Chicanos who stress their Mexican-Indian heritage. The initial enrollment of 60 students was evenly divided between the two groups. The institution was initially operated on a grant from the federal Office of Economic Opportunity, and offered courses in Indian and Chicano history, in tribal business administration, economic development, and the native arts. It is too soon to know if this university will thrive.

An international separatist Indian movement may have been started at a Symposium on Inter-ethnic Conflict in South America which met in Barbados (West Indies) in 1971, under the auspices of the Commission on International Affairs of the World Council of Churches. At this symposium, an International Work Group for Indigenous Affairs (IWGIA) was created and the group issued the *Declaration of Barbados: For the Liberation of Indians.*

The declaration was formulated by a group of 11 anthropologists, mostly from South America, and mostly without Indian ancestry. It calls for the creation of a "truly multi-ethnic state in which each ethnic group possesses the right to self-determination and the free selection of available social and cultural alternatives." It proposes that each national government should:

1. Guarantee to all the Indian populations by virtue of their ethnic distinction, the right to be and to remain themselves, living according to their own customs and moral order, free to develop their own culture.
2. Recognize that Indian groups possess rights prior to those of other national constituencies. The State must recognize and guarantee each Indian society's territory in land, legalizing it as perpetual, inalienable collective property, sufficiently extensive to provide for population growth.
3. Sanction Indian groups' right to organize and to govern in accordance with their own traditions. Such a policy would not exclude members of Indian society from exercising full citizenship, but would in turn exempt them from compliance with those obligations that jeopardize their cultural integrity. (IWGIA, p. 4)

The declaration calls also for the suspension of all missionary activity by European and American religious bodies.

SEPARATISM, PLURALISM, AND CONFLICT

If there are diverse subcultures in a city or community, and if children of these different groups attend the same school, any conflicts between adult groups are likely to be reflected in the school.

Racial Conflicts

In both northern and southern cities, as black students have entered schools that were formerly all-white, there have been a large number of ugly conflict incidents which have frequently required the help of police. A study of 670 high schools in the 45 cities with 300,000 or more population revealed that in 1968–69 about 30 percent of these schools responded *Yes* to the question: "During the past two school years, has there been a conflict situation involving two or more groups with opposing points of views that required resolution?" Twenty-one percent of the schools reported such conflicts between groups of students, and 24 percent of the schools reported cases of physical confrontation between students and staff. The frequency of student-student confrontation was highest in working-class schools which had a black-white mixture of students, and it was least in the schools that were all-black or all-white. The same trends were present with respect to student-faculty confrontations. (Havighurst, Smith, and Wilder. Chapter 8)

Such conflicts may be necessary steps on the road to a peaceful pluralism, but proponents of separatism tend to cite these conflicts as evidence in favor of separate schools for different racial and ethnic groups.

Discrimination in Reverse

As sections of certain cities turn black, the whites become a minority group in the schools, as in Newark, New Jersey, where blacks were 54 percent, and Puerto Ricans 13 percent of the population in 1971. Blacks took political control and the black mayor's black appointees to the Board of Education became a majority. The percentage of white Newark high school graduates going to college dropped to 45 percent in 1970, while the proportion of black graduates going to college rose to 52 percent. A reporter said:

> At Barringer high school, white-teenagers—who make up about one-fourth of the student body—find themselves engulfed by a whirlwind of blackness: black history, black literature, black culture, black pride, all the components of self-assertion and identity that have been hailed as healthy for a people enslaved and beaten down and brutalized over the centuries. . . . It is not so healthy for whites. . . . Whites stay out of the cafeteria, which is black turf, they don't go to basketball games, since the team is black. And just as blacks used to avoid dances at school. . . now whites avoid them. (Shipler, 1972, p. 79)

A white minister who was trying to organize the whites so that they could be effective participants in a democratic pluralism said wistfully of his white constituency, "If they felt they had a voice. . . . The great victory is to get the Board of Education to deal with the people and not deal with the stereotype—it's awfully hard. Now it's a problem of trying to convince the black majority to be humane and just toward the white minority." (Shipler, 1972, p. 80)

The Ethics of Pluralism

This example tells something about the all-important problem of the ethics of pluralism. Small minority groups are nearly always perceived to be in a superior position morally. Neutral observers of a competitive situation generally favor the underdog, the apparently weaker competitor. So it was with the early Christians in the Roman Empire, the Jews in European ghettoes, the American Indians on their reservations, and the southern sharecroppers and the Chicano migrant workers. As long as minority groups are weak, they win the sympathy of the liberal and the neutral, even when they make mistakes in their strategy for self-improvement. But as the minority group gains opportunity and power, its moral position may deteriorate.

The pluralistic solution to the problem of intergroup relations is likely to be ethically sound because it distributes power in a relatively equitable way. Even though various groups in a pluralistic democratic society act on the principle of self-interest, none is likely to gain enough power to dominate the others.

This chapter has documented the drive for separatism and ethnic identity which has been a powerful social force between 1965 and 1975 for most ethnic and racial groups in the United States. The authors of this book believe there are great economic and social and moral advantages to a greater degree of integration than now exists, and we look to a policy of democratic cultural pluralism, to be aided by the educational system.

EXERCISES

1. What are the principal intergroup conflicts (economic, ethnic, religious, or racial) in your community? in your school or college? Interview members of each of the groups in question and obtain their views regarding the ways in which conflict could be alleviated.

2. Write a paper describing your own position on the integration-pluralism-separatism continuum, and indicating how you think this area of human relations will develop over the next 10 years.

3. Select a particular minority group in which you are interested and write a paper on the treatment of this group in the public schools in your community. Include a description of the strategy (explicit or implicit) of this group for achieving its goals in the community.

SUGGESTIONS FOR FURTHER READING

1. To get some perspective on the extent of democratic pluralism in the United States at various times within the past century, read one of the following: *Up from Slavery*, by Booker T. Washington; *The Americanization of Edward T. Bok*, by Edward T. Bok; *Giants in the Earth*, by Rölvaag; *Forty Years at Hull House*, by Jane Addams; *The Newcomers*, by Oscar Handlin. Compare it with the picture presented by the "revisionists" in: *The Great School Legend*, by Colin Greer; or "Immigrants and the Schools" by David K. Cohen.

2. For a sympathetic report on the educational system preferred by a separatist group (the Amish) see the article, "Compulsory Education: The Plain People Resist," by Stephen Arons in *Saturday Review* for January 15, 1972.

3. For further treatment of minority groups and their tendencies toward separatism, students will find useful the following articles in *Readings in Society and Education*, edited by Havighurst, Neugarten, and Falk: Preston Wilcox, "Integration or Separatism in Education;" Robert J. Havighurst, "The Education of American Indians."

4. Students with an interest in white European ethnic groups will be interested in Michael Novak's book, *The Rise of the Unmeltable Ethnics*, which is a spirited defense of the "hardhat ethnics," who he feels are put down by the middle-class intellectuals.

5. The book by Milton Gordon, *Assimilation in American Life* gives a good historical and sociological treatment of intergroup relations in the United States.

6. The future of relations between ethnic and racial groups in the United States is predicted in an interesting and controversial way by John A. Morsell in his chapter on "Ethnic Relations of the Future" which appears in *The Annals* for July, 1973.

7. A useful treatment of cultural pluralism from the point of view of education is provided in the book *Cultural Pluralism*, edited by Edgar G. Epps. His concluding essays on "Schools and Cultural Pluralism" is especially good for clarification of the issues.

8. Ornstein has written an extended analysis of black nationalism or black separatism as opposed to integration in chapter 5 of *Race and Politics in School/Community Organizations*.

CHAPTER 18

Women in Education*

During the decade just past, Americans have witnessed a resurgence of interest in feminism unparalleled in scope and fervor since the first major wave of concern for women's rights, which developed concurrently with the abolitionist movement of the nineteenth century. Indeed, now as formerly, feminists trace their changing perceptions of their own position in society to their experience in the civil rights movement. As they participated in efforts to eliminate discriminations against American blacks or took part in student movements for greater control over educational institutions, they became sensitive also to injustices against women as a group.

There are many complex factors which came together to produce the women's movement that began in the 1960s. One underlying factor has been the dramatic increase in level of education of women; another, the changing concepts of marriage and parenthood that have been hastened by the development of modern methods of contraception and the increased control over parenthood; another, the changing concepts of sex roles, with an increasing minority of women who no longer look to motherhood as the necessary core of feminine identity; another, the increasing demand for women in the labor force and the growing proportions of women who work outside the home at one or more periods in their lives, thereby creating new role models for their daughters.

The women's movement has taken many forms and has given rise to a wide range of advocacy positions, ranging from conservative to radical. Beginning in 1963 with Betty Friedan's book, *The Feminine Mystique,* there has been an enormous growth of literature, both scientific and popular, written by, for, and about women. Some of the women's organizations have worked primarily for changes in education, in the law, and in the workplace to create more equality of opportunity for women. Others have taken more extreme

*This chapter was prepared with the assistance of Dr. Betty Goldiamond.

views calling for new sex roles and new forms of family organization, and have used techniques such as "consciousness-raising" groups to free women from the traditional views which they regard as self-defeating. They believe that important changes in the direction of equality between the sexes cannot be accomplished without fundamental changes in society, economic and political as well as social, whereby women will be freed from the traditional duties of childrearing.

Recognizing this wide range of views, it is nevertheless true that, in general, the feminist movement which came into being in the 1960s focuses on the special characteristics and needs of women, and the promotion of social change to support their development. And despite the wide diversity of perspectives just mentioned, the major figures in the women's liberation movement agree that women occupy a "minority" status in contemporary American society. They agree also that "feminine" traits and motivations that have been so widely accepted in the past are due only in small part to underlying biological differences, but are due in large part to our socialization practices— that is, to what girls are taught directly or indirectly as they grow up. Many believe that our formal educational system, as it carries out both its socialization and its sorting and selecting functions, helps to develop what they perceive as the "sexist" society. Although their sharpest criticism is reserved for the socialization experiences that occur within the family, most feminists also see the schools as part of the problem, and they accordingly look to the schools to become part of the solution.

One spokeswoman says, for example, "... it is significant that the general level and style of higher education for women ... is closer to that of Renaissance humanism than to the skills of mid-twentieth-century scientific and technological society. . . . While modern patriarchies have, fairly recently, opened all educational levels to women, the kind and quality of education is not the same for each sex. This difference is of course apparent in early socialization but it persists and enters into higher education as well." (Millett, 1969). This same writer goes on to argue that most of our educational institutions maintain a division between "masculine" and "feminine" subject matter, assigning the humanities and certain social sciences to women, and science and technology, the professions, business and engineering to the male.

While such allegations ignore, or blur over, the very real changes in the education of women which has occurred during the past century, there is evidence, some of it presented later in this chapter, that supports these views. Many feminists are now studying how our schools and colleges function, trying to pinpoint the ways in which sex-related discrimination may operate. They are trying also to discover just why women cooperate to the extent they do in their routing through the system, or why they fail, when they do, in efforts to acquire education for careers considered appropriate "for men only."

CHANGES IN WOMEN'S ROLES

Whatever the speed of social change that lies ahead, and whatever the opinions presently being set forth, the feminist writers and their supporters address themselves to issues having broad implications for educational theory and practice, just as, in turn, educators are looking to the broader social context when they deal with the changing educational scene for women. The latter point is well illustrated in the opening statement of the report by the Carnegie Commission on Higher Education, *Opportunities for Women in Higher Education* (1973), which reads:

> "The second most fundamental revolution in the affairs of mankind on earth is now occurring. The first came when man settled down from hunting, fishing, herding, and gathering to sedentary agricultural and village life. The second is now occurring as women, no longer so concentrated on and sheltered for their childbearing and childrearing functions, are demanding equality of treatment in all aspects of life, are demanding a new sense of purpose."

The Changing Family Cycle

The great majority of American women get married and the great majority bear at least one child. While there is a present trend toward smaller families, and while birthrates have dropped dramatically since 1957 (see Chapter 14), the reductions in birthrate are primarily with regard, not to first births, but with regard to third and fourth births. We cannot yet assess the long-term effects of the current women's movement upon marriage rates or numbers of children; nor can we yet assess the long-term effects of improved methods of family planning, changing education for women, or changing economic conditions and patterns of labor participation that have been going on for the past two decades. This is so because we cannot know the outcomes for women who are presently young and who may still marry or bear more children. If, however, we look at women born in successive decades since the turn of the century (those born from 1900 to 1909, from 1910 to 1919, and so on) and if we look only at those who are now age 35 or older, then the trends are clear—namely, that over time a *higher* proportion have married, and except for the years of the Depression, a *higher* proportion have borne children. For example, for women born 1930 to 1939, only 10 percent remained childless, as compared to 23 percent childless women born in 1880 to 1889. Also over the past 70 years, the median age at marriage has shown a downward trend dropping from 22 in 1890 to 20 in 1970.

Over the past decades, there have been other changes in timing of the events of the family cycle as age at marriage has dropped, as the first child is born earlier in the marriage, as children are spaced closer together, and as the duration of marriage has increased with increased longevity. The trend is toward a more rapid rhythm of events through most of the family cycle, then an extended interval (now some 16 years) when husband and wife are the remaining members of the household. Widowhood occurs much later, and the total life span for women has lengthened enormously.

The general trends are not expected to be reversed, even though today we are witnessing a slight upturn in median age of marriage for women (it is 20.8 rather than 20.2), more unmarried families, more commmunal and other experimental forms of family life. While the family cycle runs its course a few years later for women at higher-than-average levels of education, the general pattern of historical change just described is the same for highly educated as for poorly educated women.

Over the past 80 years an interesting and important difference has been developing between men and women with respect to the timing of family and work cycles. No longer does marriage signify that the man is ready to be the breadwinner, nor even that the period of his formal education and occupational training has ended. With the needs of the American economy for technical and professional workers, the length of time devoted to education has increased for more and more young persons, but there has not been an accompanying delay of marriage. An increasing proportion of men attending college, and particularly of men attending graduate school, are married. The accompanying phenomenon is the young wife who works to support her husband through school.

The changing sex-role patterns are reflected in the rising proportion of young married women in the labor force. In 1890, only 6 percent of married women aged 14–24 were employed, but in 1970, it was 31 percent. While these figures reflect marriages in which husbands are working as well as those in which husbands are still in school, they show not only that young wives are increasingly sharing the economic burdens of new households but also that women are doing so at younger ages. The age of economic maturity has been deferred for men but not for women.

Women at Work

It is clear that American women have been developing life patterns that combine family and work responsibilities. As has been shown, the woman of today as compared to her mother or grandmother has many more years of life when she is free from childrearing. On the average, mothers are in their early thirties when they see their last child off to school. They then have ahead of them about 40 years, or more than half of their lives. Increasingly they use their time to work outside the home. The overall picture is given by U.S. Department of Labor studies showing that nine out of ten women work outside the home at some time in their lives. In the given year 1970, of all women aged 14 and over, 40 percent were in the labor force (it was 26 percent in 1940).

(It is interesting to note that women are working in roughly the same proportions in other industrialized countries, although the numbers are somewhat higher in Soviet bloc countries. It is estimated that women constitute about 45 percent of the labor force in Rumania and Czechoslovakia; about 40 percent in the Soviet Union and in Austria; about 37 percent in the United States and in West Germany; about 34 to 35 percent in Great Britain and France; but less than 30 percent in Italy).

The major change is not only in the numbers of women who work, but even more dramatically, in the characteristics of women who work. During the 30-year period from 1940 to 1970, the numbers of working women more than doubled, but the numbers of working mothers increased eightfold. To put this point in different words, in 1940 one out of ten mothers in the United States was in the labor force; in 1960, it was three out of ten; in 1970, it was four out of ten. (Of all women workers, about 60 percent are married and living with their husbands; the rest are single, widowed, divorced, or separated.)

The *ages* at which women are most likely to be working have also changed. If we look at the composition of the labor force in 1920 and compare it with 1970, then at both periods women were most apt to be working when they are age 20 to 24. But then the patterns diverge. In the earlier period of history, the proportion of women who were working decreased steadily in successive age groups, so that in the age group 45 to 54, only a small percent were workers. By 1970, however, the proportions drop off only a little after age 25, then rise again so that in the age-group 45 to 54 there is a second peak when more than half of all women in the age group are in the labor market. Thus today middle-aged women are working in the same high proportions as young women.

All this adds up to the fact that increasing millions of American women have chosen to marry, raise children, *and* work, and to work at more than one point in their lives. The implications for women's education should be obvious, even though these facts are not often made available in high school and college counseling systems.

The major reason that women work, whether they are single or married, whether they are mothers or not, whether they are young or middle-aged, is an economic reason. It is significant that the greatest growth in women workers in the past few decades has taken place among well educated wives from families with moderate incomes. Before World War II married women workers came almost exclusively from low-income families, but this picture has changed so that by now it is just as likely for a middle-class wife to be employed as for a working-class wife.

Furthermore, there is a direct relationship between women's educational levels and their labor force participation. The more education a woman has received, the greater the likelihood that she will be working, as shown in Table 18.1. The table refers to all women as a group, but the same general trends are present if the data are broken down for different age groups. Whether women are in their twenties or in their fifties, it is still true that the more education, the more likely the woman will be working outside the home.

Findings such as these, and findings from other studies of why women work, make it clear that there are other than economic reasons that propel women into the labor market. Especially at higher educational levels, women work for intellectual and social stimulation, for opportunities for service, for self-development, and because they find the work intrinsically satisfying and rewarding.

It is similarly true, of course, that there are other than economic reasons that propel women into higher education. Women seek education for self-enrichment, for becoming better mothers, for becoming more interesting to their husbands, for contributing to community betterment—in short, not only for its value in the marketplace, but for its value in enhancing the quality of life.

Occupational Status

Table 18.2 shows the changing proportions of women in various occupational categories. In some occupations the proportions have gone up over the past few decades; in others, down. Despite the increase in overall proportions of women workers (as shown in the first row of the table), it can be seen that women were more likely to be employed at the lower levels of the economic ladder in 1970 than in 1950—as sales workers, clerical workers, operatives, and service workers. At the other end of the ladder, the proportions of professional workers who are women have increased only slightly.

The actual numbers of women in the professions alone (not shown in the table) has been increasing. There are now almost three times as many women in the professions as there were in 1940, but because the number of men has increased at a more rapid rate, the gap has widened between men and women. Also, within the professions, women are concentrated at the less prestigious levels and the concentration is intensifying. If we consider all *women* as the base, rather than all *persons in the occupation* as the base, this

TABLE 18.1.   *Percentage of Women in the Labor Force, by Educational Level (1972)*

Eight years of school	28
High school graduate	51
One to three years of college	49
College graduate	57
Five or more years of college	68

Source: U.S. Bureau of Labor Statistics, 1972, p. A-11.

becomes much clearer. Two-thirds of all women in the professions are nurses and noncollege teachers, for example, but only a small proportion are physicians or lawyers.

The changes in employment patterns shown in Table 18.2 do not reflect however, the changes that have been occurring in the most recent years, for the proportions of women now entering medical school, law school, or business school, and the numbers being awarded degrees in such fields as physical sciences and mathematics have been on the sharp increase. Similarly, data on the career choices of entering college freshmen shows that women are increasingly choosing to enter the traditionally "men's" fields. Thus, the occupational distribution may shift markedly in 1980 or 1990, as younger women—those who are probably being most affected by the women's movement—finish their schooling and move into the labor force. But just as is true of predictions regarding rates of marriage and childbearing, it is too soon to assess the long-range effects of the women's movement as it interacts with other social and economic factors in influencing the work lives of women.

Not only are women presently concentrated in the lesser skilled, lesser paid jobs, but their earnings reflect inequality of pay for equal work as compared with men. The book, *Work in America,* a report of a Presidential Advisory Panel which appeared in 1973, indicated that the gap between men's and women's earnings had widened rather than narrowed from 1955 to 1970. The picture of inequality in pay is changing, however, and probably more rapidly than has yet shown up in the overall data for women workers. For one thing, the situation for women in the higher salary brackets has already shown improvement. In 1968, only 3 percent of women working year-round and full time earned $10,000 or more, as compared with 28 percent of men. But the 1970 census showed that in the 10-year period from 1960, the number of women earning $10,000 or more had increased seven times compared to an increase of four times for men.

For another thing, the federal Equal Pay Act of 1963, which established the principle that employers shall not discriminate on the basis of sex in paying employees for equal work on jobs that require equal skill, is being enforced now more than in the 1960s. And the potential effects of Title VII of the 1964 Civil Rights Acts, which prohibited sex discrimination in employment and established an Equal Employment Opportunity Commission to enforce the law, are likely to be profound. Many past patterns of sex-based job allocations are beginning to yield under this legal pressure. In addition, in 1967, Presidential Executive Order 11246, which had earlier established a policy of nondiscrimination in government employment, was amended by the addition of "sex" as a prohibited type of discrimination. At present, all firms doing business with the government are required to prepare and use "affirmative action plans" for hiring and promoting women.

All in all, women have not only gained a substantial position as competent wage earners in our highly industrialized society; but their situation

TABLE 18.2.   Women as a Percentage of all Persons in the Occupation

	1950	1960	1970
Total workers	28	33	38
All professional and technical workers	39	38	40
Accountants	15	17	26
Architects	4	2	4
Engineers	1	1	2
Lawyers and judges	4	4	5
Librarians	89	85	82
Pharmacists	9	8	12
Physicians	7	7	9
Registered nurses	98	98	97
Health technicians	57	68	70
Social workers	69	63	63
Teachers, elementary	—	86	84
Teachers, secondary	—	49	49
Teachers, college and university	22	24	29
Scientists (biological and physical)	11	9	14
Scientists (social)	33	25	23
Managers and administrators, salaried	14	14	16
Sales workers	34	36	39
Clerical and kindred workers	62	68	74
Operatives	27	29	32
Service workers	58	62	60

Source: Adapted from Economic Report of the President (1973, pp. 155–159).

vis-a-vis men is now undergoing rapid change for the better.

The mass movement of women into the labor force has had a variety of consequences with regard to relations between the sexes and between parents and children. For instance, there is evidence that home and childcare responsibilities are being redistributed among family members, with the roles of fathers as well as mothers becoming more diverse. Various studies have also shown that the role models available to young children have altered and that daughters of working mothers grow up showing greater assertiveness and less attachments to the values of traditional femininity. For the first time in history, almost half the adolescent girls in the country have examples in their own homes of women who are combining outside employment with motherhood. In addition, women's experience in the labor force has contributed greatly to what has been called in the Report of the New York City Commission on Human Rights (1972) the "revolution of rising expectations." Women, like members of minority groups we have discussed in the preceding chapters of this book, are learning what their capabilities are; they are developing the motivation and the skills to enter and to succeed in all the various occupa-

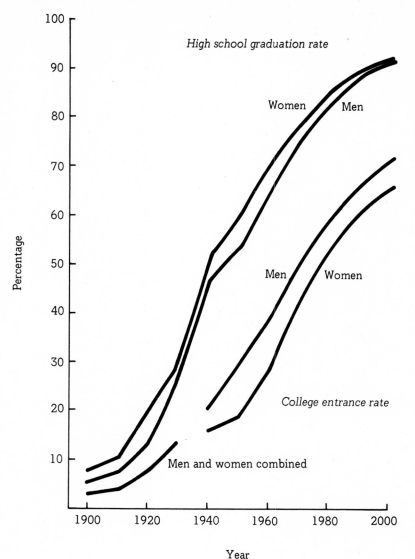

High school graduation rate

Women   Men

Men   Women

College entrance rate

Men and women combined

Year

FIGURE 18.1   Percentage of relevant age group graduating from high school and percentage entering college in the following year. (Source: Carnegie Commission on Higher Education, 1973c, p. 36. Reprinted with permission. Copyright © 1973 by the Carnegie Foundation for the Advancement of Teaching. All rights reserved.)

tional areas; and as they are being more equitably rewarded, they are closing the economic gaps that have existed between men and women workers.

THE EDUCATION OF WOMEN

The changing patterns of work and family life for women have been both the cause and the effect of changes in the education of women that have occurred over the past century.

College Attendance

The changing proportions of women and men graduating from high schools and entering college from 1900 onward are shown in Figure 18.1. Using the *total age group as the base,* it should be noted that at each point in time a higher percentage of the women than of the men graduated from high schools, although the gap between the sexes in this respect is expected to narrow to the vanishing point in the next two decades. The opposite is true for college entrants, where it has been (and is expected to continue to be) a noticeably higher proportion of the men than of the women who enter college. In 1970, of the total age group, 53 percent of men but only 41 percent of women were entering college.

It might also be noted that the college entrance rate for women has accelerated and decelerated in different historical periods, associated with fluctuations in age of marriage and in birthrates. It is not clear, however, what is cause and what is effect when the attempt is made to disentangle these factors, to say nothing of other underlying factors such as economic and technological changes, the effects of World War I and World War II upon the supply and demand of manpower both in education and in the labor force, the overall growth of higher education, and so on.

If we look at the picture from a somewhat different perspective, and use all the *persons at a selected educational level* as the base, the differences between the sexes becomes even clearer. As shown in Table 18.3, as one moves up the educational ladder, the smaller is the proportion of all persons who are women. The funnelling effect shown in the table is present despite the facts that women, on the average, earn better grades and score higher on academic achievement tests in high school (College Entrance Examination Board, 1970); and, while their overall performance on college entrance tests is slightly below that of men, women have better undergraduate records in college irrespective of their field of study (Folger, Astin, and Bayer, 1970). Undoubtedly the decision to marry deters many talented girls from continuing their education. (See, for instance, the case of Laura Carter, reported in Chapter 3, and the data on River City High School graduates, also reported

TABLE 18.3.   *Women as a percentage of persons at selected educational Levels (1970)*

High school graduates	50.4
B.A. degrees	43.1
Master's and doctor's degrees (combined)	36.5
Doctor's degrees	13.4
Faculty in colleges and universities	24.0
Full professors	8.6

Source: Adapted from Carnegie Commission on Higher Education, 1973c, p. 2.

in Chapter 3.) In addition, some of the differential in college attendance is due to lack of financial backing, for when families are faced with a choice between investing limited resources in the college education of sons or of daughters, it is more often the son who wins out. Nevertheless, there can be little doubt that college admissions policies favoring men have also contributed heavily to the loss of bright young women from the educational system. In 1969, the Presidential Task Force on Women's Rights and Responsibilities found that higher admission standards for women than for men were widespread in undergraduate schools *(A Matter of Simple Justice,* 1970).

A substantial fraction of all those who enroll in college fail to complete a bachelor's or first professional degree, but during the past 20 years, college attrition rates for women have been somewhat higher than those for men. Further, women have continued to be concentrated in college courses and degree programs which prepare them for the traditional women's roles and traditional women's occupations. The choice of fields changed somewhat for women between 1950 and 1970, but the changes accentuated the traditional patterns, with women increasingly taking degrees in education (as the demand for public school teachers grew) and in humanities and arts. In very recent years, however, there are signs of a reversal. With the market for teachers declining, and new concerns with urban problems and the environment affecting both sexes, women are increasing their enrollments in architecture, agriculture, business, and urban study, and to a slight degree also in physical sciences and engineering. Here again the 1970s and 1980s may reflect more dramatically the new outlook that seems to be developing among college women.

Graduate Education

At the point of admission to graduate schools, sex differences become even more apparent. Differences in marital status and age of men and women graduate students are important factors. Women in graduate schools are more likely than men to be single, more likely to be enrolled as part-time students, and more women than men are in their thirties or older. A larger proportion of women than men expect to take terminal M.A. degrees rather than to proceed toward the doctorate, a function of the fact that more women than men are taking graduate work in fields like education and social work where the M.A. is the important credential and where relatively few students take doctor's degrees.

Here again, attrition rates for women are higher than for men. It is difficult to document the extent of discrimination against women in graduate and in professional schools, but many who have studied the problem believe it exists to a significant degree. The situation is complicated: applicants are usually selected by individual departments making it difficult to "enforce" a common standard across a university; the cost of educating a graduate student in many universities (especially in fields like medicine) greatly exceeds tuition and creates a greater concern lest places be taken by women who will not finish (because of marriage) or who will not pursue subsequent careers as effectively as men; some faculty believe women graduate students are therefore not as "dedicated" as men; most graduate schools make it difficult to enroll part-time rather than full-time, and so on.

While attitudes are changing rapidly in most institutions of higher education, and while recent laws prohibiting discrimination are having their effects, it is probably still fair to say that women are generally disadvantaged as compared to men in pursuing higher degrees. In part, the disadvantage stems from factors which, lumped together, can be called "discrimination," but in part it stems also from the personal decisions made by women themselves. While the latter are often explained by the fact that women have been "taught" to set their standards unnecessarily low, it must also be said that most women face a genuine range of options regarding the balance they wish to create between family and career responsibilities, and related thereto, the financial commitments they wish to make to continued education. Thus the lack of motivation for graduate work may be a more significant and a more "real" factor for women than for men.

Motivation is, of course, a complicated question. There has been a recent discussion among educators and psychologists of the possibility that college women, rather than fearing failure, fear success. Horner (1969) has carried out studies indicating that in addition to the obvious social rejection that a competitive and achieving girl may experience, there is also an internal anxiety, and a fear, conscious or unconscious, that outstanding academic or other achievement may be equated with a loss of femininity. Girls who have this fear are not likely to pursue higher education.

Socialization in the schools

Whatever the complex underlying factors, many women lack motivation for pursuing advanced education and for moving into occupational roles that are demanding in terms of time, money, and effort spent in preparation. The result is that many capable women are lost to the upper levels of the academic and professional worlds, and that women in general represent an unused pool of talent.

What happens to girls as they grow up in America that has produced career expectations more limited than those of men? In particular, do the schools reinforce the sex-typing which begins in infancy, in the child's home and neighborhood?

It should be said first that there is an enormous scientific literature on sex differences, a literature that grows out of biology, psychology, sociology, and anthropology as well as education, and a literature that cannot possibly be summarized here. Suffice it to say that while nobody doubts the presence of important biological differences between the sexes, there is a wide variety of interpretations regarding which, if any, of these biological differences make a significant difference in the ways boys and girls learn or in the abilities that are needed to fulfill most of the occupations of the modern industrialized society. Whatever the inherent biological differences, nobody doubts however, that much of the difference in behavior observed between boys and girls, later between men and women, stems from differences in the socialization experiences that occur from earliest infancy onward. In short, in most families boys are treated differently from girls from the very first days of life; these differences become reinforced over time as the child meets the expectations of parents, teachers, and peers, and as these expectations become internalized.

To quote only one example of what is meant by differential socialization experiences, Moss (1967) studied mother-infant interactions during the first and third months of life and found that mothers tended to stimulate male infants significantly more than female infants and to arouse them to a higher activity level. On the other hand, they imitated girl babies significantly more frequently than boy babies, especially their vocalizations. Perhaps such differences in the treatment of infants are involved in the differences observed later when youngsters reach school age, when boys show higher general activity levels than girls and when girls show greater verbal skills than boys.

That socialization experiences in the school are also different for the two sexes can hardly be doubted. To illustrate, in a study by Sears and Feldman (1966), more than half the teachers interviewed said they differentiated in their behavior towards boys and girls even though their educational aims for the sexes were identical. While boys receive more disapproval and blame than girls, they also have more interaction with teachers along other dimensions such as approval, instruction-giving, and being listened to (Meyer and Thompson, 1963). In another study, teachers made more supportive remarks to girls and more critical remarks to boys (Lippitt and Gold, 1959); and in still another study, teachers rewarded the creative behavior of boys three times as much as the creative behavior of girls (Torrance, 1962).

There are numerous ways in which the content of the curriculum reinforces stereotyped sex differences. DeCrow (1972) has pointed, for instance, to the textbooks and readers used in elementary school grades, and makes her point in the provocative title of her article, "Look, Jane, Look! See Dick Run and Jump! Admire him!"

In high school students may find themselves segregated by sex, either by different schools or within a given school. In some large cities, for example, a specialized science and math school may admit only boys; and boys' vocational schools may teach electronics, plumbing, carpentry, printing, and other "male" trades while the girls' schools prepare students to be secretaries, beauticians, and health aides. Where school districts do not maintain separate high schools for such purposes, they may use intraschool tracking systems which prepare boys and girls for different careers. The influence of high school counselors is also important. The observation that counselors often reinforce the stereotypes in attempting to help boys and girls make career choices is confirmed by at least one study (Friedensdorf, 1969). In that study it is of interest that male counselors had attitudes that were more traditional with regard to girls' careers, while women counselors had attitudes that expanded the traditional images.

These examples can easily be multiplied, but they should be sufficient to demonstrate that school systems have in many ways—and often unthinkingly—been providing differential socialization for the two sexes. It is because of such practices that, as we said earlier, feminists see the schools as part of the problem for modern women and why they look to the schools to become part of the solution.

DIRECTED SOCIAL CHANGE

In the past decade the activities of feminists, both male and female, have already set into motion programs of change which fall roughly into two categories: the abolition of discriminations against women, whether they be *de facto* or *de jure,* and the modification of attitudes, both those held by the larger society and those that women have about themselves.

Public Policy

Perhaps the most fundamental of these changes are those taking place on the level of public policy, which provides the legal framework for further situational modification. The Equal Rights Amendment to the Constitution, which reads simply: "Equality of rights under the law shall not be denied or abridged by the United States or any state on account of sex," has been passed by both houses of Congress and has already been ratified in 33 states. When approved by 38 states, it will become the 27th Amendment to the Constitution. The amendment will affect behavioral patterns in all our major social institutions:

395

in the family, in the schools, and in the economic arena, including employment, financial practices, property ownership, and taxation.

We have already mentioned more specific legislative and administrative actions such as the federal Equal Pay Act of 1963, Title VII of the 1964 Civil Rights Act, and the amended Presidential Executive Order 11246. Of greatest importance to educators is the Higher Education Act of 1972, which provides in its Title IX for sex equality both in employment in educational institutions and in education itself. The Act applies to almost all schools receiving federal grants and loans—preschools, elementary and secondary schools, vocational and professional schools, and both public and private undergraduate and graduate institutions. It prohibits discrimination in admissions, financial assistance, use of facilities, and other areas. (Private undergraduate and single-sex public institutions are exempted from the admissions requirements of the Act, though they are subject to all its other antidiscrimination provisions.)

Educational Innovations

One federal agency which has assumed a leadership role in the effort to extend the education of women, and to overcome institutional and psychological barriers so that women can move into new occupations, is the Women's Bureau of the U.S. Department of Labor. Elizabeth Koontz (1972), the director of the Women's Bureau, recently summarized information about continuing education programs, the "open" university and "external degrees," education for nontraditional professions, career education, emerging occupations, and efforts to promote attitudinal changes—all with reference to their special implications for women.

Continuing education programs for women, an innovation of the late 50s and early 60s, have had special benefits for women who have interrupted their education to marry and rear children, but who wish to reenter the labor force. Although the design and focus of such programs vary from college to college, they generally include one or more of the following features: enrollment on a part-time basis, flexible course hours, short-term courses, counseling services for adult women, financial aid for part-time study, limited residence requirements, removal of age restrictions, liberal transfers of course credits, curriculum geared to adult experiences, credit by examination, refresher courses, reorientation courses, information services, child care facilities, relaxation of time requirements for degrees, and job placement assistance.

Still in the developmental stage, other plans for educational reform are variously designated by such terms as "external degrees," "the open university," and "university without walls." These plans incorporate fundamental changes in the whole educational system as they relate to instruction, examination, transfer of credits, and certification. Learning outside the conventional instruction program would utilize such facilities as television and correspondence courses, apprenticeships, and other innovations. While such programs are open to both men and women, they might well benefit more women than men in at least the immediate future when there appears to be more "undereducated" adult women than men.

Several activities are underway to extend women's penetration into the "men's professions" as well as to strengthen women's status in all professional fields. For example, by the early 1970s, more than 35 professional associations have an official committee or caucus group concerned about the status of women in their respective field. Generally these associations seek to abolish dual standards of admission and quota systems and to increase scholarship and other financial assistance to women who wish to acquire professional education. The Professional Women's Caucus, which is an interdisciplinary organization, has several task forces, including one on education. Their targets have included the revision of sexist textbooks and educational materials, provision of career incentives, and the promotion of educational opportunities for various vocations.

The Office of Education has recently developed a new focus on career education for every young person, aiming to insure that each boy and girl leaving high school has skills sufficient either to obtain employment, pursue further career education, or enter higher levels of education.

In the past few years there has been a sudden growth of courses and programs in women's studies. The Carnegie Commission on Higher Education reported that in the fall of 1972 there were some 1,300 single courses relating to women being offered in some 800 to 1,000 colleges. Another report (Robinson, 1973) indicated that there were some 32 women's studies programs in various colleges, where a "program" means an undergraduate major or an organizational unit responsible for women's studies. Two of these programs were offering B.A. degrees; and three, M.A. degrees.

Many of these innovative programs which were reviewed and described by Koontz are still in the early stages of development, but there is reason to believe that some, at least, will prove valuable to women and worthy of extensive replication.

EXERCISES

1. Obtain copies of the readers used in the first and second grades of your local school system. Analyze their content with regard to images of women and men.
2. Interview your mother and your grandmother regarding their life histories. What were the attitudes toward women's roles that prevailed when they were young women? What were their own views? Have those views changed recently?
3. Interview several of your instructors. What do they report regarding the status of faculty women in your institution?

4. Talk wih three or four mothers of young children. What are their aspirations for their sons? for their daughters? Do these mothers report agreement of disagreement with their husbands on these issues?

SUGGESTIONS FOR FURTHER READING

1. Schneir's *Feminism: The Essential Historical Writings* is, as indicated by the title, a collection of major writings on the feminist movement.

2. For historical perspective regarding education, Mabel Newcomer's *A Century of Higher Education for American Women* is an excellent reference. Anderson's *Sex Differences and Discrimination in Education* is a collection of brief and lively articles on various aspects of women's current status in the educational system. A varied and excellent group of papers regarding the psychology of women and women in education appeared as a special issue of *The School Review* for February, 1972.

3. The women's liberation movement of the 1960s and 1970s gave rise to a flood of books and magazine articles setting forth a wide range of views. Friedan's *The Feminine Mystique* was an early and highly influential book. For a radical view, Firestone's book, *The Dialect of Sex: the Case for Feminist Revolution,* Morgan's *Sisterhood is Powerful*, or Millett's *Sexual Politics* are of special interest. For more conservative views, Komisar's *The New Feminism*, Chafe's *The American Women*, or the New York City Commission on Human Rights' *Women's Role in Contemporary Society* are excellent references.

4. A comprehensive review of the present legal status of women is to be found in Kanowitz, *Women and the Law: The Unfinished Revolution.*

5. For a look at women in the academic professions, Bernard's book *Academic Women*, is excellent as is the Carnegie Commission on Higher Education's *Opportunities for Women in Higher Education.* For women in other high-level occupations, see Astin's *The Woman Doctorate in America*, Epstein's *Woman's Place: Options and Limits in Professional Careers*, or Kreps' *Sex in the Marketplace.*

6. A recent book summarizing much of the literature pertinent to the issue of biological vs. social influences on the development of women is Bardwick's *Psychology of Women: A study of Bio-cultural Conflicts*. While Bardwick does not take an "anatomy is destiny" view, she recognizes that the two sexes are influenced in distinctive ways by biological factors.

7. An excellent review of the effects of sex differences upon teachers' behavior appears as a chapter, "The Influence of the Sex of the Teacher and Student on Classroom Behavior," in Brophy and Good's book, *Teacher-Student Relationships.*

PART
V

The Teacher

CHAPTER 19

The Social Characteristics
of Teachers

There are many different factors involved in choosing an occupation. For some persons teaching may be regarded as a highly respectable occupation, one that will increase the individual's prestige in the community. For others, it may be seen as an opportunity to lead a life of service. For still others, teaching may be seen primarily as an occupation that offers short working hours, long vacations, and long-term security.

THE CHOICE OF TEACHING AS
AN OCCUPATION

Some persons select teaching as their occupational goal relatively early in life and plan their college years accordingly. Others make their decision relatively late, and seem—at least, from a superficial point of view—to enter teaching almost by accident. This is often the case with the wife of a graduate student who goes into teaching for a few years as a means of helping her husband through school.

Interaction of Factors Determining Choice

Whatever the particular factors that operate in any individual instance, there is always a variety of psychological and social factors interacting to produce a vocational choice, as is illustrated in this man's case:

As far back as I can remember I was interested in mechanical devices and enjoyed working with tools. At first I worked with simple things such as toys, roller skates, and bicycles, forever taking them apart and repairing them. As I grew older my interest centered on more complex machines. I worked with electricity and electrical gadgets. For several years my main interest was radio.

When I was fifteen I became intensely interested in automobiles and their repair. At this point my father and mother began to object. They could not tolerate the grease and dirt, and they worried about the dangers involved in working on these heavy machines. My father was a businessman and he felt that I belonged in business with him when I had finished school.

"Why do you want to become an auto mechanic? No one in our whole family has ever been a mechanic! Manual labor is not what we want you to do," they stormed. They cited as examples some of the mechanics and tradesmen we knew, and I must admit some of them were pretty rough characters. But this did not deter me. I worked part time after school in a neighborhood garage.

By the time I graduated from high school I had definitely decided that automechanics was my future. My parents were furious.

"Why don't you go to college like your two brothers did?" they demanded. "Don't you want to be somebody?"

I guess I was pretty obstinate because instead of going to college I got a full-time job as a mechanic. After about a year my enthusiasm began to wane. I still was interested in automobiles, but the working conditions of 30 years ago were poor. I found that I could not tolerate these drawbacks: (1) The people I had to work with used foul language. (2) There were many heavy drinkers on this job. (3) The physical strain was great. My hands were a mess. I couldn't possibly keep them clean, and I was embarrassed when I went out on a date. (4) The dangers were real. Several times I nearly lost a finger. (5) There was little security.

I knew that I would have to do something else; yet I wanted to remain in the automotive field because I still found it the most interesting. The answer came when I met a young high school teacher who taught shop in the city school system. He pointed out that I could probably be placed as an autoshop teacher if I could meet the requirements. I went to the Board of Education and was told what I would have to do to become a shop teacher. I registered at the University and started my preparation. My parents were happy again. I too was happy because now I could work with people like myself and still use my skills to best advantage.

Within society as a whole, there are economic and social factors that influence persons in their choice of teaching as an occupation. One is the need for teachers. As the need increases, more effort is made to recruit teachers through high school and college career orientation programs, through radio and television programs, and through newspapers, and magazines. In the decade of the 1960s, with the growth of international aid programs, such as the Peace Corps, and government programs to combat poverty, many persons elected teaching as an effective means of serving underdeveloped or underprivileged groups and helping to bring about social change. In the early 1970s, some young persons chose to teach in the so-called "free schools."

The decade of the 1970s sees an oversupply of young graduates for most white-collar jobs, including teaching. This is forcing a good deal of soul-searching on the part of young people, though the profession of teaching, being by far the largest in numbers, seems to offer more and more varied opportunities than do some of the other professions.

Another of the social factors that affects motivation is that of social status. Teaching is more or less attractive to persons of different social levels; and the teaching profession in America has drawn, at different periods of time, different proportions of people from various social backgrounds.

HETEROGENEITY IN SOCIAL-CLASS ORIGINS

For example, in the decades prior to 1920, teachers were recruited in large numbers from middle-class urban families, and from rural families of upper-middle and lower-middle class. Relative to the general population, persons who entered the teaching field had large amounts of formal schooling and more often than not were persons who regarded teaching as a calling. In those years, teaching was one of the few occupations available to respectable and educated women; as the schoolmaster made way for the schoolma'am, a sizable number of teachers were women from upper-middle-class and upper-class backgrounds. While teaching has always offered an avenue of opportunity for certain groups of young people, especially rural groups, the overall proportion of teachers who came from lower-status levels was probably smaller some decades ago than at present.

As America became increasingly urban; as the educational system mushroomed, with greater need for teachers, with the growth of teacher-training institutions, and with an increasing proportion of young people obtaining college education, and as more occupations became available to women, the social composition of the teaching profession changed.

A number of studies have been made of various groups of teachers and of various groups of students preparing to be teachers. These studies show that the overall majority is coming increasingly from lower-middle and upper-working classes.

A few such studies may serve as illustrations: As early as 1927, in a study of students attending midwestern teachers' colleges, it was found that over half came from working-class and farm backgrounds (Whitney, 1927). By 1939, Elsbree, in his book *The American Teacher,* was describing teachers as being predominantly lower-middle-class in origin (Elsbree, 1939). In 1941, Greenhoe's study of over 9,000 public school teachers, selected as a national sample, showed 38 percent whose fathers were farmers, 26 percent whose fathers were engaged in small businesses, 18 percent whose fathers were day laborers, and only 4 percent whose fathers were professional men (Greenhoe, 1941). In 1948, a study of seniors in education at the University of Michigan showed a bare majority coming from white-collar families (Best, 1948). In 1950, studies of students in a teachers' college in Chicago showed a majority coming from lower-middle-class families (Valentine, 1950; Wagenschein, 1950).

In more recent years, there has been a further increase in the heterogeneity of social backgrounds. The most pronounced change has been a drop in the number of teachers from farm families and an increase in the number from urban working-class families.

Table 19.1 shows the distribution by age and family origin of a national sample of teachers drawn in 1961 and for a sample drawn in 1971. In 1961, 27 percent came from farm families and 30 percent from blue-collar families (i.e., their fathers were unskilled, semiskilled, or skilled workers), while 10 years later, only 19 percent came from farm families, but 34 percent from blue-collar families. These proportions are quite different in different age groups. Age breakdowns are not shown for 1971, but are for 1961. For example, of the oldest teachers, those aged 56 and over, almost 40 percent came from farm families; while of the youngest teachers, those under age 26, only 20 percent came from farm families.

These figures are for the country at large. Differences exist between large school systems and small. In the largest school systems, the proportion of teachers who come from farm families is much lower and the proportion from urban working-class families is much higher than the national averages. As can be seen from the detailed listing of fathers' occupations of teachers in the Chicago public schools in 1964, shown in Table 19.2, five percent came from farms while almost half came from working-class homes.

SOCIAL MOBILITY AMONG TEACHERS

The social origin of a teacher is not, of course, synonymous with his social status as an adult. It is one thing to describe the social status of the families from which teachers come; another thing to describe the social status that teachers occupy once they have become established in the teaching profession.

Factors Affecting Social Status

When judged in terms of social participation, the social status of the teacher will vary to some extent, depending upon a number of factors—his social origin, the community in which he teaches, the extent and type of his social interactions, the extent to which he participates in community affairs, and so on. A teacher who comes from a working-class family and who teaches in the same city in which he was born may continue to participate almost entirely with working-class people and may, by this criterion, be said to have

TABLE 19.1. Distribution of Teachers by Father's Occupation and by Age. 1961 and 1971

	Percentages						
	Age Distribution for 1961					1961	1971
Occupation of Teacher's Father	56 or Older	46–55	36–45	26–35	Under 26	Total	Total
Farmer	39	35	29	14	20	27	19
Unskilled worker	2	5	5	11	8	7	8
Skilled or semiskilled worker	14	23	24	28	24	23	26
Managerial or self-employed	24	19	22	25	22	22	22
Professional or semiprofessional	12	14	15	14	20	15	19
Clerical or sales worker	9	5	6	9	6	7	6
Number reporting	263	464	387	509	237	1,860	1,533

Source: National Education Association, April, 1963, p. 16 (adapted). NEA, Research Report 1972-R-3, for 1971 data.

Note: Samples for 1961 and 1971 were separate.

TABLE 19.2. Father's Occupation of Chicago Public School Teachers, 1964

	Percentage of Teachers					
	Elementary School			Secondary School		
Occupation of Teacher's Father	Men	Women	Total	Men	Women	Total
Semiskilled and unskilled	26	15	17	20	9	14
Farm laborer or renter	1	1	1	1	1	1
Skilled worker, foreman, or similar	33	31	31	30	24	27
Farm owner	3	3	3	4	4	4
Clerical and small business	17	23	22	20	26	23
Professional and managerial	20	27	26	25	36	31
Number	720	4,430	5,150	1,123	1,250	2,373

Source: Adapted from Robert J. Havighurst, The Public Schools of Chicago, Chicago: Board of Education, 1964, pp. 417–18.

remained in the working class. A woman teacher in a small southern city who comes from an upper-class family may continue to occupy an upper-class position in the community.

While there are occasional exceptions of these kinds, by and large most teachers in America see themselves as middle-class people; they participate with others of the middle class and hold middle-class attitudes and values.

Frequency of Mobility

Because most teachers are middle-class it follows that a large proportion are upward-mobile persons, with many having moved up from working-class backgrounds.

For example, Table 19.2 indicates that more than 70 percent of the Chicago teachers came from working-class or clerical or small-business-owning families. But on a scale of social status, the teaching profession is located at a higher level than these, at about the lower level of professional and managerial groups. Therefore, half or more of the Chicago teachers have been upward-mobile. Similar findings have emerged from studies in Michigan and in Kansas.

It is likely that mobility occurs more frequently among teachers in metropolitan areas than in small towns. Again using the data for Chicago, Table 19.2 shows that teachers from working-class families were somewhat more likely to be teaching in elementary schools than in secondary schools. In other words, the higher the level of instruction, the higher the teacher's socioeconomic background. The table shows also that more men than women had achieved mobility through the teaching career.

Perceived Social Mobility

Up to now we have called teachers upward-mobile if their fathers' occupations were at a socioeconomic level below that of teaching. This is quite different from saying that teachers themselves feel they have been socially mobile. There is evidence, however, that teachers indeed perceive a social ladder, and perceive their own positions on that ladder. For instance, Colombotos (1962) asked the high school teachers in a large industrialized suburban community to place their parents and then themselves into one of five social classes. The findings are shown in Table 19.3.

From this table it can be seen that those teachers who described themselves as coming from lower-middle or upper-middle-class backgrounds were most likely to see themselves as having the same social position as their parents, while teachers who saw themselves as coming from working-class families were most likely to see their present social class as higher than that of their parents. For this latter group, then, a teaching career has brought with it social advancement.

TABLE 19.3. Subjective Intergenerational Mobility of Teachers: Social-Class Background as Perceived by the Respondents (in percents).

Present Social Class Compared to that of Parents	Men				Women			
	Upper-Middle	Lower-Middle	Upper-Working	Lower-Working	Upper-Middle	Lower-Middle	Upper-Working	Lower-Working
Higher than that of parents	10	39	62	73	13	32	56	90
The same as that of parents	71	56	34	27	72	63	44	10
Lower than that of parents	19	5	4	0	15	5	0	0
Number of respondents	48	112	104	49	48	78	32	10

Social Class of Parents

Source: Colombotos, John L. Sources of Professionalism: a study of high school teachers. U.S. Office of Education Cooperative Research Project No. 330. Ann Arbor: Department of Sociology, University of Michigan, 1962, p. 67 (adapted).

407

There is evidence (see Table 19.4) that suggests also that people of different social origins are somewhat differently oriented toward teaching and plan their careers differently. The Colombotos data showed that men from upper-middle-class backgrounds were seldom interested in leaving classroom teaching for an administrative position. Among men from working-class backgrounds, on the other hand, as many wished to advance through the educational administrative hierarchy as wished to remain in the classroom. It is likely that most of the upper-middle-class men were attracted to the profession because they wished literally to teach, while many of the working-class teachers chose teaching as a means to an administrative position.

The differences among the women teachers were less striking. Those with working-class backgrounds were, however, more likely to think of teaching as a full-time career, and less likely, if they planned to leave teaching to raise a family, to think of retiring altogether. It is possible that this last difference is due primarily to economic reasons.

Relatively few women in this study showed interest in achieving mobility through a career; and of this sample, only a few, all of middle-class background, expressed an interest in moving into an administrative position. The typical woman teacher, no matter what her background, saw her teaching career as beginning and ending in the classroom.

The actual frequency of upward mobility among teachers cannot be definitely established for the country at large, but the evidence is that the frequency is high, with as many as two or possibly three of every five teachers having experienced a move of at least one level in a five-level social structure. It is likely, furthermore, that the frequency of upward-mobile persons in the teaching field has been increasing in the past 50 years.

SOCIAL ORIGIN AS A FACTOR IN TEACHING PERFORMANCE

It is important to know something of the social origin of any given teacher if we are to understand his performance in the teaching role. In this connection, however, we must look at social origin in relation to personality. It has been said, for instance, that social origin is the single most important fact in predicting a teacher's behavior. This is a gross oversimplification. Although a given teacher's social origin may have had an important influence upon his or her personality, it is virtually impossible to cite generalized effects that would be true for all teachers of any single origin. For example, a teacher who comes from a middle-class family is not necessarily ineffective in dealing with lower-class children. Some middle-class teachers, coming from fairly relaxed home environments, may emerge as adaptive personalities, who readily take on the color of their social surroundings. For them, it would be relatively easy to get

TABLE 19.4. *Teachers' Career Plans by Social-Class Background (in percents).*

| | Social-Class Background | | | | | | | |
| | Men | | | | Women | | | |
Career Plans	Upper-Middle	Lower-Middle	Upper-Working	Lower-Working	Upper-Middle	Lower-Middle	Upper-Working	Lower-Working
To leave education for a job in something else	6	7	6	6	2	6	3	0
To advance in education . . . . principal, superintendent, supervisor, coordinator	17	22	30	45	2	2	0	0
To leave teaching, raise a family, then return to teaching	0	0	0	0	35	23	39	18
To leave teaching, raise a family, and not return to teaching	0	0	0	0	20	13	12	9
To stay in teaching	77	71	64	49	41	56	46	73
Number of respondents	48	111	101	49	49	79	33	11

Source: Colombotos, 1962, p. 68 (adapted).

along sympathetically with children and parents quite different from themselves. In another group, whose rigid upbringing might give them a tendency to panic when faced with the strange or unusual, prejudices may be easily aroused. Some of these persons may cling to their own ways as the only right or proper ones. They could easily drift toward treating with disdain children or parents who are of different races, religions, nationalities, or economic circumstances.

Middle-Class Backgrounds

Some teachers with middle-class backgrounds do a very good job of teaching children who come from status-levels lower than their own. They have a broad and sympathetic understanding of children and of society, and they enjoy working with socially disadvantaged pupils if the school structure is reasonably stable. Another teacher from a middle-class home may be dissatisfied and frustrated in the same situation. For example, one teacher said of her first teaching assignment.

> The impressions of my very first day of teaching are still vivid. I saw a girl from the eighth grade who was several months pregnant. At first I thought she was a very young mother bringing her child to school, but I found out that she was a thirteen-year-old pupil. (When she appeared in this obvious condition she was immediately withdrawn from school, but I now know schools where a pregnant eighth-grader is not asked to withdraw.)
>
> My other experiences that first day included listening to a dialect that was unfamiliar and almost incomprehensive to me and to language that was shocking (most terms I had never heard before), and watching one seven-year-old boy emerge from the dressing room without any clothes on. When I went back with him to see that he dressed, I found his underwear was filthy and ragged and held together with a large rusty safety pin that the boy claimed had been sticking him.
>
> I tried—I really tried my best. I remembered how I had to be tolerant, and how these were just children who didn't know any better. I remembered how I wanted to be a teacher, and how I wanted to succeed on my first assignment. But I simply couldn't take it. I applied for a transfer after a few weeks, deciding that I had to get into a different school or withdraw from teaching altogether. I did stick it out for the rest of that year, but I never could overcome my feelings.
>
> I've been in a middle-class school since then, and I'm happy with teaching now. But I still feel guilty and somehow ashamed of myself. I wish I could have been different. But at the same time, a person has to be honest with herself, and has to be comfortable in what she's doing, or she can't do anything at all. . . .

It is, of course, not only middle-class teachers dealing with lower-status children who can provide us with varying examples of how social origin and personality interact in influencing teaching behavior. Some teachers have difficulty in working with children whose families are of higher social levels than their own. An example of this general type is to be seen in the following paragraphs, taken from a longer account written by a teacher entitled "Analysis of a Failure."

Last year I was a teacher in a private school for boys in a large city. Despite my pleasant anticipation of the job, and my desire to be a better teacher than I had been in my first five years, I found myself very unhappy with the situation. . . .

The students came from families of wealth. A few athletes were there on scholarships, but in the elementary school almost all the children came from socially prominent families. Most of these boys transferred to eastern boarding schools in the ninth or tenth grade. The high school was therefore smaller, with many new students from somewhat less socially secure families admitted to fill the gaps. There were only two black students. Jewish students were admitted, but kept below a certain percentage in each grade and in the school as a whole. This percentage was not disclosed, not even to the faculty. . . .

I was hired by the Headmaster. The first interview that I had with him perhaps set the tone for the year to come more than I realized at the time. My credentials from the teachers' agency were already before him. Rather than evaluating me as a person, he seemed to be basing his decision on the prestige value of the institutions at which I had been trained. The facts that I had graduated from a well-known eastern college, that I had taught at Quaker boarding schools, and that he had a high regard for the Quaker educators he had known, seemed to be enough. I can only suppose that he had some vague hopes that I would help to give the school some atmosphere of "easterness" that both he and the parents prized. I, on the other hand, expected to be evaluated as an individual trying to be a good teacher. . . .

I felt uneasy with my students; their habits and values were different from mine. This in turn was a factor in the difficulties I had in the classroom. The majority expected me to keep strict order and to be explicit about what they should study, how they should study it, how they should write down what they knew, and so on. I had never been authoritarian in my teaching, and I was probably even less so that year as a result of the graduate work I had done the year before. I did not wish to become authoritarian. I wanted to interest the boys in the subject matter. But for them, school, and later college, were merely stepping stones to social and business success in the adult world. They intended to learn enough to get into a good college, but no more; and in the meantime they could try to enjoy school by playing the game with the teacher. Her role was to keep order; theirs to disrupt it. . . .

I had very little contact with parents. I did see them en masse at the two or three evening meetings of the parent-faculty organization and at the spring Carnival where they made $14,000 in one evening to buy new equipment for the school. The offhand way many parents treated us teachers made the cartoon seem quite real, in which the mother says to the principal, "I can't understand why the teachers can't get along with Johnny; all the other servants

*can." I felt far removed from parents in terms of values and standard of liv-
ing. I found I did not want to become like them, although I probably envied
and resented their wealth . . . and I think they had no desire for me to be a
model for their children. . . .*

*All of us—myself, the students, the parents, the Headmaster—were glad to
see the year come to an end and to find me moving on to a different teaching job. . . .*

The range of teaching behaviors in middle-class black teachers is probably as great as among white teachers. Some enjoy teaching working-class
children, black or white; others do not; some become active civil rights
workers; others stay aloof from problems of black-white relations.

Working-Class Backgrounds

Among teachers coming from lower-status families, we also see differing patterns. One, for example, tortured by inner feelings of inferiority, may regard
his origin as something to be lived down. Another, having a powerful identification with father and older siblings, may so conduct himself as to retain
and exemplify his family's social rank, and in so doing ally himself with
pupils and parents of similar origin. A third, imbued wth strong achievement
drives, may seek to deny his origin by accepting middle-class standards and
by being unusually strict, if not actually punitive, against the children and
parents from whose ranks he sees himself as having risen by dint of self-
denial. These illustrations, of course, do not by any means exhaust the
possibilities.

Jim Mallory is an example of a teacher who has moved a long way up
the social ladder, and whose flexible personality has made him unusually
successful:

*Jim Mallory was born in the state of Washington. His family's income was
derived mainly from fruit picking, and each member was responsible for some
aspect of the family endeavor. It was often Jim's lot to do the cooking and the
family wash. Since the Mallory's lived in a tent much of the time, it was also
his job to erect the tent at the fruit picking locations and to "keep house" in
all aspects.*

*Because fruit picking was seasonal work and the father was not too steady
a provider, responsibility for food and money often fell on the shoulders of
the children. At one time Jim spent five hours each evening setting pins in a
bowling alley at a nearby army base. If he told the soldiers he was hungry
they would bring him food from their mess hall. This food plus the money
earned from pin setting was for a time the sole family subsistence.*

*When Jim was 16 he joined the army but was given a medical discharge a
year later. He stayed with his family for about two weeks subsequent to his
discharge, and then stowed away on a fruit truck and went to Texas. There*

he got a job and enrolled in a junior college. After two years, he entered a large university. He received his bachelor's degree shortly after the war. He then went into graduate work in psychology, where he specialized in counseling and guidance. He became an avid student of "nondirective" counseling and "student-centered" teaching, finding this general approach in keeping with his implicit world view. He is never so delighted as when he is discussing the conflicting values of American culture, especially those of the middle-class in general and of school administrators in particular.

Jim's values are apparent in his attitudes toward his own children. They are allowed to solve their own personal and social problems, and the limits on their behavior are kept to the absolute minimum. This attitude is not always approved by his neighbors and colleagues, but it poses no special problems in Jim's eyes. . . .

Jim has been a successful teacher in high school and is now one of the most popular and admired teachers on a college faculty. His unique teaching methods in the classroom, and his sympathy and permissiveness in the counseling situation—his ability to give the student a sense of worth—this combination is one that appears strongly to almost all his students. . . .

Alice Davis is another kind of teacher:

Alice Davis grew up under the care of her grandmother, a black woman who did "day work" for middle-class white families. Alice was born when her mother was 18 years old and unmarried. The baby was given to the grandmother to rear, and the mother worked in a factory until she married at 20. This marriage did not last, and she married another man, who left her after two more children were born. She thereupon applied for Aid to Dependent Children and lived on this money with the two children and with two others that were born later.

Alice never lived with her mother, but she often saw her on Sundays. She remembers that her grandmother warned her not to play with her half-brothers and sisters and kept telling her that her mother was "not fit to bring up children." The grandmother spent evenings reading to Alice and always took her to church on Sunday.

Alice found school a wonderful place. She learned to read promptly and was the favorite of her teachers. After school she went to a neighborhood center where there was a club leader whom she liked very much. This woman kept in touch with Alice and encouraged her to finish high school and go on to the local teachers college. Alice was never so proud of herself as when she got her diploma, and looked down at her grandmother, sitting in the audience and smiling.

Alice teaches now in a working-class school where all the children are black. She runs her room strictly and punishes her pupils for the least infraction of rules. She gives out homework and insists on its being done. She often tells her children that they are lucky to have such a good school and that they must work hard to show their appreciation. She will not tolerate lying or copying.

About a fourth of her pupils come from homes where there is no father

present. She is especially strict with these children and will not accept any-
thing but the most conscientious work from them. To those who do well she
devotes much time, and she gets them properly enrolled in church groups and
in settlement houses. Those pupils who do not do well in school find her a
merciless taskmaster. When she meets physical resistance or active hostility
from such a pupil, Alice becomes so anxious that she sometimes gets sick. Her
principal has learned to help her with a few such children each year by re-
moving them to a class of another teacher who can tolerate this kind of be-
havior better than Alice.

A recent study of the role orientations of high school teachers in Chicago indicated that social-class background does not operate alone to influence teaching behavior but interacts with other variables, particularly urban-rural origins, to affect a teacher's style and goals. (Kornacker, 1966). One finding was that teachers who grew up as members of lower-status ethnic groups (Jewish and Polish) tended to emphasize subject matter knowledge and cognitive goals in their teaching, but teachers from middle-class backgrounds (primarily black, in this study) tended to have a nurturant, child-centered orientation which emphasized affective aspects of learning. Teachers who grew up in ethnic subcultures with recent rural origins (Italian and southern black) tended to be nurturant, while teachers whose ethnic backgrounds were predominantly urban in nature (Irish and Jewish) tended to favor subject-centered goals. Although these findings cannot necessarily be extended to other grade levels and other situations, they do underline the fallacy of simplistic assumptions. For example, not all teachers of middle-class background are indifferent to the emotional difficulties experienced in school by disadvantaged students, and not all teachers whose economic or ethnic backgrounds are similar to their pupils are necessarily successful with those pupils.

Personality as a Determining Factor

Each individual's personality will determine, then, the effects of his social background on his teaching behavior. There is a wide range of personality patterns within each social class and in each ethnic and racial group. Even though some modes of childraising and some personality patterns are more typical of one group than another, in each group there is a wide variety. No social class and no racial or ethnic group is barren of adaptive individuals, or of well-adjusted men and women of strong conscience, or of adventuresome pioneers.

At the same time, from the range of individuals who grew up in each social group, teaching probably draws only a fraction. From less well-situated economic groups, teaching may be expected to draw a good number of ambitious, striving people. By contrast, the upper-class boy or girl with a strong achievement drive is unlikely to choose teaching as a career. From the middle classes, education probably draws a range of personality types; among them those who want to be reformers or agents of social change. In the slum areas and working-class districts, the educational profession would seem more attractive to relatively isolated youngsters who set themselves apart from the bulk of their classmates.

Social origin may have a different influence upon a teacher's behavior during his first years of teaching than at a period later in his career. Thus a person who had felt teaching represented a step upward in social prestige might gradually find that his childhood friends who had made other choices are now gaining greater income or higher position; he might eventually feel he had made a poor occupational choice.

The effects of social origin may take different forms in the older teacher than in the newcomer to the profession. A special case exists where population change has altered the type of child a school serves. Thus, we have the experience of teachers who were drawn to a school in a "good" neighborhood and stayed in that school while the surrounding area turned into a slum. For a middle-class teacher with strong latent prejudices, this can be a demoralizing experience.

In summary, then, factors related to social origin interact with personality factors in influencing a teacher's behavior. It is also evident that both in turn are influenced by the particular school setting in which the teacher finds himself.

TEACHERS AS A HETEROGENEOUS GROUP

We have seen that teachers presently represent a wide range of social-class origins. There are other ways in which teachers are an increasingly heterogeneous group. There are more Catholic and more Jewish teachers in public schools than in earlier years, not only in large cities, but also in smaller communities. There is more diversity in marital status. Not only have the barriers against married women rapidly disappeared in all parts of the country, but there are more divorced persons being employed as teachers. There are more teachers who are mothers, especially in the present period when numbers of older women are returning to the teaching field. There are more male teachers than there were a few decades ago. (In 1971, 55 percent of high school teachers were men.)

There is a greater diversity of ethnic and racial backgrounds. Since World War II, for instance, there has been a substantial flow of Japanese men and women into teaching positions in western and midwestern cities, and teachers of Japanese ancestry abound in Hawaii. Puerto Ricans are now coming into the profession in noticeable numbers.

The black group is different from the other ethnic groups in the teaching profession due to the segregated school system in the South and in some border states prior to 1954, which created a substantial group of black teachers in black schools. The largest group of black teachers is still to be found either in the South teaching in *de facto* segregated black schools or in inner-city schools in metropolitan areas in the North and West. Black teachers are relatively highly represented also on the teaching staff in border cities such as Kansas City, St. Louis, Louisville, Washington, and Baltimore. In 1965, 28 percent of the public school teachers of Kansas City were blacks compared with about 18 percent blacks in the city population. In Chicago in 1971, 32 percent of the teachers were black, although more than half of the pupils were black.

In the country at large the assignment of black teachers is largely to schools with a predominance of black pupils, but this practice is slowly changing. For example, Philadelphia in 1965 worked out an arrangement between the teacher's union and the school administration whereby 40 white teachers went into schools that were mainly black in pupil and staff composition, while 40 black teachers transferred to schools that were mainly white. Detroit in 1965 announced a "balanced staff" policy, saying that it is educationally desirable for children in all schools to come into contact with teachers who are young and old, male and female, black and white; and the Detroit school administration worked out a plan with the teachers' organizations for teacher assignment and transfer that would work toward the goal of a balanced staff. These instances are multiplying in cities all over the country.

Effects on Teacher-Pupil Interaction

The growing diversity of teachers, and plans such as Detroit's balanced staff, mean that American school children are coming into contact with a greater variety of adult personalities. Among other things, there are now more teachers, especially at the secondary level, who know first-hand the attitudes and values of working-class children, and who know the problems of the black or the Puerto Rican or the Mexican-American child. Of the total number of teachers encountered by a child as he goes through school, he is now likely to meet a greater range of types and to experience a greater range of interpersonal relations with teachers.

Effects on Teacher-Teacher Interaction

The greater heterogeneity also affects the interaction between teachers. In many schools, new problems are created as the attitudes of old teachers come into conflict with those of younger. The following account illustrates this point.

There has been considerable change in education during my 25 years of teaching at North High School. When I first came here I was very much impressed with the social status of the teachers and the very high caliber of the students. The botany and zoology courses that I was to teach were organized on a near-collegiate level....There were honor clubs in every subject; and students and teachers stayed many hours after school doing club work.... Pupils trained for scholarship examinations. At that time probably a greater percent of students from North went to colleges and universities than from any other high school in the city. The principal and the assistant principal were both Ph.D.'s from top universities. The teachers were remarkably able scholars. To illustrate, Mr. A was a real southern gentleman. Miss B was a foreign diplomat's daughter who was as much at home in European countries as in the United States. Miss C came from a line of well-known educators. Mr. D was the author of several textbooks used in high schools all over the country. Miss E was a native Parisian who had been decorated by the French government for her work. Miss F has a doctorate in science. And so it went, right on through our faculty.

Most of these early teachers have left now, either through retirement or death. The teachers who followed were different. There are many more now who come from teacher's colleges; who have never traveled; some, but fewer, are from families of educators. They come from a different social class, and they reflect it in their teaching and social attitudes.

The older teachers get separated from the younger and newer ones. Respect for experience has dwindled. Many of the newer teachers will not take charge of clubs after school. They refuse to do extra work. They call us old-fashioned and resent the fact that we are willing to give a bit more than their idea of a day's work. All they seem to be interested in is shorter hours and more pay. Many frown on homework for pupils because it means more work for the teacher. And when they take over luncheon duty and corridor discipline, they act more like policemen than like teachers.

This teacher is giving a personal view that is undoubtedly biased by an age differential between her and her colleagues, as well as by a social-class differential. Nevertheless, differences and possible conflicts are bound to occur among teachers as heterogeneity increases in the teaching profession.

Heterogeneity of teaching staff within a given school is likely to be greater in large cities than in smaller communities; even though it is increasing to some extent in small school systems, too. Due to employment policies, the differences between teachers in small communities arise less often from ethnic or racial differences than from differences in religion, age, and marital status.

THE CAREER PATTERN

In viewing the career pattern of the teacher we may look first in broad outline at the salient features that distinguish teaching from other occupations and professions.

The teacher's clients are his pupils, and the school as a whole is built around the teacher-pupil relationship. The teacher has also a secondary, or indirect, group of clients, the parents of pupils. Beyond these, the teacher's immediate contact is with colleagues and with administrators. Thus, the teacher's relationships are primarily with four groups of people—pupils, their parents, fellow-teachers, and administrators.

The teacher works in an organization that is relatively bureaucratic. At the same time, the separateness of each classroom makes direct and continuous supervision impossible, and the teacher is himself in an administrative position. Although there is a great degree of structure and routine in the work setting (with time, space, and duties allotted in regular and scheduled ways), the routinization is in terms of the administrative system and not in terms of relationships with clients.

Compared with other occupations (although not with other professions) teaching involves a relatively long period of preparation, followed at once by full membership in the profession. A teacher takes on full status with his first regular teaching assignment, and, while informally he may be regarded as a novice for a few years by his older and more experienced colleagues, there is no formal period of apprenticeship once the first job placement is made, nor is there a period when participation and responsibility are only partial.

For the classroom teacher (omitting administrators or college teachers), the career is not, as in another occupation, characterized by movement from one to another level in a hierarchy. While it is true that many men and women who enter the teaching field move from classroom to administrative levels, or to affiliated professional service positions such as school psychologist or master teacher, the majority of teachers remain at the level of classroom teaching for the full length of their careers. Progress for most teachers is measured by relatively small and regular increments attained with age and experience—choicer assignments, more autonomy, more security, more salary, more prestige—but all these gains are within the same hierarchical level within the school structure.

Entering the Field

We have already spoken of the fact that persons choose to enter the teaching field for a great variety of reasons and that these reasons influence subsequent career patterns. Thus the person for whom entrance into teaching itself constitutes a clear and major step in upward social mobility may not exert himself greatly to move upward within the teaching hierarchy. In another case, the opposite may be true. In a third instance, the person who enters teaching with a strong sense of mission and dedication may be concerned with moving from one position to another primarily in terms of finding the place where he can be of greatest service to children. For many teachers, the initial decision was to enter college rather than to enter teaching, and a teacher-training institution, being conveniently located and relatively inexpensive, was chosen. Those who enter the teaching field in this way may have careers quite different from those who had a different entry.

Initial Adjustment

Having once chosen to become a teacher, and having obtained the requisite preparation, the teacher enters the second major phase of his career when he takes his first regular teaching position. For many persons, the first teaching experience requires considerable readjustment in personal and social life (Shaplin, 1961). Many beginning teachers experience what has been called "reality shock." The middle-class teacher described in the preceding pages who was shocked to see pregnant eighth-graders is a good example of a young woman who found herself in a situation at marked variance with her preconception of the teaching role. In large cities, where beginning teachers are often assigned to "poorer" schools, the reality shock, when it occurs, often arises from problems encountered in dealing with disadvantaged children and parents, or from encountering the more hardened orientations of older teachers and administrators.

This phenomenon of reality shock does not occur in all cases, of course. The persons, for example, who come from families of educators and who have considerable advance knowledge of the teaching career (and this is a large number) may find relatively little for which they are unprepared. The teacher who begins his career in the same type of community in which he was reared, whether small town or city neighborhood, may similarly make the transition into teaching smoothly and uneventfully.

Nor does reality shock necessarily come at the beginning of the teaching career. In a study of experienced high school teachers in Kansas City, for instance, it occurred for many, not at the point of their first teaching job, but at the point of entering the large city system. There the major readjustment was due to (1) the failure to anticipate the lack of community recognition given teachers in a large city: (2) the more impersonal tone of the interaction between teacher and pupil; and (3) the problems of paper work and clearance of routines that are involved in the larger and more bureaucratic system (Peterson, 1959).

Commitment to the Profession

Becoming committed to teaching as a career occurs at various times and to varying degrees for different people.

Some persons seem to drift into teaching; only later do they become strongly committed to it. Others select teaching as a career while still in high school and plan every move carefully. Miss Allison, for example, the daughter of a school superintendent in a small midwest town, had decided at an early age to become a teacher. She completed a B.A. degree before taking her first teaching job, taught in a small town high school for one year, then moved to a small city for one year, then entered a large city system at the age of 24. She says, "Going into the profession wasn't just an impulsive thing, with me. I haven't been like many teachers I know, moving from one place to another. I improved myself with every move."

Another teacher, by contrast, is Miss Thorburn, a teacher now in the same city high school as Miss Allison. Miss Thorburn, who also grew up in a small town, took her first teaching job in a one-room rural school, as soon as she finished high school. She moved after two years to another rural school; then to a small town of 2,000 population; then to a second, and a third small town. After eight years, she moved to a small city of 10,000; and after several more moves within communities of approximately the same size, entered the large city system at the age of 40. "I've done a lot of moving around," she says, "and I'm not always sure why. I wasn't even sure for a long time if I really wanted to stay in teaching. Oh, one thing I've gotten out of it, of course, is different kinds of experience. I taught in Colorado, and in Texas, and in Wisconsin. And I went to several different universities in the summers before I finished my bachelor's degree."

For those who enter teaching without strong commitment in advance, it has happened more frequently than not that the major commitment occurs after several years of experience and when the teacher is in the age range 30 to 40. While the timing of this commitment is affected by a variety of influences, an important factor in the past has stemmed from the fact that most people who entered the teaching field were young unmarried women. By their mid-thirties many had married and left the profession. Those who had not withdrawn from the field tended, at this age, to commit themselves to teaching as their life work.

It is likely that this "age of commitment" varies more now, since the persons who are teachers are now a more varied group of people and especially since women are no longer forced to choose between marriage and a career.

There is, on the other hand, a strong pressure for early commitments stemming from another source, that of increasing professionalization. The requirements for entering the teaching field are rising, they are becoming standard from state to state, and the teacher's education is becoming increasingly specialized. As a result, movement in and out of the teaching field tends to diminish. Some people have deplored this situation, ". . . we have all seen what has happened to teaching when the teachers' colleges and professional bodies forced those who entered it to make a career commitment, which has meant expulsion from teaching of those gifted amateurs for whom it could be a way station on the road to something else. . . ." (Riesman, 1955, p. 232.)

The trend toward early commitment was in some measure counteracted in the 1950s and 60s when the shortage of teachers was particularly acute. At that time the schools recruited a large number of broadly educated persons holding the bachelor's degree, who had had no thought of preparing for teaching while doing undergraduate work.

During periods of teachers shortages, then, persons enter the field who have not had prior commitments to teaching. Teacher training institutions have facilitated their entry by developing intensive summer-school courses and fifth-year professional training programs, such as the Master of Arts in Teaching (MAT) program. Still, as professionalization continues, the long-term trend is to increase the pressures for early commitment to the field.

Movement Along the Career Line

Although the large majority of teachers do not move from classroom teaching to administrative levels, there is considerable movement within classroom teaching: geographical movement, where the teacher goes from one community to another; movement from one grade level to another (usually from elementary to high school); and movement from one school to another within the same city system.

The Earlier Career Line. In the first half of the century, the traditional career for a school teacher was to start teaching in a rural school after one or two years of post-high school preparation. After a few years the teacher went back to college and completed a four-year course; then went to work in the schools of a small city. Often the line of progress was from grade school to high school as well as from small town to larger town.

Peterson (1956, 1964) studied the careers of women school teachers in the Kansas City school system. In the early 1950s the Kansas City system had been stable in numbers for a decade, as had other cities, due to the low birth-rate of the 1930s; and like other central cities, Kansas City had adopted a policy of employing only experienced teachers. Thus in 1953, of the women high school teachers, 78 percent were over 40 years of age. The general direction of the career movement for these teachers had been from smaller to larger towns, from grade school to high school, from lower to higher salaries, from unstable to stable teaching conditions, from poorer to wealthier communities.

> Unmarried rural-reared teachers typically began teaching in a country school near their home at the age of 17 or 18; moved to a small town school after about two years of experience and some additional education in summer school; secured a B.S. in education at about the age of 24; made two additional moves to large schools in larger towns; entered the Kansas City system at about the age of 31; moved twice within the Kansas City system; secured their current placement within the city system at the age of 35; and, in the course of continued summer school education, received an M.A. degree at about the age of 38.

The unmarried teachers from small towns followed much the same path. However, they tended to be somewhat older when they began teaching, because they often did some other kind of work in their home towns before going to school. Since many of the rural girls looked upon country school teaching as a way of earning money for further education, there is some similarity between country girls and town girls in this respect. There were, among unmarried teachers from the smaller towns, several who, like rural girls, began teaching in a country school when out of high school, saving their money for further education.

The early career phases of unmarried, urban-reared teachers are noticeably different from the others. As a rule, urban-born teachers completed their degrees before beginning to teach, taught in small town schools for a much shorter period, and entered the urban system when younger. They were not, however, much younger than teachers from small towns and farms in moving to present positions within the city system, perhaps because "settling" within the city system is more closely affiliated with age. (Peterson, 1956, pp. 75–77.)

An alternative career line existed in a few large cities, mainly in the East. Here the teachers were more likely to come from working-class and lower-middle-class families in the central city. They went from the local high school to a municipal teachers' college or university and then began teaching in the city schools. After a two or three-year probationary period they secured tenure and began looking for a school that was conveniently located near the area in which they wanted to live. They would transfer once or twice until they found a school where they liked the principal, the pupils, and the neighborhood. A subgroup, of course, worked for promotion to administrative positions.

The Contemporary Career Line. Since 1950 a new career line has developed for teachers in metropolitan areas. The majority come from the central city and attend a local teachers' college or state college. Upon securing a bachelor's degree and a teaching certificate, they start teaching in the central city system.

Many teachers secure a master's degree through part-time study. Those who want to be administrators then start preparing for examinations and get a variety of teaching experience. The others look for a school assignment that will be best for them.

The beginning teacher runs the risk of being assigned initially to an unsatisfactory school, since schools that have many vacancies and no teachers requesting transfer to them are those in which something is "wrong." Schools in the lower socioeconomic areas tend to be such "transfer vacuums." For example, in 1964 11 percent of the teachers in Chicago's slum schools had only one year of teaching experience, and only 16 percent had more than 16 years' teaching experience. In contrast, in upper-middle-class schools only 2 percent of the teachers had been teaching only a year, while 58 percent had more than 16 years' experience. A few teachers found teaching in the slums a rewarding and challenging experience, but most had, through the transfer system, moved on to "better" schools. (Havighurst, 1964)

There are, of course, a variety of reasons why teachers request transfers. In the Chicago study, only 16 percent of the elementary and 12 percent of high school teachers wished to transfer because of dissatisfaction with pupils or with the local community. The most frequent reason given was personal convenience—distance from home, for example. A teacher may also transfer for reasons of professional advancement; for example, to gain experience in another type of school, or a better position; or a teacher may be dissatisfied with his principal, or with certain aspects of his assignment that he feels mitigate against professional service. Nevertheless, more teachers request transfers from slum schools than from other schools in Chicago.

This career line leads increasingly often from a city to a suburban school system. Since the suburbs have been growing rapidly they cannot secure many teachers who were born in suburbs. They recruit from the central city or from the towns or cities outside the metropolitan area.

Thus there has developed a teacher career line in which more and more teachers are following their entire professional lives within a particular metropolitan area, teaching in a wide variety of schools in the area.

EXERCISES

1. How did you decide to become a teacher? How was your decision related to factors in your own social background?

2. Persons who enter the teaching profession are today more heterogeneous in terms of social origins than were past groups. What effects is this likely to have, when one thinks of the school as an agency affecting social mobility? Do you think the effects will be to increase mobility or to decrease it in the society at large? Why?

3. Select a teacher whom you know. Describe how his social background is affecting his teaching behavior.

4. Describe a situation in which differences in the social backgrounds of the teacher and the parent had an effect upon the child's learning. What was the effect upon the child?

5. Describe a situation in which interaction between a teacher and the principal, or the teacher and a supervisor, was influenced by factors relating to their social origins.

6. Make a study of the social origins of the people in your college class, or the teachers in your school. How many come from rural backgrounds? How many social classes are represented in the group? How many ethnic groups? Religious groups?

7. If you have colleagues who are members of minority groups, describe their attitudes toward teaching socially disadvantaged children. Can you relate differences among them to differences in their personalities?

8. Choose two teachers who have had outstanding career lines. Describe the careers of each. What was the reason underlying each move the teacher made?

SUGGESTIONS FOR FURTHER READING

1. See the selections by Wattenberg *et al.* and by Bush in *Society and Education: A Book of Readings* (Havighurst, Neugarten, and Falk) for further discussion of the social origins of teachers and the relations between social-class origin and teaching performance.

2. For questionnaire studies of the characteristics of public school teachers, see *The American Public School Teacher, 1970–71*, published by the Research Division of the NEA; and Chapter 16 and Appendix A of Havighurst's *The Public Schools of Chicago*.

3. For an interpretation of the place of the teacher in American society, read Barzun's *The Teacher in America*. Caplow's *The Academic Marketplace* is a description of some of the problems in the teachers' position in higher education (colleges and universities). Dreeben's book on *The Nature of Teaching* describes the teacher's work in a useful way.

CHAPTER 20

The Teacher in
The Community
and Classroom

The teacher is a resident of a community: a citizen, a worker, perhaps a parent. Because he is a teacher, people in the community expect him or her to behave "like a teacher." What is it, to behave like a teacher?

To answer this question, the concept of *social role* is useful. A social role is a pattern of behavior that is expected of people who fill a certain position in society. Policemen, for example, even though they are all different individuals, have a certain set of behaviors in common, and our society has a set of common expectations about their behavior. Thus we speak of the social role of the policeman; and, in the same way, of the social roles of mother or father or pupil or teacher.

Every person fills a whole set of social roles. A teacher assumes the roles of worker, husband or wife, parent, church member, club member, and citizen. The role of teacher is itself made up of a cluster of subroles, some that refer primarily to the teacher's behavior in relation to the wider community, and others that refer primarily to the teacher's behavior in relation to pupils. In real life the subroles are neither separate nor distinct, but for purposes of analysis we may focus our attention upon one after another.

THE TEACHER'S ROLES IN THE COMMUNITY

At different times in history there have been different images of the school teacher in American society: the strict schoolmaster, bending over the heads of perspiring pupils, rod in hand; the Puritanical schoolmarm, straitlaced and humorless; the absent-minded professor; and in Waller's terms, the sacred object:

> For some reason, the school has become almost equally with the church the repository of ideals. The teacher, like the minister, possesses a high degree of social sacredness. He must be a little better than other men. . . . It is his part to enjoy the finer things of life, literature, art, and the best music. He must likewise be interested in all good causes, that is, in all such causes as do not upset important vested interests in the community. . . . Like the minister, the teacher excites very real reverence and people regard him as slightly ridiculous. (Waller, 1942, p. 217.)

There were positive as well as negative images of the teacher: the revered scholar; the self-sacrificing idealist; the sympathetic advisor of youth. Margaret Mead, for example, offers the following description:

> . . . when the American hears the word "schoolteacher" . . . the image will be something like this. He will think of a grade school teacher who teaches perhaps the third or fourth grade; this teacher will be a woman of somewhat indeterminate age, perhaps in the middle 30's neither young nor old, of the middle class and committed to the ethics and manners of the middle-class world. In the emotional tone which accompanies the image there will be respect, a little fear, perhaps more than a little affection, an expectation that she will reward his efforts to learn and conform, and a spate of delighted memories of those occasions when he himself perpetrated feats of undetected mischief. . . . (Mead, 1951, p. 5.)

Whatever the prevailing image of the teacher at different times and at different places, it has always contained contradictory elements. Furthermore, as the society has increased in complexity, the images of teachers have increased in variety. As teachers have become a more heterogeneous group of people, the stereotypes about teachers are being broken down and discarded; and it has become increasingly difficult to generalize about "the" image of the teacher held by Americans.

Ascribed Status of Teachers

It is generally true that teachers as a group have been awarded somewhat less social status than other professional groups in America. In Warner's ranking of occupations according to social prestige, the public school teacher ranked lower than the other professions (Warner, Meeker, and Eells, 1960). In a list of ninety occupations, North and Hatt reported that teaching in 1947 ranked thirty-sixth, not far above the average for all occupations (North and Hatt, 1949); and a repeat study in 1963 indicated that no real change in prestige of teaching had occurred (Hodge, Siegel, and Rossi, 1964). When judged in terms of level of education required, or in terms of income earned, teaching does not compare favorably with other occupations. In these ways, the society may be said to hold an image of the teacher that is not commensurate with teachers' claims to full professional status and recognition.

This situation is partly due to the unresolved question in the minds of many Americans as to whether or not the public school teacher should be regarded as a professional person in the same way that a lawyer or a physician is regarded. On the one hand, this question may be answered affirmatively, since teaching is a legally recognized and regulated occupation; one that requires a high level of intellectual and social competence; and one that has its own professional organization that develops standards of competence—criteria commonly used to disinguish professions from other occupations.

On the other hand, the question is often answered negatively, since the teacher's social role is less specialized than that of other professionals. The teacher acts as an agent of the society in socializing children, and in this sense teachers perform a role more similar to that of parents than to that of professionals. Their responsibility is to all children, not to the selected few who need a specialized service. Teachers, accordingly, are regarded as public servants in a quite different way from other professional persons.

Herein, then, lies part of the ambiguity with which teachers are regarded in the society: They are experts with a professional know-how of their own; yet they are also, in their role of public servant, subject to the dictates of public opinion.

The teacher's role in the community involves a number of different subroles, only a few of which can be discussed here.

The Participant in Community Affairs

Since the teacher is an educated person and possesses certain skills that are useful in conducting the affairs of the community, teachers have been in demand for church work (teaching Sunday school classes, singing in the choir), for volunteer jobs with the Red Cross and other welfare organizations, and for other useful community services. Vidich and Bensman have characterized teachers as being, in this respect, "a replacement pool for spare talent as it is needed for various organizational jobs." (Vidich and Bensman, 1958, p. 270.) This role has, however, been circumscribed; it is usually limited to the "safe," noncontroversial community affairs and to activities to which little prestige is attached. There is likely to be resistance and criticism, especially in small towns, if the teacher takes an active part in politics or starts a business "on the side." Women teachers in many communities find it difficult to be accepted in the more prestigious women's clubs. The few men teachers who are accepted in the service clubs of the community are usually principals or superintendents or athletic coaches.

In a study of over 1,100 teachers in 66 communities in Pennsylvania,

Buck (1960) found that one-third participated in community organizations at or above the rate of top business and professional people (the latter group has consistently ranked highest, as compared with other occupational groups, with regard to participation in community affairs), and 80 percent had participation scores higher than the average for white-collar workers. Rates of participation were approximately the same in large as in small communities.

Because a majority of the teachers had grown up in homes where community participation was low, the implications are that many teachers change their life styles to meet the expectation that the teacher will take part in community life beyond the school.

More recently, in a nationwide sample, four out of every five teachers were found to be active in one or more organizations, and half of the active members belonged to one or more groups besides church. (NEA Research Report, 1972-R-3)

Table 20.1 reports the experience and attitudes toward the local community of public school teachers who were studied at five-year intervals after 1956. There has been relatively little change, during these 20 years, in the general participation of teachers in community affairs, except for decreased membership in political party organizations. At the same time, there has been increased political *activity* by teachers as a group, which will be discussed later in this chapter, and much more *professional* activity, as will be discussed in the next chapter. As the number of teachers from lower-middle and working-class levels increases, teacher participation in community life may well become more varied.

Community Leadership and Political Activity

While over the past two decades, teachers, like other professional groups, have probably become more actively concerned over civil rights, efforts to eliminate poverty, and other national and international problems, it is unlikely that the overall picture concerning organizational *leadership* will be reversed. Earlier studies showed that teachers participated in community affairs, but usually not as leaders. There are, of course, various factors that interact to produce this pattern, only one being the prevailing attitude in the community as regards the teacher's qualifications for leadership. Another factor that operates to curtail the teacher's participations, especially in political and economic affairs, is the expectation that the teacher as a public servant should remain neutral on controversial issues. Possibly this is the reason why only two or three percent of the teachers in the NEA samples reported in Table 20.1 had ever run for public office. In many communities, teachers are barred by state law or by local requirement from participation in political activities. On the other hand, the growing teacher militancy of the 1960s has brought teachers increasingly into local politics. For example, the California Teachers Association created a Political Education Department in

TABLE 20.1.   Teacher Participation in the Local Community

Identity with the Community	Percentages			
	1956	1961	1966	1971
Have lived here since childhood	33	33	30	29
Came as an adult; feel I "belong"	51	51	51	49
Have lived here too short a time to "belong"	9	11	15	15
Have been here some time; still an outsider	7	5	4	8
Members of:				
Church or synagogue	92	87	86	78
Youth-serving group	—	21	20	16
Political party organization	—	31	22	13
Fraternal or auxiliary group	—	33	19	15
Have been a candidate for an elective public office	3	2	3	3

Source: Questionnaire sent to a national sample of Public School Teachers.
NEA Research Report 1972-R-3. Tables 51, 53, 56.
The American Public School Teacher: 1970–71.
Copyright © 1972 by National Education Association. All rights reserved.

1971 to work on behalf of certain candidates for school board membership. The CTA supported 335 candidates in 185 school districts in the election of April, 1973. Teacher-supported candidates won 68 percent of the races in which they engaged. (Fadem and Duffy, 1973)

When asked in a 1970 NEA Survey to indicate their political philosophy, a national sample of public school teachers responded: conservative, 17 percent; tending toward conservatism, 44 percent; tending toward liberal, 28 percent; and liberal, 12 percent.

The Sociological Stranger

At the same time that teachers are expected to participate in the community, there has been the contrasting social expectation that teachers will be "sociological strangers" in the community. The teacher has often been regarded as a person who is in, but not of, the community, one who seldom sinks roots into the community.

This role of the stranger has, again, resulted from various factors. One is the expectation that teachers are a group apart, with cultural interests and cosmopolitan tastes that differentiate them from the community at large. Another is the desire to maintain the neutrality of the teacher—the theory that he will be more objective in his teaching if he is neither too well acquainted with the families of his pupils nor too much involved in local problems. Another is the view of the teacher as the sacred object or the idealist or the social reformer, whose sights are set upon goals that transcend the immediate and the present; the theory that, should he become too closely identified with the local community, his effectiveness would be diminished.

Another set of factors stems from the fact that, traditionally, teachers have been a transient group, not usually committed to the particular community in which they find themselves. Many teachers move from one community to another in search of new experience, better salaries, or better working conditions. This transiency is true of teachers in large cities as well as those in small towns, since the city teacher tends to move from one school to another and, as is still true, often teaches in a different neighborhood from the one in which he lives. Teacher placement policies are such that young teachers are often specifically advised, after completing their training, not to return to their home communities to teach.

The role of stranger is probably a declining one for teachers. In a study of Detroit teachers in the 1950s, the overwhelming majority of younger teachers were native Detroiters (Wattenberg et al., 1957, I). In Chicago in 1963, 70 percent of the elementary and 69 percent of the high school teachers had grown up in Chicago (Havighurst, 1964). A nationwide sampling of teachers in the 1960s showed that over 80 percent identified with their communities and one-third had lived in the community in which they were teaching since childhood (Table 20.1). The teacher's role of "stranger" is on the decline, furthermore, as teachers are becoming a more heterogeneous group, and as they can no longer be singled out as a group separate and apart from the community in terms of social origins, family patterns, or educational and cultural interests.

Other Community Roles of the Teacher

As is evident from the preceding sections, there are various subroles that constitute the role of the teacher in the community in addition to *community participant* and *sociological stranger.* We have already mentioned briefly the teacher as *sacred object,* as *social reformer,* and as *public servant.* We may list several others that are usually of importance in describing the teacher's behavior, although it should be kept in mind that any such list is not exhaustive, that the subroles are not mutually exclusive, and that terms other than the ones given here might be equally descriptive.

The teacher is the *surrogate of middle-class morality.* Parents often expect the teacher to be a better model of behavior for their children than they are themselves. Although parents may smoke, drink, and gamble, they want the teacher to avoid any behavior that they think might be bad for children to imitate. In this respect, parents may be following a sound principle, for the teacher, especially the young teacher dealing with adolescents, is often a more effective model for youth than is the parent. As a consequence, the teacher is expected to practice the personal virtues of the middle class—

correct speech, good manners, modesty, prudence, honesty, responsibility, friendliness, and so on. At the same time, certain other middle-class virtues, such as competitiveness, striving for financial rewards, or independence of authority, are less likely to be valued in teacher behavior.

The teacher is also expected to be a *person of culture,* with more refined tastes than the general population. He is expected to be widely read and widely traveled and to be sophisticated in outlook.

The teacher is a *pioneer in the world of ideas,* the seeker for truth. While this role is more often accorded to college professors than to public school teachers, still there is a tradition in America that educators as a group should be explorers in the world of knowledge, should be leaders in formulating the values and ideals of the society, and should work for the continual improvement of the society.

Teachers are expected to be not only fountainheads of knowledge but also *experts in regard to children,* a source of information and guidance with respect to the best methods of child rearing and the understanding of child development.

Conflict in Role Expectations

Certain of these subroles are contradictory, of course. The cautious and colorless public servant is not the bold adventurer in the world of ideas. The full participant in community affairs is not the neutral and objective stranger. There also may be conflict, not only among the roles themselves, but also between certain role behaviors and self-concept. The teacher, for example, who sees himself as a cosmopolitan person—one who has seen Paris, who has a store of worldly wisdom—may be irked by the demands put upon him to be the conservative example for children. Similarly teachers who, as a group, place such high premium upon professional status, responsibility, and freedom in their work may well find it difficult to conform to the role of safe and colorless public servant.

Yet the apparent contradictions in roles should not be overemphasized. In the first place, the teacher is not different from other people in being faced by a variety of social expectations and a variety of roles to fill. The same type of analysis that has been made above can also be made for other occupational groups, and many of the same subroles would emerge. The physician also is expected to be a cosmopolitan person at the same time that he is a surrogate of middle-class morality.

Teachers are in a particularly sensitive relation to the community because they are dealing with the community's children. They are, accordingly, under more constant public scrutiny than other groups, and may well have developed a greater degree of self-consciousness. It does not follow, however, that teachers have more complex or more conflict-laden roles to perform in the community than do other professionals.

In the second place, the presence of contradictory demands does not necessarily produce personal conflict. The teacher, like any other person, fills a variety of roles at different periods of the day or at different periods in his life. The teacher can be, in some respects, the participant—in other respects, the stranger. Most teachers, like most other people, work out a successful integration of their various role expectations.

THE TEACHER'S ROLES IN THE SCHOOL

If we shift our focus from the teacher's role in the community to the teacher's role within the school setting, we may describe the latter also as a set of subroles.

There are, first, the roles that describe the teacher in relation to other adults in the school system. The teacher is in the role of *employee* in relation to the school board. He is also in the role of *subordinate* to the principal, of *advisee* to the supervisor, of *colleague* to his fellow-teachers. That these roles are not always performed smoothly has been illustrated at earlier points in this book. Within the network of adult interaction, the teacher is in some respects in the role of *follower;* in other respects, in the role of leader or innovator. It is, however, the teacher's roles in relation to pupils that we wish to consider in more detail.

Mediator of Learning

The teacher's main role in relation to pupils, indeed the most significant of all his roles, is that of *mediator of learning*. In this role, he transmits knowledge and directs the learning process. In somewhat different terms, the main role of the teacher is to induce socially valued change in his pupils. This is at once the crux of the teaching profession and the most important criterion of the teacher's success.

In contrast to the other roles that we shall discuss presently, it is in the role of mediator of learning that the teacher tends to be most sure of himself. What is to be taught and how it is to be taught are the teacher's main stock in trade. Most of his professional training has prepared him for this role: his courses in curriculum, in methods, and in educational psychology. It is also within this role, as contrasted with others, that the teacher's behavior is the most highly ritualized and formalized. There are rules to follow and a structure within which to work. Subject matter can be defined and divided, lesson plans can be followed. There are well-defined criteria for measuring success in this role: the child can be tested and graded; and the teacher's own success is often measured in terms of the pupil's progress.

Disciplinarian

It has been said that if the teacher is to be successful in this role of facilitating learning, he must dominate the classroom situation. Domination may or may not be an integral element in the role of mediator of learning; but there is no denying that the teacher must keep some kind of order in the classroom if he is to teach, and that a second role that teachers occupy in relation to pupils is the role of *disciplinarian.*

It is this role that seems to present the most problems, especially for beginning teachers. Some complain that nowhere in their professional training were they prepared for the real problems related to maintaining order in the classroom. "Even though I had my share of practice teaching," says one young woman, "and even though there were other problems in my first year of teaching, it was my total unpreparedness in knowing what to do about discipline that was my big nightmare."

Keeping order is generally easy in a high-status or a conventional type of school, but it may be very difficult in an inner-city school that serves deprived children. Some teachers end a day with the feeling that they have used up most of their energy just in keeping order and that they have not had time for much real teaching. The problem of the teacher in such a situation is illustrated in the following paragraphs:

> *Fighting: howling and tearing at each other in the halls. Raw emotion, all on the surface. Corridor fighting needles the children in the room. Anything goes. "I went home for lunch and there wasn't no lunch, the gas was off. Virgil wouldn't let me in the lunch line, then he laid for me, beat me when I got back!" "That's all right, you hog all the food. I'll take y'on again if y'come on, come on!" "I ain' giving it back. It ain't yours." "I'll getcha, Bucky Blackie, I'll come back and getcha. I said you could have it yesterday, give it back, I didn't say today." "Hatchet Head! It ain't hardly yours it's Vernon's and he stoled it." And almost every child leaves in the morning with something gnawing him. Vernon is 11 and has eight brothers and sisters. Mrs. Weiss tells me this mother just returned from the hospital with a baby and at noon I say, "I hear you have a new baby brother, Vernon." He stares me straight in the eye, tears starting into his. "I do not," he answers.*
>
> *Mutual misery, mutual attack. Some cry all day; stay out in the hall crying, won't come in and can't tell you why. Malcolm: "Teacher, Reggie's hurtin' on Donald." Donald (hastily, scared): "No he isn't, teacher."*
>
> *Choking gutteral noises outside—not loud. In the corridor a third grade girl, low-slung, stocky, is slugging a fifth grade boy. Her eyes are cloudy; she drives her fists at him,"——off, buddy," but he gets her head and beats it against the wall. My kids rush to the door behind me, Reggie's eyes gleaming. But for once it looks so deadly, most kids are scared. The boy and girl are ringed. A boy says, "She turnin' him on, let her get what he give her. She gotta learn to defend herself." The boy is socking her in the throat. (Greene and Ryan, 1965, pp. 170–171.)*

An eighth grade teacher says,

The emotional problems that these kids have are beyond the scope of the schools. Each moment I have to spend just sitting on them. To tell you the truth, they get to the seventh and eighth grade and the teachers just can't handle them. It's not that we don't understand the reasons for their behavior. Sure, we understand the reasons for their behavior. Even though we have all the understanding in the world, the behavior in the classroom hinders the teacher and this is the most important part.

In only some classrooms, of course, does the problem of discipline take the acute forms just described; but the role of disciplinarian troubles teachers in other types of situations as well. Whether a teacher is strict or lenient is not so much the issue; in more general terms it is the problem of role definition: How is the teacher to regard himself in the role of disciplinarian? What is desirable and what is undesirable behavior in the role? Questions such as these seem to be a main source of preoccupation among teachers, especially in schools that serve the so-called disadvantaged child.

Parent Substitute

A third role in interacting with children is that of *parent substitute*. This role comes to the foreground especially in the behavior of most primary teachers: helping the child with his clothing, comforting him, showing affection, praising or censuring various types of social and emotional behavior. The role is also present to greater or lesser degree in dealing with older children and adolescents.

The role of parent substitute has received increasing attention in recent years. The male teacher probably acts as often in the role of father as does the female teacher in the role of mother. One of the reasons that men have been urged to enter the teaching profession in greater numbers, especially at the elementary levels, is the belief that children stand to benefit from the presence of both father and mother figures in the school setting.

Judge

The teacher acts also in the role of *judge*. He has authority and he maintains discipline; he gives out grades and he promotes or does not promote the child. The role of judge is never confined, however, to the area of learning and academic progress. It carries over into many other aspects of the child's behavior.

As a biology project, the class had set some seeds to grow, and we had put the dishes in a dark place in the basement. One day, we went down to check.

There were several dishes on the floor that at the time seemed to have no owners—at least their owners seemed to lose interest in the sluggishly germinating seeds. I asked whether one of these owners would like to give up his dish so that Jim, who had been absent, could have his own project, too. No one immediately volunteered, but Jim turned to me and said, "Here's one that doesn't belong to anyone."

"You're sure?" I questioned, looking around for an owner to claim it.

"Sure, it's OK," said Jim.

"OK," I told him and began showing him how to prepare the dish. Just as he finished and had the seeds and blotting paper well wetted down and carefully fitted into the dish, Arthur accosted him.

"That's my dish," he cried belligerently.

"It is not, it's mine," retorted Jim.

"That's my dish, Miss Troller," Arthur cried, turning to me.

"Jim told me it didn't belong to anyone," I replied. "We found it with nothing in it and no one would claim it."

"It's mine, and I want it," pouted Arthur.

"Well, you can't have it," replied Jim. Arthur looked at me, and I made it clear I was going to uphold Jim's claim. Arthur's face fell, he hunched his shoulders in the manner of a man unfairly beaten, and left the room. A short time later, upon returning to the classroom, I found Arthur huddled with dejection in a chair far across the room from where the other boys were working. "You gave him my dish!" he accused me.

There are more colorful terms that have been used to describe the behavior of teachers as judges or disciplinarians. Thus Redl and Wattenberg have described the roles of the teacher as being, at times, that of the *referee*, or *detective*, or *policeman* (Redl and Wattenberg, 1951).

Confidante

Somewhat opposed to the roles of disciplinarian and judge is the role of friend and *confidante*. Teachers are expected to be the friends of children; to be so supportive that children will place trust and affection in the relationship; to be so sympathetic that children will confide in them.

Surrogate of Middle-Class Morality

We have spoken in the preceding section of the teacher's role in the community as a *surrogate of middle-class morality*. This is a role that the teacher is expected to uphold, not only in his personal life outside the school, but particularly in his relations with his students. This role, as any other, stems not only from the expectations held by parents and other adults in the community, but also from the expectations held by teachers and students themselves.

I took my boys one day to the Garfield Park Conservatory. We visited the Desert Room, which was full of cactuses. Many of the boys tried to find out how much the burrs on the cactuses hurt, and I neither approved nor disapproved of their attempts. Ronnie, however, gave me a few uncomfortable glances when he noticed the signs, "Do not touch or damage plant material."

Later, we were in the Palm Room, and I tried to illustrate relatedness among plants, making specific comparisons to the palm growing next to the cycad and the ferns that were growing at our feet. I turned the fern leaves over to look for spores, but there were none on these particular specimens. Remembering that a Boston fern at the door had very obvious spores, I walked the boys over to look. Turning the leaf over so the brown spots were visible, the boys remarked, "Oh, yeah!" and seemed a little impressed.

As we walked toward the door to the Jungle Room a few minutes later, Ronnie read aloud one of the several signs in the conservatory, "Do not touch or damage plant material."

"How come we were touching the plants when the sign said definitely not to?" he asked. Floyd, Eugene, and Alton looked at me quizzically.

"Yes, that's right," I answered him ambiguously.

"Well, how come you were touching the plants?" he demanded.

I told him it was permissible for the boys to do it occasionally when they were in a class with me and had a good purpose in doing so.

Ronnie could not understand my attitude, and my behavior obviously distressed him more and more until we left the greenhouse.

Individuality in Role Performance

Any given teacher will fulfill varying role expectations in a unique manner. One teacher will stress the role of disciplinarian above all others; a second will see himself primarily in the role of friend and counselor to children; a third will attempt to eliminate all but the role of mediator of learning. For every teacher, factors of personality, factors related to social origin, and factors present in the particular school setting will interact to produce comfort in one role, discomfort in another.

Not only will every teacher work out his own pattern of behavior, but individuality will even go so far as to create new and unusual roles for the teacher. This may be seen in the case of Miriam Goldman, where a unique combination of personal and social factors was involved in producing the role of gang leader:

Miriam's immigrant parents owned a small dry goods store on the lower East side of New York, and the family lived in an apartment above the store. Her parents believed in hard work, education, and social improvement. This caused her home environment to be at sharp variance with the neighborhood culture.

Miriam was the last of eight children, physically unattractive and sensitive in temperament. In an otherwise close family unit she soon won the position of ugly duckling. Frustrated by lack of parental and sibling warmth, she became hostile to the world. Her defensive aggressiveness, quick temper, and "hard" behavior, made her an accepted leader of a neighborhood gang. The new behavior patterns that she learned coincided with her deepest personality drives. Miriam's resentment of her family led to increasingly antagonistic behavior. She continued to be frustrated by lack of personal recognition; jealousy and bitterness made her more of a fighter and less acceptable to her family.

Upon graduation from high school, an uncle sent her to teachers college. He believed that her sharp mind and keen sense of humor could, in a better environment, overcome her present difficulties. Through her college friendships she joined a clique of intellectuals. She married and had a child, only to be deserted by her husband a few months later.

Faced with the need to support a son, Miriam turned to teaching. She was given an assignment teaching delinquent boys in a lower-working-class public school. This situation was one that provided challenge, utilized her skills, and rewarded her personality traits. In her own words, she "found herself."

Her social background enabled her to understand working-class motivation. She understood the obstacles to learning—how the slum child fears being taken in by the teacher or of being a softie, and, how studying can be considered a disgraceful activity.

Discipline was the major problem. At first the boys tested her by pulling knives, threatening and physically molesting her. She responded with courage, humor, and fierce anger. In time she won the respect of the class leaders. Her aggression, quick tongue, and caustic wit made her acceptable to these boys. Miriam became a most effective teacher in this siutation. To a degree she won the position of older female leader of a male gang. She could then move ahead to teaching, and to the attempt to awaken dormant intellects in these boys.

Role performance is, as we have seen, greatly influenced by various personality factors. One of these factors is age. The relation between age of teacher and age of pupil is a variable that has diverse ramifications in role performance. On the one hand, the teacher grows older while the age of his pupils tends to remain the same (as with the teacher who continues to teach in the fourth grade, year after year). Unlike the family situation, where change goes on in both parent and child simultaneously, the difference in age between teacher and child tends to increase with length of teaching experience. This affects more than one of the teacher's roles.

It is likely that the relationship between the teacher's age and his teaching success varies tremendously, depending upon the needs of a particular group of children and the types of persons who can serve them as models.

THE TEACHER AS SOCIALIZING AGENT

The teacher is the key figure in the educational system. It is the teacher's behavior in the classroom situation that must eventually be the focus of our attention if we are to understand how society through its agent, the school,

and, in turn, the school through the person of the classroom teacher, influences the lives of children. The issues we have discussed in previous
chapters of this book—how family, school, and peer group interact in the
socialization process, how the school promotes social mobility or social stability, how the teacher himself is influenced by social forces—take on reality
in terms of particular teachers interacting with particular children.

There are countless examples that could be used to illustrate how
teachers act to socialize children. Here is an example in which a teacher
taught interracial tolerance while at the same time handling a difficult problem of discipline.

*Richard returned to school after having been kept out for four months by his
father who disapproved of the fact that there were black children in our
school. The boy returned because of a court order. Although he was successful in concealing his hostile feelings in the schoolroom, he formed cliques to
fight the black children on the playground.*

*At home he reported to his father how he was attacked daily by groups of
black children. The father was enraged and came to school to complain. We
decided that the children would be observed in order to get a true picture of
the situation.*

*The first day of observation proved rewarding. A group of boys joined Rich-
ard and they ambled over to a group of black children who were playing marbles. Richard pushed Kenneth, a black boy, while his companions kicked the
marbles over the playground. There was a tussle until the teacher on duty
interfered.*

*This was reported to their home room and both sides had a chance to ex-
plain what had happened.*

"Richard and his gang pushed Kenneth and kicked our marbles around."

*"I did not. You and your gang are always jumping us and we gotta fight,"
retorted Richard.*

*Aside, Richard was told that he had been seen, and it was known that he
had started the fight. He admitted that this was true.*

*Finally the entire group was taken into the discussion. It was a delicate
subject, but a necessary one. It so happened that one little girl named Donna
volunteered to say that her father wanted her to go to our school because he
felt that his daughter should know black children. He did not want his child
to be prejudiced. Other children related stories that helped to build up good
feeling.*

*It turned out well. The black children learned that hostile feelings
existed only among a few, and that most of us liked them. The white children
became conscious that the black children had a problem, and they offered
their sympathy. The culmination was unexpected. Richard openly apologized
to the children and promised that he would not fight them again. We had no
further problems in this area for the rest of the semester.*

In this instance, the teacher has taught at least two lessons in addition to the lesson in interracial understanding: one, that the guilty person

must not shift the blame to an innocent person; second, that group discussion is an effective means of solving problems.

The following is an example taken from a guidance lesson in a fourth grade class for the intellectually gifted in a slum school in New York City. The school was dedicated to helping lower-working-class children enter into middle-class ways of life and was deliberately trying to train these children for a separation from the private world of the family to the public world outside of the school.

> Mrs. Smith, the teacher, now asks the class the following question. "A couple of weeks ago, what did you do about taking photographs?" A child replies, "First, the man told us to smile." Mrs. Smith says, "Yes, true. Where did your preparation for the picture start?" A child says, "You had to make sure you were dressed properly." A second child says, "You had to comb and brush your hair." A third child replies, "You had to ask your mother whether she wanted you to take the photograph."
>
> Mrs. Smith accepts all of these answers and comments that they are very good. "What you have told me, children, comes under the heading of GROOMING." As she speaks, she writes this word on the blackboard in capital letters. She asks the children to pronounce the word, which they do in unison. She asks them if they have ever used that word before, and many of the children indicate that they have. Mrs. Smith now writes the following heading on the blackboard: "For a good photograph we need." Under the heading, she prints the words, grooming, washing, dressing, combing, and smiling. (Eddy, 1967)

The above examples have been selected, not because they illustrate desirable or undesirable behavior in teachers, but because they illustrate the point that the teacher, in direct or indirect ways transmits not only information and knowledge, but also a wide variety of cultural values and attitudes. It is in this sense that the teacher is a potent socializing agent in the life of the child and adolescent.

LEADERSHIP IN THE CLASSROOM

The school is both an instructional institution and a custodial institution. Since school attendance is compulsory at least until midadolescence, and students are under considerable social pressure to remain in school until age 18 or 20, it is likely that some pupils will attend school under duress, and will not attempt very vigorously to learn what the school attempts to teach. Thus the school, and the teacher, have two very different functions—to control the behavior of the student and to instruct the student.

Some new teachers find that the task of controlling behavior of pupils is too difficult or too unwelcome, and they drop out of teaching. Other teachers seek positions where the task of controlling behavior is very easy, and they can concentrate most of their attention on the tasks of instruction.

The Problem of Social Control

In the case of the school, the control of students by teachers and administrators may take place in one or another of three ways:

1. Through *coercion*. The school or its representatives may control the student through punishment or threat of punishment, or through rewards such as high grades or certificates which help the student to get employment. This method does not succeed very well in achieving stable and cooperative social arrangements between teacher and pupils.
2. Through *persuasion*. In this case the teacher discusses the situation and attempts to influence the student to comply with school requirements on the basis of the student's voluntary decision. The status difference between staff and students is reduced by this method, and the conditions of school life become open to negotiation between teachers and students. However, a state of continual negotiation about the conditions of the school, the courses to be taught, the rules of class attendance, of dress, of the student press, etc., tends toward confusion and instability. It is not favored by people concerned with rational planning and efficiency of the school operations.
3. Through *legitimacy* (respect). A better solution of the problem of social control has been advocated by the German sociologist, Max Weber, and is applied to the problem of teacher-student relations by William Spady (1974). This consists of establishing the teacher in a position of *legitimate authority* in the eyes of the student. The student obeys the suggestions or demands of the teacher because he is convinced that the teacher *deserves* respect and obedience. The power to grant authority to the teacher lies with the students, and they do this on the basis of their experience with teachers and with the school. Spady's analysis of legitimacy of teacher authority will be summarized here.

The Nature of Legitimacy

The teacher gains legitimacy for his control over students through a combination of four factors—charisma, expertise, tradition, and legal authority. Every successful teacher makes his own combination.

Charisma.   A teacher with charisma has a sense of mission and an ability to use his abilities to meet the needs of his pupils. His pupils must believe that they need him. He must have great sensitivity and empathy for his students.

Expertise.   The expertise of the teacher gives him legitimacy in the eyes of his pupils because he has demonstrated to them his knowledge and technical competence. This is probably best seen in teachers of the secondary school and college level, where they are teaching subject matter that requires a great deal of study and training.

Tradition.   This rests on a respect and reverence by students for established customs and institutions. A school rule is honored by students on the basis that it has endured for a long time. Certain church schools and private schools have this kind of legitimacy in the eyes of students and their parents, perhaps more than public schools. This is a conservative influence, and has less force, currently, than the other bases of legitimacy.

Legal Authority.   An institution which has operated successfully on the basis of law or rules has legitimacy because the rules are established and have worked in the past. The school or teacher which relies on this sort of legitimacy has a clearly stated set of rules which have been worked out through experience and thus have a rational, realistic base. Students and parents who believe in law and order give legitimacy to the school and the teacher when the school meets these conditions.

Classroom Organization

Although a classroom or a school may be organized and operated on the basis of legitimacy, or persuasion, or coercion, it seems clear that legitimacy is the best basis. Because we live in a period of rapid change, legitimacy is likely to maximize expertise and charisma rather than tradition and law.

Spady (1974) has taken a different perspective, and whatever the teacher's style may be, he summarizes the qualities of an effective teacher in the modern classroom by saying that the teacher must:

1.   have something of substance and interest to say;
2.   be capable of saying it clearly and accurately;
3.   be capable of saying it in a stimulating and exciting fashion;
4.   base this communication directly on a concern for the personal welfare of each student.

Presumably from this perspective, the only forms of social control that are likely to be effective in promoting genuine student development and achievement must involve voluntary rather than involuntary compliance; and this comes most fully when the teacher's role is legitimated by both charisma and expertise.

However, almost every school will contain some pupils who will not grant legitimacy to certain teachers or to the school as a whole, even though the majority do so. The compliance of the majority is voluntary and almost automatic, but individual students will require persuasion and/or coercion.

For example, there is always a problem of maintaining legitimacy for the school or the teacher in the eyes of students who do not succeed very well in their school work. Some students are likely to refuse to give legitimacy to the school if they are continually bombarded with low grades.

For other students, there are other reasons. The student protests of the late 1960s, both in college and high school, resulted from a refusal by groups of students, usually not a majority, to believe that their needs were being met by the school or by certain teachers. In addition, some protests were ways of showing student dissatisfaction with the socio-political situation outside of the school or college. Some teachers and school administrators sided with the students in these protests. In these instances, both students and teachers refused to give legitimacy to certain larger socio-political institutions, and then demonstrated this refusal by taking time away from their classes to exert pressure on the socio-political institutions. The "vacations" that some schools and colleges granted to students in the two weeks before the November, 1970 national elections were an example, as were the "teach-ins" held in many colleges and schools relative to the war in Vietnam.

Teaching Styles

As one watches teachers in different classrooms, one can see that each teacher has a style of his own not only for maintaining social control, but for carrying out other roles. Thelen has described in colorful terms a number of models that teachers seem to use:

1. *Socratic discussion.* The image is of a wise, somewhat crusty philosopher getting into arguments with more naive people. The issues discussed are known to both parties, and the arguments are primarily to clarify concepts and values.
2. *The town meeting.* The image is of a group of citizens meeting together to decide on courses of action required to solve problems.
3. *Apprenticeship.* The image is of a young person's life being "taken over" by an older person. The apprentice identifies with and imitates the master. According to this image, the child is in school to learn how to be like the teacher.
4. *Boss-employee, or army model.* The image here is of a teacher who has a higher status than pupils, and who has the power to reward or punish. He tells others what to do and how to do it; then sees that it gets done; and finally, evaluates how good a job he thinks it is. According to this image, the relationship between teacher and pupils need not be harsh or unfriendly, but it is necessary that the subordinate be dependent upon the "boss."
5. *The business deal.* This is essentially the "contract plan" in which the teacher makes the best deal he can with each individual student and consults with him as the work proceeds.
6. *The good old team.* The image is of a group of players listening to the coach between quarters of the football game.

7. *The guided tour.* The image here is of a group of interested children following closely behind a mature guide, who, from time to time, calls their attention to objects he wants to tell them about. He gives information, stories and opinions; he also answers questions. He maintains order, and sees to it that the number of children who arrive home equals the number who set out in the morning. (Adapted from Thelen, 1954, pp. 36–39.)

Fulfilling the Roles of the Teacher

The foregoing analysis of the teacher's job has stressed the complexities of the various roles and subroles that teachers carry out in the school. Here, as before, the important point is not so much the conflicts that may arise from this complexity, but the resolution of conflict and the integration of varying role expectations. Waller, who differentiated between what he called the authoritative role of the teacher, on the one hand, and the personal roles of the teacher, on the other, stated this point well:

> When we analyze the classroom activities of a good teacher, we find that he alternates the authoritative role with personal roles, and *lengthens and shortens the rubber band of social distance* with consummate art [italics ours].
>
> The good teacher makes such adjustments as we have described without reflection and almost without awareness. As if by a sort of instinct, he knows when to be cold and distant and when to be warm and personal, when to tighten up and when to relax, when to pat a boy on the back and when to be ruthlessly severe. He also knows what kind of classroom deviation he must suppress as likely to disrupt equilibrium and threaten control and what kinds he can afford to tolerate. He knows when to enforce his rules and when to look the other way. But it is not really instinct that guides him, nor yet reason; it is habit. From a thousand trials and a hundred errors, from a thousand crises met and mastered, he has gained the sort of unreflective wisdom that is better than conscious principle as a guide to action, better because it acts quicker and more surely. In other words, the good teacher has so completely absorbed the teacher's roles that his personality is perfectly adjusted to the classroom situation. It has become as natural and easy for him to teach and to control a class as to breathe or eat his dinner. Only when the teacher has attained this complete adjustment of his personality to his job can we say that he has really learned his art. (Waller, 1942, pp. 212, 214.)

RESEARCH ON TEACHING BEHAVIOR

The past 15 years have seen a great deal of systematic study of behavior of teachers in the classroom, related to student behavior and to student achievement. Working independently, Bush and Ryans studied the classroom behavior of hundreds of teachers in elementary and secondary schools. Using different statistical methods, they emerged with three very similar *patterns* of teacher behavior. These are:

	Ryans	*Bush*
X	Warm, understanding, friendly vs. aloof, egocentric, restricted	Affection, personality-oriented
Y	Responsible, businesslike, systematic vs. unplanned, evading, slipshod	Intellectual, subject matter-oriented
Z	Stimulating, imaginative, cheerful vs. dull, routine	Creative, expressive-oriented

Barak Rosenshine reviewed more than 50 correlational studies of relationships between teacher behaviors and student achievement. He grouped the teacher behaviors into what appeared to be logical categories and came out with groups very similar to those of Ryans and Bush. Also, student cognitive achievement was related to these patterns generally in the expected way. For example, Rosenshine found 17 research studies that dealt with teacher approval or disapproval-criticism. This is a part of Ryans' pattern X and Bush's affection, personality-oriented pattern. Of the 17 research studies, Rosenshine found that 12 revealed a negative relationship between frequency of teacher disapproval or criticism and student achievement; three studies gave doubtful results; and two studies showed positive relationships between teacher disapproval and student achievement.

The teacher behaviors can also usefully be grouped into three *domains* of behavior and teaching strategy. These are:

1. Social-emotional domain: indicating teacher's use of praise, punishment, creativity, and friendliness.
2. Cognitive domain: indicating teacher's intellectual emphasis and subject-matter orientation.
3. Organizational domain: indicating teacher's decisions about use of physical equipment, space, and structure of the class into work groups.

From this overview, it seems that teaching is a variegated set of activities which should depend on the personal qualities of the teacher as well as on the characteristics of the students and the type of community. There is no one *correct* way to teach. On the other hand, successful teaching requires a battery of skills and teaching methods which the teacher possesses and enjoys using. Two very different teachers are likely to teach in different ways, and they may both be successful.

Commitment to Teaching

Finally we turn to the question of teachers' morale, or satisfaction with their job. Table 20.2 reports the attitudes toward teaching of samples of public school teachers in 1961 and 1971, and indicates that more than 75 percent say they would become teachers again if they were to start their college work over. In a study of Chicago school teachers in 1964, 72 percent reported their attitudes toward their present positions as *very favorable* or *favorable*. (Havighurst, 1964, p. 344)

EXERCISES

1. Describe briefly two or three instances in which you or a teacher you know behaved toward the class in such a way as to fit the role of "surrogate of middle-class morality."

2. What do you think is the single most important role for the elementary school teacher to fulfill? Why?

3. Many educators see their role as maintainer of the status quo so far as the social-class system is concerned. Do you think this is a proper role for the educator? Why, or why not?

4. Select any two of the roles discussed in this chapter and describe how they have created a conflict for you at one time or another. What happened? How did you resolve the conflict?

5. Give an example of how a middle-class teacher became a model for a working-class child. What did the teacher do? What did the child do? Be specific.

6. Give an example at the high school level in which a teacher promotes conformity in a group of students. Be specific. Give an example in which the high school teacher promotes competitiveness.

SUGGESTIONS FOR FURTHER READING

1. For a good summary of recent research on teacher behavior in the classroom as related to student achievement, read the article by Barak Rosenshine in the *Review of Educational Research.*

2. The activity of teacher groups in local school politics is described in a book entitled *Pedagogues and Power* by Alan Rosenthal.

3. Read chapters 10 and 13 in *Mental Hygiene in Teaching* by Fritz Redl and William Wattenberg for further discussion of the teacher's roles in dealing with classroom groups. See also "The Teacher's Roles," by Willard Waller (chapter 10, in *Sociological Foundations of Education,* by J.S. Roucek and Associates); or "Role Functions of the Teacher in the Instructional Group," by William Clark Trow, chapter 3 in the NSSE 59th Yearbook, *The Dynamics of Instructional Groups.*

TABLE 20.2.   *Commitment to Teaching, by Sex and School Level. 1961 and 1971 Percentages*

Questionnaire Item: Suppose you could go back to your college days and start over again; in view of your present knowledge, would you become a teacher?

	All Teachers		Men		Women		Elementary		Secondary	
	1961	1971	1961	1971	1961	1971	1961	1971	1961	1971
Certainly would become a teacher	50	45	35	33	57	51	57	50	40	39
Probably would become a teacher	27	30	27	28	27	30	26	30	29	29
Chances about even for and against	13	13	19	17	10	11	10	10	16	16
Probably would not	8	9	13	16	6	5	5	7	11	11
Certainly would not	3	4	6	6	1	2	2	3	4	5
Number Responding—1961	1863		585		1278		1060		803	
1971	1502		515		987		791		711	

Source: NEA Research Report 1972-R-3, Table 35.
Status of the American Public School Teacher.
Copyright © 1972 by National Education Association. All rights reserved.

4. The paper by Getzels in *Society and Education: A Book of Readings* (Havig- hurst, Neugarten, and Falk) describes some of the contrasting roles which the teacher must assume and which produce inevitable conflicts.

5. A recent bestseller is the humorous book by Bel Kaufman, *Up the Down Staircase*, which describes the ups and downs of an inexperienced high school teacher in a large urban school trying to meet administrative directives as well as students' expectations as she reformulates her concept of the teacher's role. This book is the basis for a very effective motion picture film.

6. The chapter by Withall and Lewis, "Social Interaction in the Classroom," in the book edited by Gage, *Handbook of Research on Teaching*, is an excellent review of the findings from various studies of teacher-pupil interaction. See also the chapter by Medley and Mitzel, "Measuring Classroom Behavior by Systematic Observation," in the same book.

7. A new Yearbook of the National Society for the Study of Education, *The Psychology of Teaching Methods* (1976) reports research of the most recent years on the methods of classroom teaching.

8. Section 4, 5, and 6 of the book, *Readings in the Social Psychology of the Classroom*, edited by Charters and Gage, include a number of studies of teacher-student interaction in the classroom, including studies of classroom management, the control of hostility and the relief of anxiety over examinations.

CHAPTER 21

The Teaching Profession

The teaching profession has the largest membership among all professions. There are today about 22 million teachers in the world. This is approximately 1.3 percent of the world's population of people aged 20–64.

In the United States, the number of teachers is approximately 2.7 percent of the 20–64 age group.

The entire teaching corps is moving toward the conditions which will mark it as a *profession,* namely:

1. A process of formal training;
2. A body of specialized knowledge;
3. A procedure for certification or validation of membership in the profession;
4. A set of standards of performance—intellectual, practical, and ethical— which are defined and enforced by members of the profession.

When one applies these criteria to the people who are actually teaching, one sees that teachers of young children and even of adolescents could hardly be called professionals anywhere in the world before the twentieth century. It was more an art or a craft than a profession. Relatively young and untrained women and men held most of the jobs. They could "keep school" and "hear lessons" because they had been better than average pupils themselves, and had learned their art by observing and imitating their own teachers. Only the university professor and perhaps a few teachers in elite secondary schools might be called members of a profession in somewhat the same sense that medical doctors, lawyers, or priests were professionals. In their work attitudes, their relations with their clients, and their rules of ethics were different from property owners, entrepreneurs, bureaucrats, manual workers, peasant proprietors, and craftsmen.

Through the expansion and application of knowledge, the twentieth century has seen a proliferation of professions with the addition of architects, engineers, chemists, physicists, agronomists, dentists, accountants, and public administrators to the category of professional. This "professionalization" of work, or the intellectualization and rationalization of work, has not only vastly increased the proportion of people who are professionals in a modern society, but has given them a central position in the conduct of government, business, industry, and organized religion. Professionalization is a twentieth century phenomenon.

To examine the profession of teaching it is useful to answer the following questions: (1) What is the status of the profession? (2) How is the profession organized?

THE STATUS OF TEACHERS IN VARIOUS COUNTRIES

Teaching enjoys average to high status, depending on the amount of time and study devoted to preparing for it. Since preparation ranges from relatively few to many years of study in various countries and school systems and for various levels of education, there is a range of social status and a range of economic status for teachers of various kinds. Generally speaking, however, the other professions have higher salaries and higher social status than teaching.

It is customary and useful to speak of teaching students at three age levels—primary, secondary, and higher. Although the age boundaries vary from one country to another, there is enough agreement to set the division point between primary and secondary education at about age 14, and between secondary and higher education at 18 or 19.

Using these crude dividers, the UNESCO Yearbook for 1972 indicates that the teaching profession is distributed 58, 32, and 10 percent, respectively, among the three levels. These are very rough figures. They do not take account of China, with one-fifth of the world's population, nor of teachers who teach only adults, nor of other smaller groups with special teaching functions. There is also a good deal of variation in these proportions among various countries and continents. For instance, the proportions in America are 43, 35, and 22; in the Soviet Union they are approximately 70, 20, and 10; in Africa 75, 22, and 3; and in Europe 50, 42, and 8.

Economic Status

The salaries of primary and secondary school teachers have generally been relatively low until the period after 1955, when salaries increased sharply in many countries.

About 1900, primary school teachers were generally paid about the same wages as semiskilled laborers. For example, in 1890 the *maximum* salary of a primary school teacher in the Chicago public schools was $775 for a nine-month year, while the maximum for a secondary school teacher was three times as much. At that time a university professor might start with a salary of $1200 and move up with seniority and evidence of scholarship to about $3,500. By 1922, the salary scale for primary school teachers in Chicago was from $1,500 for beginning teachers to a maximum of $2,500, and for secondary school teachers the range was $2,000 to $2,800. At this time the purchasing power of the dollar was less than it had been in 1890. Still, Chicago salaries were relatively high. A study of a national sample of classroom teachers in primary and secondary schools in 1927 showed their average salary to be $1,300, compared with an average of $2,000 for all employed persons in the United States.

Teachers' salaries in Europe were relatively better than in America in 1900, partly due to the fact that many primary school teachers in Europe were men, with families to support. In general it appears that very low salaries have been paid all over the world to primary school teachers who were women and who had little training for the job. For instance, in Brazil in 1957, the average annual salary of a teacher in the official state primary school system was the equivalent of $850, while the average in private schools was $523, and the average for primary school teachers in the locally financed municipal schools was only $231. The school day in primary schools was from three to five hours, unless the school operated on a double or triple shift with multiple teachers. Thus a woman teacher, often a married woman, could look after her family and her home while holding down a teaching job.

The poorest countries have continued with relatively low teachers' salaries right up to the present. For example, in India there are many village schools with poorly trained teachers who are paid only about one-tenth as much as teachers in select city schools.

Japan is not a poor country, but its primary school teachers are paid about as much as a bank clerk, an office worker, or a salesperson in a department store. Teachers' salaries in present-day United States are discussed below.

Women and Men as Teachers

In most parts of the contemporary world there are more women than men in the teaching profession. Of the 22 million teachers, a crude estimate indicates that two-thirds are women. Most of them are primary school teachers. Only incomplete estimates are available for several countries, but Table 21.1 gives the percentages of women at the beginning of the 1970s.

Until recent years the secondary school teacher had a higher social status as well as a substantially higher salary than the primary school teacher. Secondary education was highly selective, designed for only a small fraction of the youth group, and secondary school teachers were generally university-

TABLE 21.1.   Women in the Teaching Profession: 1969

Country	Percentages of Women	
	Primary Schools	Secondary Schools
Argentina	92	60
Australia	68	48
Brazil	90 (est.)	53
England–Wales	62	40 (est.)
France	56	40
Germany–Federal Republic	54	32
Italy	77	55 (est.)
Japan	50	22
Luxembourg	52	26
Netherlands	50	22
Scotland	86	43
Soviet Union	80	68
United States	84	46

Source: UNESCO Yearbook, 1972.

trained, whereas primary school teachers were generally trained in "normal schools" often operating at the age level of secondary schools. However, in most modern countries, where universal schooling is extending into the secondary level, the distinctions in status between primary and secondary school teachers grow less. More secondary school teachers are needed and are therefore drawn from less highly educated groups. At the same time, primary school teachers are steadily increasing their training, and therefore their salary and status levels. In a growing number of countries, including Germany, England, and the United States, primary school teachers must have as much university-level training as secondary school teachers, and a single salary scale has been established, based on amount of training and years of experience. For example, in 1971 the average annual salary of elementary school teachers in the United States was 96 percent of the secondary school teachers' average. In this country the occupational status differential is being wiped out. On the other hand, France maintains two different systems of training, and has different names for the primary school teacher, "instituteur," and the secondary school teacher, "professeur."

Teachers Organizations

In most countries there is one major teachers' organization to which all or nearly all teachers belong and pay dues. Sometimes membership is obligatory, sometimes voluntary. Thus there is the National Union of Teachers in England, the Japanese Teachers Union, the relatively young Federation Generale de Enseignement in France, the Australian Teachers Union, the National Education Association in the United States. In the Soviet Union, where much of the political and social life of the people is organized around unions, there are three teachers' unions—for preschool teachers, primary and secondary school teachers, and teachers in higher education.

CHARACTERISTICS OF TEACHERS IN THE UNITED STATES

Looking at teachers the world over, we see that teaching is a heterogeneous profession. This is due to the wide differences of investment in education among various countries, as well as to variation of the individual teacher's status within a society in relation to the age level taught, the type of school or university, and the amount of training the teacher possesses. Tables 21.2, 21.3, and 21.4 give some useful information concerning the teaching profession in the United States. There has been substantial growth in numbers. The number of teachers without at least a four-year university course was down to three percent in 1971. The median age of all teachers had gone down six years between 1961 and 1971, due, of course, to the rapid expansion of en-

TABLE 21.2.   *Numbers of Teachers in the United States*

| | (thousands) | | | |
	1969	1971	1973	1980 (est.)
Elementary schools:				
Total	1,255	1,294	1,260	1,362
Public	1,108	1,124	1,120	1,241
Nonpublic	147	170	140	121
Secondary schools:				
Total	986	1,044	1,076	989
Public	906	956	1,002	918
Nonpublic	80	88	74	71
Higher education:				
Total*	390	422	433	551

* The numbers for higher education are full-time equivalents, for faculty members at the level of instructor or higher, giving instruction to resident students working toward a degree.

Source: U.S. Office of Education. *Digest of Educational Statistics, 1972, 1973 Projections of Educational Statistics to 1981–82.* 1972 Edition.

rollments which have required large numbers of new teachers. The proportion of male teachers has increased slightly in the elementary schools, but not in secondary schools. Very few women have become school administrators, though 20 percent of elementary school principals were women in 1972. On the whole, the teaching profession has been gaining status, due to more advanced training and salary gains. However, in the United States the teachers now face a crisis due to the oversupply of trained and licensed teachers.

TABLE 21.3.   Characteristics of United States Public School Teachers: 1961–71

	Percentages		
	1961	1966	1971
Highest degree			
Less than Bachelor's	15	7	3
Bachelor's	62	70	70
Master's or six years study	23	23	27
Doctors	0.4	0.1	0.4
Teaching for the first time			
Men	11	8	10
Women	7	10	9
Race			
Black	—	—	8
White	—	—	88
Other	—	—	4
Median age			
All	41	36	35
Men	34	33	33
Women	46	40	37
Contract salary mean, current dollars			
All	$5,264	$6,253	$9,261
Men	5,568	6,639	9,854
Women	5,120	6,077	8,953
Total years of teaching experience			
1	8	9	9
2	6	9	8
3–4	13	14	16
5–9	19	22	24
10–14	15	14	16
15–19	10	10	10
20 plus	28	21	18

Source: Adapted from NEA Research Report 1972-R-3. Tables 1, 5, 38, 46, and Highlights. Sample size, N = 1533. Percent responding = 84. Copyright © 1972 by National Education Association. All rights reserved.

The Oversupply of Teachers

The year 1970 saw a surplus of beginning teachers for the first time in the memory of most teachers. Basically, this was due to the fact that the postwar bulge in birthrate produced a crop of 3,800,000 twenty-two-year-olds in 1969, compared with approximately 3 million per year during the previous five years. Thus there was a sudden increase of 25 percent in the size of the age-cohort from which the college graduates come, and there was a comparable increase in the numbers of college graduates prepared to teach. But enrollments in elementary and secondary schools were not balancing off this increase. Actually, the elementary school enrollment was decreasing, due to a decreasing birthrate from 1962 to 1970. And the secondary school enrollment was due to decrease after 1973.

TABLE 21.4.   Comparison of Men and Women in United States Public School Teaching. 1961–71

| | Percentage of All Teachers | | | | | |
| | Elementary | | | Secondary | | |
Sex and Marital Status	1961	1966	1971	1961	1966	1971
Men	12	10	16	57	54	55
Men living with spouse	10	8	12	45	42	45
Women	88	90	84	43	46	45
Women living with spouse	57	60	57	25	28	30
Number reporting	1,071	1,229	807	810	1,112	726

| | Percentage, 1972 | | |
Job Assignments	Men	Women	Total Number
Classroom teachers	34	66	2,110,368
Principals			
Elementary	80	20	48,196
Junior high	97	3	9,374
Senior high	99	1	15,827
Assistant principals			
Elementary	69	31	6,483
Junior high	92	8	7,817
Senior high	94	6	13,289
Librarians	8	92	40,540
Counsellors	53	47	49,770

Source: NEA Research Report 1972-R-3. Table 40.
NEA Research Report 1973-R-5. Table 2.

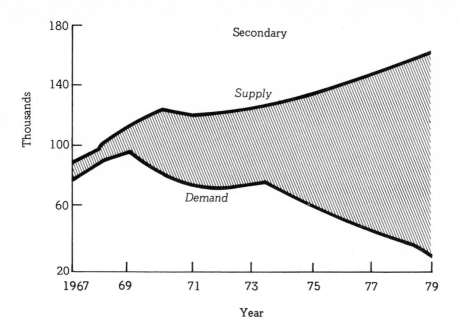

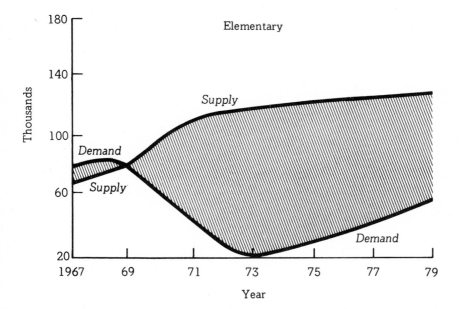

FIGURE 21.1   National supply and demand estimates for beginning teachers in public schools: 1972–1979. (*Source:* NEA *Research Bulletin*, October, 1971, Table 2, p. 71.)

The numbers of new college graduates with teachers' licenses was increasing in the 1960s and 1970s. These numbers grew from 129,000 in 1961 to 306,000 in 1971 and have been estimated to reach 397,000 in 1978. Roughly one-fourth of these people do not actually seek teaching jobs when they graduate, but this still leaves a much greater supply of people seeking jobs as teachers than the number of teaching jobs that are open. Figure 21.1 shows the relations between supply and demand for new teachers in the public elementary and secondary schools starting in 1967 and estimated to 1979. This contrasts with some 20 years of teacher shortages before 1970. The supply of beginning teachers was 88 percent of the demand in 1952, decreased to only 51 percent in 1955, then reached 99 percent in 1968. The supply is twice the demand in 1972–73, and promises to be almost three times the demand for new teachers in 1980.

Table 21.5 shows how this situation affects the young people who graduate from teacher-training institutions and are prepared to enter classrooms the following September. Normally, approximately one-fourth of this group do not seek a teaching job immediately. Some of the women get married and have children. Some of the women and men continue with graduate study or take another kind of job. But by 1970, there was a sharp drop in the proportions who secured teaching jobs with only 69 percent entering elementary and 54 percent entering secondary classrooms, and the situation was becoming worse. Clearly, this situation has an important bearing on the economic status of the teaching profession, and upon the activity of teachers' organizations.

TABLE 21.5.   Beginning Teachers in Public Schools: 1950–1972

Year	Teacher Graduates as Percent of Total Graduates with Bachelor's and First Professional Degrees			Percent of Teacher Graduates Entering Classrooms Immediately Following Graduation	
	Elementary	Secondary	Total	Elementary	Secondary
1950	6.6	20.1	26.7		
1956	13.2	18.3	31.5	81	63
1960	13.5	19.9	33.5	82	68
1966	14.1	22.2	36.3	81	67
1968	13.7	21.5	35.2	79	65
1970	13.2	21.4	34.6	69	54
1971	14.0	21.9	36.0	61	48
1972	13.7	22.4	36.1		

Source: NEA Research Report 1972-R-8. Page 9 and Table 8.
Teacher Supply and Demand in Public Schools: 1972.

THE ECONOMIC STATUS OF THE TEACHER

Teachers' salaries, in general, have been increasing markedly in recent years. From 1939 to 1960 the average annual salary of all classroom teachers increased 269 percent. For the 10 years 1949–1959, the percent of salary increase for teachers (73 percent) was greater than that for employees in manufacturing (69 percent); or for all wage and salary workers (60 percent) (NEA, May, 1960; March, 1961 II).

Salaries must be considered in relation to the purchasing power of the dollar. (Purchasing power is measured by indexes that show the change in prices from one specified date to another. Most commonly used is the Consumer Price Index of the U.S. Bureau of Labor Statistics.) Where comparisons are based upon changes in "real" purchasing power, it has been shown that there was a half century, from 1904 to 1953, in which deterioration occurred in the relative purchasing power of educators as compared to industrial workers and other occupational groups; but in the decade of the 1950s this deterioration ended (Tickton, 1961).

Table 21.6 shows how public school teachers' salaries compared with the earnings of the large group of Americans who work for salary or wages. These data are expressed in 1970–71 dollars, or dollars of constant purchasing power. It is clear that teachers have improved in salary very much since 1930, both in terms of dollars, and in relation to other members of the work force.

There were a variety of factors operating, of course, to produce this change. One was the shortage of teachers, the need to attract qualified persons to the teaching field rather than to lose them to other occupational fields. Another is that teachers have shown an increasingly higher quality of preparation over the years, and these higher standards have gained fuller public recognition.

Salaries and Other Occupational Factors

Teaching salaries must be considered, not only in overall comparisons with other occupational groups, but also in terms of their relation to other factors *within* the teaching profession.

Omitting administrators and college teachers, the difference that used to exist between elementary and secondary school teachers is disappearing as the single salary schedule is becoming the standard practice in school systems. Thus by 1954–1955, 96 percent of all school systems in communities over 2,500 in population were using salary schedules; of these, 98 percent were using the single schedule, one where salary is based upon training and experience and is not affected by grade level taught, by sex, or by marital status.

As standards are being raised for elementary teachers, and as all states

457

TABLE 21.6. *Salaries of Public School Teachers and other Workers. (In 1970–1971 Dollars)*

	1929–30	1939–40	1949–50	1959–60	1969–70*	1970–71*
Average annual salary of members of instructional staff	$3293	$4093	$5046	$6991	$9291	$9570
Average annual earnings of full-time workers for wages or salary	3214	3641	4912	6258	7704	7800
Ratio: teachers/all earners	1.02	1.13	1.03	1.12	1.20	1.23

* Partially estimated.

Source: U.S. Office of Education: *Statistics of State School Systems. Fall Statistics of Public Schools,* 1971.
  U.S. Dept. of Commerce. Office of Business Economics, *Survey of Current Business,* July issues, 1962, '66, '69, '71.

require a bachelor's degree for an elementary school certificate, the salary difference between elementary and high school teachers has narrowed. In 1950 the average annual salary of elementary school teachers was 82 percent of that of high school teachers; by 1964, it had increased to 93 percent, and in 1972 it was 95 percent. (NEA, 1973-R-3)

Differences exist between small and large communities. Teachers in the largest school systems once enjoyed a great advantage in salary over their colleagues in smaller systems; yet in recent years it has been teachers in small communities who have enjoyed the greatest gains, so that the gap is narrowing. In 1964–65, beginning teachers in school systems with over 100,000 pupils received salaries that were on the average only six percent higher than those of beginning teachers in schools of 1,200 to 2,999 pupils (NEA, October, 1964, p. 5). There are still substantial differences between salaries paid in the very largest and in the very smallest school systems, however, reflecting the inability of the smallest districts to employ fully qualified teachers.

There are also wide salary variations among the different regions of the United States, with the far West and the Midwest showing higher averages than the Southeast or the Great Plains areas. Part of these regional differences is due to the larger number of very small school districts in the less industrialized areas that accept partially prepared teachers.

Another factor is the length of time it takes the average classroom teacher to arrive at the maximum salary in the salary schedule. This period is now usually 11 or 12 years at the bachelor's degree level, 13 or 14 years at the master's level or above (NEA, December, 1964, p. 5).

In the 1950s, in an attempt to overcome teacher shortages, greater salary increases were given to beginning teachers than to experienced teachers, thus reducing the difference between minimum and maximum salaries within a given salary class. Beginning in 1960, however, while both minimum and maximum salaries were increasing, higher percents of increase were scheduled for experienced rather than for beginning teachers. Many cities also added salary classes for higher levels of preparation for those beyond the master's degree and gave greater salary recognition for experience.

At the moment, salary schedules for teachers still operate to make the teaching profession different from such other occupations as law and medicine. In the latter, after long initial periods of relatively low income, the largest economic gains tend to come in the middle and late years of the occupational career. While teachers do not typically have the long period of apprenticeship or the "early career phase" that is characteristic of many other professional groups, neither do they have the relatively large increments of income in their later years of teaching.

There has been a good deal of discussion in recent years over modifying salary schedules by adopting quality-of-service or "merit" provisions. Such plans attempt to reward the superior teacher by accelerating his movement up the salary scale, by placing him in a special, better paying category, or by paying him a bonus. On the whole, merit plans have proved difficult to administer, and many school systems have never implemented them or have abandoned them, largely because of difficulties in evaluating performance and because of the resentment and misunderstanding they created among the professional staff (NEA, March, 1961 I). Teachers' organizations on the whole have taken the position that such provisions are unfair and demoralizing to the profession.

Nonwage Benefits

Nonwage benefits, or so-called "fringe benefits," are another important factor in economic status. Here the teaching profession has made marked gains in recent years. In 1971, 58 percent of public school teachers had provisions that protected them from arbitrary dismissal before retirement age, and another nine percent had contracts which continued automatically from one year to the next unless explicitly terminated. Although the laws vary considerably in the protection they provide against dismissal, demotion, or reduction of salary, they nevertheless offer considerable security to an increasing proportion of teachers. Teachers in large city systems still have a decided advantage in this respect over teachers in small communities, since most large cities provide tenure that is wider in coverage and that offers a greater degree of protection than that provided in the state at large. Other security features such as pension plans and retirement plans also are growing in number at both local and state levels.

At the same time, fringe benefits have lagged as compared to those of other occupational groups. Pension and welfare funds, insurance, and other such benefits have increased much more rapidly for other groups, so that while the trend is for increased economic security for teachers, both teachers' salaries and nonwage benefits are far from equal to those of similarly qualified personnel.

PROFESSIONALIZATION

At the beginning of this chapter we called teaching a profession, but in fact, because there are varying definitions of a profession, there are differences of opinion concerning the degree to which education can properly be regarded as a profession.

Criteria for Professionalization

Usually the following criteria are used for an occupation to be considered a profession:

1. It requires high skill and intellectual effort.
2. It requires extensive formal education.
3. It involves primarily the exchange of service or advice in return for a fee or a salary, rather than the sale of goods for profit.
4. It has acquired traditions of group dignity and resistance to commercialism.

In applying these particular criteria, there can be little question that public school teaching is a profession.

Another way to look at the question of professionalization is in terms of how the work of a professional person differs from that of a nonprofessional. Because teachers are, for the most part, public employees who are not self-employed nor remunerated on the basis of fees rather than salary (the traditional position of, say, physicians or attorneys) a more salient comparison is with other similarly qualified personnel who are employed in large organizations. Table 21.7 shows the differences between a nonprofessional position in a large bureaucratic organization (such as that of cashier in a bank) and a professional position (such as that of resident physician or industrial scientist) according to the characteristics of the two types of work.

TABLE 21.7.   *Differences Between Bureaucratic and Professional Positions*

Bureaucratic	Professional
1. High degree of standardization: (a) stress on uniformity of clients' problems (b) personnel treated interchangeably (c) highly specific and uniform rules and work procedures	1. Low degree of standardization: (a) stress is upon uniqueness of clients and (b) of skills of personnel (c) diffuse and alternative rules and procedures
2. Decision-making is highly centralized: (a) little responsibility of employees for decision making (b) primary responsibility to the organization and the administration	2. Decision-making is decentralized: (a) responsibility of professional employees for making policy decisions (b) primary loyalty to clients and colleagues rather than to the organization
3. Specialization is task-oriented: (a) based primarily on practice or experience (b) involves primarily the accomplishment of a set of tasks (c) stresses efficiency and technique	3. Specialization is client-oriented: (a) based primarily on theoretical knowledge rather than practice (b) stresses competence in aiding clients rather than efficiency or technique

Source: Corwin, 1965, pp. 229–247 (adapted by the authors).

According to this analysis, the work of the professional as compared to the nonprofessional is less standardized, less centralized, and more specialized; the emphasis is upon the uniqueness of the client (in the case of the teacher, the primary client is the child); there is responsibility for policy decisions; and the work depends primarily on competence in aiding the client rather than upon the worker's efficiency or techniques.

From this point of view, it is somewhat less clear whether or not classroom teaching is to be regarded as a profession. Most of the time the teacher is on his own in the classroom and is generally free to develop his own teaching techniques. At the same time, he is bound to a standard curriculum, his work is evaluated by an administrator or administrative staff, and, as an employee, he is obligated to implement the policies of the administration and the board of education, policies which, in the typical case, he had little or no voice in determining.

The Professional Organization

Still another criterion for a profession is that there be a responsible association to set standards for admission and exert control over members, based upon a code of ethics and a concept of competency. This criterion, too, is becoming applicable to the teaching profession through the growth of the National Education Association (whose membership includes school administrators as well as classroom teachers), and various other local, state, and national organizations of teachers. Of the two million teachers in American public elementary and secondary schools in 1971, 75 percent were members of state teachers' associations affiliated with the NEA, and 57 percent held membership directly in the national organization. (NEA, 1972-R-3)

On the other hand, the NEA has only recently moved to limit its active membership to qualified professionals. Before August, 1964, active membership was open to "any person actively engaged in educational service." Since that date, new active members must be qualified for full certification, must possess at least a bachelor's degree, and must be "actively engaged in educational work of a professional nature."

While current standards reflect the NEA's views concerning minimum requirements for teaching, the organization does not set minimum standards for employment. This matter rests with state boards; thus the NEA does not act to control entry into teaching. Neither does the NEA have the power to discipline teachers for professionally unethical conduct. In these ways, education is said to fall short of being a full-fledged profession.

The movement of the National Education Association toward gaining professional status for teachers has clearly made great progress since 1950, and one major factor in this progress has been the shortage of teachers. Corwin says: "Professionalism represents the efforts of a vocation to gain full control over its work and to enhance its social and economic position in the society in the process " (p. 222). The teacher shortage placed the teachers' associations in a strong bargaining position. But the teacher shortage was also a disadvantage to the professional association because it forced the employment of people who lacked full professional preparation. Now, with a teacher surplus, it may be more difficult to make economic gains, but easier to make gains in other areas of professionalization.

Trends Toward Increasing Professionalization

In recent years teachers' organizations have become much more energetic. The *New York Times*, in January, 1964, noted:

> A resurgence of militancy among the nation's public school teachers marked the year of 1963. There was mounting evidence that teachers are no longer content to rule only the classroom to which they are assigned. They want a hand in the assignment and a voice in the policy that controls their professional lives. They are not asking to run the schools, but they want their views heard and heeded.

An Office of Education bulletin, in commenting that this new militancy continued to mount during the spring of 1964, said:

> New terms have evolved for the educator's vocabulary—strikes, sanctions, mediation, professional negotiation, collective bargaining, appeal, and arbitration.

> The growing importance of the teacher organization as a vigorous, articulate, and forceful element in the improvement of working conditions for teachers is well recognized. Today's teachers are interested and increasingly active through their organizations in such matters as civil rights, academic freedom, manpower needs, and international affairs. Quite recently they have become vitally concerned about their rights and responsibilities in participating in the development of the policies and regulations which determine the conditions under which they work. (Steffensen, 1964, p. 2.)

For one thing, teachers' organizations have been asserting the right of professional educators to a voice in determining educational policy at both the state and the local level. In 1959 a special task force of the NEA's National Commission on Teacher Education and Professional Standards began drafting recommendations for further professionalization of teaching (the New Horizons Project). The final report of this group said:

> A clear distinction must be drawn between the public's responsibility for decisions on education as public policy and the public's relation to execution of that policy. When it comes to determining the means for accomplishing purposes agreed upon by the public and the profession, the public should,

with complete confidence, give autonomy to the profession. (Lindsey, 1961, pp. 22–23.)

The Representative Assembly of the NEA passed in 1962 two resolutions that read in part:

> The National Education Association insists on the right of professional associations, through democratically selected representatives using professional channels, to participate with boards of education in the determination of policies of common concern, including salary and other conditions of professional service. . . .
>
> The National Education Association believes that, as a means for preventing unethical or arbitrary policies or practices that have a deleterious effect on the welfare of the schools, professional sanctions should be invoked. These sanctions would provide for appropriate disciplinary action by the organized profession. (NEA Handbook, 1962–63, p. 64.)

These resolutions have provided the basis for the National Education Association through its state and local affiliates to move into *collective bargaining* and the use of the *teachers' strike.* Thus the NEA has confronted squarely the teachers' union in competition for the allegiance of the classroom teachers of the country.

Teachers' Unions

Although teachers' unions have been in the limelight only since the early 1960s, they have a history in the United States which spans the entire twentieth century. They arose out of situations where teachers were in dire economic and professional need. It happens also that their early development was as much a result of the leadership and initiative taken by women teachers as taken by men.

An example is seen in the creation and development of the Chicago Teachers' Federation. Founded in 1897, this began as a group of women primary teachers in the Chicago public schools. At that time there was no job tenure; there was a two-year-old pension system which was obviously actuarily unsound, and primary school salaries were very low. The leader was Margaret Haley, a dynamic Irish woman, aged 36, who had been teaching in Chicago public schools for 10 years. Within the next 15 years the Chicago Teachers' Federation made a name for itself, as it fought in the courts and in political elections to improve the economic status of Chicago teachers. In 1902, the Federation affiliated with the Chicago Federation of Labor, thereby losing some of its earliest members who could not conceive of joining a labor union. Margaret Haley was the central and controversial figure of the Federation for about 40 years. Writing in 1915 in his publication, *The Daybook,* Carl Sandburg referred to her latest victory:

Margaret Haley wins again! . . . For fifteen years, this one little woman has flung her clenched fists into the faces of contractors, school land lease-holders, tax dodgers and their politicians, fixers, go-betweens and stool pigeons. . . . Over the years the *Tribune*, the *News* and the ramified gang of manipulators who hate Margaret Haley have not been able to smutch her in the eyes of the decent men and women of this town who do their own thinking.

The American Federation of Teachers was founded in 1916, and by 1920 had 180 local branches with more than 10,000 members. But the "red scare," fear of communism that followed World War I, produced a climate of opinion that was antagonistic to organized labor, and AFT membership dropped to less than 4,000 in 1923. A few years later the tensions of the Depression brought members into the teachers' union locals, and the AFT was reorganized to facilitate further growth. In 1937, five separate local teachers groups in Chicago were fused into the Chicago Teachers Union, which became Local Number One of the American Federation of Teachers. Local Number Two was the United Teachers Federation of New York City.

By the 1950s, a number of teachers' unions as well as a number of local teachers' associations affiliated with the NEA were asking for collective bargaining with their school boards. The school boards resisted, at first, but most of those in the large and medium-sized cities eventually agreed. In many places, there was only one teachers' association, either affiliated with the NEA or with the AFT. But in some cities an election was required to determine which of two or three organizations should have the power to negotiate on behalf of all teachers. A major controversy took place in New York City in December 1961, when the United Federation of Teachers (AFT) defeated the Teachers' Bargaining Organization (NEA). The teachers' union grew stronger during the 1960s.

From this time on, collective bargaining became more and more frequent, with the bargaining agency being either a local union or a local affiliate of the State Education Association or the NEA. By 1971, approximately 70 percent of the nation's teachers were covered by collective agreements.

During the decade of the 1960s, the National Education Association and its local affiliates came to act more and more like a labor union. The NEA became more explicitly a classroom teachers' organization. Whereas before 1960 NEA national and state officers had often been school or college administrators, classroom teachers now took these positions. Administrators were seen as employers or managers, and therefore on the side of the "management." In time, the American Association of School Administrators and the National Association of Secondary School Principals changed their relationships to the NEA to one of loose "association" rather than close integration. The NASSP built its own building in a suburb of Washington, D.C., and moved out of its offices in the NEA building.

Teachers' Strikes

A strike by a group of teachers was almost unheard of before 1920, but between that year and 1960 there were a number of scattered and brief work
stoppages. These were not explicitly authorized by the NEA. Then, in 1962,
the NEA announced a policy of *professional negotiations* and *professional
sanctions* which soon were translated into *collective bargaining* and the
teachers' strike. It was clear that the threat of a strike was needed to put
power behind the teachers' representatives at the bargaining table. In 1963,
the union, the American Federation of Teachers, rescinded its no-strike policy
and recognized the right of locals to strike under certain circumstances. There
followed a threatened strike of New York teachers in 1963 and of Chicago
teachers in 1965, with generally favorable outcomes for the union. In 1964–65,
six AFT locals used the strike as a weapon in negotiations with school boards.

In response to growing militancy by teachers, the American Association of School Administrators, the National Association of Secondary School
Principals, and the National Association of Elementary School Principals
joined forces in 1970 to publish a bulletin known as *The Administrative Team.*
The second issue of that bulletin reported on "Work Stoppages and the School
Administrator." Summarizing the record of collective bargaining activity in
the 1960–70 decade, it reported three teacher strikes in 1960–61 and 180
strikes during the 1969–70 school year, with a total of 500 strikes during the
decade. More than half a million teachers took part in the strikes and more
than five million man-days of instruction were involved. Thirty-three states
and the District of Columbia experienced at least one teacher strike. Seven
states—California, Illinois, Michigan, New Jersey, New York, Ohio, and
Pennsylvania—accounted for 74 percent of the strikes. Five states experienced statewide teacher strikes: Utah, Kentucky, Florida, Pennsylvania, and
Oklahoma. The number of work stoppages in 1970–71 was 130. New York
City teachers were out on strike more than 50 school days in 1967 and 1968.
Philadelphia and Detroit suffered bitter and drawn-out strikes in 1972 and
1973 respectively.

Effectiveness of Collective Negotiations.   It has been seen in Table 21.6
that teachers' salaries increased substantially after 1955 relative to the
salaries and wages of most employed persons. This increase continued right
up to 1972. Allen W. Smith found that the ratio of public school instructional
staff salaries to the average annual earnings of production or nonsupervisory
workers rose from 1.15 in 1951–52 to 1.33 in 1961–62, when the drive for
collective negotiations by teachers began. This ratio then rose to 1.54 in
1970–71 (Smith, 1972). It is a question whether the teacher shortage alone
could have accounted for these increases, especially since the shortages
terminated rather abruptly in 1969–70. Teachers' salaries have continued to
rise since 1970, and teachers have gone on strike to support their collective
bargaining power. The effectiveness of this process will be tested severely

during the decade of the 1970s given the large surplus of teachers that will be available.

In other aspects of the teachers' work there has also been a drive to increase the power of teachers through collective bargaining. In 1962 the New York City teachers' union first established a committee to develop a plan for making recommendations on school and class size, teacher specialists, racial integration, community relationships, and instructional materials and techniques. This drive toward establishing a stronger position in the determination of educational policy and practice has become more and more significant. Problems which teachers' experience in their work now turn up at the bargaining table. For example, a survey of teachers in 1968 showed that they regarded the following problem areas to be of major importance, in the following order, for big city as against suburban districts: large class size, inadequate salary, lack of public support for schools, inadequate fringe benefits, ineffective grouping of students in classes, classroom discipline and management, inadequate assistance from specialized teachers, ineffective testing and guidance program. Collective bargaining in the 1970s is concerned with attempts to solve all of these problems.

NEA–AFT: MERGER?

Since 1961 the American Federation of Teachers has grown substantially in numbers. Its membership was 61,000 in 1961 (Megel, 1961), 110,000 in 1965, and 250,000 in 1972 (Lieberman, 1972). Membership data for 1974 are not official, but it was estimated that the AFT had about 400,000 members at that time. The National Education Association in 1971 had 1,100,000 dues-paying members and another 600,000 did not belong officially to the NEA, but belonged to state associations affiliated with the NEA.

The major strength of the AFT was in several large cities, especially New York and Chicago. Merger of AFT locals with local NEA-affiliated teachers' organizations began in 1969 in Flint, Michigan. The following year the Los Angeles AFT Local 1021 combined with the Los Angeles Association of Classroom Teachers to form the United Teachers of Los Angeles with 14,000 members. Then, in 1972, the New York City AFT merged with the New York State Teachers Association to form the New York State United Teachers. Talk of mergers in other states followed, and was regarded by pro-merger forces as the most effective way to proceed. The merger issue came into prominence in the annual meetings at the NEA in 1972 and 1973. The NEA Convention in June, 1972 voted 2 to 1 against a national merger and at the same time barred its state and local affiliates from joining with any unit of AFT which involved cooperation in the AFL-CIO. In other words, the NEA did not want to become a functioning part of the national trade union organization.

In 1973 the NEA Convention faced the issue again, in several forms. The candidates for president-elect were clear in their stands on merger. Elected by a majority of the delegates was James Harris of Iowa, who had stated his belief that "an NEA–Union merger is not in the best interests of the united teaching profession." At the same time, the NEA convention approved the *beginning* of formal discussion of merger with the AFT. Clearly, a dominant issue would be the relationship of a merged teachers' association with the AFL-CIO. The discussion was broken off in February, 1974 without a settlement.

Myron Lieberman, a professor of education in the City University of New York, has been a longtime proponent of collective bargaining and has generally been favorable but not uncritical of the AFT. In a comprehensive essay on "The Future of Collective Negotiations," he suggests that the following developments will predominate in the 1970s.

1. The widespread acceptance of collective negotiations in higher education and in nonpublic schools.
2. A trend toward regional and statewide bargaining.
3. Greater scrutiny and public regulation of the internal affairs of teacher organizations.
4. An intensive effort to organize paraprofessionals in education.
5. Greater negotiating and legislative emphasis upon organizational security, especially agency shop clauses.
6. A major effort to enact federal legislation regulating collective negotiations by state and local public employees.
7. A tendency to avoid substantial organizational expenditures for curriculum, teacher education, and other activities not central to negotiations, and a corresponding effort to have nonrepresentational services financed by the government.
8. The clarification and resolution of issues relating to elected and appointed personnel of teacher organizations; the trend will be toward the election of full-time policy-making officers and the appointment of those below the policy-making and political level.
9. A growing concern with performance contracting, voucher systems, and other institutional changes that appear likely to undermine traditional employment relationships in education.
10. Widespread internal as well as external conflict over organizational activity intended to protect teachers from discrimination by race or sex. (Lieberman, 1971, p. 215–16)

CONCLUSION

The teaching profession at the elementary and secondary school levels in the United States made important strides after 1960 toward greater economic advantages and toward power in the making of educational policy. This was due partly to the shortage of teachers which placed the teachers' organiza-tions in a favorable bargaining position. Historians will probably argue over the relative importance of the teacher shortage as against the other factors in producing the organization drive of the 1960s—factors such as the need for teachers to respond to the situation created by the civil rights movement, the entry of the federal government into the field of compensatory education for children of low-income families, and the controversy over decentralization of school government in the big cities.

In effect, in this period of great change in the educational system, the teachers put their organizations squarely behind the propositions that the profession should govern itself and should assume the responsibility for de-cisions that could best be made by professionals.

There are two contrasting views of the nature of teaching which tend to determine the importance placed on the movement toward greater profes-sionalism. They depend on the answer one gives to the question: How much difference do schools make in the lives of children and in adult outcomes? If one sees the school as primarily a convenient place for families to place their children for routine training in the basic mental skills, then the teachers' organization becomes an agency for protection and enhancement of the teach-ers' economic status. But if one sees the school as a place in which there is a complex cognitive-affective interaction between teachers and students, an interaction which has an important influence on the students' personality, intellectual development, and present and future life satisfaction, then the teachers' organization becomes professional in a much broader sense. Then it must proceed on the basis of research on teacher behavior, teaching methods, and human development, and it will necessarily become involved in the controversial areas of educational policy.

EXERCISES

1. What tenure provisions for teachers are there in your state? In your city? Describe in detail.

2. What are your views regarding teachers' unions? What are their advantages, and what are their disadvantages?

3. How do you evaluate the teachers' organizations you know best, (or the teachers' organization in your home community) in relation to the various criteria for professionalism?

4. Read the Code of Ethics of The Education Profession formulated by the Na-tional Education Association (pp. 66–68 in the NEA Handbook, 1965–66). What do you consider the most important points in the code? Why?

5. Write out the outlines for the two sides of a debate on the issue of merger of the NEA and the AFT.

6. It has been proposed that the teachers' organizations become central in a new

organization of public service employees to include such groups as post office employees, and employees of city, state, and federal governments. This new organization would not be affiliated with the AFL-CIO. How would you evaluate this kind of development?

SUGGESTIONS FOR FURTHER READING

1. The writings of Myron Lieberman give a broad base for understanding the development of teaching as a profession. One could well start by reading his *Education as a Profession*.

2. The book *Society and Education: A Book of Readings* (Havighurst, Neugarten, and Falk) includes two papers dealing with the relations of the National Education Association and the American Federation of Teachers. The one by Lieberman predicts a merger of the two organizations. The paper by Stinnett presents the case for the professional association, but balances this with an objective account of union achievement.

3. For questionnaire studies of school teachers see *The American Public School Teacher, 1970–71*, published by the Research Division of the National Education Association, and chapter 16 and appendix A of *The Public Schools of Chicago*, by Havighurst.

4. The chapter, "Teachers as Professional Employees," chapter 8 in Corwin's *A Sociology of Education*, is a penetrating discussion of various issues in professionalization. It makes the point that a fundamental tension exists between the professional's principles and the bureaucratic principles of organization that teachers are expected to follow.

Bibliography*

Abrams, Charles (1965), *The City Is the Frontier.* New York: Harper & Row, Publishers. (p. 246)

Ahlstrom, Winton M. and Robert J. Havighurst (1971), *400 Losers: Delinquent Boys in High School.* San Francisco: Jossey-Bass. (pp. 132, 204, 208, 211)

Aichhorn, August (1935), *Wayward Youth.* New York: The Viking Press, Inc.

Alexander, C. Norman, Jr., and Ernest O. Campbell (1964), "Peer Influences on Adolescent Aspirations and Attainments," *American Sociological Review, 29,* 568–75. (p. 164)

Allerbeck, Klaus R. and Leopold Rosenmayr, eds. (1971), *Aufstand der Jugend? Neue Aspekte der Jugend soziologie.* Munich: Juventa Verlag. (p. 211)

Alloway, Lawrence (1972), *Violent America: The Movies 1946–1964.* New York: Museum of Modern Art. (p. 131)

American Civil Liberties Union (1965, 1968, 1973), *Academic Freedom and Civil Liberties of Students in Colleges and Universities, 1965. Academic Freedom in the Secondary Schools, 1968. Civil Liberties of Students in Elementary Schools, 1973.* New York: American Civil Liberties Union. (p. 173)

Amidon, Edmund J., and Ned A. Flanders (1961), "The Effects of Direct and Indirect Teacher Influence on Dependent-prone Students Learning Geometry." *Journal of Educational Psychology,* 1961, 52, 286–291.

Amidon, Edmund J., and Ned A. Flanders (1963), *The Role of the Teacher in the Classroom: A Manual for Understanding and Improving Teachers' Classroom Behavior.* Minneapolis: Paul S. Amidon & Associates, Inc., 1963.

Anderson, Nels (1959), *The Urban Community: A World Perspective.* New York: Holt, Rinehart, & Winston, Inc. (p. 247)

Anderson, Scarvia, ed. (1972), *Sex Differences and Discrimination in Education.* Worthington, Ohio: Charles A. Jones Publishing Company. (p. 398)

Andersson, Bengt-Erik (1973), "Project YG—A Study of a Group of Swedish Urban Adolescents," in *Topics in Human Development,* Thomas (ed.). Basel/New York: Karger. (p. 166)

Armor, David J. (1972), "The Evidence on Busing," *The Public Interest,* 28:90–126, Summer. (p. 327)

*The page number in the brackets indicate where these references are found in the book. Where no page is cited, the reading is useful but not referred to specifically in the text.

Bibliography

Armstrong, Clairette P., and A. James Gregor (1964), "Integrated Schools and Negro Character Development: Some Considerations of the Possible Effects." *Psychiatry*, 27, 69–72.

Armstrong, W. Earl, and T. M. Stinnett (1964), *A Manual on Certification Requirements for School Personnel in the United States*. Washington, D. C.: National Commision on Teacher Education and Professional Standards, National Education Association of the United States.

Ashton-Warner, Sylvia (1972), Spearpoint: *Teacher in America*. New York: Alfred A. Knopf.

Aspira (1968), Report of the First National Conference of Puerto Ricans, Mexican-Americans, and Educators on "The Special Educational Needs of Urban Puerto Rican Youth." New York City. (pp. 364, 377)

Association of American Colleges (1974), "U.S. Laws Against Discrimination on the Job," Project on the Status and Education of Women. *Ms.*, 2 (9), March.

Astin, Alexander W. (1969), "Folklore of Selectivity," pp. 57–59 in *Saturday Review*, 52, December 20, 1969. (pp. 97, 334)

Astin, Helen S. (1970), *The Woman Doctorate in America*. New York: Russell Sage Foundation. (p. 398)

Avorn, Jerry L. *et al.* (1969), *Up Against the Ivy Wall: A History of the Columbia Crisis*. New York: Atheneum. (pp. 204, 210)

Bachman, Jerald (1971), *Youth in Transition, II: The Impact of Family Background and Intelligence on Tenth-Grade Boys*. Ann Arbor, Mich.: Survey Research Center. (p. 146)

Bagdikian, Ben H. (1964), *In the Midst of Plenty: The Poor in America*. Boston: Beacon Press. (p. 38)

Bailey, Stephen K. (1970), *Disruption in Urban Public Schools*. Reston, Va.: National Association of Secondary School Principals. (p. 172)

Bailey, Stephen K.; Macy, Francis U.; and Donn F. Vickers, (1973), *Alternative Paths to the High School Diploma*. Reston, Va.: National Association of Secondary School Principals. (p. 210)

Bailey, Wilfrid C. (1953), "The Status System of a Texas Panhandle Community," *Texas Journal of Science*, 5, 316–331. (p. 22)

Bailyn, Bernard (1960), *Education in the Forming of American Society*. New York: Vintage. (p. 85)

Ball, Samuel and Gerry Ann Bogatz (1970), *The First Year of Sesame Street: An Evaluation*. Princeton, N.J.: Educational Testing Service. (p. 130)

Banfield, Edward C. (1970), *The Unheavenly City*. Boston: Little, Brown.

Banks, James A., ed. (1973), *Teaching Ethnic Studies: Concepts and Strategies*, 43d Yearbook. Washington, D.C.: National Council for the Social Studies.

Banks, James A. (1974), *Ethnic Studies: Strategies of Teaching*. Boston: Allyn and Bacon. (p. 362)

Baratz, Joan C. (1969), "Teaching Reading in an Urban Negro School System." pp. 92–116 in *Teaching Black Children to Read*, ed. by Joan C. Baratz and Roger W. Shuy. Washington, D.C.: Center for Applied Linguistics.

Baratz, Steven S. and Joan C. Baratz (1970), "Early Childhood Intervention: The Social Science Basis of Institutional Racism," *Harvard Educational Review*, 40, 29–50. (p. 152)

Bard, Bernard (1972), "Is Decentralization Working?" *Phi Delta Kappan* 54:238—253 December, 1972.

Bardwick, Judith M. (1971), *Psychology of Women: A Study of Biocultural Conflicts.* New York: Harper and Row. (p. 398)

Barker, Roger G. (1960), "Ecology and Motivation," *Nebraska Symposium on Motivation, 1960,* Marshall R. Jones, ed. Lincoln: University of Nebraska Press. (p. 127)

Barker, Roger G., and Herbert F. Wright (1951), *One Boy's Day: A Specimen Record of Behavior.* New York: Harper & Row, Publishers. (pp. 127, 133)

Barker, Roger G., and Herbert F. Wright (1954), *Midwest and Its Children: The Psychological Ecology of an American Town.* New York: Harper & Row, Publishers. (pp. 22, 127)

Barker, Roger, *et al.* (1962), *Big School—Small School: Studies of the Effects of High School Size Upon the Behavior and Experience of Students.* Department of Psychology, University of Kansas. (p. 142)

Baroni, Msgr. Gino C. (1970), *Labor Day Statement.* Washington, D.C.: United States Catholic Conference, Division for Urban Life. (p. 369)

Barr, Robert (1973), "Whatever Happened to the Free School Movement?" *Phi Delta Kappan,* 54, 454—457. (p. 279)

Barzun, Jacques (1954), *The Teacher in America.* Garden City, N.Y.: Doubleday and Company, Inc. (p. 424)

Becker, Gary S. (1964), *Human Capital.* New York: Columbia University Press. (p. 101)

Bell, Norman, and Ezra Vogel (1961), *A Modern Introduction to the Family.* New York: The Free Press.

Bendix, Reinhard, and Seymour Lipset (1953), *Class, Status, and Power: A Reader in Social Stratification.* New York: The Free Press. (p. 37)

Berdie, Ralph F., William L. Layton, Theda Hagenah, and Edward D. Swanson (1962), Who Goes To College? Minnesota Studies in Student Personnel Work, No. 12. Minneapolis: University of Minnesota Press. (pp. 90, 97)

Bereiter, Carl (1971), "A Time to Experiment with Alternatives to Education," pp. 15—24 in *Farewell to Schools???,* edited by Daniel U. Levine and Robert J. Havighurst. Worthington, Ohio: Charles A. Jones Publishing Co. (p. 217)

Berelson, Bernard (1960), *Graduate Education in the United States.* New York: McGraw-Hill Book Company. (p. 111)

Berg, Ivar (1970), *Education and Jobs: The Great Training Robbery.* New York: Praeger. (pp. 101, 106, 111)

Berger, Bennett M. (1960), *Working Class Suburb.* Berkeley and Los Angeles: University of California Press. (p. 38)

Berkinow, Louise (1972), "Heaven Won't Protect the Working Girl," *Ms.,* Spring.

Bernard, Jessie (1964), *Academic Women.* University Park, Pa.: Pennsylvania State University Press. (p. 398)

Bernard, Jessie (1966), *Marriage and the Family among Negros.* Englewood Cliffs, N.J.: Prentice-Hall, Inc. (p. 159)

Bernard, Jessie (1971), *Women and the Public Interest: An Essay on Policy and Protest.* Chicago: Aldine-Atherton.

Bernstein, B. (1961), "Social Class and Linguistic Development: A Theory of Social Learning," *Education, Economy and Society,* A. H. Halsey, J. Floud, and C. A.

473

Anderson (eds.). New York: The Free Press. (p. 146)

Bernstein, B. (1962), "Linguistic Codes, Hesitation Phenomena, and Intelligence," *Language and Speech*, 5, 31—46.

Bernstein, Basil and D. Henderson (1969), "Social Class Differences in the Relevance of Language to Socialization." *Sociology*, 3, 1—20. (p. 146)

Bernstein, Basil (1971, 1972), *Primary Socialization, Language, and Education*. A series of Monographs, including an Overview by Bernstein, titled *Language, Social Class, and Education*. Beverly Hills, Calif.: Sage Publications.

Bernstein, Basil (1971, 1973), *Class and Control, I: Theoretical Studies towards a Sociology of Language. Class, Code and Control, II: Applied Studies towards a Sociology of Language*. London: Routledge and Kegan Paul.

Bernstein, Mildren R. H. (1959), "A Study of Teachers' Role-Expectations and Role-Perceptions of a Principal, Superintendent, and Board of Education, and the Relationship between Convergence and Divergence of Role-Expectation and Role-Perception and Teacher Morale." Unpublished doctoral dissertation, New York University.

Best, John Wesley (1948), "A Study of Certain Selected Factors Underlying the Choice of Teaching as a Profession," *Journal of Experimental Education*, XVII, 201—259. (p. 404)

Bettelheim, Bruno (1959), "Feral Children and Autistic Children," *American Journal of Sociology*, LXIV, 455—467.

Billingsley, A. (1968), *Black Families in White America*. Englewood Cliffs, N. J.: Prentice Hall. (p. 159)

Binzen, Peter (1970), *Whitetown, USA*. New York: Random House. (p. 38)

Blau, Peter M. and Otis D. Duncan (1967), *The American Occupational Structure* New York: John Wiley, pp. 423—39. (p. 56)

Blauner, Robert (1970), "Black Culture: Myth or Reality?" pp. 47—57 in Readings in Society and Education, edited by Havighurst, Neugarten, and Falk. Boston: Allyn and Bacon, 1971. Also in *Afro-American Anthology, Contemporary Perspectives*, edited by Norman E. Whitten, Jr. and John F. Szwed. New York: The Free Press, 1970.

Bleecker, Ted (1965), "New York City's Effective Schools Make History," *American Teacher Magazine*, 49, No. 4.

Bloom, Benjamin S. (1964), *Stability and Change in Human Characteristics*. New York: John Wiley & Sons, Inc. (pp. 110, 133, 145)

Bloom, Benjamin S., Allison Davis, and Robert D. Hess (1965), *Compensatory Education for Cultural Deprivation*. New York: Holt, Rinehart, and Winston, Inc. (p. 133)

Blum, Richard H. and Associates (1969), I. *Society and Drugs;* II. *Students and Drugs*. San Francisco: Jossey-Bass. (p. 211)

Blum, Richard H. and Associates (1972), *Horatio Alger's Children: Role of the Family in the Origin and Prevention of Drug Risk*. San Francisco: Jossey-Bass (p. 211)

Bogue, Donald J. (1959), *The Population of the United States*. New York: The Free Press. (p. 309)

Bollens, John C., and Henry J. Schmandt (1965), *The Metropolis*. New York: Harper & Row, Publishers. (pp. 246, 287)

Bonilla, Eduardo Seda (1972), "Cultural Pluralism and the Education of Puerto Rican Youths," *Phi Delta Kappan*, 53, 294—296, January. (p. 376)

Brim, Orville G., Jr. (1958), *Sociology and the Field of Education*. New York: Russell Sage Foundation.

Brittain, Clay V. (1963), "Adolescent Choices and Parent-Peer Cross Pressures," *American Sociological Review,* 28, 385–391.

Brogan, Denis W. (1944), *The American Character*. New York: Alfred A. Knopf, Inc.

Bronfenbrenner, Urie (1960), "Freudian Theories of Identification and Their Derivatives," *Child Development,* 31, 15–40. (p. 123)

Bronfenbrenner, Urie, (1961), "The Changing American Child—A Speculative Analysis," *Merrill-Palmer Quarterly,* 7, 73–84.

Bronfenbrenner, Urie (1970), *Two Worlds of Childhood: U.S. and U.S.S.R.* New York: Russell Sage Foundation. (p. 166)

Brophy, Jere E. and Good, Thomas L. (1974), *Teacher-Student Relationships*. New York: Holt, Rinehart, & Winston. (p. 398)

Brown, B. Frank (1973), *The Reform of Secondary Education*. New York: McGraw-Hill. (pp. 172, 210)

Bruner, Jerome S. (1971), "Poverty and Childhood." Ch. 9 in *The Relevance of Education*. New York: W. W. Norton. (p. 159)

Buck, Roy C. (1960), "The Extent of Social Participation among Public School Teachers," *Journal of Educational Sociology,* 33, 311–319. (p. 428)

Buehring, Leo E. (1958), "New Pattern: Community Schools," *The Nation's Schools*. January. (p. 221)

Burgess, Ernest W., Harvey J. Locke, and Mary Margaret Thomas (1963), *The Family*. 3rd edition. New York: American Book Co.

Burton, Roger V., and John W. M. Whiting (1961), "The Absent Father and Cross-sex Identity," *Merrill-Palmer Quarterly,* 7, 85–95. (p. 123)

Bush, Robert N. (1954), *The Teacher-Pupil Relationship*. Englewood Cliffs, N.J.: Prentice-Hall. (p. 444)

Callahan, Raymond E. (1962), *Education and the Cult of Efficiency*. Chicago: University of Chicago Press. (p. 141)

Campbell, Roald F. (1945), "Are School Boards Reactionary?" *Phi Delta Kappen,* 27, 82–83, 93.

Campbell, Roald F. (1965), "Community Extension," pp. 155–62 in *White House Conference on Education*. Washington, D.C.: U.S. Government Printing Office. (p. 284)

Caplow, Theodore (1958), *The Academic Marketplace*. New York: Basic Books, Inc. Publishers. (p. 424)

Carlson, Richard O. (1962), *Executive Succession and Organizational Change*. Chicago: Midwest Administration Center, The University of Chicago.

Carnegie Commission on Higher Education (1970a), *A Chance to Learn: An Action Agenda for Equal Opportunity in Higher Education*. New York: McGraw-Hill. (p. 111)

Carnegie Commission on Higher Education (1970b), *The Open-Door Colleges: Policies for Community Colleges*. New York: McGraw-Hill. (p. 111)

Carnegie Commission on Higher Education (1971), *New Students and New Places: Policies for the Future Growth and Development of American Higher Education*. New York: McGraw-Hill. (pp. 94, 97, 100, 104, 111)

Carnegie Commission on Higher Education (1973a), *College Graduates and Jobs:*

Adjusting to a New Labor Market Situation. New York: McGraw-Hill. (pp. 19, 111, 125)

Carnegie Commission on Higher Education (1973b), *Priorities for Action: Final Report of the Commission*. New York: McGraw-Hill. (p. 111)

Carnegie Commission on Higher Education (1973c), *Opportunities for Women in Higher Education*. New York: McGraw-Hill. (pp. 111, 384, 390, 392)

Carter, Thomas P. (1970), *Mexican Americans in School: A History of Educational Neglect*. Princeton, N.J.: College Entrance Examination Board. (p. 362)

Cartter, Allan M. (1971), "Scientific Manpower for 1970–85," *Science*, 172, 132–140.

Caughran, Roy W. (1956), "A Study of the Socio-Economic Backgrounds and the Attitudes of Illinois Public School Board Members." Unpublished doctoral dissertation, Northwestern University.

Cerych, Ladislav (1972), "A Global Approach to Higher Education," Occasional Paper No. 3. International Council on Educational Development. (p. 309)

Chafe, William H. (1972), *The American Woman: Her Changing Social, Economic, and Political Roles, 1920–1970*. New York: Oxford University Press. (p. 398)

Charters, W. W., Jr. (1963), "The Social Background of Teaching," Chapter 14 in *Handbook of Research on Teaching*, N. L. Gage, ed. Chicago: Rand McNally and Co.

Charters, W. W., Jr., and N. L. Gage (1963), *Readings in the Social Psychology of Education*. Boston: Allyn and Bacon, Inc. (pp. 85, 447)

Chinoy, Ely (1955), *Automobile Workers and the American Dream*. New York: Doubleday & Company, Inc. (p. 38)

Citizens Schools Committee of Chicago (1972), *Report*, May, p. 1.

Clapp, Elsie Ripley (1939), *Community Schools in Action*. New York: The Viking Press, Inc.

Clapp, Elsie Ripley (1952), *The Use of Resources in Education*. New York: Harper & Row, Publishers. (p. 224)

Clark, Burton R. (1960), *The Open Door College: A Case Study*. New York: McGraw-Hill. (pp. 96, 97)

Clark, Burton R. (1962), *Educating the Expert Society*. San Francisco: Chandler Publishing Co. (p. 144)

Clark, Kenneth (1965), *Dark Ghetto: Dilemmas of Social Power*. New York: Harper & Row, Publishers. (p. 151)

Clark, Kenneth B. (1971), "Educating the Disadvantaged," pp. 31–43 in *Papers on Educational Reform*. Vol. II. LaSalle, Ill.: Open Court Publishing Co. (p. 336)

Clausen, John A., and Judith R. Williams (1963), "Sociological Correlates of Child Behavior," Chapter 2 in *Child Psychology*, The 62nd Yearbook of the National Society for the Study of Education, Part I. Chicago: University of Chicago Press. (p. 132)

Clausen, J. A. (1966), "Family Structure, Socialization and Personality," pp. 1–54 in *Review of Child Development Research*, Vol. 2, edited by M. L. and L. W. Hoffman. New York: Russell Sage Foundation. (p. 158)

Clinard, Marshall B. ed. (1964), *Anomie and Deviant Behavior*. New York: The Free Press. (p. 211)

Cloward, Richard A., and Lloyd E. Ohlin (1960), *Delinquency and Opportunity: A Theory of Delinquent Gangs*. New York: The Free Press. (pp. 208, 211)

Cohen, Albert K. (1955), *Delinquent Boys: The Culture of the Gang*. New York: The

Free Press. (pp. 208, 211)

Cohen, David K. (1970a), "Immigrants and the Schools," *Review of Educational Research*, 40, 13—27. (pp. 64, 84, 380)

Cohen, David K. (1970b), "Politics and Education: Evaluation of Social Action Programs in Education," *Review of Educational Research*, 40, 213—238.

Cole, Charles C., Jr. (1955), *Encouraging Scientific Talent*. A Report to the National Science Foundation. New York: College Entrance Examination Board.

Coleman, James S. (1959), "Academic Achievement and the Structure of Competition," *Harvard Educational Review*, 29, 331—351. (p. 142)

Coleman, James S. (1960), "The Adolescent Subculture and Academic Achievement," *American Journal of Sociology*, 65, 337—347. (pp. 142, 165)

Coleman, James S. (1961a), *The Adolescent Society*. New York: The Free Press. (p. 181)

Coleman, James S., with the assistance of Kurt Johassohn and John W. C. Johnstone (1961b), *Social Climates in High Schools*. Cooperative Research Monograph No. 4, U.S. Office of Education. Washington, D.C.: U.S. Government Printing Office. (p. 165)

Coleman, James S. *et al.* (1966), *Equality of Educational Opportunity*. Washington, D.C.: U.S. Government Printing Office. (pp. 83, 346, 354)

Coleman, James S. *et al.* (1974), *Youth: Transition to Adulthood*. Report of the Panel on Youth of the President's Science Advisory Committee. Chicago and London: University of Chicago Press. (pp. 166, 183, 210)

Coleman, Richard P. and Bernice L. Neugarten (1971), *Social Status in the City*. San Francisco: Jossey-Bass. (pp. 24, 37, 55, 60)

Coleman, Richard P. (1971), "Social Mobility in a Midwestern City," pp. 30—41 in *Society and Education: A Book of Readings*, ed. by Havighurst, Neugarten, and Falk. Boston: Allyn and Bacon. (p. 60)

Coles, Robert; Brenner, Joseph H. and Dermot Meagher (1971), *Drugs and Youth: Medical, Psychiatric, and Legal Facts*. New York: Liveright. (p. 201)

College Entrance Examination Board (1970), *Report of the Commission on Tests: I. Righting the Balance*. Princeton, N.J.: The College Entrance Examination Board. (pp. 89, 391)

Colombotos, John L. (1962), *Sources of Professionalism: A Study of High School Teachers*. U.S. Office of Educational Cooperative Research Project No. 330. Ann Arbor: Department of Sociology, University of Michigan. (pp. 407, 409)

Commission on School Integration (1963), *Public School Segregation and Integration in the North*. Washington, D.C.: National Association of Intergroup Relations Officials.

Committee for Economic Development (1973), *The Management and Financing of Colleges*. New York: Committee for Economic Development. (p. 109)

Conant, James B. (1959), *The American High School*. New York: McGraw-Hill Book Co.

Conant, James B. (1961), *Slums and Suburbs*. New York: McGraw-Hill Book Co.

Conant, James B. (1963), *The Education of American Teachers*. New York: McGraw-Hill Book Co.

Conference on Economic Progress (1962), *Poverty and Deprivation in the United States*. Washington, D.C.: Conference on Economic Progress. (p. 38)

Cook, Lloyd A., and Elaine F. Cook (1950), *A Sociological Approach to Education*.

2nd edition. New York: McGraw-Hill Book Co.

Corwin, Ronald G. (1965), *A Sociology of Education.* New York: Appleton-Century-Crofts. (pp. 461, 470)

Craig, Maude M., and Selma J. Glick (1963), "Ten Years' Experience with the Glueck Social Prediction Table," *Crime and Delinquency,* July, 249–261.

Craig, Maude M., and Selma J. Glick (1964), *A Manual of Procedures for Application of the Glueck Prediction Table.* New York City Youth Board. (p. 204)

Cremin, Lawrence (1961), *The Transformation of the School.* New York: Alfred Knopf. (p. 85)

Cremin, Lawrence (1965), *The Genius of American Education.* New York: Vintage Press. (p. 85)

Cross, K. Patricia (1971), *Beyond the Open Door: New Students to Higher Education.* San Francisco: Jossey-Bass.

Cross, K. Patricia (1972), "Planning for New Students to Higher Education in the 70s," pp. 144–152 in *Educational Research: Prospects and Priorities.* Washington, D.C.: U.S. Government Printing Office. (p. 91)

Cruse, Harold (1960), *The Crisis of the Negro Intellectual.* New York: William Morrow.

Cutright, Phillip (1960), "Students' Decision to Attend College," *Journal of Educational Sociology,* 33, 292–299.

Daedalus (1962), "Youth: Change and Challenge," Winter, *Journal of the American Academy of Arts and Sciences.*

Darley, John G. (1962), "Distribution of Scholastic Ability in Higher Education." Unpublished manuscript, Center for the Study of Higher Education, University of California, Berkeley. (p. 90)

Davidson, Helen H. and Judith W. Greenberg (1969), *School Achievers from a Deprived Background.* New York: City College of the City University of New York. (p. 150)

Davis, Allison (1948), *Social-Class Influences upon Learning.* Cambridge, Mass.: Harvard University Press. (p. 84)

Davis, Allison, and John Dollard (1940), *Children of Bondage.* Washington, D.C.: American Council on Education. (p. 132)

Davis, Allison, Burleigh B. Gardner, and Mary R. Gardner (1940), *Deep South.* Chicago: University of Chicago Press.

Davis, Allison, and Robert J. Havighurst (1947), *Father of the Man.* Boston: Houghton-Mifflin Co. (p. 158)

Davis, Kingsley (1947), "Final Note on a Case of Extreme Isolation," *American Journal of Sociology,* LII, 432–437.

Davis, Susan (1972), "Organizing from Within—Justice on the Job," *Ms.,* 1 (2), August.

DeCrow, Karen (1972), "Look, Jane, Look! See Dick Run and Jump! Admire Him!" in Scarvia Anderson (ed), *Sex Differences and Discrimination in Education.* Worthington, Ohio: Charles A. Jones Publishing Co. (p. 395)

Denison, Edward F. (1964), "Measuring the Contribution of Education to Economic Growth," in *The Residual Factor and Economic Growth.* Paris: Organization for Economic Cooperation and Development. (p. 101)

Detroit Area Study (1960), "Family Income in Greater Detroit: 1951–1959." Ann

Arbor: Survey Research Center, University of Michigan.

Deutsch, Martin (1965), "The Role of Social Class on Language Development and Cognition," *American Journal of Orthopsychiatry,* 35, 78—88.

Deutsch, Martin and Bert Brown (1964), "Social Influences in Negro-White Intelligence Differences," *Journal of Social Issues,* 20, 24—35. (p. 138)

Dewey, John (1904), "The Significance of the School of Education," *Elementary School Teacher,* 4, 441—453.

Dewey, John (1915), *School and Society,* 2nd edition. Chicago: University of Chicago Press. (p. 218)

Dewhurst, J. Frederic, and Associates (1955), *America's Needs and Resources: A New Survey.* New York: The Twentieth Century Fund. (pp. 292, 309)

Dobriner, William M., ed. (1958), *The Suburban Community.* New York: G. P. Putnam's Sons. (pp. 38, 246)

Dobriner, William M. (1963), *Class in Suburbia.* Englewood Cliffs, N.J.: Prentice-Hall, Inc.

Doll, Russell (1965), "Categories of Elementary Schools in a Big City." Unpublished Working Paper. University of Chicago, Department of Education. (p. 239)

Dollard, John (1937), *Caste and Class in a Southern Town.* New Haven, Conn.: Yale University Press.

Drake, St. Clair, and Horace R. Cayton (1945), *Black Metropolis.* New York: Harcourt, Brace and World, Inc.

Dreeben, Robert (1970), *The Nature of Teaching.* Glenview, Ill.: Scott, Foresman, & Co. (p. 424)

Drucker, Peter (1971), "The Surprising Seventies," *Harper's Magazine,* July, pp. 35—39. (pp. 11, 104, 305)

Dublin, Louis I., Alfred J. Lotka, and Martin Speigelman (1949), *Length of Life.* New York: The Ronald Press. (p. 309)

Eaton, Harold E. (1956), "The Social Composition of and Attitudes toward Educational Planning of County Boards of Education in West Virginia." Unpublished doctoral dissertation, University of Pittsburgh.

Eckland, Bruce (1964), "Social Class and College Graduation: Some Misconceptions corrected, "*The American Journal of Sociology,* LXX, 36—50.

Economic Report of the President (1973), Washington, D.C.: U.S. Government Printing Office. (p. 389)

Eddy, Elizabeth M. (1965, 1967), *Walk the White Line.* New York: Doubleday & Company, Inc. (p. 439)

Educational Testing Service (1971a), "Commission on Non-Traditional Study Develops Action Program," *ETS Developments,* Vol. 18, Spring. (p. 88)

Educational Testing Service, (1971b), *Integration in Evanston, 1967—71: A Longitudinal Evaluation.* Jayjai Hsia, ed. Princeton, N.J.: ETS. (p. 323)

Eells, Kenneth, *et al.* (1951), *Intelligence and Cultural Differences.* Chicago: University of Chicago Press. (pp. 23, 69)

Elsbree, Willard S. (1939), *The American Teacher.* New York: American Book Company. (p. 403)

English, Raymond (1971), "The Split Self-Image of the United States, and Its Implications for Education," pp. 59—77 in *Papers on Educational Reform,* Vol. II. LaSalle, Ill.: Open Court Publishing Co.

Epperson, D.C. (1964), "A Reassessment of Indices of Parental Influence in 'The Adolescent Society,' " *American Sociological Review*, 29, 93—96.

Epps, Edgar G. (1972), *Black Students in White Schools*. Worthington, Ohio: Charles A. Jones Publishing Co. (p. 329)

Epstein, Cynthia F. (1971), *Woman's Place: Options and Limits in Professional Careers*. Berkeley, Calif.: University of California Press. (p. 398)

Etzioni, Amitai (1971), *Toward Higher Education in an Active Society: Three Policy Guidelines*. Parts II—IV. New York: Center for Policy Research, Columbia University. (p. 88)

Fadem, Joyce and Charles A. Duffy (1973), "The CTA Proves that Teachers Can Win at Politics." *Phi Delta Kappan*, 55, 51—54, September. (p. 429)

Fantini, Mario and Marilyn Gittell (1969), "The Ocean Hill—Brownsville Experiment." *Phi Delta Kappan*, 50:442—445. (p. 253)

Fantini, Mario; Marilyn Gittell and Richard Magat (1970), *Community Control and the Urban School*. New York: Praeger.

Fantini, Mario (1972), "Learning Options," p. 3 in *Changing Schools: An Occcasional Newsletter in Alternative Schools*. No. 002. (p. 279)

Fantini, Mario (1973), *Public Schools of Choice: Alternatives in Education*. New York: Simon and Schuster. (p. 279)

Fauman, Joseph (1958), "Occupational Selection among Detroit Jews," pp. 124—137 in *The Jews, Social Patterns of an American Group*. Marshall Sklare, ed. New York: The Free Press. (p. 53)

Featherman, David L. (1971), "The Socioeconomic Achievement of White Religio-ethnic Subgroups: Social and Psychological Explanations," *American Sociological Review*, 36, 207—222.

Firestone, Shulamith (1970), *The Dialect of Sex: The Case for Feminist Revolution*. New York: William Morrow and Co., Inc. (p. 398)

Fischer, John (1970), "Black Panthers and Their White Hero-worshippers." A review of Bobby Seale's book, *Seize the Time: The Story of the Black Panther Party and Huey P. Newton. Harper's Magazine*, August, pp. 18—26. (p. 374)

Flanagan, John C. *et al*. (1964), *The American High School Student*. Project TALENT Office, University of Pittsburgh, Pittsburgh, Pa. (p. 65)

Flanders, Ned A. (1960, 1964), "Teacher Influence on Pupil Attitudes and Achievement. Final Report, 1960." University of Minnesota, Project 397; U.S. Dept. of Health, Education, and Welfare. Cooperative Research Program, Office of Education. In Bruce J. Biddle and William J. Elena (eds.) *Contemporary Research on Teacher Effectiveness*. New York: Holt, Rinehart, & Winston, Inc.

Folger, John K., Helen S. Astin and Alan E. Bayer (1970), *Human Resources and Higher Education*. Staff Report of the Commission on Human Resources and Advanced Education. New York: Russell Sage Foundation. (pp. 85, 309, 391)

Folk, Hugh (1968), *The Transition from School to Work*. Princeton, N.J.: Woodrow Wilson School of Political and International Affairs, Industrial Relations Section. (p. 188)

Fortune, Editors of (1957), *The Exploding Metropolis*. Garden City, N.Y.: Doubleday Anchor Books. (p. 246)

Frazier, E. Franklin (1939), *The Negro Family in the United States*. Chicago: University of Chicago Press. (p. 159)

Friedan, Betty (1963), *The Feminine Mystique*. New York: Dell Publishing Co., Inc. (pp. 382, 398)

Friedenberg, Edgar Z. (1959), *The Vanishing Adolescent*. Boston: Beacon Press. (p. 181)

Friedensdorf, N. W. (1969), A Comparative Study of Counselor Attitudes toward the Further Educational and Vocational Plans of High School Girls. Purdue University Ph.D. Thesis (reproduced by University Microfilms, Inc., Ann Arbor, Michigan). (p. 395)

Fuchs, Estelle and Robert J. Havighurst (1972), *To Live on This Earth: American Indian Education*. Garden City, N.Y.: Doubleday and Company. (pp. 353, 354, 362)

Fusco, Gene C. (1964), "School-Home Partnership in Depressed Urban Neighborhoods," Bulletin No. 20, U.S. Office of Education. Washington, D.C.: U.S. Government Printing Office.

Gage, N. L., ed. (1963), *Handbook of Research on Teaching*. Chicago: Rand, McNally, & Co. (p. 447)

Gage, Nathaniel, ed. (1976), *Psychology of Teaching Methods,* NSSE Yearbook. Chicago: University of Chicago Press. (p. 447)

Galbraith, John K. (1958), *The Affluent Society*. Boston: Houghton-Mifflin Company. (pp. 13, 38)

Gallaher, Art, Jr. (1961), *Plainville Fifteen Years Later*. New York: Columbia University Press. (p. 37)

Gallup, George (1971), "Third Annual Survey of the Public's Attitudes toward the Public Schools, 1971," *Phi Delta Kappan,* 53, 33–48.

Gans, Herbert J. (1962), *The Urban Villagers*. New York: The Free Press. (p. 60)

Gans, Herbert (1967), *The Levittowners*. New York: Pantheon Books, Random House. (p. 38)

Gardner, John W.(1961), *Excellence*. New York: Harper & Row, Publishers. (p. 111)

Getzels, Jacob W., and E. G. Guba (1955), "The Structure of Roles and Role Conflict in the Teaching Situation," *Journal of Educational Sociology,* 29, 30–40. (p. 447)

Getzels, Jacob W. (1963), "Conflict and Role Behavior in the Educational Setting," pp. 309–318 in *Readings in the Social Psychology of Education,* W. W. Charters, Jr., and N. L. Gage, eds. Boston: Allyn and Bacon, Inc. (pp. 267, 447)

Getzels, J. W. (1972), "On the Transformation of Values: A Decade After Port Huron." *School Review,* 80, 505–519. (p. 10)

Gibbs, James E., Carl J. Sokolowski, August W. Steinhilber, and William C. Strasser, Jr. (1965), *Dual Enrollment in Public and Non-Public Schools*. Washington, D.C.: U.S. Office of Education. (p. 287)

Glaser, Nathan, and Daniel P. Moynihan (1963), *Beyond the Melting Pot*. Cambridge, Mass.: The MIT Press. (p. 60)

Glass, David V., ed. (1955), *Social Mobility in Britain*. New York: The Free Press. (p. 58)

Glasser, William (1972a), "The Civilized Identity Society," *Saturday Review,* February 19, pp. 26–31. (p. 194)

Glasser, William (1972b), *The Identity Society*. New York: Harper and Row. (p. 191)

Glazer, Nathan (1958), "The American Jew and the Attainment of Middle-Class Rank: Some Trends and Explanations," pp. 138–146 in *The Jews, Social Pat-*

terns of an American Group, Marshall Sklare, ed. New York: The Free Press. (p. 53)

Glidewell, John C., Mildren B. Kantor, Louis M. Smith, and Lurene H. Stringer (1966), "Socialization and Social Structure in the Classroom," in Review of Research in Child Development, edited by Martin and Lois Hoffman, 2, 221–256. New York: Russell Sage Foundation. (pp. 169, 181)

Glueck, Sheldon, and Eleanor T. Glueck (1950), Unraveling Juvenile Delinquency. New York: Commonwealth Fund. (p. 204)

Glueck, Sheldon, and Eleanor T. Glueck (1956), "Early Detection of Juvenile Delinquents," Journal of Criminal Law, Criminology, and Police Science, 47, 174–182. (p. 204)

Goldberg, M. L. et al. (1966), The Effects of Ability Grouping. New York: Teachers College Press, Columbia University. (p. 85)

Goldbloom, Maurice J. (1969), "The New York School Crisis," Commentary, 43–58, January. (p. 259)

Golden, Mark; Birns, Beverly; Bridger, Wagner; and Abigail Moss (1971), "Social Class Differentiation in Cognitive Development among Black Preschool Children." Child Development, 42, 37–45. (p. 71)

Goodman, Mitchell, ed. (1971), The Movement Toward a New America: The Beginnings of a Long Revolution. New York: A. A. Knopf. (p. 210)

Goodman, Paul (1970), The New Reformation: Notes of a Neolithic Conservative. New York: Random House. (pp. 285, 288)

Gordon, C. Wayne (1957), The Social System of the High School. New York: The Free Press. (pp. 143, 181)

Gordon, Milton M. (1964), Assimilation in American Life: The Role of Race, Religion, and Origins. New York: Oxford University Press. (pp. 38, 60, 365, 370, 381)

Gossett, Thomas F. (1963), Race: The History of an Idea in America. Dallas: Southern Methodist University Press. (p. 338)

Gottlieb, David, and Warren D. TenHouten (1965), "Racial Composition and the Social Systems of Three High Schools," Journal of Marriage and the Family, 27, 204–217.

Gottman, Jean (1961), Megalopolis: The Urbanized Northeastern Seaboard of the United States. New York: Twentieth Century Fund. (p. 246)

Great Cities' Program for School Improvement (1964), Promising Practices from The Projects for the Culturally Deprived. Chicago: Research Council of the Great Cities Program for School Improvement.

Greeley, Andrew M. (1963), Religion and Career. New York: Sheed and Ward. (p. 38)

Greeley, Andrew M. (1971), Why Can't They Be Like Us?: America's White Ethnic Groups. New York: E. P. Dutton. (p. 60)

Green, Robert L. (1974), "Northern School Desegregation: Educational, Legal, and Political Issues." Chapter 10 in Uses of the Sociology of Education, ed. by C. Wayne Gordon. Chicago: University of Chicago Press. (p. 265)

Green, Thomas (1968), Work, Leisure, and the American Schools. New York: Random House. (p. 210)

Greene, Mary Frances and Orletta Ryan (1965), The Schoolchildren: Growing Up in the Slums. New York: Pantheon Books, Inc. (p. 433)

Greenhoe, Florence (1941), *Community Contacts and Participation of Teachers*. Washington, D.C.: American Council on Public Affairs.

Greer, Colin (1970), *Cobweb Attitudes: Essays in American Education and Culture*. New York: Teachers College Press, Columbia University.

Greer, Colin (1972), *The Great School Legend: A Revisionist Interpretation of American Public Education*. New York: Basic Books. (pp. 64, 84, 380)

Griliches, Zvi (1973), "Economic Problems of Youth," in *Youth: Transition to Adulthood*, edited by James S. Coleman. Washington: U.S. Government Printing Office. (p. 188)

Gronlund, Norman E. (1959), *Sociometry in the Classroom*. New York: Harper & Row, Publishers.

Grotberg, Edith H. (1972), "Institutional Responsibilities for Early Childhood Education," Ch. 14 in NSSE Yearbook, *Early Childhood Education*. Chicago: University of Chicago Press. (p. 133)

Guthrie, James W.; Kleindorfer, George B.; Levin, Henry M.; and Robert T. Stout (1971), *Schools and Inequality*. Cambridge, Mass.: MIT Press.

Halsey, A. H., Jean Floud, and C. Arnold Anderson, eds. (1961), *Education, Economy, and Society*. New York: The Free Press.

Handlin, Oscar (1959), *The Newcomers*. Cambridge, Mass.: Harvard University Press. (pp. 60, 228, 380)

Handlin, Oscar and Mary F. Handlin (1971), *The American College and American Culture: Socialization as a Function of Higher Education*. New York: McGraw-Hill. (p. 111)

Hare, Nathan (1969), Comments in "Black Leaders Speak Out on Black Education," *Today's Education, NEA Journal*, pp. 29–30, October. (p. 332)

Harlem Youth Opportunities Unlimited, Inc. (1964), *Youth in the Ghetto*. New York:

Harrington, Michael (1962), *The Other America*. New York: Macmillan Company. (p. 38)

Harrington, Michael (1968), "The Freedom to Teach: Beyond the Panaceas," the *village VOICE*, October 3. (p. 258)

Harvey, James (1972a), "Ph.D.'s and the Marketplace," *Research Currents*, Feb., ERIC Clearinghouse on Higher Education. Washington, D.C.: American Association for Higher Education. (p. 305)

Harvey, James (1972b), "Minorities and Advanced Degrees," pp. 1–6, June 1, *Research Currents*, ERIC Clearinghouse on Higher Education. Washington, D.C.: George Washington University.

Haskins, Kenneth W. (1969), "The Case for Local Control," *Saturday Review*, Vol. 52, January 11. (p. 371)

Havighurst, Robert J. (1953), *Human Development and Education*. New York: Longmans, Green, & Company.

Havighurst, Robert J. (1960), *American Higher Education in the 1960s*. Columbus: Ohio State University Press.

Havighurst, Robert J. (1964), *The Public Schools of Chicago, A Survey for the Board of Education of the City of Chicago*. Chicago: The Board of Education of the City of Chicago. (pp. 237, 238, 405, 423, 424, 430, 445, 470)

Havighurst, Robert J., ed. (1968a), *Metropolitanism: Its Challenge to Education*. Chicago: University of Chicago Press.

Havighurst, Robert J. (1968b), "Requirements for a Valid 'New Criticism' ". *Phi Delta Kappan*, 50, 20–26, September.

Havighurst, Robert J. (1970a), "Minority Subcultures and the Law of Effect," *American Psychologist*, 25, 313–322.

Havighurst, Robert J. (1970b), "The Values of Youth," pp. 3–21 in Arthur M. Kroll, ed. *Issues in American Education*. New York: Oxford University Press.

Havighurst, Robert J. (1971a), "The Culture of Poverty," pp. 57–60 in Havighurst, Neugarten, and Falk, eds. *Society and Education: A Book of Readings*. Boston: Allyn and Bacon. (pp. 38, 159)

Havighurst, Robert J. (1971b), "Social Class Perspectives on the Life Cycle," *Human Development*, 14, 110–124. (p. 19)

Havighurst, Robert J. (1971c), "Prophets and Scientists in Education," pp. 83–93 in Levine and Havighurst, eds., *Farewell to Schools???* Worthington, Ohio: Charles A. Jones Publishing Co.

Havighurst, Robert J. (1972), "Educational Leadership for the Seventies," *Phi Delta Kappan*, 53, 403–6 March.

Havighurst, Robert J. (1973), "Opportunity, Equity, or Equality," an essay review of Jencks, *et al., Inequality, School Review*, 81, 618–633. (p. 60)

Havighurst, Robert J., and Rhea Hilkevitch (1944), "The Intelligence of Indian Children as Measured by a Performance Scale," *Journal of Abnormal and Social Psychology*, 39, 419–433.

Havighurst, Robert J., and H. G. Morgan (1951), *The Social History of a War-Boom Community*. New York: Longmans, Green, & Co. (p. 22)

Havighurst, Robert J., and Lindley J. Stiles (1961), "National Policy for Alienated Youth," *Phi Delta Kappan*, XLII, 283–291. (See also Havighurst, Neugarten, and Falk, 1967).

Havighurst, Robert J., Paul H. Bowman, Gordon F. Liddle, Charles V. Mathews, and James V. Pierce (1962), *Growing Up In River City*. New York: John Wiley & Sons, Inc. (pp. 23, 47, 84, 174, 175)

Havighurst, Robert J., Bernice L. Neugarten, and Jacqueline Falk (1967), *Society and Education: A Book of Readings*. Boston: Allyn and Bacon, Inc. (p. 38)

Havighurst, Robert J., Bernice L. Neugarten, and Jacqueline Falk (1971), *Society and Education: A Book of Readings*. 2d Edition. Boston: Allyn and Bacon. (pp. 133, 159, 210, 265, 288, 338, 381, 424, 470)

Havighurst, Robert J., Frank L. Smith and David E. Wilder (1971), "A Profile of the Large City High School," *Bulletin of the National Association of Secondary School Principals*, edited by Warren Seyfert, No. 351. (pp. 84, 210, 379)

Havighurst, Robert J., and Daniel U. Levine (1971), *Education in Metropolitan Areas*, 2d ed. Boston: Allyn and Bacon.

Havighurst, Robert J., and Philip H. Dreyer, eds. (1975), *Youth 74th Yearbook of the National Society for the Study of Education*. Chicago: University of Chicago Press.

Heath, G. Louis (1972), *Red, Brown, and Black Demands for Better Education*. Philadelphia: Westminster Press. (p. 362)

Heber, Rick; Garber, Howard; Harrington, Susan; Hoffman, Caroline; and Carol Falender (1972), *Rehabilitation of Families at Risk for Mental Retardation*. Madison, Wisconsin: Rehabilitation Research and Training Center in Mental Retardation, University of Wisconsin. (p. 122)

Hechinger, Fred M. (1971), "The Challenge: De-bureaucratizing without De-schooling," *Perspectives on Education*, Teachers College, Columbia University, pp. 1–4, Fall. (p. 286)

Henderson, Vivian W. (1971), "The black college: a look down the road," *Bulletin*, American Association of Colleges for Teacher Education, 24, 1–6. (p. 330)

Henry, Jules (1955), "Docility, or Giving Teacher What She Wants," *Journal of Social Issues*, XI, 33–41.

Henry, Jules (1963), *Culture Against Man*. New York: Random House, Inc.

Henry, William E. (1965), "Social Mobility as Social Learning: Some Elements of Change in Motive and in Social Context," in *Mobility and Mental Health*, Mildred B. Kantor, ed. New York: Charles C. Thomas.

Hentoff, Nat (1968), "Ad hoc Committee on Confusion," *the village VOICE*, Sept. 26. (p. 258)

Hentoff, Nat (1969), "Ocean Hill–Brownsville and the Future of Community Control," *Civil Liberties*, No. 260, February. (p. 258)

Herriott, Robert E., and Nancy Hoyt St. John (1966), *Social Class and the Urban School*. New York: John Wiley & Sons, Inc. (p. 84)

Hernstein, R. J. (1973), *I.Q. in the Meritocracy*. Boston: Little, Brown. (p. 85)

Hess, Robert D., and Gerald Handel (1959), *Family Worlds*. Chicago: University of Chicago Press. (p. 158)

Hess, Robert D., and David Easton (1960), "The Child's Changing Image of the President," *Public Opinion Quarterly*, 24, 632–644.

Hess, Robert D., and Virginia C. Shipman (1965), "Early Experience and the Socialization of Cognitive Modes in Children," in *Child Development*, 36, No. 4, 869–886. (pp. 145, 147)

Hess, Robert D., and Judith Torney (1967), *The Development of Political Attitudes in Children*. Chicago: Aldine. (pp. 124, 132)

Hillson, Henry T. (1963), *The Demonstration Guidance Project*. George Washington High School, New York: Board of Education.

Himmelweit, Hilde T. (1961), "The Role of Intelligence in Modifying Social Class Differences in Outlook," *Acta Psychologica*, 19, 273–281.

Hodge, Robert W., Paul M. Siegel, and Peter H. Rossi (1964), "Occupational Prestige in the United States, 1925–63," *American Journal of Sociology*, 70, 286–302. (p. 426)

Hodges, Harold M., Jr. (1968), "Peninsula People: Social Stratification in a Metropolitan Complex," pp. 1–30 in *Permanence and Change in Social Class*, edited by Clayton Lane. Cambridge, Mass.: Schenkman Publishing Company. (pp. 24, 26, 27, 28, 29, 31, 37)

Hoffman, Lois W. (1961), "The Father's Role in the Family and the Child's Peer-Group Adjustment," *Merrill-Palmer Quarterly*, 7, 97–105.

Hoffman, Martin L., and Lois W. Hoffman, eds. (1964), (1966), *Review of Child Development Research*, Vol. 1 and 2. New York: Russell Sage Foundation. (pp. 132, 181)

Hollingshead, August B. (1949), *Elmtown's Youth*. New York: John Wiley & Sons, Inc. (pp. 22, 84)

Hollinshead, Byron S. (1952), *Who Should Go to College?* New York: Columbia University Press.

Holt, John (1971), *The Underachieving School*. New York: Penguin Books.

Bibliography

Hood, Albert B., and Ralph F. Berdie (1964), "The Relationship of Ability to College Attendance," *College and University*, 39, 309–318. (p. 90)

Hoover, Edgar M., and Raymond Vernon (1959), *Anatomy of a Metropolis*. Cambridge, Mass.: Harvard University Press. (p. 246)

Horner, Matina S. (1969), "Fail: Bright Women," *Psychology Today*, 3(6), November. (p. 393)

Howe, Florence (1973), "No Ivory Towers Need Apply: Women's Studies," *Ms.*, 2, (3), September.

Hoyt, Donald P. (1965), "The Relationship between College Grades and Adult Achievement. A Review of the Literature," *ACT Reports*, No. 7. Iowa City, Iowa: American College Testing Program. (p. 105)

Hughes, Everett C. (1958), *Men and Their Work*. New York: The Free Press.

Hulburd, David (1951), *This Happened in Pasadena*. New York: The Macmillan Company. (p. 224)

Hurst, Charles G. (1969), *President's Newsletter*, Vol. 2, October 20. Chicago: Malcolm X College. (p. 332)

Husen, T., ed. (1967), *International Study of Achievement in Mathematics: A Comparison of Twelve Countries*. Vols. I and II. New York: Wiley. (p. 149)

International Work Group for Indigenous Affairs (1971), *Declaration of Barbados*. IWGIA, Frederiksholms Kanal 4A. DK 1220 Copenhagen, Denmark. (p. 378)

Jackson, Philip W. (1968), *Life in Classrooms*. New York: Holt, Rinehart, and Winston.

Jacob, Philip E. (1957), *Changing Values in College: An Exploratory Study of the Impact of College Teaching*. New York: Harper & Row, Publishers. (p. 111)

Jacobs, Jane (1961), *The Death and Life of Great American Cities*. New York: Random House, Inc.

Jamarillo, Mari-Luci (1972), "Using Cultural Differences to Improve Educational Opportunities." *Intergroup*. Newsletter of the Institute for Integration, University of California at Riverside. Vol. 2, March.

Jayasuria, D. L. (1960), "A Study of Adolescent Ambition, Level of Aspiration, and Achievement Motivation." Unpublished doctoral dissertation, London School of Economics, University of London. (p. 49)

Jencks, Christopher, and David Riesman (1968), *The Academic Revolution*. New York: Doubleday and Co.

Jencks, Christopher (1968), "Private Schools for Black Children." *New York Times Magazine*. Nov. 3, p. 30, 132–137. (p. 373)

Jencks, Christopher (1970), *A Report on Financing Elementary Education by Grants to Parents*. For the Office of Economic Opportunity, pp. 151–221 in *Education Vouchers: From Theory to Alum Rock*, edited by Mecklenburger and Hostrup. (p. 276)

Jencks, Christopher, et al. (1972), *Inequality: A Reassessment of the Effect of Family and Schooling in America*. New York: Basic Books. (pp. 50, 60, 62, 106, 111)

Jensen, Arthur R. (1968), "Social Class, Race, and Genetics: Implications for Education," *American Educational Research Journal*, 5, 1–42. (p. 70)

Jensen, Arthur R. (1969), "How Much Can We Boost IQ and Scholastic Achievement?" *Harvard Educational Review*, 39, 1–123. (p. 70)

Jensen, Arthur R. (1973), "Level I and Level II Abilities in Three Ethnic Groups," *American Educational Research Journal,* 10, 263–276. (p. 70)

Johnson, Lyndon B. (1965), Speech to Graduates of Howard University on June 4. (p. 317)

Johnson, Norman J., and Peggy R. Sanday (1971), "Subcultural Variations in an Urban Poor Population," *American Anthropologist,* 73, 128–143. (p. 315)

Johnstone, John (1961), "Social Structure and Patterns of Mass Media Consumption." Unpublished doctoral dissertation, University of Chicago.

Kagan, Jerome (1958), "The Concept of Identification," *Psychological Review,* 65, 296–305. (p. 123)

Kahl, Joseph A. (1953), "Education and Occupational Aspirations of 'Common Man' Boys," *Harvard Educational Review,* 23, 186–203.

Kahl, Joseph A. (1957), *The American Class Structure.* New York: Holt, Rinehart & Winston, Inc. (pp. 20, 37, 56, 57)

Kallen, Horace M. (1924), *Culture and Democracy in the United States.* New York: Boni and Liveright. (p. 367)

Kanowitz, Leo (1969), *Women and the Law: The Unfinished Revolution.* Albuquerque: University of New Mexico Press. (p. 398)

Katz, Irwin (1964), "Review of Evidence Relating to Effects of Desegregation on the Intellectual Performance of Negroes," *American Psychologist,* XIX, 381–399. (pp. 318, 338)

Katz, Michael (1972), *Class, Bureaucracy, and Schools: The Illusion of Educational Change in America.* New York: Praeger. (pp. 84, 101, 286)

Kaufman, Bel (1964), *Up the Down Staircase.* New York: Avon Books. (p. 447)

Keeton, M. T. (1971), *Models and Mavericks: A Profile of Private Liberal Arts Colleges.* For the Carnegie Commission on Higher Education. New York: McGraw-Hill. (p. 111)

Kelly, Delos H. (1971), "School Failure, Academic Self-Evaluation, and School Avoidance and Deviant Behavior," *Youth and Society,* Vol. 2, No. 4, 489–503.

Keniston, Kenneth (1972), *Youth and Dissent.* "Prologue" and "Epilogue." New York: Harcourt, Brace, Jovanovich. (pp. 183, 194, 209, 210)

Keppel, Francis (1966), *The Necessary Revolution in American Education.* New York: Harper & Row, Publishers.

Kerber, August, and Barbara Bommarito (1965), *The Schools and the Urban Crisis: A Book of Readings.* New York: Holt, Rinehart & Winston, Inc.

Kimball, Solon T., and James E. McClellan (1962), *Education and the New America.* New York: Random House, Inc. (p. 84)

Kinney, Lucien B. (1964), *Certification in Education.* Englewood Cliffs, N.J.: Prentice-Hall, Inc.

Klopf, Gordon, John and Israel A. Laster, eds. (1963), *Integrating the Urban School.* New York: Teachers College, Columbia University, Bureau of Publications. (p. 338)

Koerner, James D. (1963), *The Miseducation of American Teachers.* Boston: Houghton Mifflin Company.

Kohlberg, Lawrence (1966), "Moral Education in the Schools: A Developmental View," *School Review,* 74, 1–29. (p. 181)

Kohlberg, Lawrence (1973), "Implications of Developmental Psychology for Education: Examples from Moral Development," *Educational Psychologist*, 10, 2—14. (p. 184)

Kohn, Melvin L. (1959, I), "Social Class and the Exercise of Parental Authority," *American Sociological Review,* 24, 352—366.

Kohn, Melvin L. (1959, II), "Social Class and Parental Values," *American Journal of Sociology*, LXIV, 337—351.

Kohn, Melvin L. (1963), "Social Class and Parent-Child Relationships: An Interpretation," *American Journal of Sociology,* 68, 471—480. (p. 149)

Komisar, Lucy (1972), *The New Feminism.* New York: Warner Books, Inc. (p. 398)

Koontz, Elizabeth D. (1972), *Plans for Widening Women's Educational Opportunities.* Washington, D.C.: U.S. Department of Labor, Women's Bureau. (p. 396)

Kopan, Andrew, and Herbert Walberg, eds. (1974), *Rethinking Educational Opportunity.* Berkeley, Calif.: McCutchan Publishing Corporation. (p. 85)

Kratzmann, Arthur (1963), "The Alberta Teachers' Association: a Prototype for the American Scene?" *Administrator's Notebook,* XII, No. 2.

Krauss, Irving (1964), "Sources of Educational Aspirations among Working-Class Youth," *American Sociological Review,* 29, 867—879.

Kreps, Juanita (1971), *Sex in the Marketplace.* Baltimore: Johns Hopkins University Press. (p. 398)

Krug, Mark M. (1972), "White Ethnic Studies: Prospects and Pitfalls," *Phi Delta Kappan,* 53, 322—324, January. (p. 368)

Krug, Mark M. (1973), *White Ethnic Groups in America: Unity in Diversity.* New York: Doubleday and Co. (p. 368)

Kvaraceus, William D., and William E. Ulrich (1959), *Delinquent Behavior: Principles and Practices.* Washington, D.C.: National Education Association.

Kvaraceus, William D., and Walter B. Miller (1959), *Delinquent Behavior: Culture and the Individual.* Washington, D.C.: National Education Association. (pp. 205, 207, 211)

Labov, William (1972a), "Academic Ignorance and Black Intelligence," *Atlantic Monthly,* pp. 59—67, June. (p. 159)

Labov, William (1972b), *Language in the Inner City: Studies in the Black English Vernacular.* Philadelphia: University of Pennsylvania Press.

Ladd, Edward T. (1973), "Regulating Student Behavior Without Ending Up in Court," *Phi Delta Kappan,* 54, 304—309. (p. 180)

Landes, Ruth (1965), *Culture in American Education.* New York: John Wiley & Sons, Inc. (p. 38)

Landis, Paul T., and Paul K. Hatt (1954), *Population Problems.* New York: American Book Company. (p. 309)

Lane, Robert E. (1959), *Political Life.* New York: The Free Press. (p. 124)

Lawrence, Jerome, and Robert E. Lee (1955), *Inherit the Wind.* New York: Random House, Inc.

Lee, Rose Hum (1955), *The City.* Philadelphia: J. B. Lippincott Co. (p. 247)

Lenski, Gerhard (1961), *The Religious Factor.* New York: Doubleday and Co. (p. 38)

Levin, Henry M.; James W. Guthrie; George B. Kleindorfer; and Robert T. Stout (1971), "School Achievement and Post-School Success: A Review," *Review of Educational Research,* 41, 1—16. (p. 62)

Levin, Henry M. (1971), "Capital Embodiment: A New View of Compensatory Education," Education and Urban Society, 3, 301–322. May. See also Guthrie, James W. et al. (1971), Schools and Inequality. Cambridge, Mass.: MIT Press. (p. 153)

Levine, Daniel U., Edna S. Mitchell, and Robert J. Havighurst (1970), Opportunities for Higher Education in Metropolitan Area: A Study of High School Seniors in Kansas City, 1967. Bloomington, Indiana: Phi Delta Kappa. (pp. 73, 75, 92, 171)

Levine, Daniel U. (1971), "Schools in Metropolitan Kansas City," pp. 107–123 in A Profile of the Large-City High School, edited by Warren C. Seyfert. Bulletin of the National Association of Secondary School Principals, Vol. 55, No. 351.

Lewis, Claudia (1946), Children of the Cumberland. New York: Columbia University Press. (p. 138)

Lewis, Oscar (1961), Children of Sanchez. New York: Random House. (p. 137)

Lewis, Oscar (1966), La Vida. New York: Random House. (p. 137)

Lewis, Oscar (1969), "Culture and Poverty." A critical review of Charles Valentine's book with this title, Caribbean Review, No. 1, p. 5–6. (p. 138)

Lewis, W. Arthur (1969), "Black Power and the American University," University: A Princeton Quarterly, No. 40, Spring. Princeton, New Jersey. (p. 333)

Lieberman, Myron (1956), Education as a Profession. Englewood Cliffs, N.J.: Prentice-Hall, Inc. (p. 470)

Lieberman, Myron (1960), The Future of Public Education. Chicago: University of Chicago Press. (p. 470)

Lieberman, Myron (1971), "The Future of Collective Bargaining," Phi Delta Kappan, 53, 214–216, December. (p. 468)

Lieberman, Myron (1972), "The Union Merger Movement: Will 3,500,000 Teachers Put It All Together?" Saturday Review, June 24, pp. 50–56. (p. 467)

Lieberman, Myron (1973), "The 1973 NEA Convention: Confusion is King," Phi Delta Kappan, 55, 3–5, September.

Lieberson, Stanley (1963), Ethnic Patterns in American Cities. New York: The Free Press. (p. 60)

Liebow, Elliott (1967), Tally's Corner. Boston: Little, Brown.

Lindsey, Margaret (1961), New Horizons for the Teaching Profession: a Report of the Task Force on New Horizons in Teacher Education and Professional Standards. Washington, D.C.: National Commission on Teacher Education and Professional Standards, National Education Association. (p. 463)

Lippitt, Ronald, and Ralph K. White (1943), "The 'Social Climate' of children's Groups," Chapter 28 in Child Behavior and Development, Roger G. Barker, Jacob S. Kounin, and Herbert F. Wright, eds. New York: McGraw-Hill Book Company.

Lippitt, R., and Gold, M. (1959), "Classroom Social Structures as a Mental Health Problem," Journal of Social Issues, 15. (p. 394)

Lipset, Seymour M., and Reinhard Bendix (1959), Social Mobility in Industrial Society. Berkeley and Los Angeles: University of California Press.

Lombardi, John and Edgar A. Quimby (1971), "Black Studies as a Curriculum Catalyst," ERIC Clearinghouse for Junior Colleges. Topical Paper No. 22, May. Los Angeles: University of California at Los Angeles.

Lynn, Laurence E., Jr. (1973). The Effectiveness of Compensatory Education: Summary and Review of the Evidence. Unpublished Report of the Assistant

Secretary for Planning and Evaluation, U.S. Department of Health, Education and Welfare, Washington, D.C. (pp. 156–157)

Lyons, Eugene (1966), *David Sarnoff*. New York: Harper & Row, Publishers. (p. 60)

McConnell, T. R. (1961), "Problems of Distributing Students among Institutions with Varying Characteristics," *North Central Association Quarterly*, 35, 226–238.

McConnell, T. R. (1962), *A General Pattern for American Public Higher Education*. New York: McGraw-Hill Book Company. (p. 111)

McElheny, Victor K. (1970), "Aspen Technology Conference Ends in Chaos," *Science*, 169, 1187, September.

McGuire, Carson, and George D. White (1957), "Social Origins of Teachers—Some Facts from the Southwest," Chapter 3 in *The Teacher's Role in American Society*, Lindley J. Stiles, ed. 14th Yearbook of the John Dewey Society.

McKelvey, Troy V. ed. (1973), *Metropolitan School Organization*, Vol. 1. *Basic Problems and Patterns*. Vol. 2. *Proposals for Reform*. Berkeley, Calif.: McCutchan Publishing Corporation. (p. 246)

Maas, Henry S. (1951), "Some Social-Class Differences in the Family System and Group Relations of Pre- and Early Adolescents," *Child Development*, 22, 145–152.

Maccoby, Eleanor E. (1951), "Television: Its Impact on School Children," *Public Opinion Quarterly*, 15, 421–444. (p. 133)

Maccoby, Eleanor E. (1958), *Readings in Social Psychology*. New York: Holt Rinehart, & Winston, Inc. (p. 158)

Marden, Charles F. (1968), *Minorities in American Society*, 3d edition. New York: American Book Company. (p. 362)

Marin, Peter (1972), "The Free School Movement: Has Imagination Outstripped Reality?" *Saturday Review*, Vol. 55, No. 30, pp. 40–44, July 22.

Marin, Peter and Allen Y. Cohen (1971), *Understanding Drug Use. An Adult's Guide to Drugs and the Young*. New York: Harper & Row. (pp. 201, 211)

Martin, John M., and Joseph P. Fitzpatrick (1965), *Delinquent Behavior: A Redefinition of the Problem*. New York: Random House, Inc. (p. 211)

Martin, William E., and Celia Burns Stendler (1959), *Child Behavior and Development*. New York: Harcourt, Brace, & World, Inc.

Matza, David (1964), *Delinquency and Drift*. New York: John Wiley & Sons, Inc. pp. 207, 211)

Mayer, Kurt (1963), "The Changing Shape of the American Class Structure," *Social Research*, XXX, 458–468. (p. 32)

Mayer, Martin (1969), *The Teachers' Strike: New York, 1968. New York Times Magazine*, Feb. 2. New York: Harper and Row. (p. 254)

Mayor's Advisory Panel on Decentralization of the New York City Schools (1969), *Reconnection for Learning: A Community School System for New York City*. New York: Praeger. (pp. 260, 265)

Mead, Margaret (1951), *The School in American Culture*. Cambridge, Mass.: Harvard University Press. (p. 426)

Mead, Margaret and Martha Wolfenstein (1955), *Childhood in Contemporary Cultures*. Chicago: University of Chicago Press.

Mead, Margaret (1970), *Culture and Commitment: A Study of the Generation Gap*. New York: Doubleday and Co. (pp. 166, 210)

Mead, Margaret (1971), "Early Childhood Experience and Later Education in Complex Cultures," pp. 67–90 in *Anthropological Perspectives on Education,* edited by Murray Wax, *et al.* New York: Basic Books.

Mecklenburger, James A. and Richard W. Hostrup, eds. (1972), *Education Vouchers: From Theory to Alum Rock.* Homewood, Ill.: ETC Publications. (p. 276)

Medley, Donald M., and Harold E. Mitzel (1963), "Measuring Classroom Behavior by Systematic Observation," in *Handbook of Research on Teaching,* N. L. Gage, ed. Chicago: Rand, McNally, & Co.

Megel, Carl J., and Administrative Staff (1961), *Report to the Convention of the American Federation of Teachers, Philadelphia, Pennsylvania.* Chicago: American Federation of Teachers. (p. 467)

Mercer, Jane R. (1973), *Labelling the Mentally Retarded.* Berkeley: University of California Press. (p. 71)

Meriam, Lewis, ed. (1928), *The Problem of Indian Administration.* Baltimore: The Johns Hopkins Press.

Merton, Robert K., Leonard Broom, and Leonard S. Cottrell, Jr., eds. (1959), *Sociology Today.* New York: Basic Books, Inc.

Meyer, W. J. and Thompson, G. G. (1963), "Teacher Interactions with Boys as Contrasted with Girls," in Kuhlen, R. G., and Thompson, G. G. (eds.) *Psychological Studies of Human Development.* New York: Appleton. (p. 394)

Michael, Donald N. (1962), *Cybernation: The Silent Conquest.* Santa Barbara, Calif.: Center for the Study of Democratic Institutions. (p. 309)

Miles, Michael W. (1971), *The Radical Probe.* New York: Atheneum Press. (p. 210)

Miller, Daniel R., and Guy E. Swanson (1958), *The Changing American Parent.* John Wiley & Sons, Inc. (pp. 136, 158)

Miller, Herman P. (1964), *Rich Man, Poor Man: The Distribution of Income in America.* New York: Thomas Y. Crowell Company. (pp. 30, 31, 38)

Miller, S. M.; Rein, Martin; Raby, Pamela; and Bertram M. Gross (1967), "Poverty, Inequality, and Conflict," *Annals of the American Academy of Political and Social Science,* Vol. 373, 16–52.

Miller, S. M. (1969), Review of the book by Sar A. Levitan, *The Great Society's Poor Law* in *The Annals of the American Academy of Political and Social Science,* No. 385, September.

Miller, S. M. and Frank Riessman (1969a), *Social Class and Social Policy.* New York: Basic Books.

Miller, S. M. and Frank Riessman (1969b), "The Credentials Trap," pp. 69–78 in S. M. Miller and Frank Riessman, eds., *Social Class and Social Policy.* New York: Basic Books.

Miller, Walter B. (1967), *City Gangs: An Experiment in Gang Behavior.* New York: John Wiley and Sons, Inc. (p. 211)

Millett, Kate (1969), *Sexual Politics.* New York: Avon Books. (p. 383)

Mills, C. Wright (1951), *White Collar.* New York: Oxford University Press, Inc. p. 38)

Mills, Nicolaus (1974), "Community Schools: Irish, Italians, and Jews," *Society,* 11,(3), 76–84, March/April.

Minzey, Jack (1972), "Community Education: An Amalgam of Many Views," *Phi Delta Kappan,* 54, 150–153, November.

Moorefield, Thomas E., and Robert J. Havighurst (1964), "Early Marriage and Social

Mobility among Girls," Journal of the National Association of Women Deans and Counselors, XXVII, No. 4, 160–71. (p. 49)

Morgan, Robin (ed.) (1970), Sisterhood Is Powerful: An Anthology of Writings from the Women's Liberation Movement. New York: Random House, Inc. (p. 398)

Morrisett, Lloyd N. (1973), "Television Technology and the Culture of Childhood," Educational Researcher, Vol. 2, No. 12, pp. 3–5, December. (p. 131)

Morrison, J. Cayce (1958), The Puerto Rican Study. Brooklyn: New York City Board of Education.

Morsell, John A. (1973), "Ethnic Relations of the Future," pp. 84–93 in The Annals of the American Academy, Vol. 408, July. (p. 381)

Moss, Howard A. (1967), "Sex, Age, and State as Determinants of Mother-Infant Interaction," Merrill-Palmer Quarterly, 13 (1). (p. 394)

Mosteller, Frederick and Daniel P. Moynihan (1972), On Equality of Educational Opportunity. New York: Random House.

Moynihan, Daniel P. (1967), "Education of the Urban Poor," Harvard Graduate School of Education Bulletin, p. 3–13, Vol. 12. (p. 83)

Mumford, Lewis (1961), The City in History. New York: Harcourt, Brace, & World, Inc. (p. 247)

Muuss, Rolfe, ed. (1971), Adolescent Behavior and Society: A Book of Readings. New York: Random House. (p. 181)

Nam, Charles B., and Mary G. Powers (1965), "Variations in Socioeconomic Structure by Race, Residence, and the Life Cycle," American Sociological Review, 30, No. 1, 97–103.

National Academy of Sciences (1967), "Racial Studies: Academy Position on Call for New Research," Science, 158, 892–893. (p. 71)

National Advisory Commission on the Education of Disadvantaged Children (1969), Title I—ESEA. A Review and a Foreward Look. Washington, D.C.: U.S. Government Printing Office. (p. 155)

National Association of Secondary School Principals (1971), A Profile of the Large-City High School, by Robert J. Havighurst, Frank L. Smith, and David E. Wilder. Bulletin of the National Association of Secondary School Principals, No. 351, January. (pp. 232, 233, 235)

National Education Association (1951), "Schools and the 1950 Census," Research Bulletin, 29, No. 4, December. Washington, D.C. National Education Association.

National Education Association (1960), "Economic Status of Teachers in 1959–60," Research Report R8, May. Washington, D.C.: National Education Association. (p. 457)

National Education Association (1961 I), "Why Have Merit Plans for Teachers' Salaries Been Abandoned?" Research Report R3, March. Washington, D.C.: National Education Association. (p. 460)

National Education Association (1961 II), "Economic Status of Teachers in 1960–61," Research Report R4, March. Washington, D.C.: National Education Association. (p. 457)

National Education Association (1962), NEA Handbook for Local, State, and National Associations, 1962–63. Washington, D.C.: National Education Association. (p. 464)

National Education Association (1963a), *The American Public School Teacher, 1960–61*. Research Monograph 1963-M2, April. Washington, D.C.: Research Division, NEA. (p. 453)

National Education Association (1963b), *Guidelines for Professional Negotiation.* Washington, D.C.: National Education Association. (p. 464)

National Education Association (1964a), "Selected Statistics of Local School Systems, 1962–63," *Research Report R11*, August. Washington, D.C.: National Education Association.

National Education Association (1964b), "Salary Schedules for Classroom Teachers, 1964–65," *Research Report R13*, October. Washington, D.C.: National Education Association. (p. 459)

National Education Association (1964c), *Research Bulletin 42*, No. 4, December. Washington, D.C.: National Education Association. (p. 459)

National Education Association (1965a), *NEA Handbook for Local, State and National Associations, 1965–66*. Washington, D.C.: National Education Association. (p. 469)

National Education Association (1965b), *Research Bulletin*, "De Facto Segregation," 43, 35–37. Washington, D.C.: National Education Association.

National Education Association (1965c), "Oklahoma Sanctions Lifted," *The Urban Reporter*, IV, No. 2, October. Washington, D.C.: National Education Association.

National Education Association (1971a), *Schools and Cable Television*. Washington, D.C.: Division of Educational Technology, National Education Association. (p. 130)

National Education Association (1971b), *Code of Student Rights and Responsibilities*. Washington, D.C.: National Education Association. (p. 181)

National Education Association (1971c), "Teacher Job Shortage Ahead," *Research Bulletin*, October, pp. 69–74. (p. 455)

National Education Association (1972a), *Teacher Supply and Demand in Public Schools, 1972–R8*. Washington, D.C.: Research Division, National Education Association. (p. 456)

National Education Association (1972b), The American Public School Teacher, 1970–71, *NEA Research Bulletin R3*, Vol. 50, No. 1, March. (pp. 405, 424, 428, 429, 446, 453, 454, 462, 470)

National Education Association (1973), *Economic Status of the Teaching Profession: 1972–73*, Research Report 1973–R-3. Washington, D.C.: National Education Association. (p. 459)

National Education Association Journal (1969), "Black Leaders Speak Out on Black Education," *Today's Education*, October, pp. 25–32.

National Science Foundation (1971a), "Unemployment Rates for Scientists, Spring, 1971," *Science Resources Studies Highlights*. NSF 71–26. Washington, D.C.: National Science Foundation, July 2. (p. 305)

National Society for the Study of Education (1953), The Community School. Fifty-second Yearbook, Part II. Chicago: University of Chicago Press. (p. 224)

National Society for the Study of Education (1972), *Early Childhood Education*, ed. by Ira J. Gordon. Chicago: University of Chicago Press.

National Society for the Study of Education (1974), *Uses of the Sociology of Education*, ed. by C. Wayne Gordon. Chicago: University of Chicago Press. (p. 265)

National Society for the Study of Education (1975), *Youth*, ed. by Robert J. Havighurst and Philip H. Dreyer. 74th Yearbook. Chicago: University of Chicago Press. (p. 210)

National Society for the Study of Education (1976), *The Psychology of Teaching Methods*. Seventy-fifth Yearbook. Chicago: University of Chicago Press.

Neugarten, Bernice L. (1949), "The Democracy of Childhood," Chapter 5 in *Democracy in Jonesville*, W. Lloyd Warner and Associates. New York: Harper & Row, Publishers. (p. 168)

Newman, Frank (ed.) (1971), *Report on Higher Education*. Washington, D.C.: U.S. Government Printing Office. (pp. 106, 111)

Newmann, Fred M. and Donald W. Oliver (1967), "Education and Community," *Harvard Educational Review*, 37, No. 1, 61–106, Winter.

New York City (1959), *Sixtieth Annual Report of the Superintendent of Schools, School Year 1957–58*. Statistical Section. Brooklyn: Board of Education of the City of New York. (p. 230)

New York City Commission on Human Rights (1972), *Women's Role in Contemporary Society*. New York: Avon Books. (pp. 389, 398)

New York Civil Liberties Union (1969), *The Burden of Blame: A Report on the Ocean Hill—Brownsville School Controversy*. New York: Civil Liberties Union, 156 Fifth Avenue. (p. 258)

Newcomer, Mabel (1959), *A Century of Higher Education for Women*. New York: Harper and Row. (p. 398)

Nichols, Robert C. (1965), "The Financial Status of National Merit Finalists," *Science*, 149, 1071–1074. (p. 108)

Nixon, Richard (1970, 1972), Public Statements on School Desegregation. *New York Times* and other newspapers, March 25 and March 17. (p. 326)

Nobile, Philip, ed. (1971), *The Con III Controversy: The Critics Look at the Greening of America*. New York: Pocket Books. (pp. 13, 38)

Noel, Edward Warren (1962), "Sponsored and Contest Mobility in America and England: a Rejoinder to Ralph H. Turner," *Comparative Education Review*, 6, 148–151.

North, Cecil, and Paul Hatt (1949), "Jobs and Occupations: a Popular Evaluation," pp. 464–473 in *Sociological Analysis*, Logan Wilson and William A. Kolb, eds. New York: Harcourt, Brace, & World, Inc. (p. 426)

Notre Dame Journal of Education (1970), *Drugs and Education*, Special Issue, Vol. 1, No. 4, Winter. (p. 211)

Novak, Michael (1971), *The Rise of the Unmeltable Ethnics*. New York: Macmillan Co. (pp. 195, 357, 369, 381)

Odell, William R. (1965), *Educational Survey Report*. Philadelphia: Board of Education. (p. 338)

Ogden, Jean, and Jess Ogden (1947), *These Things We Tried*. Charlottesville: University of Virginia Extension, 25, No. 6 (p. 224)

Olson, Clara M., and Norman D. Fletcher (1946), *Learn and Live*. New York: Alfred P. Sloan Foundation. (p. 220)

Orfield, Gary (1973), "School Integration and Its Academic Critics: Busing Studies, Their Validity Uses," *Civil Rights Digest*, Vol. 5, No. 5, Summer. (pp. 327, 338)

Ornstein, Allan C. (1974), *Race and Politics in School/Community Organizations.* Pacific Palisades, Calif.: Goodyear Publishing Company. (p. 265)

Padilla, Elena (1958), *Up from Puerto Rico.* New York: Columbia University Press. (p. 60)

Parnes, Herbert, *et al.* (1970), *National Longitudinal Survey of Employment of Youth.* Columbus, Ohio: Ohio State University.

Parsons, Talcott, and Edward A. Shils, eds. (1952), *Toward a General Theory of Action.* Cambridge, Mass.: Harvard University Press. (p. 266)

Parsons, Talcott, and Robert F. Bales (1955), *Family Socialization and the Interaction Process.* New York: The Free Press. (p. 137)

Parsons, Talcott (1959), "The School Class as a Social System: Some of Its Functions in American Society," *Harvard Educational Review,* 29, 297–318.

Passow, A. Harry (1963), *Education in Depressed Areas.* New York: Bureau of Publications, Teachers College, Columbia University.

Passow, Harry, ed. (1971), *Urban Education in the 1970s.* New York: Teachers College Press, Columbia University. (p. 133)

Perkins, James A. (1970), "Higher Education in the 1970s," *Education Record,* 51, 246–252. (p. 87)

Peterson, Warren A. (1956), "Career Phases and Inter-Age Relationships: The Female High School Teacher in Kansas City." Unpublished doctoral dissertation, Department of Sociology, University of Chicago. (pp. 419, 421, 422)

Peterson, Warren A. (1964), "Age, Teacher's Role and the Institutional Setting," Chapter IX in *Contemporary Research on Teacher Effectiveness,* Bruce J. Biddle and William J. Elena, eds. New York: Holt, Rinehart & Winston, Inc. (p. 421)

Pettigrew, Thomas F. (1964), *Profile of the Negro-American.* Princeton, N.J.: D. Van Nostrand Co., Inc.

Pettigrew, Thomas F., and Patricia J. Pajonis (1964), "Social Psychological Considerations of Racially-Balanced Schools." Unpublished working paper prepared for the New York State Commissioner of Education. (p. 318)

Pettigrew, Thomas F. (1971), *Racially Separate or Together?* New York: McGraw-Hill. (pp. 338, 375)

Pettigrew, Thomas F.; Useem, Elizabeth L.; Normand, Clarence; and Marshall Smith. (1973), "Busing: A Review of the 'Evidence,' " *The Public Interest,* 30, 88–118, Winter. (p. 327)

Phi Delta Kappa (1963), "Educating the Culturally Deprived in the Great Cities," *Phi Delta Kappan,* 45, November.

Phi Delta Kappa (1971), "Third Annual Survey of the Public's Attitudes toward the Public Schools, 1971," *Phi Delta Kappan,* 53, 33–48, September.

Phi Delta Kappa (1972a), "The Imperatives of Ethnic Education," *Phi Delta Kappan,* Special Issue, January, Bloomington, Indiana: Phi Delta Kappa. (p. 362)

Phi Delta Kappa (1972b), "Special Issue on Community Education," *Phi Delta Kappan,* Vol. 54, No. 3, November. (p. 224)

Piaget, Jean (1932), *The Moral Judgment of the Child.* New York: Harcourt, Brace, & World, Inc. (p. 181)

Pifer, Alan (1973), *The Higher Education of Blacks in the United States.* New York: Carnegie Corporation. (p. 338)

Bibliography

Pitts, Jesse R. (1973), "On Communes: A Survey Essay," *Contemporary Sociology,* Vol. 2, No. 4, pp. 351–359. (p. 210)

Pittsburgh Board of Public Education (1965), "The Quest for Racial Equality in the Pittsburgh Public Schools," *The Annual Report for 1965.* Pittsburgh, Pa.: Board of Public Education.

Pohlmann, Vernon C. (1956), "Relationship between Ability, Socioeconomic Status, and Choice of Secondary School," *Journal of Educational Sociology,* 29, 392–397.

Pois, Joseph (1964), *The School Board Crisis: A Chicago Case Study.* Chicago: Aldine Publishing Company.

President's Task Force on Women's Rights and Responsibilities (1970), *A Matter of Simple Justice: The Report of the President's Task Force on Women's Rights and Responsibilities.* Washington, D.C.: Superintendent of Documents. (p. 392)

Project Talent (1964), *The American High School Student.* Pittsburgh: University of Pittsburgh. (p. 65)

Pugh, R. W. (1948), "A Comparative Study of the Adjustment of Negro Students in Mixed and Separate High Schools," *Journal of Negro Education,* 12, 607–616.

Rainwater, Lee, Richard P. Coleman, and Gerald Handel (1959), *Workingman's Wife.* New York: Oceana Publications, Inc. (p. 38)

Raths, Louis E., and Stephen Abrahamson (1951), *Student Status and Social Class.* Bronxville, N.Y.: Modern Educational Service.

Raup, Bruce (1936), *Education and Organized Interests in America.* New York: G. P. Putnam's Sons. (p. 224)

Reagan, Barbara B. and Maynard, Betty J. (1974), "Sex Discrimination in Universities: An Approach Through Internal Labor Market Analysis," *AAUP Bulletin,* 60, (1), March.

Redl, Fritz, and William Wattenberg (1951), *Mental Hygiene in Teaching.* New York: Harcourt, Brace & World, Inc. (pp. 435, 445)

Regier, Herold G. (1972), *Too Many Teachers: Fact or Fiction?* Bloomington, Indiana: Phi Delta Kappa.

Reich, Charles (1970), *The Greening of America.* New York: Random House. (pp. 7, 13, 38, 210)

Reissman, Leonard (1973), *Inequality in American Society: Social Stratification.* Glenview, Ill.: Scott, Foresman, and Co. (pp. 7, 60)

Richards, Louise D. (1971), "Drug-Taking in Youth," *The United Teacher,* pp. 13–20, October 31. (pp. 201, 211)

Riesman, David, *et al.,* (1950), *The Lonely Crowd,* New Haven, Conn.: Yale University Press. (pp. 12, 26, 38)

Riesman, David (1955), *Individualism Reconsidered,* New York: Free Press. (p. 421)

Riessman, Frank (1962), *The Culturally Deprived Child.* New York: Harper & Row, Publishers. (pp. 9, 133)

Roberts, Ron (1971), *The New Communes.* Englewood Cliffs, N. J.: Prentice-Hall. (p. 136)

Robinson, L. H. (1973), *Women's Studies: Courses and Programs in Higher Education,* ERIC/Higher Education Research Report No. 1, American Association for Higher Education, Washington, D.C. (p. 397)

Rogers, David (1968), *110 Livingston Street*. New York: Random House.

Rohrer, John H., and Munro S. Edmonson (1960), *The Eighth Generation*. New York: Harper & Row, Publishers. (p. 132)

Rokeach, Milton and Seymour Parker (1970), "Values as Social Indicators of Poverty and Race Relations in America," pp. 97–111 in *Annals of the American Academy of Political and Social Science*, No. 368, March.

Roper, Elmo (1949), *Factors Affecting Admission of High School Seniors to College*. Washington, D.C.: American Council on Education. (p. 111)

Rosen, Bernard C. (1959), "Race, Ethnicity, and the Achievement Syndrome," *American Sociological Review*, 24, 47–60. (p. 53)

Rosenshine, Barak (1971), *Teacher Behavior and Student Achievement*. London: National Foundation for Educational Research in England and Wales. (p. 444)

Rosenshine, Barak (1974), "Experimental Classroom Studies of Teacher Training, Teacher Behavior, and Student Achievement," *Review of Educational Research*. (in Press) (p. 445)

Rosenthal, Alan (1973), *Pedagogues and Power: Teacher Groups in School Politics*. Syracuse, New York: Syracuse University Press. (p. 445)

Rossi, Peter H. and Alice S. Rossi (1961), "Some Effects of Parochial School Education in America," pp. 300–328 in *Daedalus*, 90, No. 2, Spring. (p. 38)

Roszak, Theodore (1969), *The Making of a Counter Culture*. New York: Doubleday and Co. (p. 210)

Roszak, Theodore (1972), *Where the Wasteland Ends: Politics and Transcendence in Postindustrial Society*. New York: Doubleday and Co.

Ryans, David G. (1960), *Characteristics of Teachers*. Washington, D.C.: American Council on Education. (p. 444)

Sacks, Seymour (1972), *City Schools/Suburban Schools: A History of Fiscal Conflict*. Syracuse, New York: University of Syracuse Press. (p. 246)

Saltzman, Henry (1963), "The Community School in the Urban Setting," in *Education in Depressed Areas*, A. Harry Passow, ed. New York: Teachers College, Columbia University.

Samora, Julian, ed. (1966), *La Raza, Forgotten Americans*. South Bend, Indiana: University of Notre Dame Press. (p. 362)

Sanday, Peggy R. (1972), "On the Causes of IQ Differences between Groups and the Implications for Social Policy Considerations." Unpublished Paper. Pittsburgh, Pa.: School of Urban and Public Affairs, Carnegie-Mellon University. (pp. 70, 85)

Sanford, Nevitt, ed. (1962), *The American College: A Psychological and Social Interpretation of the Higher Learning*. New York: John Wiley & Sons, Inc. (pp. 97, 111)

Sargent, S. Stansfeld (1953), "Class and Class-Consciousness in a California Town," *Social Problems*, 1, 22–27.

Saturday Review (1972), "Washington Must Do More for the Arts," Editorial, April 22, p. 18.

Scanzoni, J. H. (1971), *The Black Family in Modern Society*. Boston: Allyn & Bacon. (p. 159)

Scarr-Salapatek, Sandra (1971), "Race, Social Class, and IQ," *Science*, 174, 1285–1295. (p. 85)

Bibliography

Schmid, Calvin F., and Charles E. Nobbe (1965), "Socioeconomic Differentials among Non-White Races," *American Sociological Review,* 30, 909–922.

Schmuch, Richard (1963), "Some Relationships of Peer Liking Patterns in the Classroom to Pupil Attitudes and Achievement," *School Review,* 71, 337–359. (p. 169)

Schneir, Miriam (ed.) (1972), *Feminism: The Essential Historical Writings.* New York: Vintage Books. (p. 398)

School Review (1972), "Women and Education," Special issue, Vol. 80, No. 2, February. (p. 398)

Schrag, Peter (1972), *The Decline of the Wasp.* New York: Simon and Schuster. (p. 210)

Schramm, Wilbur, Jack Lyle and Edwin B. Parker (1960), *Television in the Lives of Our Children.* Stanford, Calif.: Stanford University Press. (pp. 130, 133)

Schultz, Theodore W. (1960), "Capital Formation by Education," *Journal of Political Economy,* 68, 571–583. (p. 269)

Schultz, Theodore W. (1961), "Education and Economic Growth," Chapter 3 in *Social Forces Influencing American Education,* Sixtieth Yearbook, Part II, National Society for the Study of Education. (p. 101)

Schultz, Theodore W. (1963), *The Economic Value of Education.* New York: Columbia University Press. (p. 269)

Scribner, Sylvia and Michael Cole (1973), "Cognitive Consequences of Formal and Informal Education," *Science,* 182, 552–559. (p. 140)

Sears, Pauline and Feldman, D. H. (1966), "Teacher Interactions," *The National Elementary Principal,* 46 (2). (p. 394)

Sears, Robert R., Eleanor E. Maccoby, and Harry Levin. (1957), *Patterns of Child Rearing.* Evanston, Ill.: Row, Peterson, & Company. (p. 158)

Seay, Maurice F. (ed) (1974) *Community Education: A Developing Concept,* Midland, Michigan: Pendell Publishing Company. (p. 224)

Seligman, Daniel (1969), "A Special Kind of Rebellion," *Fortune,* 69, January, 1969. (pp. 193, 210)

Sewell, William H., Archibald O. Haller, and George W. Ohlendorf (1970), "The Educational and Early Occupational Status Achievement Process: Replication and Revision," *American Sociological Review,* 35, 1014–1027. (pp. 85, 91)

Sewell, William H. (1971), "Inequality of Opportunity for Higher Education," *American Sociological Review,* 36, 793–809. (pp. 91, 111)

Sexton, Patricia (1961), *Education and Income.* New York: The Viking Press, Inc.

Sexton, Patricia (1965), *Spanish Harlem.* New York: Harper & Row, Publishers. (p. 60)

Shanker, Albert (1969), "The Real Meaning of the New York City Teachers' Strike," *Phi Delta Kappan,* 50, 434–441.

Shaplin, Judson T. (1961), "Practice in Teaching," *Harvard Educational Review,* 31, 33–59. (p. 419)

Shipler, David K. (1972), "The White Niggers of Newark," *Harper's Magazine,* 77–83, August. (p. 379)

Short, James F., Jr., and Fred L. Strodtbeck (1965), *Group Process and Gang Delinquency.* Chicago: University of Chicago Press. (p. 211)

Shostak, Arthur B., and William Gomberg, eds. (1964), *Blue-Collar World.* Englewood Cliffs, N.J.: Prentice-Hall, Inc. (p. 38)

Silberman, Charles E. (1964), *Crisis in Black and White.* New York: Random House, Inc.

Silberman, Charles E. (1970), *Crisis in the Classroom.* New York: Random House.

Silberman, Charles E. (1970), "Murder in the Schoolroom: How the Public Schools Kill Dreams and Mutilate Minds," *Atlantic Monthly,* June, July, August.

Sizemore, Barbara A. (1972), "Is There a Case for Separate Schools?" *Phi Delta Kappan,* 53, 281–284. (p. 372)

Skeels, Harold M., and H. B. Dye (1939), "A Study of the Effect of Differential Stimulation on Mentally Retarded Children," *Proceedings and Addresses of the American Association of Mental Deficiency,* 44, No. 1, 114–136. (p. 119)

Skeels, Harold M. (1966), *Adult Status of Children with Contrasting Early Life Experiences.* Monograph of the Society for Research in Child Development, 31, No. 6, Serial 105. Chicago: University of Chicago Press. (pp. 119, 133)

Skinner, B. F. (1973), "The Free and Happy Student," *Phi Delta Kappan,* 55, 13–17. (p. 278)

Skolnick, Arlene S. and Jerome H. Skolnick, eds. (1971), *Family in Transition.* (p. 158)

Slater, Philip E. (1970), *The Pursuit of Loneliness: American Culture at the Breaking Point.* Boston: Beacon Press, 1970.

Smilansky, Sara (1973), "Comments on relative values of work with parents and work in school for compensatory education," *Phi Delta Kappan,* 54, 362, January. (p. 153)

Smith, Allen W. (1972), "Have Collective Negotiations Increased Teachers' Salaries?" *Phi Delta Kappan,* 54, 268–270, December. (p. 466)

Smith, Bob (1965), *They Closed Their Schools: Prince Edward County, Virginia, 1951–64.* Chapel Hill: University of North Carolina Press. (p. 338)

Snyder, Solomon H. (1971), *Uses of Marijuana.* New York: Oxford University Press. (pp. 201, 211)

Spady, William G. (1974), "The Authority System of the School and Student Unrest: A Theoretical Exploration," Chapter in *Sociological Bases of Education* ed. by Wayne Gordon, 73d Yearbook of the National Society for the Study of Education. Chicago: University of Chicago Press. (p. 440)

Spectorsky, Auguste C. (1955), *The Exurbanites.* Philadelphia: J. B. Lippincott Co. (pp. 38, 246)

Spindler, George D., ed. (1963), *Education and Culture.* New York: Holt, Rinehart, & Winston, Inc. (p. 133)

Stanley, Julian C. (1973), *Compensatory Education for Children: Recent Studies in Educational Intervention.* Baltimore: Johns Hopkins University Press.

Stanley, William O., et al. (1956), *Social Foundations of Education: A Book of New Readings.* New York: The Dryden Press. (pp. 224, 288)

Steffenson, James P. (1964), *Teachers Negotiate with Their School Boards.* Bulletin No. 40. Washington, D.C.: Office of Education. (p. 463)

Stern, George C. (1963), "Characteristics of the Intellectual Climate in College Environments," *Harvard Educational Review,* 33, 5–41. (p. 97)

Stetler, Henry G. (1949), *College Admission Practices with Respect to Race, Religion, and National Origin of Connecticut High School Graduates.* Hartford, Conn.: State Interracial Commission.

Stevens, Shane (1970), "Black Handwriting on the White Wall." A review of Bobby

Seale's book, *Seize the Time: The Story of the Black Panther Party and Huey P. Newton.* Random House, 1970, in The Progressive, Sept., p. 45-47. (p. 374)

St. John, Nancy H. (1970), "Desegregation and Minority Group Performance," *Review of Educational Research,* 40, 111–113. (p. 338)

Stiles, Lindley Joseph, ed. (1957), *The Teacher's Role in American Society.* Fourteenth Yearbook of the John Dewey Society. New York: Harper & Row.

Stivers, Eugene H. (1958), "Motivation for College in High School Boys," *School Review,* LXVI, 341–350.

Stivers, Eugene H. (1959), "Motivation for College in High School Girls," *School Review,* LXVII, 320–334.

Strauss, Anselm L. (1961), *Images of the City.* New York: The Free Press. (p. 247)

Strayer, George D. (1932), *Report of the Survey of the Schools of Chicago, Illinois,* Vol. III, New York: Bureau of Publications, Teachers College, Columbia University. (p. 283)

Strodtbeck, Fred L. (1958), "Family Interaction, Values and Achievement," Chapter 4 in *Talent and Society,* David C. McClelland, Alfred L. Baldwin, Urie Bronfenbrenner, and Fred L. Strodtbeck. Princeton, N.J.: D. Van Nostrand Co., Inc. (p. 53)

Strommen, Merton P., ed. (1971), *Research on Religious Development.* New York: Hawthorn Books, Inc. (p. 181)

Sugarman, Barry (1967), "Involvement in Youth Culture, Academic Achievement and Conformity in School: An Empirical Study of London Schoolboys," *British Journal of Sociology,* 18, 151–164. (p. 170)

Sugarman, Barry (1968), "Social Norms in Teenage Boys' Peer Groups: A Study of Their Implications for Achievement and Conduct in Four London Schools," *Human Relations,* 21, 41–58. (p. 170)

Sutherland, Robert L. (1942), *Color, Class and Personality.* Washington, D.C.: American Council on Education.

Taeuber, Conrad, and Irene Taeuber (1958), *The Changing Population of the United States.* New York: John Wiley & Sons, Inc. (pp. 297, 309)

Tannenbaum, Abraham J. (1962), *Adolescent Attitudes Toward Academic Brilliance.* New York: Teachers College, Columbia University.

Tapp, June L., ed. (1971), "Socialization, the Law, and Society," *Journal of Social Issues,* Vol. 27, No. 2. (p. 132)

Terman, Frederick E. (1971), "Supply of Scientific and Engineering Manpower: Surplus or Shortage," *Science,* 173, 399–405.

Thelen, Herbert A. (1954), *Dynamics of Groups at Work.* Chicago: University of Chicago Press. (p. 443)

Thompson, W. S., and D. T. Lewis (1965), *Population Problems.* Fifth edition. New York: McGraw-Hill Book Company. (p. 309)

Thornburg, Hershel (1973), "The Adolescent and Drugs: An Overview," *Journal of School Health,* 43, 640–644. (p. 211)

Thorndike, R. L. (1973), *Reading Comprehension in Fifteen Countries.* New York: Wiley. (p. 149)

Tickton, Sidney G. (1961), *Teaching Salaries Then and Now—A Second Look.* New York: Fund for the Advancement of Education. (p. 457)

Today's Education—NEA Journal (1969), "Students and Drug Use," 16 pp. Special

Feature prepared by the Center for Studies of Narcotic and Drug Abuse, National Institute of Mental Health. (p. 211)

Torrance, E. P. (1962), *Guiding Creative Talent*. Englewood Cliffs, N.J.: Prentice-Hall. (p. 394)

Turner, Ralph (1960), "Sponsored and Contest Mobility," *American Sociological Review*, 25, 855–867.

Udry, J. Richard (1960), "The Importance of Social Class in a Suburban School," *Journal of Educational Sociology*, 33, 307–310.

UNESCO Courier, 3, No. 6–7 (1950), Quotation occurs also in the *United Nations Bulletin*, 9, 105.

U.S. Bureau of the Census (1971a), "Characteristics of American Youth: 1970," *Current Population Report*, Series P-23, No. 38. Washington, D.C.

U.S. Bureau of the Census (1971b), "Social and Economic Status of Negroes in the United States," *Current Population Report*, Series P-23, No. 38. Washington, D.C.: U.S. Government Printing Office. (p. 314)

U.S. Bureau of Labor Statistics (1965a), *Indexes of Output per Man-Hour for the Private Economy, 1947–64*. Washington, D.C.: U.S. Government Printing Office. January 29. (p. 293)

U.S. Bureau of Labor Statistics (1965b), *Employment and Earnings in the United States, 1909–65*. Bulletin 1312–3, December. Washington, D.C.: U.S. Government Printing Office.

U.S. Bureau of Labor Statistics (1972), "Educational Attainment of Workers," Special Labor Force Report No. 148, Washington, D.C. (p. 387)

U.S. Commission on Civil Rights (1972), *The Excluded Student: Educational Praccial Labor Force Report No. 148, Washington, D.C.

U.S. Commission on Civil Rights (1967a), *Racial Isolation in the Public Schools*, Vol. 1. Washington, D.C.: U.S. Government Printing Office.

U.S. Commission on Civil Rights (1967b), *Appendices to Racial Isolation in the Public Schools*, Vol. 2. Washington, D.C.: U.S. Government Printing Office.

U.S. Commission on Civil Rights (1971a), *The Unfinished Education: Outcomes for Minorities in the Five Southwestern States*. (Mexican-American Educational Series, Report II), Washington, D.C.: U.S. Government Printing Office. (p. 359)

U.S. Commission on Civil Rights (1971b), *Civil Rights Digest*, Vol. 4, No. 4, December.

U.S. Commission on Civil Rights (1971c), *Annual Review for 1971*, Vol. 4, No. 4. Washington, D.C.: U.S. Commission on Civil Rights. (p. 324)

U.S. Commission on Civil Rights (1972), *The Excluded Student: Educational Practices Affecting Mexican Americans in the Southwest*. (Mexican American Educational Series, Report III), Washington, D.C.: U.S. Government Printing Office. (p. 344)

U.S. Commission on Civil Rights (1973), *School Desegregation in Ten Communities*. Clearinghouse Publication 43.

U.S. Department of Labor (1965), *The Negro Family: The Case for National Action*. March. Washington, D.C.: U.S. Government Printing Office. (pp. 159, 336)

U.S. Department of Labor (1972), "Who Are the Working Mothers?" Women's Bureau, Employment Standards Administration, Leaflet 37 (rev.).

U.S. Government (1972), Public Law No. 92-318, Sec. 401-53. (p. 356)

U.S. Office of Education (1963), *Programs for the Educationally Disadvantaged.* Bulletin No. 17. Washington, D.C.: U.S. Government Printing Office.

U.S. Office of Education (1964), *The 1963 Dropout Campaign.* Bulletin No. 26. Washington, D.C.: U.S. Government Printing Office.

U.S. Office of Education (1965 and 1973), *Digest of Educational Statistics.* Bulletin No. 4. Washington, D.C.: U.S. Government Printing Office.

U.S. Public Health Service, Panel of Scientists (1972), *Report to the Surgeon-General on Television Violence.* Washington, D.C.: U.S. Government Printing Office. (p. 131)

U.S. Reports, Vol. 333 (1948), *Cases Adjusted in the Supreme Court at October Term, 1947,* pp. 203–256. Washington, D.C.: U.S. Government Printing Office. (p. 272)

U.S. Senate, Special Subcommittee on Indian Education (1969), *Indian Education: A National Tragedy—A National Challenge.* Washington, D.C.: U.S. Government Printing Office. (p. 355)

U.S. Senate, Special Committee on Aging (1971), *Elderly Cubans in Exile.* Washington, D.C.: U.S. Government Printing Office, November. (p. 347)

United States, 86th Congress (1960), *Report on Juvenile Delinquency.* Washington, D.C.: U.S. Government Printing Office. (p. 208)

United States, 89th Congress (1965), *Higher Education Act of 1965.* Hearings before the Special Subcommittee on Education of the Committee on Education and Labor, House of Representatives. Washington, D.C.: U.S. Government Printing Office. (p. 273)

Upjohn Institute for Employment Research, The W. E. (1972), *Work in America.* Report of a Special Task Force to the Secretary of Health, Education, and Welfare. Cambridge, Mass.: MIT Press. (p. 388)

Valentine, Charles A. (1968), *Culture and Poverty.* Chicago: University of Chicago Press.

Valentine, Earl C. (1950), "The Occupational Expectations of Three Normal School Student Groups." Unpublished masters thesis, Department of Sociology, University of Chicago. (p. 404)

Van den Berghe, Pierre L. (1967), *Race and Racism: A Comparative Perspective.* New York: John Wiley & Sons. (p. 338)

Vernon, Raymond (1959), *The Changing Economic Function of the Central City.* New York: Committee for Economic Development.

Vernon, Raymond (1961), *Metropolis, 1985.* Cambridge, Mass.: Harvard University Press. (p. 246)

Vidich, Arthur J., and Joseph Bensman (1958), *Small Town in Mass Society.* Princeton, N.J.: Princeton University Press. (pp. 224, 427)

Vieg, John A. (1939), *The Government of Education in Metropolitan Chicago.* Chicago: University of Chicago Press. (p. 282)

Walizer, Michael H. and Robert E. Herriott (1971), *The Impact of College on Students' Competence to Function in a Learning Society.* Research Report No. 47, Iowa City, Iowa: American College Testing Program.

Walker, Charles R., and R. H. Guest (1952), *The Man on the Assembly Line.* Cambridge, Mass.: Harvard University Press. (p. 38)

Waller, Jerome H. (1971), "Achievement and Social Mobility: Relations in Two Generations," *Social Biology*, 18, 252–259.

Waller, Willard (1942), "The Teacher's Roles," Chapter 10 in *Sociological Foundations of Education*, J. S. Roucek and Associates, eds. New York: Thomas Y. Crowell Company. (pp. 426, 443)

Wallerstein, Immanuel and Paul Starr (1971), *The University Crisis Reader*. New York: Random House. (p. 210)

Warner, W. Lloyd, Buford H. Junker, and Walter A. Adams (1941), *Color and Human Nature*. Washington, D.C.: American Council on Education.

Warner, W. Lloyd, and Paul S. Lunt (1941), *The Social Life of a Modern Community*. New Haven, Conn.: Yale University Press. (pp. 23, 37)

Warner, W. Lloyd, and Associates (1949), *Democracy in Jonesville*. New York: Harper & Row, Publishers. (pp. 22, 37)

Warner, W. Lloyd (1953), *American Life: Dream and Reality*. Chicago: University of Chicago Press. (p. 37)

Warner, W. Lloyd, and James C. Abegglen (1955), *Big Business Leaders in America*. New York: Harper & Row, Publishers. (p. 55)

Warner, W. Lloyd, Marchia Meeker, and Kenneth Eels (1960), *Social Class in America*, new ed. New York: Harper Torchbooks. (pp. 20, 22, 25, 37, 426)

Warner, W. Lloyd (1962), *The Corporation in the Emergent American Society*. New York: Harper & Row, Publishers.

Wattenberg, William *et al.* (1957, I), "Social Origins of Teachers—Facts from a Northern Industrial City," Chapter 2 in *The Teacher's Role in American Society*, Lindley J. Stiles, ed. Fourteenth Yearbook of the John Dewey Society. New York: Harper & Row, Publishers. (p. 430)

Wattenberg, William, *et al.* (1957, II), "Social Origin of Teachers and American Education," Chapter 5 in *The Teacher's Role in Amercian Society*, Lindley J. Stiles, ed., Fourteenth Yearbook of the John Dewey Society. New York: Harper & Row, Publishers. (p. 430)

Weaver, Robert C. (1964), "The City and Its Suburbs," *New City*, 2, pp. 4–6, March. (p. 244)

Weber, Max (1958), *From Max Weber: Essays in Sociology*. A variety of essays arranged and edited by H. Gerth and C. Wright Mills. New York: Oxford University Press.

Weber, Max (1961), "The Ethnic Group," p. 305 in Vol. 1 of *Theories of Society* by Talcott Parsons *et al.* Glencoe, Ill.: The Free Press.

Weikart, David P., Dennis J. DeLoria, and Sarah A. Lawser (1970), *Longitudinal Results of the Ypsilanti Perry Preschool Project*. Ypsilanti, Michigan: High Scope Educational Research Foundation. (pp. 133, 153)

Weinberg, Meyer, (1970), *Desegregation Research: An Appraisal*. Second Edition. Bloomington, Indiana: Phi Delta Kappa. (p. 338)

Wertham, Frederic (1954), *Seduction of the Innocent*. New York: Holt, Rinehart, & Winston, Inc.

West, James (1945), *Plainville, U.S.A.* New York: Columbia University Press. (p. 37)

Westinghouse Learning Corporation/Ohio University (1969), *Evaluation of Head Start Programs*. Pittsburgh: Westinghouse Learning Corporation. (p. 154)

Whelton, Clark (1969), "Civil Liberties Union: Trial from Within," *the village*

VOICE, March 27. (p. 258)

White, Burton L. (1973), "Growing Up Competent," *Carnegie Quarterly*, Summer, pp. 6–8. (p. 149)

Whitney, Frederick L. (1927), "The Social and Economic Background of Teacher College and of the University Students," *Education*, XLVII, 449–456. (p. 403)

Whyte, William Foote (1943), *Street-Corner Society*. Chicago: University of Chicago Press.

Whyte, William H., Jr. (1956), *The Organization Man*. New York: Simon and Schuster, Inc. (pp. 13, 38)

Wilcox, Preston (1972), "Selected Principles for Involving the Poor," p. 246–253 in *Education for the People*, Vol. 2. Sacramento, Calif.: Joint Committee on Educational Goals and Evaluation. (p. 381)

Wilensky, Harold (1964), "The Professionalization of Everyone?" *American Journal of Sociology*, 70, No. 2.

Williams, Roger M. (1971), "The Emancipation of Black Scholars," *Saturday Review*, Vol. 54, pp. 54–59, December 18.

Wills, Garry (1974), "The Country That Wasn't There," *Playboy*, 21: 173–4, 212, 265–6, January.

Wilson, Alan B. (1959), "Residential Segregation of Social Classes and Aspirations of High School Boys," *American Sociological Review*, 24, 836–845. (pp. 172, 241)

Wilson, Alan B. (1967), "Educational Consequences of Segregation in a California Community," Appendix C3, pp. 165–206, *Racial Isolation in the Public Schools*, Vol. 2. U.S. Commission on Civil Rights. Washington, D.C.: U.S. Government Printing Office.

Withey, S. et al. (1971), *A Degree and What Else?: Correlates and Consequences of a College Education*. New York: McGraw-Hill. (p. 111)

Witty, Paul (1956), "Annual Reports on TV," *School and Society*. Annual Reports during the 1950s.

Wolf, R. (1965), "The Measurement of Environments," in *Proceedings of the 1964 Invitational Conference on Testing Problems*, pp. 93–108. Princeton, N.J.: Educational Testing Service.

Wolfgang, Marvin E.; Figlio, Robert M.; and Thorsten Sellin (1972), *Delinquency in a Birth Cohort*. Chicago: University of Chicago Press. (p. 204)

Wolfle, Dael (1971), *The Uses of Talent*. Princeton, New Jersey: Princeton University Press. (pp. 104, 111)

Yankelovich, Daniel (1972a), "The New Naturalism," *Saturday Review*, April 1, pp. 32–37. (p. 190)

Yankelovich, Daniel (1972b), *The Changing Values on the Campus*. New York: Simon and Schuster. (p. 210)

Zangwill, Israel (1909), *The Melting Pot*. New York: Macmillan. (p. 386)

Zapoleon, Marguerite W. (1961), *Occupational Planning for Women*. New York: Harper & Row, Publishers.

Zigler, Edward F. (1970), "Social Class and the Socialization Process," *Review of Educational Research*. 40, pp. 87–110. (pp. 132, 146)

Zigler, Edward F. (1973), "Project Head Start: Success or Failure?" *Children Today*, Vol. 2, No. 6, pp. 2–7, November–December. (p. 155)

INDEX